Encounters with Modernity

Studies in German History

Published in Association with the German Historical Institute, Washington, D.C.

General Editors:

Hartmut Berghoff, Director of the German Historical Institute, Washington, D.C.

Uwe Spiekermann, Deputy Director of the German Historical Institute, Washington, D.C.

ENCOUNTERS WITH MODERNITY

The Catholic Church in West Germany, 1945–1975

Benjamin Ziemann

Translated from the German by Andrew Evans

berghahn
NEW YORK · OXFORD
www.berghahnbooks.com

Published in 2014 by
Berghahn Books
www.berghahnbooks.com

English-language edition
©2014 Benjamin Ziemann

German-language edition
© Vandenhoeck & Ruprecht GmbH & Co. KG
Originally published as
Katholische Kirche und Sozialwissenschaften 1945–1975

The translation of this work was funded by Geisteswissenschaften International –
Translation Funding for Humanities and Social Sciences from Germany, a joint
initiative of the Fritz Thyssen Foundation, the German Federal Foreign Office, the
collecting society VG WORT and the Börsenverein des Deutschen Buchhandels
(German Publishers & Booksellers Association).

Library of Congress Cataloging-in-Publication Data
Ziemann, Benjamin.
[Katholische Kirche und Sozialwissenschaften 1945–1975. English]
Encounters with modernity : the Catholic Church in West Germany, 1945–1975 /
Benjamin Ziemann ; translated from German by Andrew Evans.
pages cm. — (Studies in German history ; volume 17)
"Originally published as Katholische Kirche und Sozialwissenschaften 1945-1975."
Includes bibliographical references and index.
ISBN 978-1-78238-344-4 (hardback : alk. paper)— ISBN 978-1-78238-345-1
(ebook)
    1. Church and social problems—Germany—Catholic Church.
    2. Catholic Church—Germany.   3. Christianity and the social sciences—
Germany.   I. Title.
HN39.G3Z5413 2014
261.8'30943—dc23
                                                                2013041898

British Library Cataloguing in Publication Data

A catalogue record for this book is available from the British Library

ISBN: 978-1-78238-344-4 hardback
ISBN: 978-1-78238-345-1 ebook

CONTENTS

PREFACE

This book tries to offer a fresh interpretation of the history of the Catholic Church, and of religion more generally, during the first three decades of the Federal Republic of Germany. It does so by bringing two strands of historiography and two sets of questions together that have rarely been seen in conjunction. On the one hand, this is a history of the challenges the church faced in the postwar period: it charts the attempts the church made to understand the nature and meaning of secularization, the efforts it made to develop new pastoral programs, and it analyzes how new forms of engaging and including the laity responded to societal change. On the other hand, this is a history of the various ways in which applied social sciences, from statistics to opinion polling and organizational research, were employed by the Catholic Church and offered new vistas on the challenges of secularization. This use of social scientific knowledge was part of a larger process that can be dubbed the "scientization of the social." It is the core premise of this study that secularization and scientization were in fact two sides of the same coin. Seeing them in conjunction allows us to understand how the Catholic Church in West Germany encountered modernity in the three decades from 1945 to 1975.

The approach taken in this book and some of its conceptual premises are based on sociological theories that are still largely unfamiliar to Anglophone historians and general readers. I am convinced that they are sufficiently explained in the introduction and throughout the book, and hope that the reader will take time to engage with some of the implications of this approach. While some of the underlying ideas are derived from sociological theory, this is a genuinely historical study. Its core aim is to illuminate the nature of religious change in post-1945 West Germany, and to make a contribution to the history of the Catholic Church in this period. However, this book is also the result of an ongoing conversation with sociologists, and I do hope that the book might also appeal to all social scientists and theologians who have an interest in its more general conclusions about the place of religion in postwar society.

The book was originally published as *Katholische Kirche und Sozialwissenschaften 1945–1975* by Vandenhoeck & Ruprecht in 2007. For the translation, I have made considerable cuts, largely rewritten the introduction, and added some contextual information to most of the chapters. That this book can appear in the English language is due to the support of a number of institutions. First, I would like to thank Geisteswissenschaften International, a joint initiative by the Börsenverein des Deutschen Buchhandels, the Verwertungsgesellschaft Wort, the German Foreign Office, and the Fritz Thyssen Foundation, for the generous funding of the translation and the recognition that the inclusion in their program entails. I would also like to thank the German Historical Institute in Washington DC, and in particular its director, Hartmut Berghoff, and its deputy director, Uwe Spiekermann, for their kind offer to publish my book in the series of the GHI. My translator, Andrew Evans, has done an excellent job in rendering my German prose in the English language. I am also grateful for the crucial support that Casey Sutcliffe at the GHI Washington DC offered in copy editing the manuscript. My editor at Berghahn Books, Ann Przyzycki DeVita, offered helpful support and advice along the way.

Throughout the work on this book and beyond, I have benefited immensely from conversations, written feedback, and other exchanges with a number of colleagues and friends. As a historian, I am particularly grateful for the insights I received from sociologists, including Michael N. Ebertz, Staf Hellemans, Michael Koenig, Detlef Pollack, Rudolf Stichweh, and Hartmann Tyrell, and from theologians such as Friedrich Wilhelm Graf and Arie Molendijk. In my own discipline, I am particularly grateful for conversations with Wilhelm Damberg, Greg Eghigian, Peter Fritzsche, Andreas Gestrich, Martin H. Geyer, Stefan Ludwig Hoffmann, Patrick Houlihan—who also offered helpful feedback on a draft of the introduction—Anja Kruke, Hugh McLeod, Franziska Metzger, Bob Moore, Lutz Raphael, Mary Vincent—who offered crucial support at a very critical moment—and Siegfried Weichlein. Over many years, a number of friends have provided constant support and intellectual inspiration. I am especially indebted to Richard Bessel, Michael Geyer, Thomas Kühne, Thomas Mergel—who was the first to endorse the idea for this project, and the first to comment on the whole manuscript—and Helmut Walser Smith. Special thanks go to my close friend Moritz Föllmer, and to Chris Dols, a young researcher from Radboud University in Nijmegen who has written a similar and in many ways parallel study on the Dutch Catholic Church, and with whom I had the privilege of coauthoring two articles.

One cloudy and grey October afternoon in 1988, I walked into a lecture hall at Free University Berlin to attend a lecture on German agricultural history. When I sat down to take notes, with only three other students attending, I did not know that this moment would transform my life and shape my professional career. At this point, Josef Mooser was my lecturer and seminar tutor. He later turned into the supervisor of my PhD dissertation, and subsequently into a friend and constant interlocutor. Many of the things that I have learned about the place of the Catholic Church in modern history, I owe to conversations with him—thank you, Josef!

Parts of chapters 3 and 5 incorporate material that has been published previously. Author and publisher gratefully acknowledge the kind permission by the German History Society and by Oxford University Press to reprint copyrighted material from Benjamin Ziemann, "Opinion Polls and the Dynamics of the Public Sphere: The Catholic Church in the Federal Republic after 1968," *German History* 24, no. 4 (2006): 562–86; and Benjamin Ziemann, "The Gospel of Psychology: Therapeutic Concepts and the Scientification of Pastoral Care in the West German Catholic Church, 1945–1980," *Central European History* 39 (2006): 79–106, reprinted with kind permission by Cambridge University Press.

Benjamin Ziemann
Sheffield, June 2013

ABBREVIATIONS

ABP	Archiv des Bistums Passau
AfS	*Archiv für Sozialgeschichte*
ARedBo	Archiv des Redemptoristenklosters Bochum
BAE	Bistumsarchiv Essen
BAM	Bistumsarchiv Münster
BAOS	Bistumsarchiv Osnabrück
BDA	Bischöfliches Diözesanarchiv Aachen
BDKJ	Bund der Deutschen Katholischen Jugend (German Catholic Youth League)
CAJ	Christliche Arbeiterjugend
DAL	Diözesanarchiv Limburg
DBK	Deutsche Bischofskonferenz (German Bishops' Conference)
DGfP	Deutsche Gesellschaft für Pastoralpsychologie
EAF	Erzbischöfliches Archiv Freiburg
EBAP	Erzbischöfliches Archiv Paderborn
EOM	Erzbischöfliches Ordinariat München, Registratur
FAZ	Frankfurter Allgemeine Zeitung
FBK	Fuldaer Bischofskonferenz (Fulda Bishops' Conference)
FERES	International Federation of Catholic Social Research Institutes
FH	Frankfurter Hefte
FHH	Franz Hitze Haus
GG	*Geschichte und Gesellschaft*
GH	German History
HAEK	Historisches Archiv des Erzbistums Köln
HJb	Historisches Jahrbuch
HK	Herder-Korrespondenz
ICSW	Institut für Christliche Sozialwissenschaften Münster (Institute for Christian Social Sciences Münster)
IfAK	Institut für Absatzforschung Andreas Ketels
IfD	Institut für Demoskopie (Institute for Opinion Polling)
IKSE	Institut für Kirchliche Sozialforschung des Bistums Essen (Institute for Church Social Research of the Diocese of Essen)

KASKI	Katholiek Sociaal-Kerkelijk Instituut (Catholic Institute for Social-Ecclesiastical Research)
KDC	Katholiek Documentatie Centrum Nijmegen (Catholic Documentation Centre Nijmegen)
KDPT	Konferenz der deutschsprachigen Pastoraltheologen (Conference of German-Speaking Pastoral Theologians)
KH	Kirchliches Handbuch
KISIF	Katholisches Internationales Soziologische Institut für Flüchtlingsfragen (Catholic International Sociological Institute for Refugee Issues)
KuL	Kirche und Leben
LS	Lebendige Seelsorge
LThK	Lexikon für Theologie und Kirche
NL	Nachlass (personal papers)
PBl.	Pastoralblatt
PSI	Pastoralsoziologisches Institut Essen (Pastoral Sociological Institute of the Diocese of Essen)
RGG	Religion in Geschichte und Gegenwart
RJKG	Rottenburger Jahrbuch für Kirchengeschichte
SC	Social Compass
SIB	Sozialinstitut des Bistums Essen, Abt. Kirchliche Sozialforschung (Social Institute of the Diocese of Essen, Department of Church Social Research)
SPD	Sozialdemokratische Partei Deutschlands (Social Democratic Party)
StdZ	Stimmen der Zeit
WW	Wort und Wahrheit
ZfS	Zeitschrift für Soziologie
ZSt	Zentralstelle für kirchliche Statistik Deutschlands, Köln (Central Office for Church Statistics Germany, Cologne)
ZdK	Zentralkomitee der deutschen Katholiken (Central Committee of German Catholics)

INTRODUCTION

From 1945 to 1975, the Catholic Church in the Federal Republic of Germany faced many challenges. At the end of the Second World War, it seemed as if the church was the "victor among ruins." It was one of the few major societal institutions to survive the Nazi dictatorship more or less intact. And in the immediate postwar period, hopes were high that the devastating effects of Nazi rule would encourage a return to Christian values and beliefs and would reinvigorate the church's role in society. However, it soon became apparent that such high-flying hopes were to be disappointed. Some key indicators of organized piety—for instance, the number of churchgoers—quickly displayed a downward trajectory. Equally worrying were the clear signs of erosion and inner exhaustion among many Catholic voluntary associations. Associations for Catholic youth are an important case in point. Whereas 38 percent of Catholic youth belonged to a Catholic youth group in 1932, by 1950 the figure was 30 percent, by 1963 18 percent, and ten years later it had dropped to a mere 11 percent.[1] The demise of Catholic youth associations is only one example of a broader trend. Since about the 1880s, a dense network of voluntary associations had formed the backbone of the Catholic milieu, a tightly knit subculture that insulated Catholics from the disintegrating effects of modern society. By the mid-1960s at the latest, many of these associations had either lost the bulk of their membership or much of their momentum, or both. In the Federal Republic, the traditional Catholic milieu rapidly fell apart.

Yet at the same time, German Catholics were part of a much broader, exciting new development. The Second Vatican Council (1962–65) had ushered in a new period of church history, most tangibly introducing the vernacular into the celebration of Mass, among many other changes. Since the "Syllabus Errorum," the papal rejection of the many errors and dangers of liberalism and modernity published in 1864, and the First Vatican Council (1869/70), the Catholic Church had positioned itself in "fundamental opposition" to the core tendencies of modern society.[2] The Second Vatican Council reversed this attempt to separate and insulate Catholics from modernity, suggesting an intensive dialogue with the secular societal "world" instead.[3] The implementation of the council's recommendations in the German Catholic Church, as in other national churches, was anything but straightforward. Another challenge arose from the overlapping of the postconciliar debates with the politicization and contestation arising from certain groups of Catholics in the wake of 1968—predominantly, but by far not exclusively, students. Intensive struggles over the competing and often contradictory claims of top-down reform and bottom-up discontent with a hierarchical institution characterized the Catholic Church during the 1960s and 1970s.

Is it possible to make sense of these different and somewhat contradictory developments, and to establish a convincing historiographical narrative of the Catholic Church in the first three decades of the Federal Republic? So far, historians have basically suggested three different types of narrative. With a focus on the erosion of the Catholic milieu, the basic story line is one of demise and decline, of the ever-dwindling presence of practicing Catholics in the politics and society of the Bonn Republic. In this perspective, the burgeoning Catholic milieu of the period up to 1945 is replaced with a mere "religious vacuum."[4] This interpretation, to be sure, captures a crucial element of the story, not least because frustration over increasingly empty churches was a staple of debates in the church from the 1960s at the latest. On the other hand, as a story of decline it is highly unlikely to provide any startling insights. A second option is to embed the Catholic Church into the broader perspective of the learning curve of West Germans with regard to modern liberal democracy. In this perspective, both the decline of the traditional milieu and the contestation by Catholic students can be read as part of a broader trend toward the "liberalization" of West German society from the 1950s to the 1970s.[5]

A third option is advanced by church historians, who talk about a broadly conceived "transformation" of religion in the Federal Republic. First of all, the choice of the neutral term commendably avoids the obvious normative implications of concepts such as "liberalization." It also deliberately attempts to get away from a "simple interpretation" of religious change in these decades as "decline" or "secularization."[6] But while it is easy to see why "decline" offers a rather "simple" narrative, the contested and controversial notion of "secularization" is less clear in this regard. In addition, the first and the third narrative, in particular, struggle to offer any crucial insights into the general history of postwar Germany. Occasionally, church historians complain about the relative neglect of religion in textbook accounts and general histories of the Federal Republic. Yet when church historians do, indeed, aim to "integrat[e] religion into the historical mainstream," they may need to offer more substantial research agendas than just stories of (deplorable) decline or of (formal) transformation.[7]

Secularization: A Flawed Master Narrative?

In this book, I will take a different approach to studying the Catholic Church in the Federal Republic. I will interpret the trajectory of organized religion from the angle of the intersections between the Catholic Church and the social sciences. In this perspective, the basic story line is one of secularization, although it involves a specific interpretation of the secularization paradigm. Hardly any component of modernization theory has met fiercer resistance over the past fifteen years than the notion of secularization, both among historians and among sociologists of religion. Both groups have stated that the secularization paradigm is wrong in assuming a necessary decline of religion and piety in the modern age, as evidenced not only by the flourishing of religion in the nineteenth century but also by ultramontane Catholic piety and other religious revivals. The secularization paradigm, according to another line of critique, cannot account for the strength of religion in the undoubtedly modern society of the contemporary United States. Hence, it would be more apt to talk about a "return of the gods," as theologian Friedrich Wilhelm Graf has argued.[8] Some cultural historians level an even more fundamental criticism against the secularization paradigm. They see it as a mere Procrustean bed that restrains rather than facilitates research into the history of religion. Both in its origins around 1900, when sociologists such as Max Weber and Emile Durkheim first posited the notion of a "disenchantment" in the modern world, and in its current sociological permutations, secularization is seen as part and parcel of the master narrative of Western societies, as a deliberate attempt to eradicate the irrational aspects of religion from an idealized self-description of rational modernity.[9]

In response to these criticisms, it has to be acknowledged that the secularization theories of Max Weber and other turn-of-the-century luminaries certainly need to be situated in their historical context, and the anti-Catholic underpinnings of their ideas on religion in modern society need to be historicized. Yet, crucially, one must differentiate between the historical genesis of a theory and its systematic validity. To criticize secularization as a flawed master narrative in postmodernist fashion is inherently lopsided if there is no understanding that the postmodernist farewell to master narratives is in itself nothing other than—a master narrative.[10] Sociologists such as Steve Bruce and Detlef Pollack have recently begun to address some of the other criticisms mentioned above. They point out that secularization theory never posited an inevitable and straightforward linear decline of individual religiosity, and that it addresses the changing forms of religion in the modern age as much as the question of decline.[11] They also mention that the empirical evidence with regard to the United States has often been either misrepresented or misunderstood. Closer empirical scrutiny demonstrates that key indicators of religiosity in the United

States have, indeed, been in steady decline since 1945, and that the emergence of the fundamentalist "moral majority" in the 1970s, thus, has to be interpreted as a backlash against the loss of public presence that evangelical Christians had faced in the preceding decades.[12]

Functional Differentiation as a Challenge for the Church

For this book, I employ one of the core notions of most sociological approaches to secularization, although with a twist. Most sociologists agree that secularization is a specific consequence of functional differentiation in the religious system.[13] Functional differentiation is a form of societal differentiation that is neither hierarchical (as a society based on a layered structure of estates, classes, or social strata) nor based on a core difference between center and periphery. Rather, it is based on societal fields or subsystems that relate to specific challenges or problems, such as politics (taking collectively binding decisions), science (distinguishing between true and false assertions), the legal system (establishing justice against the backdrop of injustice), and so forth. Each subsystem develops a code of communications and operational programs to deal with the specific function. The emergence of functional differentiation can be traced to the early modern period. This fundamental process in the evolution of modern societies is one about which most of the early classic sociologists such as Herbert Spencer, Max Weber, and Georg Simmel agree with contemporary authors such as Talcott Parsons, Jeffrey Alexander, and Pierre Bourdieu.[14]

Consequently, functional differentiation as a societal process is relevant to the history of the Catholic Church, since it entails a fundamental change in religion's position in society. In a society characterized by the existence of functional subsystems, religion can no longer be seen as the pinnacle or as the all-encompassing representation of the unity of society, as it was in the Middle Ages and in most of the early modern period. In modern society, religion is an important subsystem of society, but it is only one among many. In this sense, religion and the churches are no longer on top—to use a spatial metaphor—but operating on a level playing field with other societal fields. Thus—and here comes the twist—we can understand secularization as the specific challenge that functional differentiation poses for the religious system at large and for the major organizations within it, such as the Catholic Church. This challenge is based on the functional differentiation of politics, mass media, science, and education, and on the concomitant religious neutralization of these fields. In a functionally differentiated society, newspaper editors can still write op-ed pieces on the grounds of their individual faith, just as physicists or political scientists can offer public commentary on the basis of their religious values. But the workings of these systems themselves are based on their distinctive codes—information/noninformation in the case of the mass media, true/false in the case of science. Any newspaper that would only print information that is newsworthy from a religious point of view would soon be out of business, including *L'Osservatore Romano*.

To understand this approach, it is crucial not to see secularization as a necessary or automatic adaptation of religion to the challenges of functional differentiation. This take on the secularization paradigm is not concerned with a direct causal relation between differentiation and religion. Rather, the focus is on the options that the churches had at their disposal when they started to observe the effects of functional differentiation. Properly understood, secularization only makes sense with regard to the relative position of religious observers in society and points historians to the semantic forms these observers used to describe this position.[15] In other words, modern society is only "secular" to the extent that religious observers perceive it as such. At this point, Anglo-American readers might want to invoke authors such as Charles Taylor or Brad S. Gregory, a philosopher and a historian of the Reformation, respectively. In two hefty tomes—Taylor in *A Secular Age* and Gregory in *The Unintended Reformation*—these authors voiced their discontent with traditional sociological secularization narratives, and particularly with Max Weber's notion of "disenchantment" as a key characteristic of the modern world.[16] Both authors, arguing from a liberal Catholic perspective, articulated their frustration with what Gregory describes as the "hyperpluralism of religious and secular commitments" in our time.[17] This is not the place to discuss the relative merits and substantial weaknesses of both accounts in detail.[18] Suffice it to say that my study differs from such attempts to criticize secularization both conceptually and practically.

First, I have no religious agenda to defend. In my view, the pluralism or even "hyperpluralism"—a derogatory term whose use I find problematic—of commitments in contemporary society is the inevitable result of a functionally differentiated society, in which different sets of rationalities and values apply in each subsystem. Second, although I share Taylor and Gregory's genuine interest in understanding whether and how the Catholic Church has been able to reconstruct a coherent dogmatic and pastoral position vis-à-vis such contemporary pluralism, I do not think that their bird's-eye view—a sweeping historical account across the ages, combined with a Catholic normative viewpoint—is the appropriate toolbox for answering this question. Both the challenge posed by secularization and the Catholic Church's different responses require a close-up study of pastoral reflection and practice at the "point of production": in diocesan offices and local parish communities. Third, I am convinced that it is possible to conceptualize a nonnormative interpretation of secularization that is not predicated on the notion of a wholesale "decline" of religion.

The particular take on the secularization paradigm that informs this study is influenced by the theories of German sociologist Niklas Luhmann (1927–98). Luhmann is still hardly known among English-speaking historians, although he was one of the most prolific and innovative sociologists of the postwar period. While Luhmann made some slight changes in his sociology of religion, published in two separate monographs, the notion of functional differentiation always formed the core of his understanding of modern society, and of secularization in particular.[19]

The consequences of secularization for the Catholic Church, which religious observers view as the challenges of functional differentiation, can be located in three different but related developments. When religion or religious values cease to integrate society, society appears "secular." This process is first registered on the semantic level in discourses on the autonomous workings of the various subsystems of society. At the turn of the century, German sociologists and intellectuals developed a distinctive—and unfortunately rather complicated—terminology to describe these phenomena. Around 1905, sociologist Max Weber began using the term *Eigengesetzlichkeit* to denote the inherently different value spheres that characterized politics, the arts, or the economy, and to flag the fact that these systems followed, in a literal translation of *eigengesetzlich,* their "own laws." In English, *Eigengesetzlichkeit* is usually rendered by the equally complicated term "entelechy." Starting in the 1920s, a number of Catholic intellectuals and theologians adopted the notion of *Eigengesetzlichkeit,* thus already acknowledging on a very basic semantic level that contemporary German society had to be seen as secular.[20]

Yet secularization is not only a semantic form; it is also a structural reality—the second level for registering secularization, which can be described as the "structural relevance of a privatization of religious decision-making."[21] In modern society, individuals can make their own, private decisions about inclusion in various subsystems of society. They can decide to join and play in a soccer club and be actively included in the sports system. But they can also decide to watch soccer only on television, and thus only be included in a passive audience role in the mass media. This shift toward different forms and levels of inclusion had fundamental consequences for the Catholic Church and other religious organizations, as they had to reorganize their internal structures and pastoral programs, and to redefine the distinctive roles of clergy and laity. Was it still possible in postwar Germany to describe the parish priest as the "shepherd" of his flock, thus tapping into a premodern, hierarchical version of the relation between clergy and laity? Was it still possible and legitimate to postulate a specific role for the clergy and hence to bar Catholic priests from inclusion in a nuclear family—the issue of celibacy—and if so, on what grounds? In the West German Catholic Church, these were controversial issues discussed in direct relation to the side effects of secularization as functional differentiation.

A third and often-neglected challenge of functional differentiation for the Church relates to the necessary knowledge about the "secularized" societal environment. It is almost a truism to say that modern, differentiated society is much more complex than traditional societies simply because of the increased relations between its various elements. Yet in the postwar period, bishops and clergy alike seriously asked themselves how they could continue to offer specific solutions to the many pastoral problems this highly differentiated society posed even while rapid change in the church's social environment increasingly devalued time-honored practices. Such specific solutions required detailed knowledge about the particular elements of social change—knowledge that affected the delivery of pastoral, liturgical, and other church services. One way to address this problem was to import "secular" forms of scientific knowledge from nontheological disciplines. This strategy, however, risked diluting the cognitive and cultural identity of the Catholic Church and causing it to lose sight of its proprium, that is, communication about God and the netherworld.[22]

Encounters with Modernity: The Catholic Church and the Social Sciences

At this point, we can at last fully grasp a key consequence of secularization that is crucial for the topic of this book. Functional differentiation, to be sure, had already emerged and become the dominant structure of German society in the nineteenth century. As mentioned, some Catholic intellectuals and theologians had registered its effects on religion under the rubric of entelechy as early as the 1920s, and had considered the relative legitimacy of this process. But only in the postwar period did the Catholic Church adopt and implement a broad range of empirical tools that allowed it to fully observe the dynamics of functional differentiation and develop pastoral strategies in response. These tools derived from various branches of the applied social sciences, including statistics and opinion polling but also psychoanalysis and psychotherapy. Thus, the reception and application of applied social sciences both facilitated and shaped the way the West German Catholic Church encountered modernity. To use an optical metaphor, these social sciences provided the binoculars for viewing seemingly distant social phenomena in high resolution; they offered a detailed picture of the ways differentiation affected the church. However, the binocular metaphor is misleading insofar as it suggests that their use did not affect the observer himself. Yet the use of social scientific knowledge, as noted in the third dimension of secularization above, also had the potential to jeopardize the identity of the church and effectively secularize it from the inside. Consequently, the Catholic Church's use of the social sciences provides another example of the scientization of the social, of the ways in which social scientific knowledge shaped social relations.

Looking at it this way, we can see that secularization and scientization were two sides of the same coin. In this book, I will investigate precisely these intersections between the side effects of differentiation and the Catholic Church's increasing use of social scientific knowledge. I will analyze the ways the church tried to reposition and reprogram itself in intensive encounters with the very modernity the social sciences brought to the attention of bishops, clergy, and active members of the laity. But what is meant by the "scientization of the social," a bulky yet necessary term? In the following, I adopt historian Lutz Raphael's definition from his landmark 1996 article, which describes scientization as the consequences that the "continuing presence of experts from the human sciences, their arguments, and the results of their research had in administrative bodies and in industrial firms, in parties and parliaments." In other words, these experts from the social sciences influenced the practical routines and decision-making processes in complex organizations. Yet they may also have had an impact on the discursive construction of meaning in the context of "social groups, classes and milieux" and in their everyday lives.[23]

In historiographical terms, the "scientization of the social" has supported two related aims. First, it has helped to highlight the relevance of the history of the social sciences for what is usually called "general" history, that is, the history contained in textbooks and surveys that barely ever mention developments in the social sciences. Social scientific knowledge about social configurations can thus be embedded in the history of twentieth-century Western societies more generally, and can inform the ways in which historians reflect both on the history and on the specific modernity of these societies.[24] It is important to bear in mind that such a perspective requires a detailed analysis of the key concepts, institutions, empirical tools, and everyday working practices from the social science disciplines applied in various contexts. There is no history of the scientization of the social without appropriate knowledge of the science used.[25]

Any history of scientization also allows us to conceptualize the intersections and interchanges between the science system and other social systems. This is relevant for the sociologists and historians of science who are keen to understand how social scientific knowledge is selected, represented, and distorted in other fields of society, as well as how persistent patterns of interpenetration between science and different fields emerge over time.[26] Yet it is also increasingly important for historians of modern religion to understand how sustained contact with the mass media, science, sports, politics, and other fields of society shaped the churches, and religious belief systems more generally.[27] The history of such contact is relevant for understanding how the semantics of religion responded to the irritations these influences posed. As we will see in each of the following chapters, Catholic theologians, sociologists, and psychologists had to spill a lot of ink to make the use of opinion polling, psychotherapy, and other disciplines not only intelligible to bishops and priests, but also compatible with the established standards of Catholic belief.

At each step of the application of social scientific knowledge, the truth value of this knowledge had to be legitimized; also, its truth claims often had to be corroborated by means of complicated and laborious, methodologically controlled regimes of producing and testing empirical data. This marked a decisive break with the knowledge regimes prevalent in the Catholic Church before the onset of scientization. Up to that point, knowledge had to be based on history and tradition, on theological assertions, or on norms and dogmas established by the church hierarchy, and, in the last instance, the Holy See. Thus, each newly introduced social scientific method encountered the objection that it might help to undermine or delegitimize the traditional set of Catholic norms and values, and that it hence might actually hinder the spreading of the Gospel rather than facilitate it. In this respect, the scientization of the Catholic Church was not only a struggle over values and over the appropriate response to secularization; it was also a fundamental challenge to Catholic theologians, who had to explore whether and how their own language and forms of reflection could be made compatible with a church that increasingly relied on social scientific knowledge. In the 1970s and 1980s, after more than three decades of intensive debates over the merits of various social science methods, German Catholic theologians published a couple of more systematic introductions to these issues.[28]

Toward the end of the period under investigation in this study, the controversy over the application of social sciences in the church had reached the phase of "secondary scientization."[29] From that point on, new sociological or psychological interventions in the practices of pastoral care were immediately confronted with competing blueprints and memoranda by other social scientific experts, as well as with the traces of earlier scientific approaches to reforming the church. The decades from 1945 to 1975 constitute a period of "primary scientization,"[30] which implies that phenomena previously addressed without any scientific intervention were now scrutinized and explored through social scientific knowledge. The process of primary scientization usually goes along with the buildup of new institutional resources, in our case primarily during the 1950s and 1960s, when various institutes for pastoral sociology were established in the West German Catholic Church, and when specialist theological journals dedicated their pages to social scientific knowledge.[31] Often, but not always, such processes correspond to the differentiation of new academic disciplines, or at least of new subdisciplines within existing ones. In this respect, the limits of the scientization of the Catholic Church become immediately apparent. Sociological approaches increasingly influenced pastoral theology, an established subdiscipline of Catholic theology, which made a decisive turn toward the empirical investigation of social phenomena. At the same time, the vast expansion of academic sociology at West German universities in the 1960s weakened the scientization of the church, as it led to a brain drain, with Catholic sociologists taking up regular academic teaching posts.[32]

Yet the allure of academia was not all that motivated these sociologists; in the late 1960s and early 1970s, their disappointment with the failure of substantial church reform was an additional motivating factor. Philipp von Wambolt, a sociologist employed by the diocese of Münster to assess a far-reaching plan for organizational reform that is detailed in chapter 4, is a case in point. Shortly after he finished working on this project in 1970, he took up a professorship at a technical college (*Fachhochschule*) for social work. In a somber farewell letter from 1972 to his former line manager Hermann-Josef Spital, head of the department for pastoral care, Wambolt outlined his reasons: while he insisted that he was still interested in pastoral problems despite having ceased to be a practicing Catholic, which put him in the category of "abstentious" or *abständig*, he explained that he could not find the appropriate "plug" for connecting to the church, and he had developed a "sore spot" about organizational "forms" that closed doors rather than opening them.[33]

Analyzing Postwar Church History

The foregoing discussion has already indicated that analyzing the process of scientization can open up a historical perspective that makes visible new vistas on the history of the Catholic Church in the Federal Republic. This is evident when the most important aspects of the history of the Catholic Church from 1945 to 1975—which also have a crucial place in historiography—are examined. From 1945 until the early 1950s, the dominant perception of the church was that it was a "victor among ruins." It had survived the war with its organizational structure largely intact and was morally unburdened thanks to its resistance to National Socialism. Having provided stability to many people in the rubble society of the postwar years, it recorded a large influx of members. The overfilled churches and the numbers of conversions and of people rejoining the church seemed to reflect a wave of re-Christianization.[34] Such perceptions and descriptions, however, derived in essence from church statistics, which comprised the first stage of the scientization of the Catholic Church. This web of categories and data from statistical discourse first provided the basis for Catholics' public claim that a re-Christianization of society was taking place in the immediate postwar period.[35]

In the 1950s, Catholic leaders invested great hopes in the mobilization of the laity for the apostolate. There were competing methods for achieving this. The first was to reconstruct the network of Catholic voluntary associations and of their larger overhead bodies, the *Verbände,* which the National Socialists had destroyed. Despite some concerns, this process was rapidly and comprehensively completed with the establishment in 1952 of the Central Committee of German Catholics (Zentralkomitee der deutschen Katholiken, ZdK) as the coordinating and most senior body of all lay associations.[36] The other method, which had numerous advocates, particularly among the clergy, was to bundle the activities of the laity together as part of Katholische Aktion or Catholic Action. This implied organizing people at parish level according to the so-called estates of nature (*Naturstände*, that is, married men and women on the one hand and young, unmarried men and women on the other). This model of mobilizing and integrating the laity in a hierarchical manner had already been discussed in the 1920s. In the Federal Republic, it continued to find many advocates among staff in the offices of the vicar-general in various bishoprics, and among Catholic students. However, Catholic Action failed to be implemented in practice just about anywhere. It reflected the intellectual thinking of Catholic elites far more than church practice.[37]

Both these methods of strengthening the laity's engagement faced a common problem: by as early as the late 1940s, doubts had begun to emerge about the upturn in church attendance really enabling lay mobilization in the long term. The analyses conducted with the help of sociographic research techniques soon revealed that, in reality, church participation was far from widespread among the core active, gainfully employed groups of modern society. The broad current of so-called missionary pastoral work thus demanded that the church break through the existing bureaucratic regime in order to replace "paper-based" pastoral activity with a "living" version that would take the laity's social environment into account. Sociography as a methodology of the social sciences was thus closely linked to an influential reform current in the church of the late 1940s and the 1950s, and provided decisive components for the specific perception of problems and strategies of action.[38]

The Reception of the Second Vatican Council

By the conclusion of the Second Vatican Council (1962–65), it was already evident that it represented a major caesura for the Catholic Church in the Federal Republic. This was not only the case with regard to the much-discussed and immediately tangible liturgical reform, which allowed Mass to be conducted in the national vernacular, but also, and primarily, in the sense that the council set the pace for the reception of sociological knowledge and methods. The main pastoral constitution, "Gaudium et Spes," for example, demanded that an "outside perspective"—to be provided by sociology—should form an important part of the church's self-understanding.[39] All the priests, theologians, and sociologists who had attempted to introduce sociological expertise to the church prior to 1965—from theologian and pastoral sociologist Norbert Greinacher to Bishop Joseph Höffner—had thus, in a way, anticipated the work of the council. The interpretation of the conciliar documents subsequently became an arena for progressives and traditionalists to argue about the justification for, and limits to, the scientization of the church. The examination of these debates provides a substantial contribution toward the history of the council's reception, an important "task" for historical research on postwar Catholicism.[40]

However, the reception of the council was intertwined with the politicization and polarization that had characterized the Catholic Church since the unrest and protest in the wake of the Catholic Day (Katholikentag) in Essen in September 1968, the traditional biannual gathering and showcasing of lay associations and initiatives. The protests in Essen emerged more or less at the same time as the dispute over the papal encyclical "Humanae Vitae," which firmly rejected the use of the contraceptive pill. Both events drew attention to a considerable potential for internal church conflict, which would indeed occupy it intensively in the years to come. In addition, the growing disagreement between many in the laity and the church leadership on questions of dogma and church policies came to the fore, turning the participation of the laity into a controversial issue. The discussion of "possibilities, limits, dangers" of "democracy in the church"—the title of a brochure published in 1970 by theologian Joseph Ratzinger—later Pope Benedict XVI—and Hans Maier, then the culture minister in Bavaria, climbed far up the church's agenda as a result.[41] This was the background to the first widespread use of opinion polls in the church, which reached its peak in spring 1970 with the distribution of the so-called total poll to all West German Catholics over sixteen years of age. The debate provoked on democracy within the church was closely associated with the use of opinion polls as a technology that allowed for the modeling and representation of a participatory public sphere.[42]

The Synod of the Dioceses in the Federal Republic, which took place in Würzburg from 1972 to 1975, attempted to calm the conflicts within the church. It had some success in this respect, thanks not least to its parliamentary style of deliberation. Its official task was to turn the council's texts into practical resolutions for all levels of church activity, from catechetics and adult education to the relationship between the church and mass media.[43] One issue in this context was the rearrangement of pastoral structures and the question of whether the traditional territorial, parish-based model had become obsolete. This was important not only because of the ongoing rapid change in pastoral methods and objectives but also because of the worrisome shortage of priests. The synod's resolutions on pastoral structures cannot be understood, however, without considering their prelude: the attempts at structural reform that almost all German dioceses had been discussing since 1967. In the extensive debate about the necessity and objectives of church planning, these reform attempts were indivisible from the use of methods from organizational sociology and were thus closely associated with a further aspect of the scientization of the Catholic Church.[44]

During the 1970s, a process began that would characterize the Catholic Church far beyond the end of the decade. In view of the ongoing conflicts and attention to the work of the synod, however, it went largely unnoticed by the public. As part of the expansion and differentiation of the West German welfare state, an unprecedented expansion of Catholic welfare provision took place. It can be seen most clearly in the statistics on the personnel resources of the Caritas organization, which provided these services on behalf of the Catholic Church: between 1970 and 1980, the number of full-time staff of this Catholic social services provider increased by around 48 percent from 190,000 to 283,000, making it one of the largest nongovernmental employers in Western Europe.[45] This process also marked a significant change in church history. For one thing, the emphasis of church work shifted from pastoral work in the traditional religious and spiritual sense to a secondary sector—providing assistance to persons in need. In addition, the expansion of Caritas was associated with the expansion of the provision of psychosocial counseling in the broadest sense. These counseling services, however, were based on therapeutic techniques from various branches of psychotherapy and group dynamics, whose acceptance and implementation in the church had ramifications for the traditional practice of pastoral work. The implementation of psychological concepts, which went hand in hand with the expansion of the Caritas organization, thus marks the final facet of the scientization of the Catholic Church up to that point.[46]

As these observations should make clear, the relationship between the Catholic Church and the social sciences from 1945 to 1975 was at all stages, and in all aspects, closely linked to central episodes and contemporary problems of church history. The research interest of this book, however, is to demonstrate the links between secularization and scientization by examining the context and origins of the application of concepts from the social sciences. If scientization means more than simply the use of certain methods, the consequences—intended and unintended—of using knowledge from the social sciences must also be investigated. This involves possible rationalization, bearing in mind that rationality in a church context is always a double-edged sword that can properly illuminate, but possibly also overshadow, the religious underpinnings of the church.

Also, the criteria for defining the "success" of applying social science methods were themselves controversial. Social scientists, theologians, and practitioners had different expectations and objectives than the bishops, diocese administrators, and active members of the laity—insofar as the sources shed light on the attitudes of the latter. To what extent, it should be asked, did the church approve the use of social sciences to observe functional differentiation, and what conclusions did it draw from this? Did the church use scientific knowledge in order to adapt its hierarchical structures to the imperative of functional differentiation? Which social science approaches did it take up enthusiastically, and which methods did it block? Did the lack of one method's success correlate to switching to another that seemed more promising for reforming the church and pastoral work?

As already emphasized, scientization often occurred not for its own sake but in the wake of reform efforts, debates, or conflicts within the church. The implications of these specific contexts are another area of inquiry for this study. Which conflicts within the church accompanied and influenced scientization? Did scientization lead to a politicization—that is, increasing bottom-up participation—and political instrumentalization of science? In light of the increasing number and intensity of conflicts from the late 1960s, can one still speak of a coherent process of scientization? Or did the church hierarchy simply use particular sociological methods with Machiavellian motives to retain power?

Looking beyond 1975, there is also the question of the irreversibility of scientization. The somewhat "fundamentalist" position within the church opposing functional differentiation raises the question of whether the conservative rollback from the late 1970s—which can be dated approximately to the year 1978, when John Paul II became pope—reversed the impetus of the Second Vatican Council, leading to a descientization of the church. A further question already asked by many critics at the time is whether scientization actually helped increase the church's options for dealing with social complexity. Given the consequences of functional differentiation, could the church enculturate belief to make it attractive to the laity? Or did the use of social sciences and the adjustment to societal differentiation reduce the church's ability to proclaim a rationalized and hence "watered down" Catholic faith in a form that remained compatible with tradition?

The State of Historiography

Finally, what are the implications of these findings for the social history of the Federal Republic? Much recent research on the history of the postwar period has overly simplistically painted the three decades from 1945 to 1975 as a unique "history of success."[47] Some historians use terms such as "liberalization" or "civilization" and describe the Federal Republic as triumphing over the authoritarian attitudes engendered by National Socialism and undergoing a far-reaching democratization of political culture from the early 1960s.[48] The emphatic terms and value-loaded normative statements these historians use to optimistically portray the Federal Republic's overcoming of the National Socialist legacy are problematic. In such historical narratives, there is also a strong tendency, from the perspective of modernization theory, to marginalize religion and the churches in the Federal Republic's history.[49] It is also worth asking whether contemporary history should really focus on the posthistory of past problems, that is, on the repercussions of the Nazi regime and the country's "coming to terms" with its legacy. Focusing on the afterlife of the Third Reich, historians of contemporary society miss the opportunity to contribute to an informed debate about the ambivalence and potential risks inherent in modern society. This study therefore takes to heart Hans Günter Hockerts's call to see contemporary history first and foremost as the "prehistory of today's sets of problems," and thus to focus on the background, context, and ambivalent consequences of the dynamics of modern society.[50] From this perspective, it is possible to recognize the continuing relevance of the history of the Catholic Church in the Federal Republic, even after confessional milieus had dissolved in the 1950s.

Historical research on the scientization of the social in the period after 1945 remains extremely patchy and disparate. Substantial monographs only exist for some selected topics, such as the implementation of industrial psychology, the significance of sociology for the self-description of West German society, and the effects of opinion polling on the political system and the strategies of major political parties.[51] A comprehensive study of the Catholic reception of psycho-analysis in the German-speaking countries still remains to be written, along the lines of the pathbreaking monograph by Agnès Desmazières on the same issue in France.[52] Research on the contemporary history of the Catholic Church, mean-while, has improved considerably in recent years. Wilhelm Damberg's pioneering 1997 study used the example of the diocese of Münster to cut a broad swath through the church's postwar history and, alongside fundamental issues of pas-toral strategy and diocese administration, also dealt extensively with youth work and school policy. Further important monographs have covered topics such as the social history of Catholic students and youth associations.[53]

In this study, I propose that the problems of acculturating Catholic belief in the Federal Republic should not be analyzed using the concept of the social-moral milieu, pioneered and successfully applied in research on Imperial Ger-many, but from the perspective of the church as an organization, including an examination of its pastoral strategies and internal structural problems. All these facets of organized religion developed in close conjunction with different aspects of the scientization of the Catholic Church.[54] There is, however, one important precedent for the current study, a monograph by sociologist Georg Kamphausen, who investigated the increasing influence of sociological ideas on the worldviews and practical endeavors of theologians and pastors in both the Catholic and the Protestant Churches. Published in 1986, his book is another indication that the period of "secondary scientization" was well under way at this time.[55]

Metaphors as Messengers of Meaning

Methodologically, it is particularly important for a history of the scientization of the church to comprehend the transfer of knowledge—that is, of categoriza-tions, issues, and theories—from the sphere of science into that of the church. Recent science studies have examined the special importance of metaphors as a form of language that enables and accelerates the interdiscursive placement of scientific concepts in other systems. Metaphors function as "messengers of mean-ing," making scientific meaning comprehensible without requiring users to deal with the complex scientific terminology. Metaphors can take on different func-tions. For one thing, they can illustrate scientific arguments, making them more convincing. Used heuristically, they make new perspectives on already familiar issues possible and allow users to explore them. And, used constitutively, metaphors not only transform earlier meanings and connotations, but also replace them with fundamentally new ones. The Catholic Church used metaphors in all these different functions in its scientization. However, some aspects of scientization, such as opinion polling, distinctly lacked convincing metaphoric language and thus made comparatively limited headway into the Catholic Church.[56]

The emphasis on the rhetorical power of metaphors not only forms a bridge to the approaches of conceptual history and historical semantics, but also focuses attention on the metaphorical and allegorical features of Catholic theological discourses. These derive primarily from the New Testament, which, like the Bible as a whole, represents a "dictionary of vivid metaphors." In this perspective, the scientization of the Catholic Church can be described, with a pinch of salt, as the substitution of traditional pastoral metaphors with others coined by the social sciences.[57] Scientization always involves describing social relations anew through the "lens"—to use an optical metaphor—of a specific set of terminology. Callum Brown offers a vivid example of this process in his analysis of the valence of statistical data on churchgoers in the Church of England. These statistics, first compiled in the 1851 census, were not initially intended to offer valid data on practiced piety. Rather, as Brown suggests, they were part and parcel of church "discourses on ecclesiastical machismo, national righteousness, class commentary or moral judgement . . . and require to be treated as such."[58]

Available Sources

Some characteristic gaps notwithstanding, a wide range of published and unpublished material was available for this study. Archival sources primarily comprise the holdings of various diocesan archives. Research in the archives focused on certain dioceses in southern and western areas of Germany, particularly Münster, Paderborn, and Munich-Freising, whose pioneering role in the reception of the social sciences was discussed in church circles at the time. Particularly notable are the dense and extremely accessible sources in the archive of the diocese of Münster. In addition to documents from the various departments of the office of the vicar-general, this archive also includes files from other institutions within the church, as well as from a number of Catholic associations, the diocese newspaper, and the Catholic academy Franz Hitze Haus (FHH).

The diocesan administrations, mainly the *Generalvikariate* (the office of the vicar-general in each diocese), underwent a process of rapid expansion and diversification in the Federal Republic. The diocese of Münster is a particularly good example of this general trend. In 1948, the *Generalvikariat* in this Westphalian diocese employed a mere 31 permanent staff, 15 priests and 16 laypersons. By 1974, at the end of the period under scrutiny in this study, that figure had risen to 417, by then comprising only a minority of 67 priests and members of religious orders and 350 lay employees.[59] This rapid expansion of church administration at the diocesan level was, in fact, a key precondition for the scientization of the Catholic Church, as it provided ever-increasing resources and sophistication in the planning and delivery of pastoral services. Yet, perhaps counterintuitively, this expansion of manpower was not always matched by a concomitant increase in the depth and significance of the paperwork left behind by diocesan administrators. While the image of a bureaucratically regulated, priest-led church might suggest that the daily routine of the clergy working in the offices of the vicar-general involved comprehensive written documentation, as practiced in a state administration, this was by no means the case. Many ideas and consultations took place face-to-face and either went undocumented or were recorded only in short notes and summary minutes. This is a particular problem with regard to the departments of pastoral care (*Seelsorgeamt*) in the *Generalvikariate*. *Seelsorgeämter* were mostly established after the Second World War, although some dioceses had precursors of these during the Third Reich. In the Federal Republic, these offices were the driving force behind many initiatives for the application of social sciences, but they often left a very sparse written record. (Here, the diocese of Münster is an important exception to this, as the *Generalvikariat* has ample written documentation on the work of the department of pastoral care.) Moreover, many incidents and proposals were documented by ordinariate council members (*Ordinariatsräte*) and are now located only in privately held, unarchived files.[60] Bishops, meanwhile, primarily bequeathed normative sources such as sermons and addresses in their personal papers.[61] The archives of the Secretariat of the German Bishops' Conference (Deutsche Bischofskonferenz, DBK), established in 1966, are not open to historical research as a matter of principle.[62]

In addition, I have consulted a broad spectrum of published sources. These include, first, the books and booklets published by Catholic sociologists, psychologists, and theologians who were interested in the social sciences. To those can be added the abundance of study reports and handouts compiled in the course of Catholic social research—often only mimeographed "grey literature"—which indicate the core topics, strategies, and results of empirical work by pastoral sociologists. Particular attention was, second, devoted to scrutinizing the relevant periodicals, as this was an important medium for primary scientization.[63] The periodicals used in the study include professional journals of sociology and the sociology of religion, with particular significance given to *Social Compass (SC)*, a journal edited in the Netherlands that served as a forum for international discussion of concepts and research results. Journals for a wider Catholic public were also consulted, in particular the widely read *Herder-Korrespondenz*

(HK). Journals on pastoral practice contained a wealth of relevant information and discussions. Aside from the pastoral journals and supplements of individual dioceses, *Lebendige Seelsorge (LS)* should be given special mention here. With over seventy-five hundred subscribers, it was by far the most widely circulated Catholic periodical of its type in the German-speaking countries in the period from 1950 to 1975.[64] This type of publication reached a broad swathe of clergy members engaged in pastoral work and, at least in the case of the pastoral journals, also served as a forum where they could discuss their own concerns, suggestions, and criticisms.

Structure of the Argument

The structure of this study follows the observation developed by science studies that the differentiation, implementation, and reception of concepts from the social sciences largely take place through individual methods and their empirical instruments. Methods are variable programs with which the core scientific distinction between true and false can be ascertained using a series of practical steps. They thus "transform evidence and experiences into problems" and maintain their plausibility for as long as their problem-solving capacity can be assumed. In the process of scientization, this question of the practical use-value of social scientific knowledge was decided by the church, as the beneficiary of the expert knowledge. Seen in this way, the "truth" offered by the social sciences was a "construction of the end-user."[65] As already indicated, each of the methods was connected to a central problem of the Catholic Church after 1945. It was the discussion and application of certain methods that first enabled many of these problems to be articulated in the church's internal debates.

The study begins with the efforts to establish church statistics (chapter 1). In order to understand this process properly, we have to go back to the early modern era, in which the notion of Catholic piety based on orthopraxy—that continuous pious practice is more important than theological orthodoxy—came to dominate. This was the precondition for statistically quantifying Catholics' ties to the church. The comprehensive collection and documentation of statistics on important elements of "active" pious practice initially helped the Catholic Church in the years around 1900 catch up administratively with the Protestants, who had already wielded such data since the middle of the nineteenth century. Many Catholics in the Weimar Republic interpreted the ebb and flow of the figures as a "curve of destiny," as the political scientist Johannes Schauff noted in his 1928 study on the declining electoral fortunes of the Catholic Center Party.[66] In the Federal Republic, this observation soon deepened into the perception of an all-encompassing crisis, which raised the question of what was causing the decline in ties to the church. Sociography, which was taken up in the Catholic

Church immediately after the end of the Second World War, promised to deliver crucial answers to this question (chapter 2).

The social stratification of active, practicing Catholics who attended church on Sunday and the links drawn to underlying sociostructural factors influencing their behavior were supposed to offer leverage against the social causes of secularization. As a method, sociography analyzed differences between social strata and their impact on organized piety. Yet the usual practice of sociography in the West German Catholic Church did not go so far as to examine the attitudes, hopes, and motives of church members. This latter task fell to the opinion polls, which culminated in 1969/70 in the "total poll" of all German Catholics in preparation for the Würzburg synod (chapter 3). The methodological instruments used in this case focused the church's awareness both on the resonance that church dogma and practice had among the faithful, and on the cognitive dissonance between these teachings and an increasingly secular social environment. However, this approach was of no help where the church apparatus itself was revealed to be dysfunctional and one of the causes of dissatisfaction. Organizational sociology was able to provide analytic tools for the attempt to reform church structures (chapter 4). However, this venture assumed a willingness to renew the hierarchical apparatus, which neither the bishops nor the laity possessed, not even during the short period of widespread reform optimism at the beginning of the 1970s. For this and other reasons, it seemed sensible to begin the reform of the church on an individual level among the priests and the faithful, and to reactivate the Catholic faith through a focus on personal encounters between individuals and in small groups. Psychological concepts of therapy and group dynamics, which had already been discussed critically in the church for a long period, proved helpful for this purpose (chapter 5).

The result is an investigation that makes a spiraling movement through the social space, following the attempts of clergy, social scientists, and the laity, to find the social configurations that would help to stabilize the church in its encounter with an increasingly secular modernity. The study follows the hopes of various actors as they explored a variety of approaches for understanding the conditions that would stabilize the church. It moves from the outer boundaries of the organization to the internal worlds of the individual faithful. The first step toward scientization began at the very edge of the church, where it encountered nonbelievers and people of other faiths. From there, the interest in scientization moved to the center of the church organization itself, and to the priests and other individuals who represented the organization in their professional roles. Having arrived at this point, however, further research on the church as a social body was blocked and pushed in other directions. Having exhausted approaches to scientization that focused on the church as a collective, it reached out to individual church members. By this point at the latest, the stage of "secondary scientization" had been achieved, in which a "model of therapeutic intervention" had expanded into the Catholic Church.[67] At the same time, social scientific interpretation and advice had been introduced using so many different methods, and on so many different levels, that any new studies frequently ran into the interventions of earlier experts.

Notes

1. Mark Edward Ruff, *The Wayward Flock: Catholic Youth in Postwar West Germany, 1945–1965* (Chapel Hill, NC, 2005), 200.

2. Franz-Xaver Kaufmann, "Katholizismus und Moderne als Aufgaben künftiger Forschung," in *Moderne als Problem des Katholizismus,* ed. Urs Altermatt, Heinz Hürten, and Nikolaus Lobkowicz (Regensburg, 1995), 12.

3. Elmar Klinger, "Das Aggiornamento der Pastoralkonstitution," in *Vaticanum II und Modernisierung: Historische, theologische und soziologische Perspektiven,* ed. Franz-Xaver Kaufmann and Arnold Zingerle (Paderborn, 1996), 171–87.

4. Mark Edward Ruff, "A Religious Vacuum: The Post-Catholic Milieu in the Federal Republic of Germany," in *Die Gegenwart Gottes in der modernen Gesellschaft: Religiöse Vergemeinschaftung und Transzendenz in Deutschland,* ed. Michael Geyer and Lucian Hölscher (Göttingen, 2006), 351–79; see Ruff, *Wayward Flock.*

5. Ulrich Herbert, "Liberalisierung als Lernprozeß: Die Bundesrepublik in der deutschen Geschichte—eine Skizze," in *Wandlungsprozesse in Westdeutschland: Belastung, Integration, Liberalisierung 1945–1980,* ed. Ulrich Herbert (Göttingen, 2002), 7–49.

6. Wilhelm Damberg, "Einleitung," in *Soziale Strukturen und Semantiken des Religiösen im Wandel: Transformationen in der Bundesrepublik Deutschland, 1949–1989,* ed. Wilhelm Damberg (Essen, 2011), 23–24, 32.

7. Mark Edward Ruff, "Integrating Religion into the Historical Mainstream: Recent Literature on Religion in the Federal Republic of Germany," *Central European History* 42 (2009): 307–37.

8. Friedrich Wilhelm Graf, *Die Wiederkehr der Götter: Religion in der modernen Kultur* (Munich, 2004), 69–99.

9. David Nash, "Reconnecting Religion with Social and Cultural History: Secularization's Failure as a Master Narrative," *Cultural and Social History* 1 (2004): 302–25; Manuel Borutta, "Genealogie der Säkularisierungstheorie: Zur Historisierung einer großen Erzählung der Moderne," *Geschichte und Gesellschaft (GG)* 36 (2010): 347–76. Based on dated literature, see also J. C. D. Clark, "Secularization and Modernization: The Failure of a 'Grand Narrative,'" *Historical Journal* 55 (2012): 161–94.

10. Benjamin Ziemann, *Sozialgeschichte der Religion: Von der Reformation bis zur Gegenwart* (Frankfurt, 2009), 32.

11. Detlef Pollack, "Historische Analyse statt Ideologiekritik: Eine historisch-kritische Diskussion der Gültigkeit der Säkularisierungstheorie," *GG* 37 (2011): 1–41.

12. Steve Bruce, *Secularization: In Defence of an Unfashionable Theory* (Oxford, 2011), 57–78, 157–76; see also Benjamin Ziemann, "Säkularisierung und Neuformierung des Religiösen: Religion und Gesellschaft in der zweiten Hälfte des 20. Jahrhunderts," *Archiv für Sozialgeschichte (AfS)* 51 (2011): 7–19.

13. Olivier Tschannen, "The Secularization Paradigm: A Systematization," *Journal of the Scientific Study of Religion* 30 (1991): 395–415.

14. See, with further references, Hartmann Tyrell, "Zur Diversität der Differenzierungstheorie: Soziologiehistorische Anmerkungen," *Soziale Systeme* 4 (1998): 119–49.

15. For such an approach with regard to the Church of England in the postwar period, see Peter Itzen, *Streitbare Kirche: Die Church of England vor den Herausforderungen des Wandels 1945–1990* (Baden-Baden, 2012).

16. Charles Taylor, *A Secular Age* (Cambridge, MA, 2007); Brad S. Gregory, *The Unintended Reformation: How a Religious Revolution Secularized Society* (Cambridge, MA, 2012).

17. Gregory, *Unintended Reformation*, 11.

18. For a trenchant critique of Taylor, see Martin Jay, "Faith-Based History," *History and Theory* 48 (2000): 76–84.

19. See Niklas Luhmann, *Funktion der Religion* (Frankfurt, 1977); Niklas Luhmann, *A Systems Theory of Religion* (Palo Alto, CA, 2012); on differentiation, see Niklas Luhmann, *The Differentiation of Society* (New York, 1982), and more generally his *Theory of Society*, vol. 1 (Palo Alto, CA, 2012). On historiography, see Benjamin Ziemann, "The Theory of Functional Differentiation and the History of Modern Society: Reflections on the Reception of Systems Theory in Recent Historiography," *Soziale Systeme* 13, nos. 1–2 (2007): 220–29.

20. Marc Breuer, *Religiöser Wandel als Säkularisierungsfolge: Differenzierungs- und Individualisierungsdiskurse im Katholizismus* (Wiesbaden, 2012), 269–348.

21. Luhmann, *Funktion*, 232.

22. On this third effect, see Luhmann, *Funktion*, 248–60.

23. Lutz Raphael, "Die Verwissenschaftlichung des Sozialen als methodische und konzeptionelle Herausforderung für eine Sozialgeschichte des 20. Jahrhunderts," *GG* 22 (1996): 166; see Lutz Raphael, "Embedding the Human Sciences in Western Societies, 1880–1980: Reflections on Trends and Methods of Current Research," in *Engineering Society: The Role of the Human and Social Sciences in Modern Societies, 1880–1980*, ed. Kerstin Brückweh et al. (Basingstoke, UK, 2012), 41–58.

24. See, with extensive references, Benjamin Ziemann et al., "Introduction," in Brückweh et al., *Engineering Society*, 1–40.

25. See Silviana Galassi, *Kriminologie im Deutschen Kaiserreich: Geschichte einer gebrochenen Verwissenschaftlichung* (Stuttgart, 2004), 17.

26. Peter Weingart, *Die Stunde der Wahrheit? Zum Verhältnis der Wissenschaft zu Politik, Wirtschaft und Medien in der Wissensgesellschaft* (Weilerswist, 2001).

27. Friedrich Wilhelm Graf, "Euro-Gott im starken Plural? Einige Fragestellungen für eine europäische Religionsgeschichte des 20. Jahrhunderts," *Journal of Modern European History* 3 (2005): 241–42.

28. Raimund Ritter, *Von der Religionssoziologie zur Seelsorge: Einführung in die Pastoralsoziologie* (Limburg, 1968); Norbert Mette and Hermann Steinkamp, *Sozialwissenschaften und Praktische Theologie* (Düsseldorf, 1983).

29. Raphael, "Verwissenschaftlichung," 178–179.

30. See ibid.; Galassi, *Kriminologie*, 17–19.

31. See chapter 2.

32. See ibid.

33. Philipp von Wambolt to Hermann-Josef Spital, 21 October 1972, Bistumsarchiv Münster (BAM), GV NA, A-201-379.

34. Joachim Köhler and Damian van Melis, "Einleitung der Herausgeber," in *Siegerin in Trümmern: Die Rolle der katholischen Kirche in der deutschen Nachkriegsgesellschaft*, ed. Joachim Köhler and Damian van Melis (Stuttgart, 1998), 11.

35. See chapter 1.

36. Thomas Großmann, *Zwischen Kirche und Gesellschaft: Das Zentralkomitee der deutschen Katholiken 1945–1970* (Mainz, 1991); on youth associations, see Ruff, *Wayward Flock*.

37. Wilhelm Damberg, *Abschied vom Milieu? Katholizismus im Bistum Münster und in den Niederlanden 1945–1980* (Paderborn, 1997), 128–31, 139–52; Christoph Schmidtmann,

Katholische Studierende 1945–1973: Ein Beitrag zur Kultur- und Sozialgeschichte der Bundesrepublik Deutschland (Paderborn, 2005). It is indicative of the problem that the relevant file on Catholic Action between 1939 and 1964 in the archives of the diocese of Münster contains only a handful of papers. A direct practical implementation of the idea never took place. See BAM, GV NA, A-101–261.

38. [Wilhelm Heinen] to Pfarrer Gerards in Aachen, 5 June 1948, Historisches Archiv des Erzbistums Köln (HAEK), Seelsorgeamt Heinen, 56; see Alfons Fischer, *Pastoral in Deutschland nach 1945*, vol. 1, *Die "Missionarische Bewegung" 1945–1962* (Würzburg, 1985).

39. Klinger, "Aggiornamento," 184.

40. Franz-Xaver Kaufmann, "Zur Einführung: Probleme und Wege einer historischen Einschätzung des II. Vatikanischen Konzils," in Kaufmann and Zingerle, *Vaticanum II und Modernisierung*, 21.

41. Joseph Ratzinger and Hans Maier, *Demokratie in der Kirche: Möglichkeiten, Gefahren, Grenzen* (Limburg, 1970); see also Thomas Großbölting, *"Wie ist Christsein heute möglich?" Suchbewegungen des nachkonziliaren Katholizismus im Spiegel des Freckenhorster Kreises* (Altenberge, 1997).

42. See chapter 3; Benjamin Ziemann, "Opinion Polls and the Dynamics of the Public Sphere: The Catholic Church in the Federal Republic after 1968," *German History (GH)* 24 (2006): 562–86.

43. See Manfred Plate, *Das deutsche Konzil: Die Würzburger Synode. Bericht und Deutung* (Freiburg, 1975); for an edition of the synod's documents tabled and finally agreed to, see *Gemeinsame Synode der Bistümer in der Bundesrepublik Deutschland: Offizielle Gesamtausgabe*, 2 vols. (Freiburg, 1976/77).

44. See chapter 4.

45. Benjamin Ziemann, "Zwischen sozialer Bewegung und Dienstleistung am Individuum: Katholiken und katholische Kirche im therapeutischen Jahrzehnt," *AfS* 44 (2004): 376–82; see also Andreas Henkelmann and Katharina Kunter, "Diakonie und Caritas im Traditionsabbruch? Historische Perspektiven zur Kirchlichkeit der Laien in der konfessionellen Wohlfahrtspflege," in Damberg, *Soziale Strukturen*, 71–87.

46. See chapter 5; Benjamin Ziemann, "The Gospel of Psychology: Therapeutic Concepts and the Scientification of Pastoral Care in the West German Catholic Church, 1950–1980," *Central European History* 39 (2006): 79–106.

47. Axel Schildt, *Ankunft im Westen: Ein Essay zur Erfolgsgeschichte der Bundesrepublik* (Frankfurt, 1999).

48. Herbert, "Liberalisierung"; Konrad Jarausch, *After Hitler: Recivilizing Germans, 1945–1995* (New York, 2009).

49. An important example is the way the Catholic Church is referenced and described in Hans-Ulrich Wehler, *Deutsche Gesellschaftsgeschichte*, vol. 5, *Bundesrepublik und DDR 1949–1990* (Munich, 2008), 369–73.

50. Hans Günter Hockerts, "Zeitgeschichte in Deutschland: Begriff, Methoden, Themenfelder," *Historisches Jahrbuch (HJb)* 113 (1993): 124.

51. Ruth Rosenberger, *Experten für Humankapital: Die Entdeckung des Personalmangements in der Bundesrepublik Deutschland* (Munich, 2008); Paul Nolte, *Die Ordnung der deutschen Gesellschaft: Selbstentwurf und Selbstbeschreibung im 20. Jahrhundert* (Munich, 2000); Anja Kruke, *Demoskopie in der Bundesrepublik Deutschland: Meinungsforschung, Parteien und Medien 1949–1990* (Düsseldorf, 2007).

52. Agnès Desmazières, *L'inconscient au paradis: Comment les Catholiques ont reçu la psychanalyse* (Paris, 2011); Johannes Cremerius, ed., *Die Rezeption der Psychoanalyse in der Soziologie, Psychologie und Theologie im deutschsprachigen Raum bis 1940* (Frankfurt, 1981), covers only the Protestant reception. In a wider perspective see Anthony Kauders, "'Psychoanalysis Is Good,

Synthesis Is Better': The German Reception of Freud, 1930 and 1956," *Journal of the History of the Behavioural Sciences* 47 (2011): 380–97.

53. Damberg, *Abschied*; Schmidtmann, *Katholische Studierende*; Ruff, *Wayward Flock*; for an informative survey of other studies, see Ruff, "Integrating Religion." For a general interpretation of the place of religion in postwar Germany, see Benjamin Ziemann, "Religion and the Search for Meaning, 1945–1990," in *The Oxford Handbook of Modern German History*, ed. Helmut Walser Smith (Oxford, 2011), 693–714.

54. For a comparative approach, see Benjamin Ziemann and Chris Dols, "Church Reform and Organizations Research in the Netherlands and Germany, 1950–1980," in Brückweh et al., *Engineering Society*, 293–312.

55. Georg Kamphausen, *Hüter des Gewissens? Zum Einfluß sozialwissenschaftlichen Denkens in Theologie und Kirche* (Berlin, 1986).

56. Sabine Maasen and Peter Weingart, "'Metaphors'—Messengers of Meaning: A Contribution to an Evolutionary Sociology of Science," *Science Communication* 17, no. 1 (1995/96): 9–31. On the functions, see Sabine Maasen, Everett Mendelsohn, and Peter Weingart, "Metaphors: Is There a Bridge over Troubled Waters?," in *Biology as Society, Society as Biology: Metaphors*, ed. Sabine Maasen, Everett Mendelsohn, and Peter Weingart (Dordrecht, 1995), 2.

57. On metaphors, see the classic study by George Lakoff and Mark Johnson, *Metaphors We Live By* (Chicago and London, 1980). On theological metaphors, see Gottlieb Söhngen, *Analogie und Metapher: Kleine Philosophie und Theologie der Sprache* (Freiburg, 1962), 71.

58. Callum G. Brown, "The Secularisation Decade: What the 1960s Have Done to the Study of Religious History," in *The Decline of Christendom in Western Europe, 1750–2000*, ed. Hugh McLeod and Werner Ustorf (Cambridge, 2003), 43.

59. See the graph in Damberg, *Abschied*, 166.

60. Hermann Josef Braun, "'Nachdem das Archivmaterial die Freude eines sonnigen Herbstspaziergangs genossen hat . . . ': Zur Überlieferung des Nachlasses des Mainzer Bischofs Dr. Albert Stohr (1935–1961)," in *Nachlässe* (Speyer, 1994), 94.

61. There is, for instance, no archival record of the Institut für christliche Sozialwissenschaften in Münster in the archive of the University of Münster. The institute itself holds only a few lever arch files relating to seminars held by Joseph Höffner and Wilhelm Weber. I am indebted to Professor Karl Gabriel for granting me access to these files.

62. Letter by the Sekretariat der Deutschen Bischofskonferenz to the author, 4 September 2000.

63. Galassi, *Kriminologie*, 21.

64. For the figure, see the editorial in *LS* 26 (1975): 1; interview with Dr. Alfons Fischer, the cofounder and long-standing editor of the journal *LS*, in Freiburg, 30 June 1999.

65. See Niklas Luhmann, *Die Wissenschaft der Gesellschaft* (Frankfurt, 1990), 362–468, quotes 427, 438.

66. See Johannes Schauff, *Das Wahlverhalten der deutschen Katholiken im Kaiserreich und in der Weimarer Republik: Untersuchungen aus dem Jahre 1928*, ed. Rudolf Morsey (Mainz, 1975), 191ff.

67. Raphael, "Verwissenschaftlichung," 178–79.

Chapter 1

COUNTING PIETY
Church Statistics and Its Uses

Although this study is about the scientization of the Catholic Church since 1945, this chapter must first look back to the early modern period. The persistence of the statistical discourse, which continued into the postwar Federal Republic—and the church's practical application of it, which will be discussed here—cannot be understood without the long prelude, beginning in the sixteenth century, to an understanding of the church based on orthopraxy. This held that it was not the proper belief or the orthodoxy of individual Catholics that mattered most for the well-being of the church, but the fact that they regularly performed a circumscribed set of pious acts. Already in the early modern period, these pious acts were in principle quantifiable. But it was only after 1900 that the application of statistical methods began to reshape a concept of piety that placed less emphasis on the nature of belief than on pious acts. For the purpose of the following study, statistics is defined as the aggregation of data for administrative purposes. It should be distinguished from the complex mathematical models of correlation and regression that were applied after the Second World War.[1]

In principle, the statistical aggregation of quantifiable aspects of society can be applied to any social context. Like no other method, statistics is therefore fundamental to the battle between "classification systems," which is also a "battle for a monopoly on the legitimate representation of the social world."[2] Tables and diagrams illustrate taxonomic structures that create, collate, and objectify wholes. The statistical approach neutralizes interdependencies between things and movements in the social space, creating average, homogeneous objects that can be used for any practical purpose. It makes the administrative treatment of aggregated units possible, which, ignoring coincidences, can be treated as representative of the average. This means that no form of administrative engagement with social reality can forego statistics. The advance of statistics thus marks the first important phase of the "scientization of the social."[3]

However, statistical discourse is not only important for the activities of administrative organizations. Statistics' "suggestive power" makes this discourse very symbolic.[4] The individual data are always part of an integrated network of parameters and indicators seeking to capture the social world. Repeated public discussion and use of data, however, draw attention to individual units of measurement, which may then act as generally valid representations of the state of a social crisis. The gross domestic product (GDP) growth rate, for example, is used to reflect the condition of an entire national economy. In this way, statistics becomes an important means for society to represent and describe itself.[5] Statistical modeling focusing on a symbolic date serves as a point of reference for political conflicts and social apportionment of blame, wherein figures are affirmed, their relevance is questioned, and other quantitative "facts" are probed. Problems are brought to light, while other approaches are concealed or shrouded in the semidarkness of imprecise and arbitrary qualitative description.

Delineating the Religious Field

Statistics fulfilled a specific function in the Catholic Church: it marked the outer limits of the religious field determined by the church and enabled its administrators to identify inner homogeneity. Statistics documented the extent and shape of people's ties to the church in a way that went far beyond mere church membership in the formal, legal sense.[6] By making Catholics "who could be counted on" visible, statistics fulfilled an important purpose within the church leadership.[7] They delineated the field of *Kirchlichkeit*—a term denoting different forms of practiced piety that constitute an active church member. This function could by no means be taken for granted, however. In order for statistical measures of *Kirchlichkeit* in the Catholic Church to be seen as necessary, it first had to be clear which factors could be regarded as specifically Catholic evidence of loyalty to faith and church. Once such a canon of practiced piety had been established, it could, in principle, be captured numerically. Carrying out this task provided a basis for administrative activities. Such statistical calculation could only be introduced once such norms of a quantitatively defined orthopraxy had become routine.

As will be shown here, the Catholic use of statistics for delineating *Kirchlichkeit*, which was discussed intensively around the year 1900, had a double prelude in the phenomena of Catholic confessionalization in the sixteenth century and ultramontanism in the nineteenth century. The plurality of confessions put the post-Reformation church under "competitive pressure" and forced it to define clear standards of worship. It formulated clear criteria for orthodoxy in the course of Catholic confessionalization and attempted to impose them as binding standards, substantially changing the practice of faith. Some models of church organization also became more detailed and complex. A particularly important development was that the leaders of the Lutheran, Reformed, and Catholic Churches all attempted to regulate the practice of written communication between church authorities and local parishes.[8] Certain forms of religious practice were promoted, and institutionalized models of written communication regularly monitored compliance by the faithful. These developments defined a binding model of orthopraxy.

Piety in the late Middle Ages was an extremely diverse affair at both the regional and local level. The faithful were free to choose from the many spiritual goods, popular saints, church services, and types of Mass the church provided. They could hope for heavenly salvation and worldly consolation alike, easily combining magic forms of practice with forms of faith that relied on official church doctrines.[9] The challenge of the Reformation rendered this diversity of practices problematic, leading the Council of Trent (1545–63) to seek solutions.[10] The resulting Tridentine reform centered on the worship of the Eucharist in the Sunday Mass and its core component: Holy Communion. It was, after all, differences in perspectives on the Eucharist that represented the main point of argument between the confessions.[11] With the doctrine of the real presence of Christ in the Eucharist and the teaching of transubstantiation—that bread and wine is literally changed into the body and blood of Jesus—the Council of Trent took a clear stance against the reformers and created a standard liturgy for the entire Catholic Church in the form of the "Missale Romanum" in 1570.[12]

The Catholic Church's use of Latin as the sole language of worship markedly distinguished Catholic from Reformation church services. Almost as important was the concentration on High Mass, and thus on the Eucharist, as the Christ-centered core of the ritual, the essence of Catholic Sunday worship; during the era of confessionalization, the church began to replace more diverse forms of religious practice with this. Previously, the Mass had been just "one component of [Sunday] worship," standing alongside choral prayer, processions, exorcisms, and other ritual events.[13] From 1570 on, it enjoyed a privileged status, ending the complexity of the medieval church. The Mass's new importance made it clear that all churchgoers were now required to personally attend the church service. The pre-Reformation form of Holy Mass, by contrast, was construed as a "memorial service for the death of Christ" that did not necessarily require the presence of the faithful. Rather, it owed its efficacy to the quasi-magical practice of the priest ably saying Mass properly.[14] The Council of Trent called for more intensive Eucharistic piety, an ambition that also lay behind encouraging Catholics to receive Communion more frequently. The celebration of Easter marked the annual high point of collective religious service, and many church regulations and diocese statutes after the Council of Trent required the faithful to receive Easter Communion.[15]

From the sixteenth century, Sunday Mass and Easter Communion formed two of the classic five commandments of the church. Fulfilling these commandments publicly and visibly manifested the Tridentine ideal of Catholic piety. Pious Catholics were also to observe the holy days, as well as periods of fasting and abstinence, and, at least once a year, usually at Easter, attend confession.[16] In particular, their obligation to attend Mass and Easter Communion set a high normative benchmark. To implement this regime, the church needed long-term control and discipline, particularly as parishioners did not perceive the concentration at Mass on passive "watching" and "listening" as "a compelling reason for disciplined and full attendance."[17] In the rural parishes of the prince-bishopric of Münster, full attendance on Sunday was only secured over the course of the eighteenth century. The entire parish had to attend church regularly, punctually, and properly—that is, for the entire duration of the service. The establishment of this church discipline then made it possible to define *Unkirchlichkeit*—the absence of religious observance, making it an "issue for outsiders."[18] With some regional differences in the timing, the obligation to attend Easter Communion had become established as normal practice by the late seventeenth century—considerably earlier than the definition of *Unkirchlichkeit*. Priests monitored attendance by means of the confession slips.[19]

In addition to the new norms of piety, the sixteenth-century, Counter-Reformation Catholic Church also introduced new modes of written communication for making sure that they were comprehensively implemented. In particular, the practice of visitation was improved.[20] In the medieval church, bishops or their representatives would periodically visit priests and parishes, but this practice had been rendered ineffective by numerous exemptions limiting bishops' power. Only after the Reformation and the Tridentine reforms was visitation expanded into an effective means for the administration to monitor local pastoral work and religious observance. This provided a formalized and documented procedure with which to ensure that the required orthopraxy was implemented. While the sixteenth-century focus was on monitoring the qualifications and conduct of the clergy, seventeenth- and eighteenth-century visitation protocols served more to collect data on parishes' buildings and financial circumstances. Nineteenth-century visitation reports were characterized by pessimistic descriptions of the morals of the lower classes, where population growth, an increase in extramarital births, and growing poverty had begun to change traditional village social structures.[21] Documenting participation at Easter Communion, which was based on the confession slips, remained a constant part of the visitation protocols into the twentieth century. This was easy to carry out if only a negligible number of parishioners failed to fulfill their Easter duties.[22] However, the figure thus derived was something of an educated qualitative estimate. It did not provide a robust quantitative analysis based on an identical set of questions at the diocese level, let alone across dioceses.[23]

The confessionalization of the early modern period anchored a model of piety in the Catholic Church that was based not on moral or ethical virtues or even the quality of belief but, first and foremost, on "practical acts of belief" that made individuals visible "members of their confession." This differentiated it from the Protestant model.[24] Such a demonstrative concept of piety, which favored outward acts of faith, found itself on the defensive from the late eighteenth century, particularly in western and southern areas of Germany. In the educated classes of the urban bourgeoisie, the advancing functional differentiation of autonomous social fields of activity and knowledge led belief and piety to lose their universal applicability, becoming marginalized into a particular sphere of life. The reform ideas of the Catholic enlightenment, and of the liberal clergy they influenced in the early nineteenth century, attempted to adapt the church to these consequences of social change by substituting ritualized forms of visible piety with an inner piety and proclamation of God's word. Moreover, a more reflexive form of moral development would replace a mechanical form of penitence.[25]

The countermovement within the church known as ultramontanism opposed these adaptations to visible secularization trends from the 1820s. The integralist and fundamentalist ultramontane worldview was a reaction to the threefold challenge faced by the church: from the Catholic enlightenment in spiritual, the French Revolution in political, and the secularization of ecclesiastical property in material respects. The clergy initiated and largely steered ultramontanism, yet it could only achieve its objectives by religiously and politically mobilizing broad spheres of the Catholic populace who felt disadvantaged by rapidly advancing modernization.[26] The mobilization of Catholics for the ultramontane model reached its conclusion in the Kulturkampf or cultural struggle of the 1870s, when the newly founded German nation-state tried to curb the power of the Catholic Church by passing hostile legislation and actively prosecuting any clergy and bishops who offended against it. The faithful now had to decide individually whether they wanted to be "good Catholics." This profession of an ultramontane Catholic identity destroyed the homogeneity of other social ties, as can be seen in the example of the Catholic bourgeoisie in the Rhineland. The experience of the Kulturkampf widened and solidified the chasm between the Catholic milieu and the Protestant majority in the German Reich.[27]

The Kulturkampf resulted in the ultramontane norm of piety being implemented as a compulsory model centering more on "prescribed forms of worship" and "good works" than on the "personal relationship between the Christian and God."[28] These works symbolized the unity of the Catholic Church and its powerful position against the strong antichurch current in politics and society. The clergyman and member of parliament for the Catholic Center Party, Paul Majunke, pointed unambiguously to this context while taking stock of the still-ongoing Kulturkampf in 1876 during the Katholikentag, the biannual convention that gathered all the different German Catholic lay initiatives and associations. Every attempt to eradicate Catholics, Majunke reasoned, had had precisely the opposite effect; Catholicism had achieved an "undreamt-of power." Majunke backed these claims with convincing and easily quantifiable evidence: the "results of political elections" as well as increasing circulation figures of Catholic newspapers and numbers of associations. The "spirit of 'churchliness' [*Kirchlichkeit*]" that pervaded society could also be discerned in the "almost overflowing" state of churches in communities large and small, he claimed. "Church attendance had become more frequent" and many men were returning to the confession box after many years' absence.[29]

In the latter third of the nineteenth century, a model of observation became established in which the effectiveness of church norms was measured using quantifiable criteria. Loyalty to the church manifested itself through these criteria in the piety and organizational front line of the milieu. However, this routinized form of classification did not yet correspond to any administrative methods that allowed the strength of the Catholic camp to be comprehensively determined. The mass nature of ultramontane mobilization stood in contrast to the patchy and disparate state of the texts that documented its extent. With their localized, sporadic information and absence of aggregated summaries, the newly introduced visitation protocols fitted this pattern, as did the notes on religious observance that city or parish priests wrote for their own use or for the benefit of their successors. These writings were intended foremost to document the effectiveness of a priest's own pastoral work and the unbroken piety of his parish. A quantitative "show of strength" by the faithful also served to demonstrate the invincibility of the Catholic Church as a whole, particularly in the period of intensive conflict between "belief" and "nonbelief" that the Kulturkampf of the 1870s represented to ultramontane Catholics.[30] Both objectives are visible in parish chronicles, for instance. In the chronicle Krefeld priest Laurenz Huthmacher produced during the Kulturkampf, he noted not only the increasing number of first-time communicants and the number of Easter Communions received in the entire city, but also the number of Krefeld Catholics who made a pilgrimage to Kevelaer to protest the attacks on the Catholic Church.[31]

An exact reading of such documents reveals that even in regions such as rural Bavaria, where religious observance was traditionally more intense, a growing number of men were neglecting church attendance in the last two decades of the nineteenth century and staying away from Easter Communion.[32] Before the introduction of church statistics, however, attempts to compile the data on church participation in the visitation reports into an overall, up-to-date picture at the deanery or diocese level were isolated. The city deaneries of Cologne attempted to create such an overview in 1867 at the request of the bishop. In 1875, the diocese of Mainz compared the figures on the Easter sacrament in the city for that year to those for the years since 1847.[33] Otherwise, there was the *Schematismus,* a handbook that provided aggregated data on the structures of the respective dioceses. These were drawn up based primarily on the number of priests, worshipers, and parishes. At the start of the early twentieth century, some of these *Schematismen* also contained details of the dense network of Catholic associations.[34]

Hermann A. Krose and the Beginning of Catholic Church Statistics

Church statistics, whose introduction was intensively discussed from the turn of the twentieth century, were well suited to an understanding of Catholic piety that placed primary importance on demonstrating the *Kirchlichkeit* of individuals. However, there was no guarantee that they would succeed. In fact, the breakthrough of church statistics can be attributed to a specific configuration of events. Efforts to get the Catholic Church to critically accept and adapt moral statistics coincided with the escalation of the confessional conflict in Wilhelmine Germany, as the debate about the alleged moral and cultural inferiority of Catholics made especially evident. Only against the background of these conflicts was the German episcopate willing to allow the use of statistics for administrative purposes and to give such work an institutional basis.[35]

Initially, a small group of clergy aimed to establish church statistics. They could count on the support of some influential politicians in the Center Party such as Matthias Erzberger, Adolf Gröber, Felix Porsch, and Karl Trimborn, none of whom, however, campaigned for this cause in public.[36] The initiative came from the church historian and domestic prelate of the pope, Paul Maria Baumgarten, who worked in Rome as a private scholar. Together with the dean of Trier Cathedral, Franz Jakob Scheuffgen, he brought a motion at the Osnabrück Katholikentag in 1901 advocating the establishment of a national "office for church statistics." This was in part motivated by the importance of reliable figures on the effectiveness of missionary work. The proposal did not initially find any wider resonance, although the Katholikentag supported it.[37] Soon afterward, however, Hermann A. Krose, SJ, pursued the matter further with Baumgarten.[38] Krose (1867–1949), who joined the Jesuit order in 1891, was not only the first committed public supporter of church statistics; he was also engaged in a practical sense, compiling a "Church Handbook" that was first published in 1908, and making contributions to this statistical compendium over many years.[39] His motive for pursuing statistics did not originally lie in monitoring *Kirchlichkeit*, however. Rather, his interest in moral statistics had led him to produce his first publications in 1899 and then to study statistics with Richard Böckh and Georg von Mayr.[40] This path was by no means an obvious one for a Catholic, especially at the turn of the century, because by this time, two decades had already passed since moral statistics had been a "fashionable science."[41]

The Belgian mathematician Adolphe Quételet had established moral statistics in 1830. He aimed to derive extensive conclusions about the rules and patterns of social behavior by summarizing and comparing quantitative material on the frequency and average distribution of suicides, marriages, and crimes. The deterministic approach this implied was reflected in the construction of the "homme moyen," who embodied the normal distribution of social phenomena. From the beginning, the German reception of moral statistics from the 1860s concentrated on the problem of free will inherent in this approach. The mathematical implications and difficulties, meanwhile, were given little attention. This led to a broad debate on the relationship between statistically documented causality and human freedom: one of the "eminent but forgotten debates in German social sciences in the nineteenth century."[42]

Numerous philosophers, theologians, and economists participated in the discussion, particularly in the period from 1860 to 1880.[43] Only a small number of them, such as Adolf Wagner or the statistician Ernst Engel, followed a fatalistic interpretation of Quételet's theses. The majority favored the arguments put forward by, among others, Gustav Schmoller, who vehemently criticized the reinterpretation of statistically derived probabilities as an indicator of psychological tendencies toward certain forms of behavior—an approach that, in his view, lacked proper methodological checks.[44] The debate was brought to a preliminary conclusion in 1882 by the Baltic Protestant theologian Alexander von Oettingen, who used material from the field of moral statistics to argue for a Lutheran social ethics. He did not attribute quantitatively demonstrable patterns of moral behavior to the effects of external social rules, but rather to the inner will of the individual, which acted as the driving force.[45] Catholic critics of moral statistics largely concurred with Oettingen's objections to social determinism, as they shared his traditional understanding of religious observance, even though he was a Lutheran.[46] As late as 1901, a renowned Catholic encyclopedia contained strong words against the "materialist arguments" of Quételet's followers, which, it claimed, inevitably led these scholars to "gloss over crimes against morality" by viewing them as a "product of the circumstances."[47]

Catholic critics also focused on the conceptual one-sidedness of moral statistics, which, they claimed, neglected "moral good deeds" that could truly be described as "free," but which were elusive to statistical "observation" and "calculation." After all, who counted the "daily prayers rising to heaven from pious lips," the donations made "silently," or the charitable activities of Catholic orders and associations?[48] Even Krose criticized the methodology of moral statistics, particularly regarding the "ceteris paribus" clause, which dictates, among other things, that when comparing extramarital births across different groups or even countries, sufficiently large control groups that share the same "living conditions" in legal and social terms should be chosen.[49] Many studies in moral statistics violated this requirement, he argued.

As late as 1910, when frequent counts of church attendance had already commenced, a priest from Baden justified the church's skepticism of statistics by pointing to the "criminal theory" of moral statistics and its use of average figures, which served to relativize morality.[50] Many clergy would have shared such reservations, especially when Pope Pius XII, as late as 1953, renewed his warning in a speech to statisticians that the law of numbers means nothing to "individual freedom of decision."[51] Nevertheless, moral statistics in Catholicism had to be reactivated after 1900 as a necessary theoretical and institutional step on the road to the central statistical office. This reactivation occurred when the church reform discussion about the causes of supposed Catholic inferiority was combined with the exploitation of this topic by Protestants for polemical purposes. In 1896, Georg von Hertling had initiated a debate within the church about the Catholics' detachment from the modern age in scientific and economic life. His argument that Catholics were insufficiently educated attracted attention far beyond the Görres-Gesellschaft, an association of Catholic academics, and also implicitly reflected on the status and self-understanding of the Catholic bourgeoisie in the era of ultramontanism.[52] In the atmosphere of intense confessional conflict around 1900, which mixed fear and perceived threats with feelings of cultural superiority from both sides, the dispute about the links between confession and economic performance in bourgeois society generated further polemics. It is difficult to prove, however, that it was Hermann Krose who "initiated" the conflict when he began to publish moral-statistical data on extramarital births, criminality, suicide, and divorces in several publications in 1899.[53]

Shortly before 1900, the debate on the confessional dimension of the figures Oettingen and other authors presented had already become so intense and theoretically confusing that one Protestant writer lamented a real need for a "journal of religious, church, confessional and moral statistics." The thematic breadth anticipated for such a publication reveals the extent to which moral-statistical discourse was an integral part of the debate of this time.[54] Krose himself referred to various Protestant pamphlets and presentations at meetings of the Evangelischer Bund—an anti-Catholic pressure group founded by Protestants in 1886 that orchestrated the confessional struggle against ultramontanism around the turn of the century—that discussed the "moral inferiority" of Catholics. Leaving aside criminality, Krose's evaluation of the material clearly demonstrated his conviction that Catholics had a clear advantage in moral matters.[55] Such seemingly precise evidence allowed him to recast their economic inferiority as an ethical superiority. Integralist forces, in particular, used this idea to try to blunt bourgeois Catholics' criticism of their own kind as backward and ultramontane.[56] A decisive reaction by the Evangelischer Bund was inevitable, however. The Evangelischer Bund produced various pamphlets that thoroughly refuted Krose's theses and demonstrated that, provided the "right methods of calculation" were used, Protestants had the better social and moral position overall—despite their poor results for suicide and criminality, in line with their "male character," that naturally resulted from their "greater levels of activity."[57] Faced with the parade of superficial and one-dimensional confessional polemics that made use of moral statistics, Krose concluded early on that only meticulous knowledge and analysis of the statistical data would enable Catholic scholars to use such data in the "interest of apologetics," that is, in defense of the proper (Catholic) teaching of the Gospel.[58]

The material and personal connections—in Krose's person—between the intensive confessional conflict around 1900 and the establishment of church statistics are not only evident in the debates about moral statistics. There was also a more immediate connection in the statistics themselves, as the Protestant churches in Germany had a long history of collecting data on the religious practices of their members. The social awakening of the *Vormärz* and the Inner Mission initiated by Johann Heinrich Wichern had required the collection of statistical data to paint an accurate picture of the situation to help win back the masses alienated from the church. From 1862, the Protestant *Landeskirchen* published annual figures as part of the Eisenach Church Conference. These included, among other things, the number of those who left the church, the number of divorces, and attendance at Communion. The data satisfied administrative needs. For example, it enabled the efficient use of funds for the creation of pastoral structures that had become necessary in the fast-growing cities. Statistical material also served apologist ends: for example, one could register the surplus of Catholic converts to Protestantism with great pleasure.[59]

Advocates of a central statistical office for the Catholic Church—who had been making themselves heard in the realm of theory and in various publications since the resolution of the Osnabrück Katholikentag—focused on precisely these two points: the usefulness of statistics in administration and apologetics. They emphasized the great importance well-ordered statistics had acquired for all modern state and other administrative activities.[60] In this area, they claimed, the Protestant *Landeskirchen* had a significant lead. Protestant pastor Johannes Schneider in Eberfeld had been publishing all statistical data in a "Church Yearbook" since 1873. In the competition between confessions, they argued, the Catholics needed quickly to "emulate" this example.[61] They believed that the organized use of statistics was not only essential to administrative work but could also be used to uphold the image of the church in public opinion. A statistical office belonging to the Catholic Church, they maintained, would help to "banish the notion of Catholic inferiority."[62]

Beyond administrative requirements, modernizing statistical work seemed to be important for enabling the church to chart improvements in its position. In the heated atmosphere of confessional conflict, the simple quantitative relationship between the Protestant and Catholic populace was a highly sensitive topic, as evident in a circular sent by the archbishop of Freiburg, Thomas Nörber, to his parish clergy in 1901. Nörber writes that statistical publications reporting a growth in the number of Protestants had not escaped the attention of the clergy. Pastoral work and the use of catechisms were to provide "resistance" to this "proselytizing," even though Catholics otherwise "respected the religious sensitivities of Protestants."[63] The first efforts to monitor the relationship between Catholics and Protestants using statistics centered on mixed marriages—which demonstrated the extent of confessional conflict in the nineteenth century like no other phenomenon and had been discussed intensively since the issue prompted a conflict in Cologne in the 1830s.[64] The Fulda Bishops' Conference had already addressed the importance of collecting statistics on mixed marriages in 1885. Beginning in 1886, there is documentary evidence that such statistics were collected by means of a questionnaire all parish offices had to complete annually. Neither the archdiocese of Baden nor the Fulda Bishops' Conference seems to have drawn any specific conclusions from the measure, however,[65] because the data were "very incomplete" and therefore "unusable for analytic purposes," as the member of the ordinariate in Freiburg responsible for statistics concluded every year without exception. This led to considerable uncertainty in the use of the data for pastoral work and publications, despite the original hopes of combating mixed marriages more effectively with the help of the figures.[66]

"Boasting with the Number of Conversions": The Context of Confessional Conflict

It was not only the confessional conflict surrounding mixed marriage that generated interest in statistics. Although they often resulted from mixed marriages, conversions between confessions were treated as an issue in their own right. This issue brought together all the ambivalent expectations of the future that characterized religious faith in Germany around the year 1900. A spectacular example, which was discussed intensively at the time, was the conversion of sociologist and women's rights activist Elisabeth Gnauck-Kühne, who had built up the women's group in the Protestant Social Congress from 1894 before converting to Catholicism in 1900.[67] A memorandum Hermann Krose presented at the Fulda Bishops' Conference in 1905 at the request of the central committee of the Katholikentag demonstrates the great significance conversion had for the advocates of statistics. Krose first argued that a central statistical office would give "clear insight" into the state of church life and, as a "timely modernization," would improve the church's public image. There was a specific and "urgent need in the interests of defending the church," wrote Krose, to be able to counter the "boasts of the Protestants and their yearly publications showing ever greater numbers of conversions." Such publications shattered the "confidence" of Catholics with weak faith while diverting Protestants from converting to the "true church."[68] Protestant literature, meanwhile, did indeed describe the higher numbers of conversions as an irrefutable strategic gain.[69]

At the same time, the example of conversions illustrates an ambivalent aspect of statistical discourse that delayed the full implementation of a central statistical office for several more years. Even Krose himself felt obliged to express the fear that publishing statistics on conversions for small geographical areas could be uncomfortable for individual parishes. Therefore, only aggregated figures were to be published. Nevertheless, it was claimed that even the "most fervent" Protestants would be unable to deny that the figures showed a positive outcome for the Catholic Church.[70] Meanwhile, the Protestant statistician Johannes Schneider admitted that he was unable to accurately document the number of conversions to Catholicism, while arguing that the Catholic Church would long since have published its own data were there anything to "boast about."[71] Both factors were decisive in the 1908 Fulda Bishops' Conference's explicit resolution not to publish figures on conversions when the Catholic Church took up its own statistical work from the provisional central office in Breslau.[72] Having published the relevant statistics in the first volume of his "Church Handbook" up to 1906, Krose, too, had to give in to the fear of a renewed polemic about the number of conversions. Only when the confessional dispute began to subside during the *Burgfrieden* in the First World War did the Fulda Bishops' Conference in 1917 open the gates to figures on conversions to Catholicism.[73]

The potential publication of data on active church participation also presented a significant obstacle to implementing the Katholikentag's recommendation. A small group of clergy around Krose and Baumgarten, including missionary author Anton Huonder, SJ, advocated establishing a central statistical office from behind the scenes. Likewise, a committee established by Robert Brüning, a lawyer from Trier and local Center Party politician, supported this goal.[74] It was clear to all participants that only the episcopate could establish the apparatus necessary to collect statistics from across the entire Reich. The only place with any sort of administrative forerunner was the archdiocese of Freiburg, where attendance at church and Easter Communion in the city deaneries of Mannheim, Freiburg, and Karlsruhe had been measured since 1905 and in the entire diocese since 1909.[75] Consequently, the plan set out in 1907 in a memorandum by the central committee of the Katholikentag, which proposed establishing a central statistical office in Berlin, was doomed to failure. It suggested using its own funds and those of the Volksverein (People's Association for Catholic Germany), which had wanted figures on the numbers of Catholic social associations. The central committee's proposal was a reaction to a resolution of the Fulda Bishops' Conference in 1905 that had proposed leaving such an office to the involvement of "private circles." The Fulda Bishops' Conference, in turn, rejected the new central committee proposal. Nevertheless, the bishops were prepared in 1907 to allow priests to collect the data privately.[76]

The Breslau cardinal Georg Kopp, a religious and political conservative, was particularly skeptical about publishing statistics, despite signaling approval of Krose's project in several letters. Kopp saw statistics merely as a secondary administrative aid, not as a science in its own right. To overcome these concerns, Krose suggested placing publication at the discretion of the individual ordinariates.[77] Kopp did, however, support the establishment of a provisional central statistical office, which was located in his see of Breslau. Together with Krose, one of Kopp's secretaries designed the first survey form, which was sent to all German parishes. Nonetheless, the aggregated and analyzed data was only published for some administrative districts. Krose simultaneously implemented the plan for an annual "Church Handbook" that he had pursued since 1906, but which could not yet contain any data on practiced piety that would count toward *Kirchlichkeit*. The generally positive reaction to the first volume of this handbook accelerated the establishment of the Breslau office.[78] Only after Kopp's death in March 1914, however, did the door to a central office tasked with collecting and publishing official church statistics for all German dioceses open. This Kölner Zentralstelle für kirchliche Statistik (Cologne Central Office for Church Statistics) took up its work in Cologne in August 1915 following a resolution by the Fulda Bishops' Conference.[79]

Building the Potemkin Village of Church Statistics

Church statistics provided a methodological instrument that—in the view of its advocates and the Fulda Bishops' Conference alike—was primarily useful for church administration at the diocese level. Unlike the irregular visitations or the priests' reports, which were full of "preconceived opinions," the tables of statistics made it possible to compare regions, deaneries, and parishes of the diocese, to recognize "pastoral problems," and to provide help. Statistics helped make individual priests, as well as those who worked in the offices of the vicar-generals, aware of quantitative relationships important to their pastoral work, allowing them to compare these over time or with other parishes.[80] Statistics reflected "facts," their "causes," and their "correlation" with other parameters.[81] Even so, whether the anticipated pastoral benefits were realized depended on the use and analysis of the statistics. With its focus on administrative purposes and lack of mathematical method, church statistics was, in practice, not dramatically different from older administrative models. Franz Groner, who headed the Kölner Zentralstelle from 1950, was the first to present another rationale for statistics when he claimed that the numerical analysis and use of factual information complied with the "Western ideal of the scientific method."[82]

The decisive difference from older techniques lay in the comprehensive collection and publication of numerical data from across different territorial units.

The statistics of the Kölner Zentralstelle encompassed all dioceses in the German Reich and, later, the Federal Republic.[83] Every one of the 9,350 parishes existing in 1922 and the 1,500 other pastoral areas and 700 deaneries had to complete a survey form each year.[84] The questions used were highly consistent, even though the number of questions fluctuated from fifty-four initially to a low of thirty-eight in 1919.[85] The first two blocks of questions covered the clergy living in the parish as well as the wider Catholic and non-Catholic population. The following three sections dealt with the number of civil and church marriages, baptisms of children born in and outside of wedlock, and church funerals. Then came the numbers of Communions per year in church institutions and monastery and convent churches and at Easter. This was followed by the number of church attendees on two Sundays during Lent and in September—the priest had to provide an average number here—and the number of those converting to or leaving the church.[86]

The priest was to maintain a card index that would help in the preparation of the figures on the local population. It was to include all Catholic families in the parish, with data on the type of marriage and number of children. Metal clips in different colors would enable priests to maintain an overview of problem cases and prepare house visits. The index would also provide more details on the information from the statistical surveys. Introduced for charitable work after the First World War, the parish index was intended to provide the priest with a point of reference for targeted pastoral work in a period of extremely high migration and fluctuation in numbers of parishioners.[87] All priests were required to maintain a parish index from 1919, using the help of the laity where possible to reduce the administrative burden. The Kölner Zentralstelle developed a common template to rein in the wide variety of parish indices. Priests in major cities often had their own well-equipped and staffed parish offices responsible for maintaining the parish index. As Maximilian Kaller's parish of St. Michael in Berlin included over seventeen thousand souls by the mid-1920s, his parish office was equipped with six staff members, a typewriter, and a copy machine.[88]

The largely uncontroversial questions and methods of statistical discourse changed little over time, from 1915 to the late 1960s. One topic of contention, though, was the counting of church visitors, which only began after the Fulda Bishops' Conference decided the issue in 1918.[89] A priest from Karlsruhe, where these figures had already been collected since 1905, demanded not only that such collection occur on the same date across the Reich, but also that it take place on a major religious holiday such as Easter Sunday. Church "visits on such days," he argued, showed that "many otherwise half-hearted circles do not want to cut their ties to the church."[90] The Freiburg ordinariate joined this call in 1915, arguing that attendance surveys in archdioceses had proved their worth for many years, even in major cities. In any case, the ordinariate argued that such counting was more valuable than pure estimates, which could "easily give rise to unfounded optimism." The archdiocese of Freiburg was alone in this position, however. Even the Kölner Zentralstelle considered such data collection impossible to implement at that time.[91] The Freiburg ordinariate also repeatedly demanded figures on the numbers attending Easter Communion, divided by gender. While this was normal practice in many parishes in Baden and some major cities, the Kölner Zentralstelle did not implement it, probably for practical reasons.[92] Other collected data came from statistical surveys that were never published, such as the number of secular priests giving up their occupation, which more than doubled from the end of the 1960s into the early 1970s. Franz Groner "discovered only through rumors" that Rome was collecting such data, and not even he, as the head of the Kölner Zentralstelle, could access the results.[93]

In practice, counting attendance at church and Communion posed considerable difficulties. Commenting on the work of the Kölner Zentralstelle in 1977, a "statistics working group" deployed by the Secretariat of the German Bishops' Conference bluntly stated the ineffectiveness of such a method: "A survey of the numbers receiving Communion and meeting their Easter obligations is not being carried out as this does not produce meaningful figures."[94] This conclusion drew a line under a statistical count that had been practiced for the previous six decades. In order to understand why the compilation of figures on the Easter Communions was terminated in 1977, it is necessary to examine the statistical office's methods for counting practiced piety. A distinction should be made here between technical difficulties and those caused by the hierarchical nature of the church organization, on the one hand, and those that resulted from the specifics of ultramontane piety, on the other.

"Form A" called for every parish priest to enter the numbers of overall annual Communions and those received at Easter, as well as attendance figures for Mass on two annual survey Sundays. These figures were checked and aggregated by the dean on "form B," and again by the diocese administration on "form C" when it compiled them for the whole diocese. Erroneous data or calculation mistakes could often be identified in this process at the parish level. The Kölner Zentralstelle could generally correct these, although it necessitated time-consuming inquiries.[95] However, the data collection itself seriously distorted the figures in the earliest stage. The Cologne ordinariate concluded in 1921 that the "usefulness of each and every statistic" depended largely "on the completeness and accuracy of the original material." In the same year, a Bavarian statistician judged the counting of church attendance to be "too problematic to ever deliver usable results."[96] The first head of the Kölner Zentralstelle concurred with this view, at least concerning the first survey, so that its results were only published retrospectively in the "Church Handbook" for the years since 1923.[97]

Counting posed several technical difficulties. First of all, the precise definition of a churchgoer was unclear; it needed to accommodate both church and practical criteria. According to canonical understanding, everyone who entered the church before the Eurcharist could be considered to have attended Mass. It was thus easiest to count everyone who entered up to this point and subtract those who left early. Provided the counting was carried out honestly, usually by the sexton, this method delivered relatively accurate figures.[98] For example, the 24 percent of churchgoers in the town of St. Ingbert in 1962 who arrived late and only in time for the sermon were included in the figures, even though sociographic discourse classed them as "marginal parishioners." A special survey carried out in a parish of Vienna in the 1950s showed that around 30 percent of all participants arrived after the Eucharist or left before the Communion started. This meant that around one-third of those present had not attended Mass proper from the perspective of the church.[99]

But how was one to count those "half-hearted" male churchgoers whose attendance went no further than the doorway of the church, where they would stand smoking while awaiting the end of the service? Their number was sizable both around the turn of the century and in the 1950s.[100] The student pastoral worker Robert Grosche, who was stationed in a village parish in the Rhineland, issued the following complaints about his male parishioners, and the methods used to survey them, in the church newspaper he edited in 1932:

> Furthermore, the survey figures even count those who—despite being in particular need of religious instruction—use the time during the sermon to take a walk around the church grounds. This is not to visit the graves of their loved ones—which in any case would be wrong at this time—but to burn their tobacco in the open air instead of the incense in the church. Obviously, the time available before Holy Mass is insufficient for them.[101]

The problem Grosche addressed ironically here was inherent in the statistical discourse. Its quantitative, exact approach implied a clean division between "churchgoing" and "nonchurchgoing" Catholics. Yet this type of counting was imprecise when the Kölner Zentralstelle—probably primarily for practical reasons—decided that all persons entering the church should be counted without checking how long they actually stayed. Particularly in urban parishes, the survey in the 1920s simply involved counting everyone leaving the church at the end of the service. Using this method, it was simply not possible to determine the precise number.[102] As the Freiburg ordinariate noted in 1915, the count at the end of the service also included people outside the church, at least on an estimated basis.[103] The practice thus gave up on the statistical aim to delineate the field of active religious practice as thoroughly as possible, instead opting to maximize the size of that field as far as possible by including those who did not practice according to standard. Thus, precise measurement was sacrificed in order to preserve the notion that the Catholic Church had an unshakable hold on its members.

Counting Easter Communion attendees was similarly problematic. Usually, the Communion certificates (*Kommunionzettel*) handed out at Easter time were used.

Although each person was to take only one certificate, in practice anyone who received Communion more than once was counted again (twicers). The inflation of the figures through such double counting also affected the measurement of church attendance. This figure still stood at around 5 percent in the mid-1960s in parishes in the Ruhr region.[104] Particularly in major cities, priests were only able to determine the numbers of those receiving Easter Communion with great difficulty, and even then without precise results. Confession slips (*Beichtzettel*), which generated better results, at least in villages and small towns, were only distributed by a few dioceses in southern Germany. To obtain more accurate results, Hermann Krose proposed that clergy use a confession counter. This device would have been able to identify, in addition to the last date of last confession, the significant numbers receiving Communion on more than one occasion during the Easter octave between Easter Sunday and St. Thomas Sunday the following weekend. Yet although Krose saw this as the "only means of counting Easter Communion in the major cities" properly, this technical aid was not deployed. [105]

Yet the real difficulties of statistically measuring people's relationship with the church lay not in technical problems, but in the church's hierarchical organization and in the premises of ultramontane piety. As early as 1919, the Fulda Bishops' Conference published a banal-sounding declaration to "dispel" parish clergy's "concerns" about scientific classification techniques. Church statistics, wrote the bishops, would be used "exclusively for statistical purposes."[106] The clergy's concern showed their lack of understanding of the purpose of such work and their unwillingness to invest the time associated with it. Many filled out survey forms "extremely superficially" or even put in pure estimates.[107] While priests who failed to collect the relevant data were supposed to be "courageous" enough "to admit" this in the 1920s, by the 1960s they were asked simply to provide an estimate.[108] Despite all the entreaties to make the "proper answering" of the questions a "part of the priest's professional ethos," many priests continued to regard the questionnaire as an "annoyance" and thus provided "correspondingly superficial" responses.[109]

Much more problematic than priests' reluctance to take on administrative work, however, was their fear of being monitored by the authorities. Many priests suspected that the diocese could use the information provided in the questionnaire to come to a comparative "judgment on the pastoral work of priests." Consequently, the Kölner Zentralstelle made the "accurate discovery . . . that priests knowingly provide incorrect information" in order "not to appear in a bad light."[110] This was not only due to their fear of criticism from the church authorities. The Kölner Zentralstelle rightly suspected that "some priests" maintained this head-in-the-sand policy "precisely" out of the fear that an "honest" approach would be an "eye-opener" as to the reality of their pastoral work.[111]

This report was relatively open about a problem that was otherwise taboo concerning statistical discourse. The sources only occasionally mention that many "doubted the accuracy of church surveys" even at the time.[112] As the history of the statistical apparatus makes clear, its establishment by no means aimed to provide an honest and exact evaluation of actual *Kirchlichkeit*. Rather, in the context of the confessional conflict in which it emerged, the statistical apparatus was supposed to demonstrate the inner unity and stability of Catholic piety. It was, therefore, exceptional for reports to mention the resultant shortcomings of the measuring techniques, and even then, only reports that were "not for public view" would do so. Yet these inadequacies were well-known to church statisticians.[113] The dean in the town of Villingen in Baden, for example, noted in a detailed analysis of the statistics available in 1923 that it was not possible to provide percentages without knowing the proportion of people in the parish required to attend Communion. Only once, he added, was information requested on the numbers not receiving Communion, and it was "well-known" that this figure was always too low and that doubling this number would be "nearer to the truth."[114] The Catholic electoral statistician Johannes Schauff, writing in 1928, also found it "somewhat improbable" that Bavarian dioceses such as Regensburg were still able to report participation at Easter Communion of almost 100 percent after subtracting children under the age of fifteen, who were not required to attend.[115]

In the 1950s, priests taking up work in new parishes could clearly see that their predecessors had "quite simply guessed" at the number of church attendees and communicants and provided "overly generous figures." The new incumbents at that point had to respond to critical inquiries from the dean with realistic data.[116] As the number of practicing Catholics declined toward the end of the 1960s, a growing number of urban parish priests refused to provide the façades for the Potemkin village of statistics; since the surveys did not enable "the real number of people attending Communion to be determined," these priests simply abandoned the procedure.[117] When the statistics working group announced the end of Communion surveys in 1977, it was simply ratifying existing practice.

The scarcity of personnel resources at the Kölner Zentralstelle was evident not only in the collection but also in the evaluation of statistical material. Only from 1920 onward was the head of the office joined by an assistant and an apprentice. Political science students also helped out at times with their basic knowledge of statistics.[118] In the 1950s, the Kölner Zentralstelle employed six people.[119] The most important medium for disseminating the collected data was the "Church Handbook," which the Kölner Zentralstelle itself published from 1927 on, taking over this task from Krose. Although sales were sluggish at first,[120] sales figures did not reliably gauge the level of interest in the church statistics presented by the handbook. The results were also widely discussed in the Catholic daily press, which praised the periodical as a "self-examination" of Catholicism.[121] The main church statistics were widely known among the Catholic populace.

Aside from the public discussion of the statistical material, the offices of the vicar-general tried to make it useful. This began in the archdiocese of Freiburg when church attendance began to be counted nationwide in 1909, with data initially compiled and listed by diocese. After considering "all the available figures on the religious and moral state of affairs," the office of the vicar-general then produced a list ranking the religious observance of all towns and deaneries in the diocese. When the data for all German dioceses became available for the first time in 1915, the Freiburg ordinariate could also list the position of dioceses in various categories.[122] Once church statistics had been collected for several years, it was possible to construct time lines that revealed positive and negative trends. Like many social historians of religion nowadays who take the figures of the Kölner Zentralstelle for granted, contemporary observers saw Easter Communion as a "good yardstick" of religious life. The church statistics that generated by far the "most" interest in the 1920s, however, related to interconfessional marriages.[123]

In the early 1950s, the Kölner Zentralstelle suggested that a deaf or otherwise disabled clergy member in every diocese should analyze the figures for each diocesan administrative district for publication. Given the already noticeable shortage of priests, however, not all districts could find a suitable person for this task.[124] Despite its limited personnel, the Kölner Zentralstelle tried in various ways to provide the episcopal authorities with the main results and trends. Apart from the annual reports, these included special summaries for each diocese that Heinrich-Otto Eitner (in the early 1920s) and Franz Groner (in the mid-1950s) sent to the ordinariates, although these consisted merely of a short manuscript that listed core data in the text and tables.[125] Even without such help, many vicar-generals "eagerly studied" the "Church Handbook" and—in light of the longer intervals between volumes after 1945—always sought the latest figures.[126] Deans and deanery conferences also discussed the statistical findings.[127] Particularly in the crisis around the year 1970, as growing numbers of Catholics were leaving the church, the latest data from Cologne proved indispensable to diocesan pastoral workers and heads of parish assemblies discussing the worrying "religious situation."[128]

The level of mathematical abstraction and differentiation used in analyzing the hard-won material remained low. It was not until 1954 that the ordinariate received data with participation differentiated according to settlement size. That "continuing religious secularization . . . was most evident in the cities" was "no new discovery" for experienced clergy, although the "extent of the difference certainly was."[129] Two key statistics, such as the number of attendees at church and Communion, were provided in raw form throughout and related to the total number of Catholics living in the relevant area. The statisticians were well aware that differentiating by age of population across regions and time was useful detail that, had it been provided, would have enabled them to take into account the proportion of children not yet required to receive Communion and a rough estimate of those unable to attend due to age or sickness. This would make the information "look better," but only "at the cost of its reliability."[130] Only sporadically did any analysis use the differentiation of Communion figures for convent, institutional, and pilgrimage churches. These statistics revealed whether changes affected those who received Communion frequently any differently than parishioners who only received Communion occasionally. In the dioceses of Cologne and Trier, for example, statistics helped to isolate the "religious decline" accurately to the second group, whereas believers with more intensive ties to the church experienced "stagnation" but no decline.[131]

Defending the Catholic Faith through Numbers

The Kölner Zentralstelle gave the Catholic Church in Germany an apparatus for measuring ties to the church that remained unique in the whole of Europe for many years. Only after the Second World War were comparable instruments established in Belgium, Austria, and England.[132] In Switzerland, precise information for the controversial analysis of church attendance was not available until the late 1950s. The sociographic studies carried out in the larger towns during that decade finally achieved clarity there. In the Netherlands, the Catholic Church only introduced a central survey form in 1956, which the Katholiek Sociaal-Kerkelijk Institut (KASKI, Catholic Institute for Social-Ecclesiastical Research) analyzed—this was the central sociological research institution of the dioceses in the Netherlands.[133]

At no point, however, was the integration of statistics into church work that the Kölner Zentralstelle achieved ever followed up by intensive use of statistics in pastoral work. Though it was stated in 1933 that statistical evidence of "damage" to religious life would spur the clergy to "greater vigor in their pastoral work,"[134] both statisticians and clergy felt that a clear demonstration of causal relations would have been necessary to generate such an effect. Such causal relations were only rarely spelled out, however. Already in the interwar period, for example, the lower level of religious observance in urban areas could be determined "almost with mathematical precision" using a formula that applied everywhere except to the cities of the Ruhr region: "The more residents a town has, the lower the proportionate level of church activity."[135] Only a short period later, however, there were unmistakable signals of declining religious practice in the countryside, too. Explanations concerning why this was the case and how the trend could be countered were vague. There was reference to a likely "decline in positive mechanisms of social control in village life" but not to any possible remedies.[136]

Even when the statistical material did seem to suggest a causal relationship, it did not offer the church a starting point for tailoring action to specific problems. One example was the birthrate in Germany, which had been declining since 1900 and was also reflected in falling birthrates in Catholic marriages. A dean in Baden described this trend as early as 1923 as the "sorest point of church statistics," linking it to the political discourse that had intensified since the First

World War on the declining strength of the German body politic (*Volkskraft*). Nevertheless, he thought he had found a way to prevent "such penitents" from slipping through the net of pastoral control. On major confession days, the confessors were to discuss their questions and intentions in advance for "the ease of committing sin often comes from the ease of absolution."[137] In the same period, the ordinariate in Freiburg merely explained the declining birthrate as "a crisis of obedience" and was unable to suggest any solutions.[138]

The vagueness of statistics for analyzing causal relationships is also evident in a note by Joseph Teusch dating from 1964, in which he aimed to substantiate his remarks on the "marital morals" of Catholics. The vicar-general of Cologne probably presented these to the *Geistlicher Rat,* or spiritual council of the archdiocese, which consisted of members of the cathedral chapter and the "real" spiritual councils, that is, those not simply appointed on an honorary basis. This committee, which met weekly in most German dioceses, advised the bishop and thus had considerable influence on the administration of the diocese.[139] Using the data on the relative numbers of births in Catholic, Protestant, and mixed-confession marriages available in the "Church Handbook," Teusch identified a general convergence of the birthrate in Catholic marriages toward the lower level of Protestant and mixed-confession marriages in the postwar period. Teusch attributed this to the "corrosion of public morals" and ethical concepts by the mass media and cited the Ingmar Bergman film *The Silence* (1963), with its theme of incestuous desire, as an example. He also placed the blame on "creeping" secularization. Ultimately for Teusch, however, one determined the other: "practicing bad morals in marriage immunizes [one] against sacramental life."[140]

Where such tautological arguments were avoided, statistical analysis soon led to the complaint that the collected information "was not informative enough" to solve specific pastoral problems. This was the case, for example, at the pastoral council (*Seelsorgerat*) of the diocese of Münster. This was one of the new bodies introduced across Germany in the late 1960s in the wake of the Second Vatican Council in which members of the laity cooperated with priests in governing the diocese. In 1968, at only its second meeting, the pastoral council discussed pastoral work for those "alienated from the church" using a collection of "statistics of church attendance" from 1953 to 1966. Several participants wanted more precise information, particularly on "young people who stayed away from church" and on the different reasons for abstaining from church that applied to different age groups. This was not forthcoming from the statistical approach, which was equally unable to provide a precise evaluation of subjective attitudes toward the relevance and legitimacy of church commandments among older and younger generations.[141] An analysis of the causes of the wave of people leaving the church around 1970 seemed unnecessary in any case. The diocesan press suspected a "deliberate campaign" behind the relevant reports in the daily press.[142] In the church crisis of the 1970s, members of the Catholic Church rashly formed ad hoc explanations for declining church attendance, whereas the Protestants conducted a differentiated analysis of motives on the basis of opinion surveys. Otto B. Roegele (1920–2005) was one such Catholic analyst. Working from 1949 as editor, and later as publisher, of the *Rheinischer Merkur* newspaper, Roegele was one of the most important Catholic publicists and journalists in the Federal Republic. In 1977, he attributed the "dramatic" decline in attendance at Mass first and foremost to the "uncertainty" and growing dissatisfaction that had spread throughout congregations as a result of the change in liturgical practice decided by the Second Vatican Council.[143]

The statistical discourse was also characterized by reluctance to use statistics for pastoral programs in ways that would have explicitly or implicitly conflicted with normal practice at that time. Quantitative studies of religious observance would have strayed into unacceptable territory when the statistics they presented were used to criticize not the weak faith of Catholics but rather the pastoral strategies of the church. A 1954 speech by Franz Groner presenting the findings of statistics collected in Düsseldorf to the city's clergy provides an example of the rhetorical and metaphorical strategies associated with this. The head of the Kölner Zentralstelle concluded by stating explicitly that statistics should not be "misunderstood" as containing "even a word of criticism of the church's achievements" in the city. Statistics, he indicated, had "no right to make such a criticism." Figures were only able to reveal "developmental trends" with which the church could work, just as a swimmer crossing a river "allows himself skillfully to be carried by the current" in order to reach the other side. In Groner's view, the "city's growing position as a diaspora" could help to "carry" the Catholic Church. The Düsseldorf Corpus Christi procession in 1953, for example, had "more of a declamatory character" than in towns where the Catholic milieu was still intact. He saw an "opportunity" to compensate for the loss of quantity with an "increase in the quality" of church life.[144] Statistics on church attendance, however, were far too vague to be used in making decisions about restructuring pastoral strategies. They did not provide precise information about the "all-transcending" medium of belief, but rather schematic truths about quantitative relationships.[145]

The practical function and effect of statistics in the church and Catholic milieu, thus, should not be sought in effects on pastoral work. Rather, the Catholic "faith in figures" was "typical for a social form on the defensive against the influence of modern society." In this context, church leaders utilized statistics in an effort to provide a "constant in times of deep change." Statistics' most important symbolic function lay in "demonstrating the public effectiveness" of the Catholic faith.[146] Yet this interpretation must also take account of a structural problem: that the statistical discourse was never able to fulfill its role completely. In practice, the ambivalence of the discourse made it difficult to create a picture of the church oriented toward publicly visible orthodoxy. In the diverse "language of statistics," the very things that statistics were supposed to help present as quantitatively unambiguous and positive for the church in fact appeared to be ambiguous and indicative of crisis.[147] This grew more problematic when the figures revealed an advancing process of "secularization." The ambivalence could also be heard in the voices of those who, at the very beginning of the debates on introducing church statistics, were only willing to allow statistics on the number of conversions to be introduced if they showed a positive balance for the Catholic Church.[148]

The ambiguity and ambivalence of the statistical discourse manifested itself in different forms. This initially included lack of agreement over which quantitative parameters contained the decisive elements for evaluating the homogeneity of the Catholic milieu. Hermann Krose had cautioned against taking any one measure of church statistics "by itself."[149] Yet the pastors and laity who dealt with statistics had little chance of heeding this warning. As the range of expectations in the Catholic milieu changed, particular statistics received special attention and became symbolically loaded. Despite the central importance of the church commandments, there was by no means common agreement on which aspects of orthopraxy were important for defining a "good" Catholic.

Given the origins of Catholic statistics in the confessional conflict, it was appropriate that statistics' main focus was not initially on church attendance and Communions received but rather on mixed marriages. A priest from Frankfurt, reflecting a widely held opinion, referred to this as the "saddest chapter" of church statistics. In large cities in particular, he claimed, the Catholic partner in a mixed marriage developed feelings of inadequacy compared to the Protestant counterpart, which precipitated the Catholic's decline in church activity and led mixed marriage to become a "graveyard of religious life in the big city."[150] This issue also triggered a debate on the "thorny question" of how to raise children whose parents belonged to different confessions.[151] In the 1930s, some authors regarded the increasing frequency of mixed marriages not only as tied to secularization, but also in relation to pronatalist discourse on population policies, which many priests supported. The lower birthrate created a problem for the church "from the national [*völkisch*] perspective, too." The Freiburg priest Bernhard Welte viewed mixed marriages as an "open wound" through which the Catholic "people were bleeding to death drop by drop."[152] In the Federal Republic, such emotional language later gave way to more sober descriptions of the pastoral problem. However, statistics on mixed marriages continued to be useful in monitoring the church environment after 1945. Before the Kolping Journeymen's Association began to accept women members in 1966, it carried out a survey of the marital circumstances of its members and the number of interconfessional marriages.[153]

In the latter days of the Weimar Republic, electoral statistics also became an important quantitative means for German Catholic reassurance. Johannes Schauff's 1928 treatises presented on the desertion of Center Party voters should be interpreted in this context. Given the dramatic decline in the Center Party vote in the Reichstag elections of that year, the young economist offered several reasons to the party's executive committee in a memorandum on the "curve of fate of the Center Party." Schauff not only pointed to the continual decline in votes for the Center Party since 1874, but also to the considerable preponderance of female voters, without whom the loss of support would have been much more dramatic.[154] Bernhard Letterhaus, a member of the Prussian diet and secretary of the Catholic Workers' Movement (Katholische Arbeiterbewegung, KAB), began to pursue similar interests in his writings in 1928.[155] Although neither of these men's arguments resonated much among the Center Party leadership, they nevertheless demonstrate the use of electoral statistics in the quantitative discourse on the homogeneity of the Catholic milieu toward the end of the Weimar Republic.

Closer to the core of church statistics, counting attendance at Mass and Easter Communion was one of its key components from the beginning. The first more detailed analyses in the 1920s could still soberly observe that there were major regional disparities in the decline in Communion since 1916, and some dioceses even experienced increasing numbers after the end of the First World War. Statisticians also registered the continually increasing number of Communions received per year and per Catholic as a positive factor.[156] Already by 1929, however, Wilhelm Marx felt forced to point to the decline in Easter Communions observed in major Rhineland cities as proof of the "neglect of Catholic life."[157] The more significant factor, however, remained the overall rise in the number of communicants from 1924, which reached its peak in 1935. This high point served from then on as the benchmark for the number of Easter Communions in the Federal Republic.[158]

Statistics as an Indicator of "Crisis"

Church attendance and Easter Communion only took center stage in church statistics, however, from the mid-1960s, as the fall in numbers rapidly accelerated. In 1964, for instance, the office of the vicar-general in Cologne calculated the total decline since 1935. For the archdiocese's pastoral council, the collapse in church attendance by more than one-quarter between 1968 and 1972 represented the most important indicator of the "crisis." In the view of the speakers at the council, this was no mere "adjustment process," but a "full-blown religious crisis."[159] As this declining tendency proved to be "no temporary occurrence" and continued throughout the following decades, the associated mood of crisis provoked a surfeit of "crisis talk." "Suffering, lack of success, decline, headwind"— these were the phrases that fitted the perception of religious observance in the 1970s and 1980s.[160] This is clear from the story of a priest whose church stood on the edge of an unnamed major city, who broke down in tears before the empty pews. Elsewhere, too, priests were "dismayed and depressed" by the steep fall in church attendance.[161] From the perspective of the statistical discourse, the notion of a crisis of the church, "much invoked" from the late 1960s, appeared at its core to be a "crisis" of attendance at "religious service."[162]

A similar trajectory in the attention to specific statistical figures as seen in church attendance and Easter Communion appears with regard to church leavers. By leaving altogether, these people made the most visible break with their religion. During the Weimar Republic, relatively few left the church, and such departures were usually explained with reference to the numbers of mixed marriages, which often prompted such a decision.[163] As the numbers of those leaving the church grew in the period between 1926 and 1932—and again on a greater scale from 1937—so, for the first time in the quantitative analysis of religious observance, did the interest in the figures on departees. However, there was a political context to this interest. Konrad Algermissen, the director of apologetics at the Volksverein—the umbrella organization of Catholic lay associations—took stock of church affairs in early 1933, shortly after the Weimar Republic had come to an end. His organization had devoted itself to fighting campaigns by proletarian freethinkers associations that encouraged people to leave the church. In a report to Cardinal Bertram, he interpreted such groups as an indicator of a more widespread "alienation from the church" capable of "undermining Catholic thought."[164] In this context, statistics acquired a "great significance to apologetics."[165] In the face of the enormous campaign launched against the Catholic Church by the National Socialist regime in 1936, the Kölner Zentralstelle conducted various special analyses of the numbers leaving the church, again documenting the limited success of Catholic efforts to stem the tide.[166] These statistics did not attract widespread sustained attention until around the end of the 1960s. With the "reports of negative trends," this issue then came to occupy both the wider public and church bodies, although nuanced information about people's motives for leaving the church was unavailable.[167]

Nonetheless, the ambivalence of the statistical discourse arose not only from differing views concerning the primary indicator of *Kirchlichkeit*. The interpretation of the individual indicators themselves gave rise to ambiguities that weakened the statistics' explanatory power. Some of these attempts at differentiation already point toward the more complex approach of sociographic discourse, as could be seen from an early stage in the data on attendance at church and Communion. Even before the Kölner Zentralstelle had been established, a priest in Baden stated in 1910 that a parish in which the women received Communion an average of four times a year and the men "at least" two or three times should be regarded as being in a better state of religious affairs than a parish where women attended weekly but men only at Easter. Without wanting to "in any way undervalue" the frequent Communion of pious women, he argued, it was necessary to distinguish by gender when counting the frequency of Communion.[168] With this disclaimer—a rhetorical denial of unequal judgment—the writer positioned himself within the intensive discourse that had been taking place since 1900 on the necessity of more comprehensive pastoral provision for, and appeal to, male parishioners. This discourse should be understood as a reaction to the visible familiarization and feminization of piety in the nineteenth century.[169] A survey in a parish of a major city in 1927 revealed that only 6.2 percent of the Communions outside the Easter period were received by married men, compared to 30.3 percent by married women. The rest were attributable to schoolchildren, unmarried "young men," and *Jungfrauen* or "unmarried young women."[170] One priest called for the extremely high number of Communions in places with convents to be accurately assessed and not simply recorded as evidence of the "success of parish pastoral work."[171]

After 1945, too, a range of voices wanted to use church attendance by employed men as the only statistical criterion with which to evaluate abstention from church. After all, children in confessional schools were forced to the Communion rail, and women traditionally practiced their religion more intensively. Nobody should therefore be "under any illusions" about the high number of communicants resulting from this, it was argued.[172] The large numbers of practicing Catholics attending church were also differentiated according to their inner conviction. It was largely accepted in the interwar period that individuals' levels of religious observance "normally" corresponded to their inner disposition.[173] Nevertheless, attendance at Mass in an industrial city like Dortmund was seen as "particularly valuable" since, unlike in smaller parishes, people attended on the basis of their own "conviction" rather than social pressure.[174]

From the beginning, the view of church practice and the pastoral situation from within the statistical discourse oscillated between hope and apprehension, between declaring the shortcomings and praising the successes of pastoral work. Thus, the discourse failed to fulfill its aim of protecting the Catholic Church from both "dangerous illusions" and "unwarranted pessimism."[175] Even the first statistical analyses were characterized by this ambiguity, interpreting the figures, however "unsatisfactory" they appeared, as "a promising indicator" for the future.[176] Although the "picture painted by statistics" in Dortmund in the late 1920s was a "dark" one, it was argued, Catholics had to "remain optimists like the Redeemer himself."[177] This fluctuation from one extreme to the other remained dominant in the period after the Second World War. Pastoral "optimism" was to be upheld as a "general rule" of the apostolate.[178] In the 1950s, too, the figures were interpreted as showing a "slight but steady decline" in some areas but "pleasing progress" in others. Cardinal Frings, for instance, presented the first part of his report at the Fulda Autumn Bishops' Conference in 1956 under the title "What the Figures Tell Us." He emphasized the increasing spiritual exercises, the "comforting" number of charitable associations, and the 244 Catholic newspapers in print.[179]

It was only in the 1960s that the statistical discourse began gradually to lose its ambivalence. It became clear in the course of this decade that "statistics, when it comes to the figures" would be depressing to all pastoral workers whose main interest was orthopraxy and who aimed to "win back the so-called 'abstainers' [*Abständige*]." It was also clear that this depressing trend would continue "for many years to come."[180] Many priests were "dismayed and despondent" at the negative trend. Even making use of the "Church Handbook" to correct information in the press no longer helped.[181] Monitoring statistics now represented the starting point for a discourse on the crisis of the church to the extent that it was understood as a crisis of orthopraxy. In other words, the statistical discourse no longer provided a feeling of continuity in a period of social change. One priest in Württemberg in the early 1960s, for example, despite counting church attendance three times per year instead of the usual two, saw the "same unsatisfactory result" every time, because his parishioners chose to make country excursions by car rather than attend church as they had in "earlier times."[182]

Thus, it could no longer be denied that "secularization" was causing declining church attendance.[183] As the crisis solidified, church statistics finally ceased to be characterized primarily by confessional conflict. In the late 1920s, Hermann Krose had already warned the Catholic Church not to "flaunt successful figures" vis-à-vis the Protestants.[184] This isolated confession of the church's weakness had given way by 1973 to a feeling of ecumenical solidarity. In that year, the sisterhood of the Heimatmission (Home Mission) in Munich, which had been active in preparing local statistical materials since 1922, presented its latest findings. That it also printed figures from the Protestant Church was not intended to prompt the question of which church was better. Rather, the practice was meant to make observers aware that "encounters with God and consistent discipleship are equally difficult for both confessions these days."[185] The director responsible for the Heimatmission "used the keyword 'recession'" when presenting the figures.[186]

In the 1950s, pastoral literature came to describe "habitual neglect of Sunday Mass" as a "pastoral problem." A different understanding of the model of orthopraxy was considered, particularly in discussions associated with the sociographic discourse about opportunities for "missionary pastoral work." This new understanding would no longer reduce orthodoxy to quantifiable aspects of piety alone.[187] Outside missionary pastoral work, relativizing the importance of the Sabbath, was decisively rejected at an early stage of deliberations, despite growing recognition that church attendance was "no longer the only measure of all things religious" and, when used as the only criterion, created a mere façade of "apparent piety."[188] However, in view of many priests' "serious concerns" about the continual decline in the number of practicing Catholics, desperation seems to have prompted some reactions. For example, Franz Hengsbach, the bishop of Essen, wrote a letter to the diocese in 1966 interpreting payment of the church tax as a "conscious declaration of belonging to the church." Hengsbach's remarks remained within the territory of statistical discourse, although he emphasized "that statistics can say little about people's faith and their willingness to act accordingly in everyday life."[189] The pressure of growing secularization tended to multiply further the duties that church orthopraxy imposed on the laity. The pastoral council of the diocese of Münster passed recommendations in November 1968 on the "concerns about those alienated from the church" that reinterpreted the meaning of the phrase "practicing Christian." Alongside participation in the Eucharist, "indispensable signs of Christian behavior" now included charitable acts and the "apostolate" of "responsibility for the world," that is, paying general attention to the problems of the secular world.[190]

Catholic circles rejected any deeper examination of Sunday worship as "self-Protestantization" of Catholicism. Critics did not take the view introduced in theological discussion after the Second World War, particularly by Karl Rahner, that "inner commitment" determined the value of a religious act to mean that "outward declaration of faith" was "unimportant" or even "inferior."[191] Considering that more than half of Catholics were no longer practicing, Joseph Ratzinger concluded as early as 1958 that it was necessary to sacrifice the wide "radius of church activity," which in any case involved an element of self-deception. He believed that the self-demarcation of Christianity would necessarily lead to a "small flock" in order to make the task of preaching faith "more realistic."[192] Despite many "reservations" among church members about "Sunday worship," the Würzburg Synod of the Dioceses in the Federal Republic, which met from 1972 to 1975, held fast to its view of the compulsory nature and significance of Sunday worship in its resolutions on religious service.[193] Missing the celebration of the Eucharist "without a pressing reason" was no longer seen as a "grave sin" in every individual case, but nevertheless represented a "serious transgression against God and the parish." The list of circumstances justifying nonattendance does, however, reveal that this measure of ties to the church had been somewhat relativized.[194]

Representing Orthopraxy

Already in 1928, one observer in the Catholic cultural journal *Hochland* complained about a widespread "latent misunderstanding that the church and Catholicism had a numerical character." Barely ten years after the Kölner Zentralstelle had been established, he wrote, its work had helped to create a "popularized statistics . . . with which those who worship numbers can promote their faith."[195] The institutional practice of statistical discourse had been designed and integrated into Catholicism's self-characterization within a short time. However, these developments cannot be understood without their long preludes in the history of piety. Confessionalization, which began in the sixteenth century, and the phenomenon of ultramontanism in the nineteenth century, shaped and promoted a model of participation in the church that favored publicly visible acts of orthopraxy over the true belief in orthodoxy. At the same time, measurement of such acts only became a fully quantitative model when confessional tensions regarding mixed marriages and conversions intensified in their symbolism around the year 1900. Statistics promised to present unity and strength where the Catholic Church needed an unambiguous profile in response to the confessional conflict. Statistical practices developed in the context of debates on moral statistics and of polemics that underscored the great importance of this approach amid the "scientization of the social."[196] The references Catholic writers made to the conservative Lutheran Alexander von Oettingen show, at the same time, that statistical discourse crossed the confessional divide and helped to preserve a traditional understanding of religious observance centering on liturgy on both sides.

Nonetheless, statistical practices failed to meet the church's expectations. Instead of presenting proof of the stability of the priestly church that had emerged in the nineteenth century, statistics turned out to be ambivalent, generating emotions that oscillated from hope to apprehension and feeding a pastoral discourse that swung back and forth between self-satisfied optimism and complaints about the church's inadequacies. Only the irreversible decline shown in the most important indicators from the 1960s onward ended this ambiguity and turned statistics into a visible and much-discussed barometer of the crisis in the church. Since then, the Kölner Zentralstelle–generated statistics on the life of the church have become the source of disappointment that lost heights will never be regained.

Notes

1. Alain Desrosières, *The Politics of Large Numbers: A History of Statistical Reasoning* (Cambridge, MA, 1998), 12ff., 178–88; Theodore M. Porter, *The Rise of Statistical Thinking, 1820–1900* (Princeton, NJ, 1986).
2. Pierre Bourdieu, "Leçon sur la leçon," in Pierre Bourdieu, *Sozialer Raum und "Klassen": Leçon sur la leçon: Zwei Vorlesungen* (Frankfurt, 1985), 53.
3. Raphael, "Verwissenschaftlichung," 171ff.
4. Friedrich Fuchs, "Sittlichkeit und Frömmigkeit in Ziffern?" *Hochland* 25, no. 2 (1928): 305.
5. On self-descriptions of societies, see Luhmann, *Gesellschaft der Gesellschaft*, 879–93.
6. *Lexikon für Theologie und Kirche (LThK)*, 3rd ed., 10 vols. (Freiburg, 1993–2001), vol. 6, col. 11–14, "Kirchenmitgliedschaft."
7. Heinrich Sieken, *Methoden und Ergebnisse der katholisch-kirchlichen Statistik* (Berlin, 1930), 71.
8. Wolfgang Reinhard, "Sozialdisziplinierung—Konfessionalisierung—Modernisierung: Ein historiographischer Diskurs," in *Die Frühe Neuzeit in der Geschichtswissenschaft*, ed. Nada Boškovska Leimgruber (Paderborn, 1997), 45; Richard van Dülmen, *Kultur und Alltag in der Frühen Neuzeit* (Munich, 1994), 3:108–37; Heinrich Richard Schmidt, *Konfessionalisierung im 16. Jahrhundert* (Munich, 1992); for regional case studies on Catholic confessionalization, see Thomas Paul Becker, *Konfessionalisierung in Kurköln: Untersuchungen zur Durchsetzung der katholischen Reform in den Dekanaten Ahrgau und Bonn anhand von Visitationsprotokollen 1583–1761* (Bonn, 1989); Andreas Holzem, *Religion und Lebensformen: Katholische*

Konfessionalisierung im Sendgericht des Fürstbistums Münster 1570–1800 (Paderborn, 2000); Peter Thaddäus Lang, "Die tridentinische Reform im Landkapitel Mergentheim," *Rottenburger Jahrbuch für Kirchengeschichte (RJKG)* 1 (1982): 143–70.

9. Van Dülmen, *Kultur,* 55–78.

10. On the periodization, see Holzem, *Religion,* 455–70; on the Tridentine dogmatics, see Schmidt, *Konfessionalisierung,* 26ff.; Hans Bernhard Meyer, *Eucharistie: Geschichte, Theologie, Pastoral* (Regensburg, 1989), 247–64.

11. Becker, *Kurköln.*

12. Holzem, *Religion,* 383; van Dülmen, *Kultur,* 118–19.

13. Becker, *Kurköln,* 151.

14. See van Dülmen, *Kultur,* 71, 61.

15. Becker, *Kurköln,* 166–70.

16. Heinrich Joseph Wetzer and Benedict Welte, eds., *Kirchenlexikon oder Enzyklopädie der katholischen Theologie und ihrer Hilfswissenschaften,* 2nd ed., 13 vols. (Freiburg, 1882–1903), vol. 5, col. 161–64; *LThK,* 3rd ed., vol. 5, col. 1513. The Sunday obligations only entered formal church law with the 1918 *Codex Iuris Canonici* (CIC); see Georg Troxler, *Das Kirchengebot der Sonntagsmeßpflicht als moraltheologisches Problem in Geschichte und Gegenwart* (Freiburg, 1971), 163–69, 183.

17. Holzem, *Religion,* 393.

18. Ibid., 383–98, quote 397; Becker, *Kurköln,* 148–66.

19. Holzem, *Religion,* 296–310; Becker, *Kurköln,* 167–68.

20. Peter Thaddäus Lang, "Visitationsprotokolle und andere Quellen zur Frömmigkeitsgeschichte," in *Aufriß der Historischen Wissenschaften,* vol. 4, *Quellen,* ed. Michael Maurer (Stuttgart, 2002), 302–24; Becker, *Kurköln,* 1–29.

21. Peter Thaddäus Lang, "Die katholischen Kirchenvisitationen des 18. Jahrhunderts: Der Wandel vom Disziplinierungs- zum Datensammlungsinstrument," *Römische Quartalsschrift* 83 (1988): 268; Fintan Michael Phayer, *Religion und das gewöhnliche Volk in Bayern in der Zeit von 1750–1850* (Munich, 1970) 171–72, 179, 206.

22. Becker, *Kurköln,* 168; for the nineteenth century, see Phayer, *Religion,* 29ff., 247; for the twentieth century, see Oded Heilbronner, *Die Achillesferse des deutschen Katholizismus: Die Schwarzwaldregion als Fallstudie* (Gerlingen, 1998), 235–36; visitation forms and reports in Bistumsarchiv Essen (BAE), K 406, K 544; Archiv des Bistums Passau (ABP), OA 9220.

23. Tobias Dietrich, "Zwischen Milieu und Lebenswelt: Kirchenbindung und Konfession im Hunsrück des 19. Jahrhunderts," *Monatshefte für evangelische Kirchengeschichte des Rheinlandes* 50 (2001): 42.

24. See van Dülmen, *Kultur,* 121.

25. Rudolf Schlögl, *Glaube und Religion in der Säkularisierung: Die katholische Stadt—Köln, Aachen, Münster—1770–1840* (Munich, 1995); Thomas Mergel, *Zwischen Klasse und Konfession: Katholisches Bürgertum im Rheinland 1794–1914* (Göttingen, 1994), 70–94; Irmtraud Götz von Olenhusen, "Die Ultramontanisierung des Klerus: Das Beispiel der Erzdiözese Freiburg," in *Deutscher Katholizismus im Umbruch zur Moderne,* ed. Winfried Loth (Stuttgart, 1991), 46–75; on the Catholic enlightenment, see Richard van Dülmen, *Religion und Gesellschaft: Beiträge zu einer Religionsgeschichte der Neuzeit* (Frankfurt, 1989), 124–71.

26. Thomas Nipperdey, *Deutsche Geschichte 1800–1866: Bürgerwelt und starker Staat* (Munich, 1983), 410–15; Otto Weiss, "Der Ultramontanismus: Grundlagen—Vorgeschichte—Struktur," *Zeitschrift für Bayerische Landesgeschichte* 41 (1978): 821–77; Christoph Weber, "Ultramontanismus als katholischer Fundamentalismus," in Loth, *Deutscher Katholizismus;* Werner K. Blessing, *Staat und Kirche in der Gesellschaft: Institutionelle Autorität und mentaler Wandel in Bayern während des 19. Jahrhunderts* (Göttingen, 1982), 84–98, 132–45, 181–95.

27. Mergel, *Klasse,* 253–82.

28. Weiss, "Ultramontanismus," 858.
29. Cited in Ernst Heinen, ed., *Staatliche Macht und Katholizismus in Deutschland*, vol. 2, *Dokumente des politischen Katholizismus von 1867 bis 1914* (Paderborn, 1979), 79–81.
30. Josef Mooser, "Volk, Arbeiter und Bürger in der katholischen Öffentlichkeit des Kaiserreichs: Zur Sozial- und Funktionsgeschichte der deutschen Katholikentage 1871–1913," in *Bürger in der Gesellschaft der Neuzeit: Wirtschaft—Politik—Kultur,* ed. Hans-Jürgen Puhle (Göttingen, 1991), 266.
31. Dieter Kastner, "Oberpfarrer Laurenz Huthmacher und seine Aufzeichnungen zur Krefelder Pfarrgeschichte aus der Zeit des Kulturkampfes (1865–1880)," in *Katholisches Krefeld,* ed. Adolf Duppengießer (Krefeld, 1988), 2:169–70, 172, 176ff.; cf. Hermann Joseph Schmitz, "Die Pfarrchronik von St. Dionysius in Krefeld aus den Jahren 1886 bis 1893," in *Geschichte im Bistum Aachen* (Aachen, 1994), 2:212, 214–15.
32. Blessing, "Staat," 193ff., 247–48.
33. Jürgen Herres, *Städtische Gesellschaft und katholische Vereine im Rheinland 1840–1879* (Essen, 1996), 383–84.
34. Wilhelm Liese, "Die kirchliche Statistik," *Theologie und Glaube* 7 (1915): 102–3.
35. A fundamental source of information on the backdrop to the foundation of the Kölner Zentralstelle is a manuscript by the first head of the office: [H.-O. Eitner], "Die Zentralstelle für kirchliche Statistik im katholischen Deutschland" (manuscript), 1922, DBK, Referat Statistik. The Cologne records on the prehistory and work of the Kölner Zentralstelle were destroyed in a fire at the office of the vicar-general there in July 1941. Memo, 23 December 1941, HAEK, Gen. I, 32.12, 6; Report on activities of the Zentralstelle for 1941, Erzbischöfliches Archiv Freiburg (EAF), B2–49–28.
36. These names were mentioned by [Eitner], "Zentralstelle," 2, DBK, Referat Statistik; on Trimborn, see Hugo Stehkämper, ed., *Der Nachlaß des Reichskanzlers Wilhelm Marx,* 5 vols. (Cologne, 1968–97), 3:181.
37. Paul Maria Baumgarten, *Die römische Kurie um 1900: Ausgewählte Aufsätze,* ed. C. Weber (Cologne, 1986), 3–85; Isa-Maria Betz, "Die Beziehung des Kirchenhistorikers Paul Maria Baumgarten zu Koblenz," *Jb. für westdeutsche Landesgeschichte* 26 (2000): 305–45; on Scheuffgen, see Heinz Monz, ed., *Trierer biographisches Lexikon* (Trier, 2000), 398; cf. *Verhandlungen der 48. General-Versammlung der Katholiken Deutschlands zu Osnabrück vom 25. bis 29. August 1901* (Osnabrück, 1901), 138ff., 143–44, 277–78, 469.
38. Paul Maria Baumgarten, *Römische und andere Erinnerungen* (Düsseldorf, 1927), 359–60. SJ stands for Societas Jesu.
39. Benjamin Ziemann, "Krose, Hermann A.," in *Biographisch-bibliographisches Kirchenlexikon,* vol. 24, ed. Traugott Bautz (Herzberg, 2005), 983–86.
40. Hermann A. Krose, "Moral und Moralstatistik," in *Aus Ethik und Leben: Festschrift für Josef Mausbach zur Vollendung des siebzigsten Lebensjahres,* ed. Max Meinertz and Adolf Donders (Münster, 1931), 177; Hermann A. Krose, *Der Einfluß der Konfession auf die Sittlichkeit: Nach den Ergebnissen der Statistik* (Freiburg, 1900), 561.
41. See Monika Boehme, *Die Moralstatistik: Ein Beitrag zur Geschichte der Quantifizierung in der Soziologie, dargestellt an den Werken Adolphe Quetelets und Alexander von Oettingens* (Cologne, 1971), 32–88, quote 173.
42. Horst Dreitzel, "Süßmilchs Beitrag zur politischen Diskussion der deutschen Aufklärung," in *Ursprünge der Demographie in Deutschland: Leben und Werk Johann Peter Süßmilchs (1707–1767),* ed. Herwig Birg (Frankfurt, 1986), 81.
43. See overview in Alexander von Oettingen, *Die Moralstatistik in ihrer Bedeutung für eine Sozialethik* (Erlangen, 1882), 20–40.
44. Porter, *Rise,* 167–71, 177–92; Boehme, *Moralstatistik,* 89–95; Krose, "Moral," 174–76.
45. Oettingen, *Moralstatistik,* 794ff.; Boehme, *Moralstatistik,* 111–41.

46. Oettingen, *Moralstatistik,* 610ff.
47. *Staatslexikon,* 2nd ed., vol. 5, col. 522–29, quote col. 525–26; see Krose, "Moral," 176–77; Baumgarten and Krose, "Ecclesiastical Statistics," 270; for the Catholic critique of moral statistics, see Lor Haas, "Moralstatistik und Willensfreiheit," *Jahrbuch für Philosophie und spekulative Theologie* 13 (1899): 17–40; see also the text by the Thomist theologian Konstantin Gutberlet, *Die Willensfreiheit und ihre Gegner* (Fulda, 1893), 43–102.
48. Bernhard Werneke, *Die Statistik freiwilliger Handlungen und die menschliche Willensfreiheit* (Frankfurt, 1868), 30–31; cf. Hermann Krose, "Der Einfluß der Confession auf die Sittlichkeit nach den Ergebnissen der Moralstatistik," *Historisch-politische Blätter* 123 (1899): 480; Hermann Krose, *Religion und Moralstatistik* (Munich, n.d. [1906]), 7.
49. Krose, "Sittlichkeit," 545ff., quote 547. In relation to the newly introduced church statistics, see also J. B., "Zur kirchlichen Statistik," *Oberrheinisches Pastoralblatt* 12 (1910): 87.
50. J. B., "Statistik," 85.
51. For the speech on 11 September 1953, see Arthur-Fridolin Utz and Joseph-Fulko Groner, eds., *Aufbau und Entfaltung des gesellschaftlichen Lebens: Soziale Summe Pius XII.,* 3 vols. (Freiburg, 1954–61), 1:959.
52. Josef Mooser, "Bürger und Katholik? Rolle und Bedeutung des Bürgertums auf den deutschen Katholikentagen 1871–1913" (Habil., Bielefeld, 1987), 169–96; Martin Baumeister, *Parität und katholische Inferiorität: Untersuchungen zur Stellung des Katholizismus im Kaiserreich* (Paderborn, 1987), 39–71.
53. Baumeister, *Parität,* 73–83; quote: Armin Müller-Dreier, *Konfession in Politik, Gesellschaft und Kultur des Kaiserreichs: Der Evangelische Bund 1886–1914* (Gütersloh, 1998), 399.
54. Karl Feyerabend, *Katholizismus und Protestantismus als Fortschrittsmächte* (Stuttgart, 1898), 34–53, quote 39.
55. Krose, *Sittlichkeit,* 1, 99; cf. Martin von Nathusius, *Die Unsittlichkeit von Ludwig XIV. bis zur Gegenwart* (Stuttgart, 1899); Gustav Schulze, *Der Unterschied zwischen der katholischen und evangelischen Sittlichkeit* (Halle, 1888), 24–25. On the moral statistical dimension of confessional polemics by Catholic writers, see, e.g., Ludwig von Hammerstein, *Katholizismus und Protestantismus, Teil III,* 5th ed. (Trier, 1906), 98–103, 109–23.
56. With reference to moral statistical data, see A. Neher and O. Neher, eds., *100 Jahre katholischer württembergischer Klerus und Volk: Ein Beitrag zur religiösen Heimatkunde auf statistischer Grundlage* (Riedlingen, 1928), 94; cf. Mooser, "Bürger," 196–205.
57. Johannes Forberger, *Moralstatistik und Konfession* (Halle, 1911), 87, 90; Müller-Dreier, *Konfession in Politik,* 399–402.
58. Krose, "Sittlichkeit," 561.
59. Lucian Hölscher, "Möglichkeiten und Grenzen der statistischen Erfassung kirchlicher Bindungen," in *Seelsorge und Diakonie in Berlin: Beiträge zum Verhältnis von Kirche und Großstadt im 19. und 20. Jahrhundert,* ed. Kaspar Elm and Hans-Dietrich Loock (Berlin, 1990), 42ff.
60. *Germania,* 2 September 1904; Paul Maria Baumgarten, *Kirchliche Statistik: Wie steht es um die kirchliche Statistik in Deutschland? Ein Wort über kirchliche Statistik, statistische Beschreibung der kirchlichen Verhältnisse Italiens* (Wörrishofen, 1905), 9; Hermann Krose, "Konfessionsstatistik und kirchliche Statistik im Deutschen Reich," *Allgemeines Statistisches Archiv* 8 (1914): 285.
61. Quote: *Kölnische Volkszeitung,* 12 September 1904; cf. *Kölnische Volkszeitung,* 3 April 1905; A. Braekling, "Kirchliche Statistik," *Der katholische Seelsorger* 17 (1905): 365, 407ff.
62. Quote: *Augsburger Postzeitung,* 1 March 1905; *Kölnische Volkszeitung,* 8 January 1905; Krose, "Errichtung," 833–34; Memorandum of the central committee of the Katholikentage to the Fulda Bishops' Conference, n.d. [1907], EAF, B2–49–15.
63. Archbishop Thomas Nörber, 26 December 1901, to the parish clergy, EAF, B2–47–57. Nörber was clearly referring to a questionnaire sent to all parishes on 15 November 1894 on the "Growth of Protestantism in the Archdiocese of Freiburg," EAF, B2–49–25.

64. Tillmann Bendikowski, "Eine Fackel der Zwietracht: Katholisch-protestantische Mischehen im 19. und 20. Jahrhundert," in *Konfessionen im Konflikt: Deutschland zwischen 1800 und 1970: ein zweites konfessionelles Zeitalter,* ed. Olaf Blaschke (Göttingen, 2002), 215–41.

65. For the minutes of the conference on 5/6 August 1885, see Erwin Gatz, ed., *Akten der Fuldaer Bischofskonferenz* (Mainz 1977–85), 1:655. Archbishop of Cologne, 9 December 1886, to the archbishop of Freiburg, and further materials in EAF, B2–49–29a; EAF, B2–49–30; Questionnaire in EAF, B2–49–103. State statistics on mixed marriages were published in Prussia for the first time in 1885, see Bendikowski, "Fackel," 227. The diocese of Mainz also collected figures on "mixed marriages" from 1898 and on conversions but not on communicants in a single set of statistics, *Kirchliches Handbuch (KH)* 3 (1910/11): 275ff.

66. Statistical report by Adolf Rösch, 29 December 1913, EAF, B2–49–20; cf. Antonius Liedhegener, *Christentum und Urbanisierung: Katholiken und Protestanten in Münster und Bochum 1830–1933* (Paderborn, 1997), 217–18; *Germania,* 2 September 1904; Georg Michl, *Religions- und kirchliche Statistik* (Munich, 1921), 11; Hermann Szillus, *Eine verbotene Frucht* (Essen-Ruhr, 1904), 13–34; on this hope, see Baumgarten, "Statistik," 21–22.

67. Ursula Baumann, *Protestantismus und Frauenemanzipation in Deutschland 1850 bis 1920* (Frankfurt, 1992), 96ff.

68. Cited by Hermann Krose, "Die kirchliche Statistik in Deutschland," *Bonner Zeitschrift für Theologie und Seelsorge* 2 (1925): 351–56. This memorandum was not available at the archives visited. In this and other points it is probably largely identical to Krose's more recent memorandum, n.d. [June 1915], EAF, B2–49–15; Krose, "Zur Frage der Errichtung eines Bureaus für kirchliche Statistik," *Historisch-politische Blätter für das katholische Deutschland* 134 (1904): 834; *Kölnische Volkszeitung,* 12 September 1904.

69. Feyerabend, *Katholizismus,* 69–70.

70. Ibid.

71. *Kirchliches Jahrbuch* 39 (1912): 352; similar to Paul Pieper, *Kirchliche Statistik Deutschlands* (Freiburg, 1899), 228; cf. Paul Maria Baumgarten, *Römische und andere Erinnerungen* (Düsseldorf, 1927), 363–64.

72. Ordinariate Freiburg to city dean Konstantin Brettle, 10 December 1908, EAF, B2–49–29a; H.O. Eitner, "Aus der kirchlichen Statistik," *Theologie und Glaube* 9 (1917): 513. [

73. *KH* 1 (1908): 122–33; *KH* 3 (1910): 274–75; Eitner, "Aus der kirchlichen Statistik," 513–14. A request by Klose to publish the figures on conversions was rejected in 1911, Gatz, *Akten,* 3:182, 277.

74. Baumgarten, *Erinnerungen,* 365, quote 363; *Germania,* 6 January 1905; *Kölnische Volkszeitung,* 22 January 1905; Robert Brüning, "Nochmals kirchliche Statistik," *Allgemeine Rundschau,* 19 February 1905.

75. Ordinariate Freiburg, 10 March 1910, to provisorische Zentralstelle für kirchliche Statistik Deutschlands, Köln (ZSt), 22 October 1915, to ZSt, EAF, B2–49–15; Ordinariate Freiburg to city deanery Karlsruhe, 10 March 1909, EAF, B2–49–16; Karl Rieder, "Kirchliche Statistik der Erzdiözese Freiburg," *Freiburger Diözesanarchiv* 10 (1909): 238; Adolf Rösch, "Zur kirchlichen Statistik der Erzdiözese Freiburg," *Freiburger Diözesanarchiv* 15 (1914): 339ff.

76. Quote: [Eitner], "Zentralstelle," 3–4, DBK, Referat Statistik; Gatz, *Akten,* 3:80, 93, 103; memorandum of the central committee, n.d. [1907], EAF, B2–49–15; on the central committee, see Dieter Fricke, ed., *Lexikon zur Parteiengeschichte: Die bürgerlichen und kleinbürgerlichen Parteien und Verbände in Deutschland (1789–1945),* 4 vols. (Cologne, 1983–86), 4:182–93.

77. Quote: Hermann Krose, "Die kirchliche Statistik in Deutschland," *Bonner Zeitschrift für Theologie und Seelsorge* 2 (1925): 352–53; Cardinal Kopp to the German ordinariates, 1 March 1909, EAF, B2–49–15; Baumgarten, *Erinnerungen,* 366; on Kopp, see Rudolf Morsey, "Georg Kardinal Kopp, Fürstbischof von Breslau: Kirchenfürst oder Staatsbischof?," *Wichmann-Jb. für*

Kirchengeschichte im Bistum Berlin 21–23 (1967–69). Kopp's motives for this reluctance are unclear, Krose to Felix von Hartmann, 6 April 1914, HAEK, Gen. II, 32.12, 4.

78. [Eitner], "Zentralstelle," 4ff., DBK, Referat Statistik; Stehkämper, *Marx,* 3:181; Gatz, *Akten,* 3:129; Baumgarten, *Erinnerungen,* 366ff.; Dr. C. Künstle to ordinariate Freiburg, 10 December 1908, EAF, B2–49–29a; on the reaction, see, e.g., *Pastoralblatt (PBl.)* 43 (1909): col. 187; *PBl.* 44 (1910): col. 89.

79. [Eitner], "Zentralstelle," 5–6, DBK, Referat Statistik; Gatz, *Akten,* 3:242; Felix von Hartmann, 27 August 1915, to ordinariate Freiburg, EAF, B2–49–15.

80. Hermann A. Krose, "Nutzen der Statistik," *Stimmen der Zeit (StdZ)* 127 (1934): 33–39, quotes 37–38; Franz Groner, "The Office of Ecclesiastical Statistics for Catholic Germany: Its Influence on the Pastoral Ministry," *Lumen Vitae* 6 (1951): 249; Resolution of the Fulda Bishops' Conference on 17–19 August 1915; "Gedanken über die Erhebung der jährlichen kirchlichen Statistik," n.d. [1915?], EAF, B2–49–15.

81. Krose, "Kirchliche Statistik in Deutschland," 346.

82. Groner, "Office," 249; compare Lothar Roos, "Glaube und Kirchlichkeit in der spätliberalen Gesellschaft—In memoriam Franz Groner," *Jahrbuch für Christliche Sozialwissenschaften* 34 (1993): 267–70.

83. Johannes Müller, "Die Neugestaltung der kirchlichen Statistik in Deutschland," *Allgemeines Statistisches Archiv* 20 (1930): 81.

84. [Eitner], "Zentralstelle," 10, DBK, Referat Statistik. The central office sent twenty-four thousand questionnaires of type "form A" each year, including the copies destined for the files of local parish priests; Sieken, *Methoden,* 24.

85. The high number in 1915 was due to the heading "order statistics," which was then removed straightaway and data collected directly from the religious orders. Sieken, *Methoden,* 25.

86. From the forms for the respective sample year in 1909 and 1915 (draft and printed version): EAF, B2–49–15; 1919: Michl, *Religions- und kirchliche Statistik,* 21; 1925: Sieken, *Methoden,* 16ff.; 1943: BAM, GV NA A-101–174; 1946: Diözesanarchiv Limburg (DAL), 552B; 1962: Bistumsarchiv Osnabrück (BAOS), 03–55–01–02; ZSt to ordinariate Freiburg, 20 October 1915, EAF, B2–49–15.

87. Johannes Carl Kammer, *Die Kartothek im Dienste der seelsorglichen und sonstigen amtlichen Verwaltung* (Trier, 1914); Josef Drexler, *Die Pfarr-Kartothek: Ihre Notwendigkeit für die Städte und ihre Organisation* (Cologne, 1914); Josef Spielbauer, "Warum eine Pfarrkartei?," *Laienapostolat* 2 (1956); sources in EAF, B2–47–69.

88. Gatz, *Akten,* 3:316; Maximilian Kaller, *Unser Laienapostolat in St. Michael Berlin: Was es ist und wie es sein soll* (1926), ed. Hans-Jürgen Brandt (Paderborn, 1997), xi–xii, 53ff.

89. Gatz, *Akten,* 3:277; *KH* 14 (1926/27): 319.

90. Priest Isemann, 6 February 1913, to city deanery Karlsruhe, EAF, B2–49–15.

91. Ordinariate Freiburg to ZSt, 22 October 1915, ZSt to ordinariate Freiburg, 20 October 1915, EAF, B2–49–15.

92. Ordinariate Freiburg to ZSt, 22 October 1915, ZSt to ordinariate Freiburg, 20 October 1915, EAF, B2–49–15; Ordinariate Freiburg, 10 March 1909, to city deanery Karlsruhe, EAF, B2–49–16; Ordinariate Freiburg, 1 May 1922, to ZSt, EAF, B2–49–28; Antonius Baumann, "Gedanken zur kirchlichen Statistik von Dortmund," *Jb. für die Katholiken Dortmunds 1929* (Dortmund, 1929), 57; Johannes Rüstermann, "Wie steht es mit dem katholischen Leben in der Großstadt?," *Theologie und Glaube* 19 (1927): 103.

93. Franz Groner to the Institut für Soziologie at the Universität Innsbruck, 11 January 1972, HAEK, Dep. DBK, file Allgemeine Auskünfte 1972–73; cf. Georg Siefer, *Sterben die Priester aus? Soziologische Überlegungen zum Funktionswandel eines Berufsstandes* (Essen, 1973), 76–77; *Kirche und Leben (KuL)* 24, no. 24 (1969): 5.

94. Final report of statistics working group, 19 October 1977, BAOS 03–55–01–02.

95. [Eitner], "Zentralstelle," 8–9, DBK, Referat Statistik.

96. Draft of a decree on church statistics, n.d. [1921], HAEK, Gen. I, 32.12, 6; Michl, *Religions-und kirchliche Statistik*, 22.

97. ZSt report for 1918, EAF, B2–49–15; *KH* 14 (1926/27): 319.

98. Sieken, *Methoden*, 71–72.

99. *Gebietsmission Dekanat St. Ingbert: Die Basisuntersuchung in einem Traditionsgebiet* (Ramstein, 1963), 57; Erich Bodzenta, "Religiöse Praxis: Eine Bestandsaufnahme in österreichischen Stadtpfarren," *Wort und Wahrheit (WW)* 13 (1958): 91.

100. Heinz Hürten, *Deutsche Katholiken 1918–1945* (Paderborn, 1992), 20; Otto Wimmer, *Handbuch der Pfarrseelsorge und Pfarrverwaltung* (Innsbruck, 1959), 183; note by Willi Fries, n.d. [1960], Erzbischöfliches Ordinariat München, Registratur (EOM), Pastorale Planungsstelle, Ordner Menges I.

101. Cited by Richard Goritzka, *Der Seelsorger Robert Grosche (1888–1967): Dialogische Pastoral zwischen Erstem Weltkrieg und ZweitOem Vatikanischen Konzil* (Würzburg, 1999), 119–20.

102. ZSt, 18 January 1956, to the ordinariates, DAL, 552B; ZSt, 15 January 1969, to the ordinariates, Erzbischöfliches Archiv Paderborn (EBAP), Kirchliche Statistik 1968–69; *KH* 22 (1943): 312; Sieken, *Methoden*, 72; J. Pipberger, "Statistik über einige religiöse Lebensäußerungen der Katholiken in Frankfurt am Main," in *Das katholische Frankfurt: Jb. der Frankfurter Katholiken* (Frankfurt, 1928), 22.

103. Ordinariate Freiburg, 22 October 1915, to ZSt, EAF, B2–49–15.

104. Sieken, *Methoden*, 62; Statistical work by Adolf Rösch, 29 December 1913, EBAP, B2–49–20; Rösch, "Zur kirchlichen Statistik," 339; Herbert Bergmann, "Strukturprobleme der städtischen Pfarrei, dargestellt am Beispiel einer Pfarrei im Ruhrgebiet," Münster, 1967 (manuscript), 41–42; Pipberger, "Statistik," 22.

105. Sieken, 62; Michl, *Religions- und kirchliche Statistik*, 98; quote: *KH* 6 (1916/17): 445–46; Ordinariate Freiburg to ZSt, 22 October 1915, EAF, B2–49–15.

106. Gatz, *Akten*, 3:316.

107. ZSt, 1 August 1919, to Fuldaer Bischofskonferenz (FBK), EAF, B2–49–15. Examples of estimates in EAF, B2–49–18.

108. ZSt to ordinariate Freiburg, 10 March 1922, EAF, B2–49–15; quote: Decree by GV Cologne, 10 March 1922, Wilhelm Corsten, ed. *Sammlung kirchlicher Erlasse, Verordnungen und Bekanntmachungen für die Erzdiözese Köln* (Cologne, 1929), 476.

109. Ritter, *Religionssoziologie*, 78.

110. ZSt, 1 August 1919, to FBK, EAF, B2–49–15.

111. Dr. Eitner, "Aus der kirchlichen Statistik der Erzdiözese Köln," 26 November 1920 (manuscript), HAEK, Gen. II, 32.12, 4.

112. Groner to Cardinal Frings, 4 December 1951, "Zusammenfassender Bericht über die Erhebungen der Zentralstelle für Kirchliche Statistik Deutschlands über das kirchliche Leben in Deutschland," HAEK, Nachlass (NL) Frings, 833.

113. Bernhard Scholten, "Bericht über die Mission in Marl," 11 January 1957, BAM, GV NA, A-201–260. Franz Groner, "Seelsorge und Statistik," *Im Dienst der Seelsorge* 10, no. 2 (1956): 23–24.

114. J. N. Schatz, "Konfessionsstatistik im Kapitel Villingen," 23 April 1923, EAF, B-2-49–15.

115. Johannes Schauff, *Das Wahlverhalten der deutschen Katholiken im Kaiserreich und in der Weimarer Republik: Untersuchungen aus dem Jahre 1928*, ed. Rudolf Morsey (Mainz, 1975), 138–39.

116. Quote: Ludger Kruse, priest in Warburg-Neustadt, 7 November 1956, to the GV, EBAP, Kirchliche Statistik 1945–61; Dean Kauff from Mönchengladbach, 24 April 1954, to the GV, Bischöfliches Diözesanarchiv Aachen (BDA), Gvs B 17, I.

117. Quote: Munich ordinariate to ZSt, 4 December 1969; Franz Groner to Munich ordinariate, 12 December 1969; Hans-Georg Mähner, 29 April 1975, to ZSt, HAEK, Dep. DBK, correspondence diocese of Munich 1950–77.

118. [Eitner], "Zentralstelle," 7, DBK, Referat Statistik; Joseph Sauren to Cardinal Bertram, 8 August 1923, HAEK, Gen. I, 32.12, 6.

119. Groner, "Office," 243.

120. Activity report by ZSt for 1928/29, EAF, B2–49–28; *KH* 24 (1952/56): vi.

121. Quote: *Badischer Beobachter,* 27 September 1927; see also *Freiburger Tagespost,* 27 September 1927, EAF, B2–49–35.

122. "Ergebnisse der kirchlichen Statistik vom Jahre 1911 für die Erzdiözese," n.d., (manuscript), memo Adolf Rösch, 12 December 1916, EAF, B2–49–20.

123. Various reports in EAF, B2–49–20; quote: "Aufstellung," n.d. [1923], EAF, B2–49–35; "Kirchliche Statistik des Jahres 1924," n.d. (manuscript), EAF, B2–49–35.

124. ZSt to the ordinariates, 22 January 1952, BAOS, 03–55–01–02; Ordinariate Limburg to ZSt, 17 April 1952, DAL, 552B; GV Paderborn to ZSt, 12 May 1952, EBAP, Kirchliche Statistik 1945–61.

125. ZSt to ordinariate Freiburg, 9 August 1921, EAF, B2–49–15; ZSt to Vicar-General Tuschen, 24 February 1954, EBAP, Kirchliche Statistik 1945–61.

126. Vicar-General Joseph Teusch to Franz Groner, 3 November 1962, HAEK, Dep. DBK, correspondence archdiocese of Cologne; cf. the speech by Vicar-General Ferdinand Buchwieser at the deanery conference of the archdiocese of Munich and Freising, 30 November 1949: Heinz Hürten, ed., *Akten Kardinal Michael von Faulhabers III: 1945–1952* (Paderborn, 2002), 516–17.

127. Jakob Clement to Cardinal Frings, 20 March 1963, HAEK, Gen. II, 32.12, Zugang 452/89, Ordner 103; Goritzka, *Der Seelsorger Robert Grosche,* 172.

128. Quote: *Diözesanlandseelsorger* of the archdiocese of Cologne to ZSt, 15 February 1973, HAEK, Dep. DBK, Allgemeine Auskünfte 1972–73; W. Drummer to ZSt, 6 March 1973, HAEK, Dep. DBK, Statistische Auskünfte 1966–67; A. H. from Vechta, 3 May 1971, to the editors of *Kirche und Leben,* BAM, Schriftleitung KuL, A 205.

129. "Kirchliche Statistik der Diözese Eichstätt nach zivilen Gemeinde-Größen-Klassen für das Jahr 1954" (manuscript), HAEK, Dep. DBK, Zählbogen-Korrespondenz; quote: Freiburg ordinariate to ZSt, 9 March 1957, HAEK, Dep. DBK, Korrespondenz Erzdiözese Freiburg 1950–77. These figures were first published in *KH* 25 (1957–61): 501–2, 522–23.

130. Quote: *KH* 24 (1952–56): 357; Rösch, "Zur kirchlichen Statistik," 343; Michl, *Religions- und kirchliche Statistik,* 98.

131. ZSt communications to bishops, 25 April 1922, EAF, B2–49–28.

132. François Houtart, *Soziologie und Seelsorge* (Freiburg, 1966), 40; Hermann Krose, "Kirchliche Statistik," in *Staatslexikon,* 5th ed. (Freiburg, 1929), vol. 3, col. 382; *LThK,* 2nd ed., vol. 9, col. 1022–23; Paul Michael Zulehner, *Wie kommen wir aus der Krise? Kirchliche Statistik Österreichs 1945–1975 und ihre pastoralen Konsequenzen* (Vienna, 1978), 11.

133. Zulehner, *Wie kommen wir aus der Krise?,* 11; Urs Altermatt, *Katholizismus und Moderne: Zur Sozial- und Mentalitätsgeschichte der Schweizer Katholiken im 19. und 20. Jahrhundert* (Zurich, 1989), 283–84; Joseph Poeisz, "The Organization of the Statistics of the Church," *SC* 14 (1967): 255–57.

134. For the minutes of the Fulda Bishops' Conference, 1 June 1933, see Bernhard Stasiewski, ed., *Akten deutscher Bischöfe über die Lage der Kirche 1933–1945* (Mainz, 1968), 1:208; Franz Groner, ed., *Kirchlich-statistischer und religionssoziologischer Informationsdienst,* no. 3 (December 1954): 22–23, HAEK, Seelsorgeamt Heinen, 11.

135. Groner, ed., *Kirchlich-statistischer und religionssoziologischer Informationsdienst,* no. 3 (December 1954): 22–23, HAEK, Seelsorgeamt Heinen, 11.

136. Emmeram Scharl, "Bricht der Glaube im katholischen Landvolk zusammen?," *Klerusblatt* 44 (1964): 107–8.

137. J. N. Schatz, "Konfessionsstatistik im Kapitel Villingen," 23 April 1923, EAF, B-2–49–15. In this context, see also Krose, "Geburtenrückgang und Konfession," in *Des deutschen Volkes*

Wille zum Leben: Bevölkerungspolitische und volkspädagogische Abhandlungen über Erhaltung und Förderung deutscher Volkskraft, ed. Martin Faßbender (Freiburg, 1917); Erhard Leclerc, *Katholik und Heldentum der Lebensbereitschaft: Ein statistischer Beitrag zur ernstesten Schicksalsfrage des deutschen Volkes* (Trier, 1935); Ingrid Richter, *Katholizismus und Eugenik in der Weimarer Republik und im Dritten Reich: Zwischen Sittlichkeitsreform und Rassenhygiene* (Paderborn, 2001), 31–54.

138. Statistical report, [probably *Geistlicher Rat* Ludwig Wilhelm Körner], n.d. [1923], EAF, B2–49–35. On the discussion of birth statistics, see Breitenstein, "Bevölkerungsgliederung," 284ff.

139. *LThK,* 3rd ed., vol. 4, col. 396; *LThK,* 2nd ed., vol. 4, col. 624–25.

140. Memo, Teusch, 2 March 1964, HAEK, Gen. II, Zugang 452/89, Ordner 103.

141. Bishop Josef Höffner to the members of the pastoral council, 28 November 1967, minutes of the meeting on 12 March 1968, BAM, GV NA, A-101–376.

142. "Widersprüche und Ungereimtheiten: Kirchenaustritte werden dramatisiert und hochgespielt," *KuL,* no. 36 (6 September 1970).

143. Otto B. Roegele, "Die Verwirrung in der Nachkonziliaren Kirche," in *Warum unsere Kirchen leerer werden . . . ,* Otto B. Roegele and Heinz Beckmann (Zurich, 1977), 7–20, quotes 7, 15.

144. Groner, ed., *Kirchlich-statistischer und religionssoziologischer Informationsdienst,* no. 3 (December 1954): 22–23, HAEK, Seelsorgeamt Heinen, 11.

145. Luhmann, *Funktion,* 312–13.

146. Siegfried Weichlein, "Katholisches Sozialmilieu und kirchliche Bindung in Osthessen 1918–1933," *Archiv für mittelrheinische Kirchengeschichte* 45 (1993): 388–89.

147. "Die Sprache der Statistik," *Jahrbuch 1927 für die Katholiken Mannheims,* 59–60. [

148. H.-O. Eitner, 15 August 1917, HAEK, Gen. II, 32.12, 4; Michael Keller to Freiburg ordinariate, 3 August 1916, EAF, B2–49–20.

149. Hermann Krose, "Sittlichkeit in Ziffern," *StdZ* 116 (1929): 154.

150. Pipberger, "Statistik," 17, 27–28; cf. Kaller, *Laienapostolat,* 22; quote: Baumann, "Gedanken," 54; Freiburg ordinariate to the city deanery Freiburg, 25 March 1926, EAF, B2–47–52.

151. Weichlein, "Bindung," 385.

152. Activity report by the ZSt for 1935/36, EAF, B2–49–28; Bernhard Welte, "Gedanken über die kirchliche Statistik der Erzdiözese Freiburg für das Jahr 1933," *Oberrheinisches Pastoralblatt* 36 (1934): 397–98, 400.

153. Heiner J. Wirtz, *Katholische Gesellenvereine und Kolpingsfamilien im Bistum Münster 1852–1960: Gott zur Ehre und den Gesellen zum Vorteil* (Münster, 1999), 164, 201.

154. Schauff, *Das Wahlverhalten,* viii–ix, 191–204.

155. Bernhard Letterhaus, "Wählervolk und Zentrumspartei: Eine wahlstatistische Untersuchung," 1933 (manuscript), Kommission für Zeitgeschichte Bonn (KfZG), Materialien KAB, G VI 2. The result of this study was also described as a "curve of fate" in Verbandszentrale der katholischen Arbeitervereine Westdeutschlands to Cardinal Schulte, 10 February 1933, HAEK, Gen. I, 32.12, 6.

156. ZSt, "Der Kommunionempfang in Deutschland in den Jahren 1909–1920," 1922 (manuscript), EAF, B2–49–28.

157. Wilhelm Marx to Michael Buchberger, 5 April 1929, in Stehkämper, *Marx,* 3:366.

158. [Josef Frings], "Einiges zur Situation der katholischen Kirche in Deutschland Herbst 1953 bis Sommer 1954," n.d. [1954], BAM, GV NA, A-101–206; Summary report on the investigations by the ZSt, 4 February 1951, HAEK, NL Frings, 833.

159. Memo, Josef Teusch, 11 April 1964, HAEK, Gen. II, Zugang 452/89, Ordner 103; Hanspeter Steinbach, "Die geistig-gesellschaftlichen Ursachen für die zunehmende Entfremdung von der Kirche und dem christlichen Glauben," *PBl. für die Diözesen Aachen etc.* 24 (1972): 73, 78.

160. Institut für Kirchliche Sozialforschung des Bistums Essen (IKSE), report no. 101, 1986, 3.

161. Franz Groner, "Neueste Statistiken und ihre Bedeutung für die Seelsorge," *PBl. für die Diözesen Aachen etc.* 39 (1987): 374–78; quote: memo, [Edbert Köster, OFM], n.d. [November 1968], BAM, GV NA, A-101–336.

162. Troxler, *Kirchengebot,* 250.

163. Norbert Greinacher, "The Development of Applications to Leave the Church and the Transfer from One Church to Another, and Its Causes," *SC* 8 (1961): 71.

164. Algermissen to Bertram, 31 March 1933, Bernhard Stasiewski, *Akten deutscher Bischöfe über die Lage der Kirche 1933–1945* (Mainz, 1968), 1:40ff.; Gotthard Klein, *Der Volksverein für das katholische Deutschland 1890–1933: Geschichte, Bedeutung, Untergang* (Paderborn, 1996), 253–72.

165. *KH* 17 (1930/31): 348.

166. ZSt, "Kirchenaustritte im Jahre 1937 in der Erzdiözese Köln," EAF, B2–49–28; Ulrich von Hehl, *Katholische Kirche und Nationalsozialismus im Erzbistum Köln 1933–1945* (Mainz, 1977), 136ff.

167. Quote: minutes of the deanery conference on 4 May 1971, BAM, GV NA, A-201–396; Minutes of the deanery conference on 24/25 May 1971, BAOS, 03–09–51–02; "Warum sie ihre Kirche verlassen," *Ruhrwort,* 20 September 1969; O. Mauer, "Kirchenaustritte," *Diakonia* 2 (1971): 145–50.

168. J. B., "Statistik," 87.

169. Norbert Busch, *Katholische Frömmigkeit und Moderne: Die Sozial- und Mentalitätsgeschichte des Herz-Jesu-Kultes in Deutschland zwischen Kulturkampf und Erstem Weltkrieg* (Gütersloh, 1997), 269–79; Hugh McLeod, "Weibliche Frömmigkeit—männlicher Unglaube?," in *Bürgerinnen und Bürger: Geschlechterverhältnisse im 19. Jahrhundert,* ed. Ute Frevert (Göttingen, 1988), 134–56.

170. Rüstermann, "Wie steht es mit dem katholischen Leben in der Großstadt?," 104.

171. Piontek, "Der Kommunionempfang in der Fürstbischöflichen Delegatur von 1910 bis 1914," *Schlesisches Bonifatius-Vereins-Blatt* 56 (1915): 173.

172. Anton Stonner, "Zwei Versuche der kirchlichen Erfassung der religiös Abständigen," *Seelsorge-hilfe* 5 (1953): 59; [A Layperson],, "Die Ursachen der heutigen Ungläubigkeit," *Der Seelsorger* 22 (1951/52): 389–93, quote 389.

173. Krose, "Nutzen der Statistik," 35.

174. Baumann, "Gedanken," 56.

175. Krose, "Errichtung," 831.

176. Adolf Rösch, "Zur kirchlichen Statistik der Erzdiözese Freiburg," *Freiburger Diözesanarchiv* 15 (1914): 345; "Ergebnisse der kirchlichen Statistik vom Jahre 1911," n.d., EAF, B2–49–20.

177. Baumann, "Gedanken," 60–61.

178. Franz Xaver v. Hornstein, "Optimismus und Pessimismus in der Seelsorge," *Anima* 5 (1950): 244.

179. Cardinal Frings, 27–29 September 1956 (manuscript), BDA, Gvs B 17, III; P. J. Wiederhold M.S.C., "Milieumission und ihre Anwendbarkeit auf deutsche Verhältnisse," lecture in Marl, 10–13 January 1953, BAM, GV NA, A-201–265.

180. Ernst Tewes, "Thesen zu einem Seelsorge-Konzept," pastoral conference on 20 March 1964 in the Munich ordinariate, Ordinariat des Erzbistums München-Freising (OEM), Hefter Seelsorgeamt.

181. Memo, n.d. [November 1968], on the contact mission in Marl, BAM, GV NA, A-101–336.

182. Priest Dangelmaier of Lautern to ordinariate Rottenburg, 29 December 1964, HAEK, Dep. DBK, correspondence diocese of Rottenburg, 1950–76.

183. Franz Groner, "Neueste Statistiken und ihre Bedeutung für die Seelsorge," *PBl. für die Diözesen Aachen, Berlin, Essen, Hildesheim, Köln Osnabrück* 39 (1987): 378.

184. Hermann Krose, "Sittlichkeit in Ziffern," *StdZ* 116 (1929): 154.

185. Katholische Heimatmission, ed., *Münchener Statistik: Das kirchliche Leben in der katholischen Bevölkerung Münchens* (Munich, 1973); "Vorbemerkung," n.p.; cf. Bernhard Häring, *Macht und Ohnmacht der Religion: Religionssoziologie als Anruf* (Salzburg, 1956), 231; Viktor Schurr, *Seelsorge in einer neuen Welt: Eine Pastoral der Umwelt und des Laientums* (Salzburg, 1957), 26.

186. "Entkirchlichung in der Großstadt: Münchener Statistik 1974," *HK* 29 (1975): 430.

187. A. Ryckmans, "Das Gewohnheitsmäßige Versäumen der Sonntagsmesse als Problem der Seelsorge," *Anima* 6 (1951): 249–53.

188. Otto Wimmer, *Handbuch der Pfarrseelsorge und Pfarrverwaltung* (Innsbruck, 1959), 183.

189. Letter to all Catholics in the diocese of Essen, 1 November 1966, BAM, GV NA, A-101–219.

190. *Im Dienst der Seelsorge* 23, no. 2 (1969): 40.

191. "Der Welt nicht gleichförmig: Die Katholiken zwischen Ghetto und Mimikry," *WW* 8 (1953): 886; Karl Rahner, "Die Sakramente als Grundfunktionen der Kirche," in *Handbuch der Pastoraltheologie*, ed. Franz-Xaver Arnold et al. (Freiburg, 1970), 1:362.

192. Joseph Ratzinger, "Die neuen Heiden und die Kirche," *Hochland* 51 (1958/59): 5.

193. Heinz Fleckenstein, "Für und wider die Sonntagsmeßpflicht," *Sein und Sendung* 6 (1974): 53; Troxler, *Kirchengebot*, 240ff.

194. *Gemeinsame Synode*, 1:187–225, quote 200; on the position of the Second Vatican Council, cf. Troxler, *Kirchengebot*, 216ff.

195. Fuchs, "Frömmigkeit in Ziffern," 305; M. Helm, "Wie sieht es in unseren Pfarreien aus?," *LS* 3 (1952): 65.

196. With regard to discourses on suicide, see Ursula Baumann, Vom Recht auf den eigenen Tod: Die Geschichte des Suizids vom 18. bis zum 20. Jahrhundert (Weimar, 2001), 202–26.

Chapter 2

IN SEARCH OF SOCIAL REALITY
Sociography

We should not get bogged down in highly emotional and hence romantic folklore, but have to survey and analyze the entire environment of the village folk in a sober manner, deferential to reality. Only then should we interpret and judge, and should try to come to a useful underpinning of our endeavors for the *Landvolk* [village–folk], based on the goal that is set by our conscience, to "omnia instaurare in christo." Only that which is real, is effective. Anyone who denies realities, denies God. We equally reject the rose-tinted spectacles of a romantic optimism and the gray ones of a paralyzing pessimism. Christians are ideo-realists.

—*Georg Kliesch[1]*

From the start, the use of statistics in the Catholic Church was characterized by ambivalences, expressing confidence about the vibrancy of practiced piety as much as concerns about the dwindling coherence of the Catholic religious field. From the 1960s at the latest, the use of statistics to describe and analyze the Catholic milieu from within even cemented the notion of a pervasive crisis, as evidenced by the then-rapid decline in the number of churchgoers and Holy Communions received during Easter. The application of another social scientific method, sociography, commenced under much more favorable auspices. In the immediate postwar period, when parts of the clergy and laity began to embrace the new technique, the Catholic Church could justifiably see itself as the "victor among the ruins," as historians Joachim Köhler and Damian van Melis have argued.[2] In the rubble society of 1945, the Catholic Church was the only major institution that had survived the war more or less intact. Impressive processions in bombed-out cities such as Cologne and Münster demonstrated that Catholics were among the first to use their regained freedom of expression. It also seemed as if many people were about to return to organized Christianity after the anti-Catholic policies of the Nazi regime. The number of churchgoers bounced back again, if only to a small peak in 1945/46. The number reentering the church also surged, and few asked whether many of these were, in fact, staunch Nazis who hoped to facilitate their denazification.[3]

These and other indicators of a seemingly flourishing religious life were soon embedded in a broader interpretation of Christianity's place in postwar Germany. Bishops and some Catholic intellectuals prominently advanced this interpretation, wherein a turn away from Christian morality had facilitated the rise of Nazism and driven the destructive energies of the Third Reich, and the laity generally responded positively to it. Against this backdrop, Catholics had both a right and a duty to reinstate Christian values at the core of social and institutional life in the Federal Republic. Only a comprehensive "re-Christianization" of society would redeem the mistakes of the past.[4] In this context, intense hopes for an active missionary drive underpinned the practical application of sociographic methods, which pervaded the West German Catholic Church in the late 1940s and 1950s.

Yet another postwar Catholic trend is equally crucial to understanding the significance of the church's embrace of sociography. It is neatly expressed in the quote at the beginning of this chapter, taken from a questionnaire on the "sociography of the village" drawn up in 1950 on behalf of a Catholic association for rural people in northwest Germany. The key aim of this endeavor was to "renew everything in Christ," drawing on the motto that Pope Pius X (1903–14) had used for his pontificate. But this missionary zeal had to be based on a proper investigation and sober recognition of the social realities in the countryside, and first even had to determine "the entire social environment" of the villagers. As Catholic priests and laypeople embarked on the ambitious program of investigating social realities with sociography, they did away with romanticized notions and rose-tinted perceptions of idealist motives as the underpinning of Christian faith. Consequently, Catholic engagement with sociography was part of a broader shift toward an acknowledgment of the social realities of modern societies in the early Federal Republic. The 1950s were the decade during which many people in West Germany—not only in the Catholic Church—started to come to grips with the complexity of modern society, and to revise or abandon traditional worldviews that they no longer deemed to be compatible with this complexity.[5]

Sociography: Origins and Contours

Today, the term "sociography" is hardly used even by experts on the history of empirical social research. Having never had a clear epistemological profile, sociography was taken in a variety of directions. Many social scientists working in German-speaking countries from the late nineteenth century until the 1960s labeled their work *Soziographie*. Hans Zeisel sketched out a "History of Sociography" in an afterword to the famous study *Marienthal: The Sociography of an Unemployed Community*, published with Marie Jahoda and Paul F. Lazarsfeld in 1933, which itself represents an outstanding example of the sociographic approach.[6] Sociography describes neatly circumscribed social units, placing them in the context of social forces and frameworks, so that the social factors promoting or restricting certain forms of action or models of organization can be analyzed. Sociography is thus able to describe causal assumptions and interactions that are indistinct or even invisible in the statistical discourse in more specific terms.

Sociography, in the narrow sense, is a specific technique of empirical social analysis for researching and describing the inner structure and special features of spatially defined social units, such as settlements, villages, or towns. This can, but need not, take statistical form. The use of statistical survey techniques enables sociography to attribute quantifiable parameters to certain social features. Alongside quantitative methods, qualitative description based on observation forms a second basic method of sociography, which can be complemented with empirical techniques such as questionnaires, interviews, or censuses in any possible combination.[7]

In the sociographic approach to social reality, researchers concentrate entirely on specific social frameworks that can be isolated for analytic purposes. Thus, sociography operates with the distinction between the part and the whole without seeking to conceptualize the processes and structures of the wider social world by different means. This has attracted criticism. For example, in 1956, Max Horkheimer observed that sociography's idea of a "modern city . . . compris[ing] a closed unit" was a heuristic fiction.[8] By observing and describing social relationships in a particular location, sociographers draw upon the routines and schemes of interpretation and classification that social actors living in that environment use. The approach systematizes and schematizes the spontaneous sociology of everyday consciousness. René König, a leading representative of empirical social research in Germany who worked with explicit hypotheses, remarked in 1952 that, "in terms of scientific logic," there could be no such thing as the "pure description" of facts. Thus, sociography had to draw upon sociology in order to formulate research objectives.[9] Nevertheless, the sociology underlying sociography can remain largely implicit in practice. This special nature of sociography means that it can open the door to engagement with sociological questions and problems, even in contexts far removed from the social sciences. It also facilitates practical sociographic work, as it can be carried out without prior professional knowledge. Sociography is open to the professionalization and institutionalization of sociological work, but does not require these to be in place at the start.

The sociographic approach found its way into the Catholic Church between 1945 and the 1950s. Various genealogies were developed in this process to embed sociological analysis in a long and honorable tradition, thereby compensating for its novelty and the church's hermeneutic unfamiliarity with it. For example, sociographic literature of the early 1950s made reference to Heinrich Swoboda, whose 1909 book on *Großstadtseelsorge* (Pastoral Work in Big Cities) marked the beginnings of the sociology of the priesthood.[10] With his research interest in the negative effects of urbanization on parish organization and his central proposal of reducing the number of souls per parish by redrawing the boundaries and increasing the overall number of parishes, the Vienna-based pastoral theologian was certainly part of the sociographic discourse. However, a close reading makes it clear that Swoboda's categorical framework and methodological approach to social reality were heavily influenced by the statistical discourse, too. This can be seen, for example, in his repeated references to mixed marriage as the great moral danger Catholics faced in urban life. It is equally evident in his evaluation of such alleged dangers, which used moral statistics, and his demand that the *status animarum,* or survey of residential individuals, be completed thoroughly, as it was urban pastors' most important tool.[11]

Another prominent example of the tendency to draw up specifically Catholic genealogies of sociography in the church was Joseph Höffner's lecture on "sociology and pastoral" work, which was received "with great acclaim" at the conference of deans in the diocese of Münster in 1953.[12] Höffner (1906–87) taught Christian social sciences in Münster and was head of a university institute of the same name. From 1962 to 1969, he was bishop of Münster, and from 1969 until his death, archbishop of Cologne. We will encounter him frequently in both these roles in the course of this book. Höffner's changing attitude to the social sciences make him particularly notable. In the 1950s, he was a staunch advocate of sociographic methods in the church. Yet, from the conclusion of the Second Vatican Council in 1965 at the latest, he began to grow increasingly "skeptical" concerning the council-announced modernization of the church. In his view, this process only spread "turmoil and uncertainty" throughout the church without halting secularization. His disillusionment also seems to have influenced his attitude toward social science, which then inspired a "left-wing" theology, and its application in the church. Höffner made various arguments opposing representatives of such a perspective from the late 1960s.[13]

In 1953, however, there was no trace of this skepticism. Höffner began his lecture by observing that it might seem "strange" to associate pastoral service and the mythical body of Christ with sociology—a discipline that was suspected, "not without good reason," of being the "child of positivism." In its empirical application as the "sociography of religion," however, sociology only served to improve the church's understanding of its milieu. The passage "I am the good shepherd, and know my sheep" (John 10:14) succinctly expressed this long-standing objective of pastoral work, though many interpreted it only in terms of personal acquaintance between individuals. By contrast, argued Höffner, the four

Gospels attest that Jesus was extremely well acquainted with the wider religious and social tensions in Palestine.[14] With the metaphor of the "good shepherd," Höffner placed sociography in a pastoral discourse, widespread since the Council of Trent, that saw the priest as a paternalistic, caring, and benevolent protector of the "parish children" entrusted to him.[15] The novelty of sociography—its specifically scientific methodology—was thus camouflaged. It was only in this context that Höffner was able to claim that the proven techniques of "home visits, parish files, and religious statistics" would lead to the heart of the sociographic issues.[16] Höffner argued that church statistics until then had been "too general" and, owing to their lack of social differentiation, "not very enlightening." He thus continued the attempts begun in the Weimar Republic to move beyond the statistical discourse by using the parish card indices to provide a breakdown of the parish by age and occupational group.[17]

The work of Ludwig Neundörfer represents another sociographic tradition in Germany that Catholic social research after 1945 applied. Neundörfer (1901–75) came from the Catholic youth movement. He worked until 1933 in the Kultusministerium (Ministry of Education and Cultural Affairs) in Hesse, and then as a town and social planner in Heidelberg. He developed techniques primarily to collect sociostatistical data at the household level and to conduct spatial mapping of social characteristics, receiving considerable resources for practical social research, despite his ideological opposition to the National Socialist regime. The Sociographic Institute at the University of Frankfurt, which Neundörfer directed, then applied his methods in social research for the church after 1945.[18]

The French *Sociologie Religieuse*

Sociologie religieuse, a French movement whose program was largely similar to that of sociography, influenced these German traditions.[19] The canonist Gabriel Le Bras (1891–1970) published an epochal essay in 1931 in which he drew up a program for quantitative long-term analysis of religious observance in France, differentiated by region. Analysis and aggregation of the visitation protocols and information contained in the *status animarum* reports on the intensity of church practice generated the data. At the very outset of the empirical work, Le Bras set out his typology of religious practice, which characterized three distinct groups of churchgoers: *conformists saisonniers,* completely outside the fold of the church, attended only for major rites of passage such as baptisms, marriages, and funerals; *pratiquants* attended church regularly and fulfilled their Easter obligations; and *personnes pieuses,* later termed *devots,* were members of Catholic associations and received Communion regularly.[20] From the early 1930s, Le Bras began to build up a group of colleagues who focused their interest in the sociology of religion on a research program examining the secularization of France over an extended historical period. Like Le Bras, Fernand Boulard (1898–1977), national pastor of the Christian rural youth organization Jeunesse agricole catholique (JAC), also oriented his work toward sociogeography and socioecology. From 1945, Boulard presented important studies on the secularization of rural areas. From 1954, he worked on a series of empirical studies for the episcopate on the social and religious structure of French dioceses.[21]

After 1945, Le Bras's student Jacques Petit, together with a group of clerics, presented a method later known in German church sociography as the "differentiated counting of church attendance." By distributing questionnaires to those attending Mass, Petit was able to break the statistics down by address, age, gender, and occupation. In presenting initial results, Le Bras concentrated on a finding that would remain central in all future studies: the "désertion des ouvriers" (desertion of the workers) and the comparatively high level of religious observance among the middle classes.[22] However, Le Bras and Boulard continued to base their primary explanations of religious practice on historical traditions and geographical configurations. Any influence of social class was, in their view, disrupted and differentiated by the specific regional shapes of occupational milieus.[23] In the mid-1950s, Jesuit father Émile Pin was the first to move the relationship between class and religious observance to the fore to explain the greater religious observance of the middle class.[24]

The "religious sociology" of France gained the attention of the broader German public in 1955 when a 24-year-old priest from Freiburg, Norbert Greinacher, presented his dissertation on pastoral theology. This was the oft-cited "Sociology of the Parish," which included a foreword by Gabriel Le Bras. One of the key figures in various stages of the scientization of the Catholic Church, Greinacher directed the Pastoral Sociological Institute (Pastoralsoziologisches Institut, PSI) in Essen, which played an important role in propagating the sociographic approach, from 1958 to 1962. After a research stay in Vienna, Greinacher taught in Münster from 1967 to 1969, before being appointed to a professorship of practical theology in Tübingen. From the late 1960s, he publicly opposed the church hierarchy, which placed him at the center of various controversies. He continually used his reputation as a social scientist and theologian to promote reform efforts within the church.[25]

Greinacher encountered the Mission de France and a number of worker-priests while studying in Paris in 1952/53, becoming a friend of Yvan Daniel, who, together with Henri Godin, coined the description of France as a "missionary country." So influential was Greinacher's study that many an observer wanted to see a copy of it "in the hands of every priest."[26] The study not only explained the objectives and importance of a sociographic research program under specific German conditions, but it also made it clear that sociography involved more than simply compiling a social breakdown of church visitors using Jacques Petit's counting cards. Greinacher borrowed heavily from the French model, using the historical analysis of the visitation protocols in the parish archive and the "systematic interview" as two important working methods. Alongside "sociologism," he saw the "perfunctory work" and "indiscretion" of the assistants from the laity as the main "threats" to a study's success.[27]

The Tradition of Catholic Social Doctrine

The specific tradition of Catholic teaching on social ethics (*Soziallehre*), which papal encyclicals put forward and specialized theologians elaborated on, was both a positive and negative reference point for the implementation of sociographic concepts in West German Catholicism. A number of renowned moral theologians and social ethicists called for an unbiased reception and discussion of sociological insights in the church and presented relevant concepts in various publications. In particular, they made *sociologie religieuse* known to a broad public as an important form of empirical research. In addition to Joseph Höffner's aforementioned contribution, the theologians Werner Schöllgen, Nikolaus Monzel, Gustav Ermecke, Jakob David, and Adolph Geck deserve primary notice.[28] Schöllgen (1893–1985), who taught moral theology in Bonn, became interested in sociology through Goetz Briefs. Like Bernhard Häring and Höffner, he took up the New Testament idea of the "kairos" as the decisive indicator of the "right and necessity of pastoral sociology."[29] In the New Testament, this term, translated in the profane sense as the "right time" or "opportunity," calls for people to turn, believe in, and follow Christ (Mark 1:15–20). For Schöllgen, it summarized the specific Christian belief that man was "called upon" to "fulfill God's mission at a specific time." It was precisely at the historical moment when an "act of destiny" was to be performed that "Christian sociology" would come into its own. Such sociology would take the present into account as a situation that determines the actions of Christians. This, according to Schöllgen, meant working with the help of "profane" sociology as the "science of reality" (Hans Freyer) or "science of the present" (René König), to which end the American methods of "case studies" and opinion surveys were of particular interest.[30] In this context, the "autonomy of the social" was to be accepted without reservation.[31]

In contrast to the theologians mentioned thus far, Adolph Geck (1898–1987) had received comprehensive training in the methods of industrial sociology and social psychology, studying with Goetz Briefs and Leopold von Wiese. He published several monographs between 1928 and 1938. After losing his lectureship in sociology at the Technische Hochschule Berlin during the Nazi regime, Geck began to study theology and became an anointed priest. From 1948, he was the director of the Catholic Social Institute of the Archdiocese of Cologne in Bad Honnef. Geck wrote a series of articles calling for the insights provided by the social sciences to be collated under the umbrella of a "social pastoral care."[32] This was supposed to help free pastoral workers from the now-outmoded "individualism" in healing care and sermons, as had been expressed in the phrase "save your soul." At the end of the period in which the church had embedded itself deeply into the social fabric, pastoral work faced a "secularized and uncivilized society" in which modern industrial production units, in particular, represented a "religion-free space." Having unmistakably highlighted the process of social differentiation, however, Geck sought to overcome it by postulating the objective of an "organically structured" parish social life that would make it possible to bring the atomizing effects of functional differentiation under control.[33]

It is evident here that the church's moral teaching also represents a negative reference point for the sociographic approach. This was the case where a growing number of Catholics lost their belief in the ability of the church's *Soziallehre* to serve as an orientation amid the complex reality of modern society. Such a view contrasts with some strands of historiography that posit a renaissance of natural law in the early years of the Federal Republic directly resulting from the increased influence of the Catholic *Soziallehre*. This development was seen, in part, as a response to the National Socialist dictatorship: the Nazis' positivistic instrumentalization of legislation and the legal system made it necessary to return to a proper moral foundation for the law. For some areas of politics, such as the reform of social and pension insurance or marriage and family policies, the natural law revival was indeed significant.[34] However, skeptical observers such as Gustav Gundlach, SJ, a leading proponent of the moral and social teaching of the church, identified a clear weakening of interest in the normative character of these ideas from as early as the mid-1950s.[35] Following the social encyclical "Mater et magistra" in 1961, Gundlach even concluded that the "church's social teaching stands before the ruins of its practical validity," because, for many Catholics, the "value of its social *teaching* had been destroyed in favor of a purely pastoral treatment of the problems of social life."[36]

Representatives of church social ethics were not the only ones who felt its declining validity. Others, too, were critical, particularly of the discipline's inability to draw clear distinctions on empirical grounds when analyzing social issues. Determined advocates of sociography repeatedly found common ground, as did Catholic representatives of the political Left, like the Frankfurter Hefte, practitioners of Catholic social work, and more neutral observers such as the editors of *Herder-Korrespondenz*. All complained that social ethics needed to be more than a "social philosophy," but that it had made little progress "beyond the first steps" toward considering "new developments in social life."[37] They linked this warning to a view typical of the sociographic discourse, which regards sociological analysis as essential in a social order characterized by growing complexity, differentiation, and anonymous "secondary systems." Such a society was quite unlike those of earlier times, in which priests had been able to maintain an overview of social relationships within their parishes simply based on their day-to-day encounters.[38]

In 1954, *Herder-Korrespondenz* returned to the continuing "complaints about the inefficacy of Christian social teachings." The journal reviewed arguments put forward by the moral theologian Jacques Leclercq (1891–1971), who taught at the Catholic University of Leuven in Belgium and wanted to replace the normative deduction of social structures provided by social teaching with an empirical sociology more fruitful to pastoral practice. In an attempt to dispel concerns, the editors of *Herder-Korrespondenz* added that Christians should not "fear" the "reality" presented by sociological facts, which only served "to confirm Christian social teachings."[39]

This implicitly addressed a problem that influenced the derivation of the sociographic approach from, and thus its acceptance through, its competition with the Catholic *Soziallehre*. Advocates of sociography always treated this issue quickly and with great decisiveness to dispel any concerns. They were aware that embedding church activity in a social context carried the risk of being "sociologistic," that is, making the approach absolute so that social factors could explain all "realities and relationships."[40] To prevent social research from suppressing the Holy Spirit entirely, sociography advocates aimed to maneuver in the space between the Scylla of a "completely unworldly and escapist . . . monophytism" and the Charybdis of "Nestorianism," in which what is spiritual acts as a mere "functionary and propagandist." This framework raised anew the problem of individual moral freedom within social constraints—an issue that had already dominated the Catholic debate on moral statistics.[41] Church sociographers responded with a clear and decisive rejection of any form of sociological determinism. Furthermore, they argued, sociography could only study the "natural component" of the religious act, not the "supernatural" elements that could only be understood through faith.[42]

This statement was only clear within the parameters of church politics. Its conceptual implications for social scientific research, meanwhile, remained advisedly fuzzy, although this was not a problem for any empirical work on sociographic surveys. The reticence of the circles with an interest in sociography meant that they afforded their work only the "modest status" of a "complementary discipline" or even regarded it as a servant of revelation.[43] Two decades later, in the late 1970s, Catholic pastoral theologians described this sort of relationship between the social sciences and theology as an "ancilla" paradigm, comparing it to a "maid" and thus critically highlighting the limited function of sociology within it.[44] The proponents of sociography were indeed willing to subordinate their approach to the apostolate. In the perspective of a historical sociology of knowledge, however, another question is more important: whether and in what form knowledge arising from and verified by sociological work was to be introduced into everyday church work. Linus Grond, OFM, the general secretary of the International Federation of Catholic Social Research Institutes (FERES), cast this practical function as the oft-cited "church thermometer" in 1953. This and similar metaphors—other authors used the terms "mirror" or "instrument" as opposed to "cure"—also reveal the mechanistic nature of this approach.[45] The question of how the church would integrate the "thermometer's" temperature readings into its own work and use them as a means of control went beyond the bounds of the sociographic discourse. The bureaucratic routines of the church apparatus were left untouched. No provision was made for a thermostat able to correct discrepancies and malfunctions, nor was any use made of the feedback model, which had already been systematically formulated and had risen to prominence during the 1950s in cybernetics.[46]

Overall, the scientific tradition of Catholic sociography presents a diverse and indistinct picture. The common flag of the sociographic approach grouped diverging traditions and positions on sociology, church politics, and theology. This broad spectrum also encompassed neo-scholasticism, a resolutely antimodern theological position opposed to rationalism. Barely able to concur with one another on the shape of their methodological instruments and their research objectives, church sociographers only agreed on the emphatic aim of using the tools of empirical social research to make a statement on social "reality" and its repercussions for the church and faith.

Practical Applications of Sociography

Many West German dioceses began to deploy the sociographic approach from the early 1950s, its near-comprehensive coverage ideally positioning it to advance sociological concepts in the Catholic Church. A variety of organizational factors, ultimately arising from two contexts in which the use of sociographic knowledge seemed plausible and essential after the end of the Second World War, spurred the use of these concepts. The first was a very "real" social transformation with far-reaching consequences. The second was a theoretical construction resulting from the projection of French religious affairs onto those of Germany.

The Refugee Crisis after the Second World War

The first impulse for the use of sociographic knowledge was the vast population shift that began in 1945 as Germans took flight or faced expulsion from elsewhere in Europe. Germany's confessional map dramatically changed as approximately twelve million Germans were expelled from Central Eastern and Southern Europe and the former eastern regions of Germany in the aftermath of the Second World War, and others then fled from the Soviet occupation zone and later the German Democratic Republic. By 1950, one in every six Catholics in the Federal Republic was a refugee. In that year, just 12 percent of all West German Catholics, but 33.6 percent of refugees, lived in diasporic environments in which less than one-third of the population belonged to the Catholic confession.[47]

This influx of refugees stoked social conflicts and engendered new forms of rebuilding community life; it also made different forms of piety and conflicting interpretations of the Christian faith collide with each other, particularly in rural areas. For example, the contrast between the wasteful frivolity of farmers' weddings and refugees' experience of material hardship within the same village led one observer in 1946 to ask if the farmers' families were not committing "a sin" every time they visited church. In his view, the church had placed too much "importance in church attendance," but not enough in morally "correct behavior."[48] The mutual lack of understanding among adherents of different social and religious perspectives indicated to contemporaries that a deep chasm, or even a "life-or-death crisis," had opened up beneath the surface of milieu Catholicism, which seemed to remain at least quantitatively intact thanks to the habitual nature of religious practice for many people. Such observations contradicted the picture of piety created by the Cologne statistics, which frequently quoted the numbers of people converting to or leaving the Catholic Church.[49] For many observers, the new social situation devalued the system of rules surrounding the orthopraxy-based statistical discourse.

In an oft-quoted and intensively discussed essay, publicist Otto B. Roegele commented in 1948 with respect to the refugees that "the façades in the religious view of the village" had "only now been revealed to be just that"; a "real Christian awareness" was lacking, its place taken by "a dreadful traditionalism." Continuing the familiar form of pastoral work, with its focus on mere conservation, would be tantamount, in his view, to the church committing suicide. Familiar pastoral work, thought Roegele, needed to give way to "functional pastoral work" conducted in a risk-taking "missionary spirit."[50] Roegele's essay addressed not only the program of missionary pastoral work but was also highly charged concerning church politics. For example, it revealed as unreal and unfounded in real practiced piety the claim of West German Catholics to represent one-third of the populace and thus to insist legitimately on maintaining the "confessional status quo" in the arguments over church and family policy.[51] In the defensive attitude of milieu Catholics, Roegele seemed suspicious, as he was a Catholic who seemed to be handing "useful weapons to the opponent."[52]

The Jesuit father and advisor to the pope Ivo Zeiger also took a dramatic view of the consequences of refugee movements for pastoral work in 1948. He concluded that Germany had become "in a real sense a missionary country,"[53] discussing this primarily in the context of the "missionary movement" that sought to adapt pastoral concepts from France. Roegele's controversial position inevitably triggered a search for reliable indicators. Particularly in the early years of the Federal Republic, the "appraisal of the religious, moral, and social position of the modern-day village" fluctuated "between wide extremes," not least because of the "shortage of scientifically watertight factual material." Proponents of sociology believed that such material was necessary for the church to advance from a "cloud of pessimism, optimism, and apathy" to "objective, demonstrable knowledge."[54] Authors who examined the radical change in the social form of the Catholic religion triggered by the refugee movements thus called for a "much more precise assessment of the state of the church," and "particularly of the sociological structure in the parishes." As clergy and laity alike took a sobering look behind the façade of quantifiable religious observance, especially in the years 1946 to 1950, they implicitly set out a program of empirical-sociographic analysis of the social-structural and cultural patterns of piety in West German Catholicism.[55]

The Missionary Movement

A broader discussion and implementation of sociographic forms of knowledge and strategies of classification took place in the context of the "missionary movement." Gathered together under this term was a heterogeneous current of theologians, priests, and people's missionaries who sought a comprehensive new beginning in pastoral activity. They shared a core conviction that the Catholic faith could no longer be satisfied with the routine of the prewar years, which had been based on the stable structures of milieu Catholicism. After all, they pointed out, the period after 1945 had been characterized by the "almost total dissolution of the traditional Catholicism" that had "carried the church in Germany up to the First World War." In their view, the "religious substance previously nourished by tradition and the sociological position of the bourgeoisie and peasantry had now been almost entirely eaten away."[56]

Initially, however, the decisive feature of the missionary movement's statements and strategies was not that they observed the situation in Germany, but that they reproduced a specific view of Catholicism prevalent in France, both as a disturbing vision of the future and as a model for "missionary pastoral care."[57] Missionary work in France, which would have major implications for sociography, began with the establishment of the Christian Workers' Youth movement, Jeunesse Ouvrière Chrétienne (JOC), in 1926, which was based on Abbé Joseph Cardijn's Belgian model. The French JOC, too, aimed to re-Christianize young workers and counter the socialist mobilization of working-class youth. To do so, it promoted a "révision de vie"—a transformation of individuals' private lives driven by work in small groups. This included, first and foremost, encouraging members to examine and appraise their own lives according to the maxim "see, interpret, act."[58] The "Jocist" was to observe his milieu at work and around his home and record his impressions in a notebook. He was then to take part in a debate with fellow members of the local JOC group, discussing these observations in light of the Christian worldview, and to act accordingly. In practice, the program took the form of surveys that were associated with mobilization campaigns. Local groups examined the living and working conditions or leisure time of young workers, later publishing and discussing the results in the membership magazine.[59] The Christliche Arbeiterjugend (CAJ), the German branch of the JOC, replicated this procedure in the 1950s, its members surveying new apprentices about their factory experiences and impressions, for example. The local chaplain of the CAJ in Duisburg, Julius Angerhausen, encouraged theology students working in the mining industry to complete a written report on their work experience.[60]

Two priests at the JOC, Henri Godin and Yves Daniel, set the tone for the continuing discussion on the secularization of France. From as early as the late 1920s, the country's secularism was a common topic of discussions within the church. In 1943, Godin and Daniel published a book entitled *La France, pays de mission?*, which, while adding little to the existing discussion on secularization in France and the surveys of the JOC, served to systematize and popularize the material, quickly selling 120,000 copies.[61] Like no other work, the book—whose impact can "hardly be overstated"[62]—placed the idea of France as a largely secularized missionary country firmly on the agenda for the church's internal discussions, in both France and Germany. This probably derived first and foremost from Godin's conviction in describing the ongoing lack of success of purely parish-based pastoral work and Catholic Action in its work among the urban working class. In their place, he called for autonomous communities of priests, who would be active among the working class and adapt themselves to living conditions within it.[63]

The Mission de Paris, founded by Godin in 1943, embodied this model, although the movement's priests restricted themselves to pastoral activity, not carrying out any manual work themselves. This and other groups of priests gave rise in the years that followed to the movement of "worker-priests," who were characterized by their determination to give up their normal priestly life entirely to bridge the gap between social environments—the central obstacle to parish-based pastoral work, in their view. The nearly one hundred worker-priests were housed in the workers' accommodation located in the banlieues of Paris and other industrial cities. They removed their ceremonial clothing and took up regular work in factories and shipyards, deciding for themselves whether and when to begin administering sacraments to their shop-floor colleagues. Some became members or even functionaries of the socialist and communist trade union movement, taking part in strikes. At the height of the Cold War, the media paid great attention to their work, generating enormous concern among large parts of the French episcopacy. Combined with pressure from the Vatican, this led in 1953 to strict regulation of the worker-priests' activity, which bordered on an outright ban.[64]

The German reception of this radical pastoral experiment in the missionary movement emphasized the "limits" of an "absolute focus on the milieu" that it made apparent. Nevertheless, German observers respected the movement's efforts to find a new "incarnation" of faith, which included not only adjustment to the social requirements of pastoral work, but also a special personal commitment and a search for new working methods. In practice, this had led to an extensive "naturalization of the priests," and thus—to use the terminology of the day—a form of practiced "sociologism."[65] Regardless of the political tensions worker-priests triggered in French Catholicism, many German observers expressed their great reverence for the movement's "idealism" and "zeal" and recommended it be replicated in Germany.[66] In France, "religious sociology" was drawn into the argument on worker-priests, as observers regarded it as one of that movement's intellectual foundations. In the Federal Republic, meanwhile, the two things were largely kept separate. The political engagement of the worker's priest was rejected. But neither the theoretical basis of their efforts nor the implications of their experiment for missionary work and sociography were affected by that.[67] Their call to find forms of pastoral care and religious service that "*constantly* adapted" to the societal environment remained largely uncontested.[68]

The German reception of these developments centered on "shock" at Godin and Daniel's findings, and on the fact that French Catholicism was beginning to "discover religious sociology as a methodology."[69] In this context, German observers widely understood Fernand Boulard's 1945 studies on the secularization of rural France as a "supplement" to Godin's theses. This was in part because both writers used a similar threefold typology of Christianity, although Boulard only regarded parts of modern France as truly secularized.[70] The missionary movement in Germany extended Henri Godin's dramatic diagnosis to the situation on their own side of the Rhine, making reference to Ivo Zeiger's 1948 description of Germany as a "missionary country."

Although the term "missionary country" later became no more than a buzzword, before gradually falling out of use altogether, it never lost "its provocative seriousness" about the necessity of reorienting pastoral work. Such reorientation was not a matter of "mechanically reproducing . . . finished recipes" from France, but of acquiring important "knowledge and principles" and adapting these to the conditions in Germany, even if the process of "secularization" there had "perhaps not yet advanced as far as it had in France."[71] The objective of renewal pursued in Germany was to create a "missionary," "conquering," or "living" pastoral care. Used largely synonymously, these terms contrasted with priests' previous "conservative" and "dry" pastoral work. The semantics implied replacing the familiar routine of pastoral "provision" with a "lively discussion" both between the clergy and the laity and among the priests themselves. It seemed that intensifying direct interaction would make it possible to break through the ritualized forms of work in the church bureaucracy, and to improve the coordination of pastoral care at the diocese level. What was more, the new approach promised to overcome "the despondency" that "threatened to encompass . . . everyone" involved in pastoral care.[72] Proponents of missionary pastoral care also hoped that it would reveal and explain the elements of the Christian message that serve to "promote, assist, and delight."[73] In particular, knowledge that it was "not only the twenty or thirty" but all one hundred of the well-protected flock who were entrusted to the *cura animarum,* or cure of souls, through religious sacraments and instruction, spurred the missionary perspective.[74] A comparison with the lost sheep from a flock of one hundred that the farmer goes in search of (Luke 15:3–7) rhetorically strengthened this idea: "How much more urgent" the search would be if there was not *one* "lost sheep" but "fifty, sixty, or even more."[75]

The implications of such an argument were clear to one deacon in Duisburg, who in 1960 subjected a report by the Pastoral Sociological Institute in Essen to searing criticism. In his view, the report on the recruitment of priests used statistical "syllogisms" that failed to present the "specter of the shortage of priests" in a plausible light. The "simple pastor," as he called himself, who hailed from rural milieu Catholicism close to Münster, used "simple mental arithmetic" to make a mockery of the complex statistical material of sociology. He particularly criticized the replacement of the neutral term *Priestermangel* (shortage of priests) with the word *Priesternot* (emergency of priests), which implied urgency without "a clear resolution as to the number of priests that constituted such an emergency."[76] This polemic demonstrates that the evaluation of the missionary dimension of sociographic work depended not only on "facts" or their subjective interpretation but also on what one emphasized in explaining the findings. The PSI's counterargument concentrated on just a single point. If—like the deacon—one regarded a ratio of one clergy member for every 2,500 souls as sufficient, the only plausible mode of pastoral care would be a "conservative" model interested only in the 30 to 40 percent of Catholics who came to church "of their own accord." Missionary pastoral care, by contrast, was "gravely concerned" with nonpracticing Catholics and found such a ratio "far too high for one parish pastoral worker."[77]

Even this indirect statement makes it clear that advocates of sociographic discourse had major ambitions concerning missionary objectives. They aimed to do nothing less than "win over and win back those who had been lost," to "bring them over" to a "personal decision" and ultimately to reinfuse society with Christianity.[78] The sociographic approach differed from the statistical discourse, which continued to treat practicing Catholics as a closed unit, even in a "diaspora-like environment." Franz Groner illustrated this perfectly using the "vivid language" of military strategy to describe the "hedgehog positions" of Catholicism in a speech to the parish clergy of Düsseldorf. Catholics in the hedgehog position turned their spikes—which they had to fortify in response to the declining influence of religious practice—toward a hostile social environment.[79] In the incisive and widespread use of military metaphors in pastoral discourse, the aim of sociography was to go on the offensive with "a climate of general mobilization" rather than merely "defend the trenches."[80]

The sociographic discourse thus had a discernible affinity with the triumphalist hopes of re-Christianizing society that were widespread in the early postwar years among the German episcopate and beyond.[81] In marked contrast to the bishops, however, sociographers emphasized the importance of breaking free from "traditional self-deception" about the state of pastoral care. They insisted on the need to carry out a precise examination of the factors that shaped the "secularist" trend in "mass opinion."[82] Missionary pastoral care "certainly did not want to spread pessimism," but aimed to "open people's eyes" to the "alarming signs" rather than pretending that "the church was in the best of health." After all, the latter approach would not halt the "decline of religious life."[83] While there was agreement among the proponents of missionary pastoral care that the Christian faith would soon grow in influence, there was a considerable difference in the willingness to undertake a robust analysis of the real situation that would be capable of directly influencing pastoral work.

Changing the Social Environment

To fulfill the missionary objective of pastoral care that sociology inspired and informed, its advocates regularly made recourse in the 1950s to specific metaphors for social "structures." That was already problematic, as representatives of traditional Catholic social teaching decisively rejected even the very term "structure." Proponents of parish sociography drew upon a lecture by Theodor W. Adorno to state its aim: to grasp tangible reality and make it conscious.[84] Even before engaging in any empirical work, they utilized metaphors for social order that characterized and structured knowledge about problems to be examined and the practice of sociology. For example, Redemptorist Viktor Schurr, who, along with Bernhard Häring, a fellow member of the Redemptorist order, was one of the most important representatives of missionary pastoral work and a staunch advocate of sociography, used the familiar image of the fishpond, widespread in the missionary pastoral movement in France, which Joseph Cardijn had first deployed:[85]

> If the water in a fishpond is contaminated, it is not enough to give medication to the inhabitants. It is not they who are hosting the sickness, but the water, their life element. It is this that must be cleansed. . . . In the past we tried to cure the moral weakness of Christians with all sorts of medicines, but the sickness could not be excised. It grew worse. The reason? The problem is not a multitude of isolated cases, but an all-encompassing sociological process: the environment in which we live and move has been poisoned.[86]

With these aggressive metaphors, Schurr had moved far from the contemplative idea of the "good shepherd" employed by Josef Höffner. For Schurr, the "poisoned" fishpond represented a secularized social "environment" or "milieu" that had grave implications for social attitudes.[87] The term "milieu" was associated in missionary pastoral work with the idea of a society that had fallen apart into different fields or subsystems.[88] In particular, mass media, leisure time pursuits, and consumption were regarded as potent spheres of influence with their own codes of behavior and thus the ability to determine people's behavior. In addition, many theologians, priests, and church sociographers held a spatially determined idea of social differentiation. For them, it was irrefutable that the old unity between the parish and the local community had broken apart. Pastoral activity, they believed, had to take the implications of this into account, such as the influence of commuters who brought home the interests, attitudes, and behaviors typical of their workplaces.

Missionary pastoral work discovered an autonomous social world. This discovery was based on the idea of social differentiation, that is, the decomposition or breakdown of a compact whole into separate parts.[89] Milieu pastoral care as a pastoral strategy, meanwhile, did not stop at the insight that an individual was "milieu-dependent." Instead, it drew more extensive conclusions from the *tertium comparationis,* the poisoning of the fishpond. The missionary aims of sociography, and the use of the metaphor, were extended to the "cleansing" of the water. The remedy could not be "as mechanical as filtering the water and removing debris from the aquarium." Rather, it required active human participation by an elite schooled in the "missionary spirit." There were thus "calls for an apostolic laity that would aim to bring about change in the milieu."[90]

The most important practical application of missionary pastoral work from the 1950s involved the new practice of the regional or area mission (*Gebietsmission*), informed and directed by sociography.[91] This evolved from the traditional people's mission (*Volksmission*), or revival mission, that all parishes since the mid-nineteenth century had conducted about once a decade to reenergize parish communities. During a traditional people's mission, a group of regular clergy from one of the missionary orders would come to a parish, usually for a fortnight, and conduct a tightly scheduled series of opportunities for the confessional, give public sermons, and celebrate Masses. It was first and foremost the Redemptorist priests who promoted the concept of a regional mission from 1953 onward and, despite some resistance, spread it throughout the Federal Republic. The core idea of the regional mission was to focus on an area larger than an individual parish. The social and church structures of this area would first be researched with sociographic methods before the start of the actual mission. This was supposed to involve the laity acting under its own responsibility. The aim of this sociographic work was to find starting points for a strategy to re-Christianize the region and thus to change the milieu over the medium to long term. This new form of missionary work also broke with the traditional strategy of preaching fire and brimstone, which had relied on generating a moral shock effect on individual Catholics. Instead, the new methods were to embed a new form of collective religious spirit that was adapted to sociostructural changes.[92]

The practice of the regional mission from the early 1950s faced various obstacles and objections, not least the skepticism of the parish clergy and the different ideas of the religious orders involved. Inevitably, a missionary concept with the goal of re-Christianizing society generated high expectations, which quickly emerged as the core problem. The very sociographic methods themselves threatened to dampen missionary optimism if the anticipated quantitative effects on religious practice failed to emerge. The negligible success of the regional mission around the Eucharistic World Congress in 1960 in Munich proved to be a watershed moment in the experience of the practitioners and people's missionaries involved in sociographic work. The practical preparation and execution of sociographic research had begun in 1957, more than three years before the mission itself. Once completed, the results of differentiated surveys on church attendance served only to reinforce the picture of a largely secularized city.[93] The priest responsible for the mission, the Redemptorist Father Josef Spielbauer, was forced to admit to his superiors that the area mission "faced a crisis."[94]

Even though sociographic work continued to prepare the ground for regional missions that were carried out until the late 1960s, the events in Munich caused many practitioners to reconsider the concept of "missionary" pastoral work. It is against this background that the "Theses for a Concept of Pastoral Care," which the Munich ordinariate councilor, Ernst Tewes, drew up in 1964, should be interpreted. Tewes wrote the theses in light of the "aggiornamento" called for by the Second Vatican Council, which was still underway at that time. Tewes emphasized that preaching must in future be "infused with the 'world,'" including the use of sociography and the observation and awareness of the "worldly faith" of a growing number of Catholics. As the statistics would "continue to be discouraging for many years to come"—a clear reference to the findings of the Munich mission—the concept of "missionary pastoral work" now needed to be used in a "more comprehensive sense," as a self-reflexive quality of pastoral activity. This meant accepting that those observing the church would "have an important and regulating influence" on the church's own communications. Every speaker at the council and from the church in general was thus engaged in a "secret dialogue" with the secular world.[95]

Tewes explicitly introduced the program of sociographic fact-finding as a concrete manifestation of the openness to the "world" that the council had demanded. His suggestion for reforming missionary pastoral work pointed beyond the limits of sociographic discourse as it had existed thus far. At the heart of that discourse was ultimately the attempt to attribute the intensity of church participation to certain social characteristics or parameters. This was supposed to enable the identification of socially determined patterns and, where appropriate, allow missionary action to correct them. Tewes, meanwhile, decoupled the term "missionary" from its association with a clearly defined canon of prescribed behaviors, supplementing and partially replacing it with the concept of a "dialogue" with the secular world. This pointed to a desire to introduce outside observations into the church's internal communications in a more systematic fashion. This ambition, though, was much more characteristic of the discursive uses of opinion polls in the church. In this context, the idea of "dialogue" took the place of the terms "mission" and "missionary."[96]

The Reluctant Institutionalization of Church Sociography

In principle, any parish priest could produce a parish sociography, provided he was prepared to acquire some introductory knowledge about it. From the early 1950s, pastoral literature included work plans to support such projects.[97] As the director of the diocesan pastoral office in Mainz found in 1957, the survey forms and explanations made it "easy" to conduct a normal differentiated count of church attendance in a limited area "without further instruction."[98] At that time, it may have seemed that there were more introductory guides to the sociographic approach than there were reports about "studies that had already been completed." This was partly because "amateurs" conducted many studies in various parts of Germany and often did not publish their results. Members of religious orders who had created their own schemas for regional missions on the basis of preceding sociographic studies, likewise, often failed to publish those studies.[99]

Some clergy felt that there was a tension between the uses of sociography in missionary pastoral work and in dedicated research institutes, where the methodology was more professional and routinized. Bernhard Häring, for example, argued that the sociographic approach would lose "its meaning and legitimacy" if it were turned into a "mechanism." After all, one of its objectives was to overcome the "fatal" routine in pastoral care and to create "missionary unrest" among pastoral workers and congregations.[100] Priests from religious orders who conducted people's missions still distinguished between "purely scientific" and "missionary" sociography in a September 1955 discussion. In "missionary" sociography, a study's empirical results were less important than the act of carrying out the study itself, with the help of the laity, and its feedback effect on the research object. One example of this was the sociographic work Hermann Josef Kahseböhmer undertook around 1960 to prepare for the people's mission in the Pfälzer Wald area of southwest Germany. In this model, which had much in common with "action research," social research now served only as a means to an end, aiming to awaken a lethargic congregation and to motivate people for apostolic activity.[101] Soon afterward, Kahseböhmer founded an institution to carry out sociographic work, while Häring, with his initial critique of institutionalized church social research, soon lost support for this position among his fellow Redemptorists. Viktor Schurr, for his part, believed that parish pastoral workers and their assistants in the laity could apply a "simplified version of parish sociology" but should otherwise make use of the "experts' results."[102]

In the 1950s, a series of dioceses continued to carry out sociographic research without the help of any research institutions. In the diocese of Aachen, a chaplain and former student of Nikolaus Monzel was granted leave for several months to collate statistical material on the spatial makeup of the diocesan administrative district.[103] Beginning in 1958, the diocese of Würzburg ran a research program that produced parish sociographies as part of Catholic Action. Specially trained committees comprised of laity examined their parish using sociologically defined criteria, looking at specific forms of Catholic Action work.[104] In the diocese of Osnabrück, the director of continuing education, Bernhard Schomakers, provided the impetus for and carried out sociographic research in various towns and diaspora areas in the diocese beginning in 1960. Schomaker's enduring interest in this approach is evident in his use of an annual meeting of the Bonifatiusverein, an association that worked for diaspora regions, to campaign for church social research and his regular participation in working meetings of Catholic pastoral sociologists.[105]

These and similar initiatives and projects made the sociographic approach well-known across large swaths of the West German church from 1950.[106] In the medium term, however, the decisive impetus and conditions for sociography's widespread breakthrough came from the provision of institutional research resources. From the early 1950s, institutes were founded that were dedicated in part or in their entirety to church sociography and social research. The first category included the Institut für Christliche Sozialwissenschaften (ICSW, Institute for Christian Social Sciences), founded by Joseph Höffner in 1951 at the University of Münster.[107] Höffner was actively committed to increasing networking between Catholic sociographers, and many of his ICSW students carried out practical work using this methodology. Höffner dealt with a variety of activities in teaching, research, and advising politicians beyond church sociography issues. Another institute partly dedicated to sociography was the Sociographic Institute at the University of Frankfurt, directed by Ludwig Neundörfer.

Three institutions were established that dealt in practice almost exclusively with empirical studies for church purposes. The first was the Katholische Internationale Soziologische Institut für Flüchtlingsfragen (KISIF, Catholic International Sociological Institute for Refugee Issues), founded in Königstein, in the Taunus area, in 1951. This was a branch of the church social research facility KASKI, located in The Hague under the directorship of George H. L. Zeegers.[108] KISIF, which occupied part of the Königsteiner Anstalten zur Flüchtlingsseelsorge (Königstein Institutes for Refugee Pastoral Care), initially devoted itself to refugee issues before becoming primarily involved with studies as part of regional missions. By the time chronic financial problems closed the institute in the early 1960s, it consisted only of Walter Menges (a former doctoral student of Neundörfer's, who carried out the scientific work) and a secretary.[109]

The second was the Pastoralsoziologisches Institut des Erzbistums Paderborn und des Bistums Essen (PSI, Pastoral Sociological Institute of the Archdiocese of Paderborn and the Diocese of Essen), which was created in 1958 along with the diocese of Essen. The bishop of Münster, Michael Keller, provided the initiative for the new diocese following an analysis of the pastoral situation on the southern fringes of his administrative district in the Ruhr region. Keller paid particular attention to the working class and to conducting pastoral work amid the heavy industry of this area. Pastoral structures in the region also became a focus of the PSI's work. Norbert Greinacher was tapped as an appropriately qualified clergyman to lead the institute, with two qualified sociologists as research assistants.[110]

The third institution was founded in the early 1960s: Hermann Josef Kahseböhmer's Social Team became active as a registered association in Landstuhl and later also in Adelsried, near Augsburg. Ottfried Selg led the Adelsried branch, which was particularly active in a range of work on behalf of the dioceses of Augsburg, Speyer, and Würzburg in the fields of parish sociography, adult education, and church planning.

Although the directors of the institutes in Münster, Frankfurt, Königstein, Essen, and Landstuhl/Adelsried kept regular contact, the fragmentation of the research institutions compared unfavorably to the situation in the Netherlands or Austria, which both had central institutes for Catholic social research covering the whole country. Fragmentation thus remained an important characteristic of sociography in the West German Catholic Church. One reason for this was the marked "diocesitis" that still existed in the 1950s. This presented an obstacle to coordinating fulfillment of new cross-diocese tasks in the church, and meant that existing institutions such as the Kölner Zentralstelle tended to stay put.[111]

Plans for a Federal Pastoral Institute

The need to respect existing institutions and the shortage of financial resources also combined, from the mid-1960s, to shape the ongoing discussion on the need to establish a "pastoral institute" at the federal level and, along with two further factors, to prevent the creation of a central point of contact for questions and studies relating to pastoral sociology. From the beginning, plans for a federal German pastoral institute, which was to be oriented along the lines of the Österreichische Seelsorgeinstitut (Austrian Pastoral Institute) in Vienna and the Pastoraal Instituut van de Nederlandse Kerkprovinz (Pastoral Institute of the Dutch Church Province), aimed to use the results of empirical social research. Alongside the Institut für missionarische Seelsorge (Institute for Missionary Pastoral Care) in St. Georgen near Frankfurt, which was run by Redemptorists, the working group of the episcopal pastoral offices and the Konferenz der deutschsprachigen Pastoraltheologen (KDPT, Conference of German-Speaking Pastoral Theologians), a loose network of theologians teaching pastoral theology at university, lent sustained support to this idea through their contact with the German Bishops' Conference. The objective was to improve coordination and make the implementation of pastoral concepts in the wake of the radical changes since the Second Vatican Council more reflective.[112] In terms of organizing social science research in the church, discussants agreed from the late 1960s that a "return to the autodidacticism of the early phase of church research" was no longer possible, not least because sociology had gradually shifted from being "purely illustrative sociography" to employing more complex procedures such as "researching motives and attitudes."[113]

Right up to the time of the Würzburg Synod of the Dioceses in the Federal Republic, which met from 1972 to 1975, discussion about a federal pastoral institute revolved largely around a 1968 report by the KDPT. The archbishop of Munich, Julius Cardinal Döpfner, had commissioned this report in his role as head of the Pastoral Commission of the German Bishops' Conference. Döpfner had also chaired the German Bishops' Conference since 1965 and was an important integrating figure for German Catholicism in the upheaval that followed the council. In the context of the planned federal pastoral institute, the report provided for the establishment of an independent Catholic institute for church social research in the Federal Republic. The conciliar documents also served to legitimize these ideas. After all, "Christus Dominus"—the decree on the bishops' pastoral role in the church—explicitly stated that an apostolate adapted to "current needs" not only needed to consider "spiritual and moral" issues, but also "social, demographic and economic" circumstances, and strongly advised that "offices of pastoral sociology" be utilized to study these.[114] The report, which was tailored to the situation in Germany, thus called for a "pure research institution" to describe "profane society," carry out empirical studies on the state of the church and religious practice, and conduct planning work. The report went substantially further than the church sociography that had been practiced up to that point, inquiring about the "significance of religious attitudes" even beyond those practices that were "embedded in the church." It proposed the use of scaling techniques and research on motives to analyze these, and thus put an emphasis on approaches from social psychology.[115]

Both the German Bishops' Conference and the synod commission in Würzburg responsible for the "order of pastoral structures" approved of these suggestions. However, even among committed advocates of the use of social sciences in pastoral planning, financial affordability set clear limits on the implementation of these ideas. Consequently, the commission members called for better use and coordination of the existing "mini-institutes" in Landstuhl/Adelsried, Essen, and Cologne. Norbert Greinacher correctly pointed out that the money for studies the German Bishops' Conference and individual dioceses had requested from nonchurch sociological research institutions could easily have financed a new, church-based institution. This would then have provided a core group of specialists familiar with the specific issues of church sociology. Yet his arguments did not sway the decision.[116]

As significant as the cost issue as discussions continued was the "consternation" of church offices afraid that a central pastoral institute would make them superfluous.[117] Hermann-Josef Spital, the head of pastoral care in the diocese of Münster, argued that a new institution would "soon claim an importance of its own" and would "further multiply" the "confusion of concepts" in pastoral practice. Particularly in the area of church social research, he claimed, there was no shortage of "analyses" but rather of "people to draw appropriate conclusions" from such work—not a task that could be left to parish clergy alone. Precisely this consideration, he wrote in 1971, had brought him into contact with Josef Scharrer and his Gesellschaft für christliche Öffentlichkeitsarbeit (GCÖ, Society for Christian Public Relations Work), with whose help Spital hoped to trigger a "learning process" that would lead to real "structural changes" in the medium term.[118] For Spital, the practical application of insights into public opinion and public relations was the issue, not any lofty ideas about "society" and its effects on pastoral work.

A further obstacle to implementing plans for a German pastoral institution, and one that was not specific to pastoral sociology, was the widespread concern among bishops about the public impact of university pastoral theologians. Bishops viewed the "Pastorale," published from 1970 in twenty-seven fascicles, as an important justification for their misgivings. Published by the Konferenz deutschsprachiger Pastoraltheologen with a recommendation from the chair of the German Bishops' Conference, the "Pastorale" was conceived as a "helping hand for pastoral service." On behalf of the bishops of North Rhine-Westphalia, Joseph Höffner railed against official approval of the "Pastorale" for pastoral practice, as it would give "undue authority" to the "private work of a small number of theologians." These and perhaps further interventions led the German Bishops' Conference to withdraw its support for the "Pastorale" in 1972.[119]

The form the widely debated central "Pastoral Institute" ultimately took seems wholly in keeping with these debates about the positioning of theological and sociological consultation and planning in the German church. In the course of an internal reorganization, the German Bishops' Conference created in 1975/76 a "central office for fundamental pastoral questions," which was under the direct responsibility of the bishops' plenary conference. Equipped with only a few full-time staff, this office was supposed to provide "inspiration and impetus" and take on "generally project-based" assignments from the bishops.[120] The new central office, the legitimate voice introducing the human sciences to pastoral care in the German church, thus took a position practically identical to that of the college of bishops.

In comparison to major nonuniversity sociological research institutions in Germany, such as the Social Research Centre Dortmund (Sozialforschungsstelle), the disparate and sometimes short-lived initiatives to institutionalize church pastoral sociology were negligible. On the other hand, empirical social research outside academia in general had only become institutionalized to a limited extent by the mid-1960s, with the exception of commercial market research and opinion surveys. Nonuniversity institutions repeatedly lost their best researchers to the universities.[121] This gave Catholic institutions some significance, albeit quantitatively small, within German sociology. It would be hard to overestimate the contribution they made to the questions the German Catholic Church posed, the approaches they took, and the forms of knowledge they acquired. Thus, these institutions' role in the scientization of the church can likewise hardly be overstated. The "mini-institutes" in Münster, Frankfurt, Essen, Königstein, and Landstuhl/Adelsried, more than any other source, familiarized a continually widening circle of theologians, secular and religious priests, members of ordinariates, and functionaries of Catholic associations with sociology, which in 1955 was still described as an "unknown science."[122] In all likelihood, only *Lebendige Seelsorge,* a widely circulated pastoral journal launched in 1950, had a comparable impact. Providing direct instruction on sociographic issues, it included articles written from a perspective that was consistently oriented toward social "reality."[123]

The church's failure to found a central institute for church social research rather than just an subordinate office with few staff members also marked the end of its efforts from 1950 to 1975 to create its own permanent research resources. In this 25-year period, the smaller institutions provided a range of services to Catholic social research. First, they trained sociographers who had a greater affinity with the church and whose research would be less inclined to criticize it. Second, the institutes in Essen and Königstein served to qualify a wide circle of people, the majority of whom worked in the church, in a kind of pastoral care based on sociological insights. Third, the institute staff had a multiplier effect on the spread of the sociographic approach, whether through numerous publications in pastoral newspapers of individual dioceses and in the academic journals on pastoral care, or directly through presentations and training courses. Fourth, the creation of institutes also led to closer networking between all parties with an interest in applying church sociography. Such personal contact also kindled efforts to standardize sociographic techniques, particularly those associated with differentiated surveys of church attendance.[124]

The Ambivalent Situation of Pastoral Sociologists

On the supply side, the church's widespread use of the sociographic method derived from the four aforementioned services that the institutes provided. Nevertheless, the institutionalization of church research institutions failed to create a core of qualified Catholic pastoral sociologists. By the early 1960s, the relevant group of individuals remained too small. This was evident at the PSI in Essen in 1962, where Greinacher felt obliged to name three possible successors when he wished to leave because he believed it was very "difficult" to find a "qualified, experienced sociologist of religion." Alongside Walter Menges, only two individuals came into consideration for him, both from the Netherlands: Oswald Schreuder, OFM, and Walter Goddijn, OFM, at the time a leading member of KASKI. After Menges and Goddijn declined, Egon Golomb ultimately became the PSI's director.[125] In the mid-1960s, it was already apparent that the church would not be able to compete with university research in sociology by creating research resources of its own. Franz Hengsbach, for example, felt that the PSI and its staff "almost spent more time communicating with other academic institutions" than with the church body that had commissioned it, the diocese of Essen and he himself as its bishop. In reaction, Hengsbach regrouped the PSI as the department of Church Social Research at the Sozialinstitut in Essen in 1964 and sought to integrate sociologists into the educational and pastoral work of the diocese. At the same time, he wanted to dispel any "distrust" of sociology among the clergy.[126]

Such reservations among the clergy again point to the ambivalent position of pastoral sociologists in the service of the church. Academically, they absolutely needed to embed themselves in the national and international "scientific community" of religious sociologists if they wanted to remain at the methodological forefront of their subject; such embedding also fulfilled a social psychological function for qualified sociologists, as it helped them balance out role conflicts and status problems when conducting church social research.[127] Such conflicts were not, however, a specific feature of church social research, but were widespread in applied sociology. They applied particularly to the institute-appointed roles of "practitioner" and "researcher." "Consultants," meanwhile, were only involved over the short term, their interaction with the Catholic Church generally funded by a private institution.[128]

One long-term solution to such role conflicts was the movement of sociologists into university institutions, which fed the immense demand for sociology professors in the years around 1970, particularly at universities of applied sciences.[129] Consequently, after 1970 university rather than church institutions increasingly conducted research on the sociology of religion, precipitating a brain drain in church social research institutions. The Königstein institute's dissolution in 1970 and the Essen institute's further demotion to an office of the diocese administration in 1975 were emblematic of this. Only the privately funded institutes Sozialteam and Gesellschaft für christliche Öffentlichkeitsarbeit continued to work on the same scale after 1975.[130] Catholic social research institutes in other Western European countries experienced the same development.[131] It was not the methodological stagnation of pastoral sociology that stalled the expansion of the church's research institutes. Rather, the decisive factor was the rapid expansion of academic sociology. In the face of growing university research, the church's own researchers found their ambivalent position untenable.

Direct and Indirect Consequences of Sociographic Research

In contrast to the statistical discourse, the sociographic discourse contained a sufficiently clear idea of the method's practical uses for church activities and thus of its own implications and effectiveness. To some extent, sociographic topics and insights emphasized the need to reorient pastoral activity in view of changing social realities. Sociography had not been intended to serve specific church interests, but rather to enable and legitimize missionary interests. This made it essential to point out the "importance of sociological studies" using their own "successes."[132] Advocates held hopes and specific suggestions for the implications of sociographic research in narrow and broad, direct and indirect terms. Some sociographers, for example, believed that city dwellers familiar with radio, film, and TV needed to be "addressed differently" than previously, when they had not had access to these media. They thought that one could utilize these study results directly to create a "sociologically 'targeted' sermon." Others also mentioned changes to pastoral care for the working class, far-sighted parish planning, coordination of pastoral work at the town level, and changes to the times of religious services as possible outcomes.[133] However, sociographers saw the value of their analysis not only in such specific interventions, but also hoped to "uncover general laws" with "the most intensive research" and thereby draw a comprehensive picture of the way modern society influenced the church.[134]

At the same time, they were already aware that sociological work did not always fulfill the objectives defined at the outset, and that it could have unintended consequences. In any case, it soon became evident that any sociological findings first needed to be "translated" into pastoral language to be of any help in that field. On the other hand, even rather scientifically "insignificant" studies could make considerable contributions to priests' work, for example, by revealing the "multilayered nature of the social situations" they examined. Writers warned people not to expect directly applicable "directives" to emerge from studies, as "sociology often raises more problems than it solves."[135] Thus, ideas from the human sciences increased the complexity of the church's work, becoming irritants, without necessarily generating models for capturing this complexity.

In the following, I will refer to direct and indirect consequences of sociographic work, although this should be understood as merely an exploratory and analytic distinction. Many indirect effects were, in fact, directly related to the intended outcomes. Four direct effects will be discussed, followed by indirect consequences.

Knocking Down the Potemkin Village of Statistics

The first direct effect of sociography was to break people's illusions, particularly those many parish pastoral workers had about the quantifiable aspects of religious practice in their parish or diocese. For decades, the Potemkin village of the

Kölner Zentralstelle's statistical apparatus had disguised the vanishing social basis of church-organized mass piety: even when the centrally quantifiable parameters such as church attendance showed a marked downward trend, one could always find another "consoling" statistic, such as the number of spiritual exercises completed.[136] The data produced within the sociographic approach made it possible to expose this self-satisfied, status quo–focused discourse. Sociographers directly criticized the lack of social differentiation in the Cologne statistics as a serious defect, arguing that a general "head count," which was then "perhaps rounded generously upwards," "achieved more or less nothing." The real question, they argued, was exactly who was attending church services, and, therefore, "much more importantly," which social groups were staying away.[137] This meant including other social characteristics and forms of religious participation beyond attendance at church and Easter Communion. As early as 1953, for example, Joseph Höffner complained to the dean of the diocese of Münster that statistics were "too general" and failed to give "any breakdown of family structure," or to provide the number of married women in jobs and a possible "loss of function" of the family that could result from this.[138]

In addition, the people's missionaries, in particular, complained that statistics had been used to disguise the real decline of practiced piety and, thus, had primarily fulfilled a reassuring function. In 1956, Bernhard Häring spoke of sugarcoated statistics whose "gentle analyses were only suitable to lull to sleep those fighting for the kingdom of God." Sociography's objective, by contrast, he described as developing the "courage" to hear the "alarm signals."[139] This characterization led to sociography and missionary pastoral work both being described as "male." Likewise, educators were divided into male and female types: a "male educator" presented his "messages to the world" without wondering how or by whom they were "received," whereas the "female teacher" was content "to preserve and care for" what had been entrusted to her.[140] The latter was precisely the self-satisfied pastoral style that the people's missionaries wanted to break through, with respect also to quantifiable pastoral care. Bernhard Scholten noted in 1957 that the clergy in Bocholt were still "reveling in statistics" despite the availability of precise data on the "general decline of religious life," although it was clear that pastoral workers could not be "spared this shock."[141]

Similar to the French *sociologie religieuse,* the sociographic discourse, in analyzing the findings, contained a self-reinforcing call for pastoral care to adapt to the changing social situation, partly because it perceived social reality more acutely than before. Moreover, it no longer attributed the "deviant" behavior of *Abständige*—"people who abstain" from practiced piety in church jargon; that is, those who stayed away from the church—to their individual moral deficits, but rather to a transformation emerging from the process of social differentiation. From the early 1960s, any presentation of the findings of the sociographic discourse was accompanied by the term "religious crisis." Following the word's original meaning—the openness of a "critical" situation, in which decisions can shape things either way—this "crisis" suggested that a decision could help the church "courageously overcome" the situation, that is, by implementing an "open-minded pastoral care."[142] In 1968, after almost ten years of work in the regional mission, the sociographers of the Social Team in Adelsried extrapolated the trend toward secularization in the diocese of Speyer to the year 2000. They concluded that more than four-fifths of Catholics would no longer be attached to the church by then (an accurate calculation, it turns out), which meant that if the milieu was to avoid its typical self-deception or "resignation" in the future, the church could no longer treat its pastoral structures "as unchangeable." Although "social structures" would no longer "support pastoral care" as they had in the typical village parish of the past, the milieu could not abandon the idea of a *Volkskirche* or people's church that encompassed and catered to all baptized Catholics. For it to flee resignedly to the "parish church" of few active believers would be an act of "sociological relativism and a betrayal of pastoral care."[143] When sociographic discourse introduced such statements, the Catholic Church had arrived at the stage of "secondary scientization," in which scientific experts had to debate other experts' interventions and studies clashed with counterstudies.[144]

Reshaping Pastoral Zones

The milieu's desire to extensively reorganize pastoral structures pointed to its attempts to optimize the church apparatus and to work on foresighted planning for deploying pastoral resources.[145] The first moves in this direction, which emerged from within the sociographic discourse, were largely similar to those of the French model of *sociologie religieuse,* with its focus on the regional context of social processes. Events in the archdiocese of Paderborn illustrate this second direct consequence of sociographic work. The pastoral office in Paderborn had inspired a lively interest in new pastoral practices underpinned by sociology. When Alois Nüschen assumed leadership of the office after Franz Hengsbach departed in 1959, efforts intensified to "bridge the gap between the world and the church, believers and unbelievers, those loyal to the church and those who stayed away." The impetus for this was the "fact," doubtless uncovered by sociographic work, that "only 20 percent of workers" in major cities were still "attached to the church." The diocesan conference in 1959 was a decisive turning point in combining and substantiating these approaches. Bernhard Häring gave the keynote speech at the event in place of fellow Redemptorist Viktor Schurr. Nüschen himself also spoke on "regional pastoral care and regional pastoral workers."[146]

This diocesan conference was the start of an initiative to incorporate Fernand Boulard's model of a "pastorale d'ensemble"—a "holistic pastoral care" in socio-spatial units (*zones humaines*)—into pastoral practice in Westphalia. Beyond this direct borrowing of concepts, the initiative kept its ambitions within the bounds of the sociographic approach by not intending to make any structural changes to "personal and regional pastoral care."[147] Following a sociological suggestion, the archdiocese constructed the "pastoral zone" as a new "intermediate structure" between deanery and diocese. To this end, it initially appointed a regional pastoral worker for the parishes in the district of Meschede, a young clergyman. In addition to carrying out the work in his own parish, he was supposed to investigate the region's "sociological and pastoral" environment and make his discoveries available to other parishes and usable in pastoral care. He discovered that one of the pressing issues in this region was the transition of young people into industrial employment. Hence, he commissioned a study on the topic from the PSI. The results of his work were evidently deemed encouraging enough that three further clergy members were given this role in other areas.[148]

In 1965, the pastoral office then held a series of workshops that led to its resolution to complete this model by creating seven "pastoral districts" in order to adapt "church pastoral methods to modern conditions" against the background of the tasks set by the Second Vatican Council. It appointed deans to these districts for a period of five years without setting out detailed working methods. Instead, the deans were supposed to develop these in the course of their work. As if self-evident, the resolution described the deans' primary responsibility as the "pastoral-sociological cataloguing of the district." Prohibitive costs (around DM 200,000) spoiled the plan to allow the Social Team experts from Adelsried to conduct a sociographic investigation of a selected deanery in each district, forcing staff of the statistical office in the general vicariate to do this work on their own.[149]

Insights into Social Differentiation

A third direct effect of sociographic work was its long-term success in conveying fundamental insights into the irreversible advance of social differentiation and thus into a development that characterized social "reality" and, with it, religion and the activity of the church. Many church figures likely saw this process as just as threatening and damaging as the decline in religious practice sociography had also revealed unmistakably. Yet social differentiation played a greater role in the overall dynamic of the process of scientization. All subsequent measures referred directly or indirectly to this issue. Every pastoral worker had to recognize that "modern society was no longer a straightforward entity, but a dynamic, exceptionally differentiated" complex. Concretely, this meant that the church was no longer working in a "church-centered" world of "farmers and the bourgeoisie," but "in a technological society divided into ten thousand occupations and countless organizations, with no common center to impose order."[150] While such formulations exuded the spirit of conservative cultural criticism in the 1950s, the sociological insight behind them pervaded the church in the medium term and determined the way it defined problems and designed practices. Amid the diversity and contradictory results that sociographic empirical work brought to light, a central analytic finding remained undisputed: the modern church was preaching its message to a "work-oriented society indifferent to faith and religion."[151]

One concrete example of this insight being incorporated into pastoral work was the debate on organizational strategies for studying village populations in the 1950s. Ludwig Neundörfer made a central contribution with a 1953 speech on the rural situation from a sociographic perspective. This speech launched a meeting of the Zentralkomitee der deutschen Katholiken, the umbrella organization of all lay initiatives in German Catholicism and also the body that organized the Katholikentag, the biannual, fairlike gathering of all these initiatives. Representing the interests of lay Catholics and their manifold associations, the ZdK was also a powerful player in West German politics in the 1950s and 1960s, not least through its close contacts to the then-governing Christian Democratic Union (CDU). Speaking about the "church and rural population," Neundörfer showed that the village could no longer be understood as an undifferentiated social unit defined by farming production or even by "farmers." Rather, rural regions were now largely shaped by those who worked in nearby towns and cities and by evacuees and refugees. The only features that continued to characterize rural life as such were its specific "form of living" and the major significance of a "familiar economy" detached from the market.[152] These theses, and the findings relating to the change in the character of the village, decisively spurred the ZdK to continue pursuing the path begun in 1951 with the creation of the Katholische Landvolkbewegung (Catholic Rural People's Movement) and to explicitly reject the idea of an occupational association for farmers. Instead, the movement was to focus on village life or the rural "milieu" as defined above.[153]

An alternative model, which only a few dioceses such as Münster followed, was to focus strongly on occupations when working with the rural population.[154] This tendency could, in part, be attributed in Münster to the sociological leanings of Heinrich Tenhumberg, who was responsible for rural pastoral care in the offices of the vicar-general. We will encounter Tenhumberg (1915–79) again later in this book. As bishop of Münster from 1969 and later as chairman of the Pastoral Commission of the German Bishops' Conference, he was a central figure in the German episcopate during the late 1960s and early 1970s. He sought compromise both in the sometimes-fierce conflicts in his diocese and within the whole German church. Tenhumburg recognized early on that administrative measures could not take care of left-wing Catholic criticism. In his view, the problems raised during the upheaval in the church from 1968 had a material justification, even though he did not share the critics' position.[155] It was not sociography but the formal sociology of Leopold von Wiese, which left open the possibility of "socioethical values," that guided Tenhumberg's perspective on rural pastoral care in the 1950s. Using von Wiese's tools to "examine the essence" of the village,

Tenhumberg thought that "agricultural activity and the population's ties to the land" without question no longer determined rural "character."[156]

As these alternative approaches show, different strategies for organizing the rural population depended on the sociological analysis of village social structures one assumed to be correct.

Differentiating between Types of Active Christians

As a fourth direct effect, sociographic work made it possible to categorize different types of religious practice using the results of differentiated church attendance surveys, and thus to exploit fully the insights this instrument provided in making pastoral judgments. At this point, however, the limits of sociography's usefulness also became apparent. As it used rigid quantifying data collection tools, it tended in practice to pigeonhole sociological work in a way that trivialized its own standard arguments and robbed it of its originally envisaged reform potential. A three-way typology of sociographic explanations emerged: spatial differentiation with regard to the parish, vertical differentiation according to social class, and generational differentiation based on different stages of life.

At its heart, this schema reflected the adoption of interpretive models from French *sociologie religieuse* in German sociography. With regard to parish typologies, for example, sociographers differentiated between intensities of religious practice using Gabriel Le Bras's model. Fernand Boulard and Émile Pin had adapted this schema to distinguish three types of parishes: Christian, indifferent, and missionary.[157] Other writers looking to demarcate "people who abstain" limited themselves to applying this characteristic to individual people. Utilizing Joseph Fichter's typology, which had slightly modified Le Bras's schema, German sociographers differentiated between members of the "core parish" (*Kernpfarre*), "average Catholics" (*Durchschnittskatholiken*), "marginal Catholics" (*Randkatholiken*), and "dormant Catholics" (*schlummernde Katholiken*).[158] The distinctions among different stages of life, were, likewise, borrowed from French *sociologie religieuse*. The oft-quoted notion that the church was increasingly made up of women, children, and the elderly came directly from French researchers' findings.[159] Finally, typologies of class structure also borrowed from French interpretive models, finding abstention from church primarily among the working class.[160]

By 1963, at the latest, some began to question the further usefulness of sociographic research. François Houtart, for example, by no means only rhetorically, inquired whether pastoral social research had reached a "critical point." Although sociographic knowledge had relatively quickly become "one of the spiritual tools" of each and every Catholic in both France and Germany, that also reduced the "novelty" of a priest discovering that the "religious practice of the petite bourgeoisie was better than that of the working class" in his parish. What difference could it make to such a priest's "pastoral orientation" whether "11.25 percent or 13.75 percent" of workers in his parish were "practicing Christians"?[161] At the same time, some priests recognized that sociographic discourse, with its quantitative typology of religious practice, had exhausted its potential to make adequately complex and differentiated assertions about "social reality" so that one need not study each environment anew. For example, the committee preparing the Cologne city mission in 1964 chose to simply examine existing studies for other cities from the institutes in Essen and Königstein to take account of Cologne's sociological "realities." When the main findings proved to be "largely consistent" with these studies, the committee concluded that "these phenomena" were "no different in Cologne" and adopted the results of the earlier studies.[162] In the diocese of Passau, by contrast, it was not until the early 1970s, when a new representative was appointed for the regional mission, that the many years of growing dissatisfaction with the sociographic preparation of missionary work were acknowledged. The analysis of the results had been disappointing on account of its schematic and delayed character: it was often conducted long after the mission itself. Consequently, the diocese methodically "unburdened" sociography such that, rather than setting its sights on social stratification, it would inquire into the "subjective level of identification with the faith and mission." Thus, the surveys in the diocese of Passau, which initially continued to be conducted using simple tearable slips, were moving in the direction of an opinion poll.[163]

Limits of Sociographic Research

In the course of the 1960s, then, sociographic discourse reached the limits of its ability to say something "true" and nontrivial about the social reality of the church and German society in general. Nevertheless, it continued to have indirect and unintended effects. First, the practical application of sociographic methods led to new patterns of classification in the Catholic Church. Sociography's categorical framework pushed back the discourses that had traditionally dominated in the church, particularly the dogmatic-mystical and the legal view of the church, but also ethical arguments and ultimately moral theology. As early as 1953, Joseph Höffner had already outlined the implications sociography had for church discourses. Discussing a priest's position in his parish, Höffner pointed out that neither a dogmatic-ecclesiological view, nor one purely based in church law, would do justice to the "tensions and possible conflicts" that really existed in this situation. With reference to a critique by Belgian sociologist of religion Jacques Leclercq, Höffner characterized such a formal and legal approach as "juridism" and rejected it as inadequate.[164]

Because sociography was used most frequently in the context of the people's mission, the mission exemplifies the general decline of moral discourse. The traditional people's mission centered on fire-and-brimstone preaching, which called on the faithful to confess their sins in church and thereby rescue their souls. Individual missionaries utilized their theatrical ability to enthrall audiences with "forceful imagery," "brutal existentialism," and "shudder-inducing Satanology" from the pulpit.[165] Such late forms of dramatic ultramontane piety continued to be used in the 1950s, as evident from the complaint of a priest in Bad Pyrmont. The "sentimentality and lack of style" of the Redemptorist fathers who conducted the people's mission in his parish had set back the parish's development as he had intended to shape it. In addition, it also prompted objections from "religiously educated Catholics."[166]

The explicit aims of the sociography-led regional mission included suppressing such "moralistic" missionary preaching.[167] With its focus on social circumstances, the new kind of mission sought to replace fire and brimstone, which aimed to save the individual soul, with supposedly more contemporary and realistic arguments. This required more "inductive" sermons that were better adapted "to the environment" of the respective region. Against the "emotive" tendency of the traditional mission style, the new mission sought to connect with the audience's "needs and problems, fears, and anxieties."[168] Priests taking confession were also supposed to take "religious-sociological" issues into consideration and "judge less harshly" the "weaknesses" induced by the "poisoned" milieu of the major cities. This style of mission circumvented the morally loaded code of ultramontane piety, with its starkly subjective dividing line between damnation and salvation. Instead, it replaced it with a far more sober discourse that acknowledged the sociographic idea that individuals were shaped by their milieu.[169]

This suppression of morally loaded arguments accompanied the practice of a new mode of thinking that suggested pastoral workers and those active in the church follow the classifying models of the sociographic discourse. One tool of priests had always been precise knowledge of their parishes' social environment. However, the specific perspective and categorical framework priests usually used to assess their social environment had continued, into the early 1950s, to attribute sociomoral qualities and deficits to individuals or groups. In the early 1920s, for example, a priest in Lower Bavaria had described social conditions in his parish using typical vocabulary such as "selfishness," "greed," and "hedonism."[170] In the early 1950s, this had not changed substantially: when priests were asked for the purposes of sociographic work which "social class" was the most loyal to the church, they continued to complain of "moral decay" or an "unwillingness to make sacrifices."[171]

In the medium term, the exhaustive promotion, dissemination, and application of sociographic research methods wore away such sociomoral perspectives and replaced them with a more realistic perspective. This perspective illustrated the fundamental dependence of religious practice and religious attitudes on the dynamic of an increasingly differentiated society and the existence of socioeconomic class structures. The reports priests sent to the general vicariate after the conclusion of regional missions reflected this awareness. The "modest question-naire" with statistical information on confessions and attendance patterns during the *Standespredigten*—sermons that separately addressed married and unmarried men and women—was no longer sufficient. Instead, the missionaries prepared a comprehensive set of questions to collect qualitative and quantitative data. Information on the social, economic, and demographic structure of the parish provided them with an extensive survey of religious life. With the use of these methods, the regular mission report became a short introduction to the social stratification, occupations, and commuting habits of the local areas and their consequences for parishioners' religious practice.[172] An important side effect of the sociographic discourse was the "practice" it gave missionaries in adopting the "empirical gaze," a fact-based approach to social reality that relied on empirical social research.[173] Sociography thus made a fundamental contribution to over-coming the socioromantic patterns of thought most church figures employed in perceiving the society around them up until then, when they had perceived anything at all.

Nevertheless, there is also evidence here of the "paradoxical syntheses of the modern and the antimodern" typical of Catholicism in the 1950s.[174] This can be seen, for example, in the ways in which sociography thematized the effects of urban life on religious practice. On the one hand, some protagonists of sociogra-phy attempted to help reduce the sweeping "prejudices" many priests held about the supposedly corrosive effects of city life on Catholicism. Instead of broad refer-ences to the "masses" and people's "isolation," they sought to present the essence of the urban lifestyle in a more positive light, using sociological research to point out the many individual freedoms it offered.[175] Sociographic institutes attempted to take the widespread and "more misleading than helpful idea" of "alienation from the church encouraged by the urban milieu" and transform it into a more complex explanatory approach. In the course of these efforts, they also presented concrete plans for adapting church services to the specific pastoral situation in major cities, for example, by increasing the importance of the central churches.[176]

On the other hand, clichés and judgments also found their way into socio-graphic work, pointing to the persistence of traditional ideas of community in West German Catholicism. A good example of this was the study prepared by Alfons Weyand for the ICSW as a prelude to the regional mission in Marl in 1955/56. This rapidly changing town was considered a pastoral problem area in the diocese of Münster that warranted particular attention. Weyand pre-dominantly emphasized findings suggesting that the horizontal mobility of the recently arrived residents was the most significant factor in secularization.[177] The study's methodology and its results were by no means beyond dispute, as Höffner's successor Wilhelm Weber rightly pointed out during an ICSW seminar. Weyand's presentation and analysis of the figures on church atten-dance included a mixture of descriptive, normative, and clichéd statements and explained away inconvenient findings using "ad hoc hypotheses." The study's main feature was Weyand's "ideology of rootedness," which was grounded in traditional German Catholic ideas of community. For Weyand, settledness and long-lasting communal relationships promoted participation in the church, while "urban life" and, "above all," the horizontal mobility associated with it, were intrinsically damaging to religious life.[178] "Continuity in religious practice," he claimed, "requires continuity in other areas of life, too." Although Weyand claimed to "let the facts speak for themselves" in this study, what he actually presented as its result was the articulation of an influential discourse within the church.[179] It started from the premise that only a "rooted person" could be a good Catholic, so that stable occupations such as farming, trade, and teaching provided favored social "models."[180] Already by 1955, the American Jesuit Joseph H. Fichter, a sober outside observer who argued from the perspective of the social structures typical in the United States, was highly skeptical about the possibility of a "restauration of community."[181]

The ambivalence of the sociographic enlightenment about the "realities" of modern industrial society can be seen elsewhere, too. Sociographers quickly agreed that the links between social circumstances and religious practice should no longer be analyzed using sociomoral categories, but with the concept of social "stratification," which comprised a group of characteristics such as livelihood, professional qualifications, and social status at work.[182] This approach corresponded to those social parameters observable by means of a differentiated counting of church visitors. However, the potential diversity of investigations was immediately narrowed down to a perspective that, by no means coincidentally, matched that of *sociologie religieuse*. Introductions to missionary pastoral care thus concentrated on the working class as the population group most in need of close attention. As soon as the first summary analyses of sociographic findings were available, it was possible to justify this on the grounds that it was usually the skilled and unskilled working class who had the lowest church involvement in relation to their share of the overall population.[183]

However, it was not only empirical findings that made it necessary to focus attention on the working class's abstention from church and to demand pastoral action on the basis of these "scientifically" proven facts. Even before any research on Germany was available, Norbert Greinacher, for example, pointed to studies in France, where a "constant feature" of all research results was a large discrepancy in religious practice between "socio-occupational classes." The results of a study by Yvan Daniel showing that miners represented 45 percent of the entire male population in the coalfields of Lens in northern France but only 2.55 percent of all practicing Catholics were so vivid that conclusions were easy to draw.[184] The analyses and pastoral strategies of *sociologie religieuse* and missionary pastoral care in France had already ascertained a working class estranged from the church, so that it became a clearly defined issue on the church agenda. It was enough to note that Pope Pius XI had written to Joseph Cardijn: "It is the greatest scandal of the nineteenth century that the church has lost the working class."[185]

Some advocates of sociographic approaches such as Michael Pfliegler or Walter Menges, however, criticized such an excessively schematic view of the working class. They called for further "investigations with general applicability" and attempts to refine and differentiate the empirical findings.[186] In the Catholic workers' movement, especially, however, the quoted sentence by Pope Pius XI was the key point of reference. Together with the associated quantitative findings, it continued to carry weight and offered ammunition with which to prove the relevance of modern pastoral care for the working class.[187] Sociography applied the concept of stratification to the Catholic Church during the short period in the 1950s and early 1960s before Marxist class terminology became so prevalent that it made the reception of sociological ideas of social inequality difficult, if not outright impossible.

Sociographic studies of individual districts and cities continued to be produced after 1970 and published in manuscript form. However, interest in sociography and its main instrument—differentiated counting of church attendance—began to decrease rapidly from 1970 onward.[188] This was not only because sociography's empirical findings had become redundant. By the late 1960s, one could generally assume that most parish priests and active laypeople were capable of practicing and applying the "empirical gaze" independently. Training courses on "parish analyses" and textbooks setting out the relevant questions for the most important data supported them in this.[189]

Another factor was the growing interest of parishes and councils in carrying out sociographic work. Increasingly, however, such studies no longer recorded "facts" so much as they triggered a learning process through the shared exploration of the social environment and thus raised awareness in parishes and church councils of the issue of modern pastoral working styles. This was evident, for example, in the plans for "project-oriented" training in pastoral care discussed in 1971 in the pastoral department of the diocese of Münster. Full- and part-time church workers were to receive block instruction, which utilized sociographic approaches, in project-focused work on parish development. The Gesellschaft für christliche Öffentlichkeitsarbeit, the private institute founded in 1966 by Josef Scharrer, a sociologist with a background in public relations management, took a leading role in conceptualizing this initiative. Based on the GCÖ's recommendation, this training was only supposed to take place in the context of courses on group dynamics, designed for the important task of "motivating and enabling participation." As with pastoral work itself, one had to generate an interest before starting any work with actual "facts." The sociographic discourse became frayed around the edges from the early 1970s, losing its coherence and ability to provide structure. It moved from the center of the pastoral program to the periphery, from hard "facts" to an agglomeration of working techniques that instructed and motivated those active in and for the church.[190]

The Sociographic Approach in France and Germany: A Comparison

With sociography, a form of empirical social science spread through the Catholic Church, for the first time extending beyond the statistical aggregation of data. In France, *sociologie religieuse* played an enormous role in shaping pastoral-theological thinking and the pastoral practice of Catholicism in the late 1940s and 1950s, as I have emphasized repeatedly.[191] If one considers the breadth of sociographic work produced in the 1950s and 1960s, one can make almost the same observation for the Federal Republic in those two decades. Clear regional concentrations of this new approach are discernible in northwestern Germany and in the archdiocese of Munich-Freising. In the course of conducting regional missions, however, all West German dioceses encountered the sociographic approach in this period. Staff in diocesan pastoral offices, clergy in missionary orders, deans, and parish priests, as well as many laypeople in the parishes and on the postconciliar councils, engaged with sociography. Staff at the pastoral-sociological institutes sought to create a network of those interested in such issues.

One crucial difference from France, however, can be found at the top of the church hierarchy, in the college of bishops. The French bishops had given the clergy an extensive "Directoire pastoral en matière sociale" in 1954, which contained analyses and instructions on addressing social problems in contemporary French society. It also called on priests to "urgently" inform themselves sufficiently about the social living conditions of the faithful, using "precise religious sociography."[192] German bishops presented no comparable coordinated initiative, and they were unable to agree that a central sociographic research institute for the Catholic Church was needed or that they should finance it, although they discussed such plans intensively in the early 1950s and again in the late 1960s. This inhibited the further spread and intensification of sociography. Moreover, that the upper echelons of the church did not authorize sociography, as was the case in France, explains its far-lower status in the consciousness of West German Catholicism at that time, and in earlier historiography.

The sociographic discourse opened church doors, metaphorically speaking, to new methodologies and concepts. The statistical discourse was, in a sense, situated just inside the doors. It attempted, while abstracting from any specific social analysis, to count those entering the church. Sociography, by contrast, aimed to understand where the attendees (as well as the abstainers) had come from spatially and socially, and, first and foremost, from which socioeconomic class. Sociography's main achievement was to understand the composition of church attendance as a reflection of the social structures surrounding the church and to research the causal relationships at work. For this, it had to be open to new concepts and take an interest in the problems and structures of modern secular society. Against the backdrop of ultramontane Catholicism's social and cultural isolation from modern society, this was a quantum leap. With the help, and through the lens, of sociography, West German Catholics literally encountered modernity on a broad scale and were able to grasp and acknowledge some of the key implications of functional differentiation for society. This included insights into how different strata were more or less ready to participate actively in the parish church.

In a sense, the programmatic demands of the protagonists of sociographic work anticipated the Second Vatican Council and, in particular, its pastoral constitution "Gaudium et Spes." This text marked a change in perspective wherein the church attempted systematically to introduce the "outside perspectives" of modern society into its own self-understanding and to afford them equal recognition. It did so with reference to sociological insights and an acceptance that it was necessary to take a sociological perspective into account in church pastoral work. There was also a direct connection between sociography and the council document itself. The work that representatives of French and Belgian pastoral sociology such as François Houtart carried out on "Gaudium et Spes" helped to determine its direction.[193]

Thus, sociography facilitated a substantial encounter between West German Catholics and modernity. Yet it is also necessary to stress the ambivalences of this encounter and the ways the church acknowledged the secular "world" and tried to adapt its pastoral structures to sociographic insights. The first ambivalence concerned its leading metaphors. On the one hand, the categorical framework and questions the sociographic discourse employed urged all devout Catholics not to close their eyes to the social environment and its implications for the intensity of religious practice. On the other hand, the rhetoric sociographers used to justify and legitimize the practice, with its emphatic "poisoning" metaphors, signaled the extent to which the protagonists of sociography still dismissed secular society as morally deficient. From the end of the 1950s, the traces of this imagery began to fade. This indicates that the church's traditional patterns of interpretation could only be replaced by powerful language with constitutive metaphors of its own that were capable of replacing old meanings with new ones.[194]

This ambivalence is also evident in the way that problems were interpreted. Central to Catholic sociography in the Federal Republic was the emphatic desire to penetrate social reality and orient pastoral activity around the knowledge thereby acquired. However, the leading metaphors, practical pastoral concepts such as the area mission, and the identification of the working class as a particularly potent crisis zone were all little-changed copies of the problem formulations and interpretations that French Catholicism had developed; they were principally valid in that specific context. In internal church discourse in the Federal Republic, the reference to the "missionary" impetus of *sociologie religieuse* was considered "progressive" until the Dutch model of "left-wing" Catholicism came to be extolled and attacked in equal measure from the late 1960s. There was no serious discussion, however, of whether the French strategies were truly applicable to the reality of West Germany.

Another ambivalence concerned the practical use of the observation techniques sociographic discourse utilized in classifying and regulating social factors in the church. The counting cards or tearable slips for differentiated counting of church attendance made sociography capable of studying much more complex issues than the simple techniques of the statistical discourse did. Combined with participant observation, the free and structured interview, and the analysis of historical sources and up-to-date official statistics, these tools enabled sociography to gain insight into the dynamic and social contours of religion that would meet the international standards of empirical social research.[195] However, in West German churches, the sociographic approach was almost effectively restricted to the use of counting cards alone. It was not long before this rendered sociography's empirical findings largely redundant and interchangeable, leading to its trivialization. This emphasis on quantification in German church sociography resulted from negotiations between pastoral sociologists and diocesan officials in which the institutions' scarce resources as well as church officials' interest in deploying a prestigious, modern, practice-oriented social research method figured prominently. That the West German Catholic Church reduced sociography to a technique for quantifying religious practice can only be correctly understood against the backdrop of the long-standing image of the church that centered on a clearly defined orthopraxy. Although the sociographic discourse openly criticized some of the self-deception inherent in church statistics, it ultimately remained trapped within the same categorical framework, which was based on clear parameters of religious practice such as attendance at Mass. The fact that sociography's quantitative tools met only isolated criticism—in each case concerning calculations of the number of priests—provides evidence of this.[196] The long shadow that the statistical discourse cast over sociography also helps to explain how disappointment spread throughout missionary pastoral care from 1960 at the latest because of the lack of measurable success. Given the immense expectations that missionary pastoral care would win the masses back to practicing Christianity, this was clearly a self-induced disappointment.

Notes

1. Georg Kliesch (Paderborn), on behalf of the Arbeitsgemeinschaft für katholisches Landleben in den nordwestdeutschen Diözesen, 14 July 1950, Testbogen zur Soziographie des Dorfes, EBAP, GA, Kirchliche Statistik, Beiakte zu 1945–1961.
2. Köhler and van Melis, "Einleitung der Herausgeber," 11.
3. Benjamin Ziemann, "Religion and the Search for Meaning, 1945–1990," in *The Oxford Handbook of Modern German History*, ed. Helmut Walser Smith (Oxford, 2011), 691.
4. Wolfgang Löhr, "Rechristianisierungsvorstellungen im deutschen Katholizismus 1945–1948," in *Christentum und politische Verantwortung: Kirchen im Nachkriegsdeutschland*, ed. Jochen-Chistoph Kaiser and Anselm Doering-Manteuffel (Stuttgart, 1990), 25–41.
5. See Nolte, *Ordnung*, 208–35.

6. Hans Zeisel, "Zur Geschichte der Soziographie" (1933), in *Die Arbeitslosen von Marienthal: Ein soziographischer Versuch über die Wirkungen langandauernder Arbeitslosigkeit,* Marie Jahoda, Paul F. Lazarsfeld, and Hans Zeisel (Frankfurt, 1982), 113–48. The afterword is not featured in the English translation: Jahoda, Lazarsfeld, and Zeisel, *Marienthal: The Sociography of an Unemployed Community* (London, 1972).

7. Zeisel, "Zur Geschichte der Soziographie."

8. Institut für Sozialforschung, *Soziologische Exkurse: Nach Vorträgen und Diskussionen* (Frankfurt, 1956), 133–50, quote 139.

9. René König, "Praktische Sozialforschung," in *Praktische Sozialforschung: Das Interview,* ed. René König (Dortmund and Zurich, 1952), 26.

10. Nikolaus Monzel, "Soziologie der Pfarrei: Ein Literaturbericht über vier Jahrzehnte (1909–1949)," *LS* 3 (1952): 156–60, 156–57.

11. Heinrich Swoboda, *Großstadtseelsorge: Eine pastoraltheologische Studie,* 2nd ed. (Regensburg, 1911), 117–18, 139, 202, 205, 214.

12. Minutes of the "Dechantenkonferenz," 25–27 May 1953, BAM, GV NA, A-101-381.

13. Reinhard Lettmann, "Joseph Höffner (1962–1969)," in *Das Bistum Münster,* ed. Werner Thissen (Münster, 1993), 1:320–27; Damberg, *Abschied,* 236–56, quote 255.

14. Minutes of the "Dechantenkonferenz," 25–27 May 1953, BAM, GV NA, A-101-381.

15. Ibid.

16. Ibid.; Gustav Ermecke, "Lebendige Seelsorge und Pastoralsoziologie," *LS* 3 (1952): 129–31, 129.

17. Minutes of the "Dechantenkonferenz," 25–27 May 1953, BAM, GV NA, A-101-381; Hans Mertens, "Sozialstatistische Studien zum Aufbau einer Großstadtpfarrgemeinde," *Unsere Diözese in Vergangenheit und Gegenwart* 2 (1928): 84–94, 143–48; Anton Weber, "Statistik des Gottesdienstbesuches," *Anregungen zur Seelsorge,* no. 10 (5 July 1959).

18. Carsten Klingemann, *Soziologie im Dritten Reich* (Baden-Baden, 1996), 87–102; Benjamin Ziemann, "Auf der Suche nach der Wirklichkeit: Soziographie und soziale Schichtung im deutschen Katholizismus 1945–1970," *GG* 29 (2003): 413.

19. The Jesuit Émile Pin referred to "études sociographiques." See his article "Dix ans de sociologie religieuse 1950–1960," *Revue de l'action populaire,* no. 145 (1961): 218.

20. Gabriel Le Bras, "Statistique et histoire religieuse," *Revue d'histoire de l'eglise de France* 17 (1931): 430–31; for a collection of his most important articles, see Gabriel Le Bras, *Études de Sociologie Religieuse,* 2 vols. (Paris, 1955/56), 195–218; on his source materials, see 229, 463–64.

21. François Boulard, *Problèmes missionnaires de la France rurale,* 2 vols. (Paris, n.d. [1945]); Le Bras, *Études,* 72–99.

22. Quote: Le Bras, *Études,* 601–2; Henri Desroche, "Areas and Methods of a Sociology of Religion: The Work of G. Le Bras," *Journal of Religion* 35 (1955): 49–50; Norbert Greinacher, *Soziologie der Pfarrei: Wege zur Untersuchung* (Colmar, 1955), 108–20.

23. Fernand Boulard, *Wegweiser in die Pastoralsoziologie* (Munich, 1960), 32–56, 102ff.

24. Émile Pin, *Pratique religieuses et classes sociales dans une paroisse urbaine: Saint-Pothin à Lyon* (Paris, 1956); Jean-Paul Terrenoire, "Pratique religieuse des catholiques en France 1930: Approches sociologiques globales et espaces de référence (1930–1980)," *Archives des Sciences Sociales des Religions* 87 (1994): 166–71.

25. Greinacher, *Soziologie der Pfarrei.*

26. Adolf Geck, "Die Entwicklung der im Dienste der sozialen Pastoral stehenden Religionssoziographie in Deutschland von 1952 bis 1956," *Kölner PBl.* 9 (1957): 49–54, quote 52; Pastor Werner Becker to KISIF, 8 August 1956, Katholiek Documentatie Centrum Nijmegen (KDC), 21, 4291.

27. Greinacher, *Soziologie der Pfarrei,* 101–7, 255–60.

28. In 1952, Monzel, Geck, and Ermecke organized the first meeting of the German section of the Conférence internationale de Sociologie religieuse, established in 1946. Gustav Ermecke, 28 February 1952, BAM, Franz-Hitze-Haus A 196.

29. Werner Schöllgen, "Recht und Notwendigkeit der Pastoralsoziologie im Urteil der Theologie," *Anima* 12 (1957): 16–24; Joseph Höffner, "Soziologie und Seelsorge," *Trierer Theologische Zeitschrift* 65 (1956): 218–19; Bernhard Häring, "Der biblische Begriff 'kairós' in seiner Bedeutung für die Pastoralsoziologie," *Theologie der Gegenwart* 2 (1959): 218–23.

30. Schöllgen referred to Acts of the Apostles 1:7; 2; Timothy 4:1–8; and Matthew 16:2–3. See Werner Schöllgen, "Christliche Soziologie als theologische Disziplin," *Die neue Ordnung* 1 (1946/47): 413–14. Both Freyer and König are quoted by Schöllgen.

31. Werner Schöllgen, *Die soziologischen Grundlagen der katholischen Sittenlehre* (Düsseldorf, 1953), 66, 170ff., 233, 238, 373, quote 29.

32. See Adolf Geck, "Erkenntnis und Heilung des Soziallebens: Zum Aufbau der Sozialwissenschaft," *Soziale Welt* 1 (1949/50): 3–12.

33. Adolf Geck, "Die moderne Seelsorgslage im Licht der Sozialwissenschaften," *Theologie und Glaube* 48 (1958): 423–43, quotes 431–33.

34. Franz-Josef Stegmann and Peter Langhorst, "Geschichte der sozialen Ideen im deutschen Katholizismus," in *Geschichte der sozialen Ideen in Deutschland*, ed. Helga Grebing (Essen, 2000), 798–813.

35. Anton Rauscher, "Die katholische Soziallehre im gesellschaftlichen Entwicklungsprozeß der Nachkriegszeit," in *Katholizismus: Wirtschaftsordnung und Sozialpolitik 1945–1963*, ed. Albrecht Langner (Paderborn, 1980), 23–26.

36. First quote: Gustav Gundlach to Heinrich Tenhumberg, 27 February 1962, BAM, GV NA, A-0-737; second quote: Gundlach to Temhumberg, 30 December 1961, BAM, GV NA, A-201-245 (emphasis in the original).

37. Klemens Brockmöller, *Industriekultur und Religion*, 3rd ed. (Frankfurt, 1964), 228.

38. Ermecke, "Pastoralsoziologie," 129; Geck, "Seelsorgslage," 424; Greinacher, *Soziologie der Pfarrei*, 40, 72; Josef Höffner, minutes of the "Dechantenkonferenz," 25–27 May 1953, BAM, GV NA, A-101-381.

39. *HK* 9 (1954/55): 345–47; Andrea-Isa Moews, *Eliten für Lateinamerika: Lateinamerikanische Studenten an der Universität Löwen in den 1950er und 1960er Jahren* (Cologne, 2000), 147–48.

40. Bernhard Häring, *Soziologie der Familie* (Salzburg, 1954), 40–53, quote 229; Schöllgen, *Grundlagen*, 328–35.

41. Werner Schöllgen, "Der Heilige Geist und die Sozialforschung," *LS* 7 (1956): 221–24, 223.

42. Greinacher, *Soziologie der Pfarrei*, 255–59, quote 256.

43. Boulard, *Wegweiser*, 89, 93; Greinacher, *Soziologie der Pfarrei*, 19.

44. Norbert Mette and Hermann Steinkamp, *Sozialwissenschaften und Praktische Theologie* (Düsseldorf, 1983), 166–68.

45. Linus Grond, "Das 'Thermometer' der Kirche: Aufgaben einer kirchlichen Sozialforschung," *WW* 8 (1953): 85–94; G. H. L. Zeegers to Archbishop Lorenz Jaeger, 14 November 1950, KDC, 21, 2771.

46. See William R. Ashby, *An Introduction to Cybernetics* (London, 1956), 42–72, 198–201.

47. Walter Menges, "Wandel und Auflösung der Konfessionszonen," in *Die Vertriebenen in Westdeutschland*, vol. 3, ed. Eugen Lemberg and Friedrich Edding (Kiel, 1959), 4ff.; Ian Connor, "The Churches and the Refugee Problem in Bavaria 1945–1949," *Journal of Contemporary History* 20 (1985): 403–5.

48. A. Heise to the chancellery of the bishop in Münster, 8 December 1946, BAM, GV NA, A-101-40; Connor, "Churches," 406.

49. Franz Xaver Arnold, "Die Heimatvertriebenen und die katholische Seelsorge," *Anima* 6 (1951): 238–49, 366–73, quotes 240, 244; see Joachim Köhler and Rainer Bendel, "Bewährte Rezepte

oder unkonventionelle Experimente? Zur Seelsorge an Flüchtlingen und Heimatvertriebenen," in Köhler and van Melis, *Siegerin in Trümmern,* 199–228.

50. Otto B. Roegele, "Der deutsche Katholizismus im sozialen Chaos: Eine nüchterne Bestandsaufnahme," *Hochland* 41 (1948/49): 205–33, quotes 221, 231.

51. Ibid., 228; Otto B. Roegele, "Verbotenes oder gebotenes Ärgernis?," *Hochland* 41 (1948/49): 542–57, 542.

52. Rudolf Hacker, "Ist der deutsche Katholizismus wirklich so schlecht?," *Bayerisches Klerusblatt* 29 (1949): 59–61, 60.

53. Ivo Zeiger, "Um die Zukunft der katholischen Kirche in Deutschland," *StdZ* 141 (1947/48): 241–52, 245; Köhler and Bendel, "Bewährte Rezepte," 207–9.

54. See, with reference to the discussion about Roegele, Georg Kliesch, 14 July 1950, Testbogen zur Soziographie des Dorfes, EBAP, GA, Kirchliche Statistik, 1945–1961.

55. Stefan Augsten, "Der restaurative Charakter der kirchlichen Arbeit seit 1945," *LS* 2 (1951): 14–24, quote 24.

56. Speech of the prelate Robert Grosche from Cologne during a meeting of 400 representatives from the laity in Altötting, 1950, *HK* 5 (1950/51): 2–7, quote 3.

57. On the reception in Germany, see Franz Benz, *Missionarische Seelsorge: Die missionarische Seelsorgebewegung in Frankreich und ihre Bedeutung für Deutschland* (Freiburg, 1958).

58. Marcel Albert, *Die katholische Kirche in Frankreich in der vierten und fünften Republik* (Rome, 1999), 65–68.

59. Pierre Pierrard, Michel Launay, and Rolande Trempé, *La J.O.C. Regards d'historiens* (Paris, 1984), 47–52.

60. Minutes of a conference of the pastoral sociologists from North Rhine-Westphalia, 25 February 1959, Archiv des Redemptoristenklosters Bochum (ARedBo), Ordner Soziologische Untersuchungen.

61. Henri Godin and Yvan Daniel, *La France, pays de Mission?* (Paris, 1943); the German translation appeared as: [Henri] Godin and [R.] Michel, *Zwischen Abfall und Bekehrung: Abbé Godin und seine Pariser Mission* (Offenburg, 1950); Étienne Fouilloux, "'Fille aînée de l'Eglise' ou 'pays de mission'? (1926–1958)," in *Société séculaire et renouveaux religieux (XXe Siècle),* ed. René Rémond (Paris, 1992), 185–94, figure 192.

62. On its reception, see Benz, *Missionarische Seelsorge,* 17–19, quote 17; Boulard, *Problèmes,* 1:113–14, 116–24, 137–42.

63. Godin and Daniel, *La France,* 54–59, 129–40, 154–57; Godin and Michel, *Abfall,* 243ff.

64. Gregor Siefer, *Die Mission der Arbeiterpriester: Ereignisse und Konsequenzen* (Essen, 1960), 66–107, 198–202, 219–32, quote 70–71.

65. Karl Delahaye, "Missionarische Seelsorge," *Kölner PBl.* 12 (1960): 146–51, quote 147; Adolf Geck, "Die französische Arbeiterpriester-Bewegung in der Krise," *Seelsorgehilfe* 5 (1953): 338–44, 341–42; Greinacher, *Soziologie der Pfarrei,* 42–46; Siefer, *Arbeiterpriester,* 16–17.

66. Quote: Geck, "Arbeiterpriester," 339; Anton Stonner, "Pastoraler Ertrag einer Frankreichreise," *Kölner PBl.* 9 (1957): 284–290, 328–335, 287–88; Benz, *Missionarische Seelsorge,* 44–54.

67. Friedrich Heer, "Die Arbeiterpriester in Frankreich: Ursprung und Hintergründe," *Hochland* 46 (1953/54): 326–41, 339; Siefer, *Arbeiterpriester,* 59–65.

68. Schöllgen, *Grundlagen,* 270 (emphasis in the original).

69. L. H. Parias, "Apostel für eine neue Ernte? Entwicklung, Situation und Probleme des französischen Katholizismus," *WW* 9 (1954): 409–20, 417; Klaus Scholl, "Ist Frankreich noch ein christliches Land?," *Hochland* 46 (1953/54): 164–73; Viktor Schurr, *Seelsorge in einer neuen Welt: Eine Pastoral der Umwelt und des Laientums* (Salzburg, 1957), 47–49.

70. Franz Hillig, SJ, "Zählt Frankreich noch als christlicher Faktor?," *StdZ* 140 (1947): 36–43, 38.

71. Benz, *Missionarische Seelsorge,* 120–38, quote 120–21.

72. [Wilhelm Heinen] to Pastor Gerards in Aachen, 5 June 1948, HAEK, Seelsorgeamt Heinen, 56.

73. Delahaye, "Missionarische Seelsorge," 147.
74. See the statement in the editorial "Das inhaltliche Anliegen," *LS* 2 (1951): 1; Brockmöller, *Industriekultur,* 68.
75. Greinacher, *Soziologie der Pfarrei,* 53.
76. Dean Bernhard Burdewick, Pamphlet zum Bericht Nr. 6, 25 October 1960, to Bishop Hengsbach, BAE, GV 82 14 12, vol. 1; PSI, Bericht Nr. 6, Priesternachwuchs und Klerus im Bistum Essen (February 1960), 83.
77. PSI to Joseph Krautscheidt, 25 January 1961, BAE, GV 82 14 12, vol. 1.
78. Robert Grosche, *HK* 5 (1950/51): 4.
79. Kirchlich-Statistischer und Religionssoziologischer Informationsdienst, no. 3 (December 1954), "Zur kirchlichen Statistik der Stadt Düsseldorf," 17–23, quote 20, HAEK, Seelsorgeamt Heinen, no. 11.
80. Johannes Sommer and Kosmas Wührer, OFMCap, "Seelsorgeamt und Volksmission," *Paulus* 35 (1963): 19–24, 20.
81. Löhr, "Rechristianisierungsvorstellungen," 26–31.
82. Alfons Fischer, "Katholisches Ghetto oder christliche Weltdurchdringung," *LS* 1 (1950): 78–86, 80, 85.
83. Bernhard Scholten, CSsR, to Heinrich Tenhumberg, 15 December 1957, BAM, GV NA, A-201-265.
84. Bernhard Häring, "Pfarrsoziographie und missionarische Seelsorge," *Paulus* 27 (1955): 17–26, 18; Benjamin Ziemann, "Missionarische Bewegung und soziale Differenzierung im Katholizismus: Die Praxis der Gebietsmission in der Bundesrepublik 1950–1960," *Kirchliche Zeitgeschichte* 18 (2005): 422.
85. George Michonneau, *Paroisse, communauté missionnaire: Conclusions de 5 ans d'expérience en milieu populaire* (Paris, 1946), 113.
86. Schurr, *Seelsorge,* 57.
87. Ibid., 16, 58–59.
88. Ziemann, "Missionarische Bewegung," 423–27.
89. Tyrell, "Diversität."
90. Paul Gail, "Milieuseelsorge—nur ein Modewort?," *Kölner PBl.* 13 (1961): 84–91, 116–20, 87.
91. Ziemann, "Missionarische Bewegung," 427–36.
92. Ibid.
93. "Die Münchener Volksmission 1960," *HK* 14 (1959/60): 439–43.
94. Cited in Antonia Leugers, *Interessenpolitik und Solidarität: 100 Jahre Superioren-Konferenz—Vereinigung Deutscher Ordensobern* (Frankfurt, 1999), 341.
95. Ernst Tewes, Thesen zu einem Seelsorge-Konzept, 20 March 1964, EOM, Registratur, Hefter Seelsorgeamt.
96. See chapter 3.
97. Greinacher, *Soziologie der Pfarrei,* 127–254; Carl Halfes, "Kennen Sie Ihre Pfarrei?," *LS* 3 (1952): 132–41.
98. Dietmar Westemeyer to Domkapitular J. Schwalbach, 8 March 1957, ARedBo, Ordner Soziologische Untersuchungen. Westemeyer referred to Greinacher, *Soziologie der Pfarrei,* 108–12, 297–306.
99. Walter Menges, "Pfarrsoziographische Forschung in Deutschland," *LS* 10 (1959): 65–69, quote 65; Franz Mühe, OMI, to Bernhard Scholten, 21 September 1956, AredBO, Ordner Soziologische Untersuchungen.
100. Häring, "Pfarrsoziographie," 18–19.
101. Walter Menges, Bericht über den Werkkurs für Volksmissionare in Fürstenried, 13–16 September 1955, KDC, 21, 2724.
102. Schurr, *Seelsorge,* 111.

103. See the materials in BDA, Gvs, E 1, I and II.
104. Menges, "Pfarrsoziographische Forschung," 67.
105. Bernhard Schomakers to Bishop Wittler, 12 September 1961, BAOS, 07-31-50; Bernhard Schomakers, "Die Bedeutung kirchlicher Sozialforschung für die Diaspora-Seelsorge," *Priester-Jahrheft des Bonifatiusvereins* (1962): 11–16.
106. Geck, "Entwicklung," 53ff.
107. For the following, see Benjamin Ziemann, "Die Institutionalisierung des Tatsachenblicks: Katholische Kirche und empirische Sozialforschung in der Bundesrepublik 1950–1970," *Mitteilungsblatt des Instituts für soziale Bewegungen* 34 (2005): 107–25.
108. On KASKI, see Benjamin Ziemann and Chris Dols, "Church Reform and Organizations Research in the Netherlands and Germany, 1950–1980," in Brückweh et al., *Engineering Society*, 293–312.
109. Ziemann, "Institutionalisierung."
110. Ibid.
111. Archbishop Jaeger to G. H. L. Zeegers, 30 December 1950, KDC, 21, 2771.
112. This was the recommendation of renowned Catholic pastoral sociologists in a paper entitled "Pastoralsoziologische Empfehlungen," which dated back to a meeting organized in Munich by the Institut für missionarische Seelsorge from 9 to 11 June 1965; see AredBo, Ordner Soziologie; Ergebnisprotokoll eines Treffens im Katholischen Büro Düsseldorf, 19 June 1971, and further materials in BAM, GV NA, A-0-979.
113. "Stellungnahme zum Aufbau einer kirchlichen Sozialforschungsstelle in Nordrhein-Westfalen," sent by Bishop Hengsbach to the other bishops in North Rhine-Westphalia, 1 February 1968, BAM, GV NA, A-101-219.
114. "Christus Dominus," no. 17, in *The Documents of Vatican II,* ed. Walter M. Abbott (London, 1966), 410.
115. KDPT, Report on the foundation of 1. A central German pastoral institute 2. An institute for church social research in Germany, 8 July 1968, memorandum by Ernst Tewes about a meeting of the Pastoral Commission of the German Bishops' Conference, 14/15 June 1968, BAM, GV NA, A-0-979.
116. Quote: Sachkommission IX der Synode, minutes of the meeting on 18 and 19 February 1972, BAM, Synodalbüro A 54; Memorandum des Beirates der KDPT, second draft, n.d. [1971], signed Norbert Greinacher, BAM, GV NA, A-0-979.
117. Quote: Prelate Alexander Stein, Kirchliche Hauptstelle für Männerseelsorge und Männerarbeit, to Tenhumberg, 11 March 1975, BAM, GV NA, A-0-979; and further materials in BAM, GV NA, A-0-979.
118. Hermann-Josef Spital to Heinrich Tenhumberg, 18 June 1971, ibid.
119. Quote: Joseph Höffner to Döpfner, 20 April 1970, BAM, GV NA, A-101-141; and Döpfner's reply, 25 April 1970, BAM, GV NA, A-101-141; Ergebnisprotokoll der Sitzung von Beirat und Hauptkommission der KDPT 14/15 October 1972, BAM, GV NA, A-0-978; Willy Bokler, Zentrales Deutsches Pastoralinstitut, 2 May 1972, and Laurenz Böggering to Heinrich Tenhumberg and Reinhard Lettmann, 30 May 1972, both in BAM, GV NA, A-201-45.
120. DBK, betr. Kirchliche Zentralstelle für pastorale Grundfragen, 26 August 1975, BAM, GV NA, A-0-979; *Gemeinsame Synode,* 2:247–50.
121. Johannes Weyer, *Westdeutsche Soziologie 1945–1960: Deutsche Kontinuitäten und nordamerikanischer Einfluß* (Berlin, 1984), 207–306.
122. Harry Pross, "Die unbekannte Wissenschaft," *Frankfurter Hefte (FH)* 10 (1955): 713–23.
123. File notes by Domdekan Engelbert Löhr, 28 March and 3 April 1957, DAL, 203 G, Gebietsmission 1957–1958.
124. Ziemann, "Institutionalisierung."

125. Quote: Greinacher to Hengsbach, 17 July 1962, BAE, GV 82 14 12, vol. 1; Krautscheidt to Hengsbach, 13 August 1962, BAE, GV 82 14 12, vol. 1.

126. Franz Hengsbach to Lorenz Jaeger, 7 December 1964, EBAP, GA, Kirchliche Statistik 1962–1967; Jahresbericht über die Tätigkeit des PSI im Jahre 1963, BAE, GV 82 14 12, vol. 1.

127. Adolf Holl, "Socio-Religious Research in Europe," *SC* 17 (1970): 461–68, 467.

128. On this distinction, see Robert C. Angell, "The Ethical Problems of Applied Sociology," in *The Uses of Sociology*, ed. Paul Lazarsfeld, William H. Sewell, and Harold L. Willensky (New York, 1967), 725–40.

129. Apart from Greinacher, the professional sociologists Egon Golomb, Walter Menges, and Philipp von Wambolt, who had all worked in church service, also became university professors between 1972 and 1975.

130. Interview with Egon Golomb, 2 October 2002.

131. In the Netherlands, there had been a partial movement of church sociology to the universities from as early as 1960, although KASKI remained the largest institute of its kind in Europe. Die allgemeine Politik von FERES, 13 October 1970, BAM, FHH A 232.

132. Oskar Simmel, SJ, editor of the *Stimmen der Zeit*, to Joseph Fichter, SJ, 2 January 1955, Loyola University, Special Collections, Joseph. H. Fichter Papers, Box 13, Folder 14.

133. Erich Bodzenta and Walter Suk, "Kirchliche Sozialforschung—Hilfe der Seelsorge," *Der Seelsorger* 26 (1955/56): 439–47, 445.

134. Erich Bodzenta, "Religiöse Praxis: Eine Bestandsaufnahme in österreichischen Stadtpfarreien," *WW* 13 (1958): 85–96, 89.

135. François Houtart and Jean Remy, "Die Anwendung der Soziologie in der pastoralen Praxis—heutiger Stand," *Concilium* 1 (1965): 209–26, 210–11.

136. See the annual report by Cardinal Frings for the Fulda Bishops Conference, 27–29 September 1956, BDA, Gvs, B 17, III.

137. Quote: Ludwig Neundörfer, "Methoden der Pastoralsoziologie," *Anima* 12 (1957): 29–38, 35; Menges to Zeegers, 12 September 1953, KDC, 21, 4289.

138. Höffner, minutes of the "Dechantenkonferenz," 25–27 May 1953, BAM, GV NA, A-101-381.

139. Häring, "Pfarrsoziographie," 25.

140. Alfons Auer, "Missionarisches Christentum: Eine seelsorgerliche Besinnung auf Prinzipielles," *Kölner PBl.* 9 (1957): 307–16, 311.

141. Bernhard Scholten to Tenhumberg, 15 December 1957, BAM, GV NA, A-201-265.

142. Wilhelm Dreier, "Religiöses Leben im Ruhrrevier," *Echo der Zeit*, no. 20 (19 May 1963).

143. Sozialteam Adelsried, *Die Entwicklung der Kirchlichkeit im Bistum Speyer 1950–2000* (Adelsried, 1968), quotes 20, 22–23; on the *Gemeindekirche*, or "parish church" see chapter 4.

144. Raphael, "Verwissenschaftlichung," 178–79.

145. See chapter 4.

146. Quote: [Alois Nüschen] to Archbishop Jaeger, 17 March 1959, EBAP, GA, Diözesan-Konferenzen 1957, 1959, 1962; Alois Nüschen to Viktor Schurr, 8 March 1959, EBAP, GA, Diözesan-Konferenzen 1957, 1959, 1962; *Bericht über die 17. Diözesankonferenz zu Paderborn vom 19. bis 22. Mai 1959* (Paderborn, n.d. [1959]), 11–29, 30–38.

147. Alois Nüschen, "Struktur und Aufgabenstellung des Seelsorgeamtes heute, Referat auf der Sitzung des Priesterrates am 1.3.1967," EBAP, GA, Seelsorgeamt 1945–1969; for a translation of a Boulard text, see "Ganzheits-Seelsorge," *Im Dienst der Seelsorge* 17, no. 2 (1963): 1–3.

148. "Raumgerechte Seelsorge," *Im Dienst der Seelsorge* 19, no. 4 (1965): 1–3, first quote 3; Second quote: Ernennungsschreiben des Generalvikars, 20 April 1960, EBAP, GA, Gebietsseelsorger 1958–1969; PSI, Bericht no. 21, 22, 22 A (1962).

149. Quote: Vorschlag zu einem Plan für die Bezirkseinteilung, 23 July 1965, EBAP, GA, Seelsorgsbezirke (Regionen) 1965–1969; and further materials in EBAP, GA, Seelsorgsbezirke

(Regionen) 1965–1969; file note Theodor Wilmsen, 7 February 1969, Theodor Wilmsen to Dean Henkel, 17 February 1969, EBAP, GA, Kirchliche Statistik 1968–1969.

150. Bodzenta and Suk, "Sozialforschung," 441.

151. Franz Greiner, "Die Katholiken in der technischen Gesellschaft der Nachkriegszeit," in *Deutscher Katholizismus nach 1945,* ed. Hans Maier (Munich, 1964), 109. Greiner contributed to *Herder-Korrespondenz* on sociology and was responsible for its "Soziographische Beilage" (sociographic supplement), which appeared from 1954.

152. *HK* 8 (1953/54), 91ff.; Ludwig Neundörfer, "Die soziale Situation des Landes," in *Kirche und Landvolk: Würzburger Tagungsbericht. Arbeitstagung des ZdK* (Paderborn, 1954), quotes 33, 35.

153. Schurr, *Seelsorge,* 36–38, 111–12; Emmeram Scharl, "Die Bedeutung des Milieus für die Seel-sorge," *PBl. für die Diözesen Aachen etc.* 17 (1965): 278–82.

154. Damberg, *Abschied,* 203–7; Emmeram Scharl, "Organisationsformen der Katholischen Land-volkbewegung in der Bundesrepublik," *Das Dorf* 9 (1957): 129–36.

155. On Tenhumberg, see the scattered information in Damberg, *Abschied.* The remarks on his position vis-à-vis left-wing Catholics are based on the evidence presented in chapter 4.

156. Heinrich Tenhumberg, "Grundzüge im soziologischen Bild des westdeutschen Dorfes," in *Landvolk in der Industriegesellschaft* (Hanover, 1952), 21–22.

157. Boulard, *Problèmes,* 1:108–27.

158. Diemar Westemeyer, "Wege zu denen, die von unserer heutigen Seelsorge nicht mehr erreicht werden," *Im Dienst der Seelsorge* 14 (1960): 6–9, 34–36, 34; Joseph H. Fichter, *Social Relations in the Urban Parish* (Chicago, 1954), 9–79; Alois Nüschen, "Sorge um die Fernstehenden," *Im Dienst der Seelsorge* 23, no. 2 (1969): 33–38, 33.

159. "Feminization" was ultimately an outcome of male employment in the age cohort of twenty to sixty years and could therefore also be understood as an effect of the age structure. Boulard, *Wegweiser,* 150.

160. Ziemann, "Suche," 427–29, 435–36.

161. François Houtart, *Soziologie und Seelsorge* (Freiburg, 1966), 81–82; Stellungnahme zum Auf-bau einer kirchlichen Sozialforschungsstelle in Nordrhein-Westfalen, n.d. [1968], BAM, GV NA, A-101-219.

162. Bruno Wegener, "Vorbereitung einer Stadtmission nach soziologischen Gesichtspunkten," *PBl. für die Diözesen Aachen etc.* 16 (1964): 144–53, 144.

163. Stefan Knobloch, *Missionarische Gemeindebildung: Zu Geschichte und Zukunft der Volksmission* (Passau, 1986), 126–28, 136–38, quote 136.

164. Minutes of the "Dechantenkonferenz," 25–27 May 1953, BAM, GV NA, A-101-381; Jacques Leclercq, "Soziologie und Juridismus," *Dokumente* 8 (1952): 315–28.

165. E. Kretz, CSsR, "Ein Wort zur Höllenpredigt," *Paulus* 25 (1953): 165–72, 165.

166. Parish Bad Pyrmont to Generalvikariat Paderborn, 16 January 1960, EBAP, GA, Volksmission 1959.

167. "Ende der Volksmission? Ein Gespräch über den Zustand der außerordentlichen Seelsorge," *LS* 3 (1952): 69–76, 72; Landolf Wißkirchen, "Volksmission heute und ihre Vorbereitung in der Pfarrei," *Paulus* 23 (1951): 81–89, 85–86.

168. Schurr, *Seelsorge,* quotes 351, 353.

169. Bernhard Häring, "Praktische Durchführungen der Pfarrsoziographie: Alarmsignale und der Mut sie zu hören," *LS* 7 (1956): 231–240, 238, 240.

170. There are many examples in the pastoral reports of parish priests in the diocese of Passau; for example, see the report from Peterskirchen, 1 July 1921, ABP, DekA II, Pfarrkirchen 12/I; the quotes are from Ulbering, n.d. [1921], ABP, DekA II, Pfarrkirchen 12/I.

171. Umfrage Bottrop, 1951/51, Fragebogen, Antwort Kaplan Heinrich Kaiser, 19 December 1951, BAM, GV NA, A-201-260.

172. Quote: Die Soziographie der Pfarrei für die Volksmission, n.d. [1954], ARedBO, Ordner Soziologische Untersuchungen; Seelsorgeamt Paderborn, Referat Landseelsorge und ländliche Bildungsarbeit to the parish priests, 20 July 1956, ARedBO, Ordner Soziologische Untersuchungen.

173. Wolfgang Bonß, *Die Einübung des Tatsachenblicks: Zur Struktur und Veränderung empirischer Sozialforschung* (Frankfurt, 1982).

174. Friedrich Wilhelm Graf, "Die nachholende Selbstmodernisierung des Katholizismus? Kritische Anmerkungen zu Karl Gabriels Vorschlag einer interdisziplinären Hermeneutik des II. Vatikanums," in *Das II. Vatikanum—christlicher Glaube im Horizont globaler Modernisierung*, ed. Peter Hünermann (Paderborn, 1998), 49.

175. Jakob David, "Der Mensch der Großstadt und unsere Seelsorge: Einige Erwägungen aus soziologischer Sicht," *Der Männerseelsorger* 15 (1965): 193–204, quotes 194–95, 197; François Houtart, "Die Kirche und die Großstädte," *WW* 11 (1956): 733–53, 741.

176. Walter Menges, "Pastorale Soziologie und städtische Seelsorge," *Anima* 12 (1957): 148–53, quote 149; Egon Golomb, "Seelsorgsplanung in der Großstadt," *Trierer Theologische Zeitschrift* 72 (1963): 129–49.

177. Alfons Weyand, *Formen religiöser Praxis in einem werdenden Industrieraum* (Münster, 1963), 79, 81, 145–57, 205–6.

178. See the detailed discussion in an essay by one of Weber's students: Materialien zu A. Weyand, ICSW, Ordner Prof. Weber, WS 1969/70, Ausgewählte Fragen der Kirchensoziologie.

179. Weyand, *Formen*, 201, 206.

180. On this perception, see the (anonymized) critical note, Einige Antworten auf die Fragen des Bischofs von Osnabrück, 13 April 1967, BAOS, 03-04-21-03, vol. II.

181. Joseph H. Fichter to Father Meyer, 1 February 1955, Loyola University, Special Collections, Joseph H. Fichter Papers, Box 1, Folder 9.

182. Münsteraner Diözesan-Präses der KAB, Wilhelm Wöste, Gedanken zu einem Schwerpunkt-Programm der Arbeiterseelsorge, n.d. [January 1958], BAM, GV NA, A-0-768.

183. Schurr, *Seelsorge*, 158–66; Norbert Greinacher, "Kirche und Arbeiterschaft," *Oberrheinisches PBl.* 62 (1961): 73–82, 75–76; Weyand, *Formen*, 113, table 40.

184. Greinacher, *Soziologie der Pfarrei*, 55–56; Yvan Daniel, *Aspects de la Pratique Religieuse de Paris* (Paris, 1952), 116–17. This study also comprised the main source for deliberations in the academic committee of the focal program, "pastoral care for workers". Minutes of the meeting on 7 November 1959, BAM, GV NA, A-0-770; Damberg, *Abschied*, 215–22.

185. Cited by Norbert Greinacher, "Seelsorge und Arbeiterschaft," *Kölner, Aachener und Essener Pastoralblatt* 12 (1960): 391–97, 391.

186. Michael Pfliegler, Review of Schurr, "Seelsorge," *Der Seelsorger* 28 (1957/58): 178–81, 180; quote: Josef Paulus, Geistlicher Direktor des ZdK, Gedanken zu einem Schwerpunktprogramm für Arbeiterseelsorge, n.d. [1959], BAM, GV NA, A-0-768; Walter Menges, "Entwicklung und Stand der religionssoziologischen Forschung in Deutschland," *SC* 6 (1959): 132–33.

187. Wilhelm Wöste, Standort und Selbstverständnis der KAB, Referat auf dem Verbandstag in Essen 1959, BAM, GV NA, A-0-767.

188. Erich Prokosch, *Pastoral-soziographische Analyse des Dekanates Stadtsteinach* (Bamberg, 1971); interview with Hans-Werner Eichelberger, 18 December 2002.

189. *Kirchliches Amtsblatt für die Diözese Münster* (1970), 121; Josef Schwermer, "Pfarrbeschreibung und Pfarrstatistik," *Theologie und Glaube* 59 (1969): 310–19.

190. Ziemann, "Suche," 421–22; quote: file note Ms. Fehlker for Spital, 29 September 1971, BAM, GV NA, A-201-357.

191. Albert, *Kirche in Frankreich*, 70ff.

192. *HK* 9 (1954/55): 235–38, quote 236.

193. Klinger, "Aggiornamento," 184.

194. Maasen, Mendelsohn, and Weingart, "Metaphors," 2.
195. See the exemplary study by Osmund Schreuder, *Kirche im Vorort: Soziologische Erkundung einer Pfarrei* (Freiburg, 1962).
196. Michael Pfliegler, "Bedeutung und Grenzen einer Statistik der Seelsorge," *Der Seelsorger* 28 (1957/58): 8–18, 11–14.

Chapter 3

REPRESENTATION AND CONTESTATION AFTER THE COUNCIL
Opinion Polling

Sociography made it possible for the Catholic Church to establish a detailed picture of the "active" laity, "active" being defined as participation in a highly circumscribed set of liturgical rituals. This understanding of being Catholic suited the late 1940s and 1950s, when many still had high hopes that the traditional Catholic milieu could be reconstructed, even though the figures quickly suggested otherwise. However, the sociographic approach to conceptualizing Catholic faith became increasingly outdated during the 1960s for two main reasons. First, the Second Vatican Council (Vatican II), which took place from 1962 to 1965, fundamentally altered definitions of what it meant to be Catholic. The "Dogmatic Constitution on the Church, Lumen Gentium" no longer defined the church as a hierarchical and metaphysical body, but rather inclusively as the "people of God." This implied that all church members possess "the same filial grace and the same vocation to perfection." The church was conceived of as a community where some were "made teachers, dispensers of mysteries and shepherds on behalf of others," yet all nonetheless shared "a true equality" through the act of "building up the Body of Christ."[1] Second, the recognition of the divergence and pluralism of different charismata in the church implied by this new definition had a sociostructural equivalent in the greater society: individualization, which made rapid progress in West Germany during the 1960s. An increasing plurality of lifestyles, consumption patterns, and sexual mores characterized the younger generation.[2] An increasing plurality of social habits also implied a greater plurality of normative orientations, a structural reality that an organization with a circumscribed set of norms such as the Catholic Church had to reckon with. For the observation and calculation of normative orientations and changing value systems within such a pluralistic society, another social scientific method, opinion polling, was much better equipped than sociography.

Opinion polling is defined here as all the research techniques based on the method practiced in the United States from the mid-1930s of selecting a representative "quota sample" or "random sample" to conduct empirical research into opinions, attitudes, motivations, or modes of behavior. The effects of public opinion polling on discourse has been a subject of long-running controversy in sociology and communication studies.[3] From the start, opinion polling as a research technique has been linked to the concept of the public sphere, and not only in the field of politics, where it played the biggest role. Depending on interpretation, opinion polling thus represents a way of either precisely identifying public opinion or of constructing that very opinion.

Opinion Polls and the Alleged Decline of the Public Sphere

Some see public opinion as a concept that reveals highly normative connotations and implications. In West Germany, for example, Jürgen Habermas's 1962 book *The Structural Transformation of the Public Sphere* provides the most obvious example. In the classical period of the public sphere, which Habermas identifies as the late eighteenth and early nineteenth centuries, the public sphere was, he claims, a forum for the rational exchange of substantial opinions and ideas in a reasonable discourse. This understanding is linked to the sociotheoretical idea of consensus, which, in Habermas's view, can be achieved in the forum of the public sphere, provided that those debating there are sufficiently informed.[4] Against this backdrop, Habermas sees opinion polling as a practice that has directly contributed to undermining and emptying the normatively loaded concept of the public sphere of meaning. The uninformed moods and voices that opinion polls record do not reflect public opinion. For Habermas, opinion polls are thus part and parcel of the "socialpsychological liquidation" of any substantial idea of the public sphere, which is ultimately reduced to a pale imitation of enlightened participation.[5] Habermas and other critics of opinion polling, most notably the French sociologist Pierre Bourdieu, distinguished between critique and affirmation to examine the effects of opinion polling on the structure of the public sphere, albeit giving preference to the critical side. This schema is historically understandable, as it was based on many assessments of opinion polling in the 1950s and 1960s. Today, however, it is clear that the distinction is insufficient for developing a realistic and theoretically grounded understanding of the public sphere. It is an illusion to assume that the main aim of the public sphere is to reach consensus. And it is even more unrealistic to expect an undistorted exchange of "real" reasons and motives from the mass media.[6]

In making a historical assessment of the effects of opinion polls in the scientization of the Catholic Church, as I aim to do here, I had to be careful to avoid becoming prejudiced by adopting normative positions. With this in mind,

I distinguish between operation and observation to decode the specific features of the opinion polling discourse. In the context of the Catholic Church, this means distinguishing the operative practice of religious communication from cases in which such operations are merely observed, from whatever position. The acts of praying, reading the Bible, listening to a sermon, or receiving Communion at Mass are not the same as observing these practices from outside, regardless of whether the observers engage in the same activities themselves at another point in time. With this distinction, the public sphere appears to be a multitude of observers who watch the operative practice of religion from outside. This has implications for the way we understand the significance of the public sphere for systems such as politics or religion. Members of the public can gain information about their own operative practices other than through the mirror of their self-observation. The public sphere thus allows them to observe the ways other observers see the system. The new research techniques of opinion polling served this exact function of a second-order mirror. Opinion polling is a method that can provoke and make manifest the latent observations of an anonymous public.[7] This perspective particularly enables us to understand the parallel use of opinion polling in a variety of contexts, ranging from the economy (market research) to politics (opinion polling) and mass media (as surveys of readers, listeners, and viewers). It remains to be explored in the following sections how, and with what intensity, the Catholic Church also made use of opinion polling to reflect on and observe itself as a religious organization.

The Catholic Church's relationship with the opinion polling discourse was ambivalent. While it did engage in the practice, it also had a number of reservations. Some reservations related to the specific technique of opinion polling—the anonymous questionnaire, which deliberately concealed any traces of the individual who had answered the questions. Another controversial point for many Catholics was that survey-based research made latent opinions and observations manifest, which, they believed, was not without moral implications. A final point of debate was the specific position that the "public" could have as an observing audience in and outside the church, with its hierarchical structure of organization. This also addressed the problem of responsiveness; that is, the question of whether and to what extent the church could, should, or even had to react if opinion polls deduced a climate of opinion critical of the church, its teachings, and its dogmas, or were dominated by opposing views.

Early Catholic Opinion Polls

In essence, such questions were part of the Catholic Church's wider problem in dealing with the public as a structural principle that applied in various contexts of the modern, functionally differentiated society. This is illustrated by a pastoral-theological "questionnaire" from the Weimar Republic, which made no claims of being based on a "precise scientific method."[8] In the run-up to the people's mission in Münster in 1931, the Capuchin priest Chrysostomus Schulte asked the readers of the church newsletter there to answer four questions about their view of the mission. He had not "literary use" in mind, but was simply trying to awaken the "interest" of the faithful, as had been discussed during the mission's preparation. While those who compiled the survey hoped that respondents would provide "honest answers," some clergy expressed enormous concern about this ambition, fearing that such a questionnaire would encourage the "laity . . . only to criticize."[9]

Schulte responded by insisting that the survey could have a "liberating" effect and serve as a "safety valve" through which criticisms could be made "in the right place." Furthermore, he argued that it would be a mistake for the church to continue to bury its head in the sand and refuse to appreciate the "true situation." This would only distance it further from the "people."[10] Finally, Schulte drew attention to another factor that was essential if the opinions expressed in the survey were to be fully appreciated. Although the "voices" heard in the survey were doubtless subjectively colored and often exaggerated, the church and clergy could not simply "ignore such opinions" but had to "engage with them." To support his thesis that the church also had to know and take into account the views of ordinary Catholics, Schulte pointed to one of the responses to his survey. An engineering graduate had noted that, since the end of the First World War, people had "achieved a greater degree of independence" and "therefore also made more independent judgments in religious issues" than before.[11]

The polarized arguments triggered by Schulte's survey already prefigured important aspects of the Catholic Church's discourse on opinion polling, which would reappear into the 1970s. For one thing, church leaders feared that surveys would reflect the momentary moods and exaggerations of notorious troublemakers, even as they acknowledged that only this anonymous form of questioning offered an "honest" means of discussing problems within the church. While some hoped that surveys would give them a tool for gaining a more realistic picture of the church's situation in society, others warned that it would trigger an unnecessary avalanche of overblown "criticism." Schulte himself explained why "opinion," as a specific connection of information and its evaluation, was relevant to the church: people's modern-day "independence" of judgment meant that the church had to accept and anticipate the expectations of its members as a factor that would determine its future activities. As the answers to his informal survey questions proved, there was not yet substantial "cognitive dissonance" between the stereotypical truths of catechism-based faith and the reality of life in Münster in the latter days of the Weimar Republic. Nevertheless, wrote Schulte, one could still hear the "cacophony of the unbelieving and neopagan world all around"; the polyphonic noise of a complex environment was already perceptible "from a distance." Schulte's survey was an initial attempt—albeit one completely uninterested in methodological issues and thus hardly true "opinion polling"—to turn the irritation created by this noise into selective information that could be discussed in the church.[12]

The introduction of scientific opinion polls in West Germany, however, did not occur until after the Second World War, when the reconstruction of a democratic political system after 1945 spurred their use. The three Western Allies commissioned polls of their own and licensed German polling institutes with the main aim of monitoring the possible persistence of antidemocratic attitudes in a postfascist society, and ensuring that Germans were learning to appreciate the openness of a free society as quickly as possible. In the American zone, the Office of Military Government, United States (OMGUS), established an Opinion Survey Section in October 1945. Until the founding of the Federal Republic in 1949, it conducted a large variety of polls about the political attitudes of the German population, and also began to use German interviewers. In this context, the Americans understood opinion polling emphatically as a democratic science: surveys could do more than mirror the nation's progress toward a democratic political culture in a quantitative form. They could also, through the representative sample, give a voice to the people, the political sovereigns of democracy, and make it possible to see their desires and perceptions, undistorted by the influences of mass media and political parties.[13] In addition to conducting their own surveys, the American occupiers solicited help from Germans. In 1949, the US High Commissioner (HICOG) established a Reactions Analysis Branch that also trained German staff in the techniques of survey research. A number of these soon founded their own institutions, such as the German Institute for Surveys of the People (Deutsche Institut für Volksumfragen, DIVO), established in 1951, or worked in commercial institutions under German management. From the end of the 1940s, various polling institutions covered the Federal Republic in an ever-denser web of opinion polls on a wide range of topics.[14]

This meant that issues such as belief, religion, and the church soon became the topic of opinion surveys, the results of which attracted press attention. In the run-up to the Katholikentag in Bochum in 1949, for example, the *Ruhr-Nachrichten* newspaper published a survey of one thousand Catholics in the Ruhr region of Westphalia that it had commissioned from the Bielefeld-based Emnid Institute. The headline itself brought attention to the interesting results, such as the fact that only "38.5 percent of those questioned" were regular church visitors and that "Christians in deed," who openly discussed their faith in the workplace, were "largely unknown."[15] Catholic journals such as *Hochland* or *Herder-Korrespondenz* noted the results of opinion polling studies on belief in God or the preference for a church wedding, addressing methodological problems, such as a questionnaire's precise treatment of an issue. However, they did not argue that these criticisms imperiled the method's general applicability to religious issues.[16] In the sociographic discourse, too, the "increase in awareness" provided by "opinion polling activities" found approval as, it was argued, they made it possible to map the outlines of a "Godless space that had spread into the souls of Christians."[17] Hardly anything suggested in the early 1950s that the reception of opinion polling methods in West German Catholicism would soon hit fundamental obstacles.

The Negative Reception of the Kinsey Report

This changed dramatically in 1953. Even before the German translation of the second volume of the Kinsey Report, *Sexual Behavior in the Human Female*, reached the market, *Herder-Korrespondenz* issued a warning to readers, comparing the study's effects to a highly potent drug. This triggered a flood of commentaries from Catholic writers, which set the tone in the critical discussion of the two studies.[18] What had happened? Alfred C. Kinsey was, in fact, a zoologist by trade, who had spent most of his career doing taxonomic studies on gall wasps. From 1938, however, he had conducted a large-scale survey about the sexual behavior of American men and women with some colleagues. The first volume, *Sexual Behavior in the Human Male*, appeared in 1948. Kinsey and three other interviewers subjected around twelve thousand people to detailed interviews that referred to a large spectrum of sexual practices. The subject matter, along with the magnitude of their samples, ventured into uncharted territory. Kinsey recorded and quantified the occurrence and frequency not only of marital, pre-, and extra-marital sexual activities by his volunteers, but also the practices of masturbation, intercourse with prostitutes, same-sex partners, and intercourse with animals. Studded with tables and around eight hundred pages long, this work supplied, in the bold claims of its author, a comprehensive "accumulation of scientific fact," independent of "questions of moral values and social custom," that could be used in sex education, therapy, and counseling. Science, Kinsey insisted, had to overcome any boundary imposed by "religious evaluation, social taboo and formal legislation" on an accurate study of human sexual behavior.[19]

These very methodological claims of Kinsey's works were widely criticized. Aside from the interview technique, critics especially questioned the representativeness of Kinsey's sample, which, as in earlier studies of sexuality, was made up of volunteers. As Kinsey had recruited subjects mainly in the northeastern United States, the working class and African Americans were distinctly underrepresented. On the other hand, as Kinsey himself pointed out, there was no doubt that his study was methodologically vastly superior to all its predecessors. [20] Even highly critical observers in West Germany reluctantly concluded that Kinsey did not rank among the "charlatans or dabblers."[21]

One problem for the reception of Kinsey's work was the way it utilized quota methods to model individuals scientifically as freedom-of-choice-enacting subjects in a modern consumer society. The same was true not only of market and consumer research in the narrow sense and of the observation of political preferences, but also of surveys on religious and social topics. It was especially the case when quota methods were used in sexology, and in particular with respect to the sexuality of women, which was controlled by an enormous apparatus of juridical rules and moral standards.[22] Kinsey assumed that every woman had the freedom to satisfy her sexual desire using any combination of sexual activities. The fact that not a single one of the women he interviewed represented "in all aspects the average type" seemed to be the "most important fact" in the materials available to him. Sexual consumption could be represented statistically but not attributed to a person as a type.[23] Survey research made it possible to methodically disaggregate larger samples into smaller subgroups and thereby to visualize the subjective preferences of individuals. Its advancement therefore made it possible to represent and observe the freedom of individual subjects through their patterns of consumption, without regard to their particularities as individuals and the social restrictions that affected them. It was precisely in this context, and for this reason, that the Kinsey Report marked a deep caesura in the scientization of the social in the twentieth century.

The connection between sampling and representation of subjectivity becomes even clearer if one considers an aspect of the report that was crucial to both the positive reception and the enormous criticism it met: the self-evident manner in which Kinsey claimed, on the basis of his expertise in the human sciences, to be the legitimate speaker for the private elements of human sexuality within the scope of the opinion polling discourse. The irritation and imposition that these studies represented in the contemporary discourse on sexuality emanated from his implicit "idea of man"; that is, from the anthropological premises of the study.[24] The interdiscursive coupling of a particular anthropological view and the regulation of sexuality held enormous consequences, not only for the scientization of sexuality, but also for the Catholic reception of opinion polling. Kinsey's work was a breath of liberal optimism for progressive-era enlightenment in an atmosphere dominated by the intolerance of the early 1950s, which was not only directed against communism. Kinsey himself was accused of supporting world communism by portraying homosexual behavior as acceptable, and in 1945 Republican members of Congress successfully launched a movement against the Rockefeller Foundation for its financial support of Kinsey's research. On the basis of his data, Kinsey had attacked the strict dichotomy between "heterosexuality" and "homosexuality" that pathologized the latter. He found the distinction baseless, as his evidence suggested that everyone's sexuality could be placed on a sliding scale of rare to regular homosexual activities.[25]

However, reactions to Kinsey's work went far beyond the hysterically exaggerated outbursts that represented the spirit of the McCarthy era. Numerous critical commentaries in the American mass media noted a tendency to reify and naturalize sexual behaviors, which they thought central to the report's argumentation. According to these critics, Kinsey was prone to mixing up the "normal," in the sense of a widespread practice, with the "natural," in the sense of behaviors that were both biologically possible and socially acceptable. Catholics and Catholic organizations in the United States were especially firm in opposing the report. But even liberal observers such as the literary and cultural critic Lionel Trilling (1905–75) criticized the way the data, as presented by an authority in a scientific field, encouraged "mechanical attitudes toward life." Despite the enlightening effects of the survey, which were to be welcomed in principle, Trilling saw a disastrous tendency to separate "sex"—as opposed to "love" and "lust"—from all the other manifestations of human life.[26] The American discussions thus principally questioned the repercussions of the Kinsey Report on public opinion, and thus the limits of what could be expressed on the subject of human sexuality without neglecting moral judgments.

The reception of the Kinsey Report among German Catholics took up many of the criticisms expressed in the United States. Not all reactions were worded as strongly as one printed in the journal *Orientierung,* published by the Jesuits, which described Kinsey's work as a "criminal" exploitation of scientific research results for "pornographic purposes." However, all agreed that "limits" had to "be drawn" to the validity of Kinsey's arguments.[27] These limits lay where the opinion polling discourse, with its model of representativity, collided with moral theology's claim to making universally applicable statements on human nature and its essential moral implications.

Within the Catholic moral discourse, critics judged the Kinsey Report, with its positivist and quantitative categories of sexual contacts and orgasms, on essentially three aspects.[28] The first related to the biologistic-anthropological premises implied, among other things, by Kinsey's casual, naturalistic way of presenting different sexual practices as a range of techniques for employing the sexual organs. Above all, they alleged, Kinsey, whom they always described as a zoologist, presented the material with implicit and explicit value judgments, which "isolated" and "autonomized" the "purely biological expression of sexuality." This meant that he had lost sight of the "cultural dimension" of the sex drive and thus the social norms that, in all known societies, "had an absolute character out of deep necessity."[29] The allegation that Kinsey denied the spiritual and cultural elements of humanity drew upon a view that was widespread among Catholics and liberals like Trilling. This view asserted the impossibility of describing human sexuality without referring to its connections to eroticism and love, or to the entire institutional apparatus codifying and normalizing intimate practices. Critics in the Catholic moral discourse intensified this criticism, observing that Kinsey's choice of words revealed the "pathos" he directed against any social confines imposed on the sex drive. Terms with negative connotations such as "confinement," "inhibition," "interference," or "blockage," in their assessment, indicated the study's libertarian style. Moreover, this biological approach did not even draw the line at relativizing people's "revulsion" at sexual relationships with animals, instead discounting such taboos as historical artifacts.[30]

Catholic critics claimed that Kinsey's biologistic image of man negated the personal nature of sexuality, and thus ultimately human dignity; the sexual act was an "act between individuals." This context, however, brought to light an issue that points beyond the wholesale disqualification of the report as a "biologistic" work. It is highly significant that Kinsey justified basing his statistical analysis on the orgasm on the grounds that it triggers a "physiological relaxation of sexual arousal."[31] For Kinsey, the characteristic buildup and release of "extreme tension" in the course of the sexual act does not primarily comprise the physical arousal of the body's various "erogenous zones" detailed in his report. Kinsey based his idea of the "total sexual outlet"—that is, the multitude of ways in which orgasm can be achieved—on the "expenditures of energy" associated with sexual contact. This language is unmistakably situated in discourses on energy and machine mechanics.[32] Kinsey's understanding of human sexuality was thus ultimately more mechanical than biologistic.

The second key aspect to the Catholic critique of the Kinsey Report was the matter of pseudomorality, which had already been thematized in the United States and was based on a positivistic listing of actually occurring modes of behavior. Kinsey, critics argued, made biology and statistics into "normative sciences," which denied the validity of Christian sexual morality and replaced it with the "dogmatism" of the "natural." Furthermore, his method claimed to express truths about the legitimacy of certain sexual conduct and practices from a position founded only on normative morality.[33] Kinsey himself had already discussed the correlation between religious norms and sexuality, as well as the discrepancies that existed between the two. However, an article published by the Volkswartbund (Catholic Association to Protect the People) vehemently rejected Kinsey's analysis. The association, founded in 1927, was devoted to the "fight against public immorality," and above all to petitioning under the Youth Protection Act. Kinsey's sample of Catholic women, half of whom felt no "regrets" for having premarital intercourse, could not, thought the association's writer, be counted as "devout Catholics" per se.[34] Had such information not been "sensationalized," as it was by Kinsey, the article maintained, even "bitter insights" into the "declining significance of traditional values" might still have been received somewhat positively. This was certainly the case when an article in the cultural magazine *Hochland* featured a study by Ludwig von Friedeburg establishing, among other things, that around half of the Catholic churchgoers surveyed supported birth control.[35] Friedeburg was employed by the Allensbach Institute, which, at the time, was one of the leading polling agencies in West Germany.

The final and decisive factor in the critique of the Kinsey Report, and in the negative reception of the opinion polling method by Catholic observers, was the way critics saw it as a form of "scientism" that went hand in hand with the "manic pressure for scientization." Anton Böhm, who as editor of *Wort und Wahrheit* and later chief editor of *Rheinischer Merkur* was one of the most important Catholic journalists in the Federal Republic, saw the Kinsey Report as the "classic example" of this trend.[36] "Scientism" here suggested that Kinsey, whose questionnaire represented the modern "bogeyman of dehumanization," had advanced into an area that should have remained out of bounds for research because it was essentially "unresearchable." According to Böhm, this self-aggrandizement of contemporary science allegedly followed logically from its willingness to denounce elementary moral standards in favor of questionable facts.[37] Even more important than the subjectively desired or perceived power of science was its advancing influence on everyone's everyday lives. The scientism of Kinsey's questionnaire contributed to a "sexualization of the general public." In Böhm's view, such "indiscretion" took ownership of individuals' safe refuges and private spheres, placing them at the mercy of the "faceless and formless social collective." Opinion polling would hence prove not to be an empirical research method but a new form of leadership in which the "public sphere would replace confession" and "the consciously or unconsciously venerated collective would take the place of the forgiver of sins."[38]

The Catholic view of the opinion polling discourse thus typically held that "this knowledge, this empowerment of the secret, creates power . . . over individuals" and "the workings of society" alike.[39] This fatal power of scientism was at the heart of the Catholic rejection of opinion polling when it came to the Kinsey Report. The criticism is reminiscent, both in its general direction and choice of language, of Michel Foucault's analyses of the compulsion to confess anchored in the discourse on sexuality. From these critics' perspective, the Kinsey Report's scientific stance, far from liberating individuals in their sexuality, actually subjugated them more deeply to the power of science by identifying and classifying their most intimate behavior.[40] Kinsey may have attacked a Victorian conception of generally accepted morality, but he did so in the name of a Victorian conception of scientific objectivity.[41] In contrast to Kinsey's optimistic and confident description of his work, which he hoped would have a liberating effect on society, Catholic criticism unmasked the hubris of a scientific discourse that not only lifted outdated taboos, but also, by widening the bounds of acceptable speech, extended its discursive power over individuals.

The Kinsey Report was a particularly spectacular example of the quota method in action, and one that was a source of dispute even among experts. The inevitable controversy surrounding the topic of sexuality, given Catholic moral attitudes, exacerbated the report's negative impact on the church's acceptance of this research technique.[42] However, some of the objections to opinion polling articulated with respect to the Kinsey Report can also be observed in other contexts.

They characterized the church's dealings with the opinion polling discourse up to 1969/70, when a survey was conducted in the preliminary stages of the Würzburg Synod of the Dioceses in the Federal Republic. However, they did not dominate the church's approach completely. After all, even Catholics did not dispute the legitimacy of public opinion polling in market and economic research. Questions about consumer demands and product preferences were generally regarded as fair game, in contrast to "intimate" matters and personal problems.[43]

The Normative Pitfalls of Statistics

The church continued to object to opinion polling on personal matters, partly using the same arguments that had already been put forward in its critique of the Kinsey Report. Critics continued to focus on opinion polling's quasi-normative loading of its findings. Public opinion polling was seen as a form of "statistics that had turned into a dogma" or the "slavish consultation" of a "demon"; that is, a sort of "demon polling" [*Dämoskopie*].[44] Even Pope Paul VI openly and repeatedly addressed this threat in 1969/70 and pointed to the hazardous "moral uncertainty" that he thought resulted from the inappropriate use of public opinion polling.[45] Depending on one's interpretation, this aspect of questionnaires concealed a psychology of the political unconscious or a form of democratic "absolute trust in the correctness of the 'common behavior.'" However, if commonly applied moral norms were established through a "quasi referendum," then "moral statistics"—as Anton Böhm described such survey results in 1974, making clear reference to the beginnings of the church's engagement with the social sciences—would turn into a "statistical morality." And through this self-reinforcing bandwagon effect, "universal chaos . . . would soon come knocking at the door." [46]

The contemporary term used to describe this problem was responsivenes. To what extent, the question was, should organizations respond to the findings of polls that claimed to represent public opinion? By the late 1960s, the problem of responsiveness was acute, not only with regard to moral standards, but also to the institution of the church and its pastoral strategy in general. Here, too, Catholic writers thought it necessary to set clear boundaries to the legitimate "fact-finding" of the opinion polling approach. The "absolute truths and values" proclaimed by the church, it was argued, depended on public opinion to be enforced but not to be "valid." Such "worldly opinion" would go against the words of the apostles: "Do not be conformed to this world" (Romans 12:2). This implied a clear rejection of the idea that a method as fluid and flexible as public opinion polling could adequately observe "unshakable social truths." Only the forms of preaching, rather than the message itself, were up for discussion.[47] Catholic moral theologians therefore eshewed the idea that public opinion, in the Catholic Church as in politics, was analogous to the "Holy Spirit," whose unpredictability reflected the all-encompassing contingency of observation and differentiation.[48]

A second important characteristic of opinion polling that clashed with the anthropological premises of Catholic thinking had also already surfaced in the reaction to Kinsey: the anonymity of all the statements made. This is a product of the methodology of public opinion polling: the questionnaire. Whether the questionnaires have been filled out by an interviewer visiting a "representative" subject's apartment or directly by respondents themselves, they share a common feature: the information recorded is permanently separated from the names and individual identities of the participants. From the Catholic point of view, this had a serious effect on the answers recorded by the "yes/no/don't know" formula. By depersonalizing the individual interviewee, critics argued, polling disregarded essential features of human nature such as individuality and, with it, freedom and dignity. At the time of the Kinsey Report, there was still widespread astonishment that anyone would want to undergo such an anonymous procedure posing questions about their intimate life. The very willingness to participate in the survey was seen as a puzzling "characteristic and new cultural phenomenon" of modern society, and one that could only be explained by the advancing organizational deterioration thereof, which was leading to "demystification" and "exposure."[49]

The procedure of answering questionnaires anonymously gradually asserted itself as a popular practice, also for controversial topics. However, the transformation of speech this implied continued to provoke critical commentary. One observer educated in the spirit of Catholic notions of social order was convinced that a "real question" involves necessary consequences everyone must understand and "accept" in advance. "Responsibility" for the consequences of a question, he believed, can only be ensured if respondents are implicitly compelled to be able to "defend" at any time the opinion they express in an answer. This responsibility is the essential prerequisite for answering the question appropriately, but the anonymous questionnaire releases the interviewee from this compulsion,[50] suggesting that every answer has a performative side.

With this notion, based on the Catholic modeling of the individual as a responsible subject, Catholic criticism of opinion polling also rejected the mathematical model of representativity that made its categorical framework plausible. What is the value of "lists of questions," a Catholic from Münster asked the synod office in 1970, that are put together in public opinion polling as "entirely noncommittal, anonymous writings"? These, he argued, could only reveal a "concession to the anxiety and character weaknesses" typical of the era. A small "fraction" of the number of answers, but from people willing to stand by their statements, would have had a far different power. A collection of anonymous reactions, meanwhile, was mere "chaff" fit only for burning.[51] This argument gained special pertinence against the backdrop of the "total poll" that was to be conducted during the Würzburg Synod.

Right up until the early 1970s, plainly audible Catholic voices took issue with the categorical framework of opinion polling and wanted to clearly limit surveying activities in the church. Unlike sociography, the Kinsey Report had exposed serious conceptual barriers to scientization. As we have seen, these pertained, among other things, to the discrepancies between the representative model of surveying and the Catholic idea of responsible public speaking. Despite such limits to permissible speech, the church tried out opinion polling for practical uses in the years prior to 1968. The extreme scarcity of information on these efforts results not merely from the fragmentary sources.[52] Rather, it also reflects the way the church commissioned opinon polls and discussed the results during this period. Opinion surveys as a tool for exploring public opinion were largely kept secret in the church. Only a small circle of high-ranking church personnel commissioned them and discussed the details and possible consequences. Surveys were conducted in the style of secret military commando campaigns, meaning that even extremely well-informed clerics in close contact with high-ranking bishops only learned about them in a round-about way and with considerable delay.

Secretive Polling in the Church during the 1960s

What was, in all likelihood, the first survey that a leading body of the West Ger-man Catholic Church ever commissioned from a commercial opinion polling institute, which sought to probe the church's public impact on the "views of Catholics," provides a striking example of this secretiveness. The Catholic Office in Bonn, whose job was to communicate with political authorities at the federal level, requested the survey at the beginning of 1960 from the Emnid Institute and discussed the results of the "pretest" in a working group with representa-tives of the institute. In commissioning this work, the Catholic Office seems, in fact, to have been fulfilling the wishes of the Fulda Bishops' Conference, which wanted information about the public perception of the election guidelines the bishops regularly published, the issue of Christian trade unions, and the Catholic relationship with the CDU and the Social Democratic Party (SPD).[53] Only a few copies of the three-volume study report were ever produced. The PSI in Essen, which held a copy, had to lend it out repeatedly.[54]

The study's controversial reception provides an indication of the practical lim-its opinion polling still faced in the early 1960s. The results indicated that an "open contradiction between hierarchy and people" only existed on the issue of confessional elementary schools. In a sense, the responses to many of the indi-vidual questions reflected the widespread ideal of a "tolerant, modern, open-minded" church. However, it was not evident that a large number of Catholics wanted to call "essential truths of belief" into question.[55] Joseph Krautscheidt, the vicar-general of Essen, pointed out the relativity of the results when he stated that "such surveys are only of minor importance to reliably understanding our fellow Catholics," because, as he noted,

> The attitude of the faithful to the church is today overwhelmingly defined by an inner rejection of strict church rules on marriage and marital morality. However, as no questions were posed, or permitted, on these issues, all the results of our survey are effectively falsified and only of limited value.[56]

Krautscheidt's statement first of all echoed the advocates of opinion polling who theorized that survey answers were less significant than the questions, as the latter demarcated the limits of what could be said. At the same time, the statement should also be read as a delayed echo of the cataclysms that the Kinsey Report triggered in the Catholic view of opinion polling. Given the controversial nature of the topic, even experts at the PSI declined to rebut this criticism with substantive arguments, as Krautscheid had wished them to. Instead, they emphasized that the survey had statistically demonstrated a popular desire for "Christian pastoral care" and that this represented a "genuine" task for the church. They concluded that a highly abstract "essential renewal" was needed so that the faith would no longer be proclaimed in "anachronistic language and dated forms."[57]

Despite the confidentiality of the results, insiders, at least, were aware that the bishops had access to "their private Emnid surveys."[58] Perhaps there were also other surveys in the 1960s that were destined "only for the bishops' bookcases."[59] Studying religious attitudes by opinion polling with the quota method did not gain broad public attention until 1967, when *Der Spiegel* magazine took up the topic. Under the headline "What Do the Germans Believe?," *Der Spiegel's* Christmas edition presented the results of a study jointly carried out by Emnid and the market research institution Institut für Absatzforschung Andreas Ketels (IfAK).[60] The magazine had commissioned the study itself on the initiative of Werner Harenberg, who had been the magazine's editor for church issues since 1961 and had followed developments in the Catholic Church intensively, particularly since Vatican II.[61] *Der Spiegel's* approach was in keeping with a trend emerging at that time for the mass media to commission surveys themselves, automatically ensuring mass publicity for the results.[62]

Catholics generally regarded *Der Spiegel* as a publication with a polemical relationship to the Christian faith and both major churches, not least due to the writings of its publisher, Rudolf Augstein. From the 1970s, the magazine repeatedly used surveys to attack the Catholic Church's abuse of power and excessive public prestige.[63] The report on the Emnid survey in 1967 focused on the same tendencies that the same institute had highlighted seven years earlier in its survey for the Catholic Office, but with greater intensity: recognition of the church as a pastoral authority, on the one hand, and rejection of its political influence and position as a "moral guardian," on the other. *Der Spiegel* interpreted people's sheer unfamiliarity with and ignorance of church dogmas in matters of everyday life as indicators of a growing privatization of the Christian faith—a religion that followers could observe "without the church."[64] The front-page story, too, provoked the church's well-honed reflexes against opinion polling—a technique that had the "audacity . . . shamelessly to expose" people's inner lives—and against *Der Spiegel,* whose pages were willing to air the "spirit of denial at any price."[65] The church newspaper in the diocese of Münster attempted to uncover the supposed bias in the data presented by *Der Spiegel* and to refute the magazine's argument. However, it was unable to convince readers universally. Some pointed out that the bishops were bound to reject any such public survey out of hand. Furthermore, one reader argued, the era in which the "church newspaper was accepted as Gospel" was definitively "over."[66]

This accurate assessment was reflected in the declining distribution figures for diocesan newspapers from the end of the 1960s. Against this backdrop, the German Bishops' Conference held discussions in 1966 on setting up a Catholic weekly newspaper. It was to be published with financial support from the bishops, but not in their name, and editorial independence would be maintained. Before giving the green light to this newspaper, which appeared in spring 1968 under the title of *Publik,* the church conducted a market analysis to clarify the "opportunities and risks" that the project involved. To this end, the Allensbach-based Institut für Demoskopie (IfD, Institute for Opinion Polling) carried out two surveys in 1967 on behalf of the German Bishops' Conference. These explored the reading habits of the "modern Catholic intelligentsia in the postconciliar period." The results revealed the "tendency" in these circles to discuss "basic questions about Catholic life."[67] Although this study—the first to be commissioned by German bishops from the Allensbach institute—was, in essence, a piece of market research, the links between church opinion polling and postconciliar change are unmistakable. The "discerning Catholic readers" identified as potential purchasers followed the norms of Catholic orthodox practice, and over 60 percent of them attended church regularly. Yet they envisaged a newspaper that would be independent of the bishops and provide a forum for expressing free and controversial opinions on a broad spectrum of topics both in and outside the church.[68] Meeting their hopes would be crucial to achieving good sales figures. Successful marketing for the newspaper depended on taking into account the views of the laypeople, whom Vatican II had invested with additional importance in relation to the church hierarchy.

Representing Postconciliar Change

These were some examples of the increasing use of opinion polling to probe attitudes toward religion and the church, even before the caesura of 1968. Only the medium of public opinion, ascertained through opinion polling, was able to articulate how the majority of Catholics felt about postconciliar change, and whether they were interested in its acceleration or reversal. The tables and diagrams that the studies produced with meticulous accuracy gave researchers a quantitative overview of a field of church conflict in which the balances of power and exact direction of the debate were not yet clearly recognizable just a few years after Vatican II. The surveys' clear distinction between "yes" and "no" enabled them to judge the council with a clarity not yet visible in the diocesan press.[69] Secret opinion polls, or those carried out by publications with a record of criticizing the church, were not in a position to substantially shape opinion in the church, whereas surveys in direct response to the impetus provided by the council and embedded in the church's decision-making processes could do so.

Precisely these two conditions were realized in the course of the various synods that took place at the regional level after the conclusion of the council. The diocesan synod in Hildesheim, which met from May 1968 onward, was the forerunner in this and the first to take place after the council. It distinguished itself from earlier synods at the diocese level in giving laypeople both a seat and a voice for the first time. In fact, the laity attended in even greater numbers than priests. Other novelties included the public nature of its proceedings, as well as the plan that all the faithful would contribute their "ideas, suggestions, wishes and criticisms" to the discussions. One flyer, of which one hundred thousand copies were distributed, listed a series of topics without making any claim to completeness and called for submissions to be sent to the synod secretariat. The diocese received around five hundred submissions, many of them emerging from intense family discussion, and passed these to the synod commission. However, the results were far too unstructured and the responses inadequately edited to provide a significant impetus to the commission's work.[70]

A similar initiative was carried out in the diocese of Osnabrück as part of its preparation for implementing the conciliar resolutions. Two sets of questions were distributed in Osnabrück in the run-up to the diocesan synod. One was directed at the active laity in association and parish bodies, the other at priests' conferences at the deanery level. The polling of the laity took place in two waves in 1966 and early 1968, with the second set of questions focusing more on the actual practice of Christianity. Bishop Hermann Wittler organized the poll, and a circle of parish priests and high-ranking staff of the diocese administration prepared it, emphasizing that the preformulated questions did not have an exclusive nature and that there were no "taboos."[71] Many parishes and associations discussed the topics raised in the questionnaire. Thirteen working groups formed especially for this purpose collated the answers and published the results as a manuscript in 1970. The organizers realized that they had not conducted a "representative" study, yet they defended their primary aim of initiating a "conversation" on the issues raised by the council.[72]

This subsequent relativization of the study's significance was in keeping with the main considerations during the survey's planning. For example, the protagonists described the work on the questionnaires as an "end in itself," not least because those questioned would see the surveys as "proof" of the "trust" being placed in them.[73] However, it was evident that diocesan leaders had differing attitudes about the context and benefit of the studies. Bishop Wittler, for instance, initially reacted defensively when advisors from the pastoral office presented the plan for a synod questionnaire on their own initiative. "In his experience," the postconciliar discussion up to that point had the wrong emphasis. For example, the laity primarily raised "criticisms of life within the church," whereas the council had tasked them with "serving the world of today."[74] Claus Kühn, a leading lay representative, warned that the questionnaire had to go beyond the narrow "Catholic sphere" and engage in the "argument with those who had broken silently with the church"; that is, with those whom sociographic terminology classed as "abstainers" (*Abständige*). Hamburg priest Henry Fischer revised the questionnaire, and it was widely distributed throughout the parish in an effort to address this critique.[75]

Public Opinion in the Church: The Katholikentag in 1968

The critical moment for the final breakthrough of opinion polling in the church came with the emergence of a Catholic protest movement in 1968,[76] which used the Katholikentag of 4 to 8 September 1968 in Essen, a biannual forum for lay initiatives, to make a public appearance.[77] Prompted by the recently published "Humanae Vitae" encyclical on birth control, lay Catholics had begun unmistakably to express their discontent and desire for participation in the church, and they made their voices heard at the Katholikentag. After the event in Essen, the opening up of the church to the secular "world" and the entirety of church everyday life proclaimed by the council came to be bitterly disputed, and included sensationalist coverage in the mass media. The Essen Katholikentag thus helped to shape the politicization and polarization of West German Catholicism, which increased in its wake. Already in the planning stages, the Katholikentag had begun to anticipate and shape these trends thanks to the initiative of Friedrich Kronenberg, who as executive secretary of the Central Committee of German Catholics played a decisive role in the planning of the forum. Kronenberg aimed to make the event a "questioning Katholikentag" that could take up and move forward public debate on open issues. As part of the planning process, the Central Committee of German Catholics organized a working meeting of some 500 experts from different fields, who together produced a catalogue of no fewer than 1,770 questions published in the run-up to the Katholikentag. The catalogue was intended to inspire discussion, but a leftist fringe group that called itself Critical Catholicism promptly rejected it as an "attempt at manipulation."[78]

Following the Essen Katholikentag, a wave of conflicts swept the church on the most diverse of topics, bringing in a rhetoric of "crisis" that peaked in the early 1970s. The use of the term "crisis" to describe the situation was nothing new in itself. [79] However, the word's use now spread beyond the bounds of quantifiable religious practice to encompass almost all areas of church organization and pastoral work. Crises were diagnosed everywhere, from the "crisis of faith" to the "crisis of authority," the crisis of confession, and the *Kirchenkrise*—a crisis of the whole church itself.[80]

The increasingly inflationary use of this word not only indicated the deep uncertainty that had gripped large parts of the clergy and active laity from the late 1960s. It also gathered together expectations of the future, which had a reciprocal effect on the ways problems were formulated and choices communicated. Given the original meaning of the word "crisis"—indicating a turning point or a point of separation—its use would suggest that the Catholic Church was about to cross a threshold at which existential decisions had to be made. The term "crisis" to some extent implied an eschatological dramatization of the situation, in which even small problems were stylized as existential questions by "progressives" and "conservatives" alike. For the latter, this led to the variously manifested conviction that the present developments could ultimately "bring about a division of the church."[81]

This was the backdrop against which the Würzburg Synod of the Dioceses in the Federal Republic took place, and the context in which the unprecedented use and acceptance of opinion polling in the Catholic Church should be interpreted. A few groups and individuals around the Essen Katholikentag had already discussed the possibility of holding a "pastoral synod" or "national council" that could take up and process the emerging conflicts in the context of a nationally coordinated enforcement of the conciliar resolutions. Two Catholic youth groups, the Nationalrat der Christlichen Arbeiterjugend (CAJ, National Council of Christian Labor Youth) and the Bund der Deutschen Katholischen Jugend (BDKJ, German Catholic Youth League), supported such a demand publicly for the first time in October and November 1968.[82] Here, as would be the case later, all eyes were on the (positive and negative) model of the Pastoral Council that had been meeting in the Netherlands since January 1968, at which participants cultivated the unconditionally open discussion of central controversies. This culminated in its support of the ordination of married men in January 1970. With this declaration and its previous controversies with Rome, the Dutch church and its Pastoral Council had become, throughout Europe, a noted model of a rebellious Catholicism that dared to engage in open conflict with the Holy See.[83]

The West German bishops and top officials of Catholic organizations agreed that it was necessary to carefully consider the character and consequences of the

Essen event, as well as to draw the appropriate conclusions from it. This consensus assumed concrete form in a meeting between the German Bishops' Conference and the Central Committee of German Catholics, which took place on 9 November 1968, again in Essen. In an analysis of the situation distributed as an ad hoc proposal, Friedrich Kronenberg pointed to the specific quality and dynamic of public opinion as a characteristic of the latest Katholikentag. It did not, he noted, follow the rules of "decision making that govern committees that are accountable." It was to be considered a "success" that Essen had "rendered existing opinions visible and put them up for public discussion." The general secretary of the Central Committee of German Catholics firmly contradicted those who, citing the noisy instrumentalization of the forum by the fringe group Critical Catholicism, denied that it reflected the state of opinion within the church. If the "waves of opinion" had risen too high at times, this should be attributed, Kronenberg asserted, not least to "a lack of opportunities for the development of public opinion in the church," as well as to insufficient practice in expressing it.[84] With these points, Kronenberg essentially marked the recently concluded Katholikentag as the West German church's first great experiment in opinion polling, which made it possible to make previously latent attitudes visible and thus observable. At the same time, in drawing a strict distinction between the observation of opinions and decision making in church bodies as a form of communicative operations, Kronenberg's analysis signaled a break with the traditional, exaggerated fears of responsiveness to the public.

Kronenberg had to admit, however, that the Katholikentag, while "significant for our situation," was, "strictly speaking . . . not representative" of Catholicism. This remark dealt with a theme that would become central to linking the preparations for the "national synod" to opinion polling. Since church structures needed to be brought into line with "postconciliar requirements," Kronenberg deemed the "strongest possible support" for such a forum to be essential for the joint work of episcopate and laity, even if he did not necessarily favor the form of the "national synod."[85] The discussion between the bishops and the Central Committee of German Catholics was characterized by divergent views of the laity's desire for participation, which had left such a lasting mark on the gathering in Essen. Some regarded the dominance of "competency issues" as "signs of a crisis," while others insisted that "structural issues" always also contained a substantive component, and that adjustments were needed in order to put the "conciliar content" into practice more effectively. A study group with equal representation from the German Bishops' Conference and the Central Committee of German Catholics was supposed to develop a "general line" for dealing with future demands for a pastoral synod.[86]

This study group, too, could not help but recognize the pressure of public opinion and urged the German Bishops' Conference to call a synod so that public opinion could be contained as much as possible. The study group noted that a "quick" decision was necessary if they still hoped to influence "the public discussion decisively." Only the form of the synod, as defined in canon law, could guarantee that the "noncommittal chatter of certain groups" would not manipulate the "formation of opinion." A nonbinding "pastoral conference," in contrast, would offer the bishops no "great scope" for later decisions. Its results would "in fact" be "so magnified by public opinion" that these "influences" could later "scarcely be corrected by the bishops'" own decisions. The Dutch Pastoral Council was cited as a negative example to underline the fear that nonbinding resolutions could be "manipulated by the mass media to seem quasi-binding."[87] Just four months after the Essen Katholikentag, the assembled bishops and representatives of the Central Committee of German Catholics, under the leadership of Franz Hengsbach, were forced to recognize that they could no longer ignore the structural significance of public opinion for all future decisions in the context of such a synod. Precisely because of its unpredictability and volatility, the observations of public opinion represented in the mass media were a factor whose dynamics rendered immediate decisions necessary.

Polling Opinions Ahead of the Würzburg Synod

It was thus no surprise when, following their spring meeting in February 1969, the German Bishops' Conference announced a resolution to prepare a "joint synod of the dioceses in the Federal Republic" and to hold it as soon as possible in Würzburg.[88] This was innovative in that it was the first time the laity would be permitted to participate in a national synod. The study group met several times during the first half of 1969 to review existing plans for the legal framework and discuss the themes of the synod. Two subcommittees were formed in March to attend to the detailed work. In the spring of 1969 the second committee, which was devoted to potential topics for the synod, took up the question of whether and in what form planning for the synod should be linked to an "opinion poll." At that point, the committee was considering combining such a total poll with a "targeted opinion poll," which would have to be carried out by an opinion polling institute.[89] To this end, Karl Forster, who in his dual function as secretary of the German Bishops' Conference and the Würzburg Synod enjoyed the public image of a technocratic "manager of German Catholicism" and pulled all the strings, contacted the Institut für Demoskopie in Allensbach.[90] From the beginning, Forster envisioned a total poll of all West German Catholics, which he saw as an "action by the church" intended to spur a discussion of the synod's themes. Another survey based on interviews using the methods of quota and random sampling would follow. The discussions that Forster and Kronenberg conducted with Gerhard Schmidtchen of the IfD in June 1969 made these ideas more concrete. It was assumed that seven of seventeen million distributed questionnaires would be returned.[91]

Only rarely was the public informed of the progress and results of these consultations. On the first of these occasions, a press conference on 3 September 1969, the bishops of the German Bishops' Conference announced that they would decide the topics and statutes for the synod on 10 and 11 November. They also first mentioned the plan to begin preparing immediately thereafter a survey in which "all Catholics" would have an opportunity to "effectively voice" their thoughts on the synod for the first time. Moreover, they stated their intention to conduct a representative survey that would expand on this objective. At the same time, they announced the formation of a preparatory committee. Apart from the themes and procedural rules of the synod, this 35-member body would also concern itself with the opinion polls.[92] On 20 April 1970, at a press conference in Bonn, Cardinal Döpfner proceeded to explain the motives, conduct, and aims of the surveys and presented the questionnaire for the total poll. The church hoped for journalistic support in this enterprise, particularly from the diocesan press, and provided it and other media outlets with three articles that were subsequently reprinted several times.[93]

Aside from these few publicized facts, the remaining substantive and technical preparations for the survey went on largely behind the scenes. The preparatory committee's deliberations were confidential.[94] On 8 December 1969, the committee conducted an extensive discussion on the survey project, which the German Bishops' Conference supported "in order to awaken the broadest possible interest in the synod." In keeping with the ideas of Karl Forster, they decided to establish an Opinion Poll subcommittee to resolve open questions and push ahead with the detailed work on the questionnaire.[95] This working group met with Gerhard Schmidtchen from January to September 1970. The members made final decisions about the survey questions and discussed the thrust and size of the planned surveys using the quota method and random sampling.[96]

The opinion poll on the Würzburg Synod finally took place between 1 May and 30 June 1970. In the framework of this total poll (*Totalbefragung*) of German Catholics, 21 million copies of the questionnaire that had been published in April were distributed, together with an introductory letter signed by the local bishop in each diocese. By the deadline, 4.4 million questionnaires had been returned to a data processing company in Stuttgart, which immediately transported them to Italy, where they were read and evaluated mechanically.[97] These figures made the survey not only the "largest project of religious sociology in the world" up to that point, but also the largest empirical survey by far in the history of the applied social sciences in Germany. The total poll was closely related to two other polls that the Institut für Demoskopie was simultaneously conducting at the end of 1970: a "representative control survey" with the written questionnaire of the total poll and a representative survey with a much wider set of questions based on interviews of 4,500 Catholics, respectively.[98] A written questionnaire involving all 26,000 secular priests and priests of religious orders in the Federal

Republic carried out on behalf of the German Bishops' Conference in early 1971 should also be interpreted in the context of the synod survey.[99]

While the practical planning of the synod poll went on largely behind closed doors, the application of opinion survey methods in the church had already become the subject of a growing number of public interventions. The longer deliberations on the themes and procedural rules for the synod, as well as the opinion poll, remained clandestine, the louder the demands for an appropriate involvement of the whole laity in this process became. Many observers deemed the phase of "preparation and raising awareness" to be almost more important than the synod itself.[100] In order to allow for the expression of a "plurality of opinion," one author writing in the leftist, liberal Catholic weekly *Publik* suggested that "representative opinion surveys" by a "recognized research institute" would be a good idea. To be sure, the findings might prove "shocking and sobering for some," he argued, but beyond reflecting opinion, they could also help to make the synod a matter for "all Catholics."[101]

In many parishes, the interest in a public discussion of the current problems and challenges facing the church was immense. This is evident, for example, in the statements many parish committees made in the diocese of Münster.[102] Their submissions point to the active laity's view of the diverse functions of opinion surveys. Many of them supported an opinion poll mainly to determine the themes that the synod should address.[103] Other parish committees felt that a survey of opinion on selected issues could not adequately put the hierarchy in "touch with the grassroots" and thus might provoke "even greater resignation." Consequently, they asked for more profound instruments to prompt a lasting process of "raising awareness" and to create a "smooth flow of communication from the bottom to the top and vice versa."[104] They suggested not only a survey conducted with the "methods of modern opinion polling," but also a superdiocesan institute that would initiate a "direct connection" between all levels of the church and ensure that minority votes did not simply disappear "in the usual channels."[105]

Finally, one parish committee suggested resignedly that a poll should be conducted not in preparation for the synod but in place of it—unless, at the very least, a two-thirds majority could enforce all of the synod resolutions, even against the vote of the bishops.[106] Many parish committees also suspected that the call for discussion proceeding from Münster was merely a "sham maneuver" on the part of the bishops to "smooth ruffled feathers." When the members of the preparatory committee were announced in November 1969, the head of the synod office in Münster feared that further "serious damage" could result from the impression that decisions on the themes and conduct of the survey had thereby already been made in advance.[107] The hopes for an appropriate representation of their views and an end to the accumulated reform blockage in the church—hopes that the laypersons active in the parish assemblies, at least, had placed in the synod—were very high indeed. Their request that "nothing should be prejudged or fixed" in the run-up to the synod thus assumed greater urgency.[108] Closely related to this was the demand that "open language" be used in "preparation" for the synod to keep from setting the "course" in a particular direction in advance. A "representative survey" appeared to be the best means of advancing the cause of uncompromisingly open communication in the church.[109]

The application of opinion polling methods was thus already a subject of intense discussion in the church, even before the questionnaire for the total poll was published in April 1970. A large number of public demands and informal statements had been made. It was already apparent during this phase that the controversial assessment of the synod would focus to a significant extent on the preparatory polls, especially as long as the synod itself had not yet begun work. Even before its official presentation to the public, the total poll acted as a focal point for the backlog of expectations that the active laity, in particular, placed on the synod. The Catholic Church had become a highly politicized arena after 1968, and one characterized by open conflicts. As a result, and in the course of public debates on the relevance and form of opinion polling, this research method became a focus of expectations and assessments for a public that, with the total poll, extended well beyond the circles of those active in the church. The total poll made opinion surveys a political issue within the church.

Polling between Taboo and Enlightenment

The total poll was conducted in a highly politicized and conflict-laden arena, in which opposing categories or systems of categories were used to describe the method of opinion polling. It was in this arena of communication, marked by diametrically opposite concepts, that the issue of whether, and in what form, the language of opinion polling could gain a legitimate position in the Catholic Church was decided. The ambivalences of the opinion polling discourse were particularly accentuated against the background of innerchurch conflicts and problems. This was already evident in the first distinction drawn: that between taboo and enlightenment. This referred to the above-mentioned desire for an absolutely open discussion of all imaginable subjects in order to find appropriate solutions to the oft-diagnosed crisis of the church. The actual questions contained in the final questionnaire of the total poll and the three previous draft versions had already put this problem in sharp focus. After all, regardless of how they were concretely formulated, they contained certain terms that fixed and identified religious and ecclesiastical subject matter. In postconciliar "conflicts within the church," however, there were "scarcely any terms whose traditional content remained uncontroversial, let alone universally binding."[110]

This observation applied even to such a key term as the "church." Down to the final version of the questionnaire, it was synonymous with church officials, although this was no longer in keeping with the ecclesiology of Vatican II. In this way the survey conveyed, at least implicitly, a "very one-sided" image of the church and suppressed necessary "food for thought," as Wolfgang Große, a suffragan bishop in the diocese of Essen who was quite critical of opinion polling, complained.[111] For example, on the question of the most important "tasks for the church nowadays," one could check a box stating that the church should urge "the powerful of this world to pursue justice and peace."[112] In Große's opinion, this formulation lacked "inspiration along the lines of a critique of ideology, education of the conscience, prayer schools," or "peace work," and he lamented that such appeals to the "powerful" by the church hierarchy, at least, "do not take us very far."[113] With its implicit church official–centered definition of the church, the questionnaire thus gave a wide berth to the redefinition of the church as the "people of God" proclaimed at Vatican II.[114]

The controversies surrounding the questionnaire, however, centered not on its implied definition of the church, but rather on its handling of the "hot potatoes"—the few topics that had caused intense debate in the preceding years, such as the pastoral handling of interchurch marriages or the collection of church tax by the state. There were also a few points that had heretofore largely been treated as taboo nontopics in official internal church discussion. These included, in particular, the possible lifting of compulsory priestly celibacy and the papal exercise of authority. This is precisely where various lay associations and left-wing Catholic and church-critical groups and initiatives intervened. They began to coordinate their efforts in the working group Synode 72 in January 1970, demanding that the final questionnaire address these issues. Otherwise, they maintained, people would suspect that the church was not undertaking a "genuine survey of opinion but only seeking to record preexisting agreement."[115]

The German Bishops' Conference publicly pointed out that question fourteen responded to these queries. It read, "In the near future, a joint synod of the German dioceses will take place. What are the things which ought to be discussed there by all means?" and then gave a list of fifteen different thematic fields that could be checked. According to the German Bishops' Conference, the questionnaire thus addressed "all of the hot potatoes in the current discussion," from the crisis of faith to celibacy, mixed marriages, and the church tax. The "manner of formulation," the bishops insisted, had made it clear that the synod could take up all of these issues, but must view them in their respective "thematic contexts."[116] In fact, the fourth of the fifteen listed groups of topics for the synod referred to "priestly service and life" and gave the following examples in brackets: "the new generation of priests, training, celibacy, clerical communities, and the diaconate."[117] The mass media's response to this manner of thematic selection remained ambivalent, however. For example, against the background of the German episcopate's "rigid stance" on the matter of priestly celibacy, some writers felt that the episcopate had now taken a "decisive step" toward "the repeatedly demanded democratization of the church" in the total poll.[118] Others in the media pointed out critically that the questionnaire did not ask where "the individual stood on the issue of celibacy." The questionnaire's avoidance of important topics could lead to a loss of interest in the synod, particularly among reformist forces. Finally, *Der Spiegel* noted that the church's "timidity" on such controversial issues was antiquated. The Hamburg-based magazine had commissioned an Emnid survey on the situation of religion and the churches back in 1967, whose findings it had published as a front-page story that same year. *Der Spiegel* had been the first publication to present the results of opinion polling in this field to a broader readership. And in the *Der Spiegel* study, 58 percent of practicing Catholics surveyed had supported allowing priests to marry.[119]

The total poll's avoidance of "hot potatoes" was perceived as creating taboo issues, while the nonpublic manner in which the study was edited provoked countermovements and direct interventions among the more "critical" laypeople and priests. In particular, rival or alternative surveys carried out from April 1970 undermined the German Bishops' Conference survey's claim to being the only legitimate application of opinion polling in preparation for the synod. The alternative survey that attracted the most attention across the country was presented in May 1970 by the Freckenhorst Circle (Freckenhorster Kreis), an independent solidarity group of Catholic priests in the diocese of Münster. The seventeen questions, which were also reprinted in the diocesan newspaper of Münster and in *Publik,* focused primarily on life within the church and asked laypeople directly to agree or disagree with a series of statements. As well as questions such as, "Do you think it is right to maintain the 'Sunday obligations'?" the survey also asked if the upcoming synod should be "allowed to make decisions against the dioceses."[120] With its open call for respondents to choose between alternatives, this questionnaire inevitably drew the criticism that it was calling for a plebiscite. It also served as a gathering point for the considerable dissatisfaction with the official study that had developed among high-ranking staff in the councils of the lay apostolate, at least in the diocese of Münster.

In the public use and juxtaposition of the categories of taboo and enlightenment, i.e. a rational discussion of all church-related issues, the issues excluded from the official questionnaire thus returned in another form and place. Now, however, they could only position themselves in direct opposition to the official survey. The desire to achieve a "frank," "unreserved" discussion of all problems within the church, which had emerged openly in 1968, became concentrated in the conflicts over what the survey could ask, and thus also tell. Any criticism of the form of testimony in the total poll, especially of the taboo placed on certain questions, could only be voiced in the margins, since the opinion survey had already, by its very size and proclaimed objective of including all Catholics, become positioned at the center of the church.

Those whose hopes of free speech in the church had been disappointed could transfer these desires to the representative survey conducted on the basis of random sampling and interviews. Even as determined a critic of the German Bishops' Conference as Klaus Lang—who, as chairman of the student organization Katholische Deutsche Studenten-Einigung (KDSE), was at the center of the leftist protests by Catholic students—hoped that it would "go into detail" in precisely those areas where the total poll had remained "pale and impersonal."[121] Karl Forster, who served as a quasi-official representative of the German Bishops' Conference in the groups and committees concerned with the synod, also referred to the various parallel polls utilizing random sampling. As the deadline for returning the questionnaires approached, he reassured the members of the preparatory commission by predicting that the representative survey soon to follow would "silence many a criticism of the general questionnaire," as "it asks directly about many hot potatoes."[122] In fact, the representative survey based on a more extensive questionnaire did inquire into attitudes toward priestly celibacy, finding that 62 percent of respondents wanted it lifted altogether, and only 16 percent wanted it retained without exception. The findings of the representative survey, however, met with nowhere near the public response that the total poll had.[123]

Experts and Counterexperts

The two surveys conducted by the Institut für Demoskopie based on a representative sample were closely linked to a second feature of the public opinion polling discourse in the Catholic Church: the opposition of experts and counterexperts. The scientific integrity and credibility of the surveys was at stake here, which was of decisive importance for the application of social scientific knowledge. Like every scientific discourse, the total poll provoked outrage among ordinary Catholics, who complained about the incomprehensible jargon on the form and its nonsensical categories. However, even these objections could be used to underscore the scientific respectability of the expert-designed survey, which earned all the more respect for being beyond ordinary people's understanding. Perhaps the strangest-sounding question was number twenty-two: "Who normally does the cooking in your home?" This was intended to identify employed women who also ran a household, and it was on precisely this question that experts had placed the greatest value, as the head of the synod office in Münster—himself no "expert in opinion polling"—reassured those who complained indignantly.[124]

The experts included staff at the Institut für Demoskopie, based in Allensbach, as well as all other theologians and social scientists who had been asked to share any concerns and advice they had prior to the survey. There was a growing willingness in leading circles of the Catholic Church, including the German Bishops' Conference, to utilize commercial institutions for market and opinion polling. In the case of the total poll, the personal contact between Hanna-Renate Laurien, the minister of culture and education in the state of Rhineland-Palatinate, and Elisabeth Noelle-Neumann, who held a professorship in Mainz, prompted this approach.[125] This provoked criticism from experts like Franz-Xaver Kaufmann, professor of sociology at the University of Bielefeld, who warned that surveys on religious topics required special theological knowledge and insisted that commercial institutes did not have a "clear awareness of the issue." In the total poll, it seemed clear that while the IfD had good technical experience with representative questionnaires, its expertise in this area caused it to routinely favor these over more suitable methods. However, quantitative analysis was only useful for questions that were already a matter of public discussion, argued Kaufmann. The answers to other questions depended on underlying attitudes, which Kaufmann believed could only be revealed using motive scales. If the total poll was to serve as more than "just an alibi for the [German] Bishops' Conference" and demonstrate that public opinion had been "taken into account," it would be better to let a team of theologians, vicar-generals, and social and religious psychologists work out an approach that could then be put into practice by the IfD.[126]

This resistance to the experts from Allensbach reveals the concerns and reservations many had about this new, technically defined methodology being so abruptly introduced to the Catholic Church. At the same time, the criticism found some resonance in the case of the representative survey, which sought from the beginning to analyze the value system and latent motives of Catholics.[127] It did so by combining opinion polling with various scaling techniques that could illustrate attitudes and motive clusters concerning specific issues.[128] However, the experts played more than just a technical role in planning these surveys. They also had a performative function through the advice their public opinion polling gave to the German Bishops' Conference, which was meant to increase trust in both the application and results of scientific methods.[129] Involving experts was especially important when it came to controversial topics like the synod, which were loaded with demands for political participation. Experts objectified the issues, enabling them to moderate the effects of such politicization and control the expectations expressed in public. The scientists' symbolic presence and public interventions reinforced the seriousness and legitimacy both of the total poll itself and of those who had commissioned it. This effect unfolded both backstage and in public. Even deciding what part of the process the public would be allowed to see helped to determine the effects that could be achieved.[130]

In the case of the total poll, the German Bishops' Conference initially decided to let the entire preparation run behind the scenes, but then it reversed course, emphatically seeking publicity and providing extensive information on the motives and desired effects of the campaign. Until the summer of 1970, this gave the diocesan synod office in Münster—like those in other dioceses—the opportunity to neutralize the surge of voices critical of the total poll. The office answered criticism from below that the questionnaire was unrepresentative or implied certain prior assumptions by pointing out that its design was the responsibility of the pollsters of the IfD. The representative survey, the office stated in a typical reply, would confirm the experts' conviction that these "criticisms were not justified."[131] Not only individual laypersons or parish committees but also the heads of the lay apostolate organized by the postconciliar councils were able to point rhetorically to the "experts" to keep the displeasure that had built up behind the scenes from finding its way into the public arena. This is demonstrated by the dispute that erupted a few days after the questionnaire of the total poll was published in April 1970 between Bishop Tenhumberg and the diocesan committee, also exposing differences within the latter body. Wilhelm Pötter, chairman of the diocesan committee in Münster, sent a letter to Bishop Tenhumberg in May, though it was actually written by Ferdinand Kerstiens, chairman of the synod committee (*Synodenausschuß*) of the diocesan committee (*Diözesankomitee*), whose general committee (*Hauptausschuß*) had formally approved the letter and its release without agreeing with its content on all points.[132] The letter expressed the continuing "disappointment and resignation" in the diocese over the preparations for the synod, citing the extensive "measures for securing" the status of the synod to preclude any decisions being made against the bishops' views. Instead, the relationship to the church's "grassroots," argued the letter, should be one of "dialogue," as the "active forces" might otherwise be driven "to resignation, at the very least." Tenhumberg, stated Pötter's letter, should present this view to the German Bishops' Conference and argue for the abandonment of the previous "policy of secrecy." Anticipating a possible objection, which was apparently already quite familiar from discussion with representatives of the German Bishops' Conference, the letter continued:

> In this context one will point to the opinion survey, which affords all Catholics the opportunity to express their views. However—doubtless fearing a plebiscitary statement by the Catholic people—many of the pressing problems are not mentioned, and others are so obscured and presented as false alternatives that there are few possibilities to express concrete wishes and suggestions, misgivings and demands. For that reason, one fears that the opinion poll will further intensify the existing discord.[133]

In the first draft of this letter, Kerstiens had put this thesis even more pointedly. He wrote of the "impression" that in preparing for the synod, the bishops were solely interested in using a "pseudodemocratic procedure" to give themselves an alibi, only to leave "everything essentially as it had always been," with the addition of a "few cosmetic repairs."[134]

The disagreement on the wording of the letter within the diocesan committee notwithstanding, Bishop Tenhumberg had to take it seriously. According to one observer, the general committee had declared agreement with its tone. Tenhumberg also had time to prepare a considered answer, as his vicar-general Reinhard Lettmann had already given him access to the earlier draft of the letter approved by the synod committee in late April. Those sentences that Kerstiens had suggested but were ultimately dropped were highlighted in the letter.

The vicar-general described them as the "misbehavior" later "rebuked"—using language that was typical of his paternalistic habitus, even though he was only thirty-seven years old at the time.[135] Tenhumberg admitted that the synod's public relations work had so far been inadequate and welcomed the suggestion of generating interest through local "discussion groups" along the lines of the Dutch model, provided that people would not see these as the "decisive" voice of the synod. He then attempted to explain the reason for the generally negative perception of the total poll:

> The negative response is a further example of how excessive or false expectations can lead to negative reactions. The questionnaire [of the total poll] must be seen in the context of the accompanying representative opinion survey in order to appreciate it properly. The bishops have relied here, by the way, completely on the judgment of the experts, pollsters, sociologists, political scientists and theologians, who certainly have no intention of concealing anything.[136]

With this answer, Tenhumberg was at least able to prevent the dissatisfaction with the preparation of the synod, which had accumulated in the synod committee and beyond, from reaching the public, as the committee did not take any further action.[137]

With the publication of the questionnaire of the total poll in April 1970, the stage was set for the expert who was to become associated like no other with opinion polling in the context of the synod, and in fact with the application of empirical social research to the Catholic Church and religious issues in general: Gerhard Schmidtchen, a long-standing employee of the Institut für Demoskopie in Allensbach who had recently been appointed full professor of sociology in Zurich. In June 1970, Schimdtchen discussed the synod on the public television channel ZDF with Hanna-Renate Laurien, Klaus Hemmerle, the spiritual director of the Central Committee of German Catholics and later bishop of Aachen, and the Viennese archbishop Franz Jachym.[138] Schmidtchen presented his views in newspaper articles, too, including that the "high response rate" compared to similar church polls in Austria and Switzerland constituted proof that the questions had awakened people's "interest" and would confound critics' "distrust" in the questionnaire of the total poll. Notwithstanding the fact that the results still had to be looked at in detail, Schmidtchen described the material from the total poll as "sensational." And he did not miss the opportunity to make the obligatory reference to the forthcoming poll of a representative sample with a more extensive list of questions, which would at last mean that those who had wanted "tougher questions" in the total poll would get their money's worth.[139]

Such statements brought out the counterexperts, who publicly criticized individual parts of the research program or proclaimed the entire undertaking to be academically worthless. Franz-Xaver Kaufmann, for example, took issue with some of the scientific analysis of the various questionnaires without casting doubt on the legitimacy of the study as a whole.[140] Staff at the Pastoral Sociological Institute in Essen, meanwhile, went much further. Two research assistants published a fundamental criticism of the total poll's methodology in the local diocesan newspaper. The uncontrollable way in which questionnaires were distributed and returned, they argued, made the survey reminiscent of the *Literary Digest*'s "straw polls" from the prehistory of modern opinion polling. These had failed once and for all in the US presidential election in 1936, when they had to compete with the more accurate quota method. Furthermore, they claimed, it was not difficult to recognize that the main objective of the study had been "to rule out any form of criticism by using ambiguity."[141]

The effectiveness and symbolic importance of counterexperts depended not only on the precision of their arguments but also on their prestige within the scientific community. A far more problematic critique than that of the two researchers from the PSI thus came from a more senior figure at the institute, Egon Golomb, who criticized the study in public lectures and in an internally distributed paper. His argument essentially took the same direction: the total poll asked questions that were necessarily "sweeping" and "superficial." As it lacked a theoretical concept, the "naïve empiricism" of commercial market research inevitably dominated. It was impossible to draw a sample from the responses to the total poll, even retrospectively. And the planned comparison of total and representative studies "provided material more suited to an undergraduate class on methodology."[142] Golomb's unguarded criticism, which he had also passed on to Bishop Hengsbach, triggered a multipronged reaction. First, Golomb was called to appear before the spiritual council of the diocese of Essen, where he was informed that his actions had been inappropriate. Second, another expert was deployed to repair the damage. As the proponents of the poll could not prevent Golomb's views from being disseminated, they presented his arguments alongside an extensive rebuttal by Gerhard Schmidtchen to the heads of the diocesan synod office as material for debate.[143] A final tried-and-tested strategy for neutralizing the influence of counterexperts was to invite them to participate in the study. Karl Forster therefore offered Golomb the opportunity to take part in analyzing the questionnaires.[144]

Counterexperts were best able to take a public stance if they had already clearly distanced themselves from a project. In the case of the synod, Norbert Greinacher was just such a figure. The pastoral theologian had made a name for himself "as one of the engines of resistance" since the synod's constitution had begun to take shape in the study group's discussions in summer 1969. Greinacher, a member of the Bensberg Circle (Bensberger Kreis) of left-leaning Catholics—mostly laity—and of the Freckenhorst Circle appeared as the spokesperson for both groups, demanding that theologians prepare a pastoral council as a forum for public discussion along the lines of the Dutch model. This would replace a synod based on church law, in which all decisions were subject to approval by the German Bishops' Conference.[145] Greinacher himself had called for the use of opinion surveys to help prepare the synod.[146]

What would prove decisive for the dramatic effect achieved by Greinacher as a counterexpert was the fact that he combined his criticism with practical work on a survey, which from 1970 turned increasingly into a countersurvey. In November 1969, the editors of a program on "church and life" on ZDF had called on television viewers to submit ideas and opinions to the Synod Mailbox. The idea came from the Pastoral Council in the Netherlands, where a similar campaign by Radio Hilversum had recorded the topics that concerned and frustrated the faithful. Cardinal Döpfner explicitly advocated ZDF's "mailbox" and took part in its symbolic opening. From the beginning, it was planned that a team led by Norbert Greinacher would examine and publish submissions to the mailbox, which had no prescribed topic or structure. The team used quantitative content analysis as the methodological tool for ascertaining the most important topics and problems.[147]

Behind the scenes, however, reservations grew about how representative the material was. Doubt was cast on the mailbox method, even though both Greinacher and the editors responsible at ZDF continually emphasized that the advantage of the submissions lay not in their number but in the independent, subjective viewpoints they provided on controversial topics. The conflict escalated when Karl Holzamer, director at ZDF and long-serving member of the Central Committee of German Catholics, refused to grant permission for a related book publication in early 1971. A further aggravating factor was that Holzamer found public support in this matter in Werner Brüning, the bishops' TV representative. This gave Greinacher the opportunity to suggest that Brüning was attempting to "control and censor" unfavorable programs.[148] At the same time, the group around Greinacher interpreted their analysis of the data as a first attempt to provide church communication with a much-needed "thermostat" that made it possible for feedback to be passed up the hierarchy from below. In their criticism of the various other synod surveys, they also pointed out that ZDF had not been able to bring itself to publish the results of its own representative survey commissioned from the IfAK polling institute. Highlighting this was potentially controversial, as the ZDF had deliberately concentrated on the problems and "hot potatoes" left open by the IfD's total poll questionnaire.[149]

Defining the Limits of Responsiveness:
The Synod Polls as Manipulation or Plebiscite

Thirdly, the differentiation between manipulation and plebiscite was of decisive importance to the opinion polling discourse in the Catholic Church. The participatory politicization in the church in the late 1960s overlapped with a problem inherent to opinion polling: how to react appropriately to the opinions revealed by such research techniques. Some feared that the calls for "dialogue" and discussion, and the polling of ordinary Catholics, was no more than "a diversionary tactic" by the bishops "aimed at calming people's spirits."[150] In his letter to Bishop Tenhumberg, Ferdinand Kerstiens suggested that the fear of a "plebiscitary statement" by the laypeople was an important motive for the form of questionnaire chosen. In the first draft of the letter he had gone even farther. There was a general "impression," he wrote, that the church was seeking an "alibi" in the form of a "pseudodemocratic procedure" in order to "keep everything essentially unchanged" while making a few "cosmetic changes."[151] Suspicions about the motives of the Würzburg Synod's total poll thus existed from the beginning. Submissions and resolutions alleged that those responsible for the synod, and thus, ultimately, the bishops, had only one purpose in mind in commissioning the survey: giving ordinary Catholics the (false) impression that they were actively involved in preparing the synod.

In the preparatory committee for the synod, too, balancing the suspicions of manipulative intent against the dangers of an apparently plebiscitary opinion poll also aroused misgivings and controversy, especially in light of anticipated public reactions to any specification of the issues. It was generally agreed that the total poll should awaken "interest" in the synod and initiate an "awareness-raising process." Moreover, the "point" of all polls was a "survey of opinion," which also implied an "ascertainment of facts." "We must, however, prevent the facts obtained [by the total poll] from attaining normative force, as it were," said one member. To keep the action from taking on such a "plebiscitary character," it was argued that the survey should include as few "questions involving decisions" as possible. This assertion apparently proved so controversial, however, that the subcommittee devoted to the polls was first asked to develop a concrete recommendation on this point.[152] In their submissions, the Paderborn suffragan bishop Johannes Degenhardt and the Trier vicar-general Professor Linus Hoffmann expressed concern that, because of its "general nature," the total poll could easily assume a "plebiscitary character."[153] Hoffmann, in particular, worried that the total poll might present opinions that were associated with a "conscious deviation from the church line" as "tenable," and thus also "insinuate" that they were "genuine possibilities for the synod." Regardless of the resolutions taken by the synod, the total poll would "have effects that could no longer be undone." After all, it was not addressed solely to "reasonable and conscientious persons."[154]

These concerns about the dangers of an opinion survey had their roots in many Catholics' general skepticism of plebiscitary democracy, which, in turn, derived from the damage plebiscitary elements in the Weimar Constitution had allegedly caused, casting a long shadow over the Federal Republic. Hoffmann's statement was at the same time an undisguised reference to the political psychology of the masses, whose irrational energies, once unleashed, could no longer fully be brought under control if one permitted taboos to be broken and opened particular issues up for discussion. Since the dynamism of political passions could no longer be contained once they were publicly released, Hoffmann believed that the poll had to be conceptualized "purely as a survey of opinion."[155] The vicar-general of Trier thereby pointed unmistakably to an important character-istic of the public sphere, which cannot be conceptualized in the Habermasian sense primarily as a forum for the rational exchange of appropriate arguments. However, he nevertheless ignored a further quality of public opinion: its func-tion in the selection and thematic concentration of expectations, which observers address to a system, and which the system must then incorporate into its opera-tive calculations.[156]

Karl Lehmann, then professor of theology in Mainz, intervened concerning this very point, at least implicitly, and also corrected the recently consulted min-utes of the committee meeting of 8 December 1969. According to Lehmann, the various synod polls could by no means be understood as a "wholly non-committal survey of opinion or an 'assertion of fact' without repercussions." To argue that it presumed a particular outcome in advance meant that, "despite the constant talk of 'God's people,'" one "did not take the will of the faithful seriously enough." To be sure, Lehmann acknowledged that "manipulation" could "be at play," although "the other side"—those who rejected the total poll because of its plebiscitary character—also introduced such manipulation. If the poll brought to light "difficult problems" that "do not suit some people," this would have the "positive effect of unsparingly revealing some matters on which we otherwise beat around the bush." A poll could "relentlessly illustrate the weight of many press-ing pastoral issues, which can never again be concealed." Regarding the minutes of the meeting of the preparatory committee on 8 December 1969, mentioned above, Lehmann explained further that he had objected to "empty survey ques-tions" because "intelligent Catholics" might otherwise feel that they were par-ticipating in a sham survey, and the whole thing could thus be "denounced as a game," to the detriment of the synod.[157]

In this written intervention, Lehmann referred to the context of communication within the church, which was essential to adequately understanding the planned total poll. The fear of manipulation expressed from below, from the laity at the grassroots level, stemmed not from irrational political passions but rather from earlier observations—whose rationality one could not deny out of hand—of how the church dealt with problems. Only four years after the end of Vatican II, the respected theologian felt compelled to warn against degrading the conciliar texts to mere random empty phrases. Despite his "genuine concern" about a possible plebiscitary instrumentalization of the results, Lehmann was more worried that the total poll would directly contribute to disappointment in the synod.[158]

Lehmann, who later became bishop of Mainz, cardinal, and head of the Ger-man Bishops' Conference, referred at the same time to the phenomenon of "com-municative latency" inherent in opinion polling. Every poll renders manifest latent opinions and attitudes that may not have been previously addressed in public, making them a point of departure for further observations.[159] In the context of the synod polls, this could be understood as an argument in favor of the opinion survey. Thus, a speaker from the German Bishops' Conference pointed out during the first public presentation of the survey project in April 1970 that the opinions published in the mass media, with which everyone was naturally familiar, were merely the "views and opinions . . . of certain groups," while the total poll was intended to give all an "honest offer" to express themselves. In this, the speaker interpreted the opinion survey primarily as a corrective to the latencies of the public sphere as represented by the mass media.[160]

Polling and the "Silent Majority" in the Church

This interpretation of the poll as a corrective corresponded to a scheme that several bishops had used—apparently independently of each other—in the run-up to the synod to correct the "erroneous" practice and interpretation of representation in the church. For example, in an interview with his diocesan magazine, bishop of Essen Franz Hengsbach noted that the "country's silent people," who scarcely spoke up otherwise, could express their "genuine concerns and wishes" in the total poll.[161] Bishop of Münster Heinrich Tenhumberg reacted with similar rhetoric when the diocesan committee told him about the worries of many in the laity regarding the synod in the summer of 1970. Altering and heightening the political slogan of the "silent majority" that Richard Nixon had coined in a much-noted television address of 3 November 1969, Tenhumberg pointed out that there was a "largely 'silent middle' in the church . . . who in general rarely express themselves, and yet are quite involved in their own way."[162] Against the background of increasing mass protests against the Vietnam War, Nixon used the phrase to correct the "majority" view presented by the liberal mass media, which he blamed for the public's antigovernment bias. Swimming against this tide, he stylized himself as a stalwart advocate for the true, freedom-loving, and hardworking Middle America of ordinary people.[163] Conservative priests and bishops similarly cited the "silent majority" (*schweigende Mehrheit*) to denounce the rebellion and protest on the left—which in their view did not reflect actual conditions in the church—as a phenomenon (over)dramatized by the media above all because of its loudness.[164]

Particularly when it came to the opposition between taboo and enlightenment and manipulation and plebiscite, it was not simply a matter of finding the appropriate system of categories with which to justify the church's use of the opinion polling method as legitimate, or reject it as illegitimate. The politically heated controversy even reached the questionnaire itself as the specific technical instrument with which opinion polling classified and regulated social issues.

There were a considerable number of Catholics who adorned the questionnaires of the total poll process with "obscene insults" not provided for in its yes/no formula.[165] A Catholic student congregation instructed the faithful on the most economical way to answer the questionnaire in order to submit critical concerns to the computerized evaluation process effectively.166 However, the decisive aspect turned out to be the distribution of the questionnaires, which, according to the survey's representation model, were supposed to reach every Catholic in the Federal Republic. These were not sent by mail due to the immense costs involved. Instead, the parish was supposed to be responsible for their distribution.[167] The parish of St. Peter in the Westphalian town of Waltrop was not the only place to refuse to do so, as it perceived "that no discussion was desired from the bottom up." In Warendorf, where a countersurvey was running, the priest preached from the pulpit against participation in the official questionnaire.[168] In many churches, the questionnaires were placed by the exit of the church, ready to be taken away. This again provoked the indignation of nonpracticing Catholics. Those who wanted to participate suspected a "manipulation of the survey results" when the priest informed them that all the questionnaire forms had already been taken.[169]

Cognitive Dissonance as an Effect of Functional Differentiation

Besides these controversies, Gerhard Schmidtchen had attempted, with the help of the sample-based representative poll with a more extensive questionnaire, to look at an aspect of the research that was important to both him and Karl Forster: the growing discrepancy between the church's value system and that of ordinary Catholics. Schmidtchen applied a theory from the research of social psychological attitudes that had been discussed and tested in the United States since the early 1950s. The most well-known and influential approach in this field was Leon Festinger's theory of "cognitive dissonance," presented in 1957, which also found resonance in the church's social research.[170] Instead, in the sample-based poll, Schmidtchen drew from Milton J. Rosenberg's model of "affective-cognitive consistency." Of the three components of the social psychological concepts of "attitude"—the "affective, cognitive and behavioral"—Rosenberg's model, unlike Festinger's, ignored behavioral expression toward the object of the attitude. Rather, it focused on experimentally verifying the relationships between the affective and cognitive components of attitude and the growing discrepancies between them.[171]

To implement this model, the organizers of the more extensive, interview-based representative poll used a method also employed by Rosenberg. First, all participants were given a card game containing thirty-six values, which first had to be sorted according to their meanings. In the second step, the cards were dealt once again, with the values this time being separated into those that would harm and benefit the church.[172] This allowed for the discrepancy between society's value system and that prevalent in the church to be measured quantitatively. The systematic foundation of this and many other measurements of cognitive dissonance was the tendency toward "'inauthentic' behavior," which was bound to occur in social systems with "complex role differentiations."[173] In a "functionally differentiated" society with plural "value norms," it was simply "unavoidable" over the long term that role conflicts would lead to discrepancies between church standards and individual decision making. This was, therefore, not an issue specific to the Catholic Church. For pastoral care, the crucial question was to discern the point at which the resulting "cognitive stress" became so great that it hindered the individual's ability to subjectively restore a "balance" between the cognitive and affective aspects of attitude.[174] The church could utilize opinion polling to answer this very question.

When the Institute for Journalism (Institut für Publizistik) at the University of Münster proposed a survey on the synod's impact in the parishes of the diocese in 1973, it received a dismissive answer. The previous year, the priests and chairs of the parish committees had already asked to be spared from any further such activities.[175] For one thing, Catholics' interest in opinion polling as a technique based on accurate representativity had waned significantly. For another, the obvious buildup, dramatization, and politicization of internal church conflicts had given way to a more relaxed approach to handling problems. This was especially noticeable in the proceedings of the Würzburg Synod itself, which was a parliamentary, unemotional event, albeit one that the press described as the "school parliament of German Catholicism," given its lack of decision-making power.[176] It had quickly become clear in Würzburg that the majority of Catholics were tired of the "controversies" after "the state of war in the church from 1966 to around 1972."[177] This had not been foreseeable when the total poll took place in 1970, prior to the Würzburg Synod. At this stage, church discussion was still weighed down with immense expectations directed at the synod as the Second Vatican Council's engine of implementation in the West German church and, at the same time, directed at solving the accumulated problems expressed through the unmistakable and diverse language of crisis.

Against this backdrop, preparation for the synod itself largely involved various public opinion polling activities. A symbolic indication of this was a broadcast on the forthcoming synod on ZDF television in June 1970 that reproduced the total poll questionnaire at enormous size, stretching to more than head height, and placed it on the wall of the studio.[178] In addition, many Catholics expressed their expectations of the synod in a questionnaire conducted by the German Bishops' Conference. But how did the intensive use of opinion polling affect the synod, and what side effects did the conflicts and controversies associated with the total poll have on the acceptance of opinion polling in the church? Karl Korn, the longtime coeditor of the *Frankfurter Allgemeine Zeitung (FAZ)* newspaper, attempted to answer the first question even before the polling had finished. He took issue with the variously expressed assumption that the church wanted the total poll questionnaire to release some of the pressure that had built up due to its dilatory and taboo treatment of various problems. He countered this with a view shared by some bishops that, once opened, this safety valve could never be closed again and might bring about "new movement and new unrest" at any time.[179] Only a few months later, Otto B. Roegele came to precisely the opposite conclusion. In view of the unexpectedly high response rate and the letters received by bishops, he judged the interview process "alone" to be worthwhile for its "psychotherapeutic effects of relief."[180]

After a precise analysis of the conflicts concerning the total poll and the opposing categories used to legitimize them, it is possible to agree with Roegele's analysis, provided that we apply it not to the subjective perceptions of those polled, as Roegele did, but instead to the balance of power within the church. The accusation that the church was suppressing controversial topics, the appearances by counterexperts, and the staging of countersurveys turned the total poll itself into a "hot potato." But at no point did these activities succeed in legitimizing the interest in democratizing and radically renewing the church, which a bottom-up interpretation of opinion polling was meant to articulate. This was partly because the church still held general reservations about opinion polling. The crucial point, however, was that, despite its deficiencies and half measures, the bishop-initiated total poll presented and positioned itself as a means of integrating and involving all Catholics, while at the same time implementing in contemporary fashion a postconciliar dialogue and "conversation" between the church and "the entire human family."[181] And when a dialogue was offered, those who declined to participate were ultimately at fault for doing so, not the limits of the dialogue itself.

The Synod Polls as a Dialogue

"Dialogue" was one of the "main words of the council."[182] And even though it was only in its meager beginnings, as Karl Forster himself acknowledged, the dialogue had now officially begun, namely, at the behest of the West German bishops. They had made a "fair offer to all Catholics." Those who rejected or in any way substantially criticized this offer positioned themselves on the periphery of the church's internal discussion and decision making. In a sense, the total poll turned the issue of responsiveness on its head. Even before the bishops were to consider the consequences of the various surveys, every single Catholic was presented with an opportunity, which at the same time implied a compulsory acceptance. "It consists of filling out and sending in the questionnaire," stressed Forster.[183] "Not evading answering the questionnaire," formulated Klaus Hemmerle in a similar vein, was itself "a step of the dialogue."[184] In the context of West

German Catholicism in the years 1969/70, the total poll served as an extremely effective instrument of symbolic participation.

The total poll also had immediate impacts on the work of the synod, although these are difficult to evaluate in specific terms. All concerns about the direct plebiscitary consequences of the poll's results proved to be unfounded: the constituent assembly of the synod demonstrated this right away in rejecting the motion to establish an independent expert committee for "crises of faith," even though 57.8 percent of Catholics in the total poll had selected the "crisis of faith of people today" as the most important subject matter for the synod. Instead, all commissions were to treat this issue as an "ongoing perspective."[185] Such rejection was made much easier by the fact that the synod surveys, like all polls of public opinion, left itself open to bold ad hoc interpretations of its findings that suggested immediate consequences and marked out the discursive boundaries of interpretation. Karl Forster, for example, quickly determined that "it would certainly be short-sighted to conclude from the quantitative urgency of the crisis of faith that the central themes of dogmatic theology can be neglected, or that publicly questioning the fundamental beliefs of the church would be without consequence for the existential crisis of faith."[186] Thus, he restated the significance of theological dogmas before any consideration of a crisis of faith should take place.

The various surveys were often present in the discussions and consultations at the synod, to the extent that every synod member was presented with an exemplar of Gerhard Schmidtchen's research report that detailed the findings of the more extensive questionnaire conducted with interviews. This was essential reading for all those gathered in Würzburg.[187] As the heads of pastoral offices warned in 1972, the draft memoranda received up to that point from the synod's various subpanels gave "too few answers on the main issue mentioned in the opinion surveys carried out in preparation for the synod." The members of this circle made the effort to evaluate the polls as an indicator of the "expectations of the faithful" and, thereby, to undertake a "strategic prioritization" against the "conservation of the status quo."[188] The evaluation of the data was initially a slow process in the individual expert panels, partly as a result of its accessibility and the sheer volume of information. The subpanel on pastoral services in the parish, for instance, first had to wait for the clergy to complete their evaluation of the special poll among clerics before carrying out an appropriate "situation analysis." On the other hand, one of the study groups belonging to the expert panel "Belief Situation and Proclamation" found the material insufficient. This group thought it necessary to obtain a content-specific survey with the help of further polling, but had to drop this ambition for lack of time. Beyond the forum of the synod, there were already many attempts to evaluate individual pastoral problems.[189] The members of the synod also tried to use the various surveys to communicate their work to a wider audience, since not only the public but also some synod members quickly lost track of the standpoints and topics discussed given the flood of working papers and submissions. They therefore challenged the diocesan press in 1973 to present their reports on the work of expert panels "more strongly than before in light of the information emerging from the opinion polls."[190]

More important to our argument than the direct repercussions on the synod itself, however, was the effect that the experience with the total poll had on the further use of opinion polling methods in the Catholic Church. After the release of Schmidtchen's research report, the press speculated that "aversion to social psychology and sociology in the leadership circles of the Catholic Church" would possibly become even stronger after this "sober stocktaking."[191] However, the exact opposite was the case, at least as far as the German Bishops' Conference was concerned—the most senior decision-making body of the Catholic Church in the Federal Republic. Karl Forster, who had initially had to overcome some doubts prior to the synod about the application of this instrument, was fascinated by the possibilities of public opinion polling, probably more than any other leading church functionary and theologian.[192]

Forster remained responsible for the scientific evaluation of the various surveys, even after giving up his second term as the secretary of the synod and the German Bishop's Conference to Josef Homeyer in 1971 and taking up a professorship in Augsburg, not least because of the numerous conflicts and accusations of "manipulation" against him.[193] In an entire series of publications, which were based primarily on the evaluation of opinion polling materials, Forster discussed the problem of religiousness that had distanced itself from the church.[194] For several years, Forster, essentially in his free time, undertook a painstaking secondary evaluation of the issue of "woman and church" using an extensive dataset of multitopic questionnaires from the diverse polls conducted by the Institut für Demoskopie since 1953. After Forster's death in 1981, Gerhard Schmidtchen finished this work and published it as a book.[195]

Polls and Pastoral Decision Making

Even after his departure from the German Bishops' Conference, Forster continued to work on expert reports, which were directly conceived as documents to aid decision making in the bishops' conference. One important topic, for instance, was the search for new models to guide the roles of priests and other pastoral workers, discussed intensively on account of the "priest crisis." The submission drawn up for this purpose is revealing, above all due to Forster's good understanding of the issue evident in the steps and provisos he described as essential to using social scientific knowledge in decision making. Initially, Forster emphasized that the opinion polling studies he used were mere "snapshots of a social situation," which could only provide information about "probabilities." Further causal analysis, he believed, would require "observations of changes over a period of time," such as those achieved by panel surveys in which participants had to repeatedly answer the same question on different occasions.[196] A survey conducted in 1974 with two thousand candidates for the priesthood intended to follow up on the poll conducted among the clergy in 1971 and identify a trend. The hope was clearly that this would reveal a return to a more hierarchically minded generation of young priests.[197]

In his work for the German Bishops' Conference on the changing role of the priest, Forster also pointed to the fact that none of the "'conclusions' and applications drawn from the material followed from the data themselves. Instead, they were based on motivations linked to the issue being studied and to responsible decision making." The risks necessarily associated with each decision, Forster implied, could thus in no way be diminished by integrating social scientific expertise. Forster came to the conclusion that it was more practical to highlight "concepts doomed to ineffectiveness" than to label "positive" guiding maxims as the "only possibility." Truth for Forster lay solely in identifying false methods.[198] The reaction to Forster's assessment shows that such warning signs could hardly be painted glaringly enough if they were to achieve the desired effect. Bishop Tenhumberg, who, as the chairman of the Pastoral Commission of the German Bishops' Conference, had commissioned the report, believed that by "going through Forster's text," one could immediately find a "series of important points to use in the final agenda of the [German] Bishops' Conference." At the conference's general meeting, he called it a "blessing" that the topic of priesthood was covered by a whole a series of new empirical studies. Tenhumberg identified a situation that needed to swiftly be seized upon by making decisions.[199]

From 1972 to 1983, Josef Homeyer acted as the secretary of the German Bishops' Conference. He had previously been the head of the schools department in the diocese of Münster and a member of the planning committee there, and will be encountered again in this book in the context of sociological organizations research.[200] Under Homeyer's aegis, the German Bishops' Conference maintained its intensive interest in opinion polling and continued to commission studies, especially from the Institut für Demoskopie. There is no documentary evidence of this, however. With few exceptions, such as the joint projects by Karl Forster and Gerhard Schmidtchen that drew on their collaboration in the synod polls, all the results of these surveys were declared confidential. An example of an exception was a joint study by Forster and Schmidtchen presented to the German Bishops' Council in 1980 and published in 1982 about Catholics' expectations concerning the church's commitment to third world countries.[201]

Another example concerned an examination and evaluation of the decline in active religious practice carried out by the Institut für Demoskopie in the late 1970s. This propelled opinion polling into a new role as an aid to interpretation of the statistical discourse, given that the latter's data did not offer sufficient evidence for in-depth analyses. In the evaluation of the survey data, the Allensbach-based institute floated an interpretation that did not necessarily correspond to the statistics published in Cologne: it viewed the late 1960s and early 1970s as a period of serious decline in religious practice—a collapse that had been followed by some degree of stabilization. Although not stated directly, it was impled that the protest movement of 1968 was the cause of the "dramatic" changes, especially as the younger generation exhibited a "growing distance" from the church.[202] Survey results were also published on topics that had attracted the particular attention of the German Bishops' Conference and its head since 1987, Karl Lehmann. One example was women's relationship with the church, which had changed dramatically from the early 1970s. It became clear that women could no longer be regarded as a "silent reserve" the church could simply fall back on to help it carry out its work.[203]

The Catholic practice of only sporadically publishing opinion polling results deviated dramatically from the Protestant Churches' use of such material in Germany. In 1970, faced with a dramatic rise in the numbers of people leaving the church, the Protestant Churches commissioned a comprehensive opinion poll on the attitudes and expectations of all Protestants. A team of theologians and religious sociologists worked alongside a polling institute on the study. Since then, the Protestant Churches in Germany have published results of sample-based polls among their members on a wide range of issues at approximately ten-year intervals.[204] This difference in the way that the Protestant and Catholic Churches used opinion polling cannot be understood without the influence of the synod surveys. The total poll and supplementary sampling had suddenly made opinion polling a central component of the most important postconciliar event for the positioning and policies of the West German Catholic Church.

A "politicization of science" more intensive than the Catholic Church had ever experienced accompanied the unprecedented scientization of debate within the church. This was manifested in the countersurveys and enormous criticism of the allegedly manipulative total poll.[205] The total poll ultimately acted as a safety valve, releasing the pressure for church reform that had built up. Nevertheless, the reaction to the poll within the synod's preparation must have concerned even advocates of polling in the church. The necessary consequence was that the "high offices" of the church largely mistrusted a "population susceptible to trends" who treated "facts" as if they were "norms" and thereby encouraged the surveys to be regarded as plebiscites.[206] Catholic criticism of opinion polling had already raised this issue in the 1950s. The politicization of opinion polling against the backdrop of the synod now stopped open discussion of such research techniques in the church, at least in the medium term. Opinion polling, a technique belonging to the public sphere, returned to the realm it had occupied in the 1960s: a secret part of the church's senior bodies, shielded from the media and the public view.

This did not necessarily mean that the Catholic Church used it less intensively or effectively than other institutions. The Protestant Churches' use of opinion polling, for example, in a ten-year survey of its members was condemned by management consultant Peter Barrenstein, who was advising the Protestant Church in Munich on how to rationalize and optimize its organization in the late 1990s. Calling them "completely useless instruments of market research," he claimed that they disappeared unread onto bookshelves because they were "not focused on action." They were therefore completely unusable for the concrete pastoral matters of individual municipalities or regions.[207] This was not the case, however, for polls with only a local or regional scope. The Social Team in Adelsried, but also particularly the Gesellschaft für christliche Öffentlichkeitsarbeit, or GCÖ, carried out a great number of such studies from the late 1970s. The GCÖ had been established in 1966 by the sociologist and public relations expert Josef Scharrer, who quickly moved the business from Frankfurt to Würzburg and ran it as a small private company that worked for various dioceses and other Catholic institutions. During the 1970s and 1980s, the GCÖ planned and developed more than one hundred opinion polls in various dioceses in the west and south of Germany, while the Institute for Communication Research (Institut für Kommunikationsforschung), a small polling organization based in the city of Wuppertal, often conducted the actual poll itself. These typically involved an "image analysis," which was supposed to be useful in constructing "trustworthy behavioral patterns" and identifying the "patterns of expectations" concerning the church. Sample surveys of this kind provoked no public controversy, since they were not based on the entire Catholic population in the Federal Republic. Instead, they were typically a part of local initiatives to build a core of helpers among the laity, for example, in the church's work with young people, senior citizens, or Caritas.[208]

Opinion polling also fulfilled an important function in the "contact mission"—a new form of the people's mission initially explored in 1969 in the area around the city of Marl in Westphalia. Unlike the regional mission of sociography, the more fundamental and longer-term contact mission no longer targeted specific social groups of those abstaining from church, but aimed instead to "awaken and maintain" a "global trust in the church."[209] The GCÖ prepared a pastoral plan for this purpose that the clergy of the deanery of Marl discussed in detail. Unlike many sociographic projects, this plan, which the clergy expected a great deal from, succeeded in "warming the priests to its implementation." The office of the vicar-general spoke of an atmosphere of "confidence and optimism" created by the GCÖ's work, despite the general dismay about declining church attendance. Cooperating closely with those affected was essential to the success of using opinion polling in pastoral work. The personal engagement of social scientists, who saw their task not only as making abstract calculations but also spared "no efforts, and no amount of travel and personal dedication" for the cause, was also crucial.[210]

Opinion Polls and the Economy of Speech in the Church

Alongside the German Bishops' Conference's rather arcane handling of polls in the later 1970s, another reaction to opinion polling had a negative effect on its application in the Catholic Church. This was not identical to the reservations expressed since the 1950s, which were a reaction to the first encounters with the new scientific techniques, but instead was a response to the enormous presence of surveys in the church around 1970. Consequently, it represented an effect of the comprehensive application of opinion polling. Some attribute such criticism to political motives, but this misses the mark, although some of the authors involved can perhaps be described as traditional or conservative.[211] Rather, it represented a further denial of the discursive legitimacy of opinion polling and its ability to pass comment on the reality of the Catholic Church. The church's use of polling at all ultimately can be regarded as an attempt to grapple with the experience of secularization. It systematically applied opinion polling where the increasing privatization of religious decision making made it impossible for dogmatic statements and pastoral decisions to find a stable and unproblematic resonance among the faithful.[212] Once many individual Catholics expressed a severe cognitive dissonance with the church, the bishops had to respond. The dissolution of traditional milieu structures and the associated rapid secularization increased the urgency of appropriate adjustments to pastoral care. Each of these pastoral decisions had to anticipate, in a counterfactual manner, foreseeable future observations and motivations with which individual Catholics would react to them. It was precisely this observation of external observations— this second-order mirror—that opinion polling provided. As Karl Forster noted, polling made manifest those expectations on which any "recommendations to change certain forms of church life" were based. And there could be no precise knowledge of these expectations without the help of polling.[213]

Concerning the total poll, some observers noticed that the questionnaire took insufficient account of precisely this core context. For example, the answer guidelines to question three ("There are different opinions among Catholics about what the church is there for") continued to "tread the path of outmoded catechism-based thinking." This was especially true of the first suggested answer: "that the church leads me to do good and reject evil,"[214] which implied that the church had a comprehensive ability to intervene in the lives of individuals, creating norms and regulating behavior, and also suggested that this offer would generally be taken up. Such an assumption did not reckon with the privatization of religious decision making—a core result of increasing role differentiation in society—whereby individuals could combine any selection of the various norms they thought appropriate. Instead, question three still assumed that a milieu standard would apply, as it had in the closed structures of the Catholic milieu up to 1914 and perhaps as late as 1945.

As the opinion polling discourse made it possible to observe the highly individualized expectations of pastoral work and the promulgation of the Gospel,
those who did not want to accept this discourse as an appropriate form of expression objected to it. This was not a question of taboo or plebiscite—the two
concepts that had been at the center of the political conflicts surrounding the
total poll. Rather, the criticism was rooted in the idea of an economy of speech
that church members were to observe. It was based implicitly on the distinction
between acts of religious communication, on the one hand, and the observation
of these, on the other. Auxiliary bishop of Essen Wolfgang Große addressed this
subject in questioning whether public opinion polling could be of "sufficient use"
when it came to "issues of belief and the 'mystery of the church,'" as opposed to
market research. The possible advantages had to be weighed against the "certain
damage" that "promoting the trend toward ever-present meaningless chatter"
would create.[215] Coming from a bishop, this statement could be read as resistance to excessive, and thus misunderstood, demands for democratization in the
church. Other voices, however, clarify that the context of his remarks concerned
the meaninglessness of the endless talking associated with the questionnaires. For
example, whereas the rector of the Dortmund *Kommende,* an institution dedicated to instruction in Catholic social teachings, called on participants of the
"social seminars" there to take an intensive interest in the synod and especially
the total poll, he nevertheless insisted that the result of the synod could not be
"words, just words," for the church was a "mental and spiritual phenomenon" and
"prayer its most effective language."[216] Similarly, Oskar Simmel, SJ, emphasized,
upon the initial presentation of the questionnaire of the total poll, that for all the
"speaking" that would be necessary at the synod, it was important not to forget
to "listen"; the Spirit of God could only be heard in a "fraternal dialogue" about
his revelation. In other words, the questionnaire designed to "make us speak"
should "further lead to listening" and thus to the "origin of the church" as the
"community of those who listen to Jesus Christ."[217] As a final example, a priest
in Moers wrote the following at the beginning of his notes for a talk on parish
pastoral work: "Replacement of theology by sociology—replacement of prayer by
discussion—discussing not praying church." He advocated the opposite attitude,
pointing to the early Christian depictions of the praying figures (orans) in the
catacombs. The priest said that these figures, looking imploringly to the heavens
with arms outstretched, represented a "typically Christian posture!"[218]

Opinion polling made heretofore-latent observations visible and expressible.
When this took place on a comprehensive scale, as with the total poll, it could
create the impression that the balance of expression in the church was being
disturbed. With so many words expressing various opinions, some felt as if faith
itself—the church's real concern—was being neglected. As opinion polling arbi-
trarily inflated and publicized some views and observations, critics insisted that
forms of religious communication—prayer and spiritual discussion—be treated

as the most important types of expression in the church. Since these were generally private forms of communication, critics did not believe that they should be
pushed into the public sphere through observation. The author and lay theologian
Ida Friederike Görres expressed this concern slightly differently in her critique of
the total poll. She felt that the questionnaire lacked the "church's dimension of
depth," its "mysterious realm"—that is, those parts of Christian belief that were
central to the "pious" and those who "embraced religion." She gently mocked the
supposedly "surprising aspects" of the first results of the total poll, such as the
claim that "nobody" had known how important silent prayer during mass was to
"so many believers." Görres did not reject the total poll because it unnecessarily
democratized the church, but because it neglected the church's center of faith in
order to protect the "well-known sensitivities of marginal Christians."[219] Görres
and those who held a similar position were clearly unintimidated by the risk
of further secularization. On the contrary, they directly expressed the concern
that too many deliberations and external reflections on the church's position in
the modern world rationalized the immeasurable and indescribable aspects of
belief, subjecting them to a "paralyzing fascination" with the polls.[220] In this view,
intimate prayer, not public statements of opinion, was the true language of the
church; prayer and discussions on faith did not need to be observed from outside,
but sufficed in themselves.

Observing the Differentiation of Value Systems

After the publication of the Kinsey Report, many Catholics in both the clergy
and the laity came to regard public opinion polling as a technology that irrespon-
sibly took possession of individuals, disregarding and erasing their uniqueness.
Moreover, they perceived Kinsey's portrayal of sexual behaviors that contradicted
Catholic moral teaching as a shocking example of scientific positivism leading to
moral relativism. This rejection of opinion polling was relativized after the Second Vatican Council. A more positive idea of public opinion as a social authority
the church should pay attention to gradually emerged. In the context of Christian
public relations work, opinion polling was supposed to win back lost trust. However, it was characteristic that the dynamic of public opinion only began to have
an effect on the Catholic Church when it began to resonate within the church's
own public sphere, that is, internally. This process began on a wide scale with the
Essen Katholikentag in 1968, which made visible the problems of politicization
and participation in the church. From then on, the mass media also intensified
tensions emerging about the appropriate interpretation and application of the
Second Vatican Council's ideas.

Opinion polling came into use at the very center of the postconciliar upheaval
in the wake of the Katholikentag in Essen in 1968 and during the preparation of

the Würzburg Synod. Its methodological approach fit the language of "dialogue," which bishops were now keen to nurture, and the council's theology, which conceptualized the church as the whole "people of God." The decisive factor, however, was the claim made by polling advocates that opinion polls provided a "representative" portrayal of opinions and attitudes. Furthermore, polls promised information on the scale and direction of the conflicts that had broken out since the council, providing a means of making the quick decisions needed to tackle the "crises" detected at all levels of the church. While the expectations of many laypeople and the church hierarchy came together on this point, the connection between the total poll and the quota method of research ensured that opinion polling was caught up in the wave of politicization that began in 1968. The highest in the church hierarchy feared the plebiscitary nature of the total poll and the direct responsiveness this implied, not only because they believed that those who held the magisterium and pastorate—in other words, those who had license to teach and oversee the church—needed to be defended against calls for democratization. The fear was also a spontaneous reaction to the arrival of a scientific method that seemed capable of reproducing the opinions and desires of ordinary Catholics with unimagined precision. This led the German Bishops' Conference and other official offices in the church to make regular use of opinion polling as an aid to orientation even after the synod had finished. In order to stop the politicization of opinion polls that had broken out in 1969/70, this work now took place only behind the closed doors of church committees. In the context of the synod poll based on a random sample with a more extensive questionnaire, some decision makers came close to breaking the church's last taboos regarding opinion polling. One member of the committee preparing the synod, for example, called for the interview-based questionnaire to inquire about people's attitudes to "sexual relationships before marriage"—the very issue that had provoked the most protest against the Kinsey Report.[221]

One might be tempted to interpret the Catholic Church's practical and discursive use of opinion polling as a necessary adjustment prompted by the breakdown of traditional milieu ties, which required a response. The church chose to react by importing a modern scientific method of analysis. That was indeed the rhetoric some contemporary accounts of the total poll used. Its main conclusion, they argued, was that "temporary factors had to be distinguished from the church's enduring core."[222] This notion of defensive modernization, however, reflected only the church's self-description of opinion polling, not its actual core use. Neither the distinction between traditional and modern, nor that between critical and affirmative, provides an adequate understanding of the significance and limits of opinion polling in the Catholic Church.

It seems more promising here to emphasize the distinction between operation and observation. This allows us to see that advancing functional differentiation required the church to deal with the privatization of religious decision making and thus with growing conflicts between the church's norm systems and individuals' attitudes. This generated both the conditions for, and the necessity of, reflecting the observations of Christians and non-Christians alike as a horizon of expectations. From that point on, all pastoral decisions had to be justified as religious operations against the backdrop of those expectations. Those seeking motivations for finding a new approach to discussing God had to learn beforehand about the disappearance of a "real notion of God." As a staff member of the pastoral department in Münster noted, only the 1967 *Der Spiegel* article "What Do the Germans Believe?" drew the attention of diocesan officials to this problem of observing motivations.[223] A recurring and increasingly trivial opinion poll finding in the 1970s was that there was a "competitive relationship" between the church's value system and the socially dominant norms. Catholics stressed by a cognitive-affective imbalance expected little from their church and increasingly responded by emigrating spiritually elsewhere.[224]

When it came to the Würzburg Synod, however, ordinary Catholics had great expectations—not only of the church, but also of opinion polling. They expected it both to control the implementation of the conciliar documents and to ensure grassroots participation in this process. These hopes were inevitably disappointed, not least due to the associated politicization of social science. Similar to the case of church statistics and sociography, the church's use of opinion polling demonstrates that the expectations scientization gave rise to in the Catholic Church led to self-made disappointment. This is the backdrop against which we should interpret the voices who saw prayer as the true language of the church, to which outside observations were a source of unnecessary distraction rather than enrichment. The mystery of faith, they believed, depended only on God as the universal observer. Amid the silence of an individual prayer, the "noise" of the secular social environment, which Chrysostomos Schulte had first identified in his 1931 nonrepresentative opinion poll, was only an unwelcome disturbance.

Notes

1. "Lumen Gentium," no. 32, in Abbott, *Documents of Vatican II*, 58.
2. Uta G. Poiger, "Generations: The 'Revolutions' of the 1960s," in The Oxford *Handbook of Modern German History*, ed. Helmut Walser Smith (Oxford, 2011), 640–62, provides an excellent survey.
3. For a historical approach, see Kruke, *Demoskopie*; see also Lisbeth Lipari, "Polling as Ritual," *Journal of Communication* 49 (1999): 83–102; for a sociological approach, see the important study by Felix Keller, *Archäologie der Meinungsforschung: Mathematik und die Erzählbarkeit des Politischen* (Constance, 2001).
4. Jürgen Habermas, *The Structural Transformation of the Public Sphere: An Inquiry into a Category of Bourgeois Society* (Cambridge, MA, 1991).
5. Ibid., 236–43.
6. Niklas Luhmann, *The Reality of the Mass Media* (Oxford, 2000), 42–44.

7. Niklas Luhmann, *Die Politik der Gesellschaft* (Frankfurt, 2000), 274–318; Rudolf Stichweh, "Die Entstehung einer Weltöffentlichkeit," in *Transnationale Öffentlichkeiten und Identitäten im 20. Jahrhundert*, ed. Hartmut Kaelble, Martin Kirsch, and Alexander Schmidt-Gernig (Frankfurt, 2002), 57–66.

8. Chrysostomus Schulte, *Laienbriefe: Das pastoraltheologische Ergebnis einer Umfrage* (Münster, 1931), 5.

9. Ibid., 5–6, 9.

10. Ibid., 10.

11. Ibid., 87.

12. Schulte, *Laienbriefe*, 11; on the concept of "noise" in systems theory, see Luhmann, *Wissenschaft*, 287ff.

13. Kruke, *Demoskopie*, 31–41; Anja Kruke and Benjamin Ziemann, "Observing the Sovereign: Opinion Polls and the Restructuring of the Body Politic in West Germany, 1945–1990," in Brückweh et al., *Engineering Society*, 234–51.

14. Kruke, *Demoskopie*, 42–57.

15. *Ruhr-Nachrichten*, 31 August 1949, Sonderbeilage; "Waren Sie letzten Sonntag in der Kirche?," *Westdeutsche Allgemeine Zeitung*, 13 March 1953.

16. Karl Schaezler, "Eine brennende Frage," *Hochland* 43 (1950/51): 250–62; "Kirche oder Standesamt? Ergebnisse einer Meinungsforschung in Österreich," *HK* 10 (1955/56): 204–5, 212–13.

17. Ignaz Zangerle, "Pfarrprobleme und Laienarbeit," in *Die Pfarre: Von der Theologie zur Praxis*, ed. Hugo Rahner (Freiburg, 1956), 88; see Bernhard Häring, "Eine alarmierende Erkenntnis aus der Soziographie," *Paulus* 26 (1954): 9–11.

18. "Der Kinsey-Bericht," *HK* 8 (1953/54): 475–82, quote 475. On the reception of Kinsey in West Germany more generally, see Sybille Steinbacher, *Wie der Sex nach Deutschland kam: Der Kampf um Sittlichkeit und Anstand in der frühen Bundesrepublik* (Munich, 2011), 139–56.

19. Quote: Alfred C. Kinsey, Wardell B. Pomeroy, and Clyde E. Martin, *Sexual Behavior in the Human Male* (Philadelphia, 1948), 3. I quote the report on females from the German edition: Alfred C. Kinsey, *Das sexuelle Verhalten der Frau* (Frankfurt, 1966); see Regina Markell Morantz, "The Scientist as Sex Crusader: Alfred C. Kinsey and American Culture," *American Quarterly* 29 (1977): 566–68.

20. Kinsey, Pomeroy, and Martin, *Male*, 5, 75–102; Kinsey, *Frau*, 34–38; Ludwig von Friedeburg, *Die Umfrage in der Intimsphäre* (Stuttgart, 1953), 2–4.

21. *HK* 8 (1953/54): 476.

22. Lawrence Birken correctly interpreted the rise of sexual science against the backdrop of the ideology of consumerism. However, his study falls short when it links this development to a structural change in the socially dominant production regime, which liberates women and children as consumers; Lawrence Birken, *Consuming Desire: Sexual Science and the Emergence of a Culture of Abundance, 1871–1914* (Ithaca, NY, 1988), 113–31, esp. 125. It was not until the quota method that it was possible to illustrate the individual freedom of sexual consumption and thus to articulate the interests associated with it.

23. Kinsey, *Frau*, 420. The *Herder-Korrespondenz* critic alleged a tautology precisely on this point and saw it as an attempt to "extinguish" the connection of sexuality to the individual: *HK* 8 (1953/54): 479.

24. Georg Trapp, SJ, "Das Menschenbild eines Zoologen," *Anima* 9 (1954): 155–64.

25. Morantz, "Scientist," 575.

26. Erdman Palmore, "Published Reactions to the Kinsey Report," *Social Forces* 31 (1952): 169; Lionel Trilling, "The Kinsey Report," in *An Analysis of the Kinsey Reports on Sexual Behavior in the Human Male and Female*, ed. Donald Porter Geddes (London, 1954), 223–24.

27. Otto Stöckle, "Mißbrauchte Wissenschaft," *Orientierung* 17 (1953): 211–12, quote 211; for the motive of sensationalism, see also Karl Schaezler, "Beunruhigende Intimitäten," *Hochland* 46 (1953/54): 198–200, 198.

28. For the following, see Georg Schückler, *Irrwege moderner Meinungsforschung: Zu "Umfragen in der Intimsphäre"* (Cologne, 1956); Anton Böhm, "Das Zeitalter der Indiskretion," *WW* 9 (1954): 181–93; Helmut Schelsky and Albert Mitterer, "Die Moral der Kinsey-Reporte," *WW* 9 (1954): 421–35; Schöllgen, "Moralprobleme," 319–22; *FH* 6 (1951): 183, 359; *HK* 8 (1953/54): 475–82.

29. Schelsky and Mitterer, "Die Moral der Kinsey-Reporte," 423–24.

30. Schückler, *Irrwege,* 9–10; Kinsey, Pomeroy, and Ward, *Male,* 667–69; Kinsey, *Frau,* 386–87.

31. *HK* 8 (1953/54): 481–82.

32. Kinsey, Pomeroy, and Ward, *Male,* 157–62, 193–203, 573–78, quotes 158, 193.

33. Schelsky and Mitterer, "Die Moral der Kinsey-Reporte," 425, 430; Stöckle, "Mißbrauchte Wissenschaft," 212; *HK* 8 (1953/54): 478.

34. Schückler, *Irrwege,* 11; Kinsey, Pomeroy, and Ward, *Male,* 465–87; *HK* 11 (1956/57): 101–2.

35. Schaezler, "Beunruhigende Intimitäten," 200; Friedeburg, *Umfrage,* 53.

36. Böhm, "Das Zeitalter der Indiskretion," 181, 188.

37. Schückler, *Irrwege,* 16.

38. Böhm, "Das Zeitalter der Indiskretion," 184, 188, 190; Schelsky and Mitterer, "Die Moral der Kinsey-Reporte," 426, 429–30.

39. *HK* 8 (1953/54): 479.

40. Michel Foucault, *The History of Sexuality* (Harmondsworth, UK, 1984), 1:63–64.

41. Christopher Shannon, "Sex, Science, and History," *Journal of Policy History* 12 (2000): 274.

42. Dagmar Herzog, "Desperately Seeking Normality: Sex and Marriage in the Wake of the War," in *Life after Death: Approaches to a Cultural and Social History of Europe during the 1940s and 1950s,* ed. Richard Bessel and Dirk Schumann (Cambridge, 2003), 175–79.

43. Horst Krüger, "Grenzen der Meinungsforschung," *Der christliche Sonntag* 8, no. 6 (1956): 45–46; Schückler, *Irrwege,* 13.

44. Krüger, "Grenzen der Meinungsforschung," 46; "Dämoskopie," *Rheinischer Merkur,* 21 September 1956.

45. Hans Georg Mähner, "Die Bedeutung von Meinungsumfragen in der Kirche: Grundsätzliche Untersuchung und konkrete Darstellung anhand einer Primärerhebung" (PhD diss., Universität Salzburg, 1971), 117–20.

46. Quote: Anton Böhm, *Leben im Zwiespalt: Der moderne Mensch zwischen Angst und Hybris* (Freiburg, 1974), 38–39; "Der Mythos von der Volksmeinung," *HK* 11 (1956/57): 303–5; Wilhelm Korff, "Empirische Sozialforschung und Moral," *Concilium* 4 (1968): 323–30, 326.

47. Gustav Ermecke, "Die Kirche und die Demoskopie," *Rheinischer Merkur,* 14 August 1970.

48. On this analogy, see Luhmann, *Politik,* 286.

49. *HK* 8 (1953/54): 478–79; Schaezler, "Beunruhigende Intimitäten," 198. In its survey for Ludwig von Friedeburg, the Institut für Demoskopie recorded a refusal rate of one-quarter, which was thought to be surprisingly low; Friedeburg, *Umfragen,* 9–11.

50. Krüger, "Grenzen der Meinungsforschung," 45–46.

51. Dr. M. B. to the Synodalbüro in Münster, 20 May 1970, BAM, Synodalbüro, A 6.

52. The files of the German Bishops' Conference are not yet accessible.

53. Katholisches Büro Bonn to Tenhumberg, 18 May 1960, BAM, Diözesankomitee, A 18; Jakob David, 18 February 1963, to Krautscheidt, BAE, GV 82 14 12, vol. 1.

54. Marketing Agentur von Westerholt und Wagner, 5 June 1962, to Krautscheidt, and Jakob David, 18 February 1963, to Krautscheidt, both in BAE, GV 82 14 12, vol. 1.

55. PSI, Handreichung no. 8 (1961), 7, 19.

56. Krautscheidt to Greinacher, 14 April 1961, BAE, GV 82 14 12, vol. 1.

57. PSI, Handreichung no. 8 (1961), 20–21.

58. "Weihnachtsüberraschung für *Spiegel*-Leser," *KuL* 23, no. 1 (1968).

59. The PSI in Essen had arranged for a representative poll to be conducted by the Infas Institute, that usually polled for parties including the SPD, as part of a research project being carried out since 1963 on religion in the "industrial society" of the Ruhr district and compiled an overview of various motive scales relating to this. Norbert Greinacher, "Was glauben die Katholiken?," *LS* 19 (1968): 121–25, 122; PSI, Bericht no. 42 (1966).

60. *Der Spiegel*, no. 52 (1967): 38.

61. Uwe Beck, *Kirche im "Spiegel"-Spiegel der Kirche: Ein leidenschaftliches Verhältnis* (Ostfildern, 1994), 278.

62. Kruke, *Demoskopie*, 465–95.

63. Beck, *Kirche im "Spiegel,"* 256–63.

64. *Der Spiegel*, no. 52 (1967): 38–58, quote 58. The privatization theory was also central to the evaluation of the data by Egon Golomb, "Wie kirchlich ist der Glaube?," in *Was glauben die Deutschen? Die Emnid-Umfrage: Ergebnisse und Kommentare,* ed. Werner Harenberg (Munich, 1969), 205–6. Along with Norbert Greinacher, Golomb belonged to an interconfessional group of theologians and social researchers called upon to prepare and evaluate the survey; Golomb, "Wie kirchlich ist der Glaube?," 7–8.

65. W. Z. to the editors of the journal *Kirche und Leben,* 13 January 1968, BAM, Schriftleitung KuL, A 235.

66. Quote: P. J. to the editors of *Kirche und Leben,* 31 January 1968, BAM, Schriftleitung KuL, A 235; "Weihnachtsüberraschung für *Spiegel*-Leser"; Ambrosius Stock, "Was glauben die Deutschen? Zur Glaubenskrise unserer Zeit," *Mann in der Kirche* 26 (1969): 30–33.

67. IfD-Bericht 1471, *Katholische Wochenzeitung,* Umfrage unter potentiellen Lesern und Geistlichen (1968), 1–2, IfD-Archiv.

68. IfD-Bericht 1471, 77–90, quote 18, IfD-Archiv.

69. Damberg, *Abschied,* 243–56.

70. Franz Josef Wothe, *Kirche in der Synode: Zwischenbilanz der Hildesheimer Diözesansynode* (Hildesheim, 1968), 14–25, quote 16.

71. "Besprechung über die nachkonziliare Arbeit im Bistum Osnabrück," 17 August 1966, BAOS, 03-09-51-02; Memo by Hubertus Brandenburg, n.d. [1966], BAOS, Seelsorgeamt, Akzession 4, Ordner Diözesan-Synode I.

72. *Unser Bischof befragt das Bistum: Auswertungsergebnisse des ersten Fragebogens des Bischofs von Osnabrück* (Osnabrück, 1970), 2–3.

73. "Sitzung im Bischöflichen Seelsorgeamt am 26.5.1966," BAOS, Seelsorgeamt, Akzession 4, Ordner Diözesan-Synode I.

74. Hubertus Brandenburg, "Vermerk: Besprechung beim Bischof am 27.5.1966," BAOS, Seelsorgeamt, Akzession 4, Ordner Diözesan-Synode I.

75. Quote: Claus Kühn to Hubertus Brandenburg, 19 August 1966, BAOS, Seelsorgeamt, Akzession 4, Ordner Diözesan-Synode I; "Besprechung über die nachkonziliare Arbeit im Bistum Osnabrück," 17 August 1966, BAOS, 03-09-51-02. Kühn, of Hamburg, was, among other things, a long-standing member in the committee on mass media in the Central Committee of German Catholics (ZdK).

76. On Catholic students in 1968, see Schmidtmann, *Katholische Studierende,* 316–53.

77. Großmann, *Zentralkomitee,* 210–16.

78. Ferdinand Oertel, "Aufstand der Laien: Kritik prägte den Katholikentag 1968 in Essen," *Die Politische Meinung* 378 (2001): 41; see also *1770 Forum-Fragen zu den 27 Forumgesprächen auf dem 82. Deutschen Katholikentag vom 4.–8. September 1968* (Essen, 1968), 9.

79. Joseph Höffner, "Unsere Sorge um die der Kirche Entfremdeten, Protokoll der Dechanten-Konferenz vom 19. bis 21 Mai 1964," 3–8, BAM, AD 21.

80. "Welche Ursachen führen heute zu Glaubenskrise und Gleichgültigkeit? Antworten auf die 1. Frage aus dem Rundbrief des Bischofs von Rottenburg vom November 1966," n.d. [1967], BAM, GV NA, A-201-1; Laurenz Böggering, "Visitationsbericht an Tenhumberg," 14 January 1972, BAM, GV NA, A-0-757; "Krise der Kirche oder Krise des Glaubens?," *HK* 23 (1969): 1–5.

81. "Bezirksleitung der KAB Kleve-Geldern an die Priester des Freckenhorster Kreises," 16 June 1970, BAM, GV NA, A-101-141; Hubert Jedin, "Eingabe an die Deutsche Bischofskonferenz," 16 September 1968, in Hubert Jedin, *Lebensbericht,* ed. Konrad Repgen (Mainz, 1984), 266–72, quote 269.

82. "Kommt eine deutsche Pastoralsynode?," *HK* 23 (1969): 12–15; interview by the author with Elisabeth Rickal, former chairperson of the BDKJ, 9 December 2002, in Bochum.

83. Damberg, *Abschied,* 588–602.

84. Friedrich Kronenberg, "Thesen für das Gespräch zwischen Bischofskonferenz und Zentralkomitee am 9. November 1968," 7 November 1968, Archiv des ZdK, 60/1, 1.

85. Ibid.

86. "Niederschrift des Gesprächs zwischen Bischofskonferenz und Zentralkomitee am 9.11.1968," Archiv des ZdK, 60/1, 1; for the discussion in the ZdK, see "Deutsche Pastoralsynode?," *Rheinischer Merkur,* 22 November 1968.

87. "Niederschrift der Sitzung Studiengruppe Bischofskonferenz-Zentralkomitee am 9.1.1969," Archiv des ZdK, 60/1, 1.

88. Scheduling in an excerpt from the minutes of the Full Assembly of the German Bishops' Conference, 24–27 February 1969, TOP 15, Archiv des ZdK, 60/1, 1. As a general introduction to the work of the Würzburg Synod, see Plate, *Das deutsche Konzil*; see also the official journal of the synod, *Synode,* vols. 1–6 (1970–75).

89. Karl Forster, 7 May 1969, to Elisabeth Noelle-Neumann, Archiv des ZdK, 60/1, 1; telephone interview with Friedrich Kronenberg, 14 April 2003. Kronenberg was, together with Karl Forster, Bernhard Hanssler, Karl Lehmann, and Klaus Hemmerle, a member of the subcommittee devoted to potential topics for the synod. The membership of this committee, like that of the study group, was not made public.

90. Hannes Burger, "Der Manager des deutschen Katholizismus," *Süddeutsche Zeitung,* 5/6 January 1971.

91. Quote: Elisabeth Noelle-Neumann to Forster, 3 September 1969, Archiv des ZdK, 60/1, 5; Karl Forster, 20 May and 30 June 1969, to Gerhard Schmidtchen/IfD, Archiv des ZdK, 60/1, 1.

92. Press release of the office of the German Bishops' Conference, 3 September 1969, Archiv des ZdK, 60/1, 1; *HK* 23 (1969): 501.

93. Secretariat of the synod to the chairmen of the diocesan synodal offices, 10 April 1970, BAM, GV NA, A-101–41; see Oskar Simmel, SJ, "Was will die Fragebogenaktion?," *Glaube und Leben: Katholische Kirchenzeitung für das Bistum Mainz,* 3 May 1970; Karl Forster, "Die Befragung: Ein ehrliches Angebot an alle Katholiken," *Katholisches Sonntagsblatt* 17 (1970): 10–11; Klaus Hemmerle, "Alle sind gefragt—wonach? Notizen zur Thematik der Fragebogenaktion an alle Katholiken," *Konradsblatt: Wochenzeitung für das Erzbistum Freiburg,* 3 May 1970.

94. Memo, Forster to Hengsbach, received 5 December 1969, BAE, NL Hengsbach, 1008.

95. "Niederschrift der Sitzung der Vorbereitungskommission," 8 December 1969, Archiv des ZdK, 60/1, 4.

96. Minutes were not taken. See scattered evidence in Archiv des ZdK, 60/1, 5, 60/1, 6; interview with Elisabeth Rickal, 9 December 2002.

97. For technical details, see the sources in BAM, Synodalbüro A 6.

98. Gerhard Schmidtchen, *Zwischen Kirche und Gesellschaft: Forschungsbericht über die Umfragen zur Gemeinsamen Synode der Bistümer in der Bundesrepublik Deutschland* (Freiburg, 1972), xiii–xiv.

99. Gerhard Schmidtchen, *Priester in Deutschland: Forschungsbericht über die im Auftrag der Deutschen Bischofskonferenz durchgeführte Umfrage unter allen Welt- und Ordenspriestern in der Bundesrepublik* (Freiburg, 1973); Karl Forster, "Probleme und Chancen einer missionarischen Pastoral heute: Hinweise aus den Ergebnissen der Synodenumfragen und der Befragung der Welt- und Ordenspriester," *Ordenskorrespondenz* 16 (1975): 5–19.

100. Hannes Burger, *Süddeutsche Zeitung*, 1 March 1969, printed in *Synode 72: Texte zur Diskussion um eine gemeinsame Synode der Diözesen in der Bundesrepublik Deutschland. Zusammengestellt von der Dokumentationszentrale Publik*, 3 vols. (Frankfurt, 1969/70), 1:76.

101. Franz Josef Trost, "Die Stunde der Laien," *Publik*, 7 March 1969.

102. For details, see Ziemann, "Opinion Polls," 571–72.

103. Parish committee, "Zu den Hl. Schutzengeln," Schmedehausen-Hüttrup, 13 August 1969, BAM, Synodalbüro A 3.

104. Committee of the Catholics in Ibbenbüren district, 18 July 1969, BAM, Synodalbüro A 3.

105. Parish committee, St. Josef Rheinhausen, 11 August 1969, BAM, Synodalbüro A 3.

106. Parish committee, Hl. Kreuz Merhoog, n.d., BAM, Synodalbüro A 3.

107. Karl Hürten to Tenhumberg, 23 October 1969, BAM, Synodalbüro A 1.

108. Parish committee, St. Marien Emsdetten, 21 July 1969, BAM, Synodalbüro A 3.

109. Parish committee, St. Josef Rheinhausen, 11 August 1969, BAM, Synodalbüro A 3.

110. Hannes Burger, "Die Meinungen von über vier Millionen Katholiken," *Süddeutsche Zeitung*, 4/5 July 1970; see also "Politik rangiert an letzter Stelle," *Rheinischer Merkur*, 10 July 1970.

111. Wolfgang Große to Karl Forster, 1 December 1969, BAE, NL Hengsbach 1008.

112. IfD, "2. Entwurf für die Fragebogen-Aktion zur Synode," n.d., Archiv des ZdK, 60/1, 5. See also the final version of the questionnaire in Schmidtchen, *Kirche und Gesellschaft*, 299–302.

113. Wolfgang Große to Forster, 1 December 1969, BAE, NL Hengsbach 1008.

114. See "Lumen Gentium," no. 9, in Abbott, *Documents of Vatican II*, 24–26; Hermann J. Pottmeyer, "Modernisierung in der katholischen Kirche am Beispiel der Kirchenkonzeption des I. und II. Vatikanischen Konzils," in *Vaticanum II und Modernisierung: Historische, theologische und soziologische Perspektiven*, ed. Franz-Xaver Kaufmann and Arnold Zingerle (Paderborn, 1996), 131–46, 142–43.

115. M. K. to Hengsbach, 27 January 1970, BAE, Würzburger Synode, Hefter Allgemeine Befragung. See also *In Sachen Synode: Vorschläge und Argumente des Vorbereitungskongresses*, ed. Norbert Greinacher, Klaus Lang, and Peter Scheuermann (Düsseldorf, 1970).

116. Manuscript for the press conference, 20 April 1970, BAM, GV NA, A-101–140. See also Schmidtchen, *Kirche und Gesellschaft*, 301.

117. Schmidtchen, *Kirche und Gesellschaft*, 301.

118. Comment by Robert Luchs, *Neue Ruhr-Zeitung*, 21 April 1970.

119. Comment by Franz Czerny, *Westdeutsche Allgemeine Zeitung*, 21 April 1970; Maria Kranzhoff, "Überraschende Ergebnisse? Zur großen Synodenumfrage 1970," *Katholische Frauenbildung* 72 (1971): 373.

120. "Echo," *Westfälische Nachrichten*, 23 May 1970.

121. Lang was a member of the preparatory committee that was in charge of preparing the synod. See Klaus Lang, "Bisher über 300.000 Fragebögen zurück," *Publik*, 29 May 1970.

122. Minutes of a meeting of the preparatory committee, 26 June 1970, Archiv des ZdK, 60/1, 4.

123. Schmidtchen, *Kirche und Gesellschaft*, 128–35; see also the complaints by Hubert Schöne to the editors of the diocesan newspaper *Kirche und Leben*, 28 October 1972, BAM, Schriftleitung KuL, A 229.

124. First quote: Berthold Bröker to Synodalbüro, 27 May 1970, BAM, Synodalbüro A 6; second quote: Reply by Karl Hürten, 3 June 1970, BAM, Synodalbüro A 6.

125. Interview by the author with Dr. Hanna-Renate Laurien in Berlin, 28 February 2003.

126. Quote: Franz-Xaver Kaufmann, Merkpunkte zur vorgeschlagenen Umfrage des Instituts für Demoskopie, n.d. [November 1969], Archiv des ZdK, 60/1, 5. See similar objections by the Paderborn auxiliary bishop Johannes Degenhardt, "Voten zur Fragebogenaktion und Repräsentativumfrage," n.d. [December 1969], Archiv des ZdK, 60/1, 5.

127. Minutes of a meeting of the Vorbereitungskommission on 9 March 1970, Archiv des ZdK, 60/1, 4; Gerhard Schmidtchen, "Repräsentative Kontroll- und Ergänzungsbefragung zur Fragebogen-Aktion," n.d. [22 April 1970], Archiv des ZdK , 60/1, 5.

128. For an introduction to scaling techniques applied to religious attitudes, see Sozialinstitut des Bistums Essen, Abt. Kirchliche Sozialforschung (SIB, Social Institute of the Diocese of Essen, Department of Church Social Research), Bericht no. 49 (1968).

129. Stephen Hilgartner, *Science on Stage: Expert Advice as Public Drama* (Palo Alto, CA, 2000), 3–9.

130. Ibid., 10–20.

131. Arbeitskreis Synode 72 der Pfarrei St. Theresia in Münster to Tenhumberg, 10 May 1970, BAM, Synodalbüro A 6; quote: Answer by Karl Hürten, 3 July 1970, BAM, Synodalbüro A 6.

132. See Wilhelm Pötter to Tenhumberg, 27 May 1970, BAM, Diözesankomitee, A 55.

133. Wilhelm Pötter to Tenhumberg, 26 May 1970, BAM, Diözesankomitee, A 55.

134. Draft of a letter of the diocesan committee to Tenhumberg, n.d., forwarded to Tenhumberg by Reinhard Lettmann, 28 April 1970, BAM, GV NA, A-101-141. The cited sections were later deleted by the steering committee of the diocesan committee.

135. First quote: Bernd Plettendorff to Kerstiens, 11 May 1970, BAM, Diözesankomitee A 55; second quote: Note from Reinhard Lettmann to Tenhumberg, 28 April 1970, BAM, GV NA, A-101-141.

136. Tenhumberg to Wilhelm Pötter, 1 July 1970, BAM, GV NA, A-101-141.

137. "Protokolle der Sitzungen des Sachausschusses Synode am 22.4. und 8.7.1970," BAM, Diözesankomitee A 55.

138. See the photo in *KuL,* 7 June 1970.

139. Gerhard Schmidtchen, "Mehrheit begrüßt Unruhe," *Publik,* 4 December 1970.

140. Franz-Xaver Kaufmann, "Zwischen Kirche und Meinungsforschung," *HK* 26 (1972): 505–9; see also the rejoinder by Gerhard Schmidtchen, "Zwischen Kirche und Gesellschaft," *HK* 26 (1972): 596–600; Otwin Massing, "Zwischen Kirche und Gesellschaft: Kritische Anmerkungen zur Synoden-Umfrage," *FH* 28 (1973): 409–16.

141. Ursula Boos-Nünning and F. Keller, "Hauptbestreben der Fragebogenaktion: Kritik ausschließen," *Ruhrwort,* 2 May 1970.

142. Egon Golomb, "Stellungnahme zur Umfrage für die Synode 1972," n.d., BAM, Synodalbüro A 6.

143. Egon Golomb to Ferdinand Schulte-Berge, 30 April 1970, and "Vermerk über eine Besprechung am 5.5.1970 im Geistlichen Rat," both in BAE, Würzburger Synode, Hefter Allgemeine Befragung; Karl Forster to the Synodalbüros, 9 June 1970, BAM, Synodalbüro A 6; Gerhard Schmidtchen, Erwiderung auf drei kritische Anmerkungen von Herrn Dr. Egon Golomb, n.d., Archiv des ZdK, 60/1, 5.

144. "Protokoll der Sitzung des Synodalbüros Essen v. 27.5.1970," BAE, Würzburger Synode, Hefter Protokolle der Sitzungen des Synodalbüros.

145. R. Lehmann, "Widerstand gegen geplante Synode," *Konradsblatt,* 15 September 1969, quoted from the reprint in *Synode 72,* 1:141–42. A draft of the statute was published in July 1969 due to an indiscretion; see *Synode 72,* 1:ix.

146. Lehmann, "Widerstand," in *Synode 72,* 1:141–42.

147. Press release by the Katholische Nachrichten Agentur, 29 September 1969, in *Synode 72,* 2:96.

148. Quote: Norbert Greinacher, "Postfach Synode," *Publik,* 16 July 1971; Mitteilung der Programmdirektion Kultur des ZDF, 6 January 1970, Archiv des ZdK, 60/1, 6; "4.5 Millionen Fragebogen eingegangen," *KuL,* 28 June 1970.

149. Helmut Geller, Norbert Greinacher, and Heinrich Ludwig, eds., *2000 Briefe an die Synode: Auswertung und Konsequenzen* (Mainz, 1971), 7–18, quote 12; Franz-Xaver Kaufmann, "Briefe an die Synode," *FAZ*, 5 January 1972; interview by the author with Franz-Xaver Kaufmann, Bielefeld, 27 September 2000. A copy of the report on this poll could not be located.

150. Karl Hürten to Tenhumberg, 23 October 1969, BAM, Synodalbüro A 1.

151. Draft of the letter by the diocesan committee, n.d., sent by Reinhard Lettmann to Tenhumberg, 28 April 1970, BAM, GV NA, A-101-141.

152. "Niederschrift zur Sitzung der Vorbereitungskommission am 8.12.1969," Archiv des ZdK, 60/1, 4.

153. Votes on the opinion polls, n.d. [December 1969], Archiv des ZdK, 60/1, 5.

154. Linus Hofmann, "Stellungnahme zu dem Entwurf eines Fragebogens zur Synode," n.d., Archiv des ZdK, 60/1, 5.

155. Ibid.

156. Stichweh, "Die Entstehung einer Weltöffentlichkeit."

157. Karl Lehmann, "Stellungnahme zum Ziel von Fragebogenaktion und Repräsentativbefragung," 20 December 1969, Archiv des ZdK, 60/1, 5.

158. Ibid.

159. Jürgen Bellers, "Moralkommunikation und Kommunikationsmoral: Über Kommunikationslatenzen, Antisemitismus und politisches System," in *Antisemitismus in der politischen Kultur nach 1945,* ed. Werner Bergmann and Rainer Erb (Opladen, 1991), 278–91.

160. Simmel, "Was will die Fragebogenaktion? "

161. *Ruhrwort,* 6 September 1969, quoted in *Synode 72,* 2:51.

162. Tenhumberg to Wilhelm Pötter, 1 July 1970, BAM, GV NA, A-101-141.

163. Text of the speech in *Public Papers of the Presidents: Richard Nixon 1969–1974,* vol. 1, *1969* (Washington DC, 1971), 901–909, quote 909.

164. Elisabeth Noelle-Neumann's argument about the "spiral of silence" resembles this; it can be assumed that she was inspired partly by Richard Nixon. See Elisabeth Noelle-Neumann, "Die Schweigespirale: Über die Entstehung der öffentlichen Meinung," in *Standorte im Zeitstrom: Festschrift für Arnold Gehlen zum 70. Geburtstag am 29. Januar 1974,* ed. Ernst Forsthoff and Reinhard Hörstel (Frankfurt, 1974), 299–330.

165. "Ein Besuch im Umfragebüro Stuttgart," *Katholisches Sonntagsblatt,* no. 24 (1970).

166. "AK Synode in der KSG Münster, Synodenumfrage," n.d., BAOS, Seelsorgeamt, Akzession 4, Ordner Synode Würzburg.

167. Only 71 percent of all German Catholics actually received a questionnaire, as the IfD established with a sample-based poll; *Allensbacher Berichte,* no. 17 (1970): 1.

168. Familienkreis der Gemeinde St. Peter in Waltrop to the editors of *Kirche und Leben,* 5 June 1970, BAM, Schriftleitung KuL., A 229.

169. W. S. from the city of Herten to Tenhumberg, 29 June 1970. In his 9 July 1970 reply, Karl Hürten stated that the representative survey would correct such mistakes. Both are in BAM, Synodalbüro A 6. See also Gerd Hirschauer, "Eine Synode wird gemanagt," *Werkhefte* 24 (1970): 150–53, 152.

170. PSI, Bericht no. 38 (1965), 6ff.

171. Milton J. Rosenberg, "Hedonism, Inauthenticity, and Other Goads toward Expansion of a Consistency Theory," in *Theories of Cognitive Consistency: A Sourcebook,* ed. Robert P. Abelson et al. (Chicago, 1968), 101.

172. Schmidtchen, *Kirche und Gesellschaft,* 56–92, 278–79, esp. 56–57; Rosenberg, "Hedonism," 74–75.

173. Rosenberg, "Hedonism," 101.

174. That was Karl Forster's conclusion in "Glaube-Kirche-Gesellschaft: Versuch einer theologischen und pastoralen 'Anwendung' sozialwissenschaftlicher Analysen" (1974), in *Glaube*

und Kirche im Dialog mit der Welt von heute, vol. 2 (Würzburg, 1982), 102–20, quotes 106.

175. Synodalbüro to Institut für Publizistik der Westfälischen Wilhelms-Universität, 26 April 1973, BAM, Synodalbüro A 2.

176. H. J. Herbort, "Das katholische Schülerparlament," *Die Zeit*, 8 January 1971, cited in *Synode* 2, no. 3 (1971): 21–22; "Die Katholiken üben Demokratie: Die erste Vollversammlung der Synode in Würzburg," *Publik*, 8 January 1971.

177. *Süddeutsche Zeitung*, 22 November 1974.

178. See the photo in *KuL*, 7 June 1970.

179. Karl Korn, "Katholisches Plebiszit?," *FAZ*, 18 June 1970.

180. "Professor Otto B. Roegele kommentiert vorläufige Auswertungsergebnisse der Meinungsbefragung zur Synode 72," *Kirchenzeitung für das Erzbistum Köln*, 23 October 1970.

181. Pastoral constitution "Gaudium et Spes," no. 3, in Abott, *Documents of Vatican II*, 201.

182. Pottmeyer, "Modernisierung," 139.

183. Karl Forster, "Die Befragung," 10–11.

184. Hemmerle, "Alle sind gefragt—wonach?"

185. Quote: *HK* 25 (1971): 96; "57.8 percent der Katholiken suchen Antwort auf Glaubensnot," *Die Welt*, 27 November 1970.

186. Karl Forster, "Zur theologischen Motivation und zu den pastoralen Konsequenzen der Umfragen zur Gemeinsamen Synode der Bistümer in der Bundesrepublik Deutschland," in *Befragte Katholiken: Zur Zukunft von Glaube und Kirche: Auswertungen und Kommentare zu den Umfragen für die Gemeinsame Synode der Bistümer in der Bundesrepublik Deutschland*, ed. Karl Forster (Freiburg, 1973), 19.

187. Karl Lehmann, "Allgemeine Einleitung," in *Gemeinsame Synode* 1:21–67, 45–46.

188. First quote: Minutes of the Konferenz der Seelsorgeamtsleiter, 12–14 June 1972, BAM, GV NA, A-201-464; second quote: Minutes of the Konferenz der Seelsorgeamtsleiter, 10–12 December 1973, BAM, GV NA, A-201-464.

189. Walter Kasper, "Die pastoralen Dienste in der Gemeinde: Einleitung," in *Gemeinsame Synode* 1:584; Roman Bleistein, "Glaubensschwierigkeiten junger Menschen—unvoreingenommene Analyse und pastorale Möglichkeiten," *PBl. für die Diözesen Aachen etc.* 25 (1973): 109–19.

190. Prof. Michael Schmolke, Mitglied der Sachkommission VI: Erziehung-Bildung-Information to the editors of *KuL*, 25 May 1973, BAM, Redaktion *Kirche und Leben* A 229.

191. G. Renner, "Denken anders als die Kirche," *Die Zeit*, 13 September 1972.

192. Interview with Elisabeth Rickal, 9 December 2002.

193. On the motives for this move, see "Die Chance der deutschen Synode: Publik-Gespräch mit dem Sekretär der Synode," *Publik*, 20 August 1971.

194. Forster, "Glaube-Kirche-Gesellschaft"; Karl Forster, ed., *Religiös ohne Kirche? Eine Herausforderung für Glaube und Kirche* (Mainz, 1978).

195. Gerhard Schmidtchen, *Die Situation der Frau: Trendbeobachtungen über Rollen- und Bewußtseinsänderungen der Frauen in der Bundesrepublik Deutschland* (Berlin, 1984).

196. Karl Forster, "Entscheidungen und pastorale Initiativen für die kirchlichen Berufe: Hinweise aus den Ergebnissen sozialwissenschaftlicher Untersuchungen der letzten Jahre," n.d. [1975], BAM, GV NA, A-0-966. Forster based his conclusions primarily on Gerhard Schmidtchen, *Priester in Deutschland: Forschungsbericht über die im Auftrag der Deutschen Bischofskonferenz durchgeführte Umfrage unter allen Welt- und Ordenspriestern in der Bundesrepublik* (Freiburg, 1973); Gerhard Schmidtchen, *Umfrage unter Priesteramtskandidaten: Forschungsbericht des Instituts für Demoskopie Allensbach über eine im Auftrag der DBK durchgeführte Erhebung* (Freiburg, 1975); Institut für Kirchliche Sozialforschung des Bistums Essen (IKSE), Bericht no. 88, 1975; Gregor Siefer, *Sterben die Priester aus? Soziologische Überlegungen zum Funktionswandel eines Berufsstandes* (Essen, 1973), 71–72.

197. This was according to the analysis by Karl Forster in Schmidtchen, *Umfrage unter Priesteramts-kandidaten,* 227; on "trend reversal," see Lothar Roos, "Pastoralwissenschaftliche Überlegungen zu den Reformvorstellungen der Priester," in *Priester zwischen Anpassung und Unterscheidung: Auswertungen und Kommentare zu den im Auftrag der Deutschen Bischofskonferenz durchge-führten Umfragen unter allen Welt- und Ordenspriestern in der Bundesrepublik Deutschland,* ed. Karl Forster (Freiburg, 1974), 76.

198. Forster, "Entscheidungen und pastorale Initiativen."

199. Tenhumberg to Josef Homeyer, 25 August 1975, and Tenhumberg, "Allgemeine Einführung zum Schwerpunkt-Thema der Herbst-Vollversammlung 1975," n.d, both in BAM, GV NA, A-0-966.

200. Damberg, *Abschied,* 291, 455. See also chapter 4.

201. Karl Forster and Gerhard Schmidtchen, *Glaube und Dritte Welt: Ergebnisse einer Repräsentativum-frage über weltkirchliche Aufgaben und die Motive deutscher Katholiken* (Munich, 1982), 7, 11.

202. The report on the evaluation was not published, but Joseph Höffner cited it repeatedly in his *Pastoral der Kirchenfremden: Eröffnungsreferat bei der Herbstvollversammlung der Deutschen Bischofskonferenz 1979 in Fulda* (Bonn, 1979), 31–41, quotes 35.

203. German Bishops' Conference, ed., *Frauen und Kirche: Eine Repräsentativumfrage von Katho-likinnen. Im Auftrage des Sekretariats der Deutschen Bischofskonferenz durchgeführt vom Institut für Demoskopie Allensbach* (Bonn, 1993); A. Fotzik, "Nicht länger die stille Reserve: Allens-bach-Studie zum Thema Frau und Kirche," *HK* 47 (1993): 306–11.

204. Helmut Hild, ed., *Wie stabil ist die Kirche? Bestand und Erneuerung: Ergebnisse einer Meinungs-befragung* (Gelnhausen, 1974), 8–20.

205. On these forms of structural coupling, see Weingart, *Wahrheit,* 139–51, quote 140.

206. David Seeber, "Die emanzipative Generation," *HK* 38 (1984): 527–31, 528.

207. "'Orientierung am Kunden': Ein Gespräch mit McKinsey-Direktor Peter Barrenstein," *HK* 52 (1998): 342–47, 344.

208. Quote: IfK, Abschlussbericht 3-1970, 1; IfK, Meinungsumfrage I/1968; interview with Josef Scharrer, 17 April 2003.

209. GCÖ, "Umrisse für den Plan einer Kontaktmission," 5 March 1968, BAM, GV NA, A-201-377.

210. This is the description from the office of the vicar-general in a remarkable and very positive appraisal of Scharrer's engagement. File note, n.a., n.d. [P. Edbert Köster, OFM, November 1968], BAM, GV NA, A-101-336.

211. This applies, for example, to Ida Friederike Görres (1901–71), who was still treated as a critic of the church on account of her 1946 "Brief über die Kirche" (Letter about the Church). She was later chided as "reactionary," which was equally inaccurate. Erik von Kuehnelt-Leddihn, "Weltmännisches Christentum," *FH* 18 (1963): 271.

212. On this theoretical context, see the introduction to this book.

213. Karl Forster, "Die Befragung: Ein ehrliches Angebot an alle Katholiken," *Katholisches Sonntags-blatt,* no. 17 (1970): 11.

214. F. P. Becker, "Fragen an den Fragebogen," *Bonifatiusbote: Sonntagsblatt für die Diözese Fulda,* 21 June 1970; for question three of the synod poll, see Schmidtchen, *Kirche und Gesellschaft,* 299. The Trier vicar-general also complained that this phrase was an "old catechism formula" and "sounds perjorative [today]," even though, in his opinion, it was meant in an "absolutely positive" sense. Linus Hofmann, "Stellungnahme zu dem Entwurf eines Fragebogens zur Syn-ode," n.d. [1969], Archiv des ZdK, 60/1, 5.

215. Wolfgang Große to Karl Forster, 1 December 1969, BAE, NL Hengsbach 1008.

216. Helmut Josef Patt, "Was machen die Sozialen Seminare mit der Synode?," *Im Dienst der Seel-sorge* 25, no. 1 (1971): 25. For Otto B. Roegele's similar views, see "Planen ohne Gebet," *KuL,* 3 May1970.

217. Simmel, "Was will die Fragebogenaktion?"
218. Johannes Hüneborn in Borth über Moers, "Überlegungen zur Gemeinde-Pastoral," n.d. [ca. 1970], BAM, GV NA, A-201-25.
219. Ida Friederike Görres, "Kritische Fragen über den Fragebogen: Eine betrübte Überlegung," *Rheinischer Merkur*, 21 August 1970, here quoted from a longer version in Ida Friederike Görres, *Der gewandelte Thron: Bemerkungen zur Synode und anderes* (Freiburg, 1971), 61–76, quotes 71, 73, 75–76.
220. Oskar Köhler, "Lasset uns nach Allensbach gehen," *StdZ* 192 (1974): 317.
221. "Protokoll der Vorbereitungskommission vom 1./2.5.1970," Archiv des ZdK, 60/1, 4. This suggestion referred to a draft by Schmidtchen, which inquired in question seven: "In issues of marital family life, do you feel that the church understands-supports-patronizes-abandons you or none of the above?" Gerhard Schmidtchen, "Repräsentative Kontroll- und Ergänzungsbefragung zur Fragebogen-Aktion," 22 April 1970, Archiv des ZdK, 60/1, 5. The final version of the questionnaire did not contain any question of this type; see Schmidtchen, *Kirche und Gesellschaft*, 263–98.
222. Johannes Gründel, "Kirche und moderne Wertsysteme," in Forster, *Befragte Katholiken*, 71.
223. Presentation by Karl Hürten, minutes of the pastoral conference in the deanery of Greven, 26 April 1971, BAM, GV NA, A-201-23.
224. Quote: drawing on a poll conducted for *Der Spiegel* magazine, "Die gestreßten Katholiken: Was sie von ihrer Kirche halten—Wie wenig sie erwarten," *Rheinischer Merkur*, 4 January 1980; based on an Infratest poll, "Kirche stößt auf Interesse," *Rheinischer Merkur*, 31 July 1970.

Chapter 4

PLANNING THE FUTURE OF THE CHURCH
Organizational Research

At first glance, the Catholic Church seems a highly unlikely candidate for the practical application of organizational research. In the years after 1945, official ecclesiology reaffirmed the traditional idea of the church as the "mystical body of Christ," as outlined in the encyclical "Mystici Corporis," issued by Pope Pius XII in June 1943. According to this notion, the church was more than simply a strictly hierarchical body. As a mystical body, the church was not to be understood as a worldly, man-made bureaucratic structure with changeable elements. On the contrary, it had been instituted by God and designed by him as a close-knit community and as an organism whose individual elements had to fulfill an "ascribed" (Talcott Parsons) and fixed role.[1] Consequently, there seemed to be no entry point for social scientific ideas on organizational change. The human relations movement had coined the phrase "overcoming resistance to change" as a motto for the pivotal aim of this type of organizational research.[2] Seen as a mystical body, the church was predicated precisely on the rejection of institutional change not only as a practical option but also as an inherent possibility.

Even in the Catholic Church, however, there was a discrepancy between the official artifice of dogmatic constitutions and promulgations, on the one hand, and the practical requirements of pastoral care, on the other. In the decades after 1945, this discrepancy between the façade of ecclesiological statements and daily encounters with problems and deficiencies quickly evolved into a yawning gap, opening the door for the application of organizational research. The starting point was the intensive discussion about the increasing shortage of priests, which left the remaining priests overburdened with duties. This focus on the clergy's "performance roles" (Talcott Parsons) enabled a consideration of changes within the organizational routines of the church that emerged from the late 1950s. Toward the end of the 1960s, however, another set of perceptions made a full-scale application of organizational research possible. Like leading politicians in the Federal

Republic, key circles in the church grew more optimistic about planning. In the church, planning concerned the delivery of pastoral services. Planning was a notion at the core of positive assumptions, widely held in the late 1960s, that complex organizations could become more functionally viable, as well as more open to the pervasive desire for more participation, through flexible adaptation. Planning for the future was thus key to adapting to change, and organizational research could help to inform and facilitate this adaptation.[3] Yet in the broader context of our inquiry into how the Catholic Church responded to secularization, the application of organizational research also has a wider significance, as it helps us avoid portraying the church as a passive victim of an anonymous and unstoppable process of societal change. Analyzing the encounters between Catholics and organizational research or organizational sociology—the two terms are used synonymously in the following—in the period from 1945 to 1980 helps us understand how laymen and church officials at various levels of the hierarchy actively engaged with new forms of social science knowledge in order to reinvigorate and adapt the teaching of the Gospel in a rapidly changing social environment, and thus responded to "secularization."

Organizations and Organizational Research

Organizations are communicative entities that overcome the uncertain and indefinite nature of their social environment by building complex structures. They are based on decisions that their members are expected to treat as behavioral maxims—decisions that, in turn, are based on other decisions. Organizations thus continually link decisions together. Membership itself requires one to make a decision to enter or exit the relevant organization. This gives organizations a clearly definable and visible external boundary. They can assign roles to members and link these to programs of work, as well as oblige members to be represented in social communication. This dual linkage of decisions—those concerning membership and those setting and specifying member roles—allows them to take on an important feature of formal organization: the setting and implementation of objectives that are specifically defined and follow specific rationality criteria. While older forms of organizational theory heavily influenced by Max Weber regarded this as the most important feature, new forms, since Herbert Simon's work in the 1950s, however, have moved ever more decisively away from the assumption inherent in the older forms that decision making is always an objective and goal-oriented process. Instead, they use terms such as "bounded rationality" or the "garbage can" to emphasize the uncertain, uninformed, and ambiguous nature of organizational decision making.[4] Some sociologists even regard organizations as "irrational," noting that formally irrational decisions are, in fact, better at motivating decisive action within them.[5]

The combination of the variability of decisions and the longevity of structures within organizations has made them a marker of modernity. Nowadays, a large share of all social communication takes place through and in organizations. This also applies to religious communication. Thomas Luckmann claimed in 1967 that the contemporary social form of belief was a freely floating "invisible religion." However, it has not been proven empirically that a substantial amount of religious communication takes places outside the churches. And in this debate, the "full burden of proof" lies on those who assert that the deinstitutionalized, "invisible" form of religion functions in a way "comparable" to the organizational form.[6]

The practical application of organizational sociology began shortly before the First World War with Frederick Taylor's studies on scientific management. Until well into the 1950s, almost all sociological analyses of decision-making processes and internal structure formation focused on the model of the company. Only since then has organizational research regularly been applied to many different types of organizations. Organizational research is a valuable discipline precisely because it abstracts from the specific purposes of organizations.[7] By around 1970 at the latest, the sociology of religion adopted the organizational sociological approach and cast off the traditional distinction between churches and sects, which dated back to Ernst Troeltsch and Max Weber. For one thing, this distinction was inadequate for capturing the diversity of religious groups and associations in the United States. Even more importantly, it had hindered the reception of insights from organizational research in the study of religion and had thus represented a barrier to more complex models of thinking about organized religion.[8]

The discourse of organizational research is characterized by the language of optimization, rationalization, and functionalization. Its leading categories are pragmatism rather than dogmatism, motivation rather than tradition, and objectivism rather than subjectivism. The aim of applying organizational sociology to an organization is always to minimize or remove obstacles on its path to achieving the objectives of allocating scarce resources appropriately and shaping routines and decision-making processes as efficiently as possible.[9] In seeking to best adapt an organization to its specific social environment, the sociological approach ignores historically evolved legitimacy or any normative cultivation of existing arrangements and processes. Organizational sociological thinking is not based on the premodern concept of self-sufficient *stabilitas,* but instead aims for dynamic stability. Because organizations face constant change, sociological advice has no respect for tradition. Only when a client's wishes or objections are taken into account, as is common practice in applied social research, is the work of organizational sociology restricted. In its pursuit of rationalization and effectiveness, organizational research tends to follow the impulses and interests from the top of the organization. This is a discourse of reform from above, which, in seeking to regulate social relations in practical terms, must often neutralize and overcome elements of inertia from below.[10]

The Decreasing Appeal of the Priesthood

Organizational research first arrived at the West German Catholic Church through a side door. Sociological methods were not initially applied to the church as a whole, but to priests and the roles they fulfilled. From this first application, social science methods were eventually applied to the decision-making processes within the organization of the church. This focus on the clergy was justified by the fact that priests had decisive responsibility for the church's contact with its societal environment in their daily pastoral work with the laity—their performance role (Parsons). Sociologists interpreted priests' role conflicts as indicative of a "failed integration of the social system itself," which, together with other developments, ultimately pushed the priest issue to the heart of the church's internal debates on reform.[11]

Sociological ideas were first applied to the priest's role, however, via sociography. Fernand Boulard pioneered this approach with his 1950 study on the "Rise or Decline of the French Clergy." Using extensive statistical sources, Boulard described the correlations between the number of ordinations to the priesthood in a particular region and various features of that region—such as social stratification, the degree of urbanization, school education, and the influence of the family.[12] With significant quantitative evidence, the study immediately generated intense interest in the declining attractiveness of the priestly vocation in many other Western European countries. Werenfried van Straaten and the Viennese archbishop Franz Jachym provided an initial impetus for conducting studies on this issue. Jan Dellepoort, who headed the Department for Occupations in the Clergy at KASKI in The Hague, coordinated further empirical work. A large-scale study of the "European Priest Question" appeared under his leadership in 1958, together with multiple follow-up studies on individual countries.[13] This research addressed the growing concern surrounding the continual decline in the number of ordinations, which many West German bishops had lamented in their pastoral letters since the early 1950s.[14] The studies all still followed the categorical framework of the sociographic discourse, however, interpreting the considerable decline in the number of candidates—particularly when viewed against the absolute rise in the number of Catholics—as a "structural question." This meant that they attributed the trend to macrosocial causes such as urbanization or the changed pattern of social mobility, which had largely eliminated the use of the priesthood as a means of social advancement.[15]

None of these quantitative studies sought to relate the reduced attractiveness of the priesthood to the reality of priests' pastoral work. Swiss theologian Jakob Crottogini was the first to attempt to interpret the phenomenon implicitly from this perspective. With the aid of a questionnaire sent to 621 priests in Switzerland, France, and Germany, he conducted the first empirical study of the life circumstances that led a man to the priesthood. The study also broached the subject of the priests' "occupational crisis," which consisted of them calling their career decision into question, at least temporarily, as well as the related issue of celibacy. The work generated a great deal of discussion even before its publication in 1955. However, it was immediately banned by the Congregation for the Doctrine of the Faith in the Vatican and only indirectly found its way to an interested audience over time.[16] This reaction to Crottogini's study shows unmistakably that any sociological qualitative studies on the occupational practice of priests still faced insurmountable obstacles in the Catholic hierarchy at that time.[17]

For this reason, pastoral theologians in the 1950s still looked first to palliative measures to solve the worst problems. The overburdening of priests, already discussed in the interwar period, continued to be interpreted principally as a quantitative problem. A declining number of priests were charged with continually increasing pastoral tasks, despite the advancing process of de-Christianization. This inevitably meant that many were "overburdened" with work and responsibilities—a condition prompting a series of dioceses to suggest pragmatic measures to reduce a priest's daily hours of work and enable him to concentrate on core pastoral duties. Among other things, these included limiting Sunday services and occasionally canceling sermons or restricting religious teaching at vocational schools and technical colleges. The protagonists of the sociographic discourse hoped to reduce the burden on clergy considerably by making use of the laity, especially since women from "well-to-do families" wanted to become involved in something outside the home in order to avoid "boredom." There were also suggestions to reduce the responsibilities of priests in church administration.[18] Yet despite these efforts to "simplify pastoral work," there was still a consensus in the 1950s that the rationalization of a priest's activities should be limited.[19] Drawing especially on a comparison with the classic example of rational production methods—Fordist car production—observers held fast to the view that priestly service could not be oriented primarily toward its "utility," but had to center on unity with Christ.[20]

The Sociology of the Role Set

From the mid-1960s, however, it became widely recognized that the "priest crisis" and the "overburdening of roles" experienced by priests were more than just a quantitative problem of excessive hours for the average parish priest.[21] Church sociologists now used the concept of social roles, as systematized primarily by Robert Merton in the United States, as the key to interpreting the contemporary problems of the priesthood. Ralf Dahrendorf's 1957 study *Homo Sociologicus* had made the interests and terminology of the sociology of roles familiar beyond the small circle of academic sociologists. Dahrendorf handily defined social roles as "bundles of expectations directed at the incumbents of positions in a given society,"[22] thus describing the central concern of the new direction of research. Moving away from the concept of the individual, wherein the uniqueness and completeness of each person and their actions were the focus, the role concept drew attention to the contradictions and complexities in the expectations directed at the behavior and qualities of those who held certain social positions. As professionals in complex organizations, people were no longer "individuals," but were instead understood as social units at the intersection of a set of role expectations. From as early as the late 1950s, the American Catholic sociologist Joseph Fichter, SJ, had been using the role concept to analyze spiritual vocations. He generalized this approach to social reality in a work on sociology's basic principles, which was translated into German in 1967 as *Grundbegriffe der Soziologie*. Fichter explicitly pointed out that there were narrow limits to individuals' ability to influence the nature of the role expectations directed at them. Like other pastoral sociologists, he thus emphasized that structural constellations that could be transformed in the course of social change molded social roles' specific forms.[23]

It was precisely such changing role expectations created by social transformation that were the focus of pastoral sociology's analysis of the priest's role set. Empirical studies on the views pupils at Catholic secondary schools held of priests had made it clear that they saw the priesthood as a "static occupation," only able to reach a "narrow section of society" in a highly formalized manner. In view of the social changes taking place, the traditional imagery used to describe the role of priests—for example, the idea of the "good shepherd"—had "long lost its positive effect." Newly introduced images, such as that of "God's loudspeaker," also failed to be persuasive.[24] The central idea that now shed new light on the falling number of ordinations was the growing "role uncertainty" of priests. This related, in part, to the balancing act priests had to perform between the expectations of the faithful entrusted to them, on the one hand, and those of the bishops, on the other. At the same time, priests increasingly confronted contradictory expectations, particularly in their parishes and through contact with the secular world. In a process intensified by the conciliar innovations gradually being implemented in liturgy and pastoral work, both the traditional "core parish" and the more "dynamic groups" in church and society made different demands as to how priestly service should be structured.[25]

One reason the role concept achieved growing resonance in the search for ways to solve the crisis of the priesthood was, first of all, its own imagery, particularly the associations with stage roles. Fichter insisted on distinguishing between the sociological concept and the "stage role," the latter serving as no more than an analogy to aid comprehension.[26] However, actors on the stage could, of course, be "booed off" and subjected to criticism if their performance failed to meet people's expectations, and the novel terminology is likely to have touched on similar experiences as it was applied to priests. With its ubiquitous theater imagery, the sociology of roles was able, unlike almost any other social scientific approach, to appeal to a broad, nonspecialist audience. In language that resonated, it described widespread fears of alienation and the problems of coping with increasing social complexity.[27] There were only isolated warning voices cautioning against sociologists who tried to teach priests threatened by a "loss of self-confidence" that, in a modern world, they would "play a role" only for the elderly and sick. For such theorists, the "main concern" for the kingdom of God and the church now had to be left to God himself, and the prospect of a "smaller, poorer, inward-looking and simplified church of tomorrow" was to be seen as a "sign of hope."[28] The majority of observers, however, saw this position, in which the church would survive the crisis passively by shrinking to a healthy "small flock," as an evasion of the preponderance of urgent questions. The conclusion that the clergy's "loss of status" represented a fundamental cause of the crisis was inescapable, even for a polemic conducted against sociologists whose "anthropological premises" characterized the priest's role as one of a social "outsider."[29] Nevertheless, for all the differences in the exact interpretation of causes and possible solutions, it was widely agreed from the mid-1960s that the position of the Catholic priest was characterized by increasing "role uncertainties and conflicts."[30]

A second reason sociological concepts became legitimate categories in the discourse on the priest's role set was the Second Vatican Council. The decree produced by the council, "Presbyterorum Ordinis," had addressed priests' feelings of fragmentation and inner conflict in the face of their diverse responsibilities without issuing moral reproach and admonishments. However, the behavioral maxims it suggested—observing the will of God and adhering to the rules of the church—did not provide any concrete solutions to the crisis. As a result, it was surely of little use, especially as priests were still advised to orient themselves toward the "role of the good shepherd," which many now found to be problematic.[31] Most literature on pastoral practice held that the conciliar texts had not given adequately clear and specific advice on the "urgent questions surrounding life as a priest." At most, they had provided building blocks for his new role set.[32] It thus appeared "self-evident" that a theological view of the priest issue could deliver no more than "partial insights," and that sociological categories were essential for interpretation.[33]

Third, this uncertainty corresponded to a restructuring of priestly service initiated by the conciliar resolutions: the parish priest was increasingly to be deprived of his "independence" and turned into the pastoral assistant of the local bishop. This was reflected by the move to largely abolish the irremovability of priests, especially by discontinuing the right to a benefice. Priests had, until then, usually been appointed in a particular parish for life, which offered them some protection from the pastoral requirements imposed by the church bureaucracy.[34] The new system increased the pressure on individual parish priests to conform to the pastoral strategies of their bishops, which applied across parish boundaries. At least on paper, priests had become pastoral assistants to their bishops to an extent never seen before.[35] Precisely this development, however, heightened the clergy's ambivalent situation in the conflict between their parishes' expectations and the pastoral norms defined by the bishops. One way out of this conflict of roles was for individuals to give up the priesthood and thus resign their specific role. This was the path a growing number of clergy chose in the period around 1970. Others joined forces in independent solidarity groups of priests, creating collective bargaining power to protest publicly against particularly problematic interpretations of their role. These groups intensively discussed precisely the points, such as celibacy, ecumenical work, and pastoral care relating to marriage, in which church norms were perceived as particularly inflexible.[36] In Albert O. Hirschman's terminology of 1970, the solidarity groups represented priests' ability to counteract the visible decline of their organization though a collective "voice."[37]

Investigating Priests' Roles

Alongside the direct observation of priests' daily work in the parish, it was a quantitative instrument that was first available to conduct empirical research of priests' role behavior and role conflicts: the "time budget" developed and applied by pastoral sociologists. With the aid of a diary, the priest or chaplain had, over a certain period of time, to make a note of the nature and duration of all the activities carried out in the course of the day. This allowed the scope of pastoral, liturgical, and administrative tasks, as well personal prayer, to be profiled. It enabled the different roles to be weighted and simultaneously helped in the search for possible time saving, as was appropriate to the initial concentration on priests being "overworked."[38] In preparing new forms of cooperation for pastoral work in the parish, the "time budget"—German pastoral practitioners consistently used the English term—could also serve to match interests to the work conducted. Pastoral assistants and any secretarial support available were then involved in the study. For this reason, pilot studies, which in 1970 were ready to put the *Strukturplan* discussed in the diocese of Münster into practice (which will be discussed in more detail below), were also designed to include a time budget exercise, in which priests took notes on the actual time spend for different routine tasks.[39]

If a study of priests' role behavior in practical parish work was to go beyond measuring time pressure, it would have to make use of questionnaires and unstructured interviews to achieve meaningful results. Only in this way could more precise information about the willingness of individual priests to cooperate with the laity and other priests in pastoral work be garnered. The subjective weighting of the individual areas of responsibility, and the flow of communications behind pastoral decisions, could also only be studied by directly questioning individual clergy. In view of the very extensive insight into and potential access to the personality and occupational practices of the individuals concerned, every empirical study on the role profile of Catholic clergy required the subjects to be highly motivated. This was the case, for example, in a study carried out in the early 1970s, it is believed, by the Social Team in Landstuhl on a relatively large sample of 288 priests in the Palatinate region. The study was conducted as "action research," meaning that it consciously relied on active participation by the "objects" of the study. Moreover, it was planned from the beginning that the priests would use the results to inform their working practices.[40]

The interest in the sociology of roles already pointed to the very phenomenon the study was to verify and describe: the widespread role uncertainty of priests. Both the initiative for and fate of another study for which the PSI in Essen provided professional support provides further indication of this. In March 1967, representatives of an informal group of chaplains from the archdiocese of Cologne sought an audience with the institute's head, Egon Golomb. Their ideas were still very "unclear." Golomb recommended that the chaplains carry out a role analysis and suggested Leo von Deschwanden, a young sociologist with a diploma in economics, to work on the project. Deschwanden was well qualified for the job. Working at the Wuppertal-based Institut für Kommunikationsforschung, he had participated in two studies on the priest's role by the Brussels-based pastoral sociologist François Houtart. These studies had also generated a relevant publication by Deschwanden. A plan for the role analysis began to crystallize in a series of discussions with the chaplains. The pastoral office of the archdiocese and the office of the vicar-general were also involved, not least in order to finance the study.[41]

The vicar-general and Franz Groner, who was involved as a reviewer, reacted with skepticism and negativity. Groner dismissed the research plan as "undergraduate work," though he declined to offer specific criticisms of the methodology or content. Groner judged the plan somewhat imperiously as not worth the DM 1,700 spent on it, compared to the DM 200 fee for a specialist lecture by a professor. Golomb was only able to save the project from rejection by explaining at length how sociologists translated everyday experiences into theoretical problems. That the chaplain to the bishop of the archdiocese had also expressed enormous doubts did not help matters. Golomb wanted to prevent an unnecessary "crisis of authority" and anticipated that the study would provide a useful "channel in the midst of potential communication difficulties." This was Deschwanden's main working hypothesis, as well as the wish of the chaplains in the Cologne archdiocese. Deschwanden suspected that a lack of communication and cooperation in pastoral work lay at the heart of chaplains' uncertain self-image and understanding of their pastoral role. Indeed, the Social Team in Adelsried confirmed this hypothesis in many interviews with priests in the diocese of Augsburg.[42] Like other authors, Deschwanden regarded the priesthood as a "total role" that almost fully absorbed an individual's private life. He located the central role conflict in the contradiction between functions such as administering the sacraments (which relied on the church-bestowed official charisma), and functions such as pastoral care and work with associations (which were more dependent on the individual charisma of the priest).[43]

Cardinal Josef Frings and the vicar-general of Cologne, Hermann Jansen, eventually consented to the planned study on the pastoral roles of chaplains in the archdiocese, albeit with a set of restrictive conditions. Apart from constant contact with the archdiocese commission responsible for issues of priestly life, these included the requirement that the archbishop personally approve any publications. From the outset, both men ruled out the possibility of the results being scientifically evaluated and presented in a doctoral dissertation. This eliminated one of Deschwanden's main motivations for working on this topic. Questions on personal matters were also forbidden, including the personal prayer life of the clergy, as well as the "position on women" and celibacy. Cardinal Frings had already complained that the preliminary study failed to list the planned questions. Clearly discouraged by these restrictions and a tug-of-war that lasted for months, Deschwanden preferred to take up an alternative career opportunity in his home country of Switzerland.[44] The Cologne chaplains had to make do without a sociological analysis of their role problems. The fate of this study indicates how controversial and conflict laden the use of interviews could be as a basis for research on the role conflicts of a specific group of priests. By contrast, sending questionnaires to all priests in West Germany, which was done at practically the same time as the synod's total poll, implied an anonymization and distancing from the acute presence of role problems. Questions about celibacy could also be posed in this manner.[45]

Soon after a role conflict for priests was diagnosed sociologically in general terms in the late 1960s, people began asking how the crisis could be overcome, taking the descriptions from social science into account. This question ultimately concerned the organization's willingness to increase priests' motivation by applying measures to redefine their role, and thus to attract more individuals to take up the occupation. But was the church even in the position to react appropriately to problems revealed by sociological analyses through its typical medium of decision making? In public perception and academic analysis alike, the role crises of priests and chaplains were often interpreted as a "crisis of authority," a dissatisfaction with the "decisions" of the "church authorities," and thus also as a "conflict of authority."[46] The analysis of the questionnaire priests had completed in a separate poll for the Würzburg Synod in the early 1970s also noted this problem. This analysis described it as a contradiction between a "vertical" and a "horizontal" or "functional" understanding of the priesthood. While the former was based on priests being hierarchically legitimated through ordination and the authority of the bishop, the latter model defined priests in relation to the service they provided to the parish faithful and the trust parishioners placed in them.[47]

There was no evidence, even in the tumultuous period after 1968, of a crisis of authority so great as to seriously damage the bishop's authority to impose legal decisions. Isolated cases of priests openly refusing to read out a bishop's pastoral letter to their congregation because they disagreed with the content were an exception.[48] But did the sociological analyses of the situation offer any suggestions on how priests' tensions with episcopal authority could be reduced, even if bishops were prepared to incorporate and implement the important wishes of "horizontally" oriented priests in their decisions? Karl Forster's analysis of the various surveys on the role profile of church occupations, submitted as an expert dossier to the German Bishops' Conference in 1975, provides an exemplary insight into this issue. Forster insisted that bishops had to work to relieve priests of the "pressure" caused by long-term "overburdening of roles" and thus to find "realizable concepts for cooperation between priests, deacons and the laity." The future shape of "joint responsibility" at the parish and diocese level was also "significant." "Strengthening people's sense of individual involvement," Forster claimed, could "unburden" priests faced with a conflict of roles. While he did not make specific suggestions, Forster, in this analysis, took up the major concerns of reform-willing clergy who had a "horizontal" understanding of their position.[49]

At the same time, Forster recognized that laity participation in pastoral decisions at the parish level could also lead to a "considerable additional burden on priests." Alongside the composition of decision-making bodies in the parish and the clergy's "willingness to cooperate," this depended "decisively" on the ongoing diocesan practice for dealing with specific conflicts.[50] Forster thus addressed an ambivalence in the planned reformulation of models of the priesthood, which was otherwise dealt with only implicitly. An unburdening of the priest by the parish assembly or *Pfarrgemeinderat,* which brought laity and clergy together, depended on both sides being willing to cooperate and on the absence of any serious conflicts blocking such cooperation. As an alternative to the overburdened "all-around parish clergyman" responsible for everything, cooperation with other pastoral workers and laypeople in a team was proposed, in which each individual would acquire and specialize in an area of expertise.[51] In proposing a division of labor, management consultants were advocating a principle that had considerably improved efficiency in business environments.[52]

Only rarely was it recognized, however, that teamwork, far from unburdening priests, tended initially to extend their role even further. They were now additionally expected to bring good teamwork skills to the job.[53] Moreover, clergy members and pastoral workers approached by the public now continually had to decide who was responsible for what: the parish priest or, for example, a specialist in marital advice in a neighboring parish. This arrangement may have allowed the all-around priest to withdraw from the front line, but he now had to balance the apportionment of responsibility elsewhere. The offer of specialized services always threatened to prompt laypeople to take on a "consumerist attitude."

Pastoral sociologists concluded from this that the "total" role of the priest should be blown apart, either by classifying pastoral work as a separate job, or by abolishing compulsory celibacy in order to make new role combinations possible.[54] In 1969, the French pastoral sociologist Èmile Pin made the radical suggestion of dividing the function of the priestly ministry into four parts, with separate training and occupational paths. He distinguished between theologians qualified by academic study, presbyters charged with leading congregations and the Eucharist, specially trained pastoral "advisors," and administratively experienced church "functionaries." Such extensive proposals were only occasionally given serious discussion in the West German Catholic Church, however.[55]

Priests as Team Workers

Experts informed by sociology, such as Norbert Glatzel or Karl Forster, perceived considerable problems in the idea to base the model of priesthood on teamworking ability and the division of labor. This presented new coordination problems and demanded that individual priests make constant decisions on the competencies of others and the delegation of work. The decision for a largely horizontal model of roles may perhaps have superficially alleviated the crisis of authority, but did almost nothing to unburden priests. If anything, the complexity of the clergy's roles and the need for priests to continually make decisions about other decisions—which had previously been the task of the parish assembly—increased the burden further. As priests identified "with the reality of the church," Karl Forster believed the church should avoid anything that might trigger "conflicts of identification without good reason." This meant seeking "consensus" by increasing communication. On the other hand, he wanted this to remain within tight limits: where moral norms were broken in "significant" matters, "recognizable consequences" had to follow, for nobody could identify with an "amorphous" social construct. Forster held that the "belief that this sinful church" was "the holy church of the Lord" had to be vindicated. If the impression was given that churches "could 'be made'" by man, the "primary motive" for identifying with an occupation in the church would be lost.[56] Decisions on the exact shape of the priest's role could thus not be based on faith alone, but also had to enable the church to maintain a sharp external profile as an organization.

Forster's 1975 expert dossier submitted to the German Bishops' Conference, intended as an aid to decision making in the highest bodies of the Catholic Church in West Germany, presented all of these issues. This indicates the sophistication that the scientization of the Catholic Church had reached only ten years after it began to engage with questions about the sociology of roles. However, it also illustrates the special difficulties the church as a religious organization faced in acting upon its decisions. Faith is a comparably weak medium of communication, which, in the history of modern society, has not succeeded in finding a stable form with a high probability of acceptance. It was not faith itself but confession—the formal commitment to a faith—that governed membership in the church after the Reformation and the Counter-Reformation. Faith unites God and the soul as that which lives beyond death. With ideas such as sin and the moral distinction between good and evil, individuals can order their lives and charge them with religious meaning. The medium of faith gains shape as religion permeates the ways people lead their lives. In the context of church decision making, the weakness of the medium of faith points to the difficulties in convincing people that membership in a church will have any consequence for the fate of their souls.[57]

Companies or courts, by contrast, can support their decisions with information codified in the specific media of money or the legal statute books, and make recourse to their ability to condition motives. Money in particular is not only calculable in exact accounting terms for the relevant decision, but also makes it highly probable that people will follow behavioral expectations associated with it. In light of these facts, pastoral sociologist Egon Golomb proposed a "more structured career path" for the clergy that involved improved compensation. He was able to point to a study of a controversial salary reform that Leslie Paul had presented to the Church of England in 1964.[58] However, Catholic priests with doubts about celibacy would probably not have been helped by a salary increase. Media reports suggested the exact opposite, proposing that, in addition to their celibacy, priests should also live in poverty to send the signal of a "church on a pilgrimage."[59] Of more use were specific legal changes in regulations pertaining to former priests. Many observers thought that moves could be made to improve the often-problematic position of priests who left active ministry upon becoming married. In this area, informal practice had progressed faster than the formal organization. For example, a dean in southern Germany, with the tacit support of his bishop, allowed former priests who had married to perform pastoral work on weekends.[60] Yet ultimately each priest had to be able to reconcile his lifestyle with his faith. It was therefore a "serious problem" when in the early 1970s no less than 52 percent of candidates to the priesthood believed a change in the celibate lifestyle to be necessary, even though it was "clear that no change at all was in prospect."[61] This frank appraisal by Karl Forster illustrates one of the strategies the organization used to deal with the complexity of the celibacy issue: not deciding anything at all.

The Thorny Issue of Celibacy

Most pastoral sociologists involved in reviewing the priest's role believed that compulsory celibacy would sooner or later have to be abolished, contradicting the church's strategy of inaction. They also argued that the family, like the *vita*

communis for other clergy, would present married priests with new role requirements.[62] Yet theirs was a sociological rather than a theological judgment. Forster's assessment also reflected the reality that the West German Catholic Church
was unable to make resolutions on this matter independently. There had been
a temporary but serious "crisis of confidence" at the Würzburg Synod when
the German Bishops' Conference ignored the question of the so-called *viri pro-
bati*, the admission of married men into the priesthood, in its discussions in
April 1972. The relevant committee and the full assembly of the synod at least
attempted to discuss the pros and cons of celibacy to find "criteria" for making
a future decision. Soon, however, came the "sobering recognition" that the core
of the argument could not be clearly resolved given the different theological and
ecclesiological positions, particularly in light of the generational division within
the clergy. Although from a pastoral viewpoint the issue needed to be resolved,
celibacy proved to be "unripe for decision" at the synod. Any future decision,
it seemed, could only be drawn from the "power of faith."[63] The obvious and
undisputed bottom line was that the Holy See and the bishops would ultimately
decide the celibacy issue.

Thus, the role crisis of priests, at least insofar as it concerned the celibate lifestyle, was passed back to the level of the individual. "Individuals rather than institutions have to manage this task," wrote a pastoral theologian in 1964.[64] This
revealed a typical form of reductionist thinking in which decisions about matters
of faith could be made less complex, even though faith itself was a rather unspecific
medium for decision making. The rector of the Canisian order active in the diocese
of Münster since 1854 discussed this at a pastoral conference in 1971. In addressing
the current "crisis among priests," he claimed that the more opinion polls were used
to attempt to "achieve clarification," the "more complicated the situation" became.
It was no more possible to "learn faith" through such research than by studying
theology, he argued. The rector was convinced that faith could "only" be learned
through "encounters with people" who "bear witness to faith." In other words, faith
is learned and strengthened through faith. This was the traditional formula religious organizations used to substitute for their lack of the ability to solve problems
and make decisions with regard to faith.[65]

This passing on of faith had problems of its own, as evidenced at a pastoral
conference in Rheinberg in the diocese of Münster that same year. A priest there
argued that belief was being passed "less and less from generation to generation,"
which would have immediate repercussions for the formula described above. A
decreasing number of people were learning the faith as a matter of course in childhood and following it for the rest of their lives. Rather, faith had been "assimilated into the 'continuous reflection' typical of modern consciousness." This
phrase was a direct reference to a brilliant text by sociologist Helmut Schelsky,
a key figure in empirical social research and academic sociology in West Germany. Writing in 1957, Schelsky had raised the issue of the institutionalization of

"permanent reflection" as a central topic in the modern sociology of religion. He had answered it provisionally by pointing to an intensification and institutionalization of the discussion about faith.[66] In the eyes of the priest from Münster, this meant that "small groups" such as "families, discussion circles, campaign groups," and others, rather than the "relatively anonymous large congregation," were increasingly imparting faith, without causing church "superstructures" to lose their importance.[67] This diagnosis raised the question of a new relationship between these different levels and thus led directly to organizational sociological considerations, such as those raised by the *Strukturplan* of the diocese of Münster, which will be discussed in more detail below.

Role sociology's treatment of the priesthood between 1965 and 1975 introduced a perspective on the clergy that was unfamiliar to the church and deviated from theological schemas. The application of these categories was supposed to counter the growing role uncertainty of priests. It quickly became clear, however, that this would not rapidly clarify and simplify the situation, but would instead increase the complexity of the church organization still further. The concept of the social role ultimately led to elements of undecidability, even if these were not always understood as such. It was certainly the case that conceptualizing the priesthood in terms of role sociology did not fit a simple framework for making decisions within the organization, even if some bishops hoped otherwise.

One direct impact of applying role sociology was that, for the first time, the leading decision-making bodies in dioceses and at the German Bishops' Conference had at their disposal unvarnished information about the expectations, attitudes, and living situation of the parish clergy. In officially arranged conversations between the bishops and the seminarians and priests, real problems were barely discussed. Younger priests who had been ordained since 1960 especially considered their "forced dishonesty toward their superiors" to be a "very important hindrance in their lives as priests." At meetings with their bishop, they reported, conversation was "kept deliberately trivial," so that the head of the diocese "does not know—perhaps also is not allowed to know or does not want to know—how priests really live."[68] The affected clergy members and social researchers alike hoped that a study of the priest's roles would enable information to be passed upward, where it would form the basis for informed decisions on reform. Hence, the independent solidarity groups of priests called for "workplace analysis" of the priesthood.[69]

Functionalist Descriptions of Priesthood

The most important consequence of role sociological work on the office and practice of the priest was thus initially an indirect one. The concept of the role pushed the thinking and language of functionalism into an area of church organization that had thus far been a bastion of theological ideas. These ideas emphasized the special dignity of the priesthood, including the divine nature of the office bestowed on the priest through his ordination, which made it inaccessible to normal mortals.[70] When viewed sociologically as a role bearer, the priest had to learn to avoid the concept of the "individual" to describe his social relationships. The terminology also implied that the expectations directed at priests could be compared to those directed at other professionals such as doctors or lawyers, thus robbing priests of their incomparability symbolized by the sacrament and, at least implicitly, desacralizing them. With its focus on an individual's performance rather than his value "in the eyes of others," the role concept tended to narrow the hierarchical gap between priests and laypeople.[71] The "ontological" evaluation and appraisal of the priest in a hierarchical system was replaced by a "functional" one. Personal "virtues" were replaced by "performance" and "output" at work.[72] This perspective afforded legitimacy to only those hierarchical elements of the priest's role that were based on the fulfillment of specific measurable services for the faith and the church, rather than on the paternalistic habit of the priest and the traditional deference of his "sheep."

The attempt to legitimize the application of the "new category of functionality" to the priesthood proceeded in this exact direction. Functionality not only "fitted easily into modern thinking" but also corresponded to what the Bible called "diakonia" or service, whether referring to "service to a neighbor" or more specifically to the priest's leading role in service to his parish.[73] Only through the pervasive influence of role sociology on the theological and practical conceptualization of the priesthood could priests be described as "managers" tasked with a multitude of contradictory responsibilities in stabilizing the milieu of parish residents with ties to the church. Some warned, however, that such a narrow understanding of the priesthood was likely to create more problems. In a largely secularized society, priests whose only job was to act as "functionaries of religion" would likely experience feelings of "emptiness," "ineffectiveness," and "meaninglessness."[74] Joseph Ratzinger warned in 1970 that a priest whose only role was that of a "social functionary" could be easily replaced by psychotherapists and other specialists. Despite all the calls for "specialization" and "professionalization," the Würzburg Synod thus continued explicitly to insist on the unity of preaching, administering sacraments, and diakonia to prevent priests being reduced to "mere religious functionaries."[75]

From the early 1970s, however, the main concern of all stakeholders in this debate was no longer to warn against a functional interpretation, but rather to find a rationale for defining the priesthood in a way that pointed beyond the dimension of functionality in the first place. For example, in analyzing the data from the priest survey during the Würzburg Synod on "role overburdening," particularly among younger priests, Klaus Hemmerle focused almost inevitably on the functional dimension of the priesthood—an approach he saw no need to justify. The real question was how to explain the still "indispensable vertical and ontological element" of the priesthood in a world dominated by the idea of functionality. With sociological categories dramatically reshaping the theological discourse on the priesthood, the answer was paradoxical. The priest, suggested Hemmerle, had to act as a "witness to and custodian of" that which is inaccessible to the laypeople. In other words, he was to fulfill an "antifunctional function."[76] The disjunction between the "vertical" and the "horizontal-functional" understanding of the priesthood was a self-reinforcing pattern that could not be broken even by those who saw such a "sharp distinction" as inaccurate and damaging to the church.[77] It spread from the priest surveys to the vocabulary of those surveyed, then on to the mass media and pastoral-theological literature, and from there back into church practice. Every attempt to reform the priesthood after 1970 had to reckon with this situation. The relevant resolution from the Würzburg Synod begins with precisely this distinction.[78]

The Church: An "Organization"?

The "age of the great movements is over in the church, too." These words, by Karlheinz Schmidthüs in 1956, drew a line under the mood of invigoration in the church that had been characterized since the 1920s by liturgical, Eucharistic, and youth movements. Schmidthüs believed that the changed sociological conditions would require the practice at the altar, the church's work in the world at large, and its targeted action to be combined in another form. This form was "unquestionably" that of an "organization." Yet this form in turn raised the problem of how to coordinate the "wealth" of existing organizations. Schmidthüs saw this as the mission of the Central Committee of German Catholics.[79] His remarks are typical of the understanding of "organization" that prevailed in German Catholicism until well into the 1970s. The term was used as a synonym for the numerous lay associations established since the middle of the nineteenth century. It was closely associated with an almost fantastical hope that this organizational structure would generate a surplus of social representation and negotiating power.[80]

At the same time, the terminology Catholic authors themselves used to describe the church continued effectively to refute the idea that it was an organization in which the decision to join and member roles stood in a variable relationship to one another. The dominant metaphors they used owed much to the ecclesiology of the Corpus Christi mysticum, which Pope Pius XII reemphasized in the "Mystici Corpus Christi" encyclical published in 1943. Voices from the sociographic discourse in the 1950s echoed these ideas. For them, the church as an organization constituted an "organism" whose individual parts focused on "serving as instruments (organon!)" of the whole. The church was at the same time a community whose ordering structure Catholics simply had to accept if they were to remain part of it.

Ultimately, the primacy of the whole over the parts meant that the "organization of the community lay in the hands of the hierarchy."[81]

From around the mid-1960s, the view of the church as an organization shifted beyond the rigid metaphor of the organism and promised to bring about a novel and more flexible coupling of its structural elements. Insofar as this involved reallocating and redefining tasks, the church demonstrated the classic feature of any organization from the viewpoint of organizational sociology: the variation of membership roles in order to achieve objectives. This initially involved approaches with disparate regional foci, degrees of specificity, and conceptual origins. The plan whose practical implementation extended the farthest was linked to the model of *pastorale d'ensemble* developed in the sociographic discourse. The archdiocese of Paderborn, for example, created "pastoral districts" in the period up to 1965 as an "intermediary structure" in order to recognize and work on specific pastoral needs in the region. These plans found resonance in German and Austrian pastoral sociology.[82]

Around the same time, comparable ideas emerged that aimed to redefine the pastoral responsibilities of the parish. To a certain extent, these resulted from the failed attempts to use missionary pastoral care to immunize church members against the secular influence of the social environment, as well as from the sociological insight that many people traveled between parishes to take part in church services. The widespread view that the parish could be seen as an "autarchic religious structure" had been revealed to be illusory. It was no longer enough, wrote François Houtart, "to see the parish as an organizational unit of a larger whole." Houtart instead favored the idea of a "tiered pastoral structure" at the town level that would reach beyond individual parishes.[83] This suggestion clearly represented a shift away from the traditional view of the church as an organism.

Other deliberations emphasized that even as pastoral structures became more differentiated, they should not replace the parish as the traditional center of territorial pastoral work designed to include all Catholics living in the local area. Nonetheless, centralized institutions appeared necessary, especially in large cities, to take over the work of certain functions or categories of pastoral care—for example, social and Caritas work, campaigning, workplace pastoral care, and "interparish campaigns"—and to meet the needs arising from social mobility and differentiation. In the field of "religious organization," too, a *Stadtoberhaupt* (city leader) was planned, similar to the office of mayor. Initial outlines had also already been drawn up for church "spatial planning" in rural areas.[84] At the level of diocesan leadership, the pastoral sociologist Norbert Greinacher envisaged a "pastoral unit" to help decision makers in their search for a pastoral "strategy." Greinacher openly admitted that the concept of the unit had been borrowed directly from management theory.[85]

The concept of planning was perceptible in these suggestions and blueprints for changing the structure of pastoral institutions, although there was not yet any precise description of what "planning" meant. In this way, the semantics of the political system penetrated the Catholic Church. In the political sphere, the idea of planning had taken root in the mid-1960s, particularly in the areas of education and research policy, where it had formed an important element of political sociology inspired by ideas from cybernetics.[86] Calls for planning referred in a rather general sense to the trend for society to become more dynamic and for large parts of the population to be increasingly "mobile and fluctuating." Such arguments generalized the experience of social change accelerating more rapidly than in earlier generations.[87] This perception gave rise to a more future-oriented understanding of faith and the church, as was seen everywhere in the period around 1970. Not only pastoral sociologists reflected on the church's future, but also cardinals such as Lorenz Jaeger from Paderborn and periti such as Joseph Ratzinger, the latter summarizing his concerns in the simple question: "What will the church look like in the year 2000?"[88]

This more future-oriented awareness of the church's problems indicates an increasing consciousness of the growing risks and ambivalence the church could expect to face as part of modern society. It was by now clear that religious faith could no longer rely on being passed down through stable social structures as it had been in the past. Rather, it had to reckon with a still opaque and changeable future and depended more than ever on decisions that had to be made in the present. This required the church to be understood as a decision-based organization. In the words of pastoral sociologist Lothar Roos, preparing to make such decisions meant getting to know the terrain using the social sciences in order to adapt to rapidly changing conditions. The church could no longer rely on data that was "relatively easy" to gather and interpret, such as that available to sociography. Rather, it faced the much more challenging task of using "macrosociological insights" to develop a theoretical understanding of complex processes such as "secularization," "permanent reflection," and "fundamental democratization" and of relating these to belief and the church. Against the backdrop of this complex task, "pastoral planning" proved ultimately to be part of a more general social "planning for the future."[89]

Pastoral Planning as Organizational Reform

From 1967, the language and reform intentions of pastoral planning very quickly advanced in many German dioceses from the level of pastoral blueprints to the actual work of planning departments and church bodies. From this point on, the church was characterized by an organizational debate about structures and their reform. There were two important reasons for this sudden transformation of abstract concepts into concrete reform proposals. The first was the increasing severity of the priest shortage. With every passing year, it became clearer that the shortfall would have serious effects on pastoral work in many parishes if the bishops did not respond quickly. The diocese of Münster, for example, brought this up as a matter of urgency at the conference of deans in 1965, 1966, and again in 1968. The long "repressed problem" was now addressed unambiguously.[90] This made it clear that expressions such as "demotion of parish boundaries," *Zentralpfarrei* (centralized parish authority), *nachbarschaftlicher Pfarrverband* (neighboring parish association), and "teamwork among priests," which were all taken from the pastoral-sociological discussion, could "no longer remain purely theoretical vocabulary."[91] As the canon Wilhelm Stammkötter made clear, the "absolute necessity of painful intervention" also required the typical language of pastoral care to be reevaluated. Criticizing the central pastoral metaphor of the good shepherd, which had dominated the sociographic discourse and "largely continued to command the scene," he argued that it showed "too little of the man who educated twelve apostles and seventy-two disciples, sent them out into the world and rejoiced when they returned to him after successful work."[92] The programmatic demand was no longer to care in paternalistic fashion for a limited circle, but to educate others who could spread the word.

Second, it now seemed possible to justify interparish planning and coordination by pointing to Vatican II. In its decree on the "pastoral office" of the bishops, the Second Vatican Council had prompted a redrawing of diocese boundaries in order to adjust the church's administrative districts to the wider political, administrative, economic, and social structures.[93] The council defined the church's apostolate as a mission that transcended parish boundaries. Priests were supposed to see themselves as "assistants" to bishops and to work actively together on coordinating pastoral care in the diocese as a whole.[94] These documents could be read as an encouragement for pastoral planning at the diocesan level.

Of the experiments in changing pastoral structures pursued in various dioceses from 1967, the *Strukturplan* (structural plan) of the diocese of Münster will be examined in more detail.[95] This stood out among the many new organizational concepts, in part because its implications were far-reaching and intensively discussed within the diocese.[96] It was also accompanied by intensive analysis and advice from the field of organizational research. However, it was not the only concept for reordering diocesan pastoral structures to be designed and evaluated with considerable assistance from sociologists. Academic involvement could also be seen in the formation of parish associations (*Pfarrverbände*). The parish associations drove a structural reform in the diocese of Speyer based on the data provided by a study from the Social Team in Landstuhl. In the diocese of Augsburg, the Social Team, which was also active in the town of Adelsried, drew up the basis of a plan for the "social and church analysis" of the diocese using a series of quantitative analyses in selected towns. There, however, the necessary "substructures" of the urban parishes were based almost exclusively on the results of surveys of church attendance. The reform proposals were thus overwhelmingly created using the instruments and categories of the sociographic discourse.[97]

The *Strukturplan* in the Diocese of Münster

The *Strukturplan* presented at the end of June 1969 was a fifty-page report entitled "Reflections and Suggestions on Pastoral Structures in the Diocese of Münster" (Überlegungen und Vorschläge zur Struktur der Seelsorge im Bistum Münster). The document was the product of a planning group created in 1967 under the leadership of the canon, Wilhelm Stammkötter. The group also consulted Egon Golomb, head of the PSI in Essen. The plan's aim was to ensure, as the Second Vatican Council had intended, that "all people of God" could participate in the process of opinion forming and decision making in the church. To this end, the faithful had to be involved in four "core functions" of the church, which were set out in the introduction of the Strukturplan: service to the world, proclamation of the faith, social service (diakonia), and liturgy (koinonia). The authors drew these distinctions from the New Testament. Seen in this order, however, they also bear striking similarity to the four functions of Talcott Parsons's AGIL paradigm in his general theory of action: adaptation, goal attainment, integration, and latent pattern maintenance.[98] In setting out a model of four functions from the outset, the *Strukturplan* was a child of structural functionalism, which at this time had just reached the peak of its influence in the international sociological discussion.

To implement this schema, the *Strukturplan* specified three levels. First, all four core functions of the church were to be offered from a single point by a so-called *Großpfarrei* (large parish), thus combining traditional territorial divisions with functional ones.[99] As the central project of the *Strukturplan,* the *Großpfarrei* was supposed to encompass between twenty thousand and one hundred thousand Catholics and was comparable in size to a deanery. All laypeople and priests involved in pastoral work were to be deployed based on the principle of the division of labor. A "pastoral conference" for all staff was planned to coordinate this work. The leadership of the *Großpfarrei* was to be in the hands of the parish assembly and a dean appointed for a six-year period at the council's suggestion. The existing parishes were expected to act as a "substructure" of the *Großpfarrei* and would now be described as *kirchliche Gemeinde* (church communities). A "large part" of church life was supposed to take place at this level.[100]

In the second step, the *Strukturplan* moved on to the councils that would "represent" the "people of God" at the different levels of the diocesan church. "Expert committees" were to be formed, ranging from the committee of the *kirchliche Gemeinde,* the council of the *Großpfarrei,* the regional council, and the diocesan council. Each of these "expert committees" corresponded to the four core functions and were thus supposed to enable encounters between the church and the secular "world." The diocesan council was intended to replace the bodies that had previously headed the system of diocesan councils: the diocesan committee, the council of priests, and the pastoral council. In deciding what authority the new body would have, stated the report, it had to be taken into account that the church had been "structured hierarchically from the beginning." Nonetheless, it claimed, this did not have to mean any contradiction with the shared responsibility and decision-making power of the "people of God." Third, the *Strukturplan* made suggestions for restructuring the diocesan administration based on three levels ("production, personnel, finances") adopted from administrative science; it also prompted innovations to improve cooperation and the flow of information in the office of the vicar-general.[101]

In October 1970, Josef Homeyer, head of the schools department of the diocese and member of the planning group, explained the context of the *Strukturplan* to the conference of deans. He pointed to the continual fall in church attendance for over twenty years as an indicator of the fragility of the religious practices that had characterized earlier times. The influence of mass media, education, and occupation meant that every parish effectively had an "intangible" but "extremely effective" alternative "pulpit." The important thing, he argued, was the contradictions in the church's reaction to this development. Some in the church saw this as the result of a policy targeted to push the church away from society. Others saw the secularization and more autonomous nature of different areas of life as giving more freedom to the church. Homeyer described this as "left-wing integrationalism." Still others reacted with "helplessness, resignation and uncertainty," including some priests.[102] Referring directly to a crucial passage in the pastoral constitution on the church in the modern world from the Second Vatican Council, "Gaudium et Spes," Homeyer felt that the church should respond to the situation by reflecting on the autonomy of the profane world described at Vatican II and the joint responsibility of all the "people of God" for realizing their message of salvation in the world at large. "Gaudium et Spes" was one of the most important documents of the Second Vatican Council, in which the council had accepted the "autonomy of earthly affairs" as a key prerequisite of any pastoral activity, thus acknowledging that functional differentiation was a social force the church had to reckon with. Applying this insight to the implementation of the *Strukturplan* in 1970, Homeyer concluded that it implied that the priority of core pastoral activities would shift, based on the four core functions the *Strukturplan* had envisaged.[103] These remarks make it clear that the *Strukturplan* was prompted by the discussion emerging in the late 1960s about the general crisis of the church and its institutional effectiveness. Although the plan did not address the particularly pressing problem of the priest shortage, one parish committee had the impression, not without good reason, that this issue had been "the force behind the plan."[104]

With the approval of the *Geistlicher Rat*, the spiritual council of the diocese, the recently ordained Bishop Tenhumberg distributed the plan to all parish committees and bodies in October 1969. This was supposed to initiate the "broadest possible learning process in the diocese."[105] As the discussion consequently broadened, the number of submitted statements soon overtaxed those in the planning department carrying out such work as a second job. The pastoral department thus employed two qualified sociologists for this task from the spring of 1970. The older of the two, Philipp von Wambolt, had served in the diocese of Münster for some time. Since early 1967, he had worked as a lecturer at the Catholic university in the Chilean city of Valparaíso. When the student revolts began at the university in summer 1968, the visiting lecturer from Germany witnessed the political awakening of democracy in Chile firsthand. Von Wambolt had professionally translated the new situation into a study on structural alternatives in administration and academic organization in Catholic universities in Chile.[106] With this dual experience of being an eyewitness to social revolution and applying organizational sociology, von Wambolt took up his post in Münster in a politicized and euphoric state.[107]

Changing the Structure of the Church

As with sociography and role sociology, the application of organizational sociology initially raised general concerns about transplanting unwieldy and hermeneutically unfamiliar terminology into an area in which the abstract categories of sociological functionalism were thus far unheard of. Bishops were suddenly regarded as "function bearers," and the diocesan pastoral department was compared with the "production department" of an industrial company. The parish committees saw both these developments as "unnecessary."[108] The fears they triggered of a creeping desacralization of the church centered especially on the key concept in the *Strukturplan,* namely, the "structure." Any fundamental criticism of the *Strukturplan,* it was argued, had to illuminate the "self-understanding" of the church that the plan implied. The church, wrote one critic, should be seen as "Christ's foundation" and not as "some sociological phenomenon among others, which is structured by society and changes with it. . . . That [i.e., the fact that it was founded by Christ] is where any change finds the limits of what is permissible."[109]

This placed a clear semantic barrier to the validity of the organizational sociological discourse, which had purposefully set its sights on a fundamental aspect of the concept of "structure": the idea that structure is inseparable from structural change because the elements that form a structure, and the linkages between them, are variable factors that can change in the course of the historical process.[110] Such a standpoint fundamentally contradicted the notion of the church as having been founded by Christ and thus endowed with eternal features. To its critics, the *Strukturplan* thus amply indicated that it would give free reign to "renegades, outsiders, agitators and sectarians." For one thing, the plan cautiously moved toward abolishing compulsory celibacy by suggesting that married men be ordained to work as part-time presbyters. As they perceived "absolute faith in progress" as the "subtext" of the plan, it reminded critics of the church reformer and vicar-general Ignaz von Wessenberg (1774–1860) from Constance, one of the leading proponents of Catholic enlightenment. Moreover, some questioned whether the plan's proposals could in all cases even be reconciled with canon law.[111] Critics were right to point out that, when it came to the arguments about structural reform, this legal question in particular was given little attention compared to the topics raised by sociology. This demonstrates canon law's loss of importance during the Catholic Church's process of scientization before the proclamation of the new Code of Canon Law in 1983 made it appreciate in value under more conservative auspices.[112]

Parish committees' views of the *Strukturplan* reflected the view from below; that is, those of committed members of the parish. They indicate where and why the plan's offer to reorder church organizations failed to match the expectations of ordinary church members. The first concern was that the plan constituted a complete and closed program for reordering pastoral work in a concerted manner. A "precipitous" restructuring, it was claimed, would have a damaging effect if it irreversibly changed the "basis of religious work."[113] In place of abrupt structural change, the parish committees wanted to break up the "narrow, parish-centered mode of thinking" with a gradual "change in style." This, rather than a change in the church's organization, they believed, would be decisive.[114] The parish committees still saw the church as a corporation characterized by the organizational unity of its parts rather than as an organization marked by differences and variability. The *Strukturplan* offered no convincing metaphors with which to describe such an organization, only abstract concepts from theology and organizational sociology.[115] The illustrative function of metaphors, which had made sociography and opinion polling credible to a wide audience, was lacking in the organizational sociology discourse.

Practicing Catholics in the parish committees also felt that the introduction of the *Großpfarrei* threatened to worsen a trend that was already causing difficulty, especially for the "older and infirm" members of the parish. If parts of pastoral provision were outsourced to larger units, the "lack of contact" and "anonymity of individuals" would increase further. The faithful needed to be sure of finding "acknowledgement, respect and inner sanctuary" from clergy who were "personally devoted to their parishioners."[116] At the parish level, the idea of replacing the "all-around priest" with a team of specialists was thus rejected. As one member of the pastoral department in the diocese registered with resignation, people clearly wanted to hold on to the "ideal picture of the all-knowing shepherd who could talk to them about anything and was responsible for everything."[117] Parishioners seeking advice did not want to consult a professional specialist, like they would a dentist or lawyer. Rather, they looked to the priest as an "approachable figure in whom they could place their trust."[118]

Correspondingly, pastoral care was described as personal "help" for other people within this framework. It was suggested that the German term *Seelsorge,* which described pastoral care in the sense of care for the soul, be given up entirely, since pastoral care was not only about souls but also "about care for the person as a whole."[119] It would be incorrect to interpret this as an objection to the religious concept of the "soul." In fact, it reflected a pastoral strategy that aimed to address the individual as a "whole" being. This contrasted with all other functional sub-systems of society, which only ever address the parts of a person that are relevant for their own operations: for instance, in business a customer is addressed with regard to his financial credit, and patients in the health system are addressed with regard to specific malfunctions of their bodies—unless a hospital pastor attends to their spiritual needs. In their contact with the Catholic Church, however—at least as far as the parish assemblies in the diocese of Münster were concerned—people were to be treated as complete individuals, not as the "dividuals" that are generated in the course of their inclusion in politics, education, the economy, and science. This pastoral model insisted on "total integration in service to the word and sacrament" in opposition to the anonymous fragmentation of the individual in the context of functional differentiation.[120]

The reception of the *Strukturplan* in the parishes of the diocese of Münster already hinted at the social model for the church the active laity favored. A parish committee from Marl summarized the main characteristics: "a functional Christian parish must be a manageable size, must have a center and be held together by organic, social and human ties; it must have the characteristics of a family."[121] This invoked the main characteristics and associations of the social entity described by German sociology since Ferdinand Tönnies as a community (*Gemeinschaft*). The parish committee's use of this semantics of community reveals a dimension of the church that the authors of the *Strukturplan* had not taken into account. Whereas they regarded a reorganization of roles against the backdrop of a changing social environment as necessary, the church base (*Basis*) saw such roles as a continual series of interactions among people familiar with one another.[122] This dimension of church organization was missing in the *Strukturplan*. "Informal groups" emerge in every organization due to interaction between its members. Nowhere did the *Strukturplan* recognize and consider such groups and their motivational role in the church organization. Since Elton Mayo's Hawthorne studies, however, modern organizational sociology has assumed that it is precisely these informal groups that enable an organization to function.[123]

The foregoing outlines the aspects of the *Strukturplan* that clearly demonstrate that it was an attempt to use organizational sociological concepts to respond to "secularization." As set out in the introduction to this book, secularization is defined as the *observation* of the consequences of functional differentiation manifested in an organization that is based on the medium of decision making and reflects on this specific context. The *Strukturplan* further complicated this issue by attempting to set rules on how the laity could participate in church decision making through the postconciliar councils of the lay apostolate. It also suggested a new design for these bodies. In opaque language, the plan stated that the "joint decision making" of the councils should not be seen as contradicting the church's hierarchical constitution.[124] This issue raised little interest in the parish committees, however. Only 48 of 111 comments from the diocese of Münster mentioned the decision-making powers of the lay councils at all, and of those just 10 percent were in favor of these bodies holding overall democratic responsibility for pastoral issues. For the authors of the Strukturplan, the extreme disinterest of the laity in their own responsibilities "could not be explained."[125] It is less surprising, however, when we consider that active members of church parish committees tended not to look beyond the narrow realm of their own interactions within the parish, whose ground rules they could help to shape through informal communication with the local priest.

The main result of raising the issue of participation therefore turned out to be that the *Strukturplan* also hit opposition from priests, particularly those of the older generation. After almost thirty years of parish pastoral work and verbal commitment to initiatives for the laity as part of Catholic Action, one Capuchin priest warned emphatically against giving further powers to the laity. Laypeople, he claimed, would only criticize priests, without showing any commitment themselves and with no intention of opposing the "left-wing Catholicism" of the Second Vatican Council. Many parish committees, too, identified the plan with the "typical wave of democratization" of the 1960s. It thus aroused the suspicion that it was calling for questions of belief to be put to the vote.[126] This suspicion was all the more prevalent given the intensive debate since 1968 on the dangers and opportunities of democratizing the church, which was often conducted with categories and arguments that, in the view of the bishops, created a "sociology of religion no longer conscious of its limits."[127]

Two contrary conceptions collided in the argument on democratization. On the one side were those who rejected democratization for illegitimately transplanting the principal of majority decision making from politics to the church, even when they advocated the use of public opinion and of democratic procedures in many areas of the church's work as a corrective force.[128] Opposing them were the advocates of a far-reaching democratization of the church, who saw this as a necessary consequence of the "people of God" theology of Vatican II. For them, democratization was a "fundamental concern of the council" and an overdue step toward stopping the creeping migration away from the church by breaking up hierarchical structures.[129] A notable interpretation of the council in 1972 by sociologist Franz-Xaver Kaufmann, who taught as a professor in Bielefeld, suggested that the question of participation in church decision making was probably only a secondary motive and objective of the call for democratization. More importantly, it expressed the church's need for greater "structural variability" and freedom to act. In a church that was regarded as too rigid, this was supposed to prevent the further drain of people and motivation.[130]

The problem of such democratization through an "intentional increase in complexity" was that it considerably worsened the existing problem of formal organization that had become evident in the debates on the *Großpfarrei* and the functional role of the priest: the need to react to decisions with ever more decisions.[131] Breaking decisions down into further decisions with an elaborate chain of advisory and decision-making bodies increased the need for coordination within the organization and also required each body, first of all, to deal with the problems it had itself created. Conservative critics of the *Strukturplan* had already drawn attention to the "inflationary number of conferences" and the flow of information between different authorities that would be necessary to prepare any decisions. For them, the *Strukturplan* drew a "frightening picture of a convening, advising, minute-taking, minute-sending, minute-receiving and minute-reading, self-absorbed, administrative and administered authority." The church risked suffocating in "overorganization."[132]

Aggravating the problem further, the "specialist committees" of the council bodies were supposed to enable "encounters and confrontations between the church and the world" in the same way at all levels instead of accepting functional differentiation in a vertical sense and allowing different problems to be dealt with relatively autonomously at different levels in the hierarchy. The specialist committees proposed for "adult education," "communication media," or "work with senior citizens"—all examples at the lowest hierarchical level of the "church communities"—inevitably meant that priests' offices received unfiltered information on the confusing array of contact with the social environment and had little chance of reducing its complexity.[133] Despite its basis in the theory of differentiation, the *Strukturplan* failed in its objective of providing parishes and lay councils with structures for overcoming the complexity associated with its necessary aim of opening the church more to the world.

The Prevalence of Face-to-Face Encounters

The decisive judgment of the parish committees in the diocese of Münster in favor of face-to-face interaction included a position statement on the right of all baptized Catholics to be fully included, which the church upheld for dogmatic reasons and as a worldwide organization. These active Catholics, whose own participation went beyond fulfilling the Sunday obligations, assumed either implicitly or explicitly that their own interest in and engagement with the church was sufficient in itself. From their viewpoint, the essence of the church was to be found where Catholics carried out liturgical, charitable, and social work in their community. They placed less importance on the missionary aspiration of reaching all Catholics with the Gospel and providing pastoral care to them. Issues of church organization and its possible reform lay beyond their field of vision.

At the same time, this difference between community interaction and church organization also found expression in the debate between the rival ideas of the "community church" (*Gemeindekirche*) and the "people's church" (*Volkskirche*). This ecclesiological and pastoral discussion took place between academic theologians from 1966/67. However, it quickly attracted wider interest and, with its clear conceptual distinction, soon reached many priests and active laypeople, not least through its presence at the Würzburg Synod.

It was here that Commission IX of the full assembly, which was responsible for "pastoral structures," presented the draft of a "framework for pastoral structures in the diocese" in May 1972. This contained what "for many synod members" was a "new" concept of the religious parish. The traditional concept of the parish community—the *Pfarrgemeinde*—was to be abolished. In its place would come communities, or *Gemeinde*, based on the "substructures" of the parish: territorial *Gemeinde* in residential areas would be supplemented by *Gemeinde* "relating to people's social and functional ties (occupation, leisure activities, stage of life)." When the German Bishops' Conference immediately raised "serious theological and canonical objections" to this concept of *Gemeinde*, the pastoral sociologist Lothar Roos felt compelled to add his voice to the debate. In an extensive manuscript with which he sought to influence the ongoing discussion in the German Bishops' Conference, Roos created a genealogy of the controversy that had now come to "public attention." Commission IX had sought to "prove its authority" by pointing to the *Gemeinde* (parish community) fascicle of the "Pastorale", a multi-volume manual with guidelines for pastoral service. A look at the sources cited there identifies Norbert Greinacher's 1966 book on the church in urban society, *Kirche in der städtischen Gesellschaft*, as the starting point for the concept of the "community church."[134]

In this study of the effects of urbanization on *Kirchlichkeit*, the different forms of practiced piety that constitute an active church member, and the organization of pastoral care, Greinacher had for the first time drawn the ultimate conclusions from his pastoral-sociological interest in the secular trend of modern society. Greinacher was convinced that society had become so differentiated and rationalized that the "end of the *Volkskirche* as a social form was foreseeable." Despite differing and sometimes contradictory theological underpinnings, the term *Volkskirche*, or people's church, basically encapsulated the claim of both Protestants and Catholics that the Christian churches still represented society as a whole—that they were public churches in the sense that they were entitled to speak out in public on all social, political, and cultural issues. The notion of the people's church represented the claim that the church was present in all walks of life. Yet, according to Greinacher, this assertion no longer fit reality. The societal configuration in which the church had the "function of integrating" society as a whole and assimilated itself into social structures had ended. Greinacher located the typical features of the people's church in the special importance of its "hierarchical structure" and "central authority." "Membership out of conviction" and the "personal faith" of individual Catholics were only of secondary importance to this form of organization. It was revealing that Greinacher saw the church's loss of function in the course of social differentiation as a "cleansing process" that would allow it to focus once more on its "authentic function." Only this concentration on its core business, to use an economic metaphor, would enable it to gain respect again in society at large.[135] Clearly based on the notion of functional differentiation, Greinacher's reading of the secularization process was surprisingly positive.

The contrast between Greinacher's optimistic view and the all-encompassing crisis mentality that otherwise prevailed in the church at this time can only be understood by taking into account the hopeful vision of the community church that Greinacher believed should replace the antiquated model of the people's church. His confidence in the irrevocable nature of these historic developments is clear in his assertion that the development of the community church was "unstoppable." He based this faith in the will of God on the expectation that, in its new form as a "community of love," the church would turn into an "event" rather than a structure, into something that would be celebrated as a precious moment in time. The community church was based on the "principal of volunteerism" and demanded an "openness to faith" from its members. In this model of interaction, the church was to be found everywhere people believed in Christ and was created by their act of coming together to hear his word and celebrate the Eucharist.[136] The community church offered a vision of a church that would provide space for personal interaction between Catholics and that would be carried by the mutual trust of its members and their personal relationships with one another, rather than by a hierarchy of largely unfamiliar priests.[137]

Norbert Greinacher himself criticized the *Strukturplan* in a confidential memo from the perspective of the "community church." Given the backdrop of this utopian church conceived "from the bottom up," the model of the *Großpfarrei* set out in the *Strukturplan* gave him the impression of being suspended in midair, without foundation. At best, it might have a "subsidiary" function once the "church community" was established.[138] Such conceptual disputes in the community of Catholic pastoral sociologists were marginal, however, compared to the criticism that the concept of the community church faced from church officialdom and from theologians who represented the majority position in the church. However, despite their criticism, they did accept the analysis of social development on which the concept of the community church was based and the suggestion that the church was in crisis. After all, a social scientist like Joseph Höffner could do little to dispute such findings, especially given that they were based on the sociographic discourse that he had worked to anchor in West German pastoral work since the 1950s.[139]

The criticism of the community church model was not about individual arguments, but rather about the legitimacy of a vision based on expectations of the future wholly different from those of church officialdom. The concept of a church organization built from the community upward emerged from the belief that the top-down hierarchical stewardship of the church could no longer provide any lasting integration in functionally differentiated modern society. Thus, the status quo had to be discarded, even though some of the core features such as finance still looked secure. Meanwhile, critics of the community church concept insisted that this future development was by no means inevitable and that the advocates of the community church were being too hasty. They armed their arguments with ideas taken from other social science discourses in earlier phases of scientization. Karl Forster used the data from the Würzburg Synod polls as evidence that a large number of Catholics still expected the church to be involved in areas such as peace policy and social justice. The effectiveness of providing a "united" social presence, he believed, was an argument for maintaining the structures of the people's church. Otto B. Roegele likewise claimed that the synod polls exposed the thesis of the "end of the people's church" as the "wishful thinking of a school of theology." In the spirit of sociography's missionary impetus, Lothar Roos insisted that the church should attend to those estranged from it rather than retreat into an elite community of "pure" Catholics.[140]

Farewell to an Inclusive Public Church?

To the extent that the community church was also a sociological thesis about the development of the church as an organization, it revealed a fundamental weakness of the discourse of organizational research in the Catholic Church. Following the intervention of statistics, sociography, and opinion polling, with the concomitant observations about secularization, by around 1970 the Catholic Church had reached a point at which adjustments and structural change appeared inevitable. A proposal as extensive as that of the community church, however, was left hanging, since it was not based on a fully worked-out organizational sociological analysis. Instead, it relied on the vivid metaphors of the semantics of *Gemeinschaft* that had been cultivated in the wake of sociologist Ferdinand Tönnies's work. Such use of language fell victim to sociological criticism, which, using examples from the sociology of towns and local communities (*Gemeinde* in German parlance, not *Gemeinschaft*), was able to prove that the notion of a *Gemeinschaft* based on shared emotions was factually untenable. Questions such as how a community church should deal with internal conflicts or whether it should insist on extensive "conformity" revealed the model's conceptual limits.[141]

However, whether the thesis of an unstoppable trend toward the community church was realistic was not decided by debates among pastoral sociologists and theologians, but by the decisions or nondecisions of the church as an organization. One important aspect in this was that it had to be made sufficiently clear that church membership constituted a personal decision to take part in an orga-nization. This stood in contrast to the dogmatic view of membership in the Cath-olic Church as an automatic outcome of baptism, which required no individual decision. Even formally leaving the church could not erase the Christian qualities imparted through baptism. The concept of the community church assumed that its members possessed a willingness to voluntarily join the church and engage with the faith—a willingness the church could utilize as a source of motivation in implementing its decisions.[142]

This assumption had specific consequences for the church's sacraments, par-ticularly that of confirmation. One priest in the Lower Rhine region defined confirmation as the "sacrament of maturity," which should hence only be administered within a "mature congregation." For this reason he opposed administering the sacrament in schools, even though the rite was, in any case, probably no longer conducted for all baptized Catholics. This priest spoke out against the idea that "the church should be pushed to reduce itself to a smaller, more 'healthy' size." Yet he still believed the church had inevitably to confront a "changed reality":

> The transition from people's church to community church is a painful process, but it will not be helped by ignoring or trying to disguise it. It can bring hope, provided that we do not allow our parishes to slide blindly into it, but lead them seriously, watchfully and trustfully with every step. It need be no bad thing if confirmation takes on the character of a decision, which baptism no longer has. . . . The larger the structure, the less the individual feels responsible for it.[143]

This statement not only reveals that the concept of the community church had rapidly been widely received among large segments of the laity and clergy. It also indicates the willingness of some priests to take their own path, together with their parish, without waiting for their superiors to give instructions. The need to heighten the importance of confirmation as a voluntary commitment to church membership was also raised at the Würzburg Synod. A paper on the sacraments, and especially its recommendation of a minimum age of twelve years, makes clear its ambition to turn confirmation into an individual "declaration of faith" and to emphasize its voluntary nature.[144]

If the vitality and independence of a community based on decisions of faith was favored "with clearly more enthusiastic objectives" over the apparatus of the established church, observers with a background in sociology nonetheless regarded the development of the community church concept suspiciously, per-ceiving signs of "sect formation" in the Catholic Church.[145] Community church proponents insisted that such a structure would not be a ghetto-like sect, content to leave the secular world to its own devices, but that it would have a new "sense of responsibility" and a "sense of mission to the wider world."[146] This indicates that the debate about the community church lacked what had been a particularly notable feature of the *Strukturplan* in the diocese of Münster and had set it apart from the plans of other dioceses at that time: an adequately conceptualized and worked-out plan based on organizational sociology, shaped not only by ideology and political values, but also by sociological categories.

Everyone involved in the discussion of the *Strukturplan* was conscious, however, that an important criterion—perhaps the decisive one—for thoroughly applying sociological knowledge was missing. There had been no "analysis of the situation" through empirical social research, which would have captured the actual flow of communication in parishes and the church bureaucracy, as well as the attitudes of those involved.[147] This differed significantly from both the sociographic and opinion polling discourses, which had been legitimized primarily through their empirical gaze on certain aspects of social life. For the pastoral planning that was meant to follow the *Strukturplan,* the pastoral office in Münster discussed the necessity of "surveying the base" but rejected the idea on the grounds that it would delay work on the project.[148]

Nevertheless, the planning group was far from inactive after the publication of its *Strukturplan* in summer 1969. The sociologist von Wambolt dedicated himself to analyzing the debate on the plan within the diocese. Individual members of the group worked on two linked schemes. One was a "staffing plan for a *Großpfarrei*," which would encompass the reformulation and diversification of areas of pastoral work anticipated by the *Strukturplan*. This redefinition of member roles demonstrates once more that the *Strukturplan* saw the church as an organization in the way that organizational sociologists understand the term. The staffing plan made specific suggestions for the deployment of pastoral workers and lay theologians, which awakened interest among planners in other dioceses, too. The planning group also produced a manuscript on "pastoral care in the church community" in order to flesh out the understanding of parish community (*Gemeinde*) inherent in the *Strukturplan*. Added to this were suggestions for initial experiments with the model of the *Großpfarrei,* for which the *Strukturplan* had already earmarked the new town of Wulfen, founded in the early 1960s. Also on the planning group's agenda was a concept for the advanced training of priests, an organizational plan for the office of the vicar-general, and a cost plan.[149]

The planning group soon became convinced, however, that the proposals and drafts they were putting forward beyond the original text of the *Strukturplan* were no longer wanted and that the die had long been cast against them. Their reason for drawing this conclusion was that the bishop, vicar-general, and spiritual council, as the most important collective decision-making body in the diocese, had not discussed their submissions. In fact, the planning group had not even succeeded in generating a provisional response or confirmation of receipt. Faced with the reality of the internal communication structures of a typical Catholic diocesan administration, "amazement and disquiet" spread throughout the planning group. Its members expressed their annoyance in a letter to Bishop Tenhumberg in April 1971, which they wrote in the run-up to a press conference intended to report on the results of the discussions of the *Strukturplan*. It was already clear at this stage that the ideas of the *Strukturplan* were only to be implemented selectively at best.[150]

Adapting to Functional Differentiation

As Bishop Tenhumberg announced at the press conference, the (selective) implementation of the Strukturplan was to proceed through four measures: first, the formation of parish associations—see below for more detail on this; second, the regionalization of the diocesan structure; third, the formation of a diocesan council alongside the existing diocesan committee and council of priests; and finally, a restructuring within the office of the vicar-general. Up to this point, the office had been divided along the lines of religious "estates" with differing charismatic quality. Hence, there were separate departments for priests, religiosi (i.e., members of religious orders), and the laity. The latter was again subdivided into units for married men and women and unmarried men and women, and separate pastoral services for professional groups such as peasants or artisans. This was basically a hierarchical structure reflecting the distinctive charismatic qualities of priests and the laity. It was now replaced with separate departments for pastoral care, Caritas work, schools, personnel, and administration, which followed the imperatives of functional differentiation.[151] These were not exactly the departments that the *Strukturplan* had planned for the diocesan administration. Alongside personnel and finance, the plan had placed pastoral care centrally and divided it according to the four core functions of service to the world, proclamation of the faith, social service, and liturgy.[152] Nevertheless, at least at the top of the diocesan organization in Münster, it did represent a first reaction to this form of social differentiation. The newly created departments had not, however, been given any criteria for objectives, efficiency, or rationality with which they could judge the success of their work. The *Strukturplan* measured the success of church administration in terms of whether it provided the "conditions for church life to expand." This essentially contained the tautological call to interpret the church's four core functions as its objective. It was clear only implicitly that success meant working as far as possible in accordance with the "people of God" theology that had emerged from Vatican II.[153]

None of this was especially problematic, at least from the perspective of modern organizational sociology, which recognized that organizations always pursue several objectives that to some extent contradict one another, that they can change their most important goals without substantial damage, and that the realization of self-defined core objectives does not always guarantee an organization's future.[154]

What was a problem, however, was the question of whether organizational sociology had found sufficient acceptance outside Münster for other diocesan administrations to view both the administrative changes in the administration themselves and their evaluation using criteria of rationality and efficiency as legitimate. Precisely this question was discussed in 1969 at the conference of the heads of German pastoral offices (*Seelsorgeamtsleiter*) using the slightly different example of the "Trier model." A management consultant in the diocese of Trier had divided the ordinariate into three departments responsible for information, strategy, and pastoral services, respectively. Erich Klausener, who represented the diocese of Berlin at this conference, thought that the church should avoid the corporate world's model of monitoring target fulfillment through efficiency. "Even if no one listens to us," he argued, "it does not mean that we are wrong. In the kingdom of God, one man reaps while another sows." Other participants countered that although differences needed to be acknowledged, the church could "to some extent" be seen as a service company.[155]

The view of Klausener, as head of the pastoral department in the Berlin diocese, must certainly come as a surprise. It moved, seemingly impassively, beyond quantitative *Kirchlichkeit* as the criterion for judging the success of the church's work. This criterion had acted as the central measure in the statistical, sociographic, and even opinion polling discourses, and shaped these forms of knowledge accordingly. In the context of the organizational sociological and ecclesiological thinking dominant around 1970, this preeminence now began to wane. Thus, a primary goal of the new pastoral conception had to be avoiding "Potemkin villages and waxwork figures" in pastoral care.[156] In view, too, of the crisis mentality that characterized these years and of the priest shortage as an important aspect of pastoral planning, this represented an explicit change in priorities. In the past, the goal had been to proclaim the Christian message of salvation to the wider world and thus to secure the quantifiable circle of church activity. In the context of understanding the church as an organization, many church figures were happy to imagine a future in which they could carry on as before without sustaining too much damage.

Both proponents and opponents of church planning regarded planning under different auspices from the political planning occurring at the same time. The political arena was experiencing pronounced tension between the technical viability of planning, its foundation in the social sciences, and its sociopolitical self-conception. This led from the high expectations in the reform euphoria of the late 1960s to the sobering experience of the limits of what was possible and of political control in the early 1970s.[157] With the exception of a few pastoral theologians, the church did not greet the beginning of the planning process with hopeful expectation, but rather with a diffuse yet pervasive feeling of disorientation and perhaps even despair. Josef Homeyer expressed this anxiety at the conference of deans in Münster in 1970, concluding his presentation of the

Strukturplan with the words: "To recognize or even conjecture a possible pastoral answer to our confused and confusing situation ought to perhaps bring about a little more self-confidence in our mission of salvation, a little more security and enjoyment."[158]

Once Bishop Tenhumberg held the press conference in April 1971 presenting the results of their work, the members of the Münster planning group saw their work as done. In particular, Josef Homeyer, the head of the schools department in the diocese, called for the group to be disbanded and its tasks transferred to a department dedicated to "planning issues," which in future would pay particular attention to the parish associations. As a result of these external pressures, but on its members' own initiative, the planning group was dissolved after a "final discussion" with the bishop in 1971.[159] The concept of the *Großpfarrei* and all the associated deliberations on how to react appropriately to specialization and functional differentiation in territorial pastoral care were quietly dropped. At the conference of deans in autumn 1970, Homeyer had still highlighted the special feature of the planning carried out in the diocese of Münster: they had not followed the example of other dioceses such as Aachen and moved immediately to form parish associations, instead wanting to initially discuss their own models.[160] The following contributions to the discussion by the deans in this conference made it unmistakably clear, however, that they regarded this as a superfluous detour. While some emphasized that parishes and priests needed to open up in order to overcome widespread parochial thinking, skepticism reigned as to the chances of this change in attitude actually materializing. Bishop Tenhumberg is likely to have gained the impression from this discussion that the idea of the *Großpfarrei* simply could not be implemented, especially given the extensive resistance in the parish committees. Summarizing the contributions of the deans in the conference in autumn 1970, he stated that there was a "majority will" to retain the "existing structures" of the parishes and deaneries and to establish parish associations within the deaneries.[161]

Incremental Reform through Parish Associations

The *Strukturplan* had only mentioned the parish associations, or *Pfarrverbände,* in passing, seeing them as nothing more than a possible "preliminary step" on the path to a future *Großpfarrei*. By the end of 1971 it was clear not only in Münster, but in all West German dioceses, that the traditional parish and thus the dominance of territorial pastoral care would remain untouched.[162] No fundamental reordering of the competencies or working methods of the central diocesan administrations took place anywhere. With the parish associations, the dioceses favored a model that anticipated a limited degree of cooperation between individual parishes. In the early 1970s it was thus foreseeable that structural planning in church organization would in future pursue "practical" solutions but restrict itself to options that would not seek to change the system and that were ultimately "retrospective."[163] Each parish association was composed of between three and five parishes that formed working associations legally defined by statute, yet also retained their independence. The core of this cooperation was a pastoral conference meeting every two weeks, which involved all full-time pastoral staff. These gatherings no longer included only priests, but also an increasing number of laypeople who held new or redesigned roles—for example, the lay theologians who worked as pastoral assistants. After completing a degree in theology, these individuals worked primarily in the social and charitable areas, in religious education and in catechesis, and developed groups of laity within the parish independently. The (female) professional role of the *Gemeindereferentin,* relabeled *Seelsorgehelferin* (assistant for pastoral care) in the 1920s, was taken up by qualified female assistants from professional schools and colleges, who assisted the parish clergy but could also take on independent tasks in parish work.[164]

Cooperation between a number of parishes in a parish association made it possible to set particular emphases and determine how the work would be divided. The basic model of defining pastoral responsibility in territorial terms, however, was left untouched. The church was thus everywhere set firmly on a course of using its traditional organizational structures to deal with the rapid process of secularization, the shortage of priests, and faith transmission—phenomena that were perceived as crises from the late 1960s onward. This decision in favor of the parish associations rather than deeper reforms in church organization did not mean that the process of scientization had come to an abrupt end. It was symptomatic, however, of a certain sense of disillusionment in the early 1970s following the first wave of social science–based structural reform models. The "enthusiasm for the social sciences" initially associated with planning had "cooled markedly" within just a few years. This was primarily a result of the mountains of paperwork covered in "tables, graphs, and percentages" piling up in the diocesan planning offices. Everywhere, people became convinced that the sociological calculations and models associated with total planning were grossly out of proportion to the returns achieved thus far.[165]

The fate of the *Strukturplan* in particular suggests that the comprehensive application of organizational research failed first and foremost because of the organization itself: it was due to the blatant rejection of the reform plans from active members of the laity, the open opposition of the deans, and, not least, the marginal position of the working group tasked with planning within the diocesan administration. All future planning thus had to be smaller in scale, formulate its working stages more precisely, and, above all, make its objectives more specific. By setting out the core functions of the church, the *Strukturplan* had formulated a sort of "global objective" at the most abstract level. However, this not only had to be translated into concrete working steps and instructions, but also had to be broken down at the level of everyday parish work if it was to be of any use in practice. Without these specifics, planning would remain a nonbinding blueprint.[166]

Part of the practical work of the parish associations was precisely to conduct this scaling down of overall planning objectives to a series of specific intermediate objectives adapted to their local situations. Planning departments worked in various West German dioceses from the early 1970s. They were dedicated to issues such as the need for new priests and spatial planning. With their statistical and sociogeographic instruments, they primarily provided the external framework for the development of parish associations by working on proposals for their spatial makeup and demarcation.[167] In the work of the parish associations, planning initially meant nothing more than setting priorities for pastoral care and specifying medium-term objectives to be achieved in these fields. To this end, they deployed a bundle of concepts from the social sciences. However, these no longer derived from pure organizational sociology, but constituted a colorful and flexible mixture of methods, working techniques, and scattered fragments of academic knowledge.

For example, the statute for parish associations in the diocese of Münster was accompanied by the search for continuing education and training programs in working techniques appropriate for the parish association. This was the task of a specially created six-member "team" comprising three staff of the office of the vicar-general, a pastoral assistant, a certified sociologist, and a social work educator. This team chose to work with the Gesellschaft für christliche Öffentlichkeitsarbeit in order to test various models. It also aimed to train staff in the pastoral department so that, after a certain period, they could carry out the project-based development of parish associations independently. In the diocese of Münster, the program introducing participants to the work of a parish association initially involved carrying out a local opinion survey. The results formed the basis for developing a "pastoral plan" or, "to put it more modestly," "setting out pastoral emphases," as well as a timetable for these.[168] Depending on the chosen emphasis, social scientific expert knowledge was then introduced by hiring an appropriate member of staff at the parish association level. A typical emphasis was intensifying church youth work. Until well into the 1960s, priests themselves or chaplains were in charge of church youth groups. By the early 1970s, the priests were replaced with a teacher or social worker who typically came equipped with the emancipated and critical pedagogy popular at universities in the wake of the Frankfurt School of critical theory.[169]

Employing qualified specialists was not the only way social science–influenced practices found their way into the new parish associations. There was also a fundamental reorientation of the church's training and career paths for pastoral occupations. This set in motion a radical devaluation of academic theology and, with it, the hierarchical importance and superiority of the priest as a teacher of theology in the church. This process continues to the present day. It has fundamentally changed the profile of professional performance roles in the church, as these are now conceptualized as providers of specific religious services.

Hermann-Josef Spital reflected as early as 1971 on the social foundations of this process and on the necessity of new training paths. At this time, in the diocese of Münster there was a ratio of ten pastoral workers with an academic background in theology to every nonacademic pastoral assistant (*Seelsorgehelferin*). This mirrored a social structure whose outlook was shaped by Christianity. The result, Spital wrote, was that pastoral work could largely limit itself to preaching the Gospel and administering the sacraments. In the "pluralist" world of the present, however, it had to conduct pastoral actions and organize relationships that in the past "emerged more or less spontaneously." In order to generate the necessary discussion about faith in "the most diverse groups," a model of training based primarily on preaching that attached "similarly little" value to pastoral education was no longer suitable. It was also evident that many "young people" studied theology because their process of "reflecting on their belief" was not yet complete. Intensifying pastoral work required "specially trained" but nonacademic staff who were to be educated in long-distance courses or seminars.[170]

For the practical implementation of these ideas, Spital worked with the personnel department in the diocesan administration and with the Akademie für Jugendfragen (Academy for Youth Issues), a specialist training facility in the diocese of Münster. The aim was to come up with "project-oriented" training offerings for pastoral care. This served to educate pastoral assistants in the human sciences and at the same time sharpened their career profile. Full-time church staff were trained over a four-year period in block sessions that took place three times a year. In addition, there were short-term training measures for part-time staff. The curriculum included a set of psychological, pedagogical, and group dynamics methods. These were supposed to teach pastoral assistants the soft skills thought necessary for group-based work in the parishes and a cooperative style of working. Alongside "public relations," this comprised "pastoral counseling," "nondirective counseling techniques," and a series of other techniques from group dynamics.[171] These courses found many ways to practice "forms of cooperation between different occupational groups" in order to create step-by-step the team players that the *Strukturplan* had required but been unable to provide in practical terms. Trainees were to be encouraged to develop "critical reflection of their own occupational role," and course participants were thus closely supervised.[172]

These reform plans also had consequences for the training of priests. Some seminarians and recently ordained clergy had already been calling for greater inclusion of psychology and sociology in the curriculum since the mid-1960s. The Würzburg Synod repeated this call ten years later—an indication that little had changed in practice in the meantime.[173] The diocese of Münster reacted by extending the training on offer. As well as courses for priests organized by years after ordination, further training courses were offered beginning in 1972 on specific topics and were open to priests of all levels of experience. The themes included "opportunities and limits of the sermon," "conversation techniques," and an "introduction to group dynamics from a pastoral-psychological perspective."[174]

Theological Reflections on Pastoral Planning

In the 1970s there were also initial attempts to accompany and steer the process of church planning through theological reflection; that is, to create a "theology of planning."[175] The first major analysis of this type, a book published in 1976, clearly emphasized the dangers and limits of church planning that the technocratic approach to the church as an organization posed. There was a fundamental difference, this argument proposed, between church planning and the kind of rational behavior typically seen in companies: the objective of church planning was not to "preserve the church organization" but to "live out the Christian faith" in the form of "human interaction."[176] The danger lay in the tendency of church planning, with the use of "modern technologies of social engineering," to try to control the manifestation of belief rather than create space for the "freedom" and "spontaneity" of faith to unfold. Alongside the "plurality of the church's provision," the "voluntary nature" of faith had to be the aim and starting point of all church planning.[177]

In his analysis of the diverging views on the *Strukturplan* in the parish committees, Philipp von Wambolt also attached central importance to the freedom and privatization of religious decisions. Von Wambolt placed those who sought a cautious adjustment to social structures (position A) alongside those who hoped for a complete rebuilding of the church organization (C). In between the two poles lay a compromise position (B). Von Wambolt thought this compromise insufficient and thus proposed an "A-B-C program." In essence, this stated that the "church's salvation" was to be found in the existence of "different groups of opinion." In this "pluralistic" view, the "freedom of the church's social space" had to apply to all formal and informal groups in the church and could not be limited "to a greater extent than necessary" from above.[178] From a sociological viewpoint, von Wambolt thus called decisively for a church organization based on personal freedom, individualization, and pluralism, as did later theological reflections on church planning.

Von Wambolt drew his conclusions from observing the de facto pluralism in the parishes, which he thought the church should officially approve. At the same time, the pastoral department in the diocese of Münster was experiencing difficulties in consistently applying the modern idea of freedom and acceptance of a more individualized approach to religion—a problem that is familiar to the church to this day. The department's staff were working at this time on a draft of a pastoral plan, the first version of which was discussed and approved collectively in February 1971. The ideas formulated in it later led to the *Communio* plan implemented by Bishop Reinhard Lettmann in 1980. Unlike the *Strukturplan,* this draft was no longer based on the basic functions and core structures of the church. Instead, it conceived of a society marked by "individualization and pluralization" as the backdrop for pastoral care. In response, it attempted to take account of these tendencies with a pastoral strategy based "consistently on the individual."[179]

A careful reading of the texts written in preparation for this pastoral plan shows unmistakably that the concept of individual religious freedom was only considered in a very formal sense. The introduction of one text, for example, made reference to a conciliar declaration on religious freedom, in which the individual's "right to freedom" was postulated as the "starting point" for all the church's activities and was to be respected at all times. It is of secondary importance for our purposes whether this focus on the church's activities was an appropriate interpretation of this particular conciliar text.[180] The crucial point was that the discourse on pastoral planning used the conciliar texts to legitimize a model based on the "personality" of the individual. The freedom of the individual was, however, immediately relativized again by the "truth of revelation," which "applies to all people" and has "binding force" on everyone. Although the draft text of the pastoral plan finally approved in February 1971 postulated the "development of conscience" as a future task of church pastoral care, it did not seek to forego the "obedience structure of faith." The word of the Lord could not be a matter of "personal choice," nor could faith be "reduced to an individualist piety of 'God and the soul.'"[181] An earlier version of the text even used the term *Volksgemeinschaft* (people's community), which had been a centerpiece of Nazi ideology, without any reflection on its historical connotations. In this people's community, the text stated, believers were to live as a people "chosen by God and ordered according to his wishes."[182]

The pastoral plan created in Münster in 1971 ultimately made it clear where the meaning of the appeal to individuals' religious freedom was to be found. It was by no means intended to reconceive the church as a "mere intermediary" organization with the task of "communicating" and "strengthening" individuals' preexisting faith in God.[183] Such a model based on individual faith would have matched that of the Protestant Churches, denounced here as "Pietist." The Protestants used the medium of faith that connected "God and the soul" as a motivational resource for building and stabilizing multistructured, complex forms of spiritual communication. In the Catholic Church, meanwhile, the individual's faith remained dependent on the hierarchical institution of the church as the only body that could dispense grace. Given the changing social environment, however, a "passive reception of the church's faith" could no longer suffice. This form of belief was becoming increasingly unstable and did not provide adequate motivation for members of the organization to become actively involved. The era of catechism-based faith had irreversibly come to an end. Individuals now had to be instructed to bring their "own experience (e.g., a discussion of their belief with a brother [in faith]) to the church." Understood in this sense, freedom represented nothing other than an acceptance that one's own commitment was essential. The task of pastoral planning was to provide the appropriate forms of communication—core circles, confession, and group dynamics methods of "training for working together"—so that individuals would continue to feel comfortable in the womb of the mother church in the future. After the failure of the reform plans based on organizational research, the diocese of Münster turned to methods from the social sciences to control and improve communication in small groups.[184]

Conclusion: A Functionalist Reform Agenda for the Church

From 1965, the sober language of sociological functionalism and organizational optimization found its way into the Catholic Church in the form of role and organizational sociology. Beginning with the occupational crisis of priests and the overburdening and extension of their role profile, concepts of structural adjustment found their way in just a few years to the top decision-making bodies of the West German Catholic Church. These concepts were applied in response to society's increasing functional differentiation. The attempts that had begun everywhere to reform the structures of pastoral provision were also marked by the categorical framework of functionalism. As the experience of the *Strukturplan* in the diocese of Münster shows, however, comprehensive organizational reform encompassing both the parish offices and the offices of vicar-generals was unachievable.

From the early 1970s, all West German dioceses moved to a strategy in which decisions on how to adapt to the demands of functional differentiation were made by means of measures such as the formation of parish associations and the regionalization of dioceses. New organizational structures of parish pastoral care were not linked comprehensively to the work of the offices of vicar-generals, as had been envisaged in the *Strukturplan*. With the creation of parish associations and the increased use of laypeople as professional pastoral workers, the future course of the church's scientization also shifted. No longer would scientization focus on the planning departments of the vicar-generals' offices and their project-based work; rather, in more incremental fashion, it would focus on the small groups and further educational provision of the parish associations. In formal terms, the Catholic Church remained a hierarchically structured organization even after Vatican II, both in its "internal constitution in accordance with canon law and in its ecclesiological self-interpretation." Nevertheless, it would be misleading to describe the church as a "decidedly nonmodern organization" that did not make changes in response to the socio-structural environment of functional differentiation.[185]

The assumption that the Catholic Church is a nonmodern institution reflects the fact that "much less fuss is made about the hierarchical structure of a modern business than the hierarchical structure of the church," as Wilhelm Stammkötter noted with a touch of resignation in 1972.[186] However, the modernity of an organization is not decided on the issue of centralized competencies, but on how it connects membership decisions to decisions about member roles, and thereby reacts to social differentiation by forming internal structures. If we focus on the church's legal norms and ecclesiological self-description, we underestimate the extent to which such forms of structural change took place. The latter can only be identified with the help of sociology. The modernity of the Catholic Church is not to be measured against the normative standards of Protestant theology, in which the reformer Sebastian Franck (1499–1542) first called for the fraternal community of an "invisible spiritual church."[187] Rather, it should be measured by the extent to which it dealt with the complexity resulting from its own decisions. The central question facing any modern organization is not who makes the final decision but which organizational forms can best relate the consequences of final decisions to the social environment. Posing this question reveals the unintended consequences reform attempts such as the *Strukturplan* had, even though their primary objectives were blocked. After all, parish associations, which were essentially derived from the *Strukturplan*, brought about an enormous increase in the importance of professional laypeople working in pastoral care. This not only represented an organization-specific reaction to the consequences of functional differentiation, but also fundamentally changed the priest's position in the parish. This was the case even though there was no reform of compulsory celibacy, the very issue to which role sociology had been applied in a failed attempt to reconfigure the occupational profile of the priesthood.

From a sociological viewpoint, however, the all-too-rapid leap to the parish association as the preferred form of labor division and cooperation in the early 1970s created other organizational problems. These issues seemed to indicate a shortage rather than an excess of hierarchical management. The heads of pastoral offices stated as early as 1969 that the decisive problem of church structures lay in the immense communicative gap between the diocesan authority and the parishes that served as the "production plants" of pastoral care.[188] The *Strukturplan* attempted to respond to this with a sophisticated system of information processing and distribution that would operate in both directions. In reality, the forms of membership practiced in the parishes and the rules of church organization grew less and less connected in the 1970s. This heterarchical structure led observers schooled in Weber's and Troeltsch's categories of sociology of religion to describe the Catholic Church as leaning toward becoming a "sect."[189]

In contrast to the field of role sociology, the attempts made around 1970 to anchor organizational sociology within the church, and which nowhere else reached the same level of intensity as in the diocese of Münster, could not be implemented in the long run. The decline of church organization diagnosed in the late 1970s continued apace. This was the decisive difference between church planning and political planning, which was intensively discussed and put into practice in the same period. There were wide-reaching parallels between the political sphere and the Catholic Church with regard to their social science–based models and intentions of steering social change.[190] The important difference was in the point of departure: church planning did not set off full of optimism, but with the expectation of an advancing crisis. The disillusionment with the complexity of planning merged seamlessly into the general mood of decline that already existed.

In the meantime, the "clients" and members of the church no longer expressed their discontent through "voice," as they had in 1968, but increasingly made use of the "exit" option.[191] The first to leave were those who, with a sociologically educated view, recognized that the Catholic Church no longer satisfied their need for religious communication.[192] Christians remaining in the church could console themselves with the hope that the church would exist in future as a "small community" or "small flock." Interestingly, both conservative theologians such as Joseph Ratzinger and progressive figures like Karl Rahner agreed on this point.[193] This "defensive ideology" of the "small flock" compensated for the "feelings of frustration" triggered by the continual decline in churchgoers and the number of people paying church tax, which cast a blight on all pastoral efforts in the 1970s.[194] The idea of the "small flock" thus acted as the functional equivalent of an objective sociological analysis of church organization.

Notes

1. For the text of the encyclical, see Heinrich Denzinger, *Kompendium der Glaubensbekenntnisse und kirchlichen Lehrentscheidungen,* 37th ed., ed. Peter Hünermann (Freiburg, 1991), 1046–58.

2. Cited in Amitai Etzioni, "Industrial Sociology: The Study of Economic Organizations," in *Complex Organizations: A Sociological Reader,* ed. Amitai Etzioni (New York, 1964), 130.

3. See the brilliant analysis by Michael Ruck, "Ein kurzer Sommer der konkreten Utopie—Zur westdeutschen Planungsgeschichte der langen 60er Jahre," in *Dynamische Zeiten: Die 60er Jahre in den beiden deutschen Gesellschaften,* ed. Axel Schildt, Detlef Siegfried, and Karl Lammers (Hamburg, 2000), 362–401.

4. Some introductions to organizational research include Amitai Etzioni, *Soziologie der Organisationen* (Munich, 1967); James G. March and Herbert A. Simon, *Organizations* (New York, 1958), esp. 83–111 and 136–212; Mary Jo Hatch, *Organization Theory: Modern, Symbolic and Postmodern Perspectives* (Oxford, 1997), esp. 267–81 on the premises of rationality; Robert D. McPhee and Pamela Zaug, "Organizational Theory, Organizational Communication, Organizational Knowledge, and Problematic Integration," *Journal of Communication* 51 (2001): 574–91; on religious organizations in particular, see James A. Beckford, *Religious Organization: A Trend Report and Bibliography* (The Hague and Paris, 1975); J. Kenneth Benson and James H. Dorsett, "Toward a Theory of Religious Organizations," *Journal for the Scientific Study of Religion* 10 (1971): 138–51; Luhmann, *Funktion,* 272–316.

5. See the argument by Nils Brunsson, *The Irrational Organization: Irrationality as a Basis for Organizational Action and Change* (Chichester, UK, and New York, 1985).

6. Quote: Hartmann Tyrell, "Religionssoziologie," *GG* 22 (1996): 446; Thomas Luckmann, *The Invisible Religion* (New York, 1967).

7. Etzioni, *Organisationen,* 38–82.

8. See Benson and Dorsett, *Organizations,* 138–39; Beckford, *Religious Organization,* 92–104.

9. Michael Reed, "Organizational Theorizing: A Historically Contested Terrain," in *Studying Organization: Theory and Method,* ed. Stewart R. Clegg and Cynthia Hardy (London, 1999), 27ff.

10. Ibid., 44.

11. Leo von Deschwanden, "Eine Rollenanalyse des katholischen Pfarrepriesters," *Internationales Jahrbuch für Religionssoziologie* 4 (1968): 123–57, quote 146.

12. Fernand Boulard, *Essor ou déclin du clergé français* (Paris, 1950), 97–287.

13. Jan Dellepoort, "Manuskript eines Vortrages über die Priesterfrage vor dem Kongress 'Kirche in Not' in Königstein," 22 October 1953, KDC, NL Dellepoort, 66; Jan Dellepoort, "Zu wenig Seelsorger: Enquête über den Priesternachwuchs in Europa," *WW* 14 (1959): 245–55, 245–46; *Die europäische Priesterfrage: Bericht der Internationalen Enquête in Wien, 10.–12. Oktober 1958* (Vienna, 1959); Jan Dellepoort et al., *Die deutsche Priesterfrage: Eine soziologische Untersuchung über Klerus und Priesternachwuchs in Deutschland* (Mainz, 1961).

14. *HK* 8 (1954): 301; Damberg, *Abschied,* 184–88.

15. Quote: Dellepoort, *Seelsorger,* 252ff.; Egon Golomb, "Die Situation: Zur Entwicklung der Priesterzahl," *LS* 23 (1972): 1–4.

16. Jakob Crottogini, *Werden und Krise des Priesterberufes: Eine psychologisch-pädagogische Untersuchung über den Priesternachwuchs in verschiedenen Ländern Europas* (Einsiedeln, 1955), 181–86, 219–27; "Wie sie Priester wurden," *HK* 9 (1954/55): 367–73.

17. Joseph H. Fichter had similar experiences in the United States. It was not until 1969 that he was able to carry out a study among clergy that was not obstructed and monitored by his superiors in the Jesuit order, parts of the episcopate, or Rome. Fichter, *One-Man Research: Reminiscences of a Catholic Sociologist* (New York, 1973), 160–98.

18. Quotes: Schurr, *Seelsorge,* 366–68; Simon Hirt, "Vereinfachung der Arbeit der Seelsorger im Blick auf die bestehende Priesternot und die Zunahme der Pastorationsaufgaben," *Oberrheinisches PBl.* 56 (1955): 162–75; Adolf Geck, "Laienapostolat und Legion Mariens: Möglichkeiten der Priester-Entlastung," *Kölner PBl.* 9 (1957): 219–23.

19. Hirt, "Vereinfachung," 165.

20. Klemens Tillmann, "Henry Ford und unsere Seelsorgsmethoden," *LS* 4 (1953): 129–33, 131.

21. Lothar Roos, "Pastoralwissenschaftliche Überlegungen zu den Reformvorstellungen der Priester," in *Priester zwischen Anpassung und Unterscheidung: Auswertungen und Kommentare zu den im Auftrag der Deutschen Bischofskonferenz durchgeführten Umfragen unter allen Welt- und Ordenspriestern in der Bundesrepublik Deutschland,* ed. Karl Forster (Freiburg, 1974), 87.

22. Ralf Dahrendorf, *Homo Sociologicus* (Opladen, 1977), 33, quoted by Norbert Glatzel, "Rolle des Priesters in der Leistungsgesellschaft," *Jb. für Christliche Sozialwissenschaften* 12 (1971): 163–183, 164; Linus Grond, "Soziologische Beobachtungen zur heutigen Unsicherheit des Priesters gegenüber seiner Rolle in Kirche und Gesellschaft," *Ordenskorrespondenz* 6 (1965): 162–172, 167; see also Robert K. Merton, "The Role-Set: Problems in Sociological Theory," *British Journal of Sociology* 8 (1957): 106–20.

23. Joseph Fichter, *Religion as an Occupation: A Study in the Sociology of Professions* (Notre Dame, IN, 1961), 138–61; Joseph Fichter, *Grundbegriffe der Soziologie* (Vienna, 1969), 122–34.

24. Christoph Wagner, "Das empirische Priesterbild im Wettbewerb der Berufsbilder," *Ordenskorrespondenz* 6 (1965): 173–94, quote 190.

25. Linus Grond, "Soziologische Beobachtungen zur heutigen Unsicherheit des Priesters gegenüber seiner Rolle in Kirche und Gesellschaft," *Ordenskorrespondenz* 6 (1965): 162–72, 168–71;

Walter Goddijn, "Rollenkonflikte des Priesters in der modernen Gesellschaft," *LS* 17 (1966): 136–38.

26. Fichter, *Grundbegriffe*, 129.
27. Grond, "Beobachtungen," 166.
28. Hermann-Josef Lauter, OFM, "Notizen zur Situation des Priesters heute und morgen," *PBl. für die Diözesen Aachen etc.* 23 (1971): 66–69.
29. Hermann-Josef Lauter, "Das Priesterbild in der Krise," *PBl. für die Diözesen Aachen etc.* 19 (1967): 366–73, 372.
30. Peter Lippert, CSsR, "Der Priester in der Gemeinde," *PBl. für die Diözesen Aachen etc.* 21 (1969): 71–78, quote 72; Joseph Höffner, "Das Priesterbild des Zweiten Vatikanischen Konzils, Protokoll der Dechantenkonferenz," 31 May to 2 June 1966, BAM, AD 21; Siefer, *Priester,* 9–40.
31. "Decree on the Ministry and Life of Priests, Presbyterorum Ordinis," no. 14, in Abbott, *Documents of Vatican II,* 562–63.
32. Lauter, "Priesterbild," 366; Lippert, "Priester," 75; P. Heuser, "Die Seelsorge in der Erzdiözese Köln nach dem Konzil," *PBl. für die Diözesen Aachen etc.* 18 (1966): 322–39, 325.
33. Lippert, "Priester," 74.
34. Glatzel, "Rolle," 172; "Decree on the Bishops' Pastoral Office in the Church, Christus Dominus," no. 31, in Abbott, *Documents of Vatican II,* 419–20.
35. "Presbyterorum Ordinis," no. 7, in Abbott, *Documents of Vatican II,* 549.
36. See Chris Dols and Benjamin Ziemann, "Progressive Participation and Transnational Activism in the Catholic Church after Vatican II: The Dutch and West-German Example," *Journal of Contemporary History* 50 (2015).
37. Glatzel, "Rolle," 173; Albert O. Hirschman, *Exit, Voice and Loyalty: Responses to Decline in Firms, Organizations and States* (Cambridge, MA, 1970), 30–43.
38. Benjamin Tonna, "The Allocation of Time among Clerical Activities," *SC* 10 (1963): 93–106.
39. [Bernhard Honsel], Gesamtuntersuchung/Amt Ibbenbüren, 16 September 1969, Bernhard Honsel to Reinhard Lettmann, 19 November 1970, both in BAM, GV NA, A-101-283; Karl-Erich Englert, "Entwurf zur Ausschreibung von Strukturexperimenten 30.9.1970," BAM, GV NA, A-201-365.
40. "Arbeitspapier zur Berufsrollenanalyse des Pfarrers," n.d. [ca. 1974], BAM, GV NA, A-0-966. A similar approach, including a questionnaire and intensive interviews with twenty chaplains, was also taken in SIB, Forschungsplan (1967), 9–13.
41. Egon Golomb to Joseph Krautscheidt, 20 July 1967, BAE, GV 82 14 12, vol. 1; cf. Deschwanden, "Rollenanalyse."
42. Vicar-General Jansen to Golomb, 11 August 1967, "Gutachterliche Stellungnahme Franz Groner zum Forschungsplan 11.8.1967," Golomb to Jansen, 25 August 1967, Golomb to Krautscheidt, 29 August 1967,all in BAE, GV 82 14 12, vol. 1; SIB, Forschungsplan (1967), 5; interview with Egon Golomb on 2 October 2002.
43. Deschwanden, "Rollenanalyse," 146–49, quote 125; Norbert Glatzel, "Soziologische Aspekte der Seelsorgerrolle," *StdZ* 187 (1971): 31–42, 38.
44. Jansen to von Deschwanden, 14 August 1967, BAE, GV 82 14 12, vol. 1; Jansen to von Deschwanden, 19 October 1967, BAE, GV 82 14 12, vol. 1; von Deschwanden's reply, dated 7 November 1967, BAE, GV 82 14 12, vol. 1.
45. Schmidtchen, *Priester.*
46. Quote: Franz-Josef Trost, "Mündige Kapläne," *Publik,* 18 October 1968; "'Autoritätskonflikt': Die Priester unter der Lupe der Demoskopen," *HK* 27 (1973): 460–64, 463; Kasper, "Die pastoralen Dienste," 581.
47. Schmidtchen, *Priester,* 47–51.
48. Minutes of the "Dechantenkonferenz," 15 May 1973, BAM, GV NA, A-201-396; Luhmann, *Funktion,* 295.

49. Karl Forster, Entscheidungen und pastorale Initiativen für die kirchlichen Berufe: Hinweise aus den Ergebnissen sozialwissenschaftlicher Untersuchungen der letzten Jahre, n.d. [1975], BAM, GV NA, A-0-966.

50. Ibid.

51. "Seelsorge ohne Zufall: Führt der Spezialist aus dem Dilemma des Priestermangels?," *Ruhrwort*, no. 42, 26 October 1968.

52. Management consultant Christoph Theodor Wagner, for example, gave such advice in a much-read piece, also reprinted in the *Frankfurter Allgemeine Zeitung*: "Arbeitsteilung und Kirche," PBL. *für die Diözesen Aachen etc.* 19 (1967): 374–79.

53. "Seelsorge ohne Zufall," *Ruhrwort*, no. 42, 26 October 1968.

54. Norbert Glatzel, "Die Rolle," 176–80.

55. Émile Pin, "Die Differenzierung der priesterlichen Funktion: Eine soziologische Analyse," *Concilium* 5 (1969): 177–84, 181; Lutz Hoffmann, *Auswege aus der Sackgasse: Anwendungen soziologischer Kategorien auf die gegenwärtige Situation von Kirche und Seelsorge* (Munich, 1971), 115–55.

56. Karl Forster, Entscheidungen und pastorale Initiativen für die kirchlichen Berufe: Hinweise aus den Ergebnissen sozialwissenschaftlicher Untersuchungen der letzten Jahre, n.d. [1975], BAM, GV NA, A-0-966.

57. This is Niklas Luhmann's theory as presented in, "Das Medium der Religion: Eine soziologische Betrachtung über Gott und die Seelen," *Soziale Systeme* 6 (2000): 39–51; cf. Rudolf Schlögl, "Historiker, Max Weber und Niklas Luhmann: Zum schwierigen (aber möglicherweise produktiven) Verhältnis von Geschichtswissenschaft und Systemtheorie," *Soziale Systeme* 7 (2001): 23–45.

58. Egon Golomb, "Auch die Kirche muß ihren Einsatz planen: Die notwendige Anpassung der Seelsorgsorganisation," in *Bilanz des deutschen Katholizismus*, ed. Norbert Greinacher and Heinz Theo Risse (Mainz, 1966), 60; Leslie Paul, *The Deployment and Payment of the Clergy: A Report* (Westminster, UK, 1964), esp, 115–36; on the discussion of these proposals, see the contributions in Gervase E. Duffield, *The Paul Report Considered: An Appraisal of Leslie Paul's Report*, The Deployment and Payment of the Clergy (Marcham, UK, 1964).

59. Regarding the results of the survey of priests, see "Von Frustration ist kaum zu reden: Fragebogenaktion," *Rheinischer Merkur*, no. 25, 9 July 1971; "Die bundesdeutsche Priesterumfrage," *HK* 25 (1971): 383–87, 386.

60. Horst Hohmann, "Es war einmal ein Priester: Gespräche mit Männern die ihr Gelübde aufsagten um ein bürgerliches Leben zu führen," *Christ und Welt*, 2 April 1971; *Gemeinsame Synode*, 1:631; on the resonance of this question, see Schmidtchen, *Priester*, 115.

61. A statement used by Karl Forster, cited in Schmidtchen, *Priesteramtskandidaten*, 236.

62. Siefer, *Priester*, 40; Hoffmann, *Auswege*, 145; see Paul Zulehner, "Reform des Priesterberufs? Zu den Auswertungsversuchen der Priesterumfragen im deutschen Sprachraum," *HK* 29 (1975): 88–95, 92, 95.

63. Kasper, "Die pastoralen Dienste"; "Von Frustration ist kaum zu reden: Fragebogenaktion," *Rheinischer Merkur*, no. 25, 9 July 1971.

64. With direct reference to the issue of celibacy, see Gottfried Griesl, "Krisen im modernen Priesterleben," *LS* 17 (1966): 134–36, 135.

65. "Pastoralkonferenz des Dekanates Vreden," 8 March 1971, BAM, GV NA, A-201-24; Luhmann, *Funktion*, 307–8.

66. Pfarrer Johannes Hüneborn, "Überlegungen zur Gemeinde-Pastoral, Pastoralkonferenz Dekanatskomitee Rheinberg 5.4.1971," BAM, GV NA, A-201-25; cf. H. Schelsky, "Ist die Dauerreflexion institutionalisierbar? Zum Thema einer modernen Religionssoziologie" (1957), in Matthes, *Religion und Gesellschaft*, 164–89; Hüneborn drew his arguments from Lothar Roos, "Kann man den Heilsdienst der Kirche planen?," *LS* 22(1971): 111–22, 116.

67. Hüneborn, "Überlegungen zur Gemeinde-Pastoral."
68. According to a survey at the Collegium Borromäum in Münster, Werner Thissen, "Erwartungen des jungen Klerus an Bischof und Bistumsleitung," n.d. [1975], BAM, GV NA, A-0-966; F.-J. Trost, "Weiterbildung der Priester," *Publik*, no. 46, 14 November 1969.
69. SIB, Forschungsplan (1967), 14; Karl Forster, "Entscheidungen und pastorale Initiativen für die kirchlichen Berufe: Hinweise aus den Ergebnissen sozialwissenschaftlicher Untersuchungen der letzten Jahre," n.d. [1975], BAM, GV NA, A-0-966.
70. Lippert, "Priester," 76; "Presbyterorum Ordinis," no. 2, in Abbott, *Documents of Vatican II*, 533–36.
71. Quotes: Fichter, *Grundbegriffe*, 124–25; Matthias Becker, *Die Macht in der katholischen Kirche: Kritik der hierarchischen Praxis* (Munich, 1967), 104–5.
72. Lutz Hoffmann, "Kein Dauerabonnement für Rückzugsgefechte: Der Priesterberuf in der Leistungsgesellschaft," *Publik*, 19 June 1970. The English term "output" was used in the original, again indicating how functionalist sociology was deemed to be of Anglo-Saxon origin.
73. Lippert, "Priester," 77–78; quotes: Paul Zulehner, "Reform des Priesterberufs?," *HK* 29 (1975): 90.
74. F. Graf von Westphalen, "Nur noch Funktionäre des Kultes?," *Rheinischer Merkur*, 8 August 1969; F. Graf von Westphalen, "Was denken Priester? Ein neuer Fragebogen," *Rheinischer Merkur*, 23 October 1970.
75. *Gemeinsame Synode*, 1:589; quote: Joseph Ratzinger, *Glaube und Zukunft* (Munich, 1970), 122.
76. Klaus Hemmerle, "Funktionale Interpretation des priesterlichen Dienstes?," in *Priester zwischen Anpassung und Unterscheidung: Auswertungen und Kommentare zu den im Auftrag der Deutschen Bischofskonferenz durchgeführten Umfragen unter allen Welt- und Ordenspriestern in der Bundesrepublik Deutschland*, ed. Karl Forster (Freiburg, 1974), quotes 31, 38.
77. Roos, "Reformvorstellungen," 77.
78. *Gemeinsame Synode*, 1:619.
79. Karlheinz Schmidthüs, "Weltamt und Apparat: Probleme des Wirkens der Kirche im Zeitalter der Organisation," *Rheinischer Merkur*, 16 March 1956.
80. It is worth remembering the phrase coined by Bernhard Hanssler in 1958: that which is not "organized" is "socially inexistent." Cited in Großmann, *Zentralkomitee*, 147–51.
81. Gustav Ermecke, "Organisation als soziologische Form der Seelsorge," *Theologie und Glaube* 37/38 (1947/48): 141–67, quotes 146, 148, 153; Nikolaus Monzel, "Die Kirche als Gemeinschaft," *WW* 4 (1949): 525–30.
82. Erich Bodzenta, Norbert Greinacher, and Linus Grond, *Regionalplanung in der Kirche* (Mainz, 1965), 117–41, 165–80.
83. Houtart, *Soziologie*, 57–67, quotes 57–58; cf. Egon Golomb, "Seelsorgsplanung in der Großstadt: Entwurf eines Organisationsmodells," *Trierer Theologische Zeitschrift* 72 (1963): 136–37.
84. Quote: Golomb, "Seelsorgsplanung," 139. The term *Stadtoberhaupt* was coined by Klemens Brockmöller, quoted here in Norbert Greinacher, "Soziologische und organisatorische Aspekte einer diözesanen kirchlichen Strategie," *LS* 16 (1965): 124–28, 126; Josef Stegmann, "Überlegungen zur kirchlichen Raumplanung in vorwiegend ländlichen Gebieten," *PBl. für die Diözesen Aachen etc.* 20 (1968): 334–42.
85. Greinacher, "Soziologische und organisatorische Aspekte," 126.
86. Ruck, "Ein kurzer Sommer."
87. Quote: Philipp Boonen, *Das Konzil kommt ins Bistum: Zur Diskussion um die künftige Planung und Struktur des kirchlichen Dienstes* (Aachen, 1967), 25–26; Alfred Weitmann, "Es geht nicht ohne Plan: Gedanken zur Unerläßlichkeit einer diözesanen Seelsorgekonzeption," *LS* 16 (1965): 119–24, 120; Golomb, "Einsatz," 46.
88. The title of the closing chapter in Ratzinger, *Glaube und Zukunft*, 107–25; Lorenz Jaeger, "Die Zukunft der Kirche und die Situation der katholischen Theologie," *Im Dienst der Seelsorge*

25, no. 1 (1971): 1–4; H. Schäufele, "Hat das Christentum noch eine Zukunft," *Rheinischer Merkur,* 22 October 1971.

89. Roos, "Heilsdienst," quotes 112–13; on researching the future, see Alexander Schmidt-Gernig, "Scenarios of Europe's Future—European Future Studies of the 1960s and 1970s as an Example of a Transnational Public Sphere of Experts," *Journal of European Integration History* 8 (2002): 69–90.

90. Damberg, *Abschied,* 288–89.

91. Wilhelm Stammkötter, "Fragen der strukturellen und personellen Planung, Protokoll der Dechantenkonferenz v. 4.-6.6.1968," 11–19, BAM, AD 21.

92. Wilhelm Stammkötter, "Priesterliche Zusammenarbeit in der Seelsorge, Dechantenkonferenz vom 31.5.-2.6.1966," BAM, AD 21.

93. Decree on the Bishops' Pastoral Office in the Church, "Christus Dominus," nos. 22 and 23, in Abbott, *Documents of Vatican II,* 412–13; Boonen, *Konzil,* 27–28.

94. "Christus Dominus," nos. 29 and 30, in Abbott, *Documents of Vatican II,* 275; "Errichtungs-Urkunde der Planungsabteilung, 25.11.1967," BAM, GV NA, A-101-156.

95. The essential features of this can be found in Damberg, *Abschied,* 287–301. However, Damberg engages neither with the conceptual underpinnings of the *Strukturplan* nor with organizational sociology's intensive accompaniment and analysis of it. For the following, see in more detail Benjamin Ziemann, "Organisation und Planung in der katholischen Kirche um 1970: Das Beispiel der Diözese Münster," *Schweizerische Zeitschrift für Religions- und Kulturgeschichte* 101 (2007): 185–206.

96. Josef Hofmeier, "Kirchliche Strukturplanung," *StdZ* 188 (1971): 230–46.

97. Hans Kühn, *Strukturreform im Bistum Speyer 1969–1980* (Speyer, 1992), 14–15; K. Embacher, "Strukturgerechte Seelsorge," *Jahresbericht 1968/69:* 47–54, quote 50.

98. Damberg, *Abschied,* 287–92; *Überlegungen und Vorschläge zur Struktur der Seelsorge im Bistum Münster: Strukturplan.* N.p., n.d. [Münster, 1969], 5–8, quote 7–8; Talcott Parsons, "General Theory," in *Sociology Today: Problems and Prospects,* ed. Robert K. Merton (New York, 1959), 4–16.

99. *Überlegungen,* 11–14.

100. Ibid., quotes 15, 17.

101. Ibid., 24–33, 37–44, quotes 24, 28, 37; on the council system, see Damberg, *Abschied,* 268–77.

102. [Josef Homeyer], "Einleitungsreferat zur Diskussion des Strukturplanes auf der Dechantenkonferenz am 17.9.1970," BAM, GV NA, A-201-365.

103. Ibid.; quote: "Pastoral Constitution on the Church in the Modern World, Gaudium et Spes," no. 36, in Abbott, *Documents of Vatican II,* 233.

104. Pfarrkomitee St. Marien in Bevengern, 18 October 1970, BAM, GV NA, A-201-14.

105. Minutes of the meeting of the spiritual council on 26 September 1969, BAM, GV NA, A-101-166.

106. See the letters by von Wambolt to Albrecht Beckel and to his former colleagues in the Franz-Hitze-Haus, written in 1968 and 1969, in BAM, FHH A 15.

107. See Dols and Ziemann, "Progressive Participation."

108. Minutes of the "Dekanatskomitee" Nottuln, 27 February 1970, BAM, GV NA, A-201-24; "unnecessary": opinion of St. Sixtus in Haltern, 13 October 1970, BAM, GV NA, A-201-16.

109. Dr. Bernhard Reismann, "Gedanken, Bedenken und Gegenvorschläge zum Strukturplan für das Bistum Münster," n.d. [this undated memo was sent to Spital on 4 May 1970], BAM, GV NA, A-201-365.

110. See the definition by Helmut Josef Patt, "Pfarrei-Pfarrverband-Dekanat," *Im Dienst der Seelsorge* 26, no. 2 (1972): 46–53, 47–48.

111. Reismann, "Gedanken, Bedenken und Gegenvorschläge"; cf. *Überlegungen,* 18. Ratzinger, in *Glaube und Zukunft,* 113–14, also thought—possibly after reading the *Strukturplan*—when

reading Wessenberg's works, with their "garden sheers of constructive reason," that he was in fact encountering a "progressivist from the year 1969."

112. See also the critical remarks in Knut Walf, "Das neue Kirchenrecht—das alte System: Vorkonziliarer Geist in nachkonziliaren Formulierungen," in *Katholische Kirche—wohin? Wider den Verrat am Konzil,* ed. Norbert Greinacher and Hans Küng (Munich, 1986), 78–93.

113. Pfarrkomitee St. Martinus in Elten, n.d., Pfarrkomitee St. Katharina in Dinklage, 30 October 1970, both in BAM, GV NA, A-201-14.

114. Pfarrkomitee Christus-König in Borken, 5 October 1970, BAM, GV NA, A-201-14.

115. Pfarrkomitee Heilig Geist Münster, 1 August 1970, BAM, GV NA, A-201-15.

116. Pfarrkomitee St. Josef in Dorsten, 24 September 1970, BAM, GV NA, A-201-15.

117. Pfarrkomitee St. Bartolomäus in Laer, 10 August 1970, BAM, GV NA , A-201-15; Georg Ruhmöller, "Überlegungen zum Strukturplan für das Bistum Münster, 22.3.1970," BAM, GV NA, A-201-365.

118. Pfarrkomitee St. Johannes in Eppinghoven, 18 June 1970, BAM, GV NA, A-201-14.

119. Pfarrkomitee Liebfrauen in Bocholt, 1 April 1970, Pfarramt Heilig-Geist in Oldenburg, 10 June 1970, both in BAM, GV NA, A-201-15.

120. "Minutes of the pastoral conference of the deanery of Telgte 6.7.1970," BAM, GV NA, A-201-24; on the "dividual" created through inclusion in functional subsystems, see Armin Nassehi, *Differenzierungsfolgen: Beiträge zur Soziologie der Moderne* (Opladen and Wiesbaden, 1999), 117.

121. Pfarrkomitee St. Marien in Marl, 29 May 1970, BAM, GV NA, A-201-15.

122. On the distinction between interaction and organization, see Luhmann, *Differentiation,* 69–89.

123. Emil Walter-Busch, *Das Auge der Firma: Mayos Hawthorne-Experimente und die Harvard Business School, 1900–1960* (Stuttgart, 1989), 191.

124. *Überlegungen,* 28.

125. Philipp von Wambolt, "Statistische Auswertung der Diskussion, März 1971," BAM, GV NA, A-201-368.

126. Hugo Bekkers, OFMCap, to Wilhelm Stammkötter, 4 February 1970, BAM, GV NA, A-101-156; Pfarrkomitee Heilig-Kreuz in Münster, 12 October 1970, BAM, GV NA, A-201-15; Dekanatskomitee Burgsteinfurt, 4 September 1970, BAM, GV NA, A-201-14.

127. Lorenz Jaeger, "Die Zukunft der Kirche und die Situation der katholischen Theologie," *Im Dienst der Seelsorge* 25, nos. 1/2 (1971).

128. For example, see Otto B. Roegele, "Signale aus Essen: Aufstieg oder Niedergang der Kirche," *Rheinischer Merkur,* 6 September 1968.

129. Walter Kasper, "Kollegiale Strukturen in der Kirche," *Sein und Sendung* 1 (1969): 5; "Wie ist Demokratie in der Kirche möglich?" *HK* 23 (1969): 97–101.

130. "Disput zum Thema Demokratisierung in der Kirche," *HK* 26 (1972): 30–36, 32.

131. Luhmann, *Funktion,* 310–11.

132. F. Jacobs, "Diskussionsbeitrag," *Unsere Seelsorge* 20, no. 3 (1970): 12; "overorganization": Pfarrkomitee Liebfrauen in Beckum, n.d., BAM, GV NA, A-201-14.

133. *Überlegungen,* 24–26; cf. Luhmann, *Differentiation,* 32–33.

134. Quotes: Lothar Roos, Begriff und Struktur der Pfarrgemeinde, sent to Heinrich Mussinghoff on 7 August 1975, BAM, GV NA, A-0-966; see Lothar Roos, "Gemeinde als kirchliche Wirklichkeit," *LS* 24 (1973): 27–37; Henry Fischer, Norbert Greinacher, and Ferdinand Klostermann, *Die Gemeinde* (Mainz, 1970) (=Pastorale. Handreichung für den pastoralen Dienst), especially 12–31.

135. Norbert Greinacher, *Die Kirche in der städtischen Gesellschaft: Soziologische und theologische Überlegungen zur Frage der Seelsorge in der Stadt* (Mainz, 1966), 233–40, 297–337; Norbert Greinacher, "Realutopie Gemeindekirche," *LS* 18 (1967): 177–85, quotes 178–79.

136. Greinacher, "Realutopie," 181–84. Karl Rahner's idea of the "self-realizing church" conceives of the church as a self-referential system open to its environment. Rahner drew his ecclesiological conclusions from functional differentiation's unavoidable implications for the dissolution of the old model of *societas perfecta,* which represented a closed system whose hierarchical structure drew upon isomorphic models of order in other fields (such as the paternalistic family, an autocratically managed business, a monarchical political system). Karl Rahner, "Ekklesiologische Grundlegung," in *Handbuch der Pastoraltheologie,* ed. Franz Xaver Arnold et al., (Freiburg, 1970), 1:122n1.

137. Greinacher, "Realutopie," 184–85.

138. Norbert Greinacher, Einige Bemerkungen zu den "Überlegungen und Vorschlägen zur Struktur der Seelsorge im Bistum Münster," n.d. [1970], BAM, GV NA, A-201-14.

139. Joseph Höffner, "Ende der Volkskirche?," *PBl. für die Diözesen Aachen etc.* 20 (1968): 295–96; Lothar Roos, "'Volkskirche' oder 'Gemeindekirche': Theologische und soziologische Überlegungen zu einer angeblichen Alternative," *Jahrbuch für christl. Sozialwissenschaften* 15 (1974): 9–32, 25–29.

140. Karl Forster, "Volkskirche oder Entscheidungskirche? Theologische und soziologische Aspekte zu einer Grundfrage des pastoralen Dienstes," in *Ortskirche, Weltkirche: Festgabe für Julius Kardinal Döpfner,* ed. Heinz Fleckenstein (Würzburg, 1973), 500–2; Otto B. Roegele, "Was das Kirchenvolk wirklich will: Ergebnisse aus dem Forschungsbericht 'Zwischen Kirche und Gesellschaft,'" *Rheinischer Merkur,* 22 September 1972; Roos, "Volkskirche," 17–18.

141. Karl-Erich Englert, "Gemeinde und Gemeinschaft: Überlegungen zur Gemeindesoziologie," *Unsere Seelsorge* 21, no. 4 (1971): 17–18; Hermann-Josef Lauter, OFM, "Zur Situation und Zukunft der Kirche," *PBl. für die Diözesen Aachen etc.* 24 (1972): 357–61, 361; K.-E. Apfelbacher, "Reform zwischen Utopie und Getto: Über die neuere Diskussion zum Thema Gemeindekirche," *HK* 29 (1975): 515–22, quote 516.

142. Greinacher, "Realutopie," 183. Greinacher also noted cautiously here that the administration of the sacraments was "to be rethought" from consideration of this aspect; cf. Luhmann, *Funktion,* 293–94.

143. Pfarrer Josef Perau (born 1910 in Hülm über Goch) to Tenhumberg, 20 September 1969, BAM, GV NA, A-101-376.

144. Forster, "Volkskirche," 498; cf. *Gemeinsame Synode,* 1:227–75, quote 246.

145. Wigand Siebel, "Sekten in der Kirche? Zur Frage der Gruppenbildung," *Rheinischer Merkur,* 23 September 1973. Siebel taught sociology in Saarbrücken and positioned himself especially in opposition to Karl Rahner's vehement criticism of an emancipatory, "sociologizing" theology. In the 1980s Siebel was part of a fundamentalist protest movement in the Catholic Church. R. Padberg, "Führungskrise in der Kirche? Ein Soziologe gibt Antwort," *Rheinischer Merkur,* 12 May 1972; Wigand Siebel, *Freiheit und Herrschaftsstruktur in der Kirche: Eine soziologische Studie* (Berlin, 1971).

146. Lauter, "Zukunft," 359.

147. Quote: Pfarrkomitee St. Josef Dorsten, 24 September 1970 ; Philipp von Wambolt, 29 April 1970, to Generalvikar Lettmann,both in BAM, GV NA, A-201-15.

148. "Protokoll der Dezernatskonferenz des Seelsorgereferates v. 23.4.1971," BAM, GV NA, A-201-2.

149. [Josef Homeyer], "Ergebnisse der Diskussion um den Strukturplan für das Bistum Münster, hier: Bericht über die bisherige Arbeit der Planungsgruppe," n.d. [March 1971], BAM, GV NA, A-101-156; on Homeyer's authorship of this document, see Homeyer to Wilhelm Stammkötter, 31 March 1971, BAM, GV NA, A-101-156.

150. [Homeyer], "Ergebnisse der Diskussion um den Strukturplan für das Bistum Münster, hier: Bericht über die bisherige Arbeit der Planungsgruppe," n.d. [March 1971], BAM, GV NA, A-101-156; memo Stammkötter to Tenhumberg, 1 April 1971, BAM, GV NA, A-101-156

151. Damberg, *Abschied,* 165, 296–99; "Wie soll das innere Gefüge der Diözese neu gestaltet werden?," *KuL,* 16 May 1971.

152. *Überlegungen,* 37–42.

153. Ibid., 37.

154. Luhmann, *Differentiation,* 27–28.

155. Memo by Spital on the conference of heads of pastoral offices, 9 to 11 December 1969, BAM, GV NA, A-201-463.

156. Wilhelm Stammkötter, "Überlegungen zur Personalsituation," *Unsere Seelsorge* 21, no. 1 (1971): 8.

157. Ruck, "Ein kurzer Sommer."

158. [Josef Homeyer], "Einleitungsreferat zur Diskussion des Strukturplanes auf der Dechanten-konferenz am 17.9.1970": BAM, GV NA, A-201-365.

159. [Josef Homeyer], "Ergebnisse der Diskussion um den Strukturplan für das Bistum Münster, hier: Bericht über die bisherige Arbeit der Planungsgruppe," n.d. [March 1971]: BAM, GV NA, A-101-156; "final discussion": Stammkötter to all those who had worked on the *Struktur-plan* and the *Stellenplan,* 29 April 1971, BAM, GV NA, A-101-156.

160. [Josef Homeyer], "Einleitungsreferat zur Diskussion des Strukturplanes auf der Dechanten-konferenz am 17.9.1970": BAM, GV NA, A-201-365; see Boonen, *Konzil,* 42–47; Johann Hofmeier, "Kirchliche Strukturplanung," *StdZ* 188 (1971): 230–46, 231.

161. Minutes of the "Dechantenkonferenz," 18 September 1970, BAM, GV NA, A-201-14; cf. Damberg, *Abschied,* 296; Kühn, *Strukturreform,* 102–10.

162. In the diocese of Limburg the *Großpfarrei* was "never a real alternative" to the parish associ-ation. Rolf Strüder, *Chancen und Gefährdung geplanten Wandels in der Kirche—aufgezeigt am Beispiel der Diözese Limburg* (St. Ottilien, 1993), 114.

163. *Überlegungen,* 21; Hofmeier, "Strukturplanung," 231, quote 234–35.

164. H. Löker, "Pfarrverband—Hilfe oder Last: Ein Erfahrungsbericht," *LS* 27 (1976): 345–49; Hanspeter Heinz, "Erste Erfahrungen mit Pfarrverbänden in den Diözesen Münster und Aachen," *PBl. für die Diözesen Aachen etc.* 25 (1973): 343–49; Fischer, *Pastoral,* 3:65–66, 259–62.

165. Heribert Gauly, "Seelsorgsplanung—lohnt sich der Aufwand?" *LS* 27 (1976): 325–28, 325; Ewald Berning, *Kirche und Planung: Die Frage nach der theologischen Relevanz von Theorie und Praxis außerkirchlicher Planung* (Frankfurt, 1976), 1.

166. Gauly, "Seelsorgsplanung," 326–27; on the operationalization of targets in the church, see also "'Stärkere Orientierung am Kunden': Ein Gespräch mit McKinsey-Direktor Peter Barren-stein," *HK* 52 (1998): 346.

167. For the archdioceses of Munich and Freising, see *Die Planung von heute für die Kirche von morgen: Kirchliche Raumplanung in der Erzdiözese München und Freising* (Munich, 1972); interview by the author with Dr. Karl-Hans Pauli, Munich, 13 September 1999; Kühn, *Struk-turreform,* 14–19.

168. Quote: Erfahrungen mit Pfarrverbänden, n.d., "Vorlage für den Diözesanrat am 11.5.1973," BAM, GV NA, A-101-378; Heinz, "Erfahrungen," 347–49; G. Götz, "Pfarrverband 'Obere Rhön': Der lebendigen aktiven Gemeinde näherkommen," *LS* 27 (1976): 349–53.

169. Löker, "Pfarrverband," 346; minutes of the pastoral conference of the deanery of Bocholt, 14 January 1970, BAM, GV NA, A-201-23.

170. Hermann-Josef Spital, "Gedanken zur zusätzlichen Ausbildung von Seelsorgskräften, 3.3.1971," BAM, GV NA, A-201-357.

171. Seelsorgeamt Münster, "Entwurf eines Ausbildungsvorschlages für eine berufsbegleitende pas-toral-theologische Ausbildung, Schulung B, 28.4.1971," and further materials, BAM, GV NA, A-201-357. Both "public relations" and "counseling" were English terms in the original.

172. G. Leuschner to Spital, 15 December 1971, BAM, GV NA, A-201-357.

173. Leo Waltermann, *Klerus zwischen Wissenschaft und Seelsorge: Zur Reform der Priesterausbildung* (Essen, 1966), 110–31; *Gemeinsame Synode*, 1:626.

174. Priesterfortbildung, Jahresbericht 1971, n.d., BAM, GV NA, A-201-374.

175. Luhmann, *Funktion*, 309.

176. Berning, *Kirche und Planung*, 279.

177. Ibid., 272–75. A theological reflection on planning can also be found in Strüder, *Chancen und Gefährdung*, 57–61, 291–99, 343–49.

178. Philipp von Wambolt, "Statistische Auswertung der Diskussion," March 1971, BAM, GV NA, A-201-368.

179. Damberg, *Abschied*, 301–5, quotes 304–5.

180. "Schwerpunkte der Heilssorge im Bistum Münster, 24.2.1971," BAM, GV NA, A-101-156. This text, discussed at a meeting of pastoral department staff on 19 February 1971, was written by Hermann-Josef Spital. The text refers for authorization to the Decree on Religious Freedom, "Dignitatis Humanae," no. 2, in Abbott, *Documents of Vatican II*, 678–79.

181. "Schwerpunkte der Heilssorge im Bistum Münster, 24.2.1971," BAM, GV NA, A-101-156.

182. Hermann-Josef Spital, "Diskussionsgrundlage zum 1. Entwurf eines Pastoralplans, 18.11.1970," BAM, GV NA, A-201-2.

183. Graf, "Selbstmodernisierung," 61.

184. "Schwerpunkte der Heilssorge im Bistum Münster, 24.2.1971," BAM, GV NA, A-101-156; H. Kerst, "Schwerpunkte der Heilssorge im Bistum Münster," *LS* 27 (1976): 355–59.

185. Graf, "Selbstmoderrnisierung," 61.

186. Wilhelm Stammkötter, "Schwierigkeiten und Chancen kirchlichen Leitungsdienstes," *Unsere Seelsorge* 22, no. 1 (1972): 1.

187. See van Dülmen, *Kultur*, 98.

188. Memo by Spital, 10 December 1969, BAM, GV NA, A-201-463.

189. As argued by Gerhard Schmied, *Kirche oder Sekte? Entwicklungen und Perspektiven des Katholizismus in der westlichen Welt* (Munich and Zurich, 1988).

190. Ruck, "Ein kurzer Sommer."

191. In the sense of the terminology used by Hirschman, *Exit*, 21–29.

192. In a somber letter to his former line manager, Hermann-Josef Spital, Philipp von Wambolt explained on 21 October 1972 that he was still interested in pastoral problems but would now count as "abstaining," as the appropriate "plug" was missing through which he could connect to the church: BAM, GV NA, A-201-379 .

193. Ratzinger, *Glaube und Zukunft*, 123; "small flock" (*kleine Herde*): Karl Rahner, cited in Forster, "Volkskirche," 496.

194. Philipp von Wambolt, "Durst nach menschlicher Kirche: Ideologiekritische Bemerkungen zur Strukturplandiskussion im Bistum Münster," n.d. [1971], BAM, GV NA, A-201-365.

Chapter 5

"Humane" Scientific Approaches
Psychology and Group Dynamics

Vatican II pushed as well . . . for Catholic pastoral care to urgently adopt the discoveries and methods of "healthy psychology." But where is this healthy psychology to be found? According to which criteria should one of the numerous, sometimes antagonistic schools be chosen to receive this accolade? One cannot pluck out raisins from all over the place and expect to end up with a usable cake. And everything is "therapy" these days anyway!
—*Gottfried Griesl, "Seelsorge oder Psychoanalyse?"*[1]

In the early 1970s, the "golden age of modernization" had reached its apex, and with it the social scientific belief in the potential of planning and planned reform to transform complex organizations and policy fields in accordance with societal change, to the benefit of all stakeholders.[2] The Catholic Church was, as the *Strukturplan* in the diocese of Münster demonstrated, part and parcel of these endeavors. This is a point that is worth stressing, as it demonstrates that the church was not simply a pre- or even antimodern relic, but rather that its chronology of reform and scientization ties in with developments in West German society at large. The same can be said about the turn that occurred from the early 1970s. As the certainties that had underpinned the planned reform of big structures quickly waned, a new focus on the individual subject finally came to the fore. Thus, there was a new emphasis on "ways of asserting the individual self" and on helping individuals to cope with personal crises and develop meaningful relationships with fellow human beings. With this new focus on the self, the church entered, one could argue, an "age of therapy."[3]

In some respects, this was nothing new for the Catholic Church. Like all systematic forms of religious belief, the Catholic faith encapsulated and codified knowledge on the conduct of personal life and implemented rules for the ethics that individuals were meant to follow. The Catholic Church can even be seen as a trailblazer for modern, therapeutic forms of self-thematization, as it had institutionalized the practice of confession in a long, drawn-out process reaching back to the late Middle Ages.[4] What had changed since 1945 at the latest, though, was that the established forms of Catholic pastoral care had been deemed insufficient for guiding and informing therapeutic help for highly individualized persons. Individualization is, as sociologists like Emile Durkheim and Georg Simmel first noted around 1900, a crucial corollary of the process of functional differentiation. As individuals moved with increasing flexibility between different functional subsystems of society, time-honored religious moral rules and codes of conduct no longer sufficed for them to thoroughly inspect and reflect on their personal selves. After people had lost trust in the wholesale planning of organizational change, the proponents of pastoral care in the Catholic Church turned to psychological approaches for therapeutic help.

The "Psy Sciences" as an Unstable Scientific Field

By turning to methods from psychology, psychotherapy, and group dynamics—a cluster of approaches that sociologist Nikolas Rose has labeled the "psy sciences"[5]—the Catholic Church fundamentally changed its approach to borrowing concepts from the human sciences. For all the conceptual differences in the details, the statistical and sociological approaches both had largely coherent methodological profiles that remained stable for many decades. Statistics, sociography, opinion polling, and organizational sociology had established categorical frameworks for posing and answering questions in predictable ways. Whereas the church did not apply these methods with the same intensity everywhere, their academic profile made it possible to utilize them in a variety of ways rather than presenting obstacles from the outset. After 1945, all of these approaches—with the partial exception of opinion polling, a late addition to academia—became firmly anchored in university research and teaching in the form of statistics and empirical social research. The academic institutionalization of empirical social research provided a relatively stable context for its application in the Catholic Church.

Psychology and psychotherapy, by contrast, involved an extremely heterogeneous scientific methodology. Moreover, psychology cannot always clearly be classed as a science in the first place. Many of the practical counseling concepts and tips for life crises described as psychology are explicitly distant from academic science; practitioners are consequently happy to accept the charge of being "quacks"—also because psychology has only a "low epistemological profile." The boundary between psychology's "positive" knowledge of the object of its study—the psyche—and commonplace psychological ideas is far more porous than in other disciplines.[6] Psychology also remains a fractured discipline. Various forms of neobehaviorism and thus experiment-based sociology dominate in universities, while psychoanalysis, humanist psychology, and most therapeutic approaches have no more than a marginal academic foothold, at least in Germany. Generally taught in private institutions, these latter subjects are dependent for funding on a public willing and able to pay for such services, or on the recognition of such treatments by public health insurers.[7]

If we understand scientific disciplines as communication communities, psychology only partially fits the description. Sociology has experienced repeated controversies since the 1960s, such as the positivism dispute or the Habermas/Luhmann controversy, in which competing schools of thought publicly aired their differences, sometimes expending great emotional energy. It is nevertheless evident that these controversies actually served to ritually portray and confirm the unity of sociology as an academic discipline. The arguments of the other side were listened to, even if they were fundamentally rejected and, perhaps, not fully understood.[8] Such controversies also existed in psychology, for example, in the prevalence of quantifiable research methods originating in the United States, which displaced the German tradition of Gestalt psychology. These methods, however, largely remained limited to university disciplines. If we look at psychology in the broader sense, beyond its academic form, then we see a field marked by isolated, diametrically opposed approaches unwilling to communicate with one another. In this unwillingness to communicate across schools, the discipline followed in the spirit of B.F. Skinner, for decades the decisive figure in neobehaviorism. Like Sigmund Freud, Skinner resolutely refused even to acknowledge academic criticism of his work. From the mid-nineteenth century, psychology as an academic discipline had largely applied statistical methods and favored laboratory experiments as the main techniques of psychological research. This marginalized all approaches that either did not share this self-conception of psychology, which was modeled on the natural sciences, or indeed rejected it entirely.[9]

Psychology is thus an unstable academic field, particularly when it comes to the psychoanalytic and psychotherapeutic approaches, which have put down only marginal roots in the university system. Theories for systematizing a discipline's research program usually emerge only once academic practice has already developed and differentiated itself. In psychology, methods were only explicated and codified to a rudimentary level and tended to be passed on through personal interaction between "teachers" and "pupils."[10] As the quote at the beginning of this chapter shows, Catholic supporters of utilizing psychology were sometimes exasperated about the unstable nature of the field. Writing in 1975 on the connection and competition between pastoral care and psychoanalysis, Gottfried Griesl referred to the conciliar document on the training of priests, "Optatam Totius," which had called for employing "the latest findings of a sound psychology" for that purpose.[11] Yet even Griesl had difficulty determining exactly what such a "sound psychology" looked like. And even more puzzling than the plethora of competing "schools" of psychology was the fact that almost anyone could claim to offer some form of "therapy." The lack of systematic truth criteria and proper accountability differentiated the Catholic Church's scientization in this field from its reception of sociography or opinion polling.

These characteristics of psychological practice have consequences for the historical reconstruction of this period of the church's scientization. Where knowledge of psychology did not involve experimental techniques, it was applied only to a very limited extent within the ordered routines of bureaucratic administrative practice that had been central to the implementation of sociology in the church. Psychology was largely taught and applied in spontaneous and ephemeral face-to-face interactions. Only rarely did it find expression in writing, and even then usually indirectly. In the following section, I therefore focus on reflective descriptions and model-based deliberations that marked out the claims to truth and the limits of the language of psychology in the church.

Therapy as an Attempt to Reintegrate the "Self"

All forms of the psychological and psychotherapeutic discourse based on the idea that the human "self" or personality is linked to consciousness share two common features. They all see psychology as the one form of knowledge that can be mobilized in order to explain and create the problematic unity and integrity of the self: "Wo Es war, soll Ich werden" (Where id was, there ego shall become).[12] Sigmund Freud's famous dictum reflects the psychological discourse's optimistic and harmonious vision, which aims to reconstruct the unity of individuals in the face of the contradictory impulses, desires, and demands that drive them. Modern psychology greatly expanded upon traditional prescientific knowledge about the inner conflict of the self and its neurotic tendencies to deceive and destroy itself, and developed new categories for explaining these. However, psychology ultimately gains its authority and legitimacy in imagining and finding ways for individuals to be autonomous, whole, and self-fulfilled amid modern society's fragmentation and inner alienation.[13] Catholic psychologists expressed this aim as the longing for a "psychosynthesis."[14] In seeking to reconstruct the human subject, however, psychology is unable to draw upon any central, consensual paradigm on the structure, inner conflicts, and external dynamics of personality. Psychology's main currents and their many tributaries and schools are divided on precisely these matters. Psychologists do not have any consistent anthropological premises. However, they do agree that the malleability of the individual is a core human characteristic.

The second discursive underpinning of psychology is the conviction that it is a science whose special mission, expertise, and dignity lies in molding and modeling the "healthy" and "normal" person. The structural characteristics of the psychological discourse include the way in which knowledge of the psyche takes on a practical dimension that remolds it at the same time. The unity of psychology consists in the diversity of forms with which it conducts therapy as a practice of intervention in the human self.[15]

Therapeutic discourse is characterized by its isolation of problems and symptoms and attempts to contribute to "solving" and "healing" them. Therapy provides a thematically open, problem-centered, and protected area of communication for working through problems, typically by using the asymmetrical question/answer structure. In therapy, individuals can thematize aspects of their selves that do not otherwise find a legitimate place in social communication and, from the "subject's" point of view, are not taken sufficiently seriously. Therapists intervene in the biographical meanings expressed by clients by isolating and defining the object of the intervention, offering ways to look at issues that differ from the clients' descriptions, and suggesting techniques for solving conflicts of the self.[16] Therapy can be understood in general as a form of advice offering clients new categories for observing their psychosocial problems. These serve to provoke and break through clients' routine ways of thinking about and interpreting their own suffering. For all the differences in the techniques used to solve these problems, three dimensions of mental crises can be distinguished that psychotherapy utilizes in its interventions. The first dimension is time; that is, the life history of the client, which is emphasized paradigmatically in the psychoanalytic model of "remembering-repeating-working through." The second dimension involves specific thematic concerns of individuals or a group. The focus on specific themes in "theme-centered interaction," for instance, is meant to prevent people from becoming lost in the dynamic of group interaction. Third, the focus may be on the client's social dimension. In this case, the social relationship between the client and the therapist is itself the center of attention, as in the paradigmatic example of the "client-centered therapy" of Carl Rogers.

The History of the Catholic Reception of Psychoanalysis

The experimental psychology of Wilhelm Wundt (1832–1920) had already awakened Catholic theologians' interest in the new science. Following Wundt's model, Cardinal Mercier (1851–1926) founded a psychological laboratory in Leuven where his students carried out research. In Milan and other cities, too, clergy members worked with methods of experimental psychology.[17] Central to the reception and fortunes of psychology in the Catholic Church was the psychoanalysis founded by Sigmund Freud. To this day, pastoral-psychological work is obliged to articulate its relationship to psychoanalysis and to legitimize its own objectives against the backdrop of Freud's understanding of the science and the human mind.[18] The Catholic reception of psychoanalysis differed from that of doctors, psychologists, and, indeed, Protestants, although it bore at least some similarities to the latter.[19]

The Catholic debate on psychoanalysis began during the First World War. During the early 1920s, the debate broadened as the new method seemed to become an "epidemic."[20] Initially, intellectual resistance was powerful, feeding upon three focal Catholic criticisms of Freudian psychology. These strategic criticisms continued to mark the boundaries of what psychoanalytic knowledge was allowed to say about humankind from the Weimar Republic until the 1960s. While some priests and pastoral workers advocated open-mindedness toward the new methods of "dissecting the soul" and their relevance to pastoral care, even such supporters expressed their moral outrage at what they regarded as the entirely unacceptable premises of psychoanalysis. The first point of dissent between the anthropological premises of the church and those of psychoanalysis was the latter's "fatalistic determinism." The drives-based model of the psyche, critics lamented, seemed to have no place for the individual's "ethical freedom of choice."[21] Albert Görres, one of the most committed Catholic advocates of the practical application of psychoanalytic forms of therapy, also decisively rejected this drives-based "determinism." As early as 1923, pastoral theologian Linus Bopp had stressed that the "mechanical-materialistic" theory of the human psyche unacceptably presented it as a "machine with the purpose of maximizing pleasure."[22] Catholic moral teaching, which was based on the freedom and ethical responsibility of the individual, perceived this axiomatic "despiritualization" as an unparalleled "desacralization of man."[23]

The second fundamental Catholic criticism of psychoanalysis attacked its "pansexualism." In this, Catholics were by no means alone. One of the most common objections to Freud's theory is its reductionist attribution of a sexual cause for all psychological phenomena.[24] Among Catholics, however, pansexualism almost became a synonym for psychoanalysis. This semantic coupling and the serious implications it implied were so commonplace that psychoanalysis rarely received more detailed treatment. In crude form, the term was closely associated with the allegation that Freud regarded all human ties as "sexually determined": one's relationship with one's parents (the Oedipus complex), with one's siblings (incest), and even with one's self (narcissism).[25] Most Catholic writers, however, related psychoanalysis to Freud's theory of sublimation, wherein all "cultural achievements," and thus even religion, were based on the "omnipotence of a shadowy instinctual life." "This teaching" of the "cultural power of the sex drive" was usually rejected less for scientific reasons than out of fear that it would have unwanted pedagogical effects. For the bastion of Catholic moral teaching as a means of disciplining human sexuality, Freud's theory presented a "grave danger to popular morals."[26] The causal personality model of psychoanalysis, it was suggested, was being willfully interpreted as a release from the constraints of moral finality.

Into the 1960s, the charge of pansexualism continued to be central to many Catholic theologians' and religious scholars' rejection of psychoanalysis.[27] Alongside those who engaged in such wholesale damnation, however, were voices more sophisticatedly refuting the link between religion and sublimation. These included Linus Bopp, a Weimar Republic Catholic advocate of thoroughly engaging with psychoanalysis, and the doctor Rhaban Liertz.[28] Bopp, too, emphasized the "panerotic guiding thread" of Sigmund Freud's work. Yet he knew about drive theory's reformulation since the First World War, with its addition of a so-called death drive or destruction drive.[29]

The scales tipped in favor of psychoanalysis after the Second World War. No longer at issue were the legitimacy and limits of a reception of psychoanalytic theory, but rather the practical application of the analytic methods for therapeutic purposes. The dominant reaction was no longer "shock at the theoretical excesses" of psychoanalysis, but instead the appreciation of the insight it provided into "valid experiences" that nobody involved in treating neuroses "could neglect with impunity."[30] One priest concluded from the practice of therapeutic work that "sexuality" was a "primordial fact of human existence," meaning that the "repression of sexuality" by many Christians should cease. From this greater critical distance, it was also evident that Freud's understanding of "sexuality" was much wider than the common usage of the term, generally encompassing people's "libidinous" striving toward each other. In any case, most critics of psychoanalysis, as they had to concede at this stage, had only studied it from secondary literature and had often copied each other's work.[31]

The third point in the Catholic resistance to psychoanalysis was the atheism that Freud attributed with great decisiveness to himself and to his work on psychoanalysis, which in his view was entirely free of religious illusions.[32] In 1923, Ludwig Bopp was still able to claim that psychoanalysts had at least a "pragmatic" appreciation of religion, referring in particular to the reformed Swiss priest and psychologist Oskar Pfister, who had been Freud's close friend since 1909 and tried to popularize his thinking in theology.[33] It was hard to maintain this argument after 1927, however, when, in a text entitled "The Future of an Illusion," Freud himself analyzed religion as a "rich store of ideas . . . born of the need to make tolerable the helplessness of man." In this article, Freud expressed his conviction that followers of religion were defending "a lost cause."[34] Faced with such clear hostility toward God, even Bopp concluded that Freud and his school had "soiled every domain of values" and "psychologized and relativized everything," greatly contributing to the "enormous rise" of the "third confession . . . of secularism."[35]

Neutralizing the Negative Elements of Psychoanalysis

These three core areas of criticism—determinism, pansexualism, and atheism—characterized the Catholic reception of psychoanalysis from its beginnings in the 1920s. Writers whose mission was to gather support within Catholic theology and the church for engaging more intensively with the analytic method and to draw up models for using psychoanalytic insights in pastoral care also had to respect these issues. Such authors developed strategies for neutralizing the unacceptable statements of psychoanalytic discourse and thus improving the prospects for its positive reception. The first strategy was to break psychoanalysis down into several parts that could then be assessed individually.

This procedure separated "the wheat from the chaff on the basis of the Catholic worldview" and collected the "grains of truth."[36] In general, the psychoanalytic discourse was neutralized by a simple binary distinction between "therapy" and "worldview"; that is, between the "method" and the "system," with a clean distinction thought to be entirely possible in principal.[37] "Psychoanalysis is divisible"—this was the idea at the heart of the operation that continued after 1945 to neutralize the undesirable implications of the discipline.[38] The Catholic reception thus decisively rejected Freud's tendency, particularly in his later years, to extend and generalize his insights from treating patients into a comprehensive cultural theory. This was sufficient to circumnavigate two of the most important obstacles: Freud's atheism and the pansexualism of his theories. It also drew attention to the fact that Freud's therapeutic method could "certainly achieve good successes."[39] There was already a wide-reaching consensus in the 1920s that incorporating the "many results verified by psychoanalysis" into the "Christian view of the soul" was not only possible, but indeed "urgently necessary."[40]

Different writers found different insights from psychoanalysis to be useful to the church. Freud's efforts to make the "whole person" the object of his therapeutic method were given a highly positive reception.[41] Linus Bopp identified the rediscovery of, and concentration on, the unconscious as an important service to science.[42] Given the praise of many Catholic authors for Freud's theory of the unconscious, it was of little importance how exactly psychoanalysis understood its inner makeup and functioning. It was enough to know that its existence could be proven "experimentally, so to speak," through hypnosis, as had already been shown even before Freud. In place of Freud's vivid and elaborate description of the psychological apparatus, the Catholic reception featured metaphors such as the "roots of the mental processes," which "lay hidden in the dark earth of the unconscious." What was decisive here was not theoretical precision but the "comfort" that the knowledge of the forces raging in the "dark bosom of the unconscious" could provide to all pastoral workers who occasionally despaired at the ineffectiveness of their efforts. Such metaphors outlined a place that neither the conscious will of the subject, nor even the best pastoral care, could reach.[43]

As early as the interwar period there were several strong indications that the categorical resistance to the psychoanalytic movement was waning. A relatively broad swath of Catholics and theologians had begun to engage with the ideas of Freud and his most important students. The objections to Freud's determinism, pansexualism, and atheism remained, but the increasingly stereotypical way in which they were repeated made it clear that the outright rejection of the psychoanalytic discourse was giving way to an interest in the detailed issues it examined. With a few exceptions, however, this interest remained academic and theoretical. This would not change until the early 1950s. In the meantime, the discursive front against Freud's concept of the person continued to overshadow any attempts to reconcile psychotherapy and pastoral care. Nevertheless, the dispute over concepts and their interpretations had yielded center stage to a practical interest in the new potential psychoanalysis and other therapeutic methods presented for human guidance and the formation of the person.[44]

Exploring the Therapeutic Potential of Psychoanalysis

Albert Görres (1918–96), a Catholic psychoanalyst and psychotherapist who taught medicine and psychoanalysis in Mainz, played a key role in influencing the debate on the reception of the psy sciences in the West German Catholic Church. His 1958 book, *The Method and Experiences of Psychoanalysis*, set the tone. This was the first serious and matter-of-fact monograph introducing Freud's analytic method specifically to a Catholic audience. Görres emphasized by way of introduction that he had no desire to be "Freud's faithful disciple," but could no longer summon the "pathos of moral and scientific outrage" that had characterized many earlier Catholic views. For Görres, the important thing was no longer the "sum of statements" about psychological phenomena contained in the corpus of psychoanalytic knowledge, nor was it Freud's "system of theoretical psychology," although he believed both deserved positive recognition. His interest focused far more on the "method of psychological examination" as a tool for uncovering and curing psychological disorders.[45] Other authors, too, thought it was time for the church to discard its "fearful cold distrust" of psychology and instead to base its future reception and application on the discipline's "practical benefit" in enabling priests to "influence, improve, and lead themselves and others." The changed attitude toward the psychological discourse could be seen in writers' new reactions to what they continued to perceive as Freud's distorted view of the human soul. For example, Görres did not believe that the "cure" for the "mistakes of psychoanalysis" lay "directly" in control and criticism from the watchtower of Christian anthropology. Instead, the "erroneous" psychoanalytic interpretation of some psychological phenomena had to be corrected "at the scientific level" itself.

Otherwise, one might get the impression that the Christian image of humanity contradicted the "scientific" one of "modern psychology."[46]

This clearly illustrates the shift that had taken place since the interwar period in the Catholic attitude toward the psychological discourse. Christian anthropology no longer automatically provided the yardstick for assessing ideas from the human sciences. Instead, the church now had to give leeway for science to judge, self-referentially, which concepts and terminology were most suitable to access the human psyche. This change in approach, together with many pastoral workers' growing interest in psychotherapy, provided the context for Pope Pius XII's intervention. In three addresses in 1952, 1953, and 1958, which he meant as an attempt to contain Catholics' interest in depth psychology, he successively softened the church's criticism of psychoanalytic pansexualism.[47] After the second address, Catholic psychotherapists already believed that their work had the "approval and blessing" of the pope.[48]

However, the pope's intervention came too late and failed in its intent to contain interest in psychology. Whereas isolated attempts to train clergy as "psychoanalytic specialist pastoral workers" had generated skepticism in the Weimar Republic,[49] by the post–Second World War period, "no few" Catholic priests were acquiring systematic knowledge of depth psychology and often passing it on to others. These included, for example, the senior schoolteacher Hans Böhringer from Stuttgart, whose numerous publications and speeches at conferences of priests made him known to "many pastoral workers" in the 1960s.[50] Spurred by his "helplessness" in the face of some problems raised in confession and religious teaching, Böhringer had worked with depth psychology since the late 1940s. After studying at the Institut für Tiefenpsychologie und Psychotherapie (Institute for Depth Psychology and Psychotherapy) in Stuttgart, which also included two training analyses, he passed his exam to become a psychotherapist in 1957. Alongside his day-to-day work as a teacher of religion, he now advised and treated people in "psychological distress."[51]

Thus, within fifteen years after the end of the Second World War, the Catholic Church's reception of psychoanalysis fundamentally shifted its focus compared to the interwar years. Before 1945, the legitimacy of the Freudian worldview and its categories had been up for debate, as well as the specific way in which the psychoanalytic discourse talked about the human mind. This continued to be a source of reservations about psychoanalysis in the postwar era, albeit in more moderate form. Now, however, the key issue was the form and institutional contexts in which Catholic doctors and pastoral workers applied psychoanalytic knowledge relating to the therapeutic classification of psychological problems.

By 1960, the writing was on the wall for the traditional pastoral model in which the everyday behavior of Catholics, and especially their sexuality, was addressed by a thick net of moral proscriptions and prescriptions. Highly differentiated casuistries governed their application. Notwithstanding all the differences and ambivalences in the psychoanalytic system of categorization, it was clear that psychology could help in establishing the truth of the self in a way that the traditional, morally informed pastoral discourse could not. Knowledge of psychology promised a truth effect that many observers believed could aid in dealing with pastoral problems. Yet it remained unclear where this knowledge should be used and which practices, methods, and forms should be applied. For our purposes, it also raises the question of which specific features of social change favored and contributed to the growing influence of a new toolbox of psychology in pastoral care. It is to these issues that we turn in the following section.

The Confession Box as a Site of Counseling?

Various researchers have investigated the sacrament of penance, of which the actual confession of sins is only a part. Sociologist Alois Hahn has focused on the notion of a compulsion to confess wherein confession serves as one of many forms of self-thematization individuals utilize to generate biographical knowledge, and thus as an important step in the emergence of the modern subject.[52] In the context of this study, the ritual of confession is especially interesting as a site of the practical application of a human science, in this case a form of knowledge that explores and systematizes the possibilities and forms of human guidance and the formation of the person. Focusing on this aspect not only fits this study's own research interest in the application of human sciences discourses in the Catholic Church; it also corresponds to the perception of many theologians who, at an early stage, explicitly contrasted psychology's new guidance techniques with pastoral workers' traditional approaches to ethical teaching and the moral character of individual Catholics.

This contrast not only referred to confession but also to the practice of spiritual guidance or spiritual direction (*Seelenführung*). The early influences of the psychological discourse can be seen in the breakdown of any common taxonomy for *Seelenführung* and its place in the overall complex of life-shaping pastoral care in confession, catechesis, marriage seminars, and counseling on life's turning points. Linus Bopp, for instance, writing in 1923, thought that the functions of the confessor and the spiritual director should be more closely linked. Those who wanted their life story to be one of "improvement" rather than simply being free of guilt had to entrust themselves to a "single guidance," which would examine more than just the sinful aspects of their souls.[53] When, five years later, pastoral theologian Theodor Müncker examined the links between pastoral care and psychoanalysis, he considered it self-evident that the two functions of confessor and spiritual director should be brought together in one person. He assumed that the "striving for perfection" spiritual direction implied in the search for a Christian life in practice often needed to be protected from "self-delusion and extravagance."

Knowledge of psychoanalysis could offer valuable "methodological" depth here, as the concept of the unconscious provided access to "inhibitions" and supposed feelings of guilt that spiritual directors had thus far only been able to guess at.[54] Spiritual direction was therefore also described as the "midpoint" between the sacrament of penitence and psychotherapeutic treatment. Other authors, however, insisted that the actual purpose of spiritual direction was for individuals to "orient their lives in accordance with the Gospel," which could not be reconciled with the "narcissistic self-reflection" of psychoanalytic methods.[55] However, spiritual direction did not follow a fixed program in seeking to practice and perfect a Christian lifestyle, which meant that "therapeutic" pastoral practices inspired by pastoral psychology could be brought under its roof.[56]

As the Catholic Church already possessed sophisticated techniques for guiding people in the form of confession and spiritual direction in the broader sense, it was natural to compare these practices with the new psychoanalytic method. It is not only psychoanalysts and psychotherapists who have drawn such a parallel since the 1920s, but also many theologians.[57] Some clergy noted with great satisfaction that, thanks to the intensive discussion about the methods and effectiveness of psychoanalytic therapies, confession's potentially highly "therapeutic" effect and its immense "importance to curative education" was finally being recognized again.[58] This model of confession contrasted considerably to the reality in the first half of the twentieth century. In practice, confession was usually a highly formalized ritual, which dealt with infringements of the church's commandments and norms as a matter of routine. The sixth commandment and thus the regulation of sexuality took the most important position in both child and adult confession.[59]

The typological comparison of confession and psychotherapy, by contrast, assumed a practice of confession in which the remorse those confessing expressed to the priest could release them from their "disruptive symptoms." Confession also culminates in the absolution of guilt—something no psychoanalysis can offer. Thus, confession had long before achieved the "free expression of the patient in front of the therapist—the great achievement of the psychoanalytic setting . . . in a much better form."[60] Pastoral workers could benefit from psychoanalytic insights into the early childhood etiology of neuroses and sexual urges such as masturbation. Enriching the confessor's approach with psychoanalytic knowledge, and thus making him "more understanding," would enable him to increase his "influence on those entrusted to him" even further in comparison to traditional methods of spiritual guidance.[61]

The Different Codes of Pastor and Therapist

For all the analogies they drew between psychoanalytic therapy and Catholic confession as methods of guiding people, most authors agreed that there is a fundamental difference between the two forms of communication. The confessor, wrote the French clergyman Marc Oraison, should avoid an "attempt at therapy," restricting himself instead to his role as the "minister of grace."[62] Even a staunch advocate of analytic approaches such as Albert Görres insisted that the two communicative codes of pastor and therapist should not be confused or mixed with one another.[63] He felt it was unjust to the client to describe personal disturbances and neurotic symptoms as "evil," using the pastoral code of sin and absolution. Instead, these were to be treated strictly in accordance with the code of the doctor, distinguishing between ill and healthy patients. His warning was directed first and foremost at clergy members who tended all too easily to treat most people as deeply "immature" in religious respects, despite all the hopes invested at that time in the "mature Christian." Their misjudgment, argued Görres, was the product of a negative anthropology that understood the "soul" as an organ that was "easily confused" and "easily damaged in its innermost life." It was here that Görres also located the basis of many pastors' distrust of psychoanalysis. For psychoanalysts, a neurosis was the symptom of developmental problems beyond an individual's control rather than "freely chosen," and thus could not simply be excised by clergy working within the "realm of free will."[64]

Philipp von Wambolt also set his sights on the deeply pessimistic Catholic view of man as a being in need of continual guidance in his 1971 comments on a text by Hermann-Josef Spital that centered on the topics of "orthopraxy, a demanding God, and a ban on divorce." Spital, argued the sociologist von Wambolt, assumed that individuals would develop a "strong tendency toward hedonism" if "not tamed by the strict demands of authorities." In von Wambolt's view, however, many pastors' incorrect belief that people "continually" engage in "disobedience, sensual pleasure," and "the exercise of power" caused their "frustration." The methodological advice von Wambolt gave to his superior in the diocese of Münster was no coincidence: "Read the transcripts of psychotherapeutic treatments. You will be amazed how difficult people make life for themselves and others." Although pastors should not ignore the "guilt" of the individual, they needed, in their pastoral care, to perceive and understand people at last in "all their complexity."[65] Von Wambolt effectively argued for church pastoral care to arm itself with the distinction between "sin" and "neurosis." Only then would it acquire a realistic image of man and be open to the "wealth of strengths" of the people who "are in fact its allies."[66] His intervention thus paralleled a view expressed in the Catholic reception of psychoanalysis. This held that pastoral spiritual guidance could only be wholly effective if it refrained from trying to uncover or repress the neurotic causes of spiritual distress. These neuroses, believed psychologists, were "unconscious and not clearly desired. As such, they represented neither sin nor the object of confession."[67]

These voices insisted on the strict distinction between the codes of confession and therapeutic conversation. However, this offered no guarantee that applying therapeutic concepts to pastoral care would not affect the code of confession, which was based on sin and absolution. As confession began visibly to lose its effectiveness in comparison to therapy, the issue became acute. Von Wamboldt had recognized the "general bankruptcy of 'spiritual guidance'" since the early 1970s. He believed that the causes could "obviously" not be found in the behavior or lack of will of Catholic laypeople, but rather in the structures and practices of spiritual direction itself. He cited the wide reception of "successful Catholic authors" such as Ignace Lepp and Friedrich Ernst von Gagern as a strong indicator of the change that had taken place. Both published a whole series of widely read books in the 1950s and early 1960s that explored problems of Christian ethics and lifestyle in exemplary fashion. The books included psychological categories and models of thought in both implicit and explicit form. The decline of spiritual guidance through confession was evident in this mass boom in self-help literature—a "symptomatic phenomenon" that stepped into the breach.[68]

As early as the 1950s and early 1960s, then, there were relatively specific ideas relating to auricular confession—the most important method of human guidance in the church—and its lack of individual appropriateness and psychological depth. Such issues were discussed with dramatically increased intensity and urgency beginning in the 1970s. A retrospective causal analysis was supposed to identify the most important causes of the rapid decline in one-to-one confession. The precise date one selected as the start of the decline formed part of the search for causes. Those who dated it to the late 1960s brought the "detraditionalization" associated with the 1968 generation into play.[69] A parish in Rheine, in which the number of private confessions fell by 50 percent between 1968 and 1971, supported this interpretation. Others, meanwhile, argued that the traditional practice of confession had only suffered serious decline as a result of the alternatives available from the end of the 1960s in the form of the penitential services (*Bußgottesdienste*) and penitential meditations (*Bußandachten*). A priest in Ibbenbüren, however, countered that, by 1966, he had already seen confessions decline by around one-third since 1964, while the first penitential meditations had not taken place until December 1968. In his experience, some of the congregation who regularly attended penitential services actually returned to private confessions.[70]

The Dramatic Crisis of Auricular Confession

This priest was more or less alone in his optimism, however. By 1970, nearly everyone agreed that there had been a dramatic decline in traditional, auricular confession.[71] When it became apparent that this development was irreversible, attempts to explain it ran wild. One pastoral strategy consisted of searching for the causes among the faithful and alleging that they were insufficiently "aware of their sins." The strategy of attributing the crisis of confession to the deficient consciousness of individual Catholics could hardly expect to meet broad agreement, however. It was too obvious that such an approach ignored the links between the crisis of faith and wider social developments that the sociographic and opinion polling discourses had popularized.[72]

The existing influence of the human sciences meant that a different explanatory approach that applied them to some extent could expect to meet with greater approval. The Freckenhorst Circle tried such an approach. Believing that people had simply become less aware that their sinful behavior might be considered objectionable, this group of priests reopened the question of responsibility by looking at both sociological and psychological factors. They questioned the anthropological premises held by traditional moral teaching, according to which people's ability to make self-empowered decisions was at best "accidental" or "exceptionally limited." By way of contrast, they pointed to the psychological discourse, in which "major burdens," "taboos established in early childhood," and "neurotic complexes" seriously restricted the freedom of the self. From this perspective, the "taboo-based morality" of traditional auricular confession was itself one of the factors that made individuals "unfree" and therefore not automatically accountable for their own sinful behavior.[73] The pastoral-psychological analysis thus saw the "helplessness" of spiritual guidance as a central cause of the decline in confession. Catholics no longer expected a "judicial or ritual" administration of the sacrament, but rather "assistance with their difficulties in life."[74]

These explanatory approaches cited exogenous causes for the decline of traditional confession. Whether complaining in moralizing terms about people's habitual lack of awareness of their own sins, or seeking explanations from the human sciences in the form of social theory, these strategies focused on people's motivation for going to confession in the first place rather than the actual form that the sacrament took. A further attempt at explanation, however, put the "formulaic" and routinized practice of confession under the microscope, describing the acknowledgement of sin as "far too mechanical" and the confessional conversation as "much too short." Münster bishop Heinrich Tenhumberg also put forward this view in his Lenten pastoral letter in 1971 in order to fend off other interpretations of the crisis of confession from the human sciences: "Depth psychology," "behavioral research," and "social studies," he argued, had made it clear that people's behavior was "not as independent" as usually assumed. This insight had led, for example, to the idea of rehabilitation in criminal justice. However, not only the personal guilt of the individual but also the "guilt of the whole of humanity" arising from "original sin" was up for debate. "Let nobody discuss away our sin and guilt!" he implored his readers. With this plea, Tenhumberg unintentionally revealed the feet of clay that the church's central code of sin/absolution really stood upon. Meanwhile, the discourses of the human sciences were already well on the way to "discussing away" and invalidating this code and its specific form of expression.[75]

Theologians who wished for confession to be redesigned to gain psychological insight into the personality of the penitent also supported an endogenous analysis of the causes of the crisis. Their criticism focused on the mechanical and impersonal nature of confession as structured by the confession manual, which prescribed that grown women should confess to "overindulgent eating" and fifty-year-old men to "disobedience" to their fathers. This "legalistic mode of confession," they believed, had to be replaced by the "dialogue of a real conversation" in which the confessor would take on the function of religious "life support" and would thus work as a real spiritual director.[76] Using Karl Rahner's terminology, these critics described the traditional practice of confession as "legalistic."[77] Given the decline of anonymous auricular confession, Catholic theologians and psychologists had no choice but to seek practical ways out of the crisis and a renewal or redesign of the sacrament of penance. Just like the analysis of the causes, however, a plethora of alternatives were proposed.

Alternatives to the Confession Box

The first strategy to emerge was the pluralization of the possible forms of confession. "Lay confession" and the "revision de vie," which was practiced in groups such as core circles, were cited as new possibilities for a "pluriform confessional practice" to supplement private confession. Lay confession among married couples, friends, or members of Christian groups placed "particularly high demands" on participants for obvious reasons if it raised problems with the relationship itself. According to its advocates, it was supposed to break down "hardened fronts" and overcome "resigned silence." Not least among the advantages was laypeople's greater "life experience and relevant knowledge" than priests'.[78] This optimism about such a new practice of confession already indicates the kind of effects that could be anticipated from making recourse to the psychological discourse.

The traditional understanding of the sacrament of penitence was that it took immediate effect upon being administered (*opus operatum*). This sacramental absolution was now replaced, however, by the arduous daily business of "working on relationships." There was to be no more penitence "that does not hurt, that does not expose, and in which one remains wholly anonymous." Penitents now had to make their own efforts rather than merely passively receiving the institutional grace imparted by the priest.[79] This program of lay confession as part of a married relationship unmistakably introduced the idea of therapy to the process of penitence and thus drove the "increase in self-controls" characteristic of modern therapeutic discourse. Instead of being carried by the inflated romantic notion of love, with its irreconcilable paradoxes, marriage was now to be a form of continual therapy. Constant self-monitoring through self-therapy appeared to offer the individual greater opportunities and room for self-development. The implications of being compelled to reach insincere agreement with a partner on mutual candor within a relationship, for instance, were not considered.[80]

The most intensively discussed and frequently practiced alternative to the confession box was and remains the penitential service, in which those assembled in the congregation are called upon to repent and renew their lives. This form of liturgy primarily met the needs of the middle class, whose ideas about morality had little in common with the catalogue of sins used in private confessions. A master craftswoman from Telgte demonstrated this in recalling a negative experience she had in the confession box that caused her to eschew going there for three years, until the town's implementation of penitential meditation in 1969:

> Vicar P. asked if I had anything to say about the sixth commandment. I answered no. I was in the confession box for over a quarter of an hour on Christmas Eve, since he didn't find out anything about me, he told me to attend the first Holy Mass of Christmas as penance. I didn't accept this. As I wrote earlier, our marriage is simply wonderful and extremely happy. Since the incident, confession has been taboo for us.[81]

She also recounted the town's "enthusiasm" for the penitential meditation. The penitential service leads to a joint confession of sins and appeal for forgiveness. In practice, inspired by examples from the Netherlands, a prayer of absolution by the priest often follows. Some groups of progressive laypeople and theologians, not least among them the Freckenhorst Circle, hoped these services would be recognized as a form of the penitential sacrament, believing this to be theologically justifiable. The discussion about the "equal value" of both forms of confession primarily concerned the question of whether so-called grave or mortal sins could be forgiven in a church service. Ultimately, however, the relevant resolutions of the German Bishops' Conference and the Würzburg Synod ruled out the penitential service taking on such a sacramental function.[82] The synod resolution on the pastoral sacrament described the penitential service as a forum for "exploring conscience" with regard to the "social sins" that come prior to and form the context of the sins of the individual. Such collective penitence was therefore meant to raise awareness of social scientific knowledge about the socialization of guilt and the church's moral outrage at the unequal distribution of the world's wealth. In more concrete terms, it was to illustrate clearly the "failure of small communities and whole parishes, for example, in the case of social injustices in the parish area or responsibility for the Third World."[83]

This socialization of guilt was only one answer to the crisis of the private confession, and, for all the controversy surrounding the penitential service, a rather marginal one. Updating the institutional arrangements and the form of the one-to-one confession received much more attention, with the aim of making new use of confession's potential to lead people. Another suggestion was to apply "more profane forms of penance and repentance." The religious pedagogue Felicitas Betz, for example, wanted to convince the Würzburg Synod members to increase Catholics' self-awareness and control over their own behavior by means of sensitivity training, self-experience groups, and individual analyses. God was "obviously" to be found everywhere that "repentance is really exercised," she reasoned.[84] This proposal had little chance of being realized, however.

A real change in private confession was projected into an area where priests' existing categories of judgment and models of communication had prevented them from understanding the real processes through which individuals developed their conscience—processes that were now to be examined empirically. This meant abandoning the "scholastic puppet-like morality" of existing spiritual guidance, which utilized reason and will to direct an "abstract person."[85] The prescientific terminology, with terms such as "abnormal," "without scruples," and "hysterical," was to be torn up.[86] The secret to addressing and overcoming personal guilt appropriately was to ensure that it was "expressed and acknowledged personally" rather than through the fixed forms of the confession manual. Psychoanalysis informed both the need for and the effectiveness of this strategy of "verbalizing" personal conflicts; analytic conversation provided a practical model.[87] The monologue structure of the existing sacrament, in which the priest followed the individual's confession with some encouraging words, was to be transformed into "a real conversation" addressing more general questions of personality and lifestyle.[88]

In contrast to the controversies surrounding the penitential service, theologians, priests, and bishops generally agreed that confession should take on the character of a dialogue. Differences did arise, however, in the details. For example, Karl Rahner raised the question of whether parishioners should engage in confession by free choice rather than out of "legal obligation," even if they might not confess sins.[89] Other theologians advocated the move to a "Christianity of choice" where there would be less "quantitative thinking" and piety would no longer be measured by the extent to which people followed the orthopraxy. Traditional auricular confession, they claimed, had "overmoralized" Christianity. In future, a "modern, existential confessional liturgy" would be essential, in which terms from the field of psychology such as "self-discovery" and "identification" would play a role.[90] Authors writing from the perspective of pastoral psychology advocated confessional conversation as the most important means for bringing the "therapeutic dimension" of confession to bear. Such conversation acted as a "helpful accompaniment" in the event of disturbances in individuals' spiritual, family, and working life, especially concerning the dangers of addiction and depression that were on the rise everywhere. This form of confessional conversation was no longer in the "service of a church jurisdiction," but sought to provide practical advice and early interventions in the life crises of the "sufferer."[91]

Suffering/Healing as a Therapeutic Code of Communication

Confession's characteristic code of sin/forgiveness was not wholly devalued, though it was joined by a second code that operated on the duality of suffering/healing and saw itself as a form of therapy. The latter was based on the idea of the indivisibility of the person who had been promised "healing." This meant that priests, whose job it was to "heal" those who came to them, also had to engage with the "natural" precursors to sin.[92]

A more therapeutic approach to confession not only required deep changes to the patterns of communication it used, but also an adjustment to the settings in which it took place and the attitude of the confessor. First, all churches needed a confession room to provide space for the confessional conversation in which the priest and the person making the confession could have a relaxed, face-to-face discussion without fear of being overheard. The confession box was unsuitable, as it was cramped and, on major church holidays in particular, confessions were heard in such rapid succession that longer confessions aroused suspicion. In practice, many priests had already been granting absolution in a private room outside the church for many years.[93] Second, if confession really was to turn from a "formal register of sins into a real conversation," priests would have to learn new communicative behavior and, particularly, practice a technique for which their job had left them ill-equipped: they would have to "learn to listen."[94]

Catholic pastoral psychologists believed that priests typically interrupted advice seekers within two and a half minutes and presented them with their verdict.[95] If the confessor was to become a therapist, however, he would have to set aside the habitus of the "stern judge" in favor of communicative behavior, whose attributes had already been formulated in the positive Catholic reception of therapeutic approaches.[96] First and foremost, these included "restraint" as the primary feature of a "willingness to help," as well as respect for the "inner life of the soul," which the confessional conversation had to penetrate.[97] In psychoanalytic terms, these maxims meant that the therapist should refrain from taking "any authoritarian attitude" toward the client and avoid any element of "suggestion."[98]

Formulating such therapeutic maxims was one thing. A more difficult task was giving priests the communication skills they needed for in-depth confessional conversations. They also had to understand why psychology-based conversational techniques were necessary and to learn to accept them. Otherwise, the confessional conversation, for all its widespread support, would in practice be no more than a more time-consuming version of the clergy's existing patterns of communication. To do justice to the new demands, the church needed models from the human sciences. A rapidly growing body of literature on techniques for pastoral conversations and especially Carl Rogers's concept of a nondirective, client-centered therapy provided these.[99] The practitioners of Rogers's techniques repeatedly invoked the danger that priests would merely acquire superficial knowledge of the relevant techniques from reading a few books and conduct "amateur psychotherapy" without adequate specialist training.[100] Nevertheless, the Würzburg Synod advised bishops to use regular courses to drive priests' training in "conversational methods and counseling."[101]

Around the mid-1970s, at the time of this resolution, many priests still exhibited a practical and habitual resistance to more therapeutic confessional conversation. Although most confessions by this time were, in the words of a Westphalian dean, much more "personal" than in the earlier, ritualized model of the confessional manual, a real confessional conversation was still a long way away—and not only because of a lack of training. For one thing, priests were short of the time needed for such conversations. On average, it added up to twenty to thirty minutes plus time for preparation and follow-up work. Even though Catholics were only meant to practice this form of confession once or twice a year at most instead of every four to six weeks, it raised the priests' workload considerably. Empirical studies on the work of priests showed that—including visits to the sick—they assisted only one person a week with a pastoral one-to-one conversation, and few parishioners ever had more than one such conversation with their priest.[102] In addition to the quantitative burden, communication that delved more deeply into the realm of personality demanded more concentration and emotional awareness. After no more than seven or eight confessional conversations, some priests complained that they were "completely exhausted."[103]

Many clergy also resisted the psychological dimension of the new model of communication. A "perfect 'client-centered' conversational technique"—so went the general thrust of the conference of deans in the diocese of Münster in 1975— was not of paramount importance, since confession was not about "psychology" but a "religious process." Some deans warned of the "danger of psychologization."[104] Hermann-Josef Spital, the head of the pastoral department in the diocese, also encountered such reservations in discussions with many pastors at that time, who were adamant that the confessional conversation "must on no account turn into psychological counseling or even therapy." On the other hand, there was great uncertainty and a definite willingness to learn. Spital responded by presenting a report that illustrated the new approaches to the "methodology of holding a conversation" and explained its use in confession. By way of example, he explored the possible question, "Is premarital sex allowed?"[105]

All in all, Spital's paper and the associated discussion at the conference of deans in the fall of 1975 were attempts to explain the new communicative possibilities of therapeutic conversational techniques in a form that preserved the church's interest in moral instruction amid the new "pluralistic social situation." This task could be likened to squaring a circle. Spital, for example, recommended an "inviting conversational technique" as a way of encouraging people to develop a new "feeling of self-worth." Bishop Tenhumberg summarized this technique in five "basic rules" that were supposed to direct the clergy's communicative behavior during confession:

1. Being able to listen patiently and identify the most important points.
2. Being able both to ask and answer questions in a gentle manner.
3. Being able to focus on the most important things (adhering to norms as an invitation to love and generosity).
4. Helping people to make a decision, but not taking the decision away from them.
5. Enabling and permitting a relation of trust, while directing it at Jesus Christ.[106]

The use of phrases such as "trust" and "feeling of self-worth," as well as the awareness that personal decisions could be made for others, were clearly reminiscent of Carl Rogers's client-centered methodology. Spital's text revealed the dilemma that inevitably faced the use of such therapeutic concepts in the context of penitence. On the one hand, he was categorical that "it is not the rule that needs justification, but the exception to it, to which somebody personally wants to confess." This was because God had created man, meaning that the rules of humankind could only be applied "within the collective" and not to loosely connected individuals. On the other hand, Spital knew only too well that in a pluralistic and individualistic society, it was no longer enough to treat moral questions as simple "factual matters" and thus to present them with the aim of indoctrination and conviction. First, the "question of meaning" had to be clarified in order to find "common ground for discussion." In concrete terms, this meant finding agreement on the "willingness to live a Christian life." Only then could conversational techniques be used to find out whether the participant was interested in assistance with a future moral decision, clarity about a past one, or the absolution of guilt.[107] The dilemma of social theory remained, in all cases, the same one that the philosopher Georg Wilhelm Friedrich Hegel had already analyzed as a paradox in the early modern theories of natural law. Hegel had pointed out that an agreement on moral norms, or on a social contract, as in the early modern theories, was only possible when an agreement in the matter of faith was already given as a contractual capacity. Whether in natural law or in a less asymmetrical form of confession, consensus rested on conditions external to the agreement. Confession could not create this agreement on its own, even with the most sophisticated methods of psychological conversation, unless the preconditions for it could already be found in both participants.

This example reveals some of the problems that prevented penitence from becoming the most important field for development of a more therapeutic and psychological pastoral discourse in the Catholic Church. While psychology and theology have analogous institutional arrangements and share the aim of leading people, it quickly became clear that the difference in their leading codes—sick/healthy vs. sin/forgiveness—was simply impossible to bypass. Even when the duality of sin and forgiveness inherent to penitence dramatically lost its power to persuade, this was so. Reconceptualizing confession as a conversation guided by therapeutic techniques, based in the duality of personal suffering and communicative therapy, was also problematic. First, this idea had to win the approval of the priests, who were generally hesitant or resistant to it. And even if it did win their approval, the theological objection that the real purpose of the sacrament of penitence is to grant forgiveness for an adequately defined form and number of sinful acts still pertained. This remains the case today, although forgiveness is no longer granted in a sovereign act of institutional mercy, but takes the form of a communicative "reconciliation" with God, one's fellow men, and the church. While it continues to be called "penitence," confession has turned into a "sacrament of reconciliation" that is only accidentally reminiscent of its earlier form.[108]

Strategies for "Personal Growth": Group Dynamics and Pastoral Counseling in the Early 1970s

Until well into the 1970s, it seemed the consensus view that confession would be the area in the Catholic Church that would receive privileged application of psychological methods. Later, however, it was recognized that other forms of personal communication in the church could be reformed using psychological models. With this recognition, the focus widened to encompass all forms of interaction or—to use another term for the same matter—personal encounters, that is, verbal and nonverbal communication between persons present in the same space. This resulted from applying models from an area of research generally termed group dynamics, which is not an independent discipline or method but a conglomerate of approaches from pedagogy, social work, social psychology, and psychotherapy. The common denominator of these approaches is that they all provoke and steer interactions. Group dynamics was primarily an import of practices and concepts from the United States. The sudden interest in group dynamics in both major the Protestant and Catholic churches in the Federal Republic emerged in the context of the 1968 protest movement, whose protagonists were interested in restructuring interactions, and in the therapeutic effects of doing so.[109] The question of whether this adequately explains the church's interest in group dynamics can be passed over for the time being. First, we will look at the wealth of areas to which the church applied group dynamics before we explain the most important methods, guiding models, and intended effects of group dynamics work.

Just as with sociography, it was the members of religious orders who quickly showed great interest in the social scientific concepts. Knowledge of group dynamics, it was thought, would improve community life and thus the attractiveness of the religious orders, which were in a state of crisis. What was more, the courses also addressed individual problems and religious experiences, such as questions of authority. Those with leadership roles, too, the heads of the religious orders agreed, were to undergo group dynamics training tailored specifically to their work in conflict resolution with the aim of strengthening a "we feeling." According to P. Karl Siepen, CSsR, the general secretary of the Association of German Religious Superiors (Vereinigung Deutscher Ordensobern), in 1972, there were "sometimes hysterical expectations" about the possible value of group dynamics approaches for reforming life in holy orders. Siepen thus invited Albert Görres to speak to the Circle of Religious Superiors (Kreis der Ordensobern) to demonstrate that the new panacea of group dynamics could not solve everything.[110]

It was therefore no coincidence that it was another member of a religious order, Karl Frielingsdorf, professor at the Jesuit university in St. Georgen, who, in the years around 1970, was the first to apply group dynamics methods in training priests. Priests active in parish pastoral work participated in a training week in which they performed playful cooperation tasks such as the "hexagon exercise," planning and decision-making games for solving conflicts in the community, and "life planning." This program was justified with the argument that the best theological training was of no use if a priest was too "uncertain" or "authoritarian" to nurture a good relationship with his parish and if his specialist knowledge was not evident "in his own attitudes and behavior."[111] A "study and working group for pastoral communication" led by three Redemptorist fathers in Munich offered relevant courses in the mid-1960s, with exercises in "leading the community" such as "controlled dialogue," "conversational analysis," "drawing in pairs: house, tree, dog," and a concluding "role play."[112] A document on the "community of church officials," which Paul Josef Cordes prepared for the German Bishops' Conference in 1975, used Horst-Eberhard Richter's best seller on group dynamics—*Die Gruppe* (The Group), first published in 1972—as an introduction to group dynamics and as the major authority to consult in the church's efforts to intensify community building among the clergy.[113]

Parish pastoral care presented an extremely broad field for applying models from group dynamics and social group work. Church activity at the parish level consisted of an endless series of interactions in staff discussions, parents' groups, faith seminars, pastoral conferences, meetings of voluntary workers, Bible groups, and other core circles, not to mention the meetings of the parish council and other bodies of the lay apostolate. These comprised what in principle was an open circle of laity and clergy but tended to be limited in practice. Even leaving aside interactions that were liturgical events in the narrow sense of the word—church services and devotions—this presented multiple possibilities for practicing group dynamics training.[114] In addition to priests, the rapidly growing number of laypeople involved in pastoral care was an important target group for such training.

It was these members of the laity who could be expected to be most willing to adopt approaches from the human sciences. They bore the main burden of "community-building" work and were most likely to recruit other laypeople for voluntary and part-time work in the parish. For these reasons, project-oriented training in the diocese of Münster from 1971 was directed at assistants for pastoral care, *Seelsorgehelferinnen,* deacons, and catechists. The spectrum of methods taught included "pastoral community work," "pastoral counseling, casework, nondirective conversation," and, finally, "group pedagogy." The curriculum also included practical supervision and "sensitivity training" in order to "sensitize" participants in "optimal pastoral 'self-engagement.'"[115] The use of English terminology such as "casework," "sensitivity training," and "counseling" already indicates an important point. A range of methods, including working with individuals and families as clients (casework), social group work, and community organization, that is, combating anomie and working on strengthening and re-creating collective ties in residential areas and small communities through charitable activities, had all been used since the 1920s in US social work and had been subject to intensive academic discussion.[116] To these the church added the closely related methods of pastoral counseling and nondirective therapy, which also originated in the United States.

Finally, group dynamics and pedagogical models also had an impact on religious adult education. The need for new models in this area emerged at pastoral conferences around the year 1970. Purely "theological education" was no longer sufficient, as it was based on the passive receptivity of the "pupils" and did not spur reflection on faith and its contemporary crisis. In its place, "discussions of faith issues" had to be initiated. The necessary instrument for this, the pastoral conference in the deanery of Greven hoped, at least, was the "Emeis method."[117] Psychological methods tend, not only in the church, to merge with the identities of their most well-known advocates, and this was the case here. The theologian Dieter Emeis, who had been in charge of theological adult education in the diocese of Osnabrück since the summer of 1970, promoted a new approach in Greven and elsewhere that frowned upon the rigid reading of a script, replacing this with a short lecture of around twenty minutes followed by group discussions among six to eight people sitting at a table. Emeis considered the arrangement of the tables in the room decisive in getting such discussions underway. A plenary discussion then closed the evening.[118]

Emeis intended for this system and other teaching interventions to emancipate laypeople, turning them into "mature" participants rather than childlike subjects of paternalistic priests. The group not only enabled a "renewal of church life," but was also capable of "more action" than the individual. Emeis's belief corresponded to an axiom of group dynamics that the potential of the group is always greater than that of the sum of its individual members.[119] Today this form of work is familiar to every student, but in 1970, it constituted a major break with the traditional strategies of Catholic adult education. However, in Greven at least, skepticism reigned as to whether the laity in this rural deanery would be willing to give up their reticence to articulate their own opinion in matters of faith. Such a commitment was essential if this model was to work.[120]

A general aspect of group dynamics and group pedagogical work, as well as of therapeutic work in the broadest sense, is the greater need for self-reflection compared to the daily routine in administrative and technical occupations. This applies to professional leaders as well as participants in group work. People who wish to support others in their "self-perception and self-realization" not only need a personality suited to these objectives, but must also be prepared to allow their own occupational practice to be reviewed periodically to see how well they are achieving them. This "supervision"—the English word being applied in Germany, too—emerged when social work and pastoral care adopted ideas from therapy and educational theory. The new terminology, not always easy for German speakers to grasp, pointed to the main task of such group dynamics work: overseeing the perspectives of others. In supervision, therapists who offer clients new ways to observe their own lives must themselves undergo periodic therapy in order to be able to fulfill this role.[121] It was appropriate to the pattern of practical application of group dynamics in the church that full-time assistants for pastoral care and *Seelsorgehelferinnen*—that is, the laity—carried out the first projects to supervise pastoral workers. Supervision thus functioned in the early years of group dynamics training as a theory of practice that aimed to implement the skills learned in training.[122]

The concepts used in group dynamics and psychological and therapeutic counseling and support are complex. From the early 1980s, numerous handbook-like introductions were published that enabled the clergy and laity to gain an overview.[123] The range of models presented was broad, reflecting the field's vitality: it had seen an explosive growth of new approaches since the 1960s. Not all but a great many of them could be consolidated, reaching a wide-enough audience for further reflection and dissemination.[124] By reading such handbooks, priests and parish assistants could educate themselves in psychoanalytic approaches, behavioral therapy based on neobehaviorism, client-centered psychotherapy, Gestalt therapy, or Jacob Moreno's psychodrama. In the 1950s, the latter had been rejected lock, stock, and barrel as "positivist." Today, however, it is applied "in almost all areas of pastoral care" as a "Bibliodrama" integrating "Bible interpretation and self-experience," in which church members explore their deep spiritual structures.[125] Other methods, too, such as transaction analysis, Viktor Frankl's logotherapy, and the personality models found in psychology have also found systematic use in pastoral care.[126] Only with these handbook-style compilations could pastoral care workers reflect on the comparative advantages and disadvantages of the various concepts for pastoral practice and determine their proximity to the Christian view of man.[127]

Such handbooks had yet to be written in the late 1960s and early to mid-1970s—the period in which therapeutic and group dynamics concepts came to be widely applied in the Catholic Church. This left two typical paths for the application of group dynamics models. First, pastors could "content themselves" with "uncritically adopting" the psychological content of various approaches without looking at their theological implications.[128] This was almost unavoidable given the minimal resources the church invested at this time in exploring psychological approaches to human interactions and their relevance to the needs of pastoral care. Consequently, many parishes carried out "amateurish experiments in group dynamics, sensitivity training," and self-experience groups. Those leading such events had quickly acquired the tools of the trade "by reading a few books."[129] The "mass epidemic" of group dynamics models applied abruptly and euphorically in the church generated concern both among professional theologians and social scientists, who hoped that group dynamics would help to break up the church's fossilized structures.[130]

Another possibility was to resort to the founding texts of the favored approach, or to follow the path of ecumenical cooperation by learning from the more advanced discussion of methodology taking place in Protestant Churches in West Germany and the United States. This second option is reflected in a "selection of literature" on the topics of conversation the Redemptorist father Karl Götzinger used as the basis for his courses on parish leadership in the mid-1960s. This included titles by Carl Rogers available in German translation and special issue of the journal *Lebendige Seelsorge* on group dynamics, as well as relevant books by Protestant authors such as Joachim Scharfenberg and Richard Riess.[131] Efforts to further develop and coordinate psychological work in the churches also manifested themselves in the cooperation between Protestant and Catholic pastoral psychologists, who worked together in the Deutsche Gesellschaft für Pastoralpsychologie (DGfP, German Society for Pastoral Psychology) from 1972, although it was overwhelmingly Protestant psychologists who drove the work and continue today to make up the majority of its six hundred members. The professionalization of psychotherapy for pastoral purposes in Germany is incomplete, however. This is precisely because it is embedded in diverging occupational areas such as church pastoral care, state education, and counseling under the auspices of the welfare state.[132]

The Client-Centered Approach

Of all the concepts for group dynamics and therapeutic work, two were used extensively in practice. Carl Rogers's (1902–87) nondirective or client-centered conversational therapy attracted particular interest from Catholic pastors and therapists.[133] Rogers's model could also be used as a concept for group therapy, in which guise it had a major influence on the American encounter movement.[134] Looking back, the preference for Rogers is unsurprising, as therapeutic concepts from humanistic psychology have been applied in many areas in the Federal Republic since the late 1980s and now hold a "dominant position" in psychosocial counseling and "therapy related to social fields." A study based on a sample of therapeutic psychologists in 1978 showed that, at that time, humanistic psychology still occupied a distant third place behind behavioral therapy and talking therapy.[135]

An important reason for this preference was that the client-centered method, which was well anchored in American "pastoral counseling," had been present in the church context for decades. It had established itself in the mid-1960s in the context of reform efforts in hospital pastoral care and was recognized as a subject at religious universities. The reception of Rogers centered on his method of nondirective conversation, which helped clients to develop and "update" their own personalities rather than providing authoritarian advice. A second important reason for the broad reception of nondirective counseling in church pastoral care is to be found in its content. The method was received positively because it was relatively easy to learn. What was more, it did not appear at first glance to commit the pastor to a particular view of mankind, unlike Freud's psychoanalysis.[136]

Since the mid-1960s, the German American psychotherapist Ruth Cohn had developed and applied the concept of theme-centered interaction (TCI), which aimed to get interactional processes going, and intensify and steer them, in order to ensure "living learning."[137] The theme-centered element made it possible to introduce the specific concerns of particular professional groups or learning situations into the group dynamics process. From 1970, many pastors and laypeople believed that the methods of group work and group therapy à la Rogers and Cohn were a "magic formula," "capable of solving all pastoral problems with an 'open sesame.'" They saw the special advantages of group dynamics not only in its promise to intensify and increase self-control of individual conscience and mental attitudes, but also in the opportunity it afforded for individuals to practice social "roles and virtues," enhancing their social competence and behavior within the group process.[138]

These conceptual premises of group dynamics work also gave rise to the method's first principle. Perhaps the most sought-after effect of such work consisted of "ego strengthening" and "self-realization."[139] Ruth Cohn's and Carl Rogers's models expressed this goal in various ways. In Cohn's TCI, one of the first rules to be remembered in an interaction was, "Do not say 'one' or 'we,' but 'I.'"[140] The practical use of TCI thus fulfilled one of the main criteria for applying social science concepts in the Catholic Church, which Philipp von Wambolt had formulated in his critique of the *Strukturplan*: such concepts should afford the subject and subjectivity a legitimate place in church discussion and break up impersonal discourses that displaced the subject.[141]

Alongside ego strengthening, a further aim of group dynamics was to generate credibility for those in service roles, such as priests, catechists, and teachers of religious education, as well as all who dealt with laypeople in the context of pastoral care and preaching, and thus representing the church as an organization. The key concept Carl Rogers developed that was to inform the attitude of the therapist and other professional service providers on a personal level was "being authentic." This maxim echoed widely in the corresponding behavioral maxims underlying group dynamics practices within the church. Regarding the pastor's "authenticity" as the key to his credibility also marked an implicit turn away from role sociology, which had been the dominant language for describing the priesthood since the mid-1960s. In role sociology, the priest could only fulfill his function professionally by recognizing his own partiality and the contradictory nature of his role behavior. Group dynamics, by contrast, was built upon the integrity and wholeness of the individual. This was essential to the open and "lively" interaction that was central to conveying faith.[142] While role sociology conceived of pastoral speech as emerging from the organization, group dynamics located it in the immediacy of the dialogue "from the me to the you."[143]

Beyond these basic principles, group dynamics also offered three more aspects that were less central, but highly significant given the hopes that pastoral practice had invested in them. The first was the expectation that group dynamics experiences would provide substantial help in dealing with conflicts in interactive contexts, which were part of daily life in the parish. A longer-term objective here was the ideal of the team player—the underlying premise of the Münster *Strukturplan* and its planned *Großpfarrei*, but which it had not itself been able to create. Two further intended effects of group dynamics consisted of overcoming motivational crises and awakening creativity. Practically speaking, this was a matter of "expanding one's capacity to tolerate frustration."[144] This quality was especially crucial when church attendance fell further while "resignation" and "apathy" continued to grow; it was vital to make up for the "loss of strength" that this caused.[145]

Group dynamics, however, did more than just help to maintain the motivation of full-time and voluntary workers, who were the most important resource available in the context of everyday parish pastoral work since the church's crisis in the late 1960s. It also promised to add value to this resource by increasing the combined potential of the individuals within the group. In particular, theme-centered interaction conceived of a "lively learning" in the group as "creative behavior" that best freed individuals' talents and strengths by binding them into the group in a "creative and cooperative" fashion.[146] The use of the term "creativity" in the church is noteworthy, since it has generally been associated with the world of management courses and economic innovation since the 1970s and is understood as the compulsion for individuals to act inventively and to grow and surpass themselves continually. Thus, group dynamics showed itself to be a methodologically modified continuation of the organizational reform agenda, which had made but little headway within the Catholic Church through the application of organizational sociology.[147]

Ambivalences of Therapeutic Pastoral Care

It is often claimed that the boundaries between psychological counseling and the religious formulation of biographical meaning largely dissolved in the second half of the twentieth century.[148] The possibilities for dealing with the subject that therapy and group dynamics offered and that the Catholic Church incorporated as a "doctrine of salvation" created a hybrid form between religion and the human sciences. Some see this as the central characteristic and specific form of secularization in the twentieth century.[149] This argument is able to draw upon early conceptual critiques of the application of therapeutic methods in pastoral care, which saw the metamorphosis of pastoral care into a "decidedly human form of assistance" as akin to "secularization."[150]

The works and influence of Eugen Drewermann throw a spotlight on this entanglement of therapy and pastoral care. Drewermann's numerous publications make him by far the most-read Catholic theologian in Germany since 1980. His writings and the advice he provides to his clients, which tread the line between theological and psychoanalytic interpretations of the Bible, explicitly serve to "dedifferentiate" pastoral care and therapy. With his media appearances, lectures, and counseling activities, Drewermann also aims to train people for a "religious conversion" that should ultimately lead them to join the community of followers and proselytes that the Paderborn theologian has gathered around him. Drewermann's movement represents a syncretic form of piety. It mixes Catholic and psychoanalytic symbolic forms, including their different interpretations of life, in a highly individualized way.[151] The controversy surrounding Drewermann shows that what some find objectionable is not so much the "reinterpretation of Christianity through depth psychology" itself, but rather his specific combination of a psychoanalytic, radically formulated criticism of the church with the personal charisma of a religious founder. In fact, both Drewermann and his quasi-official critics in the church largely agree on the idea of using depth psychology and therapeutic models to find new ways into faith.[152]

Regardless of such objections, it is clear that the application of therapeutic and group dynamics ideas in the Catholic Church has brought about an extensive "scientization of compassion."[153] While there is consensus about the broad effects of psychological methods in religious contexts, these findings have not yet been properly analyzed by religious or social theory. We will attempt to do this at the end of this chapter, after sketching out the most important consequences and ambivalences of psychological work in the Catholic Church.

The Compulsion to Confess

First, there are the connections between "secrecy and disguise," "concealing and revealing," which are a general feature of therapeutic processes. Patients can bear the ritual "(self-)probing" and "shamelessness" of therapeutic interactions because the discussion has no practical consequences and offers them a chance to reflect, relieving them in a special way from their everyday activities.[154]

Many Catholic observers remarked upon this aspect of therapy, emphasizing both critically and affirmatively the special nature of the therapeutic setting. Critics accused psychoanalysis, in particular, of "degrading people," "robbing" them of their secrets and "personal internal substance," and essentially "destroying their essence." The "admissions and self-accusations" demanded in therapy, they argued, were akin to the practices of totalitarian states.[155] Unlike the sacrament of penitence, in which the confessor was bound to "absolute silence" on what he had heard, the therapeutic conversation barged its way shamelessly into every "corner" of the patient's mind. The implicit "compulsion to confess" revealed the "dangers" of depth psychology when used in therapy.[156] Advocates of a pastoral reception of psychoanalysis, meanwhile, insisted that patients were only able to "reveal themselves" in an analytic setting because therapists took a "purely medical view." Thus, they ignored all aspects of the person that lay outside their code of sick/healthy, and indeed were not qualified for dealing with anything outside this code. These advocates sometimes praised the particular restraint and discretion of Catholic therapists, who, after all, were familiar with the special difficulties of uncovering secrets.[157]

Uniquely, Josef Goldbrunner argued that spiritual direction could use psychotherapeutic methods to reach those who were trying to "barricade" themselves away behind "façades" in order to avoid the call of God.[158] Moreover, the opening up of the personal intimate space was not a unique feature of individual therapy. The law of self-disclosure also applied in the much more widespread field of group dynamics and therapy. A single "imprudent" word could have "terrible consequences" there, as participants in the group revealed more of themselves than in most other interactive contexts, with the exception of the family. Mitigating these risks, which were typical of the therapeutic constitution of the subject, not only required the important resource of mutual "trust" among group members, but also professional leaders who were constantly aware of their great "responsibility."[159] Participants in group dynamics courses in the Catholic Church willingly took these risks in order to register the "secondary identity gains" that the therapeutic focus on the "authenticity" of the self promised to provide.[160]

The Tension between Self-Realization and Self-Control

A second consequence of the spread of therapeutic concepts in the Catholic Church was the tension it created between greater self-realization of individuals and groups, and greater self-control in the social spaces opened up by therapy. In these contexts, therapy acted as a technique of guidance that went hand in hand with the modern process of individualization, serving simultaneously to alleviate the implications of this social development and to extend them still further. Compared to traditional liturgy, with its fixed rituals and symbol-laden communication, therapy offered the advantage of flexibility. This meant that it could deal with people's needs for self-thematization and meaning in a more differentiated way.[161]

Albert Görres was one of many Catholic psychologists to critique such a psychological practice. Fearing that it could be misused as a "school of reckless self-realization," he recalled the Christian ascetic ideal of "self-denial" accompanying every form of self-realization. From this perspective, psychotherapy could best be compared to the self-development that had long been practiced in the form of spiritual exercises. Neither technique would bring "fundamentally new" insights into the person, but instead could help him, as Ignatius von Loyola described it, "to rid himself of disordered tendencies."[162]

This was a controversial comparison, as from the mid-1970s onward, the Catholic Church had encountered growing interest in meditation techniques from the Far East, such as Zen and yoga. In 1977, for example, the head of a nunnery that opened its doors to outsiders who wanted to participate in courses was amazed to discover a group of devotees of transcendental meditation (TM) among them in the guise of entirely ordinary-looking academic couples. Prior to this revelation, the group had been conspicuous only by their refusal to eat meat. After another visitor to the house intervened, it was decided that such a party had no place in a Catholic retreat house, and further bookings were canceled. Worried laypeople sent letters to the diocesan administration, which responded by pointing out that Christianity itself had a strong tradition of meditation and that breathing techniques from the Far East were certainly of interest. It was merely the use of Zen or TM as a "substitute for faith" that could not be accepted.[163] A clean distinction proved difficult, however, particularly since many religious and secular priests also knew and applied East Asian meditation techniques. The Oratorian priest Klemens Tillmann pithily summarized the sense that there was something missing in Christianity in asking, "Why did the Beatles go to India instead of coming to a German monastery?"[164]

Maintaining the distinction between the church and new providers of meditation techniques and self-realization was of great importance given that the church was now competing in an increasingly diffuse market for transcendental meaning. Amid all the emphasis Catholic critics placed on avoiding the tendency toward self-realization, they only rarely acknowledged the dramatic increase in the potential for self-guidance and self-monitoring that therapeutic techniques of guidance for individuals imparted. In the context of organizational sociology, parish priests had been advised to plan parish life and pastoral care in a way that utilized "methodological self-monitoring" of their own pastoral work.[165] The corresponding effects could clearly be seen in the practice of group dynamics concepts. These were a world away from the contemporary image of the completely detached and "wild" interaction often associated with the encounter groups in the United States. Indeed, the results of group dynamics pointed to the exact opposite. One priest summarized his experiences with the application of theme-centered interaction as follows: "What used to take us two meetings, we can now achieve in one meeting."[166]

One reason the church failed sufficiently to register the increase in self-control and self-discipline that human interactions shaped by therapy could provide was that it contradicted many Catholics' long-held stereotypes about the ability of institutions to steer individual behavior. It is no coincidence that the group dynamics techniques of behavioral change, with their three steps of "unfreezing-change-freezing," have often been compared to Pietism, based on Pietism's community rules wherein religious interaction is intensified by "forming groups of individuals who have been reborn."[167] The Catholic Church generally had little comprehension of this model of converting people and directing their behavior by making use of their individual psychological makeup. Richard Egenter, a theologian with an interest in psychology, had already emphasized in 1965 that therapeutic techniques would point unmistakably to the necessity of a "fully developed moral competence" even among the "healthy." Egenter knew only too well that the "crutch of total obedience to the law" on which the Catholic Church relied made it difficult for Catholics to make "objective" and "personal" life decisions.[168] Ten years later, however, and precisely in the context of a discussion about group dynamics methods, Bishop Heinrich Tenhumberg expressed his skepticism of the model of individual self-guidance. He pointed, in contemporary fashion, to "sociological studies" that showed that "Protestant Christians," who used their own conscience to make "free and totally independent decisions . . . were more likely to collapse in conflicts." Catholics focused on their church, meanwhile, "were more predisposed against and resistant to fashionable trends."[169] Yet objective analysis of the potential for self-guidance and self-control offered by group dynamics opposed such fears that the institutional church would be Protestantized by group dynamics techniques, and thus stood to lose its institutional authority.

The Drive toward an Optimistic Anthropology

A third consequence of the application of therapeutic techniques in church contexts was a creeping shift in the anthropological premises of pastoral care. This came about from the prominence of Carl Rogers's client-centered therapy in the church, where it had become the standard approach.[170] However, the optimistic promise of this therapeutic school, which holds that personal problems and life crises can be solved in a modest time frame by strengthening the client's sense of self, cannot be separated from Rogers's optimistic anthropology, which explicitly opposes the Christian notion of "original sin."[171] The starting point for the therapeutic conversation in nondirective counseling is the disjuncture between the individual's self-image and subjective experiences. This stands in stark contrast to the church's duality of sin and forgiveness, in which an individual's redemption depends upon the sacramental mercy of the institutional church.[172] The code underlying Rogers's therapy can be described as the distinction between self-alienation and congruence. Routinely applying such a communicative code in church institutions makes it effectively impossible to fully apply the Christian view of mankind's sinful nature.[173]

The Trend toward Rationalization and Verbalization

A fourth and further consequence of the psychological discourse's presence in the Catholic Church was the increasing rationalization of pastoral communication. This was closely linked to a process of therapeutization, which involved increasingly coupling the reshaping of the self of individuals to their participation in therapeutic counseling. This trend is particularly clear in the context of client-centered therapy. Therapists trained in Carl Rogers's methods aimed to enable patients to verbalize their emotional experiences, to which they could reply with more verbal observations. The therapeutic process essentially consisted in the search for words to convey feelings.[174]

The arrival of therapeutic concepts has brought a clear shift in the ideal of a pastoral worker. The all-knowing, ever-present "good shepherd" who combined the bureaucratic charisma imparted by his office with a paternalistic habitus has turned into a specialist in individual problems of faith, the personal search for meaning, and life crises. Successful pastoral activity no longer includes the power of sacramental authority or catechistic indoctrination. Instead, the "temporary partnership" of practical and professional counseling is the model.[175] "Counseling" has also imposed itself beyond a narrowly defined pastoral context. In many other church institutions, too, it is now paradigmatic of the way the church approaches people, addressing and normalizing their problems in therapeutic terms. A good indication of this is the dramatic increase in marriage, family, and life counseling that the Catholic Church and the Caritas organization provide.[176]

This increase occurred not only because counselors were interested in offering their services and pursuing their careers. It also reflected a broad consensus among the Catholic laity. Advocates of pastoral psychology repeatedly pointed to opinion polls of churchgoers. In the case of the synod survey, for example, 49 percent of those questioned on the "tasks of the church" ranked the desire that "the church offer support and assistance to those in mental distress" as the second most important. Other survey data revealed that three-quarters of all Catholics expected their priest to personally help individuals, seeing this as the "most important service" he provided. Sermons and church worship ranked much lower.[177] The same trend was also evident in the career objectives of the young generation of candidates for the priesthood, who joined the church in the 1970s. Asked how they envisioned their future career, they "almost always" answered that, in exercising their office, they primarily wanted to be there for "people in need." This preference for a single motive must have given older priests the impression that they would in future be seen only as "social workers" and "marriage and relationship counselors."[178]

Psychosocial counseling faces a curious dilemma in the context of the Catholic Church, the contours of which have been dramatically laid bare in the bitter conflict between lay initiatives, the German Bishops' Conference, and the Holy See since the mid-1990s over Catholic counseling services and the West German abortion law. This legislation permits first-trimester pregnancy termination, subject to prior counseling. The Holy See was opposed to Catholic institutions participating within this legal framework, as it implied that the counselors would and could advise in favor of termination. But this was by no means the first time the problem of Catholic counseling came to the fore.

Unlike secular counselors, church counselors were bound to the overarching values of Catholic moral teaching and its behavioral norms for marriage, raising children, and family planning. They were supposed to apply these teachings as fully as possible.[179] This authoritarian approach stood in stark contrast to nondirective therapy, whose practitioners felt it risked discouraging clients from seeking counseling altogether.[180] The resulting dilemma led to paradoxical statements, such as the assertion that an awareness of the counselor's "official position" should be expressed in a "client-centered form" during counseling.[181] The objective of helping clients give their life a religious purpose also contradicted the experience of many Catholic counselors, who realized that success depended on resisting preaching and direct advice in the therapeutic conversation. Caring for those who needed help also revealed the time pressure that the church, like all other systems in a functionally differentiated society, exerted. Instead of being oriented toward time-honored values, church communication was thus forced to make time-efficient appointments with clients.[182]

These dilemmas in church counseling gave its counselors a poor reputation at the top of the church hierarchy. They did "appalling things," such as recommending abortions or accepting extramarital relations as "admissible." The impression quickly arose that church counseling represented a "way of getting around usual morals," with many bishops worrying that this was an "obstacle" to preaching salvation.[183] However, even the protagonists and advocates of pastoral psychological work repeatedly articulated a problem the increase in counseling services in the church generated. Initially, it was possible to emphasize that pastoral care based on therapeutic techniques was not just service to fellow Christians, but also another form of propagating a religious message. In fact, priests working in marriage and life counseling found that those being counseled often articulated their expectations of the conversation from an "attitude of faith."[184] As counseling services in the church expanded dramatically and charged even the narrow area of pastoral activity with therapeutic intentions, it became clear that the church's offering was undergoing an enormous shift in value. Alongside pastoral care in the narrow sense, a broad and independent area of therapy-focused care and assistance emerged that has little connection to traditional pastoral care. An "oppressive wall of silence" separates confessors from the marital advisors working in their parish, for example, or hospital chaplains from nurses. In Germany, the development of Caritas into a large, independent organization shows this division of pastoral and social work clearly marked on the institutional level.[185] In recent years, pastoral psychology has therefore set out to reclaim the "faith experiences" in times of life crises that have "migrated" into the counseling centers. Its aim is to win them back into the fold of "normal" pastoral care in the parishes.[186]

Addressing the "Whole Human Being"

Finally, this migration of issues reveals a fifth consequence of scientization through psychological models, namely, that it strengthened an already existing trend. Church activities moved away from their primary religious function, which was directed at society as a whole, toward serving other systems in the social environment. In the course of this shift, the church did not entirely abandon its focus on the social mission of religion—that is, codifying man's relationship to God. However, as the church rapidly weakened—its decline in social importance made abundantly clear as revealed by sociography, opinion polling, and organizational sociology, particularly concerning problems of motivation—it "compensated with an increase in social activism." This shift in focus toward support services and psychological counseling is perhaps the "most important single consequence of secularization."[187]

If we take a closer look at the semantics of the psychological discourse in the Catholic Church, it becomes clear that the church's provision of therapy was a response to a problem caused by functional differentiation. Influenced by C. G. Jung, Wilhelm Kempf described the person who is "the master of himself" as the role model for psychological knowledge in the church. Such a figure possessed an inner world that could be likened to an ordered "cosmos." Kempf coined the term *Seelenkatholon* (wholeness of the soul) to describe the characteristic integrity of those influenced by this model.[188] Other authors, too, believed that the psychological discourse's special achievement was its ability to "see and address people in a wholeness that had not previously been recognized so comprehensively."[189] The special claim of church counseling services was that they dedicated themselves to the "individual's now precarious identity."[190] Group dynamics had also set itself a similar objective in church contexts and sought to overcome the "reduction" of individuals to their rationality and the "sum of their roles." To this end, its practitioners dedicated themselves to the "revitalization" of an old inheritance from

Christianity: the focus on the "whole" person.[191] The pastoral reception of Carl Rogers's humanist psychology likewise pointed to his call for a "holistic view of the person." Unlike behaviorism or psychoanalysis, Rogers was thus able to conceptualize the integration of somatic and psychological aspects in more personal terms.[192] Pastoral programming reflected these aims, with suggestions to replace the term used for pastoral care—*Seelsorge,* with its specific reference to the *Seele* or soul—with terms such as *Heilende Seelsorge* (healing pastoral care) or *Heilssorge* (care for salvation). Others proposed avoiding the use of *Seele* altogether, since pastoral work "was not just about care for the soul, but for the whole person."[193]

The program of *Heilssorge* directed by therapy and group dynamics aimed in essence at including the "whole person" in pastoral care. The term inclusion, and its opposite, i.e. exclusion, in this context describe the way communications are addressed at certain people.[194] Therapeutic pastoral care consciously positioned itself against a social trend wherein only certain aspects of people were deemed relevant targets for communication, with interaction being directed solely at such fragments. Within this perspective, modern society, in other words, is characterized not by the individual, but by the "dividual." Only highly specific fragments of the "self" are relevant to society's functional areas, such as the health and education systems, the economy, or politics. In this model of fragmented inclusion, religion alone involves the personal interaction that enables individuals, their meaningful experiences, crises, and perspectives, to be taken seriously as a whole and to be addressed as one.[195] The social system that presents itself as a useful metaphor for such wholeness is that of the family. It is thus no coincidence that the term "family" and its connotations were frequently heard in the discussions of the Münster *Strukturplan* and its vision of an intact and well-functioning church community.[196]

Obfuscating the Religious Code of Sin/Forgiveness

When it comes to the application of psychological and group dynamics models, it is tempting to interpret the scientization of the Catholic Church as a success story. This would illustrate the great speed at which Catholic theologians and doctors seized on psychoanalysis and psychotherapy, despite the deep chasm that separated the anthropological premises of psychoanalysis from those of Catholic moral teaching. After 1945, the theoretical reception of these forms of knowledge was rapidly translated into experiments at implementing them. These developments could also be interpreted as a response to the desire expressed by the church basis that close interpersonal relationships govern parish life and interaction. Group dynamics in particular would thus represent the fulfillment of needs not met by organizational sociology and the *Strukturplan*. The reception of group dynamics was certainly prompted by the cult of self-discovery and self-experience, which reached the Catholic Church in the wake of the 1968 movement. The scientization of the church thus followed a general trend in German social history, but also reacted to specific church problems. Client-centered therapy called for priests to be more communicative with laypeople and to present themselves as "open" and "honest." This spirit of partnership and cooperation helped to break down the hierarchical role models that had proven outmoded and had contributed to the crisis of the priesthood. Another positive aspect of psychological methods in the Catholic Church was that concepts developed by Protestant theologians and pastoral psychologists were received without bias. While the earlier stages of scientization in the Catholic Church had taken place in determined opposition to Protestant practice, ecumenical unity ruled the day when it came to pastoral psychology.

Such a positive reading cannot be dismissed. Modern, functionally differentiated society heaps immense problems of orientation, adjustment, and self-control upon the individual. Seeking to tackle these difficulties using knowledge of psychology is both a typical and, at first sight, promising approach. However, it is important not to overlook the subsequent problems that the use of psychotherapeutic methods created for the Catholic Church. In particular, the psychoanalytic modeling of human subjects, which posited that people are partly steered by their subconscious minds, made it more difficult to plausibly attribute blame to an individual, even within the church. This was just one aspect of a process that Carl Rogers's optimistic anthropology further encouraged. In general, it meant that culpable sin and merciful forgiveness became dramatically less applicable and persuasive categories. Catholic pastoral work was left with only the fragments of a sacrament that was central to its ability to guide people for at least half of the twentieth century. This development has had secondary effects, as it has further undermined the notion of the church as a *Gnadenanstalt*—the sole institution entitled to dispense grace.[197]

Psychological scientization contributed to a considerable amount of pastoral care becoming verbalized and rationalized, and it intensified difficulties in making the "afterlife" plausible in symbolic and ritual fashion. It was in some senses inevitable that the self-thematization that took place in therapeutic models of communication would break the church's "monopoly of rites." Church rites failed to address people's increasingly differentiated and individualized problems.[198] However, most forms of therapy used in the church placed extreme demands on clients' ability to verbalize their problems. This took Catholic pastoral care far away from its traditional ability to condense the indeterminate nature of meaning into forms of nonverbal communication through the use of rituals. Ultimately, therapy-based pastoral care further drove and legitimized the shift of the ritualistic dispensation of grace from the church's primary function to a secondary function, a shift that was already emerging as a major consequence of secularization.

Many studies on the development of therapeutic discourses assume that the use of these techniques can be described as a form of exerting power over the subject. Regulating individuals' sense of self with the help of the "psy sciences" serves to control them.[199] These discourse-based analyses of psychology as a modern form of human guidance have opened up a series of fruitful methodological perspectives. Nevertheless, I cannot share the excessive emphasis they place on the link between processes of scientization and the tools of power. In this, they borrow from Foucault's concept of "governmentality."[200] Apart from their probable overestimation of the true extent to which power over the individual was increased, they do not sufficiently explain the social causes and contexts of such power. Instead, I draw the conclusion here that the opportunities therapeutic discourses presented in the Catholic Church largely arose from the ongoing momentum of functional differentiation. This both enabled and necessitated the development of religion into a form of inclusion that communicated with the "whole" individual.

Notes

1. Gottfried Griesl, "Seelsorge oder Psychoanalyse?," *LS* 26 (1975): 150–53, 151.
2. Raphael, "Embedding the Human Sciences," 53.
3. Ibid.
4. Alois Hahn, "Zur Soziologie der Beichte und anderer Formen institutionalisierter Bekenntnisse: Selbstthematisierung und Zivilisationsprozess," Kölner Zeitschrift für Soziologie und Sozialpsychologie (*KZfSS*) 34 (1982): 407–34.
5. Nikolas Rose, *Inventing Our Selves: Psychology, Power, and Personhood* (Cambridge, 1998), 13.
6. Ibid., 60; Mitchell G. Ash, "Psychology," in *The Modern Social Sciences*, ed. Theodore M. Porter and Dorothy Ross (Cambridge, 2003), 273.
7. Duane P. Schultz and Ellen Schultz, *A History of Modern Psychology* (San Diego, 1987); Ash, "Psychology"; Nathan G. Hale, *The Rise and Crisis of Psychoanalysis in the United States: Freud and the Americans, 1917–1985* (New York, 1995); on psychology in Germany, see Mitchell G. Ash and Ulfried Geuter, eds., *Geschichte der deutschen Psychologie im 20. Jahrhundert: Ein Überblick* (Opladen, 1985); on psychoanalysis, see Geoffrey Cocks, "Repressing, Remembering, Working Through: German Psychiatry, Psychotherapy, Psychoanalysis and the 'Missed Resistance' in the Third Reich," supplement, *Journal of Modern History* (*JMH*) 64 (1992): S204–S16; Michael Schröter, "Zurück ins Weite: Die Internationalisierung der deutschen Psychoanalyse nach dem Zweiten Weltkrieg," in *Westbindungen: Amerika in der Bundesrepublik*, ed. Heinz Bude and Bernd Greiner (Hamburg, 1999); on therapeutic approaches, see Wolfgang Schmidbauer, *Vom Umgang mit der Seele: Entstehung und Geschichte der Psychotherapie* (Frankfurt, 2000), 227–419.
8. Alex Demirović, *Der nonkonformistische Intellektuelle. Die Entwicklung der Kritischen Theorie zur Frankfurter Schule* (Frankfurt, 1999), 741–855, esp. 810–11.
9. Schultz and Schultz, *History*, 252, 308; Rose, *Inventing*, 57–59; Ash, "Psychology," 269–70. On Freud's rhetorical strategy against critics, see A. John Soyland, *Psychology as Metaphor* (London, 1994), 145–46.
10. Schröter, "Zurück ins Weite."
11. Decree on the training of priests, "Optatam Totius," no. 11, in Abbott, *Documents of Vatican II*, 448.

12. Sigmund Freud, "Neue Folge der Vorlesungen zur Einführung in die Psychoanalyse (1933)," in *Studienausgabe* (Frankfurt, 1994), 1:516.

13. Rose, *Inventing*, 1–21.

14. Albert Görres, *Methode und Erfahrungen der Psychoanalyse* (Munich, 1958), 274–75.

15. Rose, *Inventing*, 59–60.

16. Sabine Maasen, *Vom Beichtstuhl zur psychotherapeutischen Praxis: Zur Therapeutisierung der Sexualität* (Bielefeld, 1988), 2–9.

17. Heinrich Pompey, "Seelsorge in den Krisen des Lebens," in *Seelsorge ohne Priester? Zur Problematik von Beratung und Psychotherapie in der Pastoral*, ed. Josef Maria Reuß (Düsseldorf, 1976), 46–47.

18. Isidor Baumgartner, *Pastoralpsychologie: Einführung in die Praxis heilender Seelsorge* (Düsseldorf, 1997), 76–81.

19. On the theological reception primarily among Protestants, see Joachim Scharfenberg, "Die Rezeption der Psychoanalyse in der Theologie," in *Die Rezeption der Psychoanalyse in der Soziologie, Psychologie und Theologie im deutschsprachigen Raum bis 1940*, ed. Johannes Cremerius (Frankfurt, 1981); on special issues of the Catholic reception, see Stefan Andreae, *Pastoraltheologische Aspekte der Lehre Sigmund Freuds von der Sublimierung der Sexualität* (Kevelaer, 1974), 211–21; Kasimir Birk, *Sigmund Freud und die Religion* (Münsterschwarzach, 1970), 77–119; Pompey, "Seelsorge," 49.

20. Johannes Lindworsky, SJ, "Zur Psychoanalyse," *StdZ* 108 (1925): 398–400, 400.

21. Theodor Müncker, "Katholische Seelsorge und Psychoanalyse," in *Krisis der Psychoanalyse*, ed. Hans Prinzhorn and K. Mittenzwey (Leipzig, 1928), 1:352; on the critique of determinism, see Franz Rudolf Faber, *Das Bild des Menschen in der modernen Medizin: Zur Kritik des biologischen, psychologischen, soziologischen und ethisch-religiösen Determinismus* (Cologne, 1959), 10–11, 24–29.

22. Albert Görres, "Heilung und Heil: Zur Kritik der Psychoanalyse," *Hochland* 45 (1952/53): 38–48, 40; Linus Bopp, *Moderne Psychoanalyse, Katholische Beichte und Pädagogik* (Munich, Kempten, 1923), 10; Linus Bopp, "Katholizismus und Psychoanalyse," in *Der Katholizismus als Lösung großer Menschheitsfragen*, ed. Akademischen Verein Logos (Innsbruck, Vienna, and Munich, 1925), 73ff.; Rudolf Allers, "Probleme der Psychotherapie," *StdZ* 117 (1929): 27–42, 35.

23. Josef Donat, "Irrtum und Schaden der Freudschen Psychoanalyse," *Schönere Zukunft* 11 (1935/36): 892–93.

24. Ludwig Eidelberg, ed., *Encyclopedia of Psychoanalysis* (New York, London, 1968), 292; on Freud's complex use of the term sexuality, see Bernd Nitzschke, "Die Bedeutung der Sexualität im Werk Sigmund Freuds," in Bernd Nitzschke, *Sexualität und Männlichkeit: Zwischen Symbiosewunsch und Gewalt* (Reinbek, 1988).

25. Schäffauer, "Die Psychoanalyse und ihre Bedeutung für Religion und Seelsorge," *Rottenburger Monatsschrift für praktische Theologie* 12 (1928/29): 326.

26. Nikolaus Gengler, "Psychotherapie," *Klerusblatt* 13 (1932): 469–71, 488–91, 470; Josef Goldbrunner, "Die Tiefenpsychologie von Carl Gustav Jung und christliche Lebensgestaltung: Eine moraltheologische Untersuchung" (PhD diss., Freiburg, 1939), 8.

27. Birk, *Freud und die Religion*, 113.

28. Bopp, *Beichte*, 19–23; on Bopp's biography, see Jörg Lichtenberg, *Ein- und Durchblicke in Leben und Gesamtwerk des Freiburger Pastoraltheologen Linus Bopp (1887–1971)* (Würzburg, 1997), 126–29.

29. Linus Bopp, "Das Schicksal der psychoanalytischen Bewegung," *Literarischer Handweiser* 61 (1925): 752–53.

30. Görres, "Heilung," 40; Allers, "Probleme," 36.

31. Hans Böhringer, *Die Tiefenpsychologie von morgen* (Hamm, 1961), 43.

32. On the significance of Freud's atheism for psychoanalysis, see Peter Gay, *"Ein gottloser Jude":
Sigmund Freuds Atheismus und die Entwicklung der Psychoanalyse* (Frankfurt, 1999).
33. Bopp, *Beichte*, 98; Bopp, "Katholizismus," 65–70; Gay, *Atheismus*, 59–68.
34. Sigmund Freud, "Die Zukunft einer Illusion (1927)," in *Studienausgabe*, 9:135–89, quotes 152, 186.
35. For "hostile to God," see Albert May, "Psychoanalyse und katholische Weltanschauung," *Das neue Blatt für die katholische Lehrerschaft* 5 (1929/30): 7-12, 7; Linus Bopp, "Das Schicksal der psychoanalytischen Bewegung," *Literarischer Handweiser* 61 (1925): 154–55; Allers, "Probleme," 36.
36. Müncker, "Seelsorge," 350–51; "Psychoanalyse und Moral," *HK* 3 (1948/49): 175–77, 175.
37. Gengler, "Psychotherapie," 470; Schäffauer, "Psychoanalyse," 356; Bopp, "Katholizismus," 60; Linus Bopp, "Das Schicksal der psychoanalytischen Bewegung," *Literarischer Handweiser* 61 (1925): 758; Alexander Willwoll, SJ, "Über Psychoanalyse und Individualpsychologie," *StdZ* 111 (1926): 401–16, 414.
38. Görres, *Methode*, 11; Görres, "Heilung," 38; E. Hammes, "Psychotherapie heute," *Trierer Theologische Zeitschrift* 66 (1957): 164.
39. Gengler, "Psychotherapie," 470.
40. Schäffauer, "Psychoanalyse," 358.
41. Allers, "Probleme," 37; Lichtenberg, *Durchblicke*, 127.
42. Bopp, *Beichte*, 31ff., quotes 33, 59; Bopp, "Katholizismus," 77; Willwoll, "Über Psychoanalyse," 411; Johannes Chrysostomus Schulte, *Was der Seelsorger von nervösen Seelenleiden wissen muß* (Paderborn, 1937), 20.
43. Bopp, *Beichte*, quotes 31, 36.
44. I borrow the notion of human guidance (*Menschenführung*) here from the studies on governmentality inspired by Foucault, without sharing all the premises of these studies. This includes techniques for systematically influencing other people's behavior and for self-control. Foucault himself interpreted the methods of church pastoral care as one of the three historical roots of modern govermentality. Michel Foucault, "Governmentality," in *The Foucault Effect: Studies in Governmentality*, ed. Graham Burchell et al. (Chicago, 1991), 102–4; Michel Foucault, "Afterword: The Subject and Power," in Hubert L. Dreyfus and Paul Rabinow, *Michel Foucault: Beyond Structuralism and Hermeneutics* (New York, 1982), 214–15.
45. Görres, *Methode*, 11, 17; Görres, "Heilung," 40–41.
46. Joseph Nuttin, "Psychologie und Priester," *Anima* 9 (1954): 216–31, 219, 223; Josef Maria Venhofen, "Von der Psychoanalyse zu einer christlichen Psychotherapie," *Hochland* 53 (1960/61): 464–70, 465; Erwin Ringel and Wenzel van Lun, "Seelsorge und Neurose," *Der Seelsorger* 22 (1951/52): 9–15, 58–62, 9.
47. Ziemann, "Gospel," 82–83; for more detail, see Agnès Desmazières, *L'inconscient au paradis* (Paris, 2011), 163–80.
48. F. Kopp, "Der Papst und die Psychotherapie," *Seelsorgehilfe* 5 (1953): 182–83, 185; Igor A. Caruso, "Rom zur Psychoanalyse," *WW* 8 (1953): 474–77.
49. Schäffauer, "Psychoanalyse," 357; Gengler, "Psychotherapie," 490.
50. Matussek, "Seelsorge heute: Aus der Sicht eines Psychotherapeuten," in *Seelsorge ohne Priester? Zur Problematik von Beratung und Psychotherapie in der Pastoral*, ed. Josef Maria Reuß (Düsseldorf, 1976), 98; Seelsorgliche Beratungsstelle der katholischen Kirchengemeinden Kölns, 28 November 1968, to the Generalvikariat Münster, BAM, GV NA, A-101-336; Hans Böhringer, *Priesterliche Selbstbesinnung: Ein mitbrüderlicher Brief* (Hamm, 1964).
51. Böhringer, *Tiefenpsychologie*, 41.
52. Hahn, "Beichte"; Rupert Scheule, *Beichte und Selbstreflexion: Eine Sozialgeschichte katholischer Bußpraxis im 20. Jahrhundert* (Frankfurt, 2002), 278–81.
53. Bopp, *Beichte*, 89.

54. Müncker, "Seelsorge," 355; Gratian Gruber, "Seelsorge und Psychotherapie," *Anima* 4 (1949): 37; Josef Miller, *Katholische Beichte und Psychotherapie* (Innsbruck, 1947), 7.

55. Philipp Dessauer, "Ärztliche Psychotherapie und priesterliche Seelsorge," *Geist und Leben* 24 (1951): 127–28; Heribert Gauly, "Was macht ein Gespräch zum Seelsorgegespräch?," *LS* 26 (1975): 137–50, 142.

56. *LThK*, 3rd ed., vol. 4, 1, col. 385.

57. See Scheule, *Beichte*, 249; Hahn, "Beichte," 413; Werner Schöllgen, "Psychotherapie und sakramentale Beichte," *Catholica* 1 (1932): 145, 155.

58. Gengler, "Psychotherapie," 489; May, "Psychoanalyse und katholische Weltanschauung," 11; Müncker, "Katholische Seelsorger," 354; Bopp, *Beichte*, 83; Johannes Lindworsky, SJ, "Die Psychoanalyse eine neue Erziehungsmethode?," *StdZ* 90 (1916): 269–87, 284.

59. Scheule, *Beichte*, 127–50, 159–94.

60. Albert May, "Psychoanalyse und katholische Weltanschauung," *Das neue Blatt für die katholische Lehrerschaft* 5 (1929/30): 12; "greatest achievement": Gengler, "Psychotherapie," 489; Bopp, *Beichte*, 84.

61. Müncker, "Katholische Seelsorger," 357–58; Josef Goldbunner, "Vertrauenskrise im Beichtstuhl," *Anima* 5 (1950): 229–38, 237–38.

62. Marc Oraison, "Sünde, Beichte und Tiefenpsychologie," *Anima* 7 (1952): 131–43, 141.

63. On the concept of communicative codes in religious history, see Benjamin Ziemann, "Codierung von Transzendenz im Zeitalter der Privatisierung: Die Suche nach Vergemeinschaftung in der katholischen Kirche, 1945–1980," in *Die Gegenwart Gottes in der modernen Gesellschaft: Religiöse Vergemeinschaftung und Transzendenz in Deutschland*, ed. Michael Geyer and Lucian Hölscher (Göttingen, 2006), 374–97.

64. Görres, "Heilung," 46–47; Görres, *Methode*, 35–38; Paul Josef Cordes, "Einzelbeichte und Bußgottesdienst: Zur Diskussion ihrer Gleichwertigkeit," *StdZ* 192 (1974): 28.

65. Philipp von Wambolt to Hermann-Josef Spital, 12 August 1971, BAM, GV NA, A-201-379.

66. Ibid.

67. Miller, *Beichte*, 8, 22–25, quote 23; Schöllgen, "Beichte," 148.

68. Quotes: Philipp von Wambolt, "Schreibhemmungen bei pastoralen Themen," n.d., BAM, GV NA, A-201-379; Matussek, "Seelsorge," 92, dates the beginning of this crisis to as early as the 1920s. Ignace Lepp, *Liebe, Neurose und christliche Moral: Fünf Aufsätze zum Verhältnis von Tiefenpsychologie und Glaube* (Würzburg, 1960); Ignace Lepp, *Psychoanalyse der Liebe* (Würzburg, 1961); Friedrich E. von Gagern, *Eheliche Partnerschaft* (Munich, 1963) (this text appeared in 1968 in its tenth edition, with a total print run of 85,000–100,000).

69. Scheule, *Beichte*, 82. It should be noted explicitly that this is only a secondary aspect of Scheule's interpretation.

70. Parish committee Ibbenbüren, 11 January 1971, BAM, GV NA, A-201-23.

71. Freckenhorst Circle, "Überlegungen zur Buße," May 1970, BAM, GV NA, A-201-290.

72. Minutes of the "Dechantenkonferenz," 4 March 1975, BAM, GV NA, A-101-383; "Beichtkrise und Bußerneuerung: Zur jüngsten Diskussion im deutschen Sprachraum," *HK* 27 (1973): 137–43, 137.

73. Freckenhorster Circle, "Überlegungen zur Buße," May 1970, BAM, GV NA, A-201-290.

74. Gottfried Griesl, "Das Beichtgespräch und seine therapeutische Wirkung," *LS* 30 (1979): 358–61, 358.

75. Heinrich Tenhumberg, "Bischofswort zur Fastenzeit," *Kirchliches Amtsblatt für die Diözese Münster* 105 (1971): 29–32.

76. W. Beine, CSsR, "Beichten heute: Gedanken zu den Problemen moderner Bußverwirklichung," *Rheinischer Merkur*, 6 February 1970.

77. Cited in Cordes, "Einzelbeichte," 17; Gottfried Griesl, "Pastoralpsychologische Betrachtungen zu unserer heutigen Bußpraxis," in *Entspricht die Beichtpraxis der Kirche der Forderung Jesu zur*

Umkehr? Eine Orientierungshilfe, ed. Josef Finkenzeller and Gottfried Griesl (Munich, 1971), 134–39.

78. Dirk Grothues, "Zeitgemäße Überlegungen zur Buße," *Sein und Sendung* 3 (1971): 50–60, 55, 57–58.
79. Beine, "Beichten heute."
80. Alois Hahn and Herbert Willems, "Schuld und Bekenntnis in Beichte und Therapie," in *Religion und Kultur,* ed. Jörg Bergmann (Opladen, 1993), 324; Niklas Luhmann, *Love as a Passion: The Codification of Intimacy* (Cambridge, 1986), 166–67.
81. Frau P. from Telgte to Bishop Tenhumberg, 3 June 1970, BAM, GV NA, A-0-500.
82. Cordes, "Einzelbeichte," 17ff.; *HK* 27 (1973): 138–42; *Gemeinsame Synode,* 1:262.
83. *Gemeinsame Synode,* 1:259, quote 262; *HK* 27 (1973): 140.
84. "Erste Arbeitssitzung der Synode in Würzburg," *HK* 26 (1972): 354–58, 357.
85. "Vorschläge zur Erneuerung des Bußsakraments," *HK* 24 (1970): 431–35, 432.
86. According to Dessauer, "Psychotherapie," 113.
87. Grothues, "Überlegungen," 54.
88. Beine, "Beichten heute"; Balthasar Gareis, *Psychotherapie und Beichte* (St. Ottilien, 1988), 24–26.
89. *HK* 24 (1970): 434; "Hirtenwort zur Fastenzeit," *Kirchliches Amtsblatt für die Diözese Münster* 106 (1972): 13–15; Josef Bommer, "Formen der Bußliturgie heute," *Liturgisches Jahrbuch* 21 (1971): 140–49, 146–47; Hermann-Josef Spital, Einige Bemerkungen zur Methodik der Gesprächsführung, 14 May 1975, BAM, GV NA, A-101-383.
90. Bommer, "Bußliturgie," quotes 147, 141, 144.
91. Griesl, "Beichtgespräch," 358, 361.
92. Griesl, "Beichtgespräch," 361; Gauly, "Seelsorgegespräch," 140; Josef Bommer, "Das Bußsakrament als Gericht und als Seelsorge: Zur therapeutischen Dimension von Buße und Bußsakrament," in *Erfahrungen mit dem Bußsakrament,* ed. Konrad Baumgartner (Munich, 1978), 2:244.
93. Pfarrer Paul Dyckmans to Spital, 12 February 1975; Minutes of the "Dechantenkonferenz," 4 March 1975, TOP 1, Arbeitskreis 2; Pfarrer Josef Berntsen, 27 February 1975, all in BAM, GV NA, A-101-383.
94. Minutes of the "Dechantenkonferenz," 4 March 1975, BAM, GV NA, A-101-383.
95. Gottfried Griesl, "Zur Gesprächsfähigkeit des Seelsorgers," *LS* 20 (1969): 101–107, 101.
96. Urs Altermatt, "Kirchengeschichte im Wandel: Von den kirchlichen Institutionen zum katholischen Alltag," *Zeitschrift für schweizerische Kirchengeschichte* 87 (1993): 29.
97. Andreas Snoeck, SJ, *Beichte und Psychoanalyse* (Frankfurt, 1960), 123.
98. Görres, "Heilung," 41.
99. From the broader literature, see Josef Schwermer, *Psychologische Hilfen für das Seelsorgegespräch* (Munich, 1974); Anton Kner, *Seelsorge als Beratung* (Freiburg, 1968); André Godin, *Das Menschliche im seelsorglichen Gespräch: Anregungen der Pastoralpsychologie* (Munich, 1972), 35–80.
100. Quote: Gauly, "Seelsorgegespräch," 145; Nuttin, "Psychologie," 220–21.
101. *Gemeinsame Synode,* 1:273.
102. Baumgartner, *Pastoralpsychologie,* 250; Fichter, *Parish,* 127; Konrad Baumgartner and Wunibald Müller, ed., *Beraten und Begleiten: Handbuch für das seelsorgerliche Gespräch* (Freiburg, 1990), 23.
103. Dechant Hans Siemen to Spital, 24 February 1975, BAM, GV NA, A-101-383.
104. Minutes of the "Dechantenkonferenz," 4 March 1975, BAM, GV NA, A-101-383.
105. Hermann-Josef Spital, "Einige Bemerkungen zur Methodik der Gesprächsführung," 14 May 1975, BAM, GV NA, A-101-383.
106. Report on the "Dechantenkonferenz," 16 September 1975, BAM, GV NA, A-101-383.
107. Hermann-Josef Spital, "Einige Bemerkungen zur Methodik der Gesprächsführung," 14 May 1975, BAM, GV NA, A-101-383.

108. Sekretariat der Deutschen Bischofskonferenz, ed., *Umkehr und Versöhnung im Leben der Kirche: Orientierungen zur Bußpastoral* (Bonn, 1997), 26–33, quote 35.

109. According to Karl-Wilhelm Dahm, "Gruppendynamik und kirchliche Praxis: Versuch einer Beziehungsklärung," in *Gruppendynamik in der kirchlichen Praxis: Erfahrungsberichte,* ed. Karl-Wilhelm Dahm and Hermann Stenger (Munich, 1974); on group dynamics in the United States, see Kurt W. Back, *Beyond Words: The Story of Sensitivity Training and the Encounter Movement* (New York, 1972). The marginal effect in practice of the German concepts of group dynamics already in place by 1967, in particular the lack of reception of the approaches suggested by Kurt Lewin, is visible in the Catholic reception of Peter R. Hofstätter, *Gruppendynamik: Kritik der Massenpsychologie,* (Reinbek 1957). Only the second edition, which appeared in 1971, was received positively; see Heinrich Pompey, "Rezension: Peter R. Hofstätter, Gruppendynamik—Kritik der Massenpsychologie: Reinbek bei Hamburg 1971," *Theologischer Literaturdienst: Beilage zum Würzburger Diözesanblatt* 4 (1972): 63–64.

110. Quotes: Leugers, *Solidarität,* 313, 325–36; Sigrun Polzien, "TZI-Kurse mit Ordensleuten und Weltpriestern," in Dahm and Stenger, *Gruppendynamik in der kirchlichen Praxis.*

111. Karl Frielingsdorf, "Berufsbezogene Gruppendynamik in der Priesterfortbildung," *Diakonia* 2 (1971): 382–96, quotes 392, 385 (the term "life planning" is in English in the original); Ulrich Krömer, "Methodische Gruppenarbeit—Chance für die Pastoral?," *LS* 23 (1972): 156–60.

112. "Programm des Kurses für Gemeindeleitung v. 25.-30.7.1976," n.a., handwritten notes, n.d., EOM, Pastorale Planungsstelle, Akte P. Wesel, Gemeindeleitung; P. Karl Götzinger, CSsR, to Hans Georg Mähner, 31 October 1976, EOM, Pastorale Planungsstelle, Akte PV-Kurs 1977.

113. Paul Josef Cordes, Zur Gemeinschaft kirchlicher Amtsträger, Vorlage zur DBK 1975, BAM, GV NA, A-0-966; Horst-Eberhard Richter, *Die Gruppe: Hoffnung auf einen neuen Weg, sich selbst und andere zu befreien* (Reinbek, 1972). Cordes was head of pastoral issues and secretary of the pastoral commission in the German Bishops' Conference from 1972.

114. Heinz J. Kersting, "Verschiedene Modelle in der Sozialen Gruppenarbeit," *LS* 23 (1972): 165–73, 165; Albert Rinse Koffeman, "Training von Priestern in den Methoden der Sozialen Gruppenarbeit," *LS* 23 (1972): 153–56.

115. Seelsorgeamt Münster, "Entwurf eines Ausbildungsvorschlages für eine berufsbegleitende pastoral-theologische Ausbildung, Schulung B," 28 April 1971, BAM, GV NA, A-201-357.

116. The literature on these approaches is boundless. On the theoretical history of social work in the United States, see, for example, Louis Lowy, *Sozialarbeit/Sozialpädagogik als Wissenschaft im angloamerikanischen und deutschsprachigen Raum: Stand und Entwicklung* (Freiburg, 1983); Leslie Margolin, *Under the Cover of Kindness: The Invention of Social Work* (Charlottesville, VA, 1997); Back, *Beyond Words,* 175–89; for introductions to case studies, see Helen Harris Perlman, *Social Casework: A Problem-Solving Process* (Chicago, 1957); Tom Douglas, *Basic Groupwork* (London, 1978); Charles F. Grosser, *New Directions in Community Organization: From Enabling to Advocacy* (New York, 1973), 3–20.

117. Minutes of the "Pastoralkonferenz" in Greven, 26 April 1971, BAM, GV NA, A-201-23.

118. Minutes of the "Pastoralkonferenz" in Greven, 18 May 1971, BAM, GV NA, A-201-23; Bishop Hermann Wittler to Dieter Emeis, 11 August 1970, BAOS, 07-31-52.

119. Dieter Emeis, "Theologische Bildungsarbeit in Gruppen und die Ziele der Synode" (manuscript), n.d. [1972], BAM, GV NA, A-201-374; Dahm, "Gruppendynamik und kirchliche Praxis," 23–24.

120. Protokoll der Pastoralkonferenz in Greven, 18 May 1971, BAM, GV NA, A-201-23.

121. Theresia Hauser, "Aspekte der Supervision für Praktiker in Gemeinde und Institution," in Dahm and Stenger, *Gruppendynamik in der kirchlichen Praxis,* 226. On the skepticism toward the traditional psychoanalytic model of supervision in Catholic pastoral care, see Baumgartner, *Pastoralpsychologie,* 324–29.

122. Marta Fehlker, AG Projektorientierte Bildung, "Ausschreibung Sozialwissenschaftlich-pastoralpsychologischer Grundkurs," 11 March 1976; Seelsorgeamt Münster, "Entwurf eines Ausbildungsvorschlages für eine berufsbegleitende pastoral-theologische Ausbildung, Schulung B," 28 April 1971; memo Johannes Killing, 6 December 1971, all in BAM, GV NA, A-201-357; Hauser, "Aspekte," 221–31; Pompey, "Seelsorge," 54.

123. Baumgartner, *Pastoralpsychologie*; Baumgartner and Müller, *Beraten und Begleiten*; Jürgen Blattner, Balthasar Gareis, and Alfred Plewa, eds., *Handbuch der Psychologie für die Seelsorge*, 2 vols. (Düsseldorf, 1992); Josef Schwermer, *Den Menschen verstehen: Eine Einführung in die Psychologie für seelsorgliche Berufe* (Paderborn, 1987).

124. For an overview, see Back, *Beyond Words*, 103–16; Cecil Holden Patterson and Edward C. Watkins, *Theories of Psychotherapy* (New York, 1996), provides an introduction to the wealth of therapeutic approaches.

125. Arthur Fridolin Utz, "Der Kampf der Wissenschaften um das Soziale," *Die neue Ordnung* 9 (1955): 201; Guido Kreppold, "Träume, Symbole und Bibel: Am Beispiel einer Selbsterfahrungsgruppe und einer Einzeltherapie," in *Psychologie hilft Glauben: Durch seelisches Reifen zum spirituellen Erwachen. Berichte, Erfahrungen, Anregungen*, ed. Peter Raab (Freiburg, 1990), 99–104.

126. Blattner, Gareis, and Plewa, *Handbuch*, 2:111–232; Baumgartner, *Pastoralpsychologie*, 331–518; Schwermer, *Verstehen*.

127. Baumgartner, *Pastoralpsychologie*, 518–43.

128. Pompey, "Seelsorge," 55.

129. Gauly, "Seelsorgegespräch," 145.

130. Hermann Steinkamp, *Gruppendynamik und Demokratisierung* (Mainz and Munich, 1973), 186.

131. P. Karl Götzinger, CSsR, "Literaturauswahl Gesprächsführung," n.d. [1976], EOM, Pastorale Planungsstelle, Akte P. Wesel, Gemeindeleitung; Joachim Scharfenberg, *Seelsorge als Gespräch: Zur Theorie und Praxis der seelsorgerischen Gesprächsführung* (Göttingen, 1972); Richard Riess, *Seelsorge: Orientierung, Analysen, Alternativen* (Göttingen, 1973). Matthias Kroeger, *Themenzentrierte Seelsorge: Über die Kombination klientzentrierter und themenzentrierter Arbeit nach C. R. Rogers und R. C. Cohn in der Theologie* (Stuttgart, 1973), was a widely read introduction published in many editions and tailored to the Protestant Churches.

132. Pompey, "Seelsorge," 49; see the materials in Akten der Deutschen Gesellschaft für Pastoralpsychologie, Ordner Unterlagen zur Gründung.

133. Arnold Mente to Heinrich Tenhumberg, 3 October 1975, BAM, GV NA, A-0-639.

134. Back, *Beyond Words*, 67, 101–2.

135. Georg Hörmann and Frank Nestmann, "Die Professionalisierung der Klinischen Psychologie und die Entwicklung neuer Berufsfelder in Beratung, Sozialarbeit und Therapie," in Ash and Geuter, *Geschichte der deutschen Psychologie*, 264–66, quote 266; on humanist psychology, see Roy Jose DeCarvalho, *The Founders of Humanistic Psychology* (New York, 1991).

136. Ziemann, "Gospel," 89–90.

137. Kroeger, *Themenzentrierte Seelsorge*, 157–222, quote 158.

138. Krömer, "Gruppenarbeit," 159.

139. Frielingsdorf, "Priesterfortbildung," 386.

140. Kroeger, *Themenzentrierte Seelsorge*, 159–60, 194.

141. See chapter 4.

142. Ziemann, "Gospel," 94–95.

143. Carl Rogers's relationship with Martin Buber should be noted here, whose dialogue principle shaped the idea of "relationship" in American pastoral counseling; Maurice North, *The Secular Priests* (London, 1972), 72.

144. Hubert Recktenwald, "Gruppendynamische Erkenntnisse und ihre pädagogische und politische Relevanz," *LS* 23 (1972): 150–153, 151.

145. *fk-Information*, no. 1 (1974): 7.

146. Marta Fehlker, AG Projektorientierte Bildung, "Ausschreibung Sozialwissenschaftlich-pastoralpsychologischer Grundkurs," 11 March 1976, BAM, GV NA, A-201-357.

147. Ziemann, "Gospel," 97–98.

148. Peter Ludwig Berger, *The Sacred Canopy: Elements of a Sociological Theory of Religion* (Garden City, NJ, 1967).

149. Mette and Steinkamp, *Sozialwissenschaften*, 106.

150. Georg Trapp, SJ, "Probleme der Seelsorge in der Begegnung mit der Psychotherapie," *Anima* 6 (1951): 200–206, 201.

151. Christel Gärtner, *Eugen Drewermann und das gegenwärtige Problem der Sinnstiftung: Eine religionssoziologische Fallanalyse* (Frankfurt, 2000), 27, 280.

152. Walter Kasper, "Tiefenpsychologische Umdeutung des Christentums," in *Tiefenpsychologische Deutung des Glaubens? Anfragen an Eugen Drewermann*, ed. Albert Görres and Walter Kasper (Freiburg, 1988), 9–25, quote 9; see also Albert Görres, "Erneuerung durch Tiefenpsychologie," in Görres and Kasper, *Tiefenpsychologische Deutung des Glaubens?*

153. Kamphausen, *Hüter des Gewissens*, 173.

154. Hahn and Willems, "Schuld und Bekenntnis," 317, 324–25.

155. Joachim Bodamer, "Die Krankheit der Psychoanalyse," *WW* 10 (1955): 183–96, 188–89; quotes: Joachim Bodamer, *Gesundheit und technische Welt* (Stuttgart, 1955), 70–71.

156. Miller, *Beichte*, 17, 23; Michael Pfliegler, "Personale Seelsorge: Zu dem gleichnamigen Werk von Josef Goldbrunner," " *Der Seelsorger* 25 (1954/55): 104–111, here 109.

157. Dessauer, "Psychotherapie," 118, quote 116; Snoeck, *Beichte und Psychoanalyse*, 123, 125.

158. Josef Goldbrunner, *Sprechzimmer und Beichtstuhl: Über Religion und Psychologie* (Freiburg, 1965), 75.

159. "Diskutieren mit Herz und Verstand: In Ibbenbüren wird ein neues Kommunikations-Modell mit Erfolg erprobt," *KuL*, 8 May 1977.

160. Hahn and Willems, "Schuld und Bekenntnis," 325.

161. Hahn and Willems, "Schuld und Bekenntnis," 321, 324; Baumgartner and Müller, *Beraten und Begleiten*, 53.

162. Albert Görres, "Kirchliche Beratung—eine dringende Antwort auf Symptome und Ursachen seelischer Krisen?," in *Kirchliche Beratungsdienste*, ed. Sekretariat der DBK (Bonn, 1987), 14, 29; Katholische Fernseharbeit beim ZDF, ed., *Die Kirche wickelt sich ab—und die Gesellschaft lebt die produktive Kraft des Religiösen: Nur 18 Thesen zum Verhältnis Kirche, Religion und Kultur* (Mainz, 1995), 22–23; Hahn and Willems, "Schuld und Bekenntnis," 324.

163. Memo Kettler for Tenhumberg, 8 June 1977, BAM, GV NA, A-0-639; Kloster St. Josef der Schwestern von der Heimsuchung Mariä to Tenhumberg, 1 September 1977, BAM, GV NA, A-0-639; quote: Dirk Grothues to L. from Borken, 23 January 1975, BAM, GV NA, A-0-639.

164. Quote: Katholische-Nachrichten-Agentur, 18 June 1975, BAM, GV NA, A-0-639; Heinrich Tenhumberg, "Transzendentale Meditation—Religionsersatz?," *KuL*, 13 July 1975. From 1970, Tillmann conducted numerous introductory courses in meditative techniques; Ida-Friederike Görres to P. Ludwig Bertsch, SJ, 14 April 1971, in Görres, *Thron*, 152–53.

165. Lutz Hoffmann, "Anpassung an die Wirklichkeit. Intuition oder Planung?," *Publik*, 27 June 1969.

166. "Diskutieren mit Herz und Verstand: In Ibbenbüren wird ein neues Kommunikations-Modell mit Erfolg erprobt," *KuL*, 8 May 1977; Back, *Beyond Words*, 78–79, 214, 224–27.

167. Dahm, "Gruppendynamik," 25; Kamphausen, *Hüter des Gewissens*, 187; *Die Religion in Geschichte und Gegenwart: Handwörterbuch für Theologie und Religionswissenschaft* (*RGG*), ed. Kurt Galling, Tübingen 1957–1965, 3rd ed., 5:370–81, quote 371.

168. Richard Egenter and Paul Matussek, *Ideologie, Glaube und Gewissen: Diskussion an der Grenze zwischen Moraltheologie und Psychotherapie* (Munich 1965), 114–15.

169. Bericht über die Dechantenkonferenz v. 16 September 1975, BAM, GV NA, A-101-383. Tenhumberg was probably referring to the results of a study by Gerhard Schmidtchen, *Protestanten und Katholiken: Soziologische Analyse konfessioneller Kultur* (Berne, 1973).

170. Mette and Steinkamp, *Sozialwissenschaften*, 151.

171. According to the Catholic theologian and social ethicist Arthur-Fridolin Utz, cited in Steinkamp, *Gruppendynamik*, 181.

172. Carl Rogers, *Die klientenzentrierte Gesprächspsychotherapie* (Frankfurt, 1983), 418–57, esp. 455–56.

173. Ziemann, "Gospel," 99–101.

174. Ibid., 102.

175. Baumgartner and Müller, *Beraten und Begleiten*, 20–30, quote 24.

176. Ziemann, "Dienstleistung," 380.

177. Schmidtchen, *Kirche und Gesellschaft*, 25; Pompey, "Seelsorge," 8; "most important service": Gauly, "Seelsorgegespräch," 31; Kamphausen, *Hüter des Gewissens*, 204.

178. Gauly, "Seelsorgegespräch," 16–17.

179. Görres, "Beratung," 30.

180. Blattner, Gareis, and Plewa, *Handbuch*, 508, quote 488; Dietrich Stollberg, *Therapeutische Seelsorge: Die amerikanische Seelsorgebewegung: Darstellung und Kritik* (Munich, 1969), 72.

181. W. Berger and H. Andrissen, "Das amerikanische Phänomen 'Pastoral Counseling' und seine Bedeutung für die Pastoraltheologie," in *Handbuch der Pastoraltheologie: Praktische Theologie der Kirche in ihrer Gegenwart*, ed. Franz-Xaver Arnold et al. (Freiburg, 1968), 3:577.

182. Ziemann, "Dienstleistung," 381.

183. Görres, "Beratung," 7; Paul Zulehner, "Was gewinnen Beratung und Seelsorge durch ihre wechselseitige Beziehung?," in *Beratung als Dienst der Kirche*, ed. Katholische Bundesarbeitsgemeinschaft für Beratung (Freiburg, 1981), 119–20.

184. Heinrich Pompey, "Seelsorge zwischen Gesprächstherapie und Verkündigung," *LS* 26 (1975): 162–69, 165; Heinrich Pompey, "Handlungsperspektiven kirchlicher Beratung," in *Kirchliche Beratungsdienste*, ed. Sekretariat der Deutschen Bischofskonferenz (Bonn, 1987), 57–58, 66.

185. Baumgartner and Müller, *Beraten und Begleiten*, 31; Ziemann, "Dienstleistung," 382–83.

186. Baumgartner, *Pastoralpsychologie*, 31.

187. Luhmann, *Funktion*, 264.

188. W. Kempf, "Versuch einer ersten Einführung in die Gedankenwelt der modernen Tiefenpsychologie," *Trierer Theologische Zeitschrift* 58 (1949): 304–5.

189. Josef Rudin, *Psychotherapie und Religion* (Olten and Freiburg, 1964), 9.

190. Mette and Steinkamp, *Sozialwissenschaften*, 147–48.

191. Steinkamp, *Gruppendynamik*, 194; Arnd Hollweg, *Theologie und Empirie: Ein Beitrag zum Gespräch zwischen Theologie und Sozialwissenschaft in den USA und Deutschland* (Stuttgart, 1971), 91–98.

192. Baumgartner, *Pastoralpsychologie*, 437.

193. Ibid., 39; Pfarramt Heilig-Geist in Oldenburg, 10 June 1970, BAM, GV NA, A-201-15.

194. Peter Fuchs, *Der Eigen-Sinn des Bewußtseins: Die Person, die Psyche, die Signatur* (Bielefeld, 2003), 24–30.

195. Nassehi, *Differenzierungsfolgen*, 117.

196. See chapter 4.

197. Michael N. Ebertz, *Erosion der Gnadenanstalt? Zum Wandel der Sozialgestalt von Kirche* (Frankfurt, 1998), 194–97.

198. Hahn and Willems, "Schuld und Bekenntnis," 321.

199. Quote: Rose, *Inventing*, 11; Sabine Maasen, *Genealogie der Unmoral: Zur Therapeutisierung sexueller Selbste* (Frankfurt, 1998), 476–77.

200. Foucault, "Governmentality."

CONCLUSION

The Scientization of the Church as an Encounter with a Dangerous Modernity

This book is neither a conventional church history, with a focus on the discussions among and high-level decision making of bishops and their advisors, or on the theological underpinnings of these decisions. Nor is it a cultural history of German lay Catholics and the ways in which they articulated or practiced their individual faith. Rather than treading these well-established paths of historiography, this book has tried to offer new insights into the intersections of religion, social sciences, and society in the postwar period. It has done so through a focus on the "scientization of the social," asking whether and how different methods from the social sciences allowed bishops, theologians, and priests to observe the side effects of functional differentiation, and to formulate pastoral responses to them. Before we take stock of the key findings of this book and summarize its core arguments, it seems worthwhile to remind the reader that the approach taken in this study is anything but tangential to core notions of organized religion in the Catholic Church. Ever since the Counter-Reformation, the Catholic Church has insisted that the Catholic faith should lead to practiced piety, that it had to materialize in identifiable acts of worship. Statistics provided a means of gathering and calculating quantitative data on the frequency of such acts of practiced piety. It was another staple of Catholic pastoral practice that the priests should be well acquainted with the livelihood of their "flock" and have an understanding of the social factors that influenced their beliefs. In the decades after 1945, sociography was the method that provided scientific insights into these issues.

Statistics and sociography provided new answers to well-established pastoral questions. In the postwar period, however, new questions came to the fore. Whereas the Catholic Church had traditionally assumed that the laity would subscribe to all core values and dogmas of its teaching, the actual resonance of orthodoxy became increasingly unclear during the 1960s. Thus, opinion polling based on random or quota samples provided a means to gauge the "cognitive dissonance" that many laypeople experienced. Ecclesiology, that is, debates on the nature of the church as a body and as an institution, was a well-established part of theological reflection and teaching. Yet as the notion of planning took center stage in politics in the late 1960s, high-ranking diocesan officials asked whether the church itself was really fit for the purpose of providing pastoral care. Role sociology and organizational research enabled answers to this question, as they effectively scrutinized the church like any other secular organization. Ultimately, then, Catholic faith and the sacrament of confession, in particular, had allowed individuals to reflect upon the principles that guided their lives, and to seek personal integrity and spiritual balance.[1] This core notion of the Catholic faith was rediscovered and rearticulated once theologians started to come to grips with psychoanalysis and other therapeutic approaches.

It is hence one of the claims of this book that analyzing the "scientization" of the Catholic Church can shed light on core aspects of organized religion in the postwar period. But before we discuss this argument more broadly, it is worth summarizing key findings with regard to the different stages of scientization, encapsulated in the social science methods that were applied between 1945 and 1975. The statistical addition and aggregation of baptisms, marriages, churchgoers, and communions initially had the effects that advocates of these methods had been hoping for since 1900. Church statistics enabled the Catholic Church to distance itself more effectively from Protestantism, clearly delimiting the church's external boundaries and making Catholic piety more coherent and visible. From the late 1940s, however, statistics moved irrevocably from demonstrating the stability of the field of Catholic piety to illustrating the unfolding "crisis" of the church, as it came to be described in the late 1960s. Both the church hierarchy and many parish clergy experienced a self-inflicted disappointment as a result of their focus on Sunday attendance figures. The intensity and persistence of this fixation on quantitative aspects of religion can only be explained by its long historical prelude following confessionalization, which anchored this way of thinking deep in the Catholic Church's self-understanding. Statistics became an important part of the church's own self-description. It left its mark on other ways in which secularization was observed, particularly sociography, but also opinion polling. Only pastoral psychology, and to a limited extent organizational sociology before it, has been able to loosen many Catholics' deep-rooted orientation to pastoral statistics as the essence of a functioning church.

The first clear signs of crisis in the figures produced by church statistics led the church to receive sociographic methods in a form that remained within the statistical paradigm, expanding it still further. Sociography could answer a question that church statistics had left open: in which class or age group were those Catholics who stayed away from Sunday church services and no longer received Easter Communion? The findings achieved with the help of sociographic data forced the church to recognize something that was not per se a new empirical phenomenon. Rather, it was a new *observation* for the Catholic Church, something that was registered in a formal and systematic fashion that earlier debates could not rely upon. The data confirmed for the first time a fundamental dissociation between the world of the church and the world of gainful employment. This made it unmistakably clear that the religious field was a separate or even self-contained social domain, decoupled in motivational terms from other areas of social activity. After the sobering experience of the regional mission conducted in advance of the World Eucharistic Congress in Munich in 1960, there could be no doubt that this process was unstoppable even by a "missionary" movement. In other words, the Catholic "milieu" was already lacking coherence before the modernization and mass culture of the 1960s affected it.[2] In spite of this, recent research has repeatedly asserted that a "re-Christianizing movement" or even "re-Catholicization" took place since the mid-1950s and represents an important trend in West German social history.[3]

This labeling would make little sense even with the caveat that such hopes had no grounding whatsoever in the stability and coherence of the Catholic religious field. Claims about the "re-Christianization" in the 1950s fail to acknowledge that the sociographic discourse of the 1950s contained more than just the hope for a missionary reconquest of lost terrain. Rather, sociography was also aware from the outset that the societal environment of the church in the form of mass media, the world of work, leisure, and consumption followed its own "secular" logic. Yet it would be a mistake to see sociography as a wholly unsuccessful stage in the scientization of the Catholic Church. Sociography failed when measured against its declared missionary objective. On the other hand, however, a small group of sociologists, theologians, and people's missionaries succeeded in comprehensively enlightening the church and Catholics about fundamental structural features of modern society. Sociography helped them to rapidly move on from corporate notions of social order and romantic ideas of an organic community. It replaced moral schemas for evaluating social behavior with more realistic ideas that related patterns of action to social structures. In this sense, sociographic ideas anticipated the Second Vatican Council, which would later proclaim the "aggiornamento," the opening up of the church to the secular "world," as its core objective. In addition, the sociographic method also changed the self-descriptions of the Catholic Church, as it acknowledged functional differentiation and thus placed it on the pastoral agenda.

Sociography left many unanswered questions that had to be posed given the lack of missionary success: What were the attitudes and motives of those Catholics who ignored the church's pastoral offers and thus could no longer be described as "active?" And what expectations did those Catholics who were still interested in the fate of their church have in the postconciliar phase of the church's transformation? These questions were addressed by the instrument of opinion polling, which the church began to apply comprehensively from the late 1960s. In this context, we can also understand the application of social sciences as an instrumental attempt by the bishops and heads of organized lay Catholicism to react to the crises of and challenge to Catholic power structures that were becoming clear in 1968. Here, the application of opinion polling provided a clear advantage. Opinion polls allowed the church to show responsiveness, that is, to demonstrate that their results were taken seriously as a statement about the prevalent desires among the laity, or the base or *basis* of the church, as many observers started to call it then. This new responsiveness was either feared or emphatically welcomed, depending on the observer's standpoint. Polling responded to the quest for participation in the church, but also allowed it to be managed. The structure of the questionnaire symbolically represented the hopes for a comprehensive reform of the church, but at the same time hedged it in by clauses and watered it down. Seen in this way, the use of opinion polling was an unmitigated success. It made a decisive contribution to defusing the "state of war within the church from 1966 to around 1972," as one journalist described it in 1974.[4] Thus, it took the sting out of the revolt of sections of the laity in the wake of 1968.

The instrumental use of opinion polling in this period of crisis and conflict was accompanied by a longer-term systematic use of opinion research. Only through the use of the random sample in polling was it possible to identify the motives of ordinary Catholics and thus to observe the privatization of religious decision making that was a fundamental consequence of functional differentiation. Opinion polling in the church revealed the extent of a "cognitive dissonance" between the attitudes of those Catholics who were formally baptized, but took no serious interest in the church (*Taufscheinkatholiken*), and the value system that the church hierarchy represented. This dissonance was a fact that none of the numerous church polls conducted in the 1970s could ignore. The discrepancy between the belief of the many and the dogmas and structures of the church could not easily be redressed. Even though many Catholics continued to express high expectations in the moral responsibility and political and social engagement of the church, the basic finding remained the same: the morality preached by the church did not fit the lifestyles and norms of modern society. This cognitive dissonance was a consequence of functional differentiation, as those priests and bishops who were keen to identify clusters of motives, and thus actively engaged polling as a method, quickly discovered.

At around the same time opinion polling was applied, the sober and neutral language of sociological functionalism found its way into the church, through the discussion of role sociology and organizational research. The application of these concepts can be understood as a preemptive answer to the aporias that opinion polling had revealed. If the value systems of ordinary Catholics collided substantially with the routine practices of the church apparatus, it was necessary to reform and adapt the structures of the church as an organization. The *Strukturplan* discussed in the diocese of Münster made the most far-reaching proposal to solve this problem. With its fundamental orientation to four basic functions of the church, the *Strukturplan* made it clear that the answer to the consequences of functional differentiation should be to restructure the church organization accordingly—its administrative and pastoral structures, decision-making processes, and the designated roles of priests and lay personnel. However, it proved impossible in Münster to implement a comprehensive reform of the diocesan administration and to replace the traditional parish-based organizational setup. This was not only because the reform was rejected by the deans, whom the plan would have downgraded to administrators of a *Großpfarrei*. Even more important was its rejection by laypeople who were active in the church. These individuals saw their parishes as an organic community—a harmonious family.

The church discovered its interest in reordering and planning church structures through organizational research at the same time that ideas from the social sciences were gaining influence in politics as planning tools. It would be a mistake, however, to draw extensive parallels here by locating church planning primarily in the climate of social reform of the late 1960s. The political discourse, especially at the time of the coalition government led by the Social Democratic Party (SPD) under Chancellor Willy Brandt from 1969, was characterized by "optimism about progress" and the "promise" of the new opportunities opened up by planning.[5] There was little evidence of this in the church, however. Those responsible for church planning—theologians, sociologists, and high-ranking staff at the offices of the vicar-generals—had a very different expectation of the future. They observed an "invisible pulpit" in the parishes, which represented the values and rationality criteria of other functional subsystems of society. This, they believed, hindered the preaching of the Gospel. Thus, the application of planning and organizational research in the Catholic Church started off from the perception of a crisis, as exemplified by the far-ranging debate about the shortage of priests that was the starting point for the planning proposals. In complete contrast to the transformative mood in the political sphere, there was little optimism about the prospect of reorganizing the church. This also makes it untenable for us to interpret the use of organizational sociology as a Machiavellian strategy to retain power by a church focused on tradition. The starting point of church planning was not adherence to tradition, but the criticism of it, and not the goal of retaining power, but rather the feeling of powerlessness in the face of the consequences of functional differentiation.

Even though there was no radical reform of the parish-based model of pastoral services or the hierarchical structure of the church organization, the discussion and application of organizational research in the church was not a complete failure. Its most important trigger—the increasing shortage of clergy—was somewhat compensated for by deploying more trained laypeople in parish pastoral care. This was something that the *Strukturplan* had explicitly envisaged. The parish association or *Pfarrverband* was in many ways a derivative form of the originally planned *Großpfarrei*. In practice, clergy and laity in the *Pfarrverbände* of the 1970s quietly pursued many of the original reform impulses of the *Strukturplan* in slightly modified form. The concept of *Gemeindekirche* or "community church" also lent support to those Catholics who were interested in decoupling the parish from the top-down organization and comprehensive "delivery" of pastoral services through the church apparatus. It is clear from interviews with active proponents of the reform current around 1970, such as the Münster priest Ferdinand Kerstiens, that they regard many of their hopes as having been fulfilled by the contemporary church of the 1980s. In their view, church life at the parish level has only marginal interest in official rules and pronouncements, and is largely carried out by Christians "who have grasped the idea that they themselves are the parish."[6] While the fundamental reform of the church organization around the year 1970 had to be rapidly shelved, a creeping organizational reform took place in the church from the 1970s in the sense that there was a heterarchical decoupling between the hierarchy and the parish "base."

At this point it is also clear how the reception of therapeutic and group dynamics models from psychology arose directly from the half-hearted and less-than-explicit use of organizational sociology. The discussion of the *Strukturplan* had made it clear that large-scale organizational reform—such as functionalizing decision-making processes and hierarchies—could not reckon with general approval. By contrast, an interest in steering and "humanizing" interactions within the organization could pay dividends, especially at the parish level. The application of psychological concepts thus did more than just tackle the frustration in church circles. It also made an important contribution to dismantling hierarchically structured forms of interaction in the church and led to a more egalitarian and cooperative tone prevailing in the parishes. Seen in conceptual terms, the widespread application of methods from psychology can also be interpreted as a reaction to the observation of functional differentiation and its effects on individual Catholics.

This should be obvious if we consider that modern society only treats certain aspects of people as relevant. The functionally differentiated society is interested not in the individual, but rather in the "dividual": that partial and selected dimension of a person that is addressed by the communication of society's functional subsystems. Politics, for instance, communicates with individuals as voters, the economy deals with them in their capacity to make payments, and even the health system, despite recurring claims and attempts to offer an integrated or holistic approach, is addressing only a "dividual"—that particular part of a person that requires health care. Therapeutic pastoral care, by contrast, aims to enculturate Catholicism anew by addressing the individual in targeted fashion as a "whole." This type of pastoral care is thereby promising to "heal" the deficiencies that arise from functional differentiation. As with the other stages of scientization, however, the ambivalences and problems stemming from such an application of pastoral psychology must also be emphasized. The use of Carl Rogers's client-centered therapy in particular verbalized and rationalized pastoral care in a way that undermined the plausibility of the church's traditional, ritual-based, nonverbal communication.

The deployment of methods from psychology drew to a close the final phase of the Catholic Church's scientization, at least in the period up to 1975.[7] It is worth asking here whether this really represented a coherent process, or whether the social sciences became far more a medium and a battleground for the increasingly heated conflicts in the church between "progressives" and "conservatives." It should be emphasized first of all that these two interpretations are not mutually exclusive. One feature of the scientization of the social is that the process of applying social sciences in practice also draws these disciplines into conflict-ridden arenas. From the perspective of science as a social system, this contributes to a "politicization of science," which is a corollary of the scientization of the social.[8] This aspect of scientization can be seen in the controversies between sociographers and representatives of the Catholic teaching of natural law, between advocates and opponents of opinion polls, and between the protagonists of the *Strukturplan* and its critics. In the case of the Catholic Church, the conclusion of the Second Vatican Council in 1965 meant that every discussion of social science also became embroiled in the conflicts over the implementation of the council's resolutions. Whether the council had legitimized and advocated the use of social scientific methods became a matter of constant concern.

Is the scientization of the Catholic Church—from statistics to psychology—best interpreted as a coherent process? One way of answering that question is to consider whether scientization is the flip side of secularization, and in that sense represents a history of loss for the church. After all, it appears that the church is no longer responsible for the moral teaching of citizens, for the control of confessional school education, for making sure that a "good" press prevails, and for making sure that social science is oriented toward the Catholic doctrine of natural law and capable of mobilizing the faithful accordingly. Based on the findings of the sociographic discourse, however, some Catholic pastoral sociologists in the 1960s pointed to the possibility that the "cleansing" of the church's functions could be seen as a "positive" outcome of secularization if one emphasized the "aspect of service to the world." In their view, the disappointment about the church's "loss of functions" expressed merely a "restoration pastoral care," and the "dogged study of religious practice" was an "outdated understanding of the church" in which the church apparatus of the *Amtskirche* (official church) "simply counts" the faithful.[9] Sociography, opinion polling, organizational sociology, and, most of all, pastoral psychology all provide strong points of reference for an interpretation capable of viewing secularization as a gain in, or rather a return to, genuine religious competencies. This is evident in the rhetorical pathos that interpreted therapeutic care and assistance for others as the essence of a true Christianity. In this view, pastoral psychology is an "external prophecy": it illuminates an important dimension of Christian teaching from the outside, almost forgotten about by the church itself. This "external prophecy" does not, however, apply at the primary level of the religious function of the church (that is, to communicate and symbolize the possibility of a world that transcends the visible reality), but rather at the secondary level of providing help to others. Nevertheless, the Catholic Church finally seems to have found or rediscovered its genuine competence in the grand narrative of success represented by "healing pastoral care." The story of the two Emmaus disciples (Luke 24:13–35) is the metaphor most frequently used to prove the authenticity and Biblical credentials of this "healing pastoral care."[10]

All in all, the process of "primary scientization" has progressively affected various aspects and activities of the church. But it would be wrong to present the scientization of the Catholic Church as a sweeping and irreversible success story. It is also necessary to point out the limits of scientization. One example is the limited professionalization of social scientific expertise in the church. During the 1970s, professionals with some social scientific expertise found widespread employment in the church and took major roles in pastoral care, particularly in the form of lay pastoral workers and as counselors who were trained in psychology. It seems, however, that the social scientific training of these groups has hindered their position in the Catholic Church in the medium term rather than promoting it, as was the case with many other academically trained experts.[11]

Limits to scientization are apparent not only in the lacking of professionalization of pastoral practitioners with social scientific background and training. They are also visible in the semantics of the self-description of the church since the 1970s. Reservations about the advance of "sociologisms" in the church, which had already been expressed with regard to sociography in particular, now widened into fundamental criticism of the way in which approaches and concepts from the social sciences were watering down church communication. Such voices were further bolstered after the end of the period that is under scrutiny here, during the pontificate of John Paul II, from 1978. Indicative of these shifts is the changing significance of canon law for disputes within the church. In the preparation for the Würzburg Synod around 1970, concerns about procedure that were based on canon law clearly lost ground to those who supported using social scientific insights into the structure of the public sphere and political participation. By contrast, the conservative revision of the Code of Canon Law (Corpus Juris Canonicus) in 1983 no longer even permitted a synod with decisive participation by laypeople along the lines of the Würzburg Synod.[12]

If we take seriously the idea that secularization is an observer-relative category, then the late 1970s and 1980s represented a period of rollback and in fact a descientization of the church. Insights into the consequences of functional differentiation for pastoral care were rejected increasingly openly in favor of belief as the center and "midst" of life. This was in large part a reaction to the earlier advance of scientization. In 1987, for example, the chair of the Deutsche Gesellschaft für Pastoralpsychologie reported that pastoral psychological work had been "becoming more difficult" for a few years. The DGfP was no longer a "child of growth" as it had been in the 1970s amid increasing interest in these approaches, she concluded resignedly. What was more, the "relationship to fundamentalist tendencies and groups" in the churches had changed. The "evangelical answer" to concepts of pastoral psychology was no longer a "polemic," but rather an attempt at an institutionalized counterattack.[13] Not only the internal perspective of pastoral sociologists interested in a "cleansing of functions," but also the external perspective of the fundamentalist critics of this strategy, point to the extensive scientization of the social between 1945 and 1975 in the Catholic Church.

With the application of social sciences, the relationship between secularization and scientization entered a new phase. In the nineteenth century it had been the natural sciences, particularly Darwinist biology and the popular materialism of Ernst Haeckel, Jakob Moleschott, or Ludwig Büchner that Catholic observers had decisively rejected as secular thought.[14] The reception and application of methods from sociology, which, with a view to issues of scientization has been rightly described as the "key science of the twentieth century," shifted the church's approach to scientization considerably.[15] The main concern was no longer to ward off and immunize the church against scientific discoveries for which the Catholic Church claimed a philosophical competence of its own. Rather, the observation of social change led the church itself to apply secular means in order to recognize the process of secularization, capture its increasing complexity, and, if possible, control it.

In conceptual terms, scientization should not be understood as a process in which systematic, reflexive forms of knowledge penetrate a field that had not previously been affected by more reflexive forms of knowledge. The completion of visitation reports, the systematization of various forms of community through Catholic social teaching, the ecclesiology of the Corpus Christi mysticum, or the casuistry of the sinful soul used in penitence all share a common characteristic: with the exception of public opinion, which the Catholic Church still did not accept as a legitimate sphere in the early 1960s, the church had in fact already applied systematic knowledge to everything that later became the object of scientization. It thus makes little sense in the case of the Catholic Church to take scientization as a synonym for rationalization, particularly given the problematic connotations of this term since Max Weber's distinction between different types of rationality. A more helpful formulation would be to describe the scientization of the church as a process in which a "scientific field of rationality" took precedence over an already existing form of rationality.[16] Even though the knowledge provided by the social sciences was subject to the testing criteria of scientific methodology, it was not inherently "more correct" or "better" than that previously used in the Catholic Church. Such truth effects certainly took place, however. Interestingly, this happened particularly where new concepts corrected the results of earlier stages of scientization—for example, with sociography's criticism of the Potemkin village built with the help of church statistics. The decisive difference, though, was another one: namely, that theological forms of knowledge systematized dogmas—and thus normative expectations—while the human sciences undertook "nothing less than a systematization of . . . human experiences," as the pastoral sociologist Norbert Mette described it.[17]

For the decades following the end of the Second World War, the scientization of the social is mostly associated with three social processes: the dynamic of capitalist mass consumption along Fordist lines, the consolidation of parliamentary democracy, and the further expansion of the welfare state. The scientization of the social thus appears as a process driven both by the large demand for information on the part of large industrial companies and, decisively, by the social democratic "reform coalition" of state and parastate institutions together with the groups of experts and social partners networked and allied with them.[18] In the case of the Catholic Church, this interpretation must be both widened and refined. The scientization of the church was founded neither in a political program of expanding welfare state politics, nor in personal or institutional networks that connected the church to state-driven modernization efforts. Instead, one important reason for applying methods from the social sciences lay more in the challenge posed by the reform and protest movements within the church from the late 1960s. Opinion polls, church planning, and conversational therapy engaged with the problems resulting from functional differentiation. However, they could expect significant interest from the church only once the postconciliar conflict, which was closely associated with the more general turmoil of the late 1960s, put these aspects of the pastoral activities of the church on the agenda. Scientization was not only a telescope with which to observe the consequences of secularization from a safe distance. As time went on, it also increasingly became a discourse of normalization that the church could deploy to "defuse" conflicts.[19]

Overall, the emphasis of the argument presented in this book is on the imperative to reform and adapt formal organizations in a rapidly changing societal environment. Just like the Catholic Church, companies, trade unions, and political parties had to make enormous efforts to retain their agency in a permanently changing society. The scientization of the social owes its energy in no small part to the necessity of keeping large organizations maneuverable in their respective subsystems of society. In 1982, the Social Democrat Peter Glotz used the metaphor of the "tanker" in order to demonstrate how difficult it is to steer these organizations through the rough waters of modern society.[20] However, there was an important difference when it came to the church's application of methods from the social sciences. Glotz was talking about the SPD and other large political parties. In companies and administrative bodies, organizational sociology was one of the most important forms of applied social science in the postwar period.[21] In the Catholic Church, however, organizational research resonated relatively weakly in comparison to its impact on industrial companies, political parties, and welfare state administrations.

Seen in this perspective, scientization was a deliberate strategy that was adopted in order to uphold the presence of the Catholic Church in West German society and to retain its collective agency as an organization. In this limited sense, this is a positive reading of scientization, as it increased the options that were at the disposal of the church hierarchy. Such a positive interpretation, however, should not lead to a streamlined success story of how the church adapted to social change in the postwar period, similar to those historiographical interpretations of the Federal Republic more generally that present a narrative of straightforward "modernization" or "liberalization" since the 1950s.[22] From the perspective of the application of social scientific knowledge, the unintended side effects and problems emanating from a process of scientization are crucial. Usage of the applied social sciences in the church was not simply a straightforward modernization. Rather, it was tantamount to making a leap into a "dangerous modernity." This modernity was "dangerous" in the sense that the much-increased chances for the inclusion of the laity were connected to increasing risks for the enculturation of the Catholic faith more generally. Sociologist Peter Fuchs first developed this argument with regard to the reform of Holy Mass in the wake of the Second Vatican Council.[23] On the one hand, the introduction of the vernacular made Mass much more accessible and thus increased its inclusive reach, that is, it modernized the church successfully. However, by abolishing the use of Latin, the ritual was also cleansed of some of the very hermetic elements that had constituted an important part of its relevance and thus also of its persuasiveness, if not to say of its "magic." In that sense, the introduction of the vernacular was a "dangerous" step, as it entailed the risk of streamlining the church with modernity and taking away its edge.

This notion of a "dangerous modernity" that the church entered when it tried to modernize its core ritual can be used to highlight the ambivalence of the scientization of the church. The use of opinion polls is an important case in point. In the heated conflicts of the late 1960s, the use of polls enabled articulation and regulation of notions of responsiveness. At that critical juncture, this was helpful, as it deemphasized the intensive conflicts between different currents and groups within the church. But the import of the political semantics of responsiveness and democratization into the religious sphere was also problematic. It did not totally overshadow the *proprium* of the church—faith and communication with God—but it at least temporarily threatened to reduce it to a second-tier problem. The application of organizational research in church planning demonstrates similar problems. Planning aimed to adapt the structures of the church apparatus to a rapidly changing societal environment, an attempt that was long overdue when it was finally tackled in the years around 1970. At the same time, however, these useful reform attempts threatened to alienate large swaths of precisely those active members of the laity whose interests they were meant to serve in the first place. Traditional Catholics resented any reorganization of the parish along functionalist lines. Progressive Catholics were disappointed by the fact that the hierarchical form of the organization was not fundamentally affected by this functionalist reform, which did not create new institutional forms for the articulation of pluralism and diversity, as Philipp von Wambolt had demanded.

Therapeutic concepts of pastoral care that were based on new forms of personal encounter and conversation are a final example of the "dangerous modernity" that the Catholic Church encountered through the use of the social sciences. Offering new forms of therapeutic pastoral discussion was an important means of engaging even those individuals who were largely detached from the church, and thus of establishing a chance to communicate the message of the Gospel to them. But through their inherent rationalization and deemphasis of nonverbal communication through ritual, they threatened to hollow out the message of the Gospel, and to render it only in reduced form, and only to those who could communicate in the "elaborate code" of therapeutic talk.

Analyzing the scientization of the Catholic Church thus helps to better understand the ambivalences of organized religion in postwar West Germany, and in Western societies more generally. The trajectory of organized Catholic religion in the three decades since 1945 can only be understood by employing the secularization paradigm. Yet this secularization was not simply a straightforward and irreversible decline, despite the increasingly dramatic drop in the number of churchgoers, communions, and ultimately also parish clergy. As we have seen throughout this book, secularization was also productive: it triggered responses and intensive efforts by pioneers in pastoral sociology and pastoral care, church officials, and engaged members of the laity, all of whom sought to adapt the organizational structures and the pastoral strategies of the church to the challenges of a functionally differentiated society. In that sense, the history of the Catholic Church in the Federal Republic was part of a larger development: the attempt to reconfigure the place of Christian religion in a modern society, and to make it "compatible with the future of modernity."[24]

Notes

1. See the important article by Hahn, "Zur Soziologie der Beichte."
2. See in more detail, with a critical discussion of the available evidence, Benjamin Ziemann, "Zur Entwicklung christlicher Religiosität in Deutschland, 1900–1960," in *Religion und Gesellschaft*, ed. Christof Wulf and Matthias Koenig (Wiesbaden, 2013): 99–122.

3. Herbert, "Liberalisierung," 21, 39; see also Peter Lösche and Franz Walter, "Katholiken, Konservative und Liberale: Milieus und Lebenswelten bürgerlicher Parteien in Deutschland während des 20. Jahrhunderts," *GG* 26 (2000): 487.

4. *Süddeutsche Zeitung*, 22 November 1974.

5. On planning in the political system, see Gabriele Metzler, *Konzeptionen politischen Handelns von Adenauer bis Brandt: Politische Planung in der pluralistischen Gesellschaft* (Paderborn, 2005), quotes 420–21; Ruck, "Kurzer Sommer."

6. Interview with Ferdinand Kerstiens, cited in Großbölting, *Suchbewegungen*, 262.

7. Only in the period after 1975 was a form of pedagogy heavily influenced by sociological ideas adopted in Catholic youth work, catechetics, and continuing education. This paradigm shift is encapsulated in the replacement of the chaplain who is responsible for youth work in a parish community with a layperson with a higher education diploma in pedagogy. See the scattered remarks in Damberg, *Abschied*, 363–83; *Gemeinsame Synode*, 1:303–6.

8. Peter Weingart, "Verwissenschaftlichung der Gesellschaft—Politisierung der Wissenschaft," *Zeitschrift für Soziologie (ZfS)* 12 (1983): 228.

9. Hans Goddijn and Walter Goddijn, *Sichtbare Kirche: Ökumene und Pastoral: Einführung in die Religionssoziologie* (Vienna, 1967), 184–87; see also the arguments by Norbert Greinacher, discussed in chapter 4; on this problem, see also Alois Hahn, "Luhmanns Beobachtung der Religion," *KZfSS* 53 (2001): 580–89.

10. See the extensive interpretation of this passage by Baumgartner, *Pastoralpsychologie*, 92–142.

11. This was not a "professionalization" in the sense that the word is generally used by social historians. On this issue, see Raphael, "Verwissenschaftlichung," 180–81.

12. Walf, "Kirchenrecht"; Ziemann, "Dienstleistung," 392–93.

13. Liesel-Lotte Herkenrath-Püschel, 9 February 1987, Akten der Deutschen Gesellschaft für Pastoralpsychologie, Ordner Unterlagen zur Gründung.

14. Owen Chadwick, *The Secularization of the European Mind in the Nineteenth Century* (Cambridge, 1975), 161–88.

15. Joachim Matthes, "Soziologie: Schlüsselwissenschaft des 20. Jahrhunderts?," in *Lebenswelt und soziale Probleme: Verhandlungen des 20. Deutschen Soziologentages zu Bremen 1980*, ed. Joachim Matthes (Frankfurt and New York, 1980), 15.

16. Maasen, *Genealogie*, 478–79.

17. Contribution to a discussion by Norbert Mette, printed in Gottfried Griesl, "Praktische Theologie zwischen Verkündigung und Psychotherapie," in *Von der Pastoraltheologie zur Praktischen Theologie 1774–1974*, ed. Erika Weinzierl and Gottfried Griesl (Salzburg, 1975), 223.

18. Raphael, "Verwissenschaftlichung," 177–78; see also Peter Wagner, "Social Science and Social Planning during the Twentieth Century," in *The Modern Social Sciences*, ed. Theodore M. Porter and Dorothy Ross (Cambridge, 2003), 601–6; on the notion of a "reform coalition," see Peter Wagner, "The Mythical Promise of Societal Renewal: Social Science and Reform Coalitions," in *A History and Theory of the Social Sciences* (London, 2001), 54–72.

19. Raphael, "Verwissenschaftlichung," 178.

20. Peter Glotz, *Die Beweglichkeit des Tankers* (Munich, 1982).

21. This point is rightly emphasized by Peter Wagner, "The Uses of the Social Sciences," in Porter and Ross, *The Modern Social Sciences*, 545–46.

22. See, for instance, Herbert, "Liberalisierung"; Jarausch, *After Hitler*.

23. See Peter Fuchs, "Gefährliche Modernität: Das zweite vatikanische Konzil und die Veränderung des Messeritus," *KZfSS* 44 (1992): 1–11.

24. Franz-Xaver Kaufmann, "Ist das Christentum zukunftsfähig?," in *Religion und Modernität: Sozialwissenschaftliche Perspektiven* (Tübingen, 1989), 235–75.

BIBLIOGRAPHY

Archives

Bischöfliches Diözesanarchiv Aachen (BDA):
- Gvs E 1, I; Gvs E 1, II; Gvs B 17, I-III

Institut für Demoskopie Allensbach, Archiv:
- IfD-Berichte 1351, 1364, 1471

Archiv des Redemptoristenklosters Bochum (ARedBo):
- Ordner Soziologische Untersuchungen; Ordner Missions-Konferenzen CSsR C 2; Ordner Missions-Konferenzen C 3; Ordner Soziologie

Archiv der Kommission für Zeitgeschichte, Bonn (KfZG):
- NL Hermann Joseph Schmitt: 1, 7
- Materialien KAB: G VI 2, G VII

Archiv des Zentralkomitees der deutschen Katholiken, Bonn (Archiv ZdK):
- 60/1, 1—60/1, 6, 2202/2

Archiv der Sozialen Demokratie, Bonn (AsD):
- NL Walter Dirks: 18, 76, 123, 126

Deutsche Bischofskonferenz, Referat Statistik, Bonn:
- [O. Eitner], Die Zentralstelle für kirchliche Statistik im katholischen Deutschland (ms., 1922)

Bistumsarchiv Essen (BAE):
- K 406, K 544, P 316
- GV 82 14 12, Bde. 1–3
- Nachlaß Kardinal Hengsbach (NL 1): 1008, 1011, 1015, 1016, 1022, 1024
- Würzburger Synode: Hefter Allgemeine Befragung, Hefter Protokolle der Sitzungen des Synodalbüros, Hefter Synode 72-Vorträge

Erzbischöfliches Archiv Freiburg (EAF):
- B2–47–52, B2–47–57, B2–47–67, B2–47–69, B2–49–15, B2–49–16, B2–49–18, B2–49–20, B2–49–25, B2–49–27, B2–49–28, B2–49–29a, B2–49–30, B2–49–35, B2–49–103

Historisches Archiv des Erzbistums Köln (HAEK):
- Depositum DBK: Allgemeine Auskünfte 1972–1973, Korrespondenz Diözese München 1950–1977, Korrespondenz Diözese Rottenburg 1950–1976, Korrespondenz Diözese Würzburg 1950–1978, Korrespondenz Erzdiözese Freiburg 1950–1977, Korrespondenz Erzdiözese Köln, Statistische Auskünfte 1966–1967, Zählbogen-Korrespondenz
- Seelsorgeamt Heinen: 11, 56, 60
- CR II: 2.19, 9
- Gen. I: 32.12, 6
- Gen. II: 32.12, 1–6, 9–10; 32.12, Zugang 452/89, Ordner 102, Ordner 103
- NL Josef Frings: 833–836, 840
- NL Adolph Geck

Diözesanarchiv Limburg (DAL):
- 203G Gebietsmission 1957/58, 203G Gebietsmission 1959, 552A, 552B

Erzbischöfliches Ordinariat München (EOM), Registratur:
- Hefter Redemptoristen bis 1988, Teil 1; Hefter Seelsorgeamt

Erzbischöfliches Ordinariat München (EOM), Pastorale Planungsstelle:
- Aktenordner zur Soziographischen Erhebung im Vorfeld des Eucharistischen Welt-kongresses 1960: Menges I; Teil II: Münchens katholische Pfarreien; Teil III: Das Münchener Kirchenvolk
- Akte P. Wesel, Gemeindeleitung; Akte PV-Kurs 1977

Bistumsarchiv Münster (BAM):
Generalvikariat Münster, Neues Archiv (GV NA)
- Bischöfliches Sekretariat (A-0): 195, 500, 639, 737, 757, 767, 768, 770, 783a, 787, 790, 805, 966, 978, 979
- Sekretariat des Generalvikars (A-101): 40, 140, 141, 155, 156, 166, 167, 174, 175, 189, 206–8, 219, 245, 261, 283, 336, 376, 378, 381, 383
- Hauptabteilung 200, Seelsorge. Geschäftsführung 201 (A-201): 1, 2, 14–16, 23–25, 260, 265, 283, 290, 357, 365, 366, 368, 374, 376, 379, 383, 396, 463
- Kommissariat Niederrhein: A 4
- Diözesankomitee Münster: A 18, A 41, A 42, A 55
- Katholische Studentengemeinde (KSG): A 136, 194
- Franz-Hitze-Haus Münster 1949–1974 und Soziale Seminare im Bistum Münster (FHH): A 15, 50, 58, 196, 232
- Schriftleitung der Bistumszeitung *Kirche und Leben*: A 205, A 229, A 235
- Synodalbüro der Gemeinsamen Synode der Bistümer in der Bundesrepublik Deutsch-land: A 1–A 6, A 54, A 59
- Amtsdrucksachen (AD): 21

Institut für Christliche Sozialwissenschaften an der Westfälischen Wilhelms-Universität Münster (ICSW):
- Aktenordner mit Seminarunterlagen: Ordner Joseph Höffner; Ordner Prof. Wilhelm Weber, WS 1969/70

Loyola University New Orleans, Monroe Library, Special Collections:
- Joseph H. Fichter Papers, Box 1, Folder 9; Box 13, Folders 13–17

Katholiek Documentatie Centrum Nijmegen (KDC):
- Bestand 21 (KASKI): 2719–2728, 2757, 2768–2772, 4288–4292, 4303
- Archief Mensen in Nood: 1184, 1540
- NL Dellepoort: 66, 102, 103, 354
- KASKI: Memorandum No. 32 (1956)
- Knipsels: G. H. L. Zeegers

Akten der Deutschen Gesellschaft für Pastoralpsychologie, Geschäftsstelle der DGfP, Nürnberg:
- Ordner Unterlagen zur Gründung

Bistumsarchiv Osnabrück (BAOS):
- 03–04–21–01/02/03, 03–04–22–01/02, 03–09–51–02, 03–55–01–01, 03–55–01–02, 07–31–50, 07–31–52
- Seelsorgeamt, Akzession 4: Ordner Diözesan-Synode I, Ordner Synode Würzburg

Erzbischöfliches Archiv Paderborn (EBAP):
- Generalakten (GA): Diözesan-Konferenzen 1957, 1959, 1962; Gebietsseelsorger 1958–1969; Kirchliche Statistik, 1945–1961; Kirchliche Statistik, Beiakte zu 1945–1961;

Kirchliche Statistik 1962–1967; Kirchliche Statistik 1968–1969; Kommende, Personal, 1947–1960; Kommende, Satzung, Kuratorium des GSI 1959–1962; Kommende, Satzung, Kuratorium des GSI 1963–1969; Seelsorgeamt 1945–1969; Seelsorgsbezirke (Regionen) 1965–1969; Volksmission 1959; Volksmission 1960–1961; Volksmission 1962

Archiv des Bistums Passau (ABP):
- OA 9220
- DekA II: Burghausen 12/I, Fürstenzell 12/I, Obernzell 12/I, Pfarrkirchen 12/I

Published Sources

Individual articles from pastoral and sociological journals published prior to 1975 are not listed again in the section *Contemporary Literature (until 1975)* of this bibliography. They are fully referenced in the endnotes of the text.

Periodicals

Allensbacher Berichte 17 (1970)
Anima: Vierteljahresschrift für praktische Seelsorge 4 (1949)–12 (1957)
Augsburger Postzeitung (1905)
Berichte und Dokumente: Published by the Zentralkomitee der deutschen Katholiken 6 (1970)–24 (1975)
Civitas 1 (1962)–10 (1971)
Concilium 1 (1965)–11 (1975)
Das Dorf: Zweimonatsschrift zur christlichen Erneuerung des Landlebens: Führungsorgan der Katholischen Landbewegung Deutschlands 5 (1953)–9 (1957)
Der christliche Sonntag: Katholisches Wochenblatt 8 (1956)
Der Seelsorger: Zweimonatsschrift für Praxis und Theorie des kirchlichen Dienstes 21 (1950/51)–31 (1960/61)
Diakonia: Der Seelsorger: Internationale Zeitschrift für praktische Theologie 1 (1970)–5 (1974)
Dokumente: Zeitschrift im Dienst übernationaler Zusammenarbeit 1 (1945/46)–20 (1970)
Echo der Zeit (1963–65)
Fk-Information: Mitteilungen des Freckenhorster Kreises (1974–76)
Frankfurter Hefte 1 (1946)–29 (1974)
Germania (1904, 1905, 1916)
Herder-Korrespondenz 1 (1946/47)–30 (1976)
Hochland: Monatsschrift für alle Gebiete des Wissens, der Literatur und Kunst 7 (1909/10)–25 (1928), 39 (1946/47)–63 (1971)
Im Dienst der Seelsorge: Beilage zum Kirchlichen Amtsblatt der Erzdiözese Paderborn 3 (1949)–28 (1974)
Informationen der Kölner Ordensprovinz CSsR 17 (1986)
Internationales Jahrbuch für Religionssoziologie 1 (1965)–8 (1975)
Jahrbuch 1927 für die Katholiken Mannheims
Jahrbuch des Instituts für christliche Sozialwissenschaft [from 9 (1968): *Jahrbuch für Christliche Sozialwissenschaften*] 1 (1960)–34 (1993)
Katechetische Blätter 85 (1960)–87 (1962)
Kirche und Leben: Bistumszeitung Münster 24 (1969)–25 (1970)

Kirche, Meinung, Medien: Tips und Informationen zur Gemeindearbeit: Published by the Gesellschaft für Christliche Öffentlichkeitsarbeit 4 (1971)–5 (1972)

Kirchliches Amtsblatt für die Diözese Münster 105 (1971)–106 (1972)

Kirchliches Handbuch für das katholische Deutschland 1 (1908)–29 (1976/86)

Kirchliches Jahrbuch für die evangelischen Landeskirchen Deutschlands 39 (1912)

Klerusblatt: Organ der Diözesan-Priestervereine Bayerns und des Bistums Speyer 13 (1932), 29 (1949), 32 (1952), 44 (1964)

Kölner, Aachener und Essener Pastoralblatt 10 (1958)–15 (1963)

Kölnische Volkszeitung (1904/5)

Lebendige Seelsorge 1 (1950)–30 (1979)

Liturgisches Jahrbuch 1 (1951)–26 (1977)

Lumen Vitae 1 (1946)–6 (1951)

Mann in der Kirche 26 (1969)–28 (1971)

Münsterisches Pastoralblatt (1914)

Oberhirtliches Verordnungsblatt für die Diözese Passau (1893)

Oberrheinisches Pastoralblatt 56 (1955), 60 (1959), 67 (1966)–75 (1974)

Ordenskorrespondenz 6 (1965), 16 (1975)

Orientierung 17 (1953)

Pastoralblatt 43 (1909)–44 (1910)

Pastoralblatt für die Diözesen Aachen, Berlin, Essen, Köln, Osnabrück 16 (1964)–27 (1975)

Paulus: Zeitschrift für missionarische Seelsorge 22 (1950)–37 (1965)

Publik: Informationen, Meinungen, Analysen und Bilder dieser Woche 1 (1968)–4 (1971)

Rheinischer Merkur (1956, 1968–74)

Ruhrwort (1969–70)

Seelsorgehilfe 1 (1949)–5 (1953)

Sein und Sendung 1 (1969)–7 (1975)

Social Compass: International Review of Sociology of Religion 1 (1954)–19 (1972)

Soziale Welt 1 (1949/50)

Stimmen der Zeit 90 (1916)–117 (1929), 139 (1946/47)–154 (1953/54), 179 (1967)–193 (1975)

Synode: Amtliche Mitteilungen der gemeinsamen Synode der Bistümer in der Bundesrepublik Deutschland 1 (1970)–6 (1975)

Theologie der Gegenwart 1 (1958)–7 (1964)

Theologie und Glaube: Zeitschrift für den katholischen Klerus 17 (1925)–23 (1931), 48 (1958)–62 (1972)

Trierer Theologische Zeitschrift 58 (1949)–77 (1968)

Unsere Seelsorge: Wegweiser und Mitteilungen für Seelsorge und Laienarbeit im Bistum Münster 3 (1953)–22 (1972)

Werkhefte 24 (1970)–26 (1972)

Wort und Wahrheit: Monatsschrift für Religion und Kultur 7 (1952)–14 (1959)

Source Collections, Published Minutes

Abbott, Walter M., ed. *The Documents of Vatican II*. London and Dublin, 1966.

Baumgarten, Paul Maria. *Die Römische Kurie um 1900: Ausgewählte Aufsätze*. Edited by C. Weber. Cologne, 1986.

Denzinger, Heinrich. *Kompendium der Glaubensbekenntnisse und kirchlichen Lehrentscheidungen*. 37th ed. Edited by Peter Hünermann. Freiburg, 1991.

Gatz, Erwin, ed. *Akten der Fuldaer Bischofskonferenz 1871–1919*. Vols. 1–3. Mainz, 1977–85.

Heinen, Ernst, ed. *Staatliche Macht und Katholizismus in Deutschland: Dokumente des politischen Katholizismus von 1867 bis 1914*. Vol. 2. Paderborn, 1979.

Hennelly, Alfred T., ed. *Liberation Theology: A Documentary History*. New York, 1990.

Hürten, Heinz, ed. *Akten Kardinal Michael von Faulhabers*. Vol. 3, *1945–1952*. Paderborn, 2002.

Protokoll des SPD-Parteitags Hannover 1973. Hannover, 1973.

Public Papers of the Presidents: Richard Nixon 1969–1974. Vol. 1, *1969*. Washington DC, 1971.

Stasiewski, Bernhard, ed. *Akten deutscher Bischöfe über die Lage der Kirche 1933–1945*. Vol. 1, *1933–1934*. Mainz, 1968.

Stehkämper, Hugo, ed. *Der Nachlaß des Reichskanzlers Wilhelm Marx*. 5 vols. Cologne, 1968–97.

Volk, Ludwig, ed. *Akten deutscher Bischöfe über die Lage der Kirche 1933–1945*. Vol. 5, *1940–1942*. Mainz, 1983.

Encyclopedias

Bautz, Friedrich-Wilhelm, ed. *Biographisch-Bibliographisches Kirchenlexikon*. Vols. 1–20. Hamm (later Herzberg), 1975–2002.

Buchberger, Michael, ed. *Lexikon für Theologie und Kirche*. 1st ed. 10 vols. Freiburg, 1930–38.

Eidelberg, Ludwig, ed. *Encyclopedia of Psychoanalysis*. New York and London, 1968.

Fricke, Dieter, ed. *Lexikon zur Parteiengeschichte: Die bürgerlichen und kleinbürgerlichen Parteien und Verbände in Deutschland (1789–1945)*. 4 vols. Cologne, 1983–86.

Galling, Kurt, ed. *Die Religion in Geschichte und Gegenwart: Handwörterbuch für Theologie und Religionswissenschaft*. 3rd ed. 7 vols. Tübingen 1957–1965.

Höffner, Joseph, and Karl Rahner, eds. *Lexikon für Theologie und Kirche*. 2nd ed. 10 vols. Freiburg, 1957–65.

Kasper, Walter, ed. *Lexikon für Theologie und Kirche*. 3rd ed. 11 vols. Freiburg, 1993–2001.

Krause, Gerhard and Gerhard Müller, eds. *Theologische Realenzyklopädie*. Berlin, 1977ff.

Kürschners Deutscher Gelehrten-Kalender. 11th ed. Berlin, 1966.

Sacher, Hermann, ed. *Staatslexikon*. 5th ed. Freiburg, 1926–32.

Wetzer, Heinrich Josef, and Benedikt Welte, eds. *Kirchenlexikon oder Enzyklopädie der katholischen Theologie und ihrer Hilfswissenschaften*. 2nd ed. 13 vols. Freiburg, 1882–1903.

Study Reports by Pastoral-Sociological Research Institutions

Pastoralsoziologisches Institut des Erzbistums Paderborn und des Bistums Essen (PSI)

Berichte (Reports)

no. 1: Bestandsaufnahme der Niederlassungen männlicher und weiblicher Orden und ordensähnlicher Kongregationen im Bistum Essen (1959).

no. 3: Pastoralsoziologische Untersuchung der Stadt Essen. Erster Teil: Zur soziologischen Struktur der Stadt Essen (1959).

no. 3 A: Pastoralsoziologische Untersuchung der Stadt Essen. Erster Teil: Zur soziologischen Struktur der Stadt Essen. Tabellen und Kartogramme (1959).

no. 4: Pastoralsoziologische Untersuchung der Stadt Essen. Zweiter Teil: Das religiöse Leben im Raume der Stadt Essen; Dritter Teil: Pastoraltheologische Überlegungen (1961).

no. 4 A: Pastoralsoziologische Untersuchung der Stadt Essen. Tabellen und Kartogramme (1961).

no. 4 B: Tabellenband zur differenzierten Kirchenbesucherzählung in Essen vom 25. Oktober 1959 (April 1961).

no. 6: Priesternachwuchs und Klerus im Bistum Essen (1960).

no. 10: Priesternachwuchs und Klerus im Erzbistum Paderborn (1961).

no. 11: Pastoralsoziologische Untersuchung der Stadt Dortmund. Erster Teil: Zur gesellschaftlichen Situation der Stadt Dortmund (1961).

no. 11 A: Pastoralsoziologische Untersuchung der Stadt Dortmund. Erster Teil: Zur gesellschaftlichen Situation der Stadt Dortmund. Tabellen und Graphiken (1961).

no. 12: Pastoralsoziologische Untersuchung der Stadt Dortmund. Zweiter Teil: Religiöse Praxis (1962).

no. 21: Jugendprobleme im Kreis Meschede/Sauerland, I. Teil: Gesellschaftlicher Hintergrund (1962).

no. 22: Jugendrobleme im Kreis Meschede/Sauerland, II. Teil: Konflikte und Probleme (1962).

no. 22 A: Jugendprobleme im Kreis Meschede/Sauerland, III. Teil (1962). [From no. 38 as: Sozialinstitut Essen. Kirchliche Sozialforschung. Berichte (SIB)].

no. 42: Zum Begriff und den sozialwissenschaftlichen Meßmethoden der Religiosität (1966).

no. 49: Skalierungsverfahren in der sozialpsychologischen Einstellungsforschung zur Religion, Essen, 1968. [From no. 64 as: Institut für Kirchliche Sozialforschung Essen (IKSE)].

no. 88: Berufsbild und Selbstverständnis von Laientheologen. Eine empirische Untersuchung unter studierenden Laientheologen an deutschen Universitäten und Erziehungswissenschaftlichen Hochschulen. Essen, 1975.

no. 101: Zur pastoralsoziologischen Situation im Bistum Essen: Daten und Überlegungen. Essen, 1986.

IKSE, Kirchliche Statistik. Jahreserhebung 2001. Essen, 2002.

SIB, Forschungsplan für eine Untersuchung über die Rolle des Kaplans als Seelsorger in der Diözese Köln, n.d. [1967].

Handreichungen (Guidance Manuals):

no. 1: Die differenzierte Kirchenbesucherzählung (1959).

no. 2: Die Pfarrkartei (February 1960).

no. 4: Aspekte der gesellschaftlichen Wirklichkeit im Raume des Bistums Essen (January 1960).

no. 8: Kurzer Kommentar zu einer Umfrage über Kirche und Öffentlichkeit (August 1961).

no. 9: Die Frage der Mischehen mit katholischer Beteiligung in Deutschland (1961).

no. 12: Zur Frage der Meßzeiten in der Essener Innenstadt (September 1961).

no. 13: Überlegungen zur Lebendigkeit des Glaubens in der Bundesrepublik (January 1962).

no. 17: Zur religiösen Praxis in der Stadt Essen. Bemerkungen zur Verläßlichkeit und zum Situationsbild der Angaben der kirchlichen Statistik (August 1963).

no. 19: Vorstellungen über den Priester. Ein Thesenkatalog (January 1964).

no. 42: Mady Layendecker-Thung, Zur Frage nach der Sozialform des Glaubens. Versuch einer Typologie kirchlicher Organisationsformen (1977).

Sozialteam, Landstuhl (Later in Adelsried)

Gebietsmission Dekanat Kitzingen: Basisuntersuchung und Pfarreitypologie, Ramstein 1963 (Strukturelle Seelsorge, no. 5).
Gebietsmission Dekanat St. Ingbert. Die Basisuntersuchung in einem Traditionsgebiet, Ramstein/Pfalz 1963 (Strukturelle Seelsorge, no. 3).
Die Entwicklung der Kirchlichkeit im Bistum Speyer 1950–2000, Adelsried 1968 (Strukturelle Seelsorge, Bd. 1).
Sozialteam, ed. Sozial-kirchliche Analyse der Stadt Augsburg, no. 1: Religiöse Praxis und zwischenpfarrliche Wanderung. Landstuhl, 1967.
Sozialteam, ed. Sozial-kirchliche Analyse der Stadt Augsburg, no. 2: Meßzeiten und Kirchenbesuch. Landstuhl, 1967.
Sozialteam, ed. Sozial-kirchliche Analyse der Stadt Augsburg, no. 7: Die Situation der Kirche in der Stadt. Landstuhl, 1969.

Institut für Kommunikationsforschung Wuppertal-Frankfurt

Bericht über das Ergebnis der Meinungsumfrage I/1968 (Primärerhebung) für die katholische Pfarrgemeinde St. Anna. Munich, 1968.
Abschlußbericht 3–1970. Primärerhebung. Image der Dienste eines Dekanates. [Munich], 1970.
Abschlußbericht I. 12–1970. Primärerhebung. Image der Dienste eines Dekanates. [Passau], 1970.

Contemporary Literature (until 1975)

1770 Forum-Fragen zu den 27 Forumgesprächen auf dem 82. Deutschen Katholikentag vom 4.–8. September 1968. Essen, 1968.
Algermissen, Konrad. "Pastorallehren aus der Statistik des Kirchenaustritts und Freidenkerbewegung der Nachkriegszeit." *Theologisch-praktische Quartalschrift* 83 (1933): 686–716.
Amery, Carl. *Die Kapitulation oder Deutscher Katholizimus heute.* Reinbek, 1963.
Angell, Robert C. "The Ethical Problems of Applied Sociology." In *The Uses of Sociology,* 2nd ed, ed. Paul Lazarsfeld, William H. Sewell and Harold L. Wilensky, 725–40. New York, 1967.
"Auf dem Weg zu einer Theologie der Diasporakirche." In *Theologische Materialien für Kontroverstheologie und Konfessionskunde* 1, nos. 3/4 (1957): 33–64.
Bauer, Clemens. "Der Deutsche Katholizismus und die bürgerliche Gesellschaft." In *Deutscher Katholizismus: Entwicklungslinien und Profile,* 28–52. Frankfurt, 1964.
Baumann, Antonius. "Gedanken zur kirchlichen Statistik von Dortmund." In *Jb. für die Katholiken Dortmunds 1929,* 49–61. Dortmund, 1929.
Baumgarten, Paul Maria. *Kirchliche Statistik: Wie steht es um die Kirchliche Statistik in Deutschland? Ein Wort über kirchliche Statistik, Statistische Beschreibung der kirchlichen Verhältnisse Italiens.* Wörrishofen, 1905.
———. *Römische und andere Erinnerungen.* Düsseldorf, 1927.
Baumgarten, Paul Maria, and Hermann A. Krose. "Ecclesiastical Statistics." In *The Catholic Encyclopedia,* ed. C. G. Herbermann, 14:269–82. New York, 1912.

Beckel, Albrecht. "Etappen auf dem Weg." In *Erfahrungen 1971: Aspekte der Akademiearbeit,* ed. Albrecht Beckel, 15–27. Münster, 1971.

Becker, Matthias. *Die Macht in der katholischen Kirche: Kritik der hierarchischen Praxis.* Munich, 1967.

Benz, Franz. *Missionarische Seelsorge: Die missionarische Seelsorgebewegung in Frankreich und ihre Bedeutung für Deutschland.* Freiburg, 1958.

Berger, W., and H. Andrissen. "Das amerikanische Phänomen 'Pastoral Counseling' und seine Bedeutung für die Pastoraltheologie." In *Handbuch der Pastoraltheologie: Praktische Theologie der Kirche in ihrer Gegenwart,* ed. Franz-Xaver Arnold, 3:570–85. Freiburg, 1968.

Bergmann, Herbert. "Strukturprobleme der städtischen Pfarrei, dargestellt am Beispiel einer Pfarrei im Ruhrgebiet." Manuscript. Münster, 1967.

Bericht über die 17. Diözesankonferenz zu Paderborn vom 19. bis 22. Mai 1959. Paderborn, n.d. [1959].

Bierbaum, Athanasius. *Warum so viele Bedenken gegen die tägliche heilige Kommunion?* Warendorf, 1913.

Biestek, Felix P., SJ. *The Casework Relationship.* London, 1961. First published 1957.

Bodamer, Joachim. *Gesundheit und technische Welt.* Stuttgart, 1955.

Bodzenta, Erich, ed. *5 Jahre Internationales Katholisches Institut für Kirchliche Sozialforschung (ICARES), Abteilung Österreich 1952–1957: Eine Festschrift.* Vienna, 1957.

Böhm, Anton. *Leben im Zwiespalt: Der moderne Mensch zwischen Angst und Hybris.* Freiburg, 1974.

Böhringer, Hans. *Die Tiefenpsychologie von morgen.* Hamm, 1961.

———. *Priesterliche Selbstbesinnung: Ein mitbrüderlicher Brief.* Hamm, 1964.

Boonen, Ph. *Das Konzil kommt ins Bistum: Zur Diskussion um die künftige Planung und Struktur des kirchlichen Dienstes.* Aachen, 1967.

Bopp, Linus. "Das Schicksal der psychoanalytischen Bewegung." *Literarischer Handweiser* 61 (1925): 749–60.

———. *Katholizismus und Psychoanalyse, Der Katholizismus als Lösung großer Menscheitsfragen.* Innsbruck, Vienna, and Munich, 1925. Published by Akademischer Verein Logos.

———. *Moderne Psychoanalyse, Katholische Beichte und Pädagogik.* Munich and Kempten, 1923.

———. "Sigmund Freuds Lebenswerk im Gericht der Zeit." *Schönere Zukunft* 7 (1931): 100–1, 132–33, 153–55.

Boulard, Fernand. *Essor ou Déclin du Clergé Français.* Paris, 1950.

———. *Problèmes missionnaires de la France rurale.* 2 vols. Paris, n.d. [1945].

———. *Wegweiser in die Pastoralsoziologie.* Munich, 1960.

Braekling, Alois. "Kirchliche Statistik." *Der katholische Seelsorger* 17 (1905): 362–69, 405–14.

Breitenstein, Desidirius, OFM. "Bevölkerungsgliederung und Seelsorge." In *Lebendige Seelsorge: Wegweisung durch die religiösen Ideen der Zeit für den Klerus deutscher Zunge,* ed. W. Meyer and P. Neyer, 275–93. Freiburg, 1937.

———. *Diaspora und Bonifatiusverein.* Hamm, 1920.

Brockmöller, Klemens. *Industriekultur und Religion.* Frankfurt, 1964.

Browe, Peter, SJ. *Die Pflichtkommunion im Mittelalter.* Münster, 1940.

Brüning, R. "Nochmals Kirchliche Statistik." *Allgemeine Rundschau,* no. 8 (19 February 1905): 86–87.

Carrier, Herve, and Emile Pin. *Sociologie du Christianisme: Bibliographie Internationale.* Rome, 1964.

———. *Sociologie du Christianisme: Bibliographie Internationale: Supplément 1962–1966.* Rome, 1968.

Connan, Francois, and Jean-Claude Barreau. *Die Pfarrei von morgen.* Lucerne and Munich, 1968.

Corsten, Wilhelm, ed. *Sammlung kirchlicher Erlasse, Verordnungen und Bekanntmachungen für die Erzdiözese Köln.* Cologne, 1929.

Croon, Helmuth. "Methoden zur Erforschung der gemeindlichen Sozialgeschichte des 19. und 20. Jahrhunderts." *Westfälische Forschungen* 8 (1955): 139–49.

Crottogini, Jakob. *Werden und Krise des Priesterberufes: Eine psychologisch-pädagogische Untersuchung über den Priesternachwuchs in verschiedenen Ländern Europas.* Einsiedeln, 1955.

Dahm, Karl-Wilhelm. "Gruppendynamik und kirchliche Praxis: Versuch einer Beziehungsklärung." In *Gruppendynamik in der kirchlichen Praxis: Erfahrungsberichte,* ed. Karl-Wilhelm Dahm and Hermann Stenger, 11–47. Munich, 1974.

Dahrendorf, Ralf. *Homo Sociologicus.* Opladen, 1977.

Daniel, Yvan. *Aspects de la Pratique Religieuse de Paris.* Paris, 1952.

Debarge, Louis. *Psychologie und Seelsorge.* Lucerne, 1969.

Dellepoort, Jan, Norbert Greinacher and Walter Menges, *Die deutsche Priesterfrage: Eine soziologische Untersuchung über Klerus und Priesternachwuchs in Deutschland.* Mainz, 1961.

Demal, Willibald, OSB. *Pastoral Psychology in Practice: Contributions to a Psychology for Priests and Educators.* Cork, 1955. First published in German as *Praktische Pastoralpsychologie,* Vienna, 1947.

Desroche, Henri. "Areas and Methods of a Sociology of Religion: The Work of G. Le Bras." *Journal of Religion* (35) 1955: 34–47.

Die Erzdiözese Freiburg während der Jahre 1922–1946 im Lichte der Statistik. Freiburg, 1946.

Die europäische Priesterfrage: Bericht der Internationalen Enquête in Wien, 10.–12. Oktober 1958. Vienna, 1959. Published by the Internationales Katholisches Institut für kirchliche Sozialforschung Wien.

Die Planung von heute für die Kirche von morgen: Kirchliche Raumplanung in der Erzdiözese München und Freising. Munich, 1972.

Donat, Josef. "Irrtum und Schaden der Freudschen Psychoanalyse." *Schönere Zukunft* 11 (1935/36): 892–94.

Drexler, Josef. *Die Pfarr-Kartothek: Ihre Notwendigkeit für die Städte und ihre Organisation.* Cologne, 1914.

Ducos, P. "Zeitgemäße Volksmission." *Werkblätter für die Seelsorge* 3 (1949): 16–21.

Duffield, Gervase E. *The Paul Report Considered: An Appraisal of Leslie Paul's Report, The Deployment and Payment of the Clergy.* Marcham, 1964.

Egenter, Richard. "Psychotherapie und Gewissen." *Münchener Theologische Zeitschrift* 8, no. 1 (1957): 33–45.

Egenter, Richard, and Paul Matussek. *Ideologie, Glaube und Gewissen: Diskussion an der Grenze zwischen Moraltheologie und Psychotherapie.* Munich, 1965.

Eitner, H. O. "Aus der kirchlichen Statistik." *Theologie und Glaube* 9 (1917): 509–15.

Ellwein, Thomas. *Klerikalismus in der deutschen Politik.* Munich, 1955.

Emmel, F. "Theologen im Ruhr- und Rheinbergbau." Manuscript, library of the ICSW Münster. Münster, 1952.

Erste Diözesansynode des Bistums Aachen, 13. bis 17. Dezember 1953. Vol. 1, *Synodalakten.* Aachen, 1955.

Etzioni, Amitai, *Soziologie der Organisationen.* Munich, 1967.

———, ed. *Complex Organizations: A Sociological Reader.* New York, 1964.

Faber, Franz-Rudolf. *Das Bild des Menschen in der modernen Medizin: Zur Kritik des biologischen, psychologischen, soziologischen und ethisch-religiösen Determinismus.* Cologne, 1959.

Faßbender, Martin, ed. *Des deutschen Volkes Wille zum Leben: Bevölkerungspolitische und volkspädagogische Abhandlungen über Erhaltung und Förderung deutscher Volkskraft.* Freiburg, 1917.

Feyerabend, Karl. *Katholizismus und Protestantismus als Fortschrittsmächte.* Stuttgart, 1898.

Fichter, Joseph H., SJ. *Grundbegriffe der Soziologie.* 2nd ed. Vienna, 1969. First published in German in 1967 and in English in 1957.

———. *One-Man Research: Reminiscences of a Catholic Sociologist.* New York, 1973.

———. *Religion as an Occupation: A Study in the Sociology of Professions.* Notre Dame, IN, 1961.

———. *Social Relations in the Urban Parish.* Chicago, 1954.

———. *Soziologie der Pfarrgruppen: Untersuchungen zur Struktur und Dynamik der Gruppen einer deutschen Pfarrei.* Schriften des Instituts für christliche Sozialwissenschaften der Westfälischen Wilhelms-Universität Münster 5. Münster, 1958.

Fischer, Alfons. *Seelsorgehilfe: Werkbuch für apostolische Schulung und Arbeit der Laien.* 2nd ed. Freiburg, 1952.

Fischer, Henry and Norbert Greinacher. *Die Gemeinde.* Mainz, 1970. (= Pastorale. Handreichung für den pastoralen Dienst).

Forberger, Johannes. *Moralstatistik und Konfession.* Halle, 1911.

Forster, Karl. "Glaube-Kirche-Gesellschaft: Versuch einer theologischen und pastoralen 'Anwendung' sozialwissenschaftlicher Analysen" (1974). In *Glaube und Kirche im Dialog mit der Welt von heute,* ed. Karl Forster, 2:102–20. Würzburg, 1982.

———. "Volkskirche oder Entscheidungskirche? Theologische und soziologische Aspekte zu einer Grundfrage des pastoralen Dienstes." In *Ortskirche, Weltkirche: Festgabe für Julius Kardinal Döpfner,* ed. Heinz Fleckenstein, 488–506. Würzburg, 1973.

———, ed. *Befragte Katholiken: Zur Zukunft von Glaube und Kirche: Auswertungen und Kommentare zu den Umfragen für die Gemeinsame Synode der Bistümer in der Bundesrepublik Deutschland.* Freiburg, 1973.

———, ed. *Priester zwischen Anpassung und Unterscheidung: Auswertungen und Kommentare zu den im Auftrag der Deutschen Bischofskonferenz durchgeführten Umfragen unter allen Welt- und Ordenspriestern in der Bundesrepublik Deutschland.* Freiburg, 1974.

———, ed. *Religiös ohne Kirche? Eine Herausforderung für Glaube und Kirche.* Mainz, 1978.

Freud, Sigmund. "Die Traumdeutung." In *Studienausgabe,* 2. Frankfurt, 1989.

———. "Die Zukunft einer Illusion (1927)." In *Studienausgabe,* 9:135–89. Frankfurt, 1994.

———. "Neue Folge der Vorlesungen zur Einführung in die Psychoanalyse (1933)." In *Studienausgabe,* 9:447–608. Frankfurt, 1994.

Friedeburg, Ludwig von. *Die Umfrage in der Intimsphäre.* Stuttgart, 1953.

Frielingsdorf, Karl. "Gruppendynamische Arbeit mit Theologiestudenten." In *Gruppendynamik in der kirchlichen Praxis: Erfahrungsberichte,* ed. Karl-Wilhelm Dahm and Hermann Stenger, 51–67. Munich, 1974.

Frye, Alfred. "Das religiös-sittliche Verhalten in der katholischen Pfarrei in Olfen." PhD diss., Münster, 1959.

Fuchs, F. "Sittlichkeit und Frömmigkeit in Ziffern?" *Hochland* 25, no. 2 (1928): 301–5.

Gagern, Friedrich E. von. *Eheliche Partnerschaft.* Munich, 1963.

Geller, Helmut, Norbert Greinacher, and Heinrich Ludwig, eds. *2000 Briefe an die Synode: Auswertung und Konsequenzen.* Mainz, 1971.

Gemeinsame Synode der Bistümer in der Bundesrepublik Deutschland: Offizielle Gesamtausgabe. 2 vols. Freiburg, 1976/77.

Gémes, Carolus. *Das Gebiet und die Methoden der Religionssoziologie nach Gabriel Le Bras.* Rome, 1955.

Goddijn, Hans, and Walter Goddijn. *Sichtbare Kirche: Ökumene und Pastoral: Einführung in die Religionssoziologie.* Vienna, 1967.

Goddijn, Walter. *Deferred Revolution: A Social Experiment in Church Innovation in Holland 1960–1970.* Amsterdam, 1975.

———. "Die katholische Pfarrsoziologie in Westeuropa." In *Soziologie der Kirchengemeinde,* ed. Dietrich Goldschmidt, Franz Greiner and Helmut Schelsky, 16–35. Stuttgart, 1960.

Godin, André. *Das Menschliche im seelsorglichen Gespräch: Anregungen der Pastoralpsychologie.* Munich, 1972.

Godin, Henri, and Yvan Daniel. *La France, pays de mission?* Paris, 1943.

Godin, Henri, and Rene Michel. *Zwischen Abfall und Bekehrung: Abbé Godin und seine Pariser Mission.* Offenburg, 1950.

Goldbrunner, Josef. "Die Tiefenpsychologie von Carl Gustav Jung und christliche Lebensgestaltung: Eine moraltheologische Untersuchung." PhD diss., Freiburg, 1939.

———. *Personale Seelsorge: Tiefenpsychologie und Seelsorge.* Freiburg, 1954.

———. *Sprechzimmer und Beichtstuhl: Über Religion und Psychologie.* Freiburg, 1965.

Goldschmidt, Dietrich, Franz Greiner and Helmut Schelsky, eds. *Soziologie der Kirchengemeinde.* Stuttgart, 1960.

Golomb, Egon. "Auch die Kirche muß ihren Einsatz planen: Die notwendige Anpasssung der Seelsorgsorganisation." In *Bilanz des deutschen Katholizismus,* ed. Norbert Greinacher and Heinz Theo Risse, 42–67. Mainz, 1966.

———. "Ergebnisse und Ansätze pfarrsoziologischer Bemühungen im katholischen Raum." In *Probleme der Religionssoziologie,* ed. Dietrich Goldschmidt and Joachim Matthes, 202–13. Cologne and Opladen, 1962.

Görres, Albert. *An den Grenzen der Psychoanalyse.* Munich, 1968.

———. *Methode und Erfahrungen der Psychoanalyse.* Munich, 1958.

Görres, Ida Friederike. *Der gewandelte Thron: Bemerkungen zur Synode und anderes.* Freiburg, 1971.

Greinacher, Norbert. *Die Kirche in der städtischen Gesellschaft: Soziologische und theologische Überlegungen zur Frage der Seelsorge in der Stadt.* Mainz, 1966.

———. "Ist Deutschland Missionsland?" *Mitteilungsblatt des Alfred-Delp-Werkes* (June 1953): 9–12.

———. *Soziologie der Pfarrei: Wege zur Untersuchung.* Colmar, 1955.

Greinacher, Norbert, Klaus Lang and Peter Scheuermann, eds. *In Sachen Synode: Vorschläge und Argumente des Vorbereitungskongresses.* Düsseldorf, 1970.

Greiner, Franz. "Die Katholiken in der technischen Gesellschaft der Nachkriegszeit." In *Deutscher Katholizismus nach 1945,* ed. Hans Maier, 103–35. Munich, 1964.

Griesl, Gottfried. "Pastoralpsychologische Betrachtungen zu unserer heutigen Bußpraxis." In *Entspricht die Beichtpraxis der Kirche der Forderung Jesu zur Umkehr? Eine Orientierungshilfe,* ed. Josef Finkenzeller and Gottfried Griesl, 117–204. Munich, 1971.

Groner, Franz. "L'etat de recherches de sociologie religieuse en Allemagne." In *Sociologie religieuse, sciences sociales: Actes du IVe Congrès Internationale,* 117–30. Paris, 1955. Published by the Conférence Internationale de Sociologie Religieuse.

Grundlagen und Perspektiven der Sozialen Arbeit. N.p., 1966. Published by the Kommende. Sozialinstitut des Erzbistums Paderborn in Dortmund-Brackel.

Gutberlet, Konstantin. *Die Willensfreiheit und ihre Gegner*. Fulda, 1893.

Haas, Lor. "Moralstatistik und Willensfreiheit." *Jb. für Philosophie und spekulative Theologie* 13 (1899): 17–40.

Habermas, Jürgen. *The Structural Transformation of the Public Sphere: An Inquiry into a Category of Bourgeois Society*. Cambridge, MA, 1991.

Hammerstein, Ludwig v. *Katholizismus und Protestantismus*. 5th ed. Trier, 1906. First published in 1894.

Hammes, E. "Psychotherapie heute." *Trierer Theologische Zeitschrift* 66 (1957): 163–68.

Harenberg, Werner, ed. *Was glauben die Deutschen? Die Emnid-Umfrage: Ergebnisse und Kommentare*. Munich, 1969.

Häring, Bernhard. *Macht und Ohnmacht der Religion: Religionssoziologie als Anruf*. Salzburg, 1956.

———. *Soziologie der Familie*. Salzburg, 1954.

Hasenfuß, Josef. *Der Soziologismus in der modernen Religionswissenschaft*. Würzburg, 1955.

Hättenschwiller, Josef, SJ. *Die öftere und tägliche heilige Kommunion nach dem päpstl: Dekrete vom 20. Dezember 1905*. 3rd ed. Innsbruck, 1909.

Hauser, Theresia. "Aspekte der Supervision für Praktiker in Gemeinde und Institution." In *Gruppendynamik in der kirchlichen Praxis: Erfahrungsberichte*, ed. Karl-Wilhelm Dahm and Hermann Stenger, 213–31. Munich, 1974.

Häußler, F., SJ. "Unsere seelsorgliche Situation im Lichte der Statistik." *Klerusblatt* 31 (1951): 266–67.

Hellgrewe, Henny. *Dortmund als Industrie- und Arbeiterstadt: Eine Untersuchung der wirtschaftlichen und sozialen Entwicklung der Stadt*. Dortmund, 1951.

Hemmerle, Klaus. "Funktionale Interpretation des priesterlichen Dienstes?" In *Priester zwischen Anpassung und Unterscheidung: Auswertungen und Kommentare zu den im Auftrag der Deutschen Bischofskonferenz durchgeführten Umfragen unter allen Welt- und Ordenspriestern in der Bundesrepublik Deutschland*, ed. Karl Forster, 27–40. Freiburg, 1974.

Hennis, Wilhelm. *Meinungsforschung und repräsentative Demokratie: Zur Kritik politischer Umfragen*. Tübingen, 1957.

Hild, Helmut, ed. *Wie stabil ist die Kirche? Bestand und Erneuerung: Ergebnisse einer Meinungsbefragung*. Gelnhausen, 1974.

Hoffmann, Lutz. *Auswege aus der Sackgasse: Anwendungen soziologischer Kategorien auf die gegenwärtige Situation von Kirche und Seelsorge*. Munich, 1971.

Höffner, Joseph. *Industrielle Revolution und religiöse Krise: Schwund und Wandel des religiösen Verhaltens in der modernen Gesellschaft*. Opladen, 1961.

———. *Pastoral der Kirchenfremden: Eröffnungsreferat bei der Herbstvollversammlung der Deutschen Bischofskonferenz 1979 in Fulda*. Bonn, 1979.

Hofstätter, Peter R. *Gruppendynamik: Kritik der Massenpsychologie*. Reinbek 1957.

Hollweg, Arnd. *Theologie und Empirie: Ein Beitrag zum Gespräch zwischen Theologie und Sozialwissenschaft in den USA und Deutschland*. Stuttgart, 1971.

Houtart, François. *Soziologie und Seelsorge*. Freiburg, 1966. First published in French in 1963.

Hyman, Herbert H., and Paul B. Sheatsley. "The Scientific Method." In *An Analysis of the Kinsey Reports on Sexual Behavior in the Human Male and Female*, ed. Donald Porter Geddes, 95–120. London, 1954.

Isambert, François André. *Christianisme et Classe Ouvrière: Jalons pour une étude de sociologie historique*. Tournai, 1961.

Jahresbericht 1968/69 des Sozialteam e.V. Landstuhl/Adelsried. Adelsried, 1969.

Jedin, Hubert. *Lebensbericht*. Edited by Konrad Repgen. Mainz, 1984.

Jordan, Max. "Deutschland, ein Missionsland." *Katholischer Digest* 4 (1950): 561–64.

Jung, Carl Gustav. "Psychotherapists or the Clergy (1932)." In *Collected Works*, ed. Carl Gustav Jung, 11:327–47. London, 1958.

Kahseböhmer, Hermann J., and Ottfried Selg. *Einstellung und Verhalten in der Volkskirche Augsburg*. Adelsried, 1969.

Kaller, Maximilian. *Aus einer Großstadtpfarrei: Erkenntnisse und Folgerungen aus einer Pfarrkartei*. Freiburg, 1923.

———. *Unser Laienapostolat in St. Michael Berlin: Was es ist und wie es sein soll*. Edited and introduced by Hans Jürgen Brandt. Paderborn, 1997. First published 1926.

Kammer, Johannes Carl. *Die Kartothek im Dienste der seelsorglichen und sonstigen amtlichen Verwaltung*. Trier, 1914.

Katholische Heimatmission, ed. *Münchener Statistik: Das kirchliche Leben in der katholischen Bevölkerung Münchens*. Munich, 1973.

Kaufmann, Franz-Xaver. *Theologie in soziologischer Sicht*. Freiburg, 1973.

[Keller, Michael]. *Die Sendung der Kirche und die soziale Ordnung: Ansprache von Bischof Dr. Michael Keller anläßlich der Einweihung des neuen Gebäudes des Franz-Hitze-Hauses zu Münster*. Münster, 1959.

Kinsey, Alfred C., Wardell B. Pomeroy and Clyde E. Martin. *Das sexuelle Verhalten der Frau*. Frankfurt, 1966. First published in English in 1953.

Kinsey, Alfred C., Wardell B. Pomeroy and Clyde E. Martin. *Sexual Behavior in the Human Female*. Philadelphia, 1953.

Kinsey, Alfred C., Wardell B. Pomeroy and Clyde E. Martin. *Sexual Behavior in the Human Male*. Philadelphia, 1948.

Kirche vor Ort: 10 Jahre Bistum Essen. Essen, 1968.

Kner, Anton. *Seelsorge als Beratung*. Freiburg, 1968.

Knöpfel, Ludwig. "Religionsstatistik." In *Die Statistik in Deutschland nach ihrem heutigen Stand*, ed. Friedrich Zahn, 1:307–23. Munich, 1911.

"Konfessionelle und kirchliche Verhältnisse im Großherzogtum Hessen." *Mitteilungen der Großherzoglich-Hessischen Zentralstelle für die Landesstatistik* 38, no. 870 (1908): 145–60.

König, René. *Materialien zur Soziologie der Familie*. Berne, 1946.

———. "Praktische Sozialforschung." *Praktische Sozialforschung: Das Interview*, ed. René König, 15–36. Dortmund and Zurich, 1952.

Kroeger, Matthias. *Themenzentrierte Seelsorge: Über die Kombination klientzentrierter und themenzentrierter Arbeit nach C. R. Rogers und R. C. Cohn in der Theologie*. Stuttgart, 1973.

Krose, Hermann A. "Der Einfluß der Confession auf die Sittlichkeit nach den Ergebnissen der Moralstatistik." *Historisch Politische Blätter* 123 (1899): 479–99, 545–61.

———. *Der Einfluß der Konfession auf die Sittlichkeit: Nach den Ergebnissen der Statistik*. Freiburg, 1900.

———. "Die kirchliche Statistik in Deutschland." *Bonner Zeitschrift für Theologie und Seelsorge* 2 (1925): 346–55.

———. "Geburtenrückgang und Konfession." In *Des deutschen Volkes Wille zum Leben: Bevölkerungspolitische und volkspädagogische Abhandlungen über Erhaltung und Förderung deutscher Volkskraft*, ed. Martin Faßbender, 207–26. Freiburg, 1917.

———. "Konfessionsstatistik und kirchliche Statistik im Deutschen Reich." *Allgemeines Statistisches Archiv* 8 (1914): 267–92, 624–45.

———. "Moral und Moralstatistik." In *Aus Ethik und Leben: Festschrift für Josef Mausbach zur Vollendung des siebzigsten Lebensjahres*, ed. Max Meinertz and Adolf Donders, 170–80. Münster, 1931.

———. *Religion und Moralstatistik*. Munich, n.d. [1906].

———. "Sittlichkeit in Ziffern." *StdZ* 116 (1929): 149–54.

———. "Zur Frage der Errichtung eines Bureaus für kirchliche Statistik." *Historisch Politische Blätter für das katholische Deutschland* 134 (1904): 830–37.

———. "Zur Frage eines statistischen Amtes für die Gesamtkirche." *Theologie und Glaube* 29 (1937): 188–95.

Laloux, Joseph. *Seelsorge und Soziologie: Eine praktische Einführung für die Gemeindearbeit*. Lucerne, 1969.

Le Bras, Gabriel. *Études de Sociologie Religieuse*. 2 vols. Paris, 1955/56.

———. "Statistique et histoire religieuse." *Revue d'histoire de l'eglise de France* 17 (1931): 425–49.

Leclerc, Erhard. *Katholik und Heldentum der Lebensbereitschaft: Ein statistischer Beitrag zur ernsten Schicksalsfrage des deutschen Volkes*. Trier, 1935.

Lepp, Ignace. *Liebe, Neurose und christliche Moral: Fünf Aufsätze zum Verhältnis von Tiefenpsychologie und Glaube*. Würzburg, 1960.

———. *Psychoanalyse der Liebe*. Würzburg, 1961.

Liertz, Rhaban. *Über Seelenaufschließung: Ein Weg zum Erforschen des Seelenlebens*. Paderborn, 1926.

———. *Wanderungen durch das gesunde und kranke Seelenleben bei Kindern und Erwachsenen*. Kempten, 1923.

Liese, Wilhelm. "Die kirchliche Statistik." *Theologie und Glaube* 7 (1915): 101–12.

Luckmann, Thomas. *Das Problem der Religion in der modernen Gesellschaft*. Freiburg, 1963.

Lutz, Hans. *Das Menschenbild der Kinsey-Reporte: Analyse und Kritik der philosophisch-ethischen Voraussetzungen*. Stuttgart, 1957.

Mähner, Hans Georg. "Die Bedeutung von Meinungsumfragen in der Kirche: Grundsätzliche Untersuchung und konkrete Darstellung anhand einer Primärerhebung." PhD diss., University of Salzburg, 1971.

March, James G., and Herbert A. Simon. *Organizations*. New York, 1958.

Matthes, Joachim. *Die Emigration der Kirche aus der Gesellschaft*. Hamburg, 1964.

———. *Kirche und Gesellschaft: Einführung in die Religionssoziologie II*. Reinbek, 1969.

———. "Soziologie: Schlüsselwissenschaft des 20. Jahrhunderts?" In *Lebenswelt und soziale Probleme: Verhandlungen des 20. Deutschen Soziologentages zu Bremen 1980*, ed. Joachim Matthes, 15–27. Frankfurt and New York, 1980.

May, Albert. "Psychoanalyse und katholische Weltanschauung." *Das neue Blatt für die katholische Lehrerschaft* 5 (1929/30): 7–12.

Menges, Walter. *Soziale Verhältnisse und Kirchliches Verhalten im Limburger Raum: Ergebnisse einer im Auftrage des Bischöflichen Ordinariates Limburg anläßlich der Gebietsmission von 1959 durchgeführten pfarrsoziologischen Untersuchung in 40 Pfarreien des Limburger Raumes*. Limburg, 1959.

Menne, F. W. "Christentum und menschliche Fruchtbarkeit: Eine Studie über christliches Wertsystem und gesellschaftliche Realität." PhD diss., FU Berlin, 1971.

Mertens, Hans. "Sozialstatistische Studien zum Aufbau einer Großstadtpfarrgemeinde." *Unsere Diözese in Vergangenheit und Gegenwart* 2 (1928): 84–94, 143–48.

Merton, Robert K. "The Role-Set: Problems in Sociological Theory." *The British Journal of Sociology* 8 (1957): 106–20.

Michl, Georg. *Religions- und Kirchliche Statistik*. Beiträge zur Statistik Bayerns 96. Munich, 1921.

Michonneau, Georges. *Paroisse, communauté missionnaire: Conclusions de 5 ans d'expérience en milieu populaire*. Paris, 1946.

Miller, Josef. *Katholische Beichte und Psychotherapie*. Innsbruck, 1947.

Mills, C. Wright. "Grand Theory." In *The Sociological Imagination*, 25–49. New York, 1959.

Mönch, A. "Statistik auf dem Pfarramte." *Pastor Bonus* 17 (1904/5): 355–60.

Monzel, Nikolaus. *Struktursoziologie und Kirchenbegriff*. 2nd ed. Cologne and Bonn, 1972. First published 1939.

———. *Was ist christliche Gesellschaftslehre? Öffentliche Antrittsvorlesung, gehalten am 16. Mai 1956 aus Anlaß der Übernahme des neu errichteten Lehrstuhles für Christliche Gesellschaftslehre und Allgemeine Religionssoziologie*. Munich, 1956.

Motte, John Francis, Henri Holstein et al. *Mission Générale: Dix ans d'expérience au C.P.M.I.* Paris, 1961.

Motte, John Francis, and Médard Dourmap, OFM. *Mission Générale—œuvre d'Église*. Paris, 1957.

Müller, Johannes. "Die Neugestaltung der kirchlichen Statistik in Deutschland." *Allgemeines Statistisches Archiv* 20 (1930): 78–81.

Müncker, Theodor. "Katholische Seelsorge und Psychoanalyse." In *Krisis der Psychoanalyse*, ed. Hans Prinzhorn and Kuno Mittenzwey, 1:350–60. Leipzig, 1928.

Nathusius, Martin v. *Die Unsittlichkeit von Ludwig XIV. bis zur Gegenwart*. Zeitfragen des christlichen Volkslebens 24. Stuttgart, 1899.

Neher, O., and A. Neher, eds. *100 Jahre katholischer württembergischer Klerus und Volk: Ein Beitrag zur religiösen Heimatkunde auf statistischer Grundlage*. Riedlingen, 1928.

Neundörfer, Ludwig. "Die soziale Situation des Landes." *Kirche und Landvolk: Würzburger Tagungsbericht: Arbeitstagung des ZdK*, 30–58. Paderborn, 1954.

Noelle-Neumann, Elisabeth. "Die Schweigespirale: Über die Entstehung der öffentlichen Meinung." In *Standorte im Zeitstrom: Festschrift für Arnold Gehlen zum 70. Geburtstag am 29. Januar 1974,* ed. Ernst Forsthoff and Reinhard Hörstel, 299–330. Frankfurt, 1974.

North, Maurice. *The Secular Priests*. London, 1972.

Oettingen, Alexander v. *Die Moralstatistik in ihrer Bedeutung für eine Sozialethik*. 3rd ed. Erlangen, 1882.

Otto, J. A., SJ. "Missionsland?" *Die Katholischen Missionen* 70 (1951): 131–35.

Parsons, Talcott. "General Theory." In *Sociology Today: Problems and Prospects,* ed. Robert K. Merton, 3–38. New York, 1959.

Paul, Leslie. *The Deployment and Payment of the Clergy: A Report*. Westminster, UK, 1964.

Perlman, Helen Harris. *Social Casework: A Problem-Solving Process*. Chicago, 1957.

Pfliegler, Michael. *Pastoraltheologie*. Vienna, 1962.

Pieper, Paul D. *Kirchliche Statistik Deutschlands*. Freiburg, 1899.

Pin, Émile, SJ. "Dix ans de sociologie religieuse 1950–1960." *Revue de l'action populaire* 145 (1961): 217–29.

———. *Pratique religieuses et classes sociales dans une paroisse urbaine: Saint-Pothin à Lyon*. Paris, 1956.

Piontek, [?]. "Der Kommunionempfang in der Fürstbischöflichen Delegatur von 1910 bis 1914." *Schlesisches Bonifatius-Vereins-Blatt* 56 (1915): 170–74, 188–92; 57 (1916): 7–11, 27–31, 41–44.

Pipberger, J. "Statistik über einige religiöse Lebensäußerungen der Katholiken in Frankfurt." In *Das katholische Frankfurt: Jahrbuch der Frankfurter Katholiken,* ed. Jacob Herr, 15–28. Frankfurt, 1928.

Pollet, J. "Zur Situation des Flüchtlings in der Diaspora." *Caritas* 52 (1951): 110–17.

Polzien, Sigrun. "TZI-Kurse mit Ordensleuten und Weltpriestern." In *Gruppendynamik in der kirchlichen Praxis: Erfahrungsberichte,* ed. Karl-Wilhelm Dahm and Hermann Stenger, 178–90. Munich, 1974.

Pompey, Heinrich. "Handlungsperspektiven kirchlicher Beratung." In *Kirchliche Beratungsdienste,* ed. Sekretariat der Deutschen Bischofskonferenz, 44–68. Bonn, 1987.

———. "Rezension: Peter R. Hofstätter, Gruppendynamik—Kritik der Massenpsychologie: Reinbek b. Hamburg 1971." *Theologischer Literaturdienst: Beilage zum Würzburger Diözesanblatt* 4 (1972): 63–64.

———. "Seelsorge in den Krisen des Lebens." In *Seelsorge ohne Priester? Zur Problematik von Beratung und Psychotherapie in der Pastoral,* ed. Josef Maria Reuß, 29–72. Düsseldorf, 1976.

Prinz, Franz, SJ. *Kirche und Arbeiterschaft: Gestern-heute-morgen.* Munich, 1974.

Prokosch, Erich. *Pastoral-soziographische Analyse des Dekanates Stadtsteinach.* Bamberg, 1971.

Rahner, Karl. "Die Sakramente als Grundfunktionen der Kirche." In *Handbuch der Pastoraltheologie,* 2nd ed, ed. Franz-Xaver Arnold and Karl Rahner, 1:356–66. Freiburg, 1970.

———. "Ekklesiologische Grundlegung." In *Handbuch der Pastoraltheologie,* 2nd ed, ed. Franz-Xaver Arnold and Karl Rahner, 1:121–56. Freiburg, 1970.

Ratzinger, Joseph. *Glaube und Zukunft.* Munich, 1970.

Ratzinger, Joseph, and Hans Maier. *Demokratie in der Kirche: Möglichkeiten, Gefahren, Grenzen.* Limburg, 1970.

Richter, Horst-Eberhard. *Die Gruppe: Hoffnung auf einen neuen Weg, sich selbst und andere zu befreien.* Reinbek, 1972.

Rieder, Karl. "Kirchliche Statistik der Erzdiözese Freiburg." *Freiburger Diözesanarchiv* 10 (1909): 237–70.

———. "Kirchliche Statistik der Erzdiözese Freiburg." *Freiburger Diözesanarchiv* 13 (1912): 265–89.

Riesman, David. *The Lonely Crowd: A Study of the Changing American Character.* New Haven, CT, 1950.

Riess, Richard. *Seelsorge: Orientierung, Analysen, Alternativen.* Göttingen, 1973.

Ritter, Raimund. *Grundfragen der Soziologie: Eine Einführung für Religionslehrer und praktische Theologen.* Zurich, 1973.

———. *Von der Religionssoziologie zur Seelsorge: Einführung in die Pastoralsoziologie.* Limburg, 1968.

Roegele, Otto B. "Die Verwirrung in der Nachkonziliaren Kirche." In Otto B. Roegele and H. Beckmann. *Warum unsere Kirchen leerer werden . . . ,* 7–57. Zurich, 1977.

Rogers, Carl R. *Die klientenzentrierte Gesprächspsychotherapie.* Frankfurt, 1983. First published in English in 1951.

———. *Die nicht-direktive Beratung.* Frankfurt, 1985. First published in English in 1942.

———. *On Becoming a Person: A Therapist's View of Psychotherapy.* Boston, 1961.

———. *Therapeut und Klient: Grundlagen der Gesprächspsychotherapie.* Frankfurt, 1983.

Roos, Lothar. "Pastoralwissenschaftliche Überlegungen zu den Reformvorstellungen der Priester." In *Priester zwischen Anpassung und Unterscheidung: Auswertungen und Kommentare zu den im Auftrag der Deutschen Bischofskonferenz durchgeführten Umfragen unter allen Welt- und Ordenspriestern in der Bundesrepublik Deutschland,* ed. Karl Forster, 73–88. Freiburg, 1974.

Rösch, Adolf. "Zur kirchlichen Statistik der Erzdiözese Freiburg." *Freiburger Diözesanarchiv* 15 (1914): 317–67.

Rosenberg, Milton J. "Hedonism, Inauthenticity, and Other Goads: Toward Expansion of a Consistency Theory." In *Theories of Cognitive Consistency: A Sourcebook,* ed. Robert P. Abelson, 73–111. Chicago, 1968.

Rudin, Josef. *Psychotherapie und Religion.* 2nd ed. Olten and Freiburg, 1964.

Rüstermann, Johannes. "Wie steht es mit dem katholischen Leben in der Großstadt?" *Theologie und Glaube* 19 (1927): 102–5.

Schäffauer, [?]. "Die Psychoanalyse und ihre Bedeutung für Religion und Seelsorge." *Rottenburger Monatsschrift für praktische Theologie* 12 (1928/29): 321–29, 353–60.

Scharfenberg, Joachim. *Seelsorge als Gespräch: Zur Theorie und Praxis der seelsorgerischen Gesprächsführung.* Göttingen, 1972.

Schauff, Johannes. *Das Wahlverhalten der deutschen Katholiken im Kaiserreich und in der Weimarer Republik: Untersuchungen aus dem Jahre 1928,* ed. Rudolf Morsey. Mainz, 1975.

Schilgen, Hardy, SJ. *Warum gehst du nicht? Gedanken über die häufige heilige Kommunion.* Kevelaer, 1935.

Schindler, Anton. "Seelsorger und Kirchenbesuch." *Der Seelsorger* 11 (1934): 51–54.

Schlund, Robert. "Pastoralplanung im Erzbistum Freiburg." In *Informationen: Berichte, Kommentare, Anregungen,* no. 3 (1970): 20–24.

Schmauch, Joachim. *Zur soziologischen Bedeutung der erwerbsmäßigen Pendelwanderung.* Münster, 1958.

Schmidtchen, Gerhard. *Priester in Deutschland: Forschungsbericht über die im Auftrag der Deutschen Bischofskonferenz durchgeführte Umfrage unter allen Welt- und Ordenspriestern in der Bundesrepublik.* Freiburg, 1973.

———. *Protestanten und Katholiken: Soziologische Analyse konfessioneller Kultur.* Berne, 1973.

———. *Umfrage unter Priesteramtskandidaten: Forschungsbericht des Instituts für Demoskopie Allensbach über eine im Auftrag der DBK durchgeführte Erhebung.* Freiburg, 1975.

———. *Zwischen Kirche und Gesellschaft: Forschungsbericht über die Umfragen zur Gemeinsamen Synode der Bistümer in der Bundesrepublik Deutschland.* Freiburg, 1972.

Schmidthüs, Karlheinz. "Die öffentliche Meinung und die Katholiken." *Deus lo vult* 4 (1954): 106–11.

Schmitt, Hermann-Joseph. "Die Binnenwanderung der katholischen Kirche als Moraltheologisches und Pastoraltheologisches Problem: Eine moraltheologische und soziologische Untersuchung." PhD diss., University of Tübingen, 1942.

Schöllgen, Werner. *Aktuelle Moralprobleme.* Düsseldorf, 1955.

———. "Christliche Soziologie als theologische Disziplin." *Die neue Ordnung* 1 (1946/47): 404–17.

———. *Die soziologischen Grundlagen der katholischen Sittenlehre.* Handbuch der katholischen Sittenlehre 5. Düsseldorf, 1953.

———. "Psychotherapie und sakramentale Beichte." *Catholica* 1, no. 2 (1932): 145–57.

Schomakers, Bernhard. "Die Bedeutung kirchlicher Sozialforschung für die Diaspora-Seelsorge." *Priester-Jahrheft des Bonifatiusvereins* (1962): 11–16.

Schreuder, Osmund. *Kirche im Vorort: Soziologische Erkundung einer Pfarrei.* Freiburg, 1962.

Schückler, Georg. *Irrwege moderner Meinungsforschung: Zu "Umfragen in der Intimsphäre."* Cologne, 1956.

Schulte, Chrysostomus, OMCap. "Können wir mit dem heutigen Sakramentenempfang zufrieden sein?" *Theologie und Glaube* 20 (1928): 232–49.

———. *Laienbriefe: Das pastoraltheologische Ergebnis einer Umfrage.* Münster, 1931.

Schulze, Gustav. *Der Unterschied zwischen der katholischen und evangelischen Sittlichkeit.* Halle, 1888.

Schurr, Viktor. *Seelsorge in einer neuen Welt: Eine Pastoral der Umwelt und des Laientums.* 3rd ed. Salzburg, 1957.

Schwer, Wilhelm. *Der soziale Gedanke in der katholischen Seelsorge: Ein Beitrag zur Geschichte der Seelsorge und der sozialen Ideen im 19. Jahrhundert.* Cologne, 1921.

Schwermer, Josef. *Den Menschen verstehen: Eine Einführung in die Psychologie für seelsorgliche Berufe.* Paderborn, 1987.

———. *Psychologische Hilfen für das Seelsorgegespräch.* Munich, 1974.

Selg, Ottfried. *Einführung zum vorläufigen Gesamtergebnis der Umfrage unter allen Katholiken, Ergebnis der Umfrage für die gemeinsame Synode der Bistümer in der Bundesrepublik Deutschland.* Informationen des Synodalbüros 2. Augsburg, 1970.

———. *Seelsorge in der Stadt: Pastoralsoziologische Überlegungen zur Organisation der Kirche in der Stadt Heidelberg.* Augsburg, 1968.

Shippey, Frederick A. "The Relations of Theology and the Social Sciences According to Gabriel Le Bras." *Archives de Sociologie des Religions* 20 (1965): 79–93.

Siebel, Wigand. *Freiheit und Herrschaftsstruktur in der Kirche: Eine soziologische Studie.* Berlin, 1971.

Siefer, Gregor. *Die Mission der Arbeiterpriester: Ereignisse und Konsequenzen.* Essen, 1960.

———. *Sterben die Priester aus? Soziologische Überlegungen zum Funktionswandel eines Berufsstandes.* Essen, 1973.

Sieken, Heinrich. *Methoden und Ergebnisse der katholisch-kirchlichen Statistik.* Berlin, 1930.

Spielbauer, Josef. "Warum eine Pfarrkartei?" *Laienapostolat* 2 (1956): 42–45.

———. *Was geht mich mein Nachbar an? Chancen und Forderungen des Wohnviertelapostolats.* Limburg, 1967.

Springer, Emil. *Haben wir Priester noch Vorurteile gegen die häufige und tägliche Kommunion der Gläubigen.* 2nd ed. Paderborn, 1910.

Steinkamp, Hermann. *Gruppendynamik und Demokratisierung.* Mainz and Munich, 1973.

Steinmetz, Rudolf. "Die Stellung der Soziographie in der Reihe der Sozialwissenschaften (1913)." In *Gesammelte kleinere Schriften zur Ethnologie und Soziologie,* 3:96–107. Groningen, 1935.

Stenger, Hermann. "Hermann, Lebendiges Lernen in Religionslehrerkursen." In *Gruppendynamik in der kirchlichen Praxis: Erfahrungsberichte,* ed. Karl-Wilhelm Dahm and Hermann Stenger, 99–112. Munich, 1974.

Stenzel, Peter. "Gruppendynamische Arbeitsformen in der ländlichen Pfarrei." *Gruppendynamik in der kirchlichen Praxis: Erfahrungsberichte,* ed. Karl-Wilhelm Dahm and Hermann Stenger, 113–28. Munich, 1974.

Stollberg, Dietrich. *Therapeutische Seelsorge: Die amerikanische Seelsorgebewegung: Darstellung und Kritik.* Munich, 1969.

Stonner, A. "Zwei Versuche der kirchlichen Erfassung der religiös Abständigen." *Seelsorgehilfe* 5 (1953): 59–66.

Sugg, M. "Katholische Fachhochschule in NRW." *Katholische Frauenbildung* 72 (1971): 676–77.

Swoboda, Heinrich. *Großstadtseelsorge: Eine pastoraltheologische Studie.* 2nd ed. Regensburg, 1911.

Synode 72: Texte zur Diskussion um eine gemeinsame Synode der Diözesen in der Bundesrepublik Deutschland: Zusammengestellt von der Dokumentationszentrale Publik. 3 vols. Frankfurt, 1969/70.

Szillus, H. *Eine verbotene Frucht.* Essen, 1904.

Tenhumberg, Heinrich. "Grundzüge im soziologischen Bild des westdeutschen Dorfes." In *Landvolk in der Industriegesellschaft,* 20–50. Hannover, 1952.

Tilanus, Cornelius. *Empirische Dimensionen der Religiosität: Zum Begriff und den sozialwissen- schaftlichen Meßmethoden der Religiosität.* Augsburg, 1972.

Trilling, Lionel. "The Kinsey Report." In *An Analysis of the Kinsey Reports on Sexual Behavior in the Human Male and Female,* ed. Donald Porter Geddes, 222–45. London, 1954.

Troschke, Paul. *Aus der Geschichte der Statistik: Aufgabe und Arbeitsweise evangelischer Kirchen- statistik.* Charlottenburg, 1929.

Überlegungen und Vorschläge zur Struktur der Seelsorge im Bistum Münster: Strukturplan. N.p., n.d. [Münster, 1969].

Unser Bischof befragt das Bistum: Auswertungsergebnisse des ersten Fragebogens des Bischofs von Osnabrück. Osnabrück, 1970.

Utz, Arthur Fridolin. "Der Kampf der Wissenschaften um das Soziale." *Die neue Ordnung* 9 (1955): 193–201.

Utz, Arthur Fridolin, and Joseph-Fulko Groner, eds. *Aufbau und Entfaltung des gesellschaftli- chen Lebens: Soziale Summe Pius XII.* 3 vols. Freiburg, 1954–61.

Waltermann, Leo, ed. *Klerus zwischen Wissenschaft und Seelsorge: Zur Reform der Priesteraus- bildung.* Essen, 1966.

Weber, A. "Statistik des Gottesdienstbesuches." *Anregungen zur Seelsorge,* no. 10 (5 July 1959).

Welte, Bernhard. "Gedanken über die kirchliche Statistik der Erzdiözese Freiburg für das Jahr 1933." *Oberrheinisches Pastoralblatt* 36 (1934): 395–401.

Werneke, Bernhard. *Die Statistik freiwilliger Handlungen und die menschliche Willensfreiheit.* Frankfurt, 1868.

Weyand, Alfons. *Formen religiöser Praxis in einem werdenden Industrieraum.* Münster, 1963.

Wimmer, Otto. *Handbuch der Pfarrseelsorge und Pfarrverwaltung.* Innsbruck, 1959.

Witz, Oskar. *Unsere Pflichten als Seelsorger bezüglich des Dekrets über die tägliche Kommunion: Mit einem Anhang über die Feier des ersten Monatsfreitags.* Saarlouis, 1909.

Wothe, Franz Josef. *Kirche in der Synode: Zwischenbilanz der Hildesheimer Diözesansynode.* Hildesheim, 1968.

Wurzbacher, Gerhard, and Renate Pflaum. *Das Dorf im Spannungsfeld industrieller Entwick- lung.* Stuttgart, 1954.

Zangerle, Ignaz. "Pfarrprobleme und Laienarbeit." In *Die Pfarre: Von der Theologie zur Praxis,* ed. Hugo Rahner, 87–96. Freiburg, 1956.

Zehn Jahre Institut für christliche Sozialwissenschaften der Westfälischen Wilhelms-Universität Münster/Westfalen 1951–1961. Münster, n.d. [ca. 1961].

Research Literature and Contemporary Literature after 1975

Albert, Marcel. *Die katholische Kirche in Frankreich in der vierten und fünften Republik.* Rome, 1999.

Altermatt, Urs. *Katholizismus und Moderne: Zur Sozial- und Mentalitätsgeschichte der Sch- weizer Katholiken im 19. und 20. Jahrhundert.* Zurich, 1989.

Andreae, Stefan. *Pastoraltheologische Aspekte der Lehre Sigmund Freuds von der Sublimierung der Sexualität.* Kevelaer, 1974.

Ash, Mitchell G. "Psychology." In *The Modern Social Sciences,* eds. Theodore M. Porter and Dorothy Ross, 251–74. Cambridge, 2003.

Ash, Mitchell G., and Ulfried Geuter, eds. *Geschichte der deutschen Psychologie im 20. Jahrhundert: Ein Überblick.* Opladen, 1985.

Ashby, William R. *An Introduction to Cybernetics.* London, 1956.

Back, Kurt W. *Beyond Words: The Story of Sensitivity Training and the Encounter Movement.* New York, 1972.

Baumann, Ursula. *Protestantismus und Frauenemanzipation in Deutschland 1850 bis 1920.* Frankfurt, 1992.

———. *Vom Recht auf den eigenen Tod: Die Geschichte des Suizids vom 18. bis zum 20. Jahrhundert.* Weimar, 2001.

Baumeister, Martin. *Parität und katholische Inferiorität: Untersuchungen zur Stellung des Katholizismus im Kaiserreich.* Paderborn, 1987.

Baumgartner, Alois. *Sehnsucht nach Gemeinschaft: Ideen und Strömungen im Sozialkatholizismus der Weimarer Republik.* Munich, 1977.

Baumgartner, Isidor. *Pastoralpsychologie: Einführung in die Praxis heilender Seelsorge.* 2nd ed. Düsseldorf, 1997.

Baumgartner, Konrad, and Wunibald Müller, ed. *Beraten und Begleiten: Handbuch für das seelsorgerliche Gespräch.* Freiburg, 1990.

Bäumler, Christof, Gerd Birk and Jürgen Kleemann. *Methoden der empirischen Sozialforschung in der praktischen Theologie: Eine Einführung.* Munich, 1976.

Beck, Uwe. *Kirche im "Spiegel"-Spiegel der Kirche: Ein leidenschaftliches Verhältnis.* Ostfildern, 1994.

Becker, Thomas Paul. *Konfessionalisierung in Kurköln: Untersuchungen zur Durchsetzung der katholischen Reform in den Dekanaten Ahrgau und Bonn anhand von Visitationsprotokollen 1583–1761.* Bonn, 1989.

Beckford, James A. *Religious Organization: A Trend Report and Bibliography.* The Hague and Paris, 1975.

Bellers, Jürgen. "Moralkommunikation und Kommunikationsmoral: Über Kommunikationslatenzen, Antisemitismus und politisches System." In *Antisemitismus in der politischen Kultur nach 1945,* ed. Werner Bergmann and Rainer Erb, 278–91. Opladen, 1991.

Bendikowski, Tillmann. "'Eine Fackel der Zwietracht': Katholisch-protestantische Mischehen im 19. und 20. Jahrhundert." In *Konfessionen im Konflikt: Deutschland zwischen 1800 und 1970: Ein zweites konfessionelles Zeitalter,* ed. Olaf Blaschke, 215–41. Göttingen, 2002.

Benson, J. Kenneth, and James H. Dorsett. "Toward a Theory of Religious Organizations." *Journal for the Scientific Study of Religion* 10 (1971): 138–51.

Berger, P. *The Sacred Canopy: Elements of a Sociological Theory of Religion.* New York, 1967.

Berning, Ewald. *Kirche und Planung: Die Frage nach der theologischen Relevanz von Theorie und Praxis außerkirchlicher Planung.* Frankfurt, 1976.

Betz, Isa-Maria. "Die Beziehung des Kirchenhistorikers Paul Maria Baumgarten zu Koblenz." *Jahrbuch. für westdeutsche Landesgeschichte* 26 (2000): 305–45.

Birk, Kasimir. *Sigmund Freud und die Religion.* Münsterschwarzach, 1970.

Birken, Lawrence. *Consuming Desire: Sexual Science and the Emergence of a Culture of Abundance, 1871–1914.* Ithaca, NY, 1988.

Blackbourn, David. *Wenn ihr sie wieder seht, fragt wer sie sei: Marienerscheinungen in Marpingen: Aufstieg und Niedergang des deutschen Lourdes.* Reinbek, 1997.

Blattner, Jürgen, Balthasar Gareis, and Alfred Plewa, eds. *Handbuch der Psychologie für die Seelsorge.* 2 vols. Düsseldorf, 1992.

Blessing, Werner K. *Staat und Kirche in der Gesellschaft: Institutionelle Autorität und mentaler Wandel in Bayern während des 19. Jahrhunderts.* Göttingen, 1982.

Boehme, Monika. *Die Moralstatistik: Ein Beitrag zur Geschichte der Quantifizierung in der Soziologie, dargestellt an den Werken Adolphe Quetelets und Alexander von Oettingens.* Cologne, 1971.

Bommer, Josef. "Das Bußsakrament als Gericht und als Seelsorge: Zur therapeutischen Dimension von Buße und Bußsakrament." In *Erfahrungen mit dem Bußsakrament,* ed. Konrad Baumgartner, 2:232–48. Munich, 1978.

Bonß, Wolfgang. *Die Einübung des Tatsachenblicks: Zur Struktur und Veränderung empirischer Sozialforschung.* Frankfurt, 1982.

Bourdieu, Pierre. "Leçon sur la leçon." In *Sozialer Raum und "Klassen": Leçon sur la leçon: Zwei Vorlesungen,* 47–81. Frankfurt, 1985.

Braun, Hermann Josef. "'Nachdem das Archivmaterial die Freude eines sonnigen Herbstspaziergangs genossen hat . . . ': Zur Überlieferung des Nachlasses des Mainzer Bischofs Dr. Albert Stohr (1935–1961)." In *Nachlässe,* 63–96. Speyer, 1994.

Breuer, Marc. *Religiöser Wandel als Säkularisierungsfolge: Differenzierungs- und Individualisierungsdiskurse im Katholizismus.* Wiesbaden, 2012.

Bröckling, Ulrich. "Kreativität: Ein Brainstorming." In *Vernunft—Entwicklung—Leben: Schlüsselbegriffe der Moderne,* ed. Ulrich Bröckling, Axel T. Paul and Stefan Kaufmann, 235–44. Munich, 2004.

Brown, Callum G. *The Death of Christian Britain: Understanding Secularization 1800–2000.* London, 2001.

———. "The Secularisation Decade: What the 1960s Have Done to the Study of Religious History." In *The Decline of Christendom in Western Europe, 1750–2000,* eds. Hugh McLeod and Werner Ustorf, 29–46. Cambridge, 2003.

Bruce, Steve. *Secularization: In Defence of an Unfashionable Theory.* Oxford, 2011.

Brunsson, Nils. *The Irrational Organization: Irrationality as a Basis for Organizational Action and Change.* Chichester, UK, and New York, 1985.

Bullough, Vern L. *Science in the Bedroom: A History of Sex Research.* New York, 1994.

Burkard, Dominik. "Zeichen frommen Lebens oder Instrument der Politik? Bruderschaften, 'Donzdorfer Fakultät' und Versuche katholischer Milieubildung." *Hohenstaufen-Helfenstein: Historisches Jb. für den Kreis Göppingen* 8 (1998): 151–86.

Busch, Nobert. *Katholische Frömmigkeit und Moderne: Die Sozial- und Mentalitätsgeschichte des Herz-Jesu-Kultes in Deutschland zwischen Kulturkampf und Erstem Weltkrieg.* Gütersloh, 1997.

Chadwick, Owen. *The Secularization of the European Mind in the Nineteenth Century.* Cambridge, 1975.

Cholvy, Gérard, and Yves-Marie Hilaire. *Histoire religieuse de la France contemporaine.* Vol. 3, *1930–1988.* Toulouse, 1988.

Clark, Jonathan. "Secularization and Modernization: The Failure of a 'Grand Narrative.'" *Historical Journal* 55 (2012): 161–94.

Cocks, Geoffrey. "Repressing, Remembering, Working Through: German Psychiatry, Psychotherapy, Psychoanalysis and the "Missed Resistance" in the Third Reich." Supplement, *JMH* 64 (1992): S204–S16.

Colonge, Paul. "L'image de la France dans 'Hochland' avant 1914." *Der Europadiskurs in den deutschen Zeitschriften (1871–1914),* ed. Michel Grunewald, 191–203. Berne, 1996.

Connor, Ian. "The Churches and the Refugee Problem in Bavaria 1945–1949." *JCH* 20 (1985): 399–421.

Cremerius, Johannes, ed. *Die Rezeption der Psychoanalyse in der Soziologie, Psychologie und Theologie im deutschsprachigen Raum bis 1940.* Frankfurt, 1981.

———. "Einleitung." *Die Rezeption der Psychoanalyse in der Soziologie, Psychologie und Theologie im deutschsprachigen Raum bis 1940,* ed. Johannes Cremerius, 7–29. Frankfurt, 1981.

Damberg, Wilhelm. *Abschied vom Milieu? Katholizismus im Bistum Münster und in den Niederlanden 1945–1980.* Paderborn, 1997.

———. "Bernd Feldhaus und die 'Katholische Gesellschaft für Kirche und Demokratie' (19681972)." *Westfälische Forschungen* 48 (1998): 117–25.

———. "Einleitung." In *Soziale Strukturen und Semantiken des Religiösen im Wandel: Transformationen in der Bundesrepublik Deutschland, 1949–1989,* ed. Wilhelm Damberg, 9–35. Essen, 2011.

DBK, ed. *Frauen und Kirche: Eine Repräsentativumfrage von Katholikinnen: Im Auftrage des Sekretariats der Deutschen Bischofskonferenz durchgeführt vom Institut für Demoskopie Allensbach.* Bonn, 1993.

DeCarvalho, Roy Jose. *The Founders of Humanistic Psychology.* New York, 1991.

Desmazières, Agnès. *L'inconscient au paradis: Comment les Catholiques ont reçu la psychanalyse.* Paris, 2011.

Desrosières, Alain. *The Politics of Large Numbers: A History of Statistical Reasoning.* Cambridge, MA, 1998.

Dietrich, Tobias. "Zwischen Milieu und Lebenswelt: Kirchenbindung und Konfession im Hunsrück des 19. Jahrhunderts." *Monatshefte für evangelische Kirchengeschichte des Rheinlandes* 50 (2001): 37–60.

Doorn, Jost van. "The Development of Sociology and Social Research in the Netherlands." *Mens en Maatschappij* 31 (1956): 189–264.

Douglas, Tom. *Basic Groupwork.* London, 1978.

Dreitzel, Horst. "Süßmilchs Beitrag zur politischen Diskussion der deutschen Aufklärung." In *Ursprünge der Demographie in Deutschland: Leben und Werk Johann Peter Süßmilchs (1707–1767),* ed. Herwig Birg, 29–141. Frankfurt, 1986.

Dülmen, Richard van. *Kultur und Alltag in der Frühen Neuzeit.* Vol. 3. Munich, 1994.

———. *Religion und Gesellschaft: Beiträge zu einer Religionsgeschichte der Neuzeit.* Frankfurt, 1989.

Ebertz, Michael N. "Die Organisierung von Massenreligiosität im 19. Jahrhundert: Soziologische Aspekte zur Frömmigkeitsforschung." *Jahrbuch für Volkskunde N.F.* 2 (1979): 38–72.

———. "'Ein Haus voll Glorie schauet . . . ': Modernisierungsprozesse der römisch-katholischen Kirche im 19. Jahrhundert." In *Religion und Gesellschaft im 19. Jahrhundert,* ed. Wolfgang Schieder, 62–85. Stuttgart, 1993.

———. *Erosion der Gnadenanstalt? Zum Wandel der Sozialgestalt von Kirche.* Frankfurt, 1998.

———. "Herrschaft in der Kirche: Hierarchie, Tradition und Charisma im 19. Jahrhundert." In *Zur Soziologie des Katholizismus,* ed. Karl Gabriel and Franz-Xaver Kaufmann, 89–111. Mainz, 1980.

Eitler, Pascal. "Politik und Religion—semantische Grenzen und Grenzverschiebungen in der Bundesrepublik Deutschland (1965–1975)." In *Neue Politikgeschichte: Perspektiven einer historischen Politikforschung,* ed. Ute Frevert and Heiny-Gerhard Haupt, 268–303. Frankfurt, 2005.

Falby, Alison. "The Modern Confessional: Anglo-American Religious Groups and the Emergence of Lay Psychotherapy." *Journal of the History of the Behavioral Sciences* 39 (2003): 251–67.

Fischer, Alfons. *Pastoral in Deutschland nach 1945.* Vols. 1–3. Würzburg, 1985–90.

Forster, Karl. "Zur Interdependenz zwischen der theologischen und der soziologischen Sicht von Glaube und Kirche und zu den theologischen Auswirkungen solcher Interdependenz." In *Politische Denaturierung von Theologie und Kult,* ed. Wilhelm Weber, 9–33. Aschaffenburg, 1978.

Forster, Karl, and Gerhard Schmidtchen. *Glaube und Dritte Welt: Ergebnisse einer Repräsentativumfrage über weltkirchliche Aufgaben und die Motive deutscher Katholiken.* Munich, 1982.

Foucault, Michel. "Afterword: The Subject and Power." In *Michel Foucault: Beyond Structuralism and Hermeneutics,* by Hubert L. Dreyfus and Paul Rabinow, 208–26. New York, 1982.

———. "Governmentality." In *The Foucault Effect: Studies in Governmentality,* ed. Graham Burchell, Colin Gordon, and Peter Miller, 87–104. Chicago, 1991.

———. *The History of Sexuality.* Vol. 1. Harmondsworth, UK, 1984.

Fouilloux, Étienne. "'Fille aînée de l'Eglise' ou 'pays de mission'? (1926–1958)." In *Société séculaire et renouveaux religieux (XXe Siècle),* ed. René Rémond, 131–252. Paris, 1992.

Frese, Matthias, and Michael Prinz. "Sozialer Wandel und politische Zäsuren seit der Zwischenkriegszeit: Methodische Probleme und Ergebnisse." In *Politische Zäsuren und gesellschaftlicher Wandel im 20. Jahrhundert,* ed. Matthias Frese and Michael Prinz, 1–31. Paderborn, 1996.

Fuchs, Peter. *Der Eigen-Sinn des Bewußtseins: Die Person, die Psyche, die Signatur.* Bielefeld, 2003.

———. "Gefährliche Modernität: Das zweite vatikanische Konzil und die Veränderung des Messeritus." *KZfSS* 44 (1992): 1–11.

Furger, Franz, ed. *Akzente christlicher Sozialethik: Schwerpunkte und Wandel in 100 Jahren "christlicher Sozialwissenschaften" an der Universität Münster.* Münster, 1995.

Fürst, Walter. "Die Geschichte der 'Praktischen Theologie' und der kulturelle Wandlungsprozeß in Deutschland vor dem II. Vaticanum." In *Die katholisch-theologischen Disziplinen in Deutschland 1870–1962: Ihre Geschichte, ihr Zeitbezug,* ed. Hubert Wolf, 263–89. Paderborn, 1999.

Fürstenberg, Friedrich, and Ingo Mörth. "Religionssoziologie." In *Handbuch der empirischen Sozialforschung,* 2nd ed., ed. René König, 14:1–84. Stuttgart, 1997.

Galassi, Silviana. *Kriminologie im Deutschen Kaiserreich: Geschichte einer gebrochenen Verwissenschaftlichung.* Stuttgart, 2004.

Gareis, Balthasar. *Psychotherapie und Beichte.* St. Ottilien, 1988.

Gärtner, Christel. *Eugen Drewermann und das gegenwärtige Problem der Sinnstiftung: Eine religionssoziologische Fallanalyse.* Frankfurt, 2000.

Gatz, Erwin. "Deutschland." *Kirche und Katholizismus seit 1945,* ed. Erwin Gatz, 1:53–158. Paderborn, 1998.

Gay, Peter. *"Ein gottloser Jude": Sigmund Freuds Atheismus und die Entwicklung der Psychoanalyse.* Frankfurt, 1999.

Glotz, Peter. *Die Beweglichkeit des Tankers.* Munich, 1982.

Goertz, Stephan. *Moraltheologie unter Modernisierungsdruck: Interdisziplinarität und Modernisierung als Provokationen theologischer Ethik—im Dialog mit der Soziologie Franz-Xaver Kaufmanns.* Münster, 1999.

Goritzka, Richard. *Der Seelsorger Robert Grosche (1888–1967): Dialogische Pastoral zwischen Erstem Weltkrieg und Zweitem Vatikanischen Konzil.* Würzburg, 1999.

Görres, Albert. "Erneuerung durch Tiefenpsychologie." In *Tiefenpsychologische Deutung des Glaubens? Anfragen an Eugen Drewermann,* ed. Albert Görres and Walter Kasper, 133–74. Freiburg, 1988.

———. "Kirchliche Beratung—eine dringende Antwort auf Symptome und Ursachen seelischer Krisen?" In *Kirchliche Beratungsdienste,* ed. Sekretariat der DBK, 5–31. Bonn, 1987.

Götz von Olenhusen, Irmtraud. "Die Ultramontanisierung des Klerus: Das Beispiel der Erzdiözese Freiburg." In *Deutscher Katholizismus im Umbruch zur Moderne,* ed. Wilfried Loth, 46–75. Stuttgart, 1991.

———, ed. *Wunderbare Erscheinungen: Frauen und katholische Frömmigkeit im 19. und 20. Jahrhundert.* Paderborn, 1995.

Graf, Friedrich Wilhelm. "Die nachholende Selbstmodernisierung des Katholizismus? Kritische Anmerkungen zu Karl Gabriels Vorschlag einer interdisziplinären Hermeneutik des II. Vatikanums." In *Das II. Vatikanum—christlicher Glaube im Horizont globaler Modernisierung,* ed. Peter Hünermann, 49–65. Paderborn, 1998.

———. "Euro-Gott im starken Plural? Einige Fragestellungen für eine europäische Religionsgeschichte des 20. Jahrhunderts." *Journal of Modern European History* 3 (2005): 231–56.

Griesl, Gottfried. "Praktische Theologie zwischen Verkündigung und Psychotherapie." In *Von der Pastoraltheologie zur Praktischen Theologie 1774–1974,* ed. Erika Weinzierl and Gottfried Griesl, 199–225. Salzburg, 1975.

Großbölting, Thomas. *"Wie ist Christsein heute möglich?" Suchbewegungen des nachkonziliaren Katholizismus im Spiegel des Freckenhorster Kreises.* Altenberge, 1997.

Grosser, Charles F. *New Directions in Community Organisation: From Enabling to Advocacy.* New York, 1973.

Großmann, Thomas. *Zwischen Kirche und Gesellschaft: Das Zentralkomitee der deutschen Katholiken 1945–1970.* Mainz, 1991.

Hahn, Alois. "Luhmanns Beobachtung der Religion." *KZfSS* 53 (2001): 580–89.

———. "Zur Soziologie der Beichte und anderer Formen institutionalisierter Bekenntnisse: Selbstthematisierung und Zivilisationsprozess." *KZfSS* 34 (1982): 407–34.

Hahn, Alois, and Herbert Willems. "Schuld und Bekenntnis in Beichte und Therapie." In *Religion und Kultur,* ed. Jörg Bergmann, Alois Hahn and Thomas Luckmann, 309–330. Opladen, 1993.

Hahn, Ulla. *Das verborgene Wort: Roman.* Stuttgart, 2001.

Hale, Nathan G. *The Rise and Crisis of Psychoanalysis in the United States: Freud and the Americans, 1917–1985.* New York, 1995.

Hartmann, P. C. *Kulturgeschichte des Heiligen Römischen Reiches 1648 bis 1806.* Vienna, 2001.

Hatch, Mary Jo. *Organization Theory: Modern, Symbolic and Postmodern Perspectives.* Oxford, 1997.

Hausberger, Karl. "'Ach, unsere Landleute können sich gar nicht helfen . . . ': Streiflichter auf die seelsorgliche, soziale und wirtschaftliche Situation im Bayerischen Wald zu Anfang unseres Jahrhunderts aus der Feder des Kooperators Dr. Johann Markstaller." *Beiträge zur Geschichte des Bistums Regensburg* 26 (1992): 257–94.

Hehl, Ulrich von. *Katholische Kirche und Nationalsozialismus im Erzbistum Köln 1933–1945.* Mainz, 1977.

Heilbronner, Oded. *Die Achillesferse des deutschen Katholizismus: Die Schwarzwaldregion als Fallstudie.* Gerlingen, 1998.

Heller, Andreas. "'Du kommst in die Hölle . . . ': Katholizismus als Weltanschauung in lebensgeschichtlichen Aufzeichnungen." In *Religion und Alltag: Interdisziplinäre Beiträge zu einer Sozialgeschichte des Katholizismus in lebensgeschichtlichen Aufzeichnungen,* ed. Andreas Heller, Theresia Bauer, and Olivia Wiebel-Fanderl, 28–54. Vienna, 1990.

Henke, Thomas. *Seelsorge und Lebenswelt: Auf dem Weg zu einer Seelsorgetheorie in Auseinandersetzung mit soziologischen und sozialphilosophischen Lebensweltkonzeptionen.* Würzburg, 1994.

Henkelmann, Andreas, and Katharina Kunter. "Diakonie und Caritas im Traditionsabbruch? Historische Perspektiven zur Kirchlichkeit der Laien in der konfessionellen Wohlfahrtspflege." In *Soziale Strukturen und Semantiken des Religiösen im Wandel. Transformationen in der Bundesrepublik Deutschland, 1949–1989*, ed. Wilhelm Damberg, 71–87. Essen, 2011.

Herbert, Ulrich. "Liberalisierung als Lernprozeß: Die Bundesrepublik in der deutschen Geschichte—eine Skizze." In *Wandlungsprozesse in Westdeutschland: Belastung, Integration, Liberalisierung 1945–1980*, ed. Ulrich Herbert, 7–49. Göttingen, 2002.

Hermans, Baldur. "Das Ruhrbistum Essen als gesellschaftlicher und sozialethischer Handlungsraum." In *Das Ruhrgebiet—Ein starkes Stück Westfalen*, ed. Rainer Bovermann, Stefan Goch and Hans-Jürgen Priamus, 127–42. Essen, 1996.

Herr, Theodor. *Patient Kirche—was ist mit der Kirche los? Eine sozialwissenschaftliche Untersuchung.* Paderborn, 2001.

Herres, Jürgen. *Städtische Gesellschaft und katholische Vereine im Rheinland 1840–1879.* Essen, 1996.

Herzog, Dagmar. "Desperately Seeking Normality: Sex and Marriage in the Wake of the War." In *Life after Death: Approaches to a Cultural and Social History of Europe during the 1940s and 1950s*, ed. Richard Bessel and Dirk Schumann, 161–93. Cambridge, 2003.

Hilgartner, Stephen. *Science on Stage: Expert Advice as Public Drama.* Palo Alto, CA, 2000.

Hirschman, Albert. *Exit, Voice and Loyalty: Responses to Decline in Firms, Organizations and States.* Cambridge, MA, 1970.

Hockerts, Hans Günter. "Zeitgeschichte in Deutschland: Begriff, Methoden, Themenfelder." *Historisches Jahrbuch* 113 (1993): 98–127.

Holm, Nils G. *Einführung in die Religionspsychologie.* Munich and Basel, 1990.

Hölscher, Lucian. "Die religiöse Entzweiung: Entwurf zu einer Geschichte der Frömmigkeit im 19. Jahrhundert." *Jahrbuch der Gesellschaft für niedersächsische Kirchengeschichte* 93 (1995): 9–25.

———. "Einleitung." In *Datenatlas zur religiösen Geographie im protestantischen Deutschland: Von der Mitte des 19. Jahrhunderts bis zum Zweiten Weltkrieg*, ed. Lucian Hölscher, 1:1–20. Berlin, 2001.

———. "Möglichkeiten und Grenzen der statistischen Erfassung kirchlicher Bindungen." In *Seelsorge und Diakonie in Berlin: Beiträge zum Verhältnis von Kirche und Großstadt im 19. und 20. Jahrhundert*, ed. Kaspar Elm and Hans-Dietrich Look, 39–59. Berlin, 1990.

Holzem, Aandreas. *Religion und Lebensformen: Katholische Konfessionalisierung im Sendgericht des Fürstbistums Münster 1570–1800.* Paderborn, 2000.

Honsel, Bernhard. *Der rote Punkt: Eine Gemeinde unterwegs.* Düsseldorf, 1983.

Hörger, Hermann. "Frömmigkeit auf dem altbayerischen Dorf um 1800." *Oberbayerisches Archiv* 102 (1978): 123–42.

———. "Stabile Strukturen und mentalitätsbildende Elemente in der dörflichen Frömmigkeit: Die pfarrlichen Verkündbücher als mentalitätsgeschichtliche Quelle." *Bayerisches Jb. für Volkskunde* (1980/81): 110–33.

Hörmann, Georg, and Frank Nestmann. "Die Professionalisierung der Klinischen Psychologie und die Entwicklung neuer Berufsfelder in Beratung, Sozialarbeit und Therapie." In *Geschichte der deutschen Psychologie im 20. Jahrhundert: Ein Überblick*, ed. Mitchell G. Ash and Ulfried Geuter, 252–85. Opladen, 1985.

Hürten, Heinz. *Deutsche Katholiken 1918–1945.* Paderborn, 1992.

Institut für Sozialforschung. *Soziologische Exkurse: Nach Vorträgen und Diskussionen.* Frankfurt, 1956.

Jacobi, Jolande. *Die Psychologie von C.G. Jung: Eine Einführung in das Gesamtwerk*. Frankfurt, 1978.

Jedin, Hubert, ed. *Handbuch der Kirchengeschichte*. Vol. VI/2. Freiburg, 1973.

Jockwig, Klemens. "Die Volksmission der Redemptoristen in Bayern von 1843 bis 1873." *Beiträge zur Geschichte des Bistums Regensburg* 1 (1967): 41–396.

Kamphausen, Georg. *Hüter des Gewissens? Zum Einfluß sozialwissenschaftlichen Denkens in Theologie und Kirche*. Berlin, 1986.

Kasper, Walter. "Tiefenpsychologische Umdeutung des Christentums." In *Tiefenpsychologische Deutung des Glaubens? Anfragen an Eugen Drewermann*, ed. Albert Görres and Walter Kasper, 9–25. Freiburg, 1988.

Kastner, Dieter. "Oberpfarrer Laurenz Huthmacher und seine Aufzeichnungen zur Krefelder Pfarrgeschichte aus der Zeit des Kulturkampfes (1865–1880)." In *Katholisches Krefeld*, ed. Adolf Duppengießer, 2:133–202. Krefeld, 1988.

Katholische Fernseharbeit beim ZDF, ed. *Die Kirche wickelt sich ab—und die Gesellschaft lebt die produktive Kraft des Religiösen: Nur 18 Thesen zum Verhältnis Kirche, Religion und Kultur*. 2nd ed. Mainz, 1995:

Kauders, Anthony. "'Psychoanalysis Is Good, Synthesis Is Better': The German Reception of Freud, 1930 and 1956." *Journal of the History of the Behavioural Sciences* 47 (2011): 380–97.

Kaufmann, Franz-Xaver. "Die Entwicklung von Religion in der modernen Gesellschaft." In *Religion-Kirche-Islam: Eine soziale und diakonische Herausforderung*, ed. Klaus D. Hildemann, 21–37. Leipzig, 2003.

———. "Ist das Christentum zukunftsfähig?" In *Religion und Modernität: Sozialwissenschaftliche Perspektiven*, 235–75. Tübingen, 1989.

———. "Katholizismus und Moderne als Aufgaben künftiger Forschung." In *Moderne als Problem des Katholizismus*, ed. Urs Altermatt, 9–32. Regensburg, 1995.

———. *Kirche begreifen: Analysen und Thesen zur gesellschaftlichen Verfassung des Christentums*. Freiburg, 1979.

———. "Zukunftsfähigkeit der Theologie: Abschließende Bemerkungen." In *Zukunftsfähigkeit der Theologie: Anstöße aus der Soziologie Franz-Xaver Kaufmanns*, ed. Karl Gabriel, Jürgen Horstmann and Norbert Mette, 157–67. Paderborn, 1999.

———. "Zur Einführung: Probleme und Wege einer historischen Einschätzung des II. Vatikanischen Konzils." In *Vaticanum II und Modernisierung: Historische, theologische und soziologische Perspektiven*, ed. Franz-Xaver Kaufmann and Arnold Zingerle, 9–34. Paderborn, 1996.

Kehrer, Günter. *Einführung in die Religionssoziologie*. Darmstadt, 1988.

Keller, Felix. *Archäologie der Meinungsforschung: Mathematik und die Erzählbarkeit des Politischen*. Constance, 2001.

Kerkloh, Werner, Franz Thalmann, Angela Sauerland and Wilhelm Weber. "Porträt einer Lehr- und Forschungsstätte: 25 Jahre Institut für Christliche Sozialwissenschaften der Westfälischen Wilhelms-Universität Münster." *Jb. für Christliche Sozialwissenschaften* 18 (1977): 11–50.

Kern, Horst. *Empirische Sozialforschung: Ursprünge, Ansätze, Entwicklungslinien*. Munich, 1982.

Kindermann, Adolf. "Religiöse Wandlungen und Probleme im katholischen Bereich." In *Die Vertriebenen in Westdeutschland*, ed. Eugen Lemberg and Friedrich Edding, 3:92–158. Kiel, 1959.

"Kinsey: A 50th Anniversary Symposium." *Sexualities: Studies in Culture and Society* 1 (1998): 83–106.

Klein, Gotthard. *Der Volksverein für das katholische Deutschland 1890–1933: Geschichte, Bedeutung, Untergang.* Paderborn, 1996.

Klingemann, Carsten. *Soziologie im Dritten Reich.* Baden-Baden, 1996.

———. "Wiederaufbauplanung als Fortsetzung der nationalsozialistischen Raumplanung am Soziographischen Institut der Universität Frankfurt." In *Stadt und Raum 1933–1949*, ed. AG Stadtgeschichte, 179–95. Kassel, 1991.

Klinger, Elmar. "Das Aggiornamento der Pastoralkonstitution." In *Vaticanum II und Modernisierung: Historische, theologische und soziologische Perspektiven*, ed. Franz-Xaver Kaufmann and Arnold Zingerle, 171–87. Paderborn, 1996.

Knobloch, Stefan. *Missionarische Gemeindebildung: Zu Geschichte und Zukunft der Volksmission.* Passau, 1986.

Köhler, Joachim, and Rainer Bendel. "Bewährte Rezepte oder unkonventionelle Experimente? Zur Seelsorge an Flüchtlingen und Heimatvertriebenen." In *Siegerin in Trümmern: Die Rolle der katholischen Kirche in der deutschen Nachkriegsgesellschaft*, ed. Joachim Köhler and Damian van Melis, 199–228. Stuttgart, 1998.

Kösters, Christoph. "Katholiken in der Minderheit: Befunde, Thesen und Fragen zu einer sozial- und mentalitätsgeschichtlichen Erforschung des Diasporakatholizismus in Mitteldeutschland und der DDR (1830/40–1961)." *Wichmann-Jahrbuch* 36/37 (1997): 169–204.

Krautscheidt, Joseph. "Gründung des Bistums Essen: Die Jahre 1951–1957." In *Zeugnis und Dienst: Zum 70. Geburtstag von Bischof Dr. Franz Hengsbach*, 29–55. Bochum, 1980.

Kreppold, Guido. "Träume, Symbole und Bibel: Am Beispiel einer Selbsterfahrungsgruppe und einer Einzeltherapie." In *Psychologie hilft Glauben: Durch seelisches Reifen zum spirituellen Erwachen: Berichte, Erfahrungen, Anregungen*, ed. Peter Raab, 97–106. Freiburg, 1990.

Kruijt, Jakob P. "Die Erforschung der protestantischen Kirchengemeinde in den Niederlanden." In *Soziologie der Kirchengemeinde*, ed. Dietrich Goldschmidt, 35–49. Stuttgart, 1960.

Kruke, Anja. *Demoskopie in der Bundesrepublik Deutschland: Meinungsforschung, Parteien und Medien 1949–1990.* Düsseldorf, 2007.

Kruke, Anja, and Benjamin Ziemann. "Observing the Sovereign: Opinion Polls and the Restructuring of the Body Politic in West Germany, 1945–1990." In *Engineering Society*, eds. Kerstin Brückweh, Dirk Schumann, Richard Wetzell and Benjamin Ziemann, 234–51. Basingstoke/UK, 2012.

Kühn, Hans. *Strukturreform im Bistum Speyer 1969–1980.* Speyer, 1992.

Küppers, Kurt. *Marienfrömmigkeit zwischen Barock und Industriezeitalter: Untersuchungen zur Geschichte und Feier der Maiandacht in Deutschland und im deutschen Sprachgebiet.* St. Ottilien, 1987.

Lakoff, George, and Mark Johnson. *Metaphors We Live By.* Chicago and London, 1980.

Lang, Peter Thaddäus. "Die katholischen Kirchenvisitationen des 18. Jahrhunderts: Der Wandel vom Disziplinierungs- zum Datensammlungsinstrument." *Römische Quartalsschrift* 83 (1988): 265–95.

———. "Die tridentinische Reform im Landkapitel Mergentheim." *RJKG* 1 (1982): 143–70.

———. "Visitationsprotokolle und andere Quellen zur Frömmigkeitsgeschichte." *Aufriß der Historischen Wissenschaften*, ed. Michael Maurer, 4:302–24. Stuttgart, 2002.

Lehmann, Hartmut. "Jenseits der Säkularisierungsthese: Religion im Prozess der Säkularisierung." In *Religion zwischen Kunst und Politik: Aspekte der Säkularisierung im 19. Jahrhundert*, ed. Manfred Jakubowski-Thiessen, 178–90. Göttingen, 2004.

Lehmann, Karl. *Sicherung künftiger Handlungsfähigkeit: Bericht zum Abschluß einer Untersuchung des Bistums Mainz mit der Unternehmensberatung McKinsey & Company am 18.6.2002.* http://www.kath.de/bistum/mainz/info/mckinsey/bericht-sicherung-18-6-02.htm (accessed 17 September 2003).

Lettmann, Reinhard. "Joseph Höffner (1962–1969)." In *Das Bistum Münster*, ed. Werner Thissen, 1:320–27. Münster, 1993.

Leugers, Antonia. *Interessenpolitik und Solidarität: 100 Jahre Superioren-Konferenz—Vereinigung Deutscher Ordensobern.* Frankfurt, 1999.

Leugers, August-Hermann. "Latente Kulturkampfstimmung im Wilhelminischen Kaiserreich: Konfessionelle Polemik als konfessions- und innenpolitisches Kampfmittel." In *Die Verschränkung von Innen-, Konfessions- und Kolonialpolitik im Deutschen Reich vor 1914*, ed. Johannes Horstmann, 13–37. Schwerte, 1987.

Liedhegener, Antonius. *Christentum und Urbanisierung: Katholiken und Protestanten in Münster und Bochum 1830–1933.* Paderborn, 1997.

Lindau-Bank, Detlev, ed. *Tanzende Steine: Festschrift für Philipp Wambolt zum 75. Geburtstag.* Berlin, 1993.

Löhr, Wolfgang. "Rechristianisierungsvorstellungen im deutschen Katholizismus 1945–1948." In *Christentum und politische Verantwortung: Kirchen im Nachkriegsdeutschland*, ed. Jochen-Christoph Kaiser and Anselm Doering-Manteuffel, 25–41. Stuttgart, 1990.

Lorenzer, Alfred. *Das Konzil der Buchhalter: Die Zerstörung der Sinnlichkeit: Eine Religionskritik.* Frankfurt, 1984.

Lösche, Peter, and Franz Walter. "Katholiken, Konservative und Liberale: Milieus und Lebenswelten bürgerlicher Parteien in Deutschland während des 20. Jahrhunderts." *GG 26* (2000): 471–92.

Lowy, Louis. *Sozialarbeit/Sozialpädagogik als Wissenschaft im angloamerikanischen und deutschsprachigen Raum: Stand und Entwicklung.* Freiburg, 1983.

Luckmann, Thomas. *Die unsichtbare Religion.* Frankfurt, 1991.

Lüdtke, Alf. *Eigen-Sinn: Fabrikalltag, Arbeitererfahrungen und Politik vom Kaiserreich bis in den Faschismus.* Hamburg, 1993.

Luhmann, Niklas. "Das Medium der Religion: Eine soziologische Betrachtung über Gott und die Seelen." *Soziale Systeme* 6 (2000): 39–51.

———. *Die Gesellschaft der Gesellschaft.* 2 vols. Frankfurt, 1998.

———. "Die Organisierbarkeit von Religionen und Kirchen." In *Religion im Umbruch*, ed. J. Wössner, 245–85. Stuttgart, 1972.

———. *Die Politik der Gesellschaft.* Frankfurt, 2000.

———. *Die Wissenschaft der Gesellschaft.* Frankfurt, 1990.

———. *The Differentiation of Society.* New York, 1982.

———. *Funktion der Religion.* Frankfurt, 1977.

———. *Love as a Passion: The Codification of Intimacy.* Cambridge, 1986.

———. *The Reality of the Mass Media.* Oxford, 2000.

———. *A Systems Theory of Religion.* Palo Alto, CA, 2012.

Maasen, Sabine. *Genealogie der Unmoral: Zur Therapeutisierung sexueller Selbste.* Frankfurt, 1998.

———. *Vom Beichtstuhl zur psychotherapeutischen Praxis: Zur Therapeutisierung der Sexualität.* Bielefeld, 1988.

Maasen, Sabine, Everett Mendelsohn, and Peter Weingart. "Metaphors: Is There a Bridge Over Troubled Waters?" In *Biology as Society, Society as Biology: Metaphors*, ed. Sabine Maasen, Everett Mendelsohn, and Peter Weingart, 1–8. Dordrecht, 1995.

Maasen, Sabine, and Peter Weingart. "'Metaphors—Messengers of Meaning': A Contribution to an Evolutionary Sociology of Science." *Science Communication* 17, no. 1 (1995/96): 9–31.

Maier-Kuhn, H. "Utopischer Individualismus als personales und säkulares Heilsangebot: Eine ideologiekritische und sozialethische Untersuchung der Gesprächspsychotherapie von Carl R. Rogers unter besonderer Berücksichtigung ihrer Adaption durch die Pastoralpsychologie." PhD diss., University of Würzburg, 1979.

Margolin, Leslie. *Under the Cover of Kindness: The Invention of Social Work*. Charlottesville, VA, 1997.

Marx, Reinhard. *Ist Kirche anders? Möglichkeiten und Grenzen einer soziologischen Betrachtungsweise*. Paderborn, 1990.

Matussek, Paul. "Seelsorge heute: Aus der Sicht eines Psychotherapeuten." In *Seelsorge ohne Priester? Zur Problematik von Beratung und Psychotherapie in der Pastoral*, ed. Josef Maria Reuß, 91–107. Düsseldorf, 1976.

McLeod, Hugh. "Weibliche Frömmigkeit—männlicher Unglaube?" In *Bürgerinnen und Bürger: Geschlechterverhältnisse im 19. Jahrhundert*, ed. Ute Frevert, 134–56. Göttingen, 1988.

McPhee, Robert D., and Pamela Zaug. "Organizational Theory, Organizational Communication, Organizational Knowledge, and Problematic Integration." *Journal of Communication* 51 (2001): 574–91.

Menges, Walter. "Wandel und Auflösung der Konfessionszonen." In *Die Vertriebenen in Westdeutschland*, ed. Eugen Lemberg and Friedrich Edding, 3:1–22. Kiel, 1959.

Mergel, Thomas. *Zwischen Klasse und Konfession: Katholisches Bürgertum im Rheinland 1794–1914*. Göttingen, 1994.

Mette, Nobert. "Religionssoziologie—katholisch: Erinnerung an religionssoziologische Traditionen innerhalb des Katholizismus." In *Zur Soziologie des Katholizismus*, ed. Karl Gabriel and Franz-Xaver Kaufmann, 39–56. Mainz, 1980.

Mette, Nobert, and Hermann Steinkamp. *Sozialwissenschaften und Praktische Theologie*. Düsseldorf, 1983.

Metzler, Gabriele. *Konzeptionen politischen Handelns von Adenauer bis Brandt: Politische Planung in der pluralistischen Gesellschaft*. Paderborn, 2005.

Meyer, Hans Bernhard. *Eucharistie: Geschichte, Theologie, Pastoral*. Regensburg, 1989.

Moews, Andrea-Isa. *Eliten für Lateinamerika: Lateinamerikanische Studenten an der Universität Löwen in den 1950er und 1960er Jahren*. Cologne, 2000.

Moltmann, Jürgen, ed. *Wie ich mich geändert habe*. Gütersloh, 1997.

Mooser, Josef. "Abschied von der Proletarität: Sozialstruktur und Lage der Arbeiterschaft in der Bundesrepublik." In *Sozialgeschichte der Bundesrepublik Deutschland*, ed. Werner Conze and M. Rainer Lepsius, 143–86. Stuttgart, 1983.

———. "Bürger und Katholik? Rolle und Bedeutung des Bürgertums auf den deutschen Katholikentagen 1871–1913." Habil., Bielefeld, 1987.

———. "Katholische Volksreligion, Klerus und Bürgertum in der zweiten Hälfte des 19. Jahrhunderts: Thesen." In *Religion und Gesellschaft im 19. Jahrhundert*, ed. Wolfgang Schieder, 144–56. Stuttgart, 1993.

Morantz, Regina Markell. "The Scientist as Sex Crusader: Alfred C. Kinsey and American Culture." *American Quarterly* 29 (1977): 563–89.

Morsey, Rudolf. "Georg Kardinal Kopp, Fürstbischof von Breslau: Kirchenfürst oder 'Staats-bischof'?" *Wichmann-Jahrbuch für Kirchengeschichte im Bistum Berlin* 21–23 (1967–69): 42–65.

Müller-Dreier, Armin. *Konfession in Politik, Gesellschaft und Kultur des Kaiserreichs: Der Evangelische Bund 1886–1914.* Gütersloh, 1998.

Nash, David. "Reconnecting Religion with Social and Cultural History: Secularization's Failure as a Master Narrative." *Cultural and Social History* 1 (2004): 302–25.

Nassehi, Armin. *Differenzierungsfolgen: Beiträge zur Soziologie der Moderne.* Opladen and Wiesbaden, 1999.

Nienhaus, Frank. "Transformations- und Erosionsprozesse des katholischen Milieus in einer ländlich-textilindustrialisierten Region: Das Westmünsterland 1914–1968." In *Politische Zäsuren und gesellschaftlicher Wandel im 20. Jahrhundert: Regionale und vergleichende Perspektiven,* ed. Matthias Frese and Michael Prinz, 597–629. Paderborn, 1996.

Nipperdey, Thomas. *Deutsche Geschichte 1800–1866: Bürgerwelt und starker Staat.* Munich, 1983.

Nitzschke, Bernd. "Die Bedeutung der Sexualität im Werk Sigmund Freuds." In *Sexualität und Männlichkeit: Zwischen Symbiosewunsch und Gewalt,* 282–346. Reinbek, 1988.

Noelle-Neumann, Elisabeth. "Über den Fortschritt der Publizistikwissenschaft durch die Anwendung empirischer Forschungsmethoden: Eine autobiographische Aufzeichnung." In *Kommunikationswissenschaft—autobiographisch: Zur Entwicklung einer Wissenschaft in Deutschland,* ed. Arnulf Kutsch and Horst Pöttker, 36–61. Opladen, 1997.

Nolte, Paul. *Die Ordnung der deutschen Gesellschaft: Selbstentwurf und Selbstbeschreibung im 20. Jahrhundert.* Munich, 2000.

Oertel, Ferdinand. "Aufstand der Laien: Kritik prägte den Katholikentag 1968 in Essen." *Die Politische Meinung* 378 (2001): 39–44.

Palmore, Erdman. "Published Reactions to the Kinsey Report." *Social Forces* 31 (1952): 165–72.

Patterson, Cecil-Holden, and C. Edward Watkins. *Theories of Psychotherapy.* 5th ed. New York, 1996.

Phayer, Fintan Michael. *Religion und das gewöhnliche Volk in Bayern in der Zeit von 1750–1850.* Munich, 1970.

Pierrard, Pierre, Michel Launay and Rolande Trempé. *La J.O.C.: Regards d'historiens.* Paris, 1984.

Plate, Manfred. *Das deutsche Konzil: Die Würzburger Synode: Bericht und Deutung.* Freiburg, 1975.

Platt, Jennifer. *A History of Sociological Research Methods in America 1920–1960.* Cambridge, 1996.

Poiger, Uta G. "Generations: The 'Revolutions' of the 1960s." In *The Oxford Handbook of Modern German History,* ed. Helmut Walser Smith, 640–642. Oxford, 2011.

Pollack, Detlef. "Historische Analyse statt Ideologiekritik: Eine historisch-kritische Diskussion der Gültigkeit der Säkularisierungstheorie." *GG* 37 (2011): 1–41.

Pompey, Heinrich. "Handlungsperspektiven kirchlicher Beratung." In *Kirchliche Beratungsdienste,* ed. Sekretariat der Deutschen Bischofskonferenz, 44–68. Bonn, 1987.

———. "Seelsorge in den Krisen des Lebens." In *Seelsorge ohne Priester? Zur Problematik von Beratung und Psychotherapie in der Pastoral,* ed. Josef Maria Reuß, 29–72. Düsseldorf, 1976.

———. "Theologisch-psychologische Grundbedingungen der seelsorglichen Beratung." In *Christliches ABC heute und morgen: Handbuch für Lebensfragen und kirchliche Erwachsenenbildung,* ed. Eckard Lade, 6: 179–209. Bad Homburg, 1986.

Porter, Theodore M. *The Rise of Statistical Thinking 1820–1900*. Princeton, NJ, 1986.

Porter, Theodore M., and Dorothy Ross, eds. *The Modern Social Sciences*. Cambridge, 2003.

Pottmeyer, Hermann J. "Modernisierung in der katholischen Kirche am Beispiel der Kirchenkonzeption des I. und II. Vatikanischen Konzils." In *Vaticanum II und Modernisierung: Historische, theologische und soziologische Perspektiven*, ed. Franz-Xaver Kaufmann and Arnold Zingerle, 131–46. Paderborn, 1996.

Poulat, Émile. *Naissance des Prêtres-Ouvriers*. Tournai, 1965.

Raphael, Lutz. "Die Verwissenschaftlichung des Sozialen als methodische und konzeptionelle Herausforderung für eine Sozialgeschichte des 20. Jahrhunderts." *GG* 22 (1996): 165–93.

Rauscher, Anton. "Die katholische Soziallehre im gesellschaftlichen Entwicklungsprozeß der Nachkriegszeit." In *Katholizismus, Wirtschaftsordnung und Sozialpolitik 1945–1963*, ed. Albrecht Langner, 11–26. Paderborn, 1980.

Reed, Michael. "Organizational Theorizing: A Historically Contested Terrain." In *Studying Organization: Theory and Method*, ed. Stewart R. Clegg and Cynthia Hardy, 25–52. London, 1999.

Reinhard, Wolfgang. "Sozialdisziplinierung-Konfessionalisierung-Modernisierung: Ein historiographischer Diskurs." In *Die Frühe Neuzeit in der Geschichtswissenschaft: Forschungstendenzen und Forschungsergebnisse*, ed. Nada Boškovska Leimgruber, 39–55. Paderborn, 1997.

———. "Was ist katholische Konfessionalisierung?" In *Die katholische Konfessionalisierung*, ed. Wolfgang Reinhard and Heinz Schilling, 419–52. Gütersloh, 1995.

Reiter, Johannes. "Die katholische Moraltheologie zwischen den beiden Vatikanischen Konzilien." In *Die katholisch-theologischen Disziplinen in Deutschland 1870–1962: Ihre Geschichte, ihr Zeitbezug*, ed. Hubert Wolf, 231–41. Paderborn, 1999.

Reuß, Josef Maria. "Vorwort des Herausgebers." In *Seelsorge ohne Priester? Zur Problematik von Beratung und Psychotherapie in der Pastoral*, ed. Josef Maria Reuß, 7–11. Düsseldorf, 1976.

Richou, Françoise. *La Jeunesse Ouvrière Chrétienne (J.O.C.): Genèse d'une jeunesse militante*. Paris, 1997.

Richter, Ingrid. *Katholizismus und Eugenik in der Weimarer Republik und im Dritten Reich: Zwischen Sittlichkeitsreform und Rassenhygiene*. Paderborn, 2001.

Rölli-Allkemper, Lukas. *Familie im Wiederaufbau: Katholizismus und bürgerliches Familienideal in der Bundesrepublik Deutschland 1945–1965*. Paderborn, 2000.

Rose, Nikolas. *Governing the Soul: The Shaping of the Private Self*. London, 1990.

———. *Inventing Our Selves: Psychology, Power, and Personhood*. Cambridge, 1998.

Rosenberger, Ruth. *Experten für Humankapital: Die Entdeckung des Personalmangements in der Bundesrepublik Deutschland*. Munich, 2008.

Ruck, Michael. "Ein kurzer Sommer der konkreten Utopie—Zur westdeutschen Planungsgeschichte der langen 60er Jahre." In *Dynamische Zeiten: Die 60er Jahre in den beiden deutschen Gesellschaften*, ed. Axel Schildt, Detlef Siegfried, and Karl Christian Lammers, 362–401. Hamburg, 2000.

Ruff, Mark Edward. *The Wayward Flock: Catholic Youth in Postwar West Germany 1945–1965*. Chapel Hill, NC, 2005.

Rutz, Oswin. *Obrigkeitliche Seelsorge: Die Pastoral im Bistum Passau von 1800 bis 1918*. Passau, 1984.

Scharfenberg, Joachim. "Die Rezeption der Psychoanalyse in der Theologie." In *Die Rezeption der Psychoanalyse in der Soziologie, Psychologie und Theologie im deutschsprachigen Raum bis 1940*, ed. Johannes Cremerius, 255–338. Frankfurt, 1981.

Schatz, Klaus. *Zwischen Säkularisation und zweitem Vatikanum: Der Weg des deutschen Katholizismus im 19. und 20. Jahrhundert.* Frankfurt, 1986.

Scheule, Rupert M. *Beichte und Selbstreflexion: Eine Sozialgeschichte katholischer Bußpraxis im 20. Jahrhundert.* Frankfurt, 2002.

Schildt, Axel. *Ankunft im Westen: Ein Essay zur Erfolgsgeschichte der Bundesrepublik.* Frankfurt, 1999.

———. *Moderne Zeiten: Freizeit, Medien und "Zeitgeist" in der Bundesrepublik der 50er Jahre.* Hamburg, 1995.

———. *Zwischen Abendland und Amerika: Studien zur westdeutschen Ideenlandschaft der 50er Jahre.* Munich, 1999.

Schlögl, Rudolf. *Glaube und Religion in der Säkularisierung: Die katholische Stadt—Köln, Aachen, Münster—1770–1840.* Munich, 1995.

———. "Historiker, Max Weber und Niklas Luhmann: Zum schwierigen (aber möglicherweise produktiven) Verhältnis von Geschichtswissenschaft und Systemtheorie." *Soziale Systeme* 7 (2001): 23–45.

Schmidbauer, Wolfgang. *Vom Umgang mit der Seele: Entstehung und Geschichte der Psychotherapie.* Frankfurt, 2000.

Schmidt, H. R. *Konfessionalisierung im 16. Jahrhundert.* Munich, 1992.

Schmidtchen, Gerhard. *Die Situation der Frau: Trendbeobachtungen über Rollen- und Bewußtseinsänderungen der Frauen in der Bundesrepublik Deutschland.* Berlin, 1984.

Schmidt-Gernig, Alexander. "Ansichten einer zukünftigen 'Weltgesellschaft': Westliche Zukunftsforschung der 60er und 70er Jahre als Beispiel einer transnationalen Expertenöffentlichkeit." In *Transnationale Öffentlichkeiten und Identitäten im 20. Jahrhundert,* ed. Hartmut Kaelble, Martin Kirsch and Alexander Schmidt-Gernig, 393–421. Frankfurt, 2002.

Schmidtmann, Christoph. *Katholische Studierende 1945–1973: Ein Beitrag zur Kultur- und Sozialgeschichte der Bundesrepublik Deutschland.* Paderborn, 2005.

Schmied, Gerhard. *Kirche oder Sekte? Entwicklungen und Perspektiven des Katholizismus in der westlichen Welt.* Munich and Zurich, 1988.

Schmitz, Gerold, OFM. *Kirche auf dem Prüfstand: Katholizismus im ausgehenden 20. Jahrhundert.* Frankfurt, 1989.

Schmitz, Hermann Joseph. "Die Pfarrchronik von St. Dionysius in Krefeld aus den Jahren 1886 bis 1893." In *Geschichte im Bistum Aachen,* 2:199–295. Aachen, 1994.

Schneider, D. M. *Johannes Schauff (1902–1990): Migration und "Stabilitas" im Zeitalter der Totalitarismen.* Munich, 2001.

Scholten, Bernhard. *Die Volksmissionen der Kölner Redemptoristen von 1945 bis zum zweiten vatikanischen Konzil: Ihr Beitrag zum Wiederaufbau des religiös-kirchlichen Lebens in der Bundesrepublik Deutschland.* Bonn, 1981.

———. *Die Volksmissionen der norddeutschen Redemptoristen zwischen den beiden Weltkriegen 1918–1939.* Bonn, 1980.

Schorske, Carl E. *Fin-de-Siècle Vienna: Politics and Culture.* New York, 1985.

Schröter, Michael. "Zurück ins Weite: Die Internationalisierung der deutschen Psychoanalyse nach dem Zweiten Weltkrieg." In *Westbindungen: Amerika in der Bundesrepublik,* ed. Heinz Bude and Bernd Greiner, 93–118. Hamburg, 1999.

Schulte-Umberg, Thomas. *Profession und Charisma: Herkunft und Ausbildung des Klerus im Bistum Münster 1776–1940.* Paderborn, 1999.

Schultz, Duane P., and Ellen Schultz. *A History of Modern Psychology.* 4th ed. San Diego, CA, 1987.

Schulz, Kristina. *Der lange Atem der Provokation: Die Frauenbewegung in der Bundesrepublik und in Frankreich 1968–1976.* Frankfurt and New York, 2002.

Schwarte, Johannes. *Gustav Gundlach J. (1892–1963): Maßgeblicher Repräsentant der katholischen Soziallehre während der Pontifikate Pius' XI. und Pius' XII.* Munich, 1975.

Sekretariat der Deutschen Bischofskonferenz, ed. *Katholische Kirche in Deutschland: Statistische Daten 2001.* Bonn, n.d. [2002].

———, ed. *Umkehr und Versöhnung im Leben der Kirche: Orientierungen zur Bußpastoral.* Bonn, 1997.

Shannon, Christopher. "Sex, Science, and History." *Journal of Policy History* 12 (2000): 265–78.

Söhngen, Gottlieb. *Analogie und Metapher: Kleine Philosophie und Theologie der Sprache.* Freiburg, 1962.

Soyland, A. John. *Psychology as Metaphor.* London, 1994.

Sperber, Jonathan. *Popular Catholicism in Nineteenth Century Germany.* Princeton, NJ, 1984.

Stäheli, Urs. *Sinnzusammenbrüche: Eine dekonstruktive Lektüre von Niklas Luhmanns Systemtheorie.* Weilerswist, 2000.

Stegmann, Franz-Josef. "Geschichte der sozialen Ideen im deutschen Katholizismus." In *Geschichte der sozialen Ideen in Deutschland,* ed. Helga Grebing and Peter Langhorst, 597–862. Essen, 2000.

Steinbacher, Sybille. *Wie der Sex nach Deutschland kam: Der Kampf um Sittlichkeit und Anstand in der frühen Bundesrepublik.* Munich, 2011.

Stenger, Hermann. "Beziehung als Verkündigung." In *Seelsorge ohne Priester? Zur Problematik von Beratung und Psychotherapie in der Pastoral,* ed. Josef Maria Reuß, 73–90. Düsseldorf, 1976.

Stichweh, Rudolf. "Die Entstehung einer Weltöffentlichkeit." In *Transnationale Öffentlichkeiten und Identitäten im 20. Jahrhundert,* ed. Hartmut Kaelble, Martin Kirsch, Alexander Schmidt-Gernig, 57–66. Frankfurt, 2002.

Strüder, Rolf. *Chancen und Gefährdung geplanten Wandels in der Kirche—aufgezeigt am Beispiel der Diözese Limburg.* St. Ottilien, 1993.

Terrenoire, Jean-Paul. "Pratique religieuse des catholiques en France 1930: Approches sociologiques globales et espaces de référence (1930–1980)." *Archives des Sciences Sociales des Religions* 87 (1994): 153–87.

Troxler, Georg. *Das Kirchengebot der Sonntagsmeßpflicht als moraltheologisches Problem in Geschichte und Gegenwart.* Freiburg, 1971.

Tschannen, Olivier. "The Secularization Paradigm: A Systematization." *Journal of the Scientific Study of Religion* 30 (1991): 395–415.

Tyrell, Hartmann. "Religionssoziologie." *GG* 22 (1996): 428–57.

———. "Zur Diversität der Differenzierungstheorie: Soziologiehistorische Anmerkungen." *Soziale Systeme* 4 (1998): 119–49.

Vogt, Karl-Heinz. "Zur Frage der Meßbarkeit religiöser Phänomene." In *Kirche und Gesellschaft heute,* ed. Franz Böckle and Franz-Josef Stegmann, 69–87. Paderborn, 1979.

Wagner, Peter. "The Mythical Promise of Societal Renewal: Social Science and Reform Coalitions." In *A History and Theory of the Social Sciences,* 54–72. London, 2001.

———. "Social Science and Social Planning during the Twentieth Century." In *The Modern Social Sciences,* ed. Theodore M. Porter and Dorothy Ross, 591–607. Cambridge, 2003.

———. "The Uses of the Social Sciences." In *The Modern Social Sciences,* ed. Theodore M. Porter and Dorothy Ross, 537–52. Cambridge, 2003.

Wahl, Heribert. "Therapeutische Seelsorge als Programm und Praxis: Praktisch-theologische Überlegungen zur Situation der Pastoralpsychologie." In *Glauben lernen—leben lernen: Beiträge zu einer Didaktik des Glaubens und der Religion,* ed. Konrad Baumgartner, Paul Wehrle, and Jürgen Werbick, 411–38. St. Ottilien, 1985.

Walf, Knut. "Das neue Kirchenrecht—das alte System: Vorkonziliarer Geist in nachkonziliaren Formulierungen." In *Katholische Kirche—wohin? Wider den Verrat am Konzil,* ed. Norbert Greinacher and Hans Küng, 78–93. Munich, 1986.

Walter-Busch, Emil. *Das Auge der Firma: Mayos Hawthorne-Experimente und die Harvard Business School, 1900–1960.* Stuttgart, 1989.

Weber, Clemens. "Ultramontanismus als katholischer Fundamentalismus." In *Deutscher Katholizismus im Umbruch zur Moderne,* ed. Wilfried Loth, 20–45. Stuttgart, 1991.

Weber, Wilhelm, ed. *Politische Denaturierung von Theologie und Kult.* Aschaffenburg, 1978.

———. *Wenn aber das Salz schal wird . . . Der Einfluß sozialwissenschaftlicher Weltbilder auf theologisches und kirchliches Sprechen und Handeln.* 2nd ed. Würzburg, 1984.

Wehler, Hans-Ulrich. *Deutsche Gesellschaftsgeschichte,* vol. 5, *Bundesrepublik und DDR 1949–1990.* Munich, 2008.

Wehr, Gerhard. *C.G. Jung: Leben, Werk, Wirkung.* Zurich, 1988.

Weichlein, Siegfried. "Katholisches Sozialmilieu und kirchliche Bindung in Osthessen 1918–1933." *Archiv für mittelrheinische Kirchengeschichte* 45 (1993): 367–89.

Weingart, Peter. *Die Stunde der Wahrheit? Zum Verhältnis der Wissenschaft zu Politik, Wirtschaft und Medien in der Wissensgesellschaft.* Weilerswist, 2001.

———. "Verwissenschaftlichung der Gesellschaft—Politisierung der Wissenschaft." *ZfS* 12 (1983): 225–41.

Weiss, Otto. "Der Ultramontanismus: Grundlagen-Vorgeschichte-Struktur." *Zeitschrift für Bayerische Landesgeschichte* 41 (1978): 821–77.

Wertheimer, Michael. *A Brief History of Psychology.* New York, 1970.

Westhoff, Hanneke, and Jan Roes. "Seelische versus geistliche Fürsorge: Die Rolle der psychohygienischen Bewegung bei der Transformation des niederländischen Katholizismus im 20. Jahrhundert." *Kirchliche Zeitgeschichte* 7 (1994): 137–60.

Weyer, Johannes. *Westdeutsche Soziologie 1945–1960: Deutsche Kontinuitäten und nordamerikanischer Einfluß.* Berlin, 1984.

Wirtz, Heiner. *Katholische Gesellenvereine und Kolpingsfamilien im Bistum Münster 1852–1960: "Gott zur Ehre und den Gesellen zum Vorteil."* Münster, 1999.

Wolf, Hugo. "Zwischen Fabriksirene und Glockengeläut: Zur Alltags-, Sozial- und Mentalitätsgeschichte der Pfarrei St. Johannes Frankfurt-Unterliederbach." *Archiv für Mittelrheinische Kirchengeschichte* 49 (1997): 179–209.

Wothe, Franz Josef. *Wilhelm Maxen: Wegbereiter neuerer Großstadtseelsorge.* Hildesheim, 1962.

Zeisel, Hans. "Zur Geschichte der Soziographie." In *Die Arbeitslosen von Marienthal: Ein soziographischer Versuch über die Wirkungen langandauernder Arbeitslosigkeit,* by Marie Jahoda, Paul Lazarsfeld, and Hans Zeisel, 113–48. Frankfurt, 1982.

Zerfaß, Rolf. "Was sind letztlich unsere Ziele? Pastoralpsychologische Thesen zur Motivationskrise in der Pastoral der Kirchenfremden." In *Erfahrungen mit Randchristen: Neue Horizonte für die Seelsorge,* ed. Katholische Glaubens-Information, 43–64. Freiburg, 1985.

Ziemann, Benjamin. "Auf der Suche nach der Wirklichkeit: Soziographie und soziale Schichtung im deutschen Katholizismus 1945–1970." *GG* 29 (2003): 409–40.

———. "Die Institutionalisierung des Tatsachenblicks: Katholische Kirche und empirische Sozialforschung in der Bundesrepublik 1950–1970." *Mitteilungsblatt des Instituts für soziale Bewegungen* 34 (2005): 107–25.

———. "The Gospel of Psychology: Therapeutic Concepts and the Scientification of Pastoral Care in the West German Catholic Church, 1950–1980." *Central European History* 39 (2006): 79–106.

———. "Krose, Hermann A." In *Biographisch-Bibliographisches Kirchenlexikon,* ed. Traugott Bautz, 24:983–86. Herzberg, 2005.

———. "Missionarische Bewegung und soziale Differenzierung im Katholizismus: Die Praxis der Gebietsmission in der Bundesrepublik 1950–1960." *Kirchliche Zeitgeschichte* 18 (2005): 419–38.

———. "Öffentlichkeit in der Kirche: Medien und Partizipation in der katholischen Kirche der Bundesrepublik 1965–1972." *Medialisierung und Demokratie im 20. Jahrhundert,* ed. Frank Bösch and Norbert Frei, 163–90. Göttingen, 2006.

———. "Opinion Polls and the Dynamics of the Public Sphere: The Catholic Church in the Federal Republic after 1968." *GH* 24 (2006): 562–86.

———. "Organisation und Planung in der katholischen Kirche um 1970: Das Beispiel der Diözese Münster." *Schweizerische Zeitschrift für Religions- und Kirchengeschichte* 101 (2007): 185–206.

———. "Religion and the Search for Meaning, 1945–1990." In *The Oxford Handbook of Modern German History,* ed. Helmut Walser Smith, 693–714. Oxford, 2011.

———. "Säkularisierung und Neuformierung des Religiösen: Religion und Gesellschaft in der zweiten Hälfte des 20. Jahrhunderts." *AfS* 51 (2011): 3–36.

———. *Sozialgeschichte der Religion: Von der Reformation bis zur Gegenwart.* Frankfurt and New York, 2009.

———. "Zwischen sozialer Bewegung und Dienstleistung am Individuum: Katholiken und katholische Kirche im therapeutischen Jahrzehnt." *AfS* 44 (2004): 357–93.

Ziemann, Benjamin, and Chris Dols. "Church Reform and Organizations Research in the Netherlands and Germany, 1950–1980." In *Engineering Society: The Role of the Human and Social Sciences in Modern Societies, 1880–1980,* eds. Kerstin Brückweh, Dirk Schumann, Richard Wetzell and Benjamin Ziemann, 293–312. Basingstoke, UK, 2012.

Ziemann, Benjamin, Richard Wetzell, Kerstin Brückweh, and Dirk Schumann. "Introduction." In *Engineering Society: The Role of the Human and Social Sciences in Modern Societies, 1880–1980,* eds. Kerstin Brückweh, Dirk Schumann, Richard Wetzell and Benjamin Ziemann, 1–40. Basingstoke, UK, 2012.

Zulehner, Paul Michael. "Was gewinnen Beratung und Seelsorge durch ihre wechselseitige Beziehung?" In *Beratung als Dienst der Kirche,* ed. Katholische Bundesarbeitsgemeinschaft für Beratung, 105–20. Freiburg, 1981.

———. *Wie kommen wir aus der Krise? Kirchliche Statistik Österreichs 1945–1975 und ihre pastoralen Konsequenzen.* Vienna, 1978.

INDEX

Aachen, Diocese of, 82, 202
abstention, 49, 93, 97
Adorno, Theodor W., 78
Algermissen, Konrad, 48
alienation from church, 48, 96, 174, 235, 252
Amtskirche, 272
Angerhausen, Julius, 75
annual communion, 38
apostolate, 10, 49, 51, 71, 84, 135, 138, 187, 192, 242
Area mission, 79–80, 100
atheism, 226, 226n32, 227, 228
Augsburg, Diocese of, 83, 176, 187
Augstein, Rudolf, 124
Austria, 43, 83, 139, 185

Baden, 32, 34, 38, 41, 43, 48
baptism, 37, 79, 198, 267
Barrenstein, Peter, 152
Baumgarten, Paul Maria, 30, 35
Belgium, 43, 71
belief, 8, 14–15, 24, 28–29, 45, 51, 69–70, 115, 123, 148, 154–55, 170, 179, 181, 186, 193, 197, 205–8, 220–21, 232, 243, 266, 269, 274
Bertram, Adolf Cardinal, 48
Betz, Felicitas, 237
Bishop, 7–8, 13, 17, 19, 27–28, 35, 40, 64, 78, 84–85, 84n113, 99, 123–25, 129–32, 134, 138, 139, 141–42, 144, 147, 153, 156, 171, 173–75, 178, 181–82, 187, 190, 193, 237, 239, 253, 266, 269
Böckh, Richard, 30
Böhm, Anton, 120
Böhringer, Hans, 229

Bonifatiusverein, 82
Bopp, Linus, 225–27, 230
Boulard, Fernand, 68, 76, 90, 93, 171
Bourdieu, Pierre, 4, 112
Brüning, Robert, 141
Brüning, Werner, 35
Büchner, Ludwig, 274
Bund der Deutschen Katholischen Jugend, 128

Canisian, 181
Cardijn, Joseph, 74, 78, 98
Caritas, 12–13, 152, 185, 200, 252, 254
Catechetics, 12, 272n7
Catholic Action, 10–11, 11n37, 75, 82, 193
Catholic Day in Essen 1968, 12
Catholic Institute for Social Ecclesiastical Research, 43
Catholic Office Bonn, 123
Catholic Social Institute of the Archdiocese of Cologne, 69
Catholic Sociological Institute for Refugee Issues, 82
celibacy, 6, 134–36, 172, 175, 177, 179–81, 181n64, 190, 209
Center Party, 18, 28, 30, 35, 46–47
Central Committee of German Catholics, 10, 127, 127n75, 129–30, 139, 141, 184
Central Office for Church Statistics Germany, Cologne, 30, 36
Christian Democratic Union (CDU), 92
Christian Labor Youth, 128
church crisis, 56
church going, 39
church handbook, 30, 35–36, 38, 41–42, 44, 50